BEN THOMPSON

PORTRAIT OF A GUNFIGHTER

Ben Thompson as he appeared at the age of twenty-nine. This was made in Wichita, Kansas, and is the earliest known image of Thompson.

Courtesy Western History Collection, University of Oklahoma. Image # 2144.

BEN THOMPSON
PORTRAIT OF A GUNFIGHTER

Thomas C. Bicknell
and
Chuck Parsons

Foreword by Robert K. DeArment

Number 20 in the A.C. Greene Series
University of North Texas Press
Denton, Texas

Printed in the United States of America.

10 9 8 7 6 5 4 3 2 1

Permissions:
University of North Texas Press
1155 Union Circle #311336
Denton, TX 76203-5017

The paper used in this book meets the minimum requirements of the American National Standard for Permanence of Paper for Printed Library Materials, z39.48.1984. Binding materials have been chosen for durability.

Library of Congress Cataloging-in-Publication Data

Names: Bicknell, Thomas C., 1952- author. | Parsons, Chuck, author.
Title: Ben Thompson : portrait of a gunfighter / by Thomas C. Bicknell and Chuck Parsons ; foreword by Robert K. DeArment.
Other titles: A.C. Greene series ; no. 20.
Description: Denton, Texas : University of North Texas Press, [2018] | Series: A.C. Greene series ; number 20 | Includes bibliographical references and index.
Identifiers: LCCN 2018014575| ISBN 9781574417302 (cloth : alk. paper) | ISBN 9781574417418 (ebook)
Subjects: LCSH: Thompson, Texas Ben, 1842-1884. | Gunfighters--Texas--Biography. | Peace officers--Texas--Biography. | Frontier and pioneer life--Texas.
Classification: LCC F391.T5125 B53 2018 | DDC 364.1092 [B] --dc23
LC record available at https://lccn.loc.gov/2018014575

Ben Thompson: Portrait of a Gunfighter is Number 20 in the A.C. Greene Series

The electronic edition of this book was made possible by the support of the Vick Family Foundation.
Maps courtesy Charles David Grear.

DEDICATIONS

For my dear wife, Karen, and our lovely daughters, Natalie, Brooke, and Laura: Thank you for your love, ideas, patience, inspiration, and encouragement throughout this entire effort.

—Tom Bicknell

Again, as always, to my wife Pat for all her help with writing and research, her encouragement, and her love.

—Chuck Parsons

CONTENTS

LIST OF ILLUSTRATIONS

FOREWORD

This is not the first biography of Ben Thompson, one of the most fascinating characters of the American western frontier. As early as 1884, the year of Thompson's death, William M. Walton (1832-1915), his friend and attorney, privately published *Life and Adventures of Ben Thompson, the Famous Texan. Including a Detailed and Authentic Statement of his Birth, History and Adventures by One Who Has Known Him Since a Child.* This book with its lengthy title has been reprinted at least three times, in 1926, 1954, and 1956. One would think that an author with the intimate knowledge of a man's life claimed in the title would have covered all bases in his presentation, especially since Walton was Thompson's lawyer and his client had a long history of conflicts with the law.

But western frontier historian Floyd B. Streeter (1888-1956) discovered enough new information about Thompson to write *Ben Thompson, Man with a Gun,* brought out by a New York publisher in 1957, and hailed by bibliophile Ramon Adams, that indefatigable critic of western outlaw/lawman literature, as "reliable" and showing "good research."

In addition to these books, countless articles in newspapers, historical journals, and popular magazines have appeared in the more than 130 years since Thompson's death, for many of the deeds and misdeeds of this intriguing character have been controversial as well as fascinating.

But now comes a new volume co-authored by Tom Bicknell and Chuck Parsons. For many years Tom Bicknell has diligently researched Ben Thompson, his trouble-prone younger brother, Billy, and the multitude of individuals who impacted their careers, and Chuck Parsons is a prolific author of books and articles dealing with frontier Texas. Together they have produced a book that provides much new information about the early life of the Thompson brothers, their activities during the Civil War, the revolutionary period in Mexico, and the violent Reconstruction age in the States that followed. In the process they have resolved many of the questions raised, but unanswered, in previous writings.

The American frontier of the nineteenth century has been called the "Wild West," then and since, in large part because of the exploits of the storied gunfighters, of whom Texas contributed far more than its share. Of the notorious Texas shootists, none was more respected (and feared) than Ben Thompson. His close friend W. B. "Bat" Masterson, no slouch in the pistol-wielding business himself, wrote in 1907: "Ben Thompson was a remarkable man in many ways, and it is doubtful if in his time there was another man living who equaled him with a pistol in a life and death struggle ... He had during his career more deadly encounters with the pistol than any man living and won out in every single instance."

Thompson's reputation in his lifetime and later was so great that in the early 1930s when Stuart Lake penned his history of Wyatt Earp, with the intention of promoting his protagonist to the highest levels of frontier stardom, he included an entirely fictional account of Earp's heroic disarming and arrest of Thompson after a gun-smoke fracas in the cattle town of Ellsworth, Kansas.

This and other factual and mythical stories about Ben and his brother Billy, including the mysterious assassination of Ben

Thompson and his crony, John King Fisher, on March 11, 1884, are dealt with in great detail by the authors of this volume, utilizing every bit of available information.

It is a book that anyone interested in this phase of American history will want to read and it will prove to be a valuable reference for future researchers and writers, for it is destined to be the *definitive* account of the life of one of the most interesting characters of the "Wild West."

Robert K. DeArment
Sylvania, Ohio
November 2016

ACKNOWLEDGMENTS

The courtesy and extraordinary efforts of librarians, archivists, government employees, and interested private citizens helped to make this book possible. It is a pleasure to acknowledge their contributions. They include ...

Marjorie (Bicknell) Shapiro for her invaluable help in editing the manuscript, Mrs. Alice Hayes and her entire staff of the Crystal Lake, Illinois Public Library, Mr. C. P. "Tom" Dearden, of Knottingley, West Yorkshire, England. The late Mr. Dearden, a local researcher, lecturer, collector, historian, and lifelong resident of Knottingley graciously contributed historical photographs and information about his hometown. In addition, Mr. Dearden painstakingly researched the Thompson family life in England, provided copies of the Thompson marriage and birth certificates, cemetery information, shipping records and ownership papers, English census data, and last will and testament documents. Jim "The Cowboy" Gray, historian and author, of Ellsworth, KS, who provided such valuable insight and expertise concerning Ben and Billy Thompson's adventures in Kansas. Rick Miller, Old West researcher and author, who shared so much primary information about the Thompson brothers, and Anne Beck, a descendent of Ben Thompson, for the family history she so freely shared.

To all friends of the Old West who immeasurably helped this process: John "Tre" Argerious, Ray Bartlett, George Bicknell, the late Ben M. Blount, Ken Blue, Mark Boardman, Dan Buck, John Curry, Robert DeArment, Jack DeMattos, the late Ernesto Dovalina Sr. and family, Bill and his son Finnegan Failey, Doug Dukes, Gary Fitterer, Charles David Grear, Frank Haslwanter, David Johnson, John J. Kuznowicz, Lisa Lach, Robert McCubbin, Elmer D. McInnes, Leon Metz, Rick Miller, Roger Myers, Christopher Penn, Marylyn (Portis) Pense, the late Joseph G. Rosa, Sandy Sagala, Richard F. Selcer, Larry Shaver, Jonathan Smith, Robert Smith, Jeff Schneider, Ron Swaitkowski, C. B. Wilson, and the late R. L. Wilson.

The following are those numerous individuals and organizations who provided further assistance: American Lending Library, Confederate States Enlistment Records, Bountiful, UT; Mary Ann Torres of the Aransas County District Clerk's office, Rockport, TX; Barbara Armstrong, Aransas County Historical Society, Rockport, TX; Karen Warren, Claire D. Maxwell, Mike Miller, Jane Montz, Rusty Huckabee of the Austin History Center, Austin, TX; Michael Burgess, Public Information Officer, Austin Police Department; Joyce Schaefer, Bastrop County Probate Division, Bastrop, TX; Dana Verrell, Bastrop Public Library, Bastrop, TX; Kelly Sinclair, Belton City Library, Belton, TX; the staff of the Bexar County District Clerk's office, San Antonio, TX; Susan Dame and Kathie Bell, Boot Hill Museum, Dodge City, KS; Ellie Fithian, Buena Vista Public Library, Buena Vista, CO; Elizabeth Holmes and Christine Houze, Buffalo Bill Historical Center, Cody, WY; Nancy M. Ross, Bryan, Texas Carnegie Library; Mary Whittington, Caldwell County Genealogical & Historical Society, Luling, TX; John T. Callahan, Arms Historian and expert on J. Stevens & Co. Firearms; Steven C. Stappenbeck, William H. Richter, Ned Brierly and Stephanie Wittenbach, Briscoe Center for American History, Austin, TX; Jennifer Bosley and Barbara Dey, Colorado Historical Society,

Denver; Margaret Rose, Corpus Christi Public Library, Special Collections; Barbara Jacob, Cuero Public Library, Cuero, TX; Julie Travis, Dallas Public Library; Alice Evett and Gary Yantis, members of the "Do Nothin' Gang," San Antonio, TX; Linda Edwards, Daughters of the Republic of Texas Library (DRT), San Antonio, TX; Dixie Foster, Denison Public Library, Denison, TX; Ester Ruiz, DeWitt County District Clerk's Office, Cuero, Texas; Jeff Sheets, Dickinson County Heritage Center, Abilene, KS; Holly Rodriguez, Eagle Pass Public Library, Eagle Pass, TX; Mike Payan, Bill Lockhart and Wayne Daniel, El Paso Public Library, El Paso; Mary E. Marston, Ellsworth County, District Clerk-Magistrate Division, Ellsworth, KS; Tyra Denny and Donna Bettenbrock, Ellsworth County Museum, Ellsworth, KS; Ellsworth Historical Society, Sara Soukul; Sharon Nelson, Ellsworth, KS ISD; Suzanne Woodward and Susan Anderson, El Progreso Memorial Library; Uvalde, TX; Joyce Schaefer, Fairview Cemetery, Bastrop, TX; Rex Pederson, Firearms Engravers Guild of America; the staff of the Fort Hayes State University, Forsyth Library, Fort Hayes, KS; the staff. of the Fort Worth Public Library; Christine McNally, Galveston County District Clerk, Galveston, TX; Linda McElvain, Goodall City Library, Ogallala, NB; Sherri French, Grayson County District Clerk's Office, Sherman, TX; the staff of the Harold Washington Public Library, Chicago, IL; Peggy Fox, Director, Hill College History Center, Hillsboro, TX; Doug Weiskopf, Houston Public Library, Texas Room; Tom Shelton, Chris Floerke and Dolores B. Olivarez, Institute of Texan Cultures, San Antonio, TX; George Fox, Knights of Pythias of Texas, Fort Worth, TX; Teresa Coble, Kansas State Historical Society, Topeka; Angela Breaux, La Fourche Parish Public Library, Thibodaux, LA; Veneta McKinney, Lake County, Colorado Genealogy and History; Joseph Moreno, Laredo Public Library, Laredo, TX; Stephen E. Ostrow, Library of Congress, Prints and Photographs Division, Washington, D.C.; the staff of the

Cudahy Library, Loyola University, Chicago, IL; Victoria Daywood and the late Aurale "Lee" Huff, Caldwell County Genealogical and Historical Library, Luling, TX; the staff of the National Archives, Great Lakes Region, Chicago, IL; Richard Rattenbury, National Cowboy Hall of Fame and Western Heritage Center, Oklahoma City, OK; Chad Wall, Nebraska State Historical Society, Lincoln, NB; the staff of the Newberry Library, Chicago; Pamela D. Arceneaux, New Orleans Public Library, Williams Research Center; Samuel Huang, Northern Illinois University, Founders Memorial Library, DeKalb, Rare Books/Special Collections, the Albert Johannsen and Edward T. LeBlanc Collections of Nickel and Dime Novels; the staff of Northwestern University Library, Evanston, IL; Kay Ann Yaklin, Oakwood Cemetery, InterCare Corporation, Austin, TX; Jacquelyn Slater Reese and Breanna C. Boss, Western History Collections, University of Oklahoma Libraries; Rita Anzaldua, Refugio County District Clerk's Office, Refugio, TX; Melba Lanhart, Refugio County Public Library, Refugio, TX; Roy Marcot, Remington firearms experts and Editor, *RSA Journal* and Leon W. Wier Jr.; the staff of the Robbins Memorial Library, Ellsworth, KS; Anna B. Peebler, Rosenberg Library, Galveston, TX; Hope Brown, San Antonio City Cemetery Records Department; Marianna C. Jones, San Antonio Conservation Society; Judy Zipp, *San Antonio Express-News*, Microfilm Library; Jo Myler and T. Matthew DeWaelsche, Texana and Genealogy, San Antonio Public Library; Lisa Struthers, San Jacinto Museum of History Association, Herzstein Library; Ann Lowry, *Sherman Herald-Democrat,* Denison Branch Microfilm Library, Denison, TX; Susan Berry, Director, Silver City Museum, Silver City, NM; James W. Goodrich, Museum Director, State Historical Society of Missouri, Columbia; the staff of the State Historical Society of Wisconsin Library, Madison, WI; Jerry Thompson, Regents Professor of History at Texas A&M International University, Laredo, TX; Larry Fitzgerald, Texas

Department of Criminal Justice, Huntsville; Dan Agler, Retired Archivist at the Texas Ranger Hall of Fame and Museum, Waco; Donaly E. Brice, Research Specialist Retired, Texas State Archives and John Anderson, Photography Dept., Texas State Archives; Derek Bateman, Travis County District Clerk's Office, Austin, TX; Patricia Smith, Travis County Clerk's Office, Misdemeanor Records Division; Jim Sylvester, Travis County Sheriff's Office, Austin; Stagg of the Travis County Probate Court, Austin; Sally Grose, University of Texas at Arlington, Special Collections; Carlos Cortez, University of Texas at San Antonio; John Y. Simon, Ulysses S. Grant Association, Southern Illinois University, Morris Library, Carbondale, IL; Charles Walker, Pembina, ND; Eric Weider, collector of western memorabilia, Ventura County, CA; Rebecca Huffstutler, Witte Museum, San Antonio, TX.

Also, a last but very special thanks to all of the researchers and authors who followed Ben Thompson's trail before us.

PROLOGUE

Jack Harris mulled over his success in the Alamo City. As a well-known, popular purveyor of vice, Harris's establishment, the Vaudeville Theatre on San Antonio's Main Plaza, was not only the most notorious showplace in the city, it also housed a saloon and gambling den that was one of the very best places in the southwest for any pleasure-seeking man to visit when wanting a night on the town. The Vaudeville offered every conceivable game of dice or cards, a wide variety of cold beer and hard-hitting drinks, an entertaining stage show, and even the momentary companionship with a woman of easy virtue. For a price, Jack Harris provided his clientele anything and everything an adventurous man could possibly want.

For many Texans, gambling was a diversion, a brief form of entertainment to be enjoyed over a few drinks with friends. To the clever men who ran the games of chance at the Vaudeville, it was their livelihood. In the 1880s, a trio of tough sporting men dominated much of the Alamo City's night life. Jack Harris and his two partners, Billy Simms and Joe Foster, were the kings of San Antonio's gambling society and they were not afraid to fight any physical or political interference to remain in control.

Ben Thompson, the city marshal of Austin, was a notorious lifelong gambler and a feared gunfighter known throughout Texas as a "Killing Gentleman." In fact, many of his contemporaries considered him a sporting man without equal who was always protective of his rights as he saw them. On one occasion, Ben was in San Antonio and strolled into the Vaudeville. That night, Thompson lost heavily to Joe Foster, accused him of cheating, and retrieved his lost money with his revolver cocked in Foster's face. Later, he proclaimed loudly to his friends and acquaintances that the men running the Vaudeville robbed their customers with dishonest games and he planned to close the place down. When Harris read Thompson's assertions in the newspapers, Jack took it as an affront and a challenge he could not tolerate. He banned Thompson from his establishment and for many months, threatened Ben Thompson's life if he ever returned to the Vaudeville. Harris must have rubbed his handicapped, limp left hand and wondered when he would be afforded the opportunity to end his troubles with Thompson.

But Ben was a man with a history of doing as he pleased, and in early July of 1882, he again decided to visit San Antonio. Instead of doing the prudent thing and avoiding the Vaudeville, Thompson dropped in and ordered a drink. While standing at the Vaudeville's bar, he was reportedly belligerent, argumentative, and armed. Word that his enemy was drinking at his place of business and intended to cause trouble quickly reached Harris. He knew he would be no match with Thompson in a fight with revolvers but rather than defusing the situation by feigning the appearance of benevolence, Harris opted to increase the odds in his favor with a deadly equalizer: a shotgun.

Jack Harris entered his business, retrieved his double-barrel shotgun from his office, and hid behind an offset in the wall by the box office. This protected vantage point gave him a clear view of the entire first floor of the saloon and anyone walking through the building's front doors. Should Thompson step off from the boardwalk and reenter the theatre, he was ready.

Patrons of the Vaudeville witnessed Harris with his shotgun, and expecting trouble, ran from the barroom hollering out, "Jack has got his gun!" Thompson realized the situation in a glance and put his hand on his revolver. The two determined men began to yell angrily back and forth at each other. Harris was furious. He had built up the Vaudeville to be the most famous establishment of its kind in Texas and now this city marshal from Austin was going to try to close him up for good. Harris knew he had to kill Ben to preserve his popularity and influence within the city he so loved, and he so close to his adversary, how could he possibly miss with a firearm he knew how to handle so well? He pulled back the hammers with determination and hatefully raised his shotgun. It was time to put an end to Ben Thompson.

Chapter 1

THE LAST OF ENGLAND

"No, I shall take my chances with you."

—Buckskin Sam Hall to Ben Thompson

The English are meticulous record keepers, and the registrar noted the birth of Benjamin Thompson to the minute. He was born on "the second of November 1843 at 25 minutes to 5 A.M. at Knottingley." A little more than three years earlier, his father, twenty-four-year-old William Thompson wed, his mother, a saddler's daughter by the name of Mary Ann Baker at Saint Giles Church.[1]

Ben Thompson's birthplace was the river-port town of Knottingley located in central England in the county of Yorkshire. In 1820, the government passed legislation approving funds for the digging of a canal from Knottingley to the River Umber that empties into the North Sea. When officially opened in June of 1826, the Knottingley & Goole Canal caused land values to soar and local shipbuilding to boom. A period of prosperity ensued which lasted for decades. Several generations of the Thompson family would have dealings with the local maritime industry.

During the 1830s, Ben Thompson's grandparents, also named William and Mary, opened a small grocery at the top of Shepherd's

Bridge, which served the eastern edge of Knottingley. As they reached middle age, their hard work and prudent investments in trading vessels placed them among the town's upper middle class. William's union with his wife produced four sons. They named their first born William, and like so many other young Knottingley men coming of age, he decided to pursue a maritime career. Official records indicate, young William learned his trade properly from the bottom up, even though his father was a ship owner of considerable prominence. William stated on his marriage license that his profession was "waterman." This simple title covered all the common laborers in Knottingley who worked the barges, docks, and boats of the inland waterway of the river and canal system leading to the North Sea. With the experience and knowledge he acquired over years of hard work, he progressed past the barges and river boats. William the mariner earned that title and became a valued crewmember of seafaring ships.[2]

On August 28, 1845, less than two years after Ben's birth, Mary Ann delivered a second healthy son named William, though few would ever call him by his formal name. As he grew older he was occasionally called Bill, but most who knew him on America's southwest frontier simply called him Billy.[3] A few days after Billy's birth, their grandfather died on September 1, 1845, at the age of fifty. He was laid to rest in Saint Botolph's Church graveyard on Knottingley's Chapel Road. William the grocer's substantial estate was valued at slightly less than one thousand pounds. While his last will and testament clearly stated that his wife was to inherit the bulk of the estate, he also remembered his friends, business associates, and other family members. For his eldest son, William the mariner, he bequeathed a yearly annuity of twenty pounds, generous enough at that time to nearly support a family. This generosity came with two strong stipulations, indicating William the mariner's poor handling of money. The will stated that the payouts would be

A view of Aire Street in Knottingley, England. The house on the left is where Ben Thompson and younger brother Billy lived until the family migrated to the United States and Texas. *Courtesy the late C.P. Dearden.*

made quarterly and the clause specifically prevented William from assigning or anticipating the annuity. Even more importantly, the payouts would cease if William ever annoyed, troubled, or inconvenienced his mother. Even from the grave, it seems the father was determined to control his son's undesirable behavior.[4]

Like most seafarers of the time, William was a proud man and a hard drinker. The English mores of the nineteenth century, within sensible limits, certainly didn't frown too much on over-indulgence, and Knottingley's most famous and enduring pub, the Buck Inn, was only a short walk from his home on The Island on Aire Street. Subsequent evidence points to William the mariner having an ongoing drinking problem, because his all too frequent drinking bouts in Texas would earn him the sobriquet of "Drunken Thompson."[5] The lure of alcohol proved to be a problem that would also plague his sons Ben and Billy throughout their lives.

William honed his seafaring skills for at least five years. He first sailed the coast and then ventured out on open water. This experience qualified him to take the helm and pilot a vessel to France, Holland, or Spain. On December 31, 1846, thirty-year-old William Thompson was appointed the new master of the *William*, a single-mast sloop.[6] This ship was designed to fit the restricted size of Knottingley's canal and river navigation, but it had a cargo hold large enough to make a voyage profitable. A ship such as the *William* required a crew of only three or perhaps four men. The sailors of nineteenth century Knottingley demonstrated their courage every time they hoisted sail in one of these simple vessels to risk the harsh and unpredictable waters of the cold North Sea. When fully loaded, these small sloops would settle very low in the water, and survival in rough weather depended upon the ability of the hatch and hold covers to remain watertight.

Mary Ann gave birth to a healthy girl they named Mary Jane on March 3, 1848, and a third child joined the Thompson family. She would go on to live ninety-two years and become the matriarch of the extended Thompson family in Texas.[7]

Four years after the death of her husband, Ben and Billy Thompson's grandmother died on September 22, 1849, at the age of fifty-one. She was buried next to her husband in the Saint Botolph's Church cemetery. In January 1850, her estate was appraised at less than 450 pounds, and most likely was not completely paid out until the spring of 1851. By her declaration of "share and share alike," she split everything between William the mariner and his three younger brothers.[8]

The 1851 English Census reveals the Thompson family had moved to a new Knottingley neighborhood by the name of Little Marsh.[9] By this time, plans for a more dramatic and distant move may have been formulating. Mary Ann's older brother, William Baker, and his wife Matilda had long since immigrated to the

United States. They left from the English port city of Liverpool, and arrived in New York on August 1834. The Bakers remained in New York for at least three or four years, and two of the six Baker children were born there. By 1840, they headed west, ultimately settling in central Texas near the state capital. In fact, the Baker home was only one mile outside of Austin. Baker earned his living as a carpenter and one of the local newspapers described him as an "industrious, worthy citizen," and his wife Matilda, a "highly esteemed ... intelligent exemplary wife and mother."[10] Over the years, Mary Ann and her brother must have corresponded regularly. William Baker may have encouraged his sister and brother-in-law to seek a new life outside of England or, perhaps sadly and shockingly, the Thompson family decided to travel to Texas to aid their suddenly orphaned nieces and nephews.

Violence came to the Baker household at sunrise on July 11, 1851. A black man rode up to their home as five of the six Baker children were sitting down to their breakfast. The oldest child, eighteen-year-old John Baker, was not at home at the time. William Baker greeted the stranger and invited him to step down from his horse. After swinging out of the saddle, he began to ask Baker for directions when E. S. C. Robertson, a notable local citizen the *Texas State Gazette* identified with the title of Colonel, rode up to the Baker homestead. Suspecting the black man was a runaway slave, Colonel Robertson began to closely question him. When he was unable to adequately explain his actions or reasons for being there, Robertson and Baker tied him up and placed him in the house. Remounting his horse, Robertson rode off in search of the sheriff or one of his deputies.[11]

A few minutes later, Baker met the runaway at the door to his home. The black man had managed to cut himself free with the large butcher knife he still carried. The two men grappled in the doorway, and the powerful man stabbed Baker three times in the back. His wife Matilda rushed to his assistance. She was stabbed once in the heart. Her death was almost instantaneous, but her husband would suffer well into the next day before expiring. The black man raced to his nearby horse and fled.

The hysterical screams of the five children caught the attention of their neighbors, and a large number of men hastily found weapons and rode off in pursuit of the killer. Medical help was summoned, but William Baker's condition was deemed hopeless and he died in agony early that Saturday morning.[12] Roughly one mile from the Baker residence, the posse discovered the fugitive's abandoned horse and his baggage hidden in a thicket. The county sheriff offered a reward of $200 for the return of the fleeing killer to Austin.[13]

The runaway slave eluded capture for fifteen days. On the twenty-sixth of July, he was spotted and apprehended near Austin. A jury of twelve slaveholders tried the man and sentenced him to death. The verdict was carried out on the spot before a large group of spectators, who witnessed what was, in effect, a lynching.[14]

One year later in Liverpool, the Thompson family stepped aboard the steamship *Granada.* It was bound for New Orleans and on July 16, 1852, it arrived at the great southern port city. The names of William and Mary Thompson appear on the ship's manifest along with their three children, eight-year-old Benjamin, six-year-old Billy and four-year-old Mary Jane.[15] After disembarking they traveled from New Orleans to Galveston, Texas, on their way to their new home in Austin.

America's Deep South was a strange place to the Thompson children. Having never seen a black person before, the three youngsters looked upon the slaves working on the wharf with both wonder and fear. Hiding behind her mother's skirt, little three-year-old Mary Jane pointed at the first black person she saw and in a tiny whisper, thinking he might be Satan himself, asked if he was "the

Old Bad Man [?]" Her mother replied "that God had made them so, and that she must be as kind and polite to them as to anyone."[16]

The Thompsons did not linger in Galveston. After loading their possessions into a horse-drawn carriage, they moved north through Houston where they ate dinner at a boarding house. Eager to have some of the interesting new cake she spied, little Mary Jane pestered her mother for a slice. Her eagerness soured with her first bite, and for more than eighty years she would recall the bitter disappointment of her initial taste of Texas cornbread.[17] Continuing their journey north, the family traveled through the fledging community of Bastrop and soon crossed the Colorado River. They found themselves standing at the south end of Austin, gazing up a long flat hill at what was to be their new home. Apparently, the flavor of cornbread made a bigger impression on Mary Jane than her first view of Texas's capital city. As her parents stared at the humble looking town, they realized in more than miles, just how far they had come from their former home in England.

As the Thompson family went up Congress Avenue, the town's main thoroughfare, they could surely savor the smell of fresh-cut lumber and hear the many carpenters pounding nails in the dozens of new residences and business establishments being constructed. The early years of the 1850s marked the beginning of a building boom in Austin that lasted until the start of the Civil War. By the middle of the decade, the town boasted a population of more than 3,500 people. Once settled, the Thompson family became members of the congregation of St. David's Episcopal Church located at the corner of Bois d'Arc (present day 7th Street) and San Jacinto. Bishop Alexander Gregg, one of Austin's leading citizens and a significant slave-owner, was the prelate.[18]

Following the tragic loss of their parents, sympathetic neighbors cared for the orphaned Baker children. Afterwards, William and Mary Ann Thompson helped their nieces and nephews, and as

Once in Texas, Austin became Ben Thompson's "home town." This image of Congress Avenue dates from the early 1860s when Thompson was a young man. Note the impressive Sampson and Henricks dry goods store where Ben's father worked as a book-keeper. Note also the state capitol building at the far north end of Congress Avenue. *Courtesy the Austin History Center. Image # C00 393.*

the years passed, the Baker children managed to stay together and remained a close family. Throughout their lives, the Bakers continued a friendship with their first cousins, the Thompson children. Ann, the eldest Baker daughter, married William C. Reager, age thirty-two, a Travis County farmer. In addition to marrying Ann, Mr. Reager on May 1, 1855, officially agreed to become the legal guardian of the younger Baker children.[19]

To support his family, William Thompson turned to what he knew best: the water. As a commercial fisherman, he worked the Colorado River. The brothers joined their father in supporting the family. Ben picked up a job driving a water cart on the streets of Austin and with younger brother Billy's help, sold their father's catch to Austin's hotels, restaurants, and boarding houses.

Later, the elder William worked as an accountant at Sampson and Henricks, a large dry goods store located in the center of town on the southwest corner of Bois d'Arc and Congress Avenue.[20]

On March 21, 1858, Mary Ann Thompson gave birth to her fourth and final child. The baby was a girl and they named her Frances but everyone would call her "Fanny." Like her older sister Mary Jane, she was destined to live a long, exemplary life. In Fanny's case, she lived beyond the halfway mark of the twentieth century.

As a youth, Ben Thompson was considered a bright, handsome boy with a future full of promise. He caught the attention of a prominent Austin attorney, and a veteran of the War with Mexico, Colonel John A. Green.[21] Colonel Green sent Ben to a formal school for one or two years at his own expense. Billy also enjoyed additional schooling through the support of Green.[22] However, even with Colonel Green's financial assistance, the Thompson brothers enjoyed a limited formal education. Besides selling fish and working the water cart as an adolescent, Ben became a printer's devil for various newspapers in Austin, including John S. "Rip" Ford's *State Times*. As a grown man, he often spoke of the time he spent pursuing that trade during the 1850s. Ben seemed to have enjoyed being a printer. In his later years he still took pride in his proficiency to set type, and throughout his life he often socialized with the printers he apprenticed and worked with as a youngster.[23] Not surprisingly, as he came of age, Billy followed his older brother into the printing profession.[24]

As a young boy Ben Thompson "felt his first great hate against the brutal oppressors of poor men." One cold night Ben left his home in search of his father and soon found him lying in the street severely injured "with his scalp almost torn from his head by the club of a brutal policeman" who for an unknown reason, left William Thompson bleeding on the ground.[25]

John Salmon "Rip" Ford (1815-1897). As a young man he edited the *Austin State Times* and hired a much younger Ben Thompson as a type setter. Ford's life proved to be as adventurous as Thompson's: he served in the House of the Ninth Congress, edited various newspapers, served in the Texas army as a spy in the Mexican War, fought Indians on the frontier, served in the Texas Senate, fought Cortina on the Mexican border, and led Confederate troops at the last battle of the Civil War in May, 1865. He also was a charter member of the Texas State Historical Association. He died in San Antonio on November 3, 1897.

Courtesy the Robert G. McCubbin Collection.

Later it was stated that the Thompson brothers grew up like most boys on the frontier, without strict guardianship on the father's side. As an adolescent, Ben spent most of his free time hunting for fun. He was known to be a fighter. Even in his early teens, Ben showed his ability as a tactician by forcing his opponent to become the aggressor and in the end, beating the fight out of his opponent. William the mariner was noted for his courage and, soon, so was Ben. Initially, he used his fists like his father, but like many other Texans, young Ben soon learned how to handle firearms and he chose to become a shootist. It was a few weeks before his fifteenth birthday when the punching stopped and the shooting began.[26]

Many Old West gunfighters had a propensity to start their shooting careers while in their early teens and Ben Thompson was no exception.[27] Stories of his violent youth abound and it is difficult to determine exactly when he began to settle his disputes with a firearm.[28] However, one teenage shooting scrape is verifiable by both a contemporary newspaper article and court documents. The Austin *Southern Intelligencer* reported a shooting involving fourteen-year-old Ben Thompson in its Wednesday, October 13, 1858, issue. The short account was headlined simply as "Shooting." The editor reported that on Saturday evening Ben Thompson and another boy, James Smith, quarreled. Smith called Thompson hard names and in response, Thompson raised his shotgun and pulled the trigger. The weapon was loaded with small shot, and the entire charge hit Smith's back, except for two pellets that struck the boy's head. Thompson was apprehended and placed before Justice E. F. Calhoun, who questioned him and then discharged the youngster without punishment. These were the facts of the matter. The reporter continued, expressing his dismay at society's acceptance of young people going about Austin so well-armed. "It is a common thing here to see boys from ten to fourteen years of age, carrying about their persons, Bowie knives and pistols. We trust this will be a warning to every parent, and that such practices, so pernicious in their tendencies, may be checked in season."

It was later said that Ben shot "Smith, a bully who attempted to lord it over [him]."[29] Longtime Austin attorney and close friend of Thompson, William M. Walton, provided an explanation of the incident in his 1884 biography of Thompson claiming Ben was taunted about his shooting ability by the other boy, who "stooped down on his all-fours" offering his rear end as an obvious target and mockingly invited Ben to "blaze away." The young man soon found his backside "peppered in fine style," and he was painfully but not seriously hurt.[30]

Upset by Justice Calhoun's decision to release Thompson unpunished, citizens complained about the lenient treatment. They demanded he make an example of Ben. He was again taken into custody, and this time, a hearing by Justice Graves allowed witnesses to testify and all of the facts to be presented. Judge Graves ordered Thompson to appear at the fall term of the District Court to have the incident reviewed by a grand jury. He was released when $300 was furnished as a security bond.[31]

On Monday, December 6, 1858, the Travis County grand jury convened, and soon young Ben found himself standing before the hard-eyed stares of presiding Judge Alexander Watkins Terrell, District Attorney A.D. McGinnis and the seventeen men who comprised the grand jury. The court's docket proved light and Thompson was indicted to answer to the serious charge of assault with the intent to kill. The case was called to trial about a month later, during the second week of January. A young lawyer, R. T. Browning, was appointed by the court to act as the council for the defendant.[32]

Austin banker James H. Raymond and Doctor C.G. Keenan, one of the physicians who treated the wounded boy, gave testimony. Drawn by yelling, Raymond found Smith by Waller Creek near where east Pecan Street (6th Street) intersects at Sabine Street. He helped the bleeding boy into a wagon that took him to the home of William H. Johnson, where Smith lived. Dr. Keenan and a second physician named Dr. Herndon, examined and treated the boy who had been struck with mixed shot varying in size from squirrel to slightly larger duck size. Smith's back, arms, and head were hit, though most of the wounds were superficial. However, two or three pellets entered so deeply the two doctors declined to make any attempt to remove them.[33]

Browning succeeded in convincing the jury there had been no intent to kill, so Ben Thompson was found guilty of the lesser crime of aggravated assault.[34] The jury fined him $100, and sentenced him to sixty days in the county jail. Because of the Thompson family's inability to pay the fine, the court extended the time to be served until April 14. Shortly after finishing his original sixty-day sentence, a group of almost seventy men, including a number of Austin's most substantial and influential citizens, placed their signed petition before Gov. Hardin R. Runnels requesting Ben Thompson be released, and the remainder of the fine forgiven. The petitioners also included all twelve of the jurors who convicted Ben.[35]

The petition pleaded its case on multiple points. "Thompson is a mere youth of the age of 16 years," and his health has been "impaired by confinement," what with the warm weather coming his further "imprisonment there becomes almost insufferable." It was apparent to all that "the dungeon of Travis County is a most filthy, vile & loathsome cell," and that "further incarceration may be dangerous to him." The signers agreed the boy had been punished enough, since he "has already stayed in jail the full sixty-days & more." The petition added that "his parents are poor indeed," and indicated he shouldn't be kept in jail simply because of their inability to pay the fine. In summation, it was asserted "that the ends of justice have already been satisfied," and asked "may your

Excellency ... remit the balance of his sentence & allow him to be released." R. T. Browning penned above his signature, the "punishment has exerted all the beneficial influence it can."[36]

On March 12, 1859, Governor Runnels agreed and Ben Thompson received the first of the two executive pardons he would receive during his career. Governor Runnels ordered Thompson be released from custody and the fine remitted.[37]

Years later, the *Statesman* correctly touched on another lifelong Thompson trait, his skill at gambling, which was second only to his ability in handling firearms. The *Statesman* recalled how "he had learned to play cards before this, and while in jail he gambled with a prisoner who had a lot of jewelry, and won it all."[38]

Once Ben was released, the Walton biography presents to his readers an unsubstantiated story depicting young Ben Thompson as a defender of the weak and misfortunate. Walton maintained Thompson was one of the first in the saddle after an Indian raiding party abducted five children on the outskirts of Austin. Hard riding put the pursuers ahead of the fleeing Indians, and "unable to restrain himself, Thompson fired his rifle shooting the leading horseman through the heart; and drawing his pistol, fought with wild reckless desperation not surpassed." Four of the five children were saved and Walton concluded his story, "still but a boy, from this day, Thompson not only regarded himself as a man, but was so regarded by the people among whom he lived."[39]

Ben returned to his trade as a printer[40] and he soon accepted the invitation of Samuel Webster Slater, a forty-seven-year-old bookbinder who was then operating his business in Austin, to travel to New Orleans and continue working as his apprentice. Many believed Slater's influence over the boy became so profound that Ben "was partly raised by Mr. Slater." The two men would become very close and remain so until Slater's death more than twenty years later.[41] Ben was not long in New Orleans before he again resorted to violence. Without Slater's permission a man came into the print shop and began to load up and take away some items. Thompson ordered the man to stop what he was doing. The intruder chose to ignore the order and continued to remove items, which Thompson naturally considered theft. Ben pulled a pistol and fired one round, inflicting a superficial wound. While the wounded man recovered, Ben had to stand trial again. When the facts of the case were presented Thompson was exonerated of committing any crime and acquitted of all charges.[42]

In discussing his early career as a newspaper type setter, Ben Thompson commented that he worked for the *True Delta,* one of the more prominent dailies published in New Orleans at that time. The *True Delta* also published a popular California edition for the seafaring passengers bound for the gold fields that was sold to news-starved Californians for whatever the market would bear. This may have sparked Ben Thompson's desire to travel beyond New Orleans to see the Pacific Slope. For several months he saved his wages and then paid for steerage passage to San Francisco. Through a misunderstanding, he missed his steamship. Upset, he boarded a public conveyance for the return trip back to his place of employment. Already on board the transport was a group of upper class young Frenchmen, and among them was one, Emil de Tour, who had consumed too much wine. Also aboard was a lone young woman who caught de Tour's eye. He chose to sit down by her and press his presence upon the lady to the point of offending her. The girl resented his advances and quietly asked him to leave. Instead, de Tour took her hand and tried to force a kiss. She again rejected his advances, and this time called out for help. Ben rose from his seat and approached the lady. Emil de Tour demanded Ben remain where he was and attend to his own business. According to Walton, Ben said, "Sir, I cannot see a lady call for help and not respond." The Frenchman scoffed and declared, "You American puppy, get away from here." Thompson stepped closer and demanded of the Frenchman, "Leave the girl. I will assume to protect her." Angry, de Tour lashed out and struck Ben in the face. Instantly, Thompson drove a small knife into the Frenchman's side in return. Blood gushed from the stab wound and in a flash, the wild, good humor ended and de Tour's friends gathered about him. Secreted weapons were drawn, and Ben Thompson was forced to jump from the bus to escape.[43]

Comparable to many other westerners of his time, Ben Thompson's life is steeped in legend where no contemporary documentation exists to corroborate adventures later attributed to him. Similar to his heroism during the unsubstantiated Indian raid, Walton expanded Thompson's protection of an unnamed American girl to include a fatal duel with the offending Frenchman. Walton described how, after a few days, the wounded Frenchman recovered and began a search for the young American who had stabbed him. It wasn't long before he found Thompson and demanded satisfaction. Dueling was not restricted to the wealthy, and it was common for lower class whites and free blacks to settle their differences at popular dueling sites. Thousands of affairs of honor were fought under the "Dueling Oaks" of Allard Plantation, or behind the St. Louis Cathedral in Pere Antoine's gardens. The practice of settling animosities on the field of honor was still quite prevalent during the decade of the 1850s. This is because no single New Orleans newspaper opposed the practice of dueling. Instead the press often published the particulars of upcoming meetings between the socially prominent and famous residents. It was rare to have government officials intervene to prevent a duel because the affair rarely resulted in a fatality. Traditional dueling pistols were notoriously inaccurate and in swordplay the drawing of a little blood usually satisfied everyone's honor.

As the challenged party, Ben called for revolvers at ten paces and insisted that the shooting would continue until one of the combatants fell from his wounds. Calling Thompson's terms "barbarous," de Tour wanted to use long swords but stated short swords would also be acceptable and hinted that no serious wounds would be inflicted. Not fooled by de Tour, and unable to properly wield a sword, Thompson declined the proposal and offered yet another alternative. Per Walton, Ben stated, "I will fight on the terms [I] already named, or, if you prefer, we will go into a dark room with daggers [and] fight until one or the other falls. If dead, all right, if not dead, the victor can spare life if he wishes. Select one of the modes, accept and fight, or admit yourself a coward."

De Tour was furious, but he accepted Thompson's alternative, and they agreed to meet at a "room … in an out of the way locality." Thompson's seconds were a handful of printer boys, while many friends surrounded de Tour. One of Thompson's friends took in the situation and wisely demanded they all retire to a distance, leaving the two duelists alone to enter the room. The Frenchman stepped in first, but Ben was so close to him that no advantage could be taken. They parted and circled in the darkened room in opposite directions, Ben going to the left and de Tour to the right.

"Are you ready?" asked Ben. The Frenchman instantly struck at Thompson's voice, however Ben changed his position as he spoke so that de Tour's sudden knife thrust missed and he lost his balance. Thompson immediately lunged forward, and drove his knife into the Frenchman inflicting a fatal wound. Stepping out of the room, Ben went to a prearranged place to meet his friends.

The Frenchman was dead, and his friends sought revenge while the New Orleans police sought to arrest Thompson. Ben, now a fugitive, fled his usual haunts and found his way to the Sicilian quarter of the city. He knew he must return to Texas to be truly safe. Ben took advantage of a failure in vigilance by the police to make a night crossing of the Mississippi River to Algiers, a notorious haven for criminals and river pirates which even the police feared to venture. There he obtained a mule, and slowly rode back to Texas.[44]

At home in Austin, Ben rejoined the printing profession, now working for Norton's *Southern Intelligencer.* By this time, his typesetting skills allowed him to "receive fair wages. [However] ... events in Texas ... were of too exciting a nature for a man of his temperament to follow so peaceful an occupation."[45] Throughout most of 1859 and 1860 the frontier of Texas was aflame in a bloody border war with the Comanche tribes.

The explosive influx of predominately German immigrants meant a large portion of the southern Comanche lands, the so-called Comancheria, was being settled. With the Comanche horse herds shrinking and their valuable animal trade dissolving, the tribe's only option lay in fighting this "human surge" of settlers they knew "they could neither stop nor escape." To protect all they had, the Comanche began a "deadly raiding war."[46] Unsurpassed masters of horsemanship, they could easily strike any section of the frontier and leave burning homesteads and death behind them.

Frustrated by Governor Runnels's inability to end these seemingly endless attacks, Texans again turned to Sam Houston to lead them. Houston delivered only one campaign speech, but by running as an Independent candidate and correctly reading the sentiments of the voters, he easily defeated Runnels. On December 21, 1859, for the first and only time, Houston became governor of the State of Texas.[47]

In his inaugural address, Houston spoke of the use of treaties and annuities to help prevent further Indian depredations. To insure that his diplomacy would be effective, and to help quell the cry of his constituency to exterminate the Comanches, Houston called for a strong force of mounted rangers to be recruited. Three new Ranger commands were immediately formed. On January 4, 1860, veteran Indian fighter Edward Burleson Jr. took command of one and called for volunteers to fill his company.[48] Leaving the printing trade behind forever, Ben quit the *Intelligencer* and became one of Captain Burleson's new recruits.[49]

Captain Burleson received orders to patrol along the Nueces River in the south. Finding the region quiet, he moved his battalion nearly two hundred miles straight north. Out for forty days, he decided to rest his men and their horses, and established a temporary camp between the North Fork of the Concho and the Red Fork of the Colorado where he found good water and grass. Game was abundant, and the men feasted on buffalo, deer, elk and turkey. Duty was light, and no one suspected the presence of Indians. Disobeying standing orders that banned gambling, Thompson often pulled out his *monte* cards and spent as much time as possible honing his card playing skills. The men rested for almost ten days before Burleson restarted the patrol. On the third day, after breaking camp, he called Ben to his side, and instructed him to choose another man and scout well out from the column. Thompson selected a twenty-one-year-old from Massachusetts by the name of Samuel Stone Hall, who, five years before, had wandered into Texas. Weighing in at one hundred and twenty-five pounds with a lean, wiry build, Hall was considered handsome and was described as having good features and dark eyes. Although he usually had a relaxed, easygoing manner, he proved to be fearless in times of danger. He was a dead shot with a rifle, a hard rider, and when liquor was available, he was an equally hard drinker. Fellow Rangers christened him "Buckskin Sam" because of his favorite clothes, and the nickname stuck to him thereafter.[50] Hall would later go on to be a celebrated author and dime novelist featuring many noted Texans and other frontiersmen as characters in his adventure stories. In several of his novels, he included the Thompson brothers as subordinate characters.

In the preface of his Thompson biography, Walton explained how Ben "consented to give a fair, candid and truthful account of some of the main incidents of his experience." Among other adventuresome episodes, Ben detailed a fast-paced account of his afternoon scout with Buckskin Sam Hall.[51]

Thompson recalled how Hall had an excellent pony, "about equal to the one I rode, Texas raised, very hardy, and fleet for his breed." The two rangers were well armed, each having a Henry repeating rifle and a pair of six-shooters. After venturing for about two miles, they decided to start riding to the top of various hills to help in surveying the countryside. Seeing nothing of concern, Ben recorded how he alone put spurs to his horse and galloped to the crest of the last hill, where "there opened to my sight a scene as awful as a man may wish to see. Up the side of the hill, right towards me ... came thousands and thousands of buffalo, with a low muttering thunder, as they rushed madly along, but in the midst of the herd or rather in the middle of a hundred herds concentrated, there were between eighty to a hundred Comanche, and they had seen me." The Comanche wanted Ben's horse and guns, so they left the herd and began to chase the lone white man. Thompson fled towards his companion but unfortunately a buffalo ran against his mount and injured the horse. Reaching the waiting Hall, the two rangers instantly gave full rein to their horses.

Now Thompson and Hall were in a race for their lives, a race that required all their skills on horseback. Ben looked back and poetically explained,

> Unfortunately, just at this moment, a buffalo ran against my horse and seriously injured him, this of course greatly lessened my chance of escape, but here they come; their long, black hair floating in the wind, their eagle feather ornaments waving from side to side as they swayed their persons this way and that on their rapidly moving horses, their faces hideously disfigured with black and red war paint, with

> lances held in hand, and bows and quivers full of arrows slung over their shoulder. These things were seen at a glance ... The picture was grand, fearful ... [and] awful. Could it have been thrown truthfully, livingly ... [painted] on canvass by Rembrant [*sic*], it would be the wonder of the world, ... [but] the original can belong to no place but hell itself.

Although gravely hurt, Thompson's mount bore himself bravely as Buckskin Sam rode beside his companion. Constantly looking over his shoulder as they fled, Ben saw how the band of Comanche was coming closer and closer. There were four or five Indians some yards in advance of the others and they became the first targets of Ben and Sam's Henry rifles. Deciding to dismount and halt for a moment to make their rifle shots count, they fired into their pursuers slowing them up. The tactic proved effective and they repeated it several more times as they continued their flight across the prairie. By now a few of the marauders were within arrow shot distance. Racing up a long grade, rising into a considerable hill, Ben could feel his horse growing weaker. Yelling out, Ben advised Hall to ride on. Instead, Hall slowed his horse, and firmly replied, "No, I shall take my chances with you."

Ben's horse was exhausted, and fell. Fortunately, as the horse collapsed a volley of arrows passed over Thompson's head. Sam leaped from his mount and rushed to Thompson, who having taken shelter behind his prostrate horse, was already firing his rifle. "We fired as rapidly as we could, but it was all over with us, so far as it depended on what we could do; but we had reached safety without knowing it. Before the Indians reached us Captain Burleson came charging over the crest of the hill, his men yelling as only Texas Rangers can yell."

With Burleson's men charging toward them, the Comanche veered off to make their escape. Sam was injured in an arm and a leg but the wounds were slight. However, Ben had looked back so often and so long during the chase that his neck became twisted and he found himself suffering from a severe strain, so much so it was two months before he would turn his head without having to turn his entire body at the same time. Due to this condition, Ben was shortly relieved from further duty. Captain Burleson's company, including Buckskin Sam was officially released from service on September 7, 1860.[52]

Risking everything when he could have ridden on, Buckskin Sam's loyalty must have made an indelible impression on young Ben Thompson. For the remainder of his life Ben would repeatedly demonstrate that same unrelenting loyalty to his friends, which often led him into an enormous amount of trouble.

On August 28, Billy Thompson celebrated his fifteenth birthday. As yet, he had not had any adventures as memorable or dangerous as his older brother. Both he and his twelve-year-old sister Mary Jane had been attending school. By now, the Thompson family had been in Texas for almost a decade and it is evident they had not prospered. In fact, the total value of their possessions in 1860 was a mere $50.[53] It appears that William Thompson's efforts as a commercial fisherman and accountant only kept him in drinking money because, as one newspaper reported, he "spent much or perhaps the greatest part of his time in ebriety [*sic*]."[54] This made Austin the second boomtown in which he failed to become successful. To help make ends meet, the Thompson family took in boarders. Travis county earmarked money to pay families who housed the poor and unfortunate, and records indicate that, for many years, a Mary Ann Thompson received county funds for housing indigents.[55]

While his eldest son was out of Austin, William Thompson had finally had enough of Texas, and decided to return to the sea. A combination of reasons may have influenced him to resume his maritime career. Descendants claim he had business in England and his mother's will states that remaining monies from a trust fund be split equally between the four sons when Samuel, the youngest, reached twenty-one years in 1859.[56] Perhaps William wanted to visit Knottingley again and see his younger brothers or maybe he simply longed for the ocean. Perhaps he saw it as his last hope for a clean start. In her later years, his daughter Mary Jane explained that her "father returned to England to attend to his interest in some property. He was induced to buy a ship, and after making several trips on it as Captain, between Liverpool and Pensacola, Florida, he was seized with that terrible scourge yellow fever, died and was buried at sea."[57] Only one fact is known for certain concerning the fate of William the mariner. He went off to sea and never returned to his family in Texas.

On Ben Thompson's return to Austin, he found his father gone making him the main supporter of his mother, brother and sisters. Having already decided he was through working as a printer, Ben investigated another well-established, but much more dangerous profession in Austin. At first, he merely gambled in a limited way but he was encouraged by winning small amounts, and he decided to "cease operat[ing] from the outside, and took his place as a banker … of games, and a dealer when monte was played." Thompson possessed many of the qualities a man needed to follow the vocation of a professional gambler. He "never [drank] when on duty as a lookout" and "was of equable temper, good humor, afraid of nothing and nobody, patient, accommodating and yet cautious" His initial success encouraged Thompson, and although he often warned others not to become involved with gambling, with the notable exception of one brief period, he remained a professional gambler and a sporting man for the remainder of his life. Biographer Walton stated "that the wild, dangerous, enchanting, bitter, adventurous, blissful, damned career of a gambler was his lot."[58]

Chapter 2

THE CIVIL WAR YEARS

"Mr. Ben, You Can't Close This Game."

—Confederate Lt. Martino Gonzales to Ben Thompson

Abraham Lincoln reached Washington on February 23, 1861, with only nine short days to prepare for the presidency. On the day he arrived in Washington, Texas voters went to their polling places and officially ratified an ordinance of secession by an overwhelming majority, with 46,129 voting in favor of the ordinance and 14,697 voting against it.

During the first week of February, prior to the vote, the state's Committee of Public Safety appointed the famous Indian fighter and former mayor of Austin, John S. "Rip" Ford, a colonel of Texas State Troops. The committee ordered him to recruit and lead an expedition to the mouth of the Rio Grande where he was to demand the surrender of Fort Brown. However, events moved faster than Colonel Ford could. On the morning of February 16, the ailing seventy-year-old Brigadier General David Twiggs, commander of the Department of Texas, arrived at San Antonio's Main Plaza to confer with a group of Texas commissioners about the Federal government's stores and military installations under his control. What he found was almost one thousand Texas State Troops surrounding him. Their officers demanded that he hand over the arsenal housed in the Alamo along with all other Federal government property in Texas. At first, he was visibly shaken and refused to comply. However, by noon that day, General Twiggs signed an agreement, which surrendered every military post and Federal soldier in the state.

As a southern sympathizer, the elderly Twiggs did not have the fortitude, or the desire, to start a civil war in Texas by fighting in the streets of San Antonio. In return for his cooperation, his troops, scattered in small detachments throughout Texas, would be allowed to leave the state unmolested taking with them only the small arms, clothing, and camp equipment they could carry. Texas had rebelled and was firmly in the hands of the fledging Confederacy before the first cannon fuse was lit at the far-off Fort Sumter.

In late March, Colonel Ford and his troops entered into Fort Brown unopposed. The military district under Ford's command stretched more than one thousand miles upriver from the Gulf of Mexico to the small town of El Paso. Remaining on the lower Rio Grande, Colonel Ford continued to enlist men into his regiment. He sent Lieutenant Colonel John Robert Baylor to protect the frontier at the upper portion of the river from Indians, Mexican partisans, and the Union soldiers stationed in New Mexico territory. Baylor detested Indians, Yankees, and any other man who disagreed with him. With seven companies of cavalry, the combative Baylor pushed north up the river valley recruiting as many Texans into his battalion as he could find.

Days after the fall of Fort Sumter, passengers arriving by ship through the port of Galveston, Texas carried word of this grave rift between the North and South. However, it would not be until Saturday, June 15, that an Austin newspaper would report the surrender of Sumter to its readers.[1] The very next day, Ben Thompson enlisted in his former employer's command, and became a member of Colonel Ford's Second Regiment Texas Cavalry. He signed on for a twelve-month tour of duty, and found himself assigned to Baylor's upriver expedition.[2] Baylor was garrisoning the now abandoned army posts of sparsely populated West Texas, establishing a defensive perimeter by protecting the overland route between Fort Clark and Fort Bliss before preparing for a Confederate invasion of New Mexico Territory.

Baylor's battalion arrived at Fort Clark in Kinney County during the last week of June. Located twenty miles northeast of the Rio Grande, Fort Clark was built in 1852 to protect travelers using the vulnerable lower government road between San Antonio and El Paso. Surveyed and laid out by military engineers, the route was formerly part of an old Comanche raiding trail until the Federal Army and Rip Ford's Rangers drove them from the area. The fort was strategically placed near spring-fed Las Moras Creek, which provided a source of fresh water year-round. Company H, commanded by Captain H. A. Hamner, a close friend of Baylor and his former partner in publishing a newspaper they named the *White Man,* was left behind to garrison the post. With few Indians in the area, the Mexicans quiet and the closest Yankees in New Mexico, Captain Hamner's company found itself with very little to do.

Later newspaper accounts detail the legendary story of how Thompson, while stationed at Fort Clark, became involved in a violent scrape, shooting and wounding (and some say killing) both a commissary sergeant named Vance and a Lieutenant Hughes of H company. It is a classic example of how a very minor incident is exaggerated through its retelling.

Walton picked up where the inaccurate newspaper accounts left off by adding many details and explaining how the argument began over Thompson's need for candles so he could deal *monte* late at night. Supposedly heated words were exchanged between Sergeant Billy Vance and Thompson when Ben supposedly helped himself to an over-issue of candles from Vance's commissary mess. Both men drew their pistols and fired simultaneously. Thompson's bullet struck and knocked down his adversary. A nearby officer identified by Walton as Second Lieutenant Haigler [*sic*],[3] drew his sword and began to swing it with the intention of cutting Thompson down. Walton described Thompson as having unbelievable quickness, maintaining he "fenced with his pistol" warding off the saber blows. Seeing the blood lust in the officer's eyes, "quick as thought [Ben] presented his pistol, fired, striking the officer in the neck, who fell, and was for the time believed to be dead." Captain Hamner then arrived on the scene, and Thompson promptly surrendered to him handing over his still smoking pistol. Again, according to Walton, Ben Thompson "was never tried for shooting the sergeant and killing his lieutenant." The incident as he described did not occur.[4] Billy Vance, the eighteen-year old sergeant who was the center of this scrape, provided his version which has the simplicity of truth to it.

Sergeant Vance later wrote, "The difficulty between Ben Thompson and myself grew out of a piece of meat, which he attempted to appropriate." A few words were exchanged between the two, then Ben went for his sidearm. Being in front of Vance and within reach allowed the sergeant to catch hold of Ben's pistol in time for him to turn the muzzle. The pistol went off; luckily for Vance the pistol ball passed over his hip and made a harmless hole in the coat he was wearing. The ball then found its way into a bystander named Nathan Browner. Ben then attempted to fire a second shot, and Vance explained, "I slapped my hand on the barrel so that when he pulled the trigger the hammer fell on my hand just between my thumb and forefinger. I wrenched the pistol out of his hand and handed it to one of the boys standing by." Ben continued the struggle by drawing his knife; however, Vance took that away, too.

"The whole thing was done in less time than it has taken me to write thus far." Vance made it clear that "Capt. Hanner [*sic*] was not on the ground; there was no Lieut. Hughes belonging to the company; I never drew my pistol, nor attempted to do so; there was but the one shot fired." With the help of one other soldier, Vance took Thompson off to the guard-house.

Vance concluded his account with, "Ben at the time was but a beardless boy, and, while he was about a year younger than me, I was about one-third larger, and furthermore, up to that moment, I never knew that Ben entertained any animosity toward me. I merely regarded him as [being] in one of his reckless, desperate moods, into which he was sometimes thrown by adverse circumstances ... Ben and I got friendly again... and were after good friends."[5]

Ben Thompson was arrested and charged with drawing "his pistol and did deliberately aim and fire at the said sergeant Vance thereby endangering the life of the sergeant and wounding at the same time Corporal Browner of Company H." The shooting scrape occurred "on or about the 31st day of December 1861." The corporal's wound was not a dangerous one and he soon recovered.[6] Thompson's punishment was incarceration until April 1862, in the military stockade at Camp Hudson in Val Verde County.[7]

In the spring of 1862, the war in the Southwest turned against the Confederacy. Baylor's Battalion, and other regiments, was driven out of New Mexico Territory. That summer, a small detachment of Union soldiers reached as far east as Fort Clark and fought a bloody little skirmish with the nearby retreating Confederates. Content to have driven the Texans away, the Yankees stopped. Ben Thompson was not involved in this fighting. His company was further east on garrison duty. The Union high command rightfully viewed Texas as too vast and uninviting to invade from the west. On June 20, at the little town of Edinburg located in the lower Rio Grande valley about fifty miles west of the Gulf, Ben re-enlisted in the same regiment. This time, his term of enlistment was two years and Thompson was promoted to the rank of sergeant. However, the promotion was short-lived. It wasn't long before he was demoted to private for being absent without leave.[8]

The disastrous Southwest campaign had taken its toll on the Second Texas Cavalry and the outfit had to be reorganized. Company I became Ben Thompson's new unit.[9] The interior of Texas was beyond the reach of the Union armies, but the 625-mile-long Gulf Coast was exposed to Federal naval power. Galveston was the principal port of Texas, and the occupation of this city would give the United States navy an excellent harbor and dry dock area to overhaul and refit vessels of its blockading squadron. On October 4, a flotilla crossed the bar and entered Galveston's harbor. The Confederate battery protecting the Island City lacked the heavy cannon necessary to drive the Federal fleet away, but by the same token, the lack of a sufficient infantry force prevented the Union forces from properly occupying the town. It was clear to everyone that the situation had settled into a stalemate.

Less than a week after the Federal fleet entered Galveston Bay the new commander of the District of Texas, Major General "Prince John" Magruder, arrived from Virginia. He was surprised to find the Confederate army scattered throughout the state, and was upset that no one had thought to assemble the hard-hitting, long-range artillery necessary to bombard the Federal fleet. For these reasons he immediately issued orders to concentrate both heavy artillery and men in Galveston. The Second Texas Cavalry was one of the units ordered to march there.

During its move, Thompson's regiment made a halt outside San Antonio. To prevent the men from visiting the city's saloons and gambling halls a strict guard was placed upon them. Not to be deterred from having a drink or two, the men chose Thompson to slip into the Alamo City and return with bottles of liquor because of his "boyish looks and beardless face."[10] His first two trips were successful. To the delight of his friends, he sneaked back into camp carrying plenty of whiskey to share. On his third foraging trip, however, he was spotted and pursued. In the race to get away, his horse fell on his leg crushing it. His injury placed him in a hospital rather than the guardhouse, and while recovering, he learned that his regiment had resumed the march towards Galveston and a possible fight with the Yankees. With the help of a pair of crutches, he hurried after and caught up with them on the banks of the San Bernard River, eighty miles west of Galveston. One of the first friends he came upon as he hobbled into camp was twenty-three-year-old Phillip Coe. Described by Walton as "six feet and some inches high, extensive of girth, commanding in appearance, Coe was a gambler by profession and a rough, overbearing jollier by habit." He was also a former 1st Lieutenant, elected by his company, who had been busted down to private for repeatedly being absent without leave.[11] The two men decided they should have some fun and so they began in earnest to go find it. They headed for the small town of Saint Bernard where they traded an old horse for a gallon of cherry-spiced whiskey. Next, they hopped a train heading to the town of Richmond twenty miles further east. When the train pulled into the station, Phil Coe, who was drinking the most, was both drunk and very sick to his stomach. Thompson and Coe finally called it a night and checked into a local hotel. The following day they were found, arrested, and returned to their regiment.[12]

As the Confederate troops gathered outside of Galveston, General Magruder was finally able to get a good look at the Texans who made up his command. An Illinoisan by the name of Thomas North was stranded in Texas during the war, and he later wrote an account of his extensive travels throughout the state. A confirmed pro-Unionist, North found little that he liked about Texas or Texans. Though obviously prejudiced, he did leave behind an interesting observation of the type of men who fought for the Lone Star State.

North noticed that "the masses of them wore spurs on their heels, generally the immense wheel-spur, and though they were not born with them on ... they might as well have been, for they not only rode in them, but walked in them, ate in them, and slept in them. Their clanking as they walked was like a man in chains." Heavy belts circled their waists "suspending one or two revolvers and a bowie knife." North admitted "they were experts in the saddle, had a reckless dare-devil look, and were always ready for whisky [*sic*] and a big chew of tobacco, and the handwriting of passion and appetite was all over them." Thomas North commented disapprovingly, "In such a flock the one that has killed his man or more is hero and leader." To North it seemed "that the 'code of honor' ... is a good deal demoralized in Texas." With the simple warning, "take care of yourself," North pointed out, "shooting a man down [from] behind his back, or in the dark, or on sight" was acceptable. He believed, "in Texas ... a man is a little nearer [to] death ... than in any other country."[13]

Finally on December 21, two Federal army transports with the 42nd Massachusetts Volunteer infantry on board sailed into Galveston Bay. On Christmas Day, a token force of two hundred sixty men went ashore and occupied a portion of the town. The remaining two-thirds of the regiment stayed on their transports, suffering from either seasickness or from a measles epidemic, which had broken out while en route. The Union hold on Galveston was so tenuous that the infantry ashore only patrolled a small section of the city during the day. At night, they erected a double row of barricades to protect the end of a 400-foot long brick pier named Kahn's Wharf and bivouacked in a two-story warehouse there under the protection of the flotilla's guns.

Magruder took full advantage of the time United States's forces allowed him. He assembled three veteran regiments plus almost five thousand men of the usually inactive militia, commonly called the Home Guards, and a powerful artillery train of twenty heavy guns. Since Texas did not have a navy, he followed the advice of one of his more imaginative subordinates and authorized the transformation of two old steamships into "cottonclads." Iron was scarce in Texas. However, cotton was plentiful, so to protect the ships, the Confederates lashed bales of cotton together with sacks of cottonseed, two and sometimes three bales deep, along the decks of both vessels. General Magruder transferred three hundred cavalrymen to the steamships to provide a storming party, and the men chose to name themselves, "Horse Marines."

General Magruder devised a three-prong attack after reconnoitering the Union position on Kahn's Wharf and the Federal fleet at anchor. First, artillery would barrage both the wharf and the fleet. Then the two cottonclads would steam into the bay, ramming and storming any Union ship they could close upon. Under that covering fire, the four companies of the Second Texas Cavalry regiment would charge upon the Federal infantry position at the end of the wharf on foot. Finally, a second assault wave consisting of other units and the remainder of the Second Texas Cavalry led by Maj. Charles L. Pyron and including Ben Thompson, was to enter the shallow water carrying scaling ladders. The Confederate attack was meant to begin at midnight on New Year's Eve.

The attack was four hours behind schedule when all the troops were finally in place. Magruder personally sighted and fired the first artillery round to signal the assault. Everything went wrong for the Confederates from the start. Their artillery batteries were blasted by the Federal gunners, the cottonclads did not emerge from their river anchorage, and the first wave attacking the fortified wharf on foot stalled and retreated. This was a baptism by fire for the Massachusetts troops, and they performed well. Their musket volleys and barricades stopped the first charge and forced Magruder to order a second assault. In the moonlight, five hundred Confederates, with Ben Thompson among them, waded into the water on either side of the wharf, their rifles and scaling ladders held high. The commanding officer leading the rush later stated that his men fought well. Even though they were forced to slowly wade in water up to their hips and face a galling fire of grape, canister, and musketry, his men did not fall back until they learned the scaling ladders they carried were too short to reach the top of the barricades. Two smaller Federal gunboats pulled in close to the wharf and with precision, fired round after round of canister into the soaking wet and frustrated Texans. Most of the Confederate casualties, twenty-six killed and 117 wounded in the battle, occurred as a result of the ill-fated wading assault on the wharf. Among the many wounded was Ben Thompson.[14]

It was now dawn and General Magruder was deeply discouraged. The battle was developing into a Confederate defeat until the cottonclads and horse marines emerged. Lumbering into the bay they rammed and boarded *Harriet Lane,* the most powerful ship of the Union flotilla. Sharpshooters stationed in the high rigging swept the deck with rifle fire, killing or wounding many of the Federal officers. Farther out in the bay, the flagship of the Union fleet mysteriously exploded, killing the naval officer in charge of the operation. With only junior officers left alive, the remnants of the Union fleet quit the fight and steamed to safety well outside of the bay. The Massachusetts Infantry was left abandoned, with no choice but to run up a white flag of surrender. Galveston was free of Federal troops, but the Union blockade of the port continued as before. Magruder had only partially succeeded.

Many of the wounded soldiers from both the North and South were taken to be nursed in a makeshift hospital at the Ursuline

Convent. More than eighty men were placed in rows where the sisters of the convent cared for them. The nuns showed no favoritism and treated the Confederate and Union soldiers alike. Despite the care, evidence indicates that Thompson's battle wound and previously injured leg took a considerable time to heal. While he recovered that spring, he once again engaged in another altercation with authority.

Ben's captain, William Tobin,[15] gave Thompson and his friend, Henry Briggs, permission to write letters in his tent. While they were so engaged, Tobin's orderly, a sergeant, entered and saw the two enlisted men loafing inside. He immediately ordered them out. Briggs and Thompson refused to leave stating they had Captain Tobin's permission to be there. The furious sergeant tore into Briggs. Thompson intervened striking the sergeant with his crutch until it broke off in his hands and the sergeant was senseless. Once again, Thompson found himself under arrest and he was marched off, limping, to the guardhouse. Two days later, the regiment was ordered to Louisiana to be part of a desperate campaign to strike at New Orleans. Rushing to march, officers either forgot or forgave Thompson's offense, as he was able to accompany his regiment when it left for Louisiana.[16]

In the spring of 1863, the last remaining Confederate strongholds in the Mississippi River Valley were Vicksburg and Port Hudson. General Ulysses S. Grant was encircling Vicksburg as General Nathaniel Banks moved upriver from his base in New Orleans to lay siege to Port Hudson. The pressure to advance and provide relief to the two garrisons was immense. The Confederate authorities in the east demanded action be taken to disrupt General Banks's communication and supply lines. The most obvious way to do this was to crush his overextended western flank. Drawing upon the available troops in East Texas, a total of three thousand Confederates split into two columns and moved into western

Louisiana's Lafourche district. The object was to sever Banks's supply lines, and with more than a bit of optimism, drive on and perhaps even recapture New Orleans.

One of the columns was made up of four regiments of cavalry, and Ben Thompson's regiment, the Second Texas, was among them. Charles Pyron, an Alabaman who settled in Texas at an early age, was now the colonel commanding the regiment. Colonel Pyron was a veteran of the Mexican War, and in addition to fighting at the Battle of Galveston Bay, this hotspur had won laurels for his aggressiveness during the failed Confederate invasion of New Mexico Territory. Prior to the outbreak of the war, he made his home near San Antonio where he was both a farmer and rancher. His exceptional ability to handle a revolver established him in the minds of many as the Alamo City's finest pistol shot.[17]

On May 1 the Second Texas Cavalry set off for Louisiana on a campaign that was doomed to fail from the outset. Billy Thompson, now seventeen, joined his older brother as a trooper with the Second Texas.[18] The Lafourche district had been so stripped of Federal troops for General Banks's sweep against Port Hudson that they were unable to field even one complete infantry regiment. The Confederate two-pronged campaign came slicing down through the bayous and waterways, capturing and brushing aside any small Union opposition they encountered.

On the morning of June 20, the Southerners surprised the Union garrison at Thibodeaux, capturing a large amount of rations, including a great deal of whiskey and many new fast-firing Enfield rifles. A few miles east of where the New Orleans, Opelousas and Great Western Railroad tracks spanned the Bayou Lafourche, a scraped-together force of eight hundred Union infantrymen and six pieces of artillery prepared a commanding defensive position. The long level field in front of the Federals afforded full play for their artillery. The tall grass was cut down to prevent any concealment and they shoveled up enough dirt to form a two-foot high firing line. On the evening of June 20, about one hundred Confederates tested and tapped the Federal position. Satisfied that they could do no more without reinforcements, they returned to their camp at Thibodeaux. The Rebels ransacked the supplies they captured and with the whiskey they found, they celebrated their easy victory throughout the night and into the next morning. At about noon the next day, a thunderstorm opened up drenching everyone and everything and flooded much of the field in front of the Union position. At 6:30 p.m., the rain stopped and Colonel Pyron, tired of waiting for reinforcements that would never come, ordered his men to drive in the Federal picket line. The Battle at Lafourche Crossings was about to begin.

Pyron could muster only 206 men, yet he still gave a bewildering order. The Second Texas Regiment, despite being outnumbered four-to-one and mostly dismounted, was to charge the Union firing line with the intent of turning the Federal right flank. Federal artillery positioned to enfilade the Rebel attack let loose a dozen rounds of canister into the ranks of the wildly charging Texans. The first shot knocked Colonel Pyron off his horse, wounding him in the thigh and breaking one of his arms. The Confederates fell back in fragments, some of them crawling off the field on their hands and knees. They soon rallied and a few minutes later, the fearsome high-pitched Rebel yell signaled another charge with the wounded Pyron seated on a horse once more leading his men. The second attack soon faltered as steady volleys from the Federal infantry prevented the Rebels from closing and coming to grips with them.

Overcome with battlefield madness, Colonel Pyron assembled the remnants of his regiment for a third time and led them in a final assault. Advancing boldly and firing continually, the coolness of the Southerners so unnerved the Federal infantry that they no longer fired in disciplined volleys, but nervously loaded and sporadically fired at will. The Union left flank began to crack and a handful of Confederates briefly poured through the opening, but it wasn't enough. At bayonet point, the Federals killed or captured whoever breached their line. By 8 p.m., the battle was over. Leaving the dead where they had fallen, Colonel Pyron took what was left of his battered regiment back to their camp at Thibodeaux. The impetuous actions of Colonel Pyron left the Second Texas Cavalry Regiment decimated, and it was never again an effective fighting force. It had sustained over fifty percent casualties. Fifty-three dead men were found on the battlefield, and the Union soldiers captured nearly sixty wounded when they reached Thibodeaux two days later. In spite of their bravery and all of the blood spilled, the Confederate thrust into lower Louisiana became a savage, costly, and pointless campaign. Elsewhere, the second column came to a grinding halt. Not one Confederate soldier stepped within fifty miles of New Orleans. The Union pressure on Vicksburg and Port Hudson only intensified. In July, both bastions ran up a white flag and surrendered.

Ben and Billy Thompson emerged from the engagement at Lafourche Crossings without receiving so much as a scratch. However, Ben's ailing leg still troubled him considerably. Walton, always professing only the most honorable actions of his subject, claimed Ben's injury made him unfit for service and he was given an indefinite furlough.[19] Actually, official records state he went absent without leave on July 28, and did not return for duty for four months. It was during this time that Ben returned to his hometown of Austin and spent the late summer and fall of 1863 courting and falling in love.[20]

Ben Thompson's head was turned by pretty Catherine "Kate" Moore and he didn't hesitate in pursuing her. Kate was the eldest of five children (four daughters and one troublemaking son named James) born to Irish immigrant Martin Moore and Alabama-born

Elizabeth White. In 1839, at the age of twenty-three, Martin Moore arrived in Texas and opened one of the first dry-goods stores in Austin. Among the city's early settlers, he was well-thought of and respected. However, he could also be a bit rowdy, and court records indicate that he was occasionally indicted for fighting, illegally selling liquor, and allowing card playing in his place of business. In a fledging frontier town where inhabitants thirsted for a little fun, this may explain his popularity. By 1849, his wife Elizabeth had inherited 521 acres of land just outside of town, and they built a farmhouse which, miraculously, still stands today. Moore moved the young family into their new home. Over the next ten years, farming and raising various livestock (cattle, hogs, oxen, and horses) proved their efforts productive. The estate had an established value of $22,000. On December 18, 1859, tragedy struck the Moore family when Martin was kicked in the head by a skittish horse causing his death. Elizabeth, with her five young children and two slaves, continued to live and work on the farm until she sold it in 1866 to distinguished Austin attorney John Hancock, a slave owner and staunch Unionist throughout the war. Remarkably, the Moore-Hancock farmhouse still stands today.[21]

Kate Moore turned seventeen in 1863 and the only life she could recall was the grinding existence of life on the farm. It is easy to see how Ben Thompson's attentions flattered her and won her heart. He was handsome, full of fun and even though he had only just celebrated his twentieth birthday, his earlier adventures and his experiences in the war had matured him beyond his years.

In the Northern states, the last Thursday of November was chosen by Abraham Lincoln to be the national day of Thanksgiving. In 1863, Thanksgiving Day fell on November 26, and this was the day Ben Thompson and Kate Moore chose to be wed. They went to St. David's Church on Bois d'Arc Street (the same church the Thompson family joined when they first arrived in Austin) where

The Moore-Hancock homestead at 481 Sinclair Avenue in Austin as it appears today. It was here that the young Ben Thompson called on his future wife, Catherine Moore. *Courtesy the Tom Bicknell Collection.*

the young couple stood before Charles Gillette, an Episcopal priest, and recited their wedding vows.[22] The newlyweds spent only one day together before Ben ended his unauthorized time away from the army and reported back on Saturday, November 28. Upon his return he was placed on detached service from his regiment and ordered to help drive a mule herd to Houston.[23]

Ben Thompson's unapproved absence from the army was similar to the behavior of thousands of other Texans. With only a toehold at the reoccupied Fort Brown, the Union army was no longer viewed as a credible threat to the security of Texas. This lull in the war convinced many Confederate soldiers to leave their units without permission. While several hundred chose to become lawless renegades loafing and causing trouble along the Mexican border, most men like Thompson, returned to their homes, businesses, and families.

General Magruder was determined to rid Texas soil of every last Yankee soldier. He wrote to Colonel Ford on December 22, 1863, suggesting another campaign be mounted against the Federals entrenched at the mouth of the Rio Grande. Though small in number, the Union troops at Fort Brown, near the city of Brownsville, along with the naval forces blockading that town's seaport of Port Isabel, prevented the importation of vital manufactured products into central Texas. Supplies of all kinds were forced to move at great expense through Brownsville's sister city, the neutral and open Mexican port of Matamoros. They were then hauled by wagon almost three hundred fifty miles north along the river to Eagle Pass before passing through the Texas customhouse there and continuing on towards San Antonio and Austin. It was estimated that the long and arduous trip added at least fifty percent to the cost of the goods. This was the main reason General Magruder and Colonel Ford were eager to drive the remaining Federals out of the state. It took Ford less than a week to respond to Magruder's plan and issue a call for recruits into his new command, which he named the "Cavalry of the West." Since desertion continued to be so rampant in the spring of 1864, General Magruder offered amnesty to any Texan who returned to his unit or joined Ford's command in an effort to help boost enlistments. Few of the renegades plaguing the Mexican border took advantage of Magruder's offer. However, on March 17, 1864, with an undermanned force of about 1,200 men consisting of mostly adolescents, old men, and draft exemptions, Colonel Ford moved out of San Antonio with the intent of sweeping Federals out of the lower Rio Grande Valley. One month later, on April 16, Ben Thompson was placed on recruiting duty for his regiment.[24] He joyfully returned to his wife and extended family, and his twenty-plus years of shooting up the city of Austin began.

James B. Gillett, the future Texas Ranger and city marshal of El Paso, was born in Austin and grew up down the street from where the Thompson family lived. Years later, writing for *Frontier Times*, Gillett described how in the spring of 1864, when he was seven-years-old and attending a private school taught by Mrs. Foster, he and his classmates heard gunfire popping about a block away. As soon as school let out, Gillett and his friends ran to find the scene of the shooting and learn what the commotion was all about. He later explained that they saw where "bullets from Ben Thompson's pistol had scraped or glanced along a store building some eight feet high and one bullet hit a post ten feet up." Earlier, Thompson's brother-in-law, sixteen-year-old Jim Moore, had stolen all of his mother's pots, lids, and skillets and for a good price, sold them to a local factory in need of iron to be molded into cannon balls. Thompson found his mother-in-law crying, and when he learned what happened, he told her he would see Jim about the matter. As he left the house, Mrs. Moore called after him begging him not to hurt her son. Ben soon met up with Moore on a small side street then named Pecan (not the fashionable street off Congress Avenue). Any conversation they may have had did not last long before Ben pulled his pistol and commenced firing. The height of the bullet marks convinced Gillett that Thompson did not intend to hurt his brother-in-law but scare him, and Gillett concluded, "it worked to perfection." Witnesses to the affair claimed Jim Moore simply flew down the street as Ben pumped shots over his head. Continuing his flight, Moore left Austin and did not return to the city until after the war had ended.[25]

Following his orders, Colonel Ford moved to attack the Federal troops in the lower Rio Grande Valley. He traveled along the north bank of the river with his "Cavalry of the West" but was greatly slowed by the severe drought plaguing Texas that spring. At this moment, Ford's cavalry was the only Confederate command in the field. Ben decided to join the expedition, and his brother Billy transferred and joined Ford's regiment as well. Ben provided a lengthy description of his adventure along the Rio Grande to his biographer Walton.[26] Ben's account begins in the Texas border-town of Eagle Pass. With seventy dollars in gold provided by his younger brother, Ben opened a *monte* game to Americans only and was soon ahead almost two hundred dollars.

He explained how this "exhausted" all of the hard currency from the men he allowed to play so he decided to open the game up to all comers.

> Success had made me bolder, and I was willing to put a harder test to fortune's kindness. Before this I had not permitted a Mexican, whether a greaser, officer or gentleman, to bet at "my game." They are experts in *monte*, from the highest to the lowest grades of men; but the game had taken in the available money of all except the Mexicans, and though hazardous, I had to close or else deal those who were educated by the originators of the game. They are indeed experts. I opened the game for them, and in less than five hours I did not have a cent. I even put up my silver spurs and the gold cord that ornamented my hat. It was of no use, money, spurs, hat, cord, and all went, and the cigarette-smoking devils grinned as they won. A picked chicken, a scalded cat, a Georgia major, each was better fitted to walk aboard than I was; but I retained my six-shooter...This is where the great losses at cards occur. When that hatless, barefooted, one-gallus thing called luck, frowns, a man sins against good gambling if he don't quit.

Crossing the river into Mexico, Ben wandered into the little adobe hamlet of Piedras Negras. He noted the caliber of men there.

> There were a great many desperate characters collected there—desperadoes, actual criminals, men who had fled for crimes committed, refugees from conscription to the army—indeed a conglomerate, if I may use the expression—out of which a ready actor could have been obtained to participate in any venture, or perform any act, from preaching a passable sermon to taking the life of a real preacher.

One of Ford's officers, Captain James A. Ware, was in Piedras Negras looking for deserters. Recognizing Ben Thompson, he ordered him to cross the Rio Grande and rejoin his regiment. Based on a very enlightened viewpoint, Ben refused, believing a superior officer did not have any authority over him in a foreign country. However, to avoid trouble, Thompson crossed over to Texas and there he claimed he received permission from Colonel Ford to continue downriver on the Mexican side.[27]

Even though he was completely broke, Thompson rejected a chance to fill his pockets.

> A proposition was made to me to take part in robbing the custom house on the American side of the river. There was then a large amount of gold on deposit there, received from export duties on cotton, great quantities of which passed at that point into Mexico, and large amounts were received from import duties on goods that found their way into the country from all markets of the world. This proposition was made to me confidentially by friends who believed my desperate fortunes would move me to engage in any undertaking by which a large sum of money could be realized. It is true I needed money very badly, but I was not willing to commit a high crime to obtain it. It was a serious question with me whether I should not advise my colonel of the intended robbery and permit him to take suitable measures to prevent it; but I become possessed of the information under specially peculiar circumstances, and could not divulge it without playing the despicable role of traitor to friends and thereby occasion their death in all probability. I could not remain at Piedras Negras, because if the robbery was perpetrated I would be charged to be connected with and held responsible for it, nor could I join the regiment because the robbery would be resisted by the troops and it would devolve on me to shoot the boys; this I had no inclination to do. As it was not possible for me to prevent this attempted, or designed robbery, I concluded to hasten my departure.

On June 19, 1864, a failed attempt by about one hundred renegades was made to rob the Confederate custom house at Eagle Pass which was successfully defended by Captain Ware, twenty-three men from his command, and a group of citizens who came to his aid.[28]

The brothers separated as Billy chose to travel down the river valley towards Brownsville on the American side. Ben came upon a young friend from Austin named Julius Brown,[29] and they decided to journey together. Regretfully, Brown was as broke as Thompson. Ben approached the stage office and found the agent amiable to letting two, well-armed young men ride free with the promise to pay upon arrival in Nuevo Laredo. It was a dangerous run and recent holdups to two prior stages by Mexican banditos probably convinced the stage manager to allow Thompson and Brown on board.

After an uneventful run, the stage arrived in the little Mexican village of Nuevo Laredo, opposite the Texas town of Laredo. There Ben came upon Joe Buck, another friend who happened to be flush with cash. Buck staked Thompson to three hundred dollars to run a *monte* game to all comers. "Mexicans or devils could come in now," Thompson explained. His luck had returned as he won from the start, pulling in over twelve hundred dollars before dawn. After paying the stage line and splitting the profits with Joe Buck, Thompson had about four hundred dollars from his efforts.

Thompson then met Colonel B. Riddle, a prominent American in northern Mexico and made friends with both Riddle and his entourage of about twenty men who were as rough and brave a band as Thompson ever knew. This was a fortunate meeting, as he would soon require their help and protection.[30]

With Julius Brown still accompanying Ben, they crossed the river back to the American side and met Billy Thompson in Laredo. Eager to add to his bank roll, Ben appealed to Dick Miller, a saloon owner, to allow him to open a *monte* game in his establishment. There were a large number of Mexicans in town who belonged to the Confederate regiment commanded by soon to be

Brigadier General Santos Benavides, an exceedingly prominent man in Laredo.[31]

The soldiers were without any ready cash but were eager to play, so they proposed to venture their side arms as collateral until payday, which was only a day away. Since weapons were such a necessity on the border, they were normally used in barter and Thompson readily accepted the terms. Ben served as dealer with Billy as the lookout and Julius Brown nearby.

The game ebbed and flowed, but by midnight all of the revolvers wagered found their way into Thompson's possession. As he won them, Thompson sent the revolvers off with Julius Brown to a place of safety. Thompson admitted, "I did not win all the pistols in the company, but I did win all that were put up … I did not know but what some difficulty might arise and the 'greasers' make a rush for my Arsenal if it remained near at hand and accessible. My action was but ordinary prudence." The game ended without incident and late in the following evening, the Mexicans drew their wages and returned to Ben's game, each with a handful of cash.

Thompson explained how "they expected in that game not only to win back their pistols, but all the money in my bank … [however] … luck was with me … at about 2 o'clock at night I had won between eighteen and nineteen hundred dollars." Not surprisingly the losers "began to manifest ill-temper; to curse in their peculiar expletives, and to murmur in low guttural tones."

Expecting to be robbed, Ben was stunned to learn that his brother was without his pistol. Quietly he told Billy to go and arm himself and hurry back, since Julius Brown was not in the saloon and Ben was now alone. Stalling until Billy returned, Ben called out to the proprietor Dick Miller for a new deck of cards. While the cards were being brought, Ben began to stuff all of his winnings into a canvas sack, and what gold coins he won into his pocket.

The Mexicans realized Ben was not waiting for new cards, but instead was closing the game.

Thompson described the final moments before gun smoke filled the room.

> I was alone, surrounded by a set of as truly, black-eyed, angry, treacherous, scoundrels and assassins, maddened by loss at play, and ready to do any deed, however dark, which would carry money into their pockets, as ever shed blood, or stole things of value. This was the fact. I could feel it, almost as a tangible thing. It is well for me that I am not greatly wedded to life. Among these Mexicans was [thirty-year old] Lieutenant Martino Gonzales,[32] one of the tallest men I ever saw, a black Mexican with the eye of a murderer, that danced in a dangerous way, while the corners of his mouth twitched spasmodically. I noted him, his action, expression, movements, and rapidity of thought, and yet as thoroughly as if I had studied him for months. I knew that I should have to kill him, he kill me or I have to give up the money I had won, and that which I had of my own, which surrender I did not mean to make. He spoke good English and said:
>
> "Mr. Ben, you can't close this game"
>
> I replied: 'The game is closed."
>
> "Then you will have to give the money back to these men, out of which you have cheated them."
>
> I smiled and said, "Lieutenant, you are not in earnest, are you?"
>
> "Yes; not only in earnest, but you shall return the pistols you took from them on yesterday. They are government arms; where are they?"
>
> Still smiling I said, "Lieutenant, I won the money fairly, and I won the pistols in the same way; the pistols are private property of the soldiers, as I am informed. Surely, under these circumstances, you will not insist on your demand."
>
> "But I do insist on it, and will see that you comply without delay."

> All the time the foregoing had been going on, and even before, I had been observing the room, trying to find some possible nook, corner, projection, table or other things that would give protection when the firing commenced, and was going on, that it would commence in a very few seconds I very well knew. I observed a sort of off-set near the door when it swung open. I decided to take advantage of the situation and protect myself as well as I could.
>
> There were two candles on the table, burning, and these furnished all the light there was in the room.
>
> The lieutenant, as he ceased speaking, instantly drew his pistol and struck at the candles with his hands, intending to put the lights out, grab the money and kill me. He missed one of the candles. His failure was fatal to him, although I could not attend to him first. When the lieutenant acted it was the signal for action to his men, or least, those of them who had pistols. Miguel Zertuche[33] drew his pistol and put it right at my heart and fired. Not knowing whether I was shot or not, I fired at Zertuche hitting him in the head, and, without pausing, I shot the lieutenant through the breast, knocked the light out and dropped down into the off-set—of which I have spoken—stooping low down, and waited for results. I was informed by a gentleman, who said he counted them, that there were eight bullet-holes in the door, but each above my head in my squatting position. There was a rush for the door, pell-mell, by the Mexicans. I thought for an instant, and concluded that my safest course would be to go with the crowd and lose myself in the confusion. To conclude, in this instance, was to act, for hesitation would be fatal. I knew they would kill me to a certainly if I was identified. Out I went. Loud oaths, groans by wounded men, the fear and excitement, created a pandemonium for a few moments, but not so long as it takes to tell it.

Emerging through the doorway Thompson was recognized by one of the many Mexicans scurrying to safety. Luckily, he was only armed with an old short, smoothbore flintlock called an Escopeta. In trying to shoot Thompson, he so startled another man nearby Thompson that he knocked Ben into a deep cistern full of water. The shot tore through Thompson's clothes, but missed his body.

Swimming under water to the far side of the cistern, Ben emerged to find his returning brother. Billy asked Ben if he was hurt. Ben did not know for sure but answered "no" since he knew he was not disabled. They fled the scene and at once were separated as Billy bolted to the opposite side of a large, long stack of baled cotton. As he ran up the street, Ben met a cavalry squad responding to the gunfire. Thompson shook his soaked hair, pretending to have been bathing. The officer in charge asked Ben if he knew the reason for the gunfire and Ben replied, he "supposed the boys were having some fun with the women," at the bawdy house near the river. When the squad went off on the false scent, Thompson ran as fast as he could to get out of the town. At first, he sought to hide in a cemetery, but the sounds of the returning cavalry spurred him towards the safety of the chaparral. Daylight was not far off, and since only Mexican Confederate troops were in Laredo, Ben determined to swim the Rio Grande and return to Colonel Riddle's house, and to his tough band of new friends.

The portion of the river he came to was deep, swift, and about three-quarters of a mile wide. No boat could be found, nor a log or even a substantial tree limb. Capture was certain if he remained where he was, so Thompson calculated his chances to swim the expanse. He gathered some bushes and lashing them with his sash, pistol belt, and leather cut from his boot tops, he made a small raft as tight as possible. Testing its buoyancy, he determined it would do. Prior to crossing, he pulled off his "tail-coat, spread it on the ground, took a *monte* deck of cards from the breast pocket, and made lay-out—the seven and four." These were the last cards wagered on before the shooting started.

> This was a foolish act of bravado, but I could not resist tantalizing the greasers. I knew very well they would find it the next day. The foolishness of the act consisted in pointing my pursuers to the river as my escape route … The bundle

> of bushes would float, and gradually sink, but very slowly. While it was on or near the surface I could lean on it and float with ease; when it sank I would draw it up by my sash rope and give it direction across the current, and thus, by successive raisings of the bundle, I slowly, but successfully, crossed the Rio Grande River. I reached the west bank very much exhausted, and about two miles below where I had entered on the east bank.

Before the sun rose Thompson entered Nuevo Laredo to find Mr. Riddle's house, hopefully without being seen.

> I walked as rapidly as I could, and before it was yet light I began to pass through its narrow crooked streets. The Mexicans, men and women, were sleeping on beef-hides, thrown down on the sides of the street, in the open air, and every third or fourth pair or bunch of them had a dog near them. My pistol had gotten wet and was unfit for service, save as a club. These dogs are fierce and snap at one as does a wolf; ... In passing along, as fast as I would get beyond the dog, he would slip up behind me, snap my leg and run off whining, and that, too, when I had not touched him. The Mexicans would lazily raise themselves up and see that I was an American and contemptuously say "Gringos, Gringos," meaning "American, American," and that it makes no difference [to them] if the dogs do eat him up or tear him to pieces. I got a few well-planted licks at some of these villainous dogs, and I can assure you that I gave them something to whine for. Not a solitary man interposed to help protect me from those brutes or to drive them off, or even rebuke or call them away. By the time that I got through the streets I had been bitten in over thirty different places, all the way from just below my hips down to my very heels. One dog, a little larger than the others, was sitting apparently unconcerned on a sort of low platform, and when I got near him I was bitten on the calf of the leg by one of the hairless pests; I turned quickly to kill him if I could, and struck him with all my power, stooping over to do so. At this moment this unconcerned looking fellow stuck his fangs in my behind, and I give you my word that I turned round and round, trying to get a lick at him, as many as four or five times; at last his hold tore out and he got off free of

> hurt. In that little moment of time I was bitten six or seven times by other dogs. I was really alarmed when I found how I had been almost literally torn to pieces by this most contemptible species of the canine race, that I would have the hydrophobia. If my pistol had been in good condition, I am nearly certain I should have shot some of these dog owners for their insulting contempt; but I was in quite enough hot water then, and I had to bear the insults of these dogs and their masters heaped upon me as best I could.
>
> I was bloody from the waist down, and as full of pain as if a strong man had taken a pair of pincers and torn out pieces of flesh. At last, however, I got to Mr. Riddle's house, knocked up the inmates, stated to them in a short way all that occurred, and asked them whether they would give me asylum for a day or two. Their response was as hearty as a man could wish. They said "yes, you can remain here and no one shall take you away against your consent until we are all dead or disabled we cannot fight." My dog wounds were dressed, washed in ammonia and bound up as well as possible, considering their locality; then I retired and slept for several hours, and rose much refreshed, but very sore, yet ready for anything that might present itself.

In the meantime, when Billy became separated from his brother, he jumped atop a pile of cotton bales and climbed until he made it to the top of an unoccupied house with a flat roof and hid there. Ben felt no fear for his brother since he had nothing whatever to do with the shooting. However, the bloody clothing of the dead and wounded men were stretched on lines along the streets to inflame the search for any gringo thought to have been involved. Wisely, Billy remained in hiding throughout the following day. He suffered from the hot sun and lack of water, but dared not reveal his hiding place. Camped outside of town was a small Confederate company of Texans under the command of Captain W. H. D. Carrington, [Austin resident and brother of former Home Guard commander, Captain L. D. Carrington] and in the evening three of Carrington's men entered Laredo. Billy was able to quietly attract their attention. Realizing Billy's precarious situation, Carrington's men schemed a simple but effective plan to help him escape. One man, Joe Owens,[34] casually loafed about until he could reach Billy and exchange clothes with him. Openly, Billy came down from his hiding place and nonchalantly mounting his friend's horse, he rode out with the two other men to Captain Carrington's camp and safety. Later, Owens, wearing Billy's clothes innocently and unmolested, calmly walked out of town and was picked up by his waiting pals.[35]

Ben was faced with a tougher challenge in his flight to safety. Without explanation, it became general knowledge where Ben was hiding. Julius Brown crossed over from Laredo, found Ben at Riddle's house and told Ben the Mexicans were determined to take him and hang him no matter the cost. Brown wasn't the only one to have crossed over. Mexicans from Benavides's regiment arrived from Laredo, and with their friends on the south side of the river, planned to assault the house. Having no desire to place his friends at risk, Thompson knew he had to reach the Texas side of the river to evade or outride pursuit. Julius Brown went back and forth across the river and arranged to have Joe Owens and a handful of others from Captain Carrington's company meet Thompson at a selected time and place. With Brown accompanying him and no boat available, Ben slipped into the river and using a log, the pair paddled toward the Texas shore. A troop of mounted Mexicans spotted them mid-river, but did not move fast enough to cut them off before they reached Owens and their other friends. Even though they found themselves outnumbered five-to-one, being mounted and armed gave Thompson confidence and the Texans made no attempt to run. The Mexican officer in charge approached, asked for a parley and suggested to Ben that he should surrender. He promised no harm would come to Ben. He would merely be turned over to the civil authorities, namely the Webb County sheriff. Thompson declined and said to him "I cannot consent to my own assassination ... now if you want me, come and take me." Thompson believed the officer to be a "good-hearted man" and no effort was then made to arrest him. The Mexicans rode back towards Laredo while the Texans went wide of the town and made for Carrington's camp, which they easily reached. Billy Thompson was there and the brothers now felt safe until Captain Carrington, who did not speak directly to Thompson, but sent word that if the civil authorities in Laredo made a demand for him, he would hand Ben Thompson over to them. Ben left the camp by himself, and he would later claim, "if I had had a chance to live though a trial before a jury I should have surrendered, but the excitement was so great, and the ... bitterness towards me so uncompromising on the part of the friends of the dead men, that any of them would have shot me down could they have caught me unarmed."

With only twenty-seven gold dollars still left in his possession Thompson took fifteen of them and purchased a "little wild Mexican mule" on which he planned to use to outride pursuit. He rigged the mule as well as he was able using odds and ends. Then Thompson mounted him, and freely confessed that before he knew it, he flew over the little mule's head.

> Though small, he had the peculiar power of "bucking" with such skill and vigor that no man could ride him, unless he was hampered and shackled so that he had no use ... except to go straight ahead. I cut a forked stick and used it as an anti-martingale, placing the forked end under the jaws of the mule, so he could not lower his head. He was then about as stiff as if he had been [made] of stone; but I hired a half breed Indian to lead him, and, by dint of deep spurring and unmerciful lashing with a quirt, I got him to move forward. He soon warmed up and gave out kindly action. These little animals, when conquered, come down to their work with a will and are seemingly tireless. They will readily travel from sixty to seventy miles a day with a man on them, weighing half as much as they do. My Indian did not accompany me

> more than ten miles. The mule admitted me to be master. I removed the stick, and away we went.

Staying off the roads, Thompson pushed his mule hard and reached another company of Texans, this one commanded by Captain William Armstrong of Travis County. Presented to Armstrong, Thompson detected the officer's nervousness. Captain Armstrong had heard of the shooting and knew of the determination of the victim's friends to capture Thompson no matter what. He informed Ben of the weakness of his company. Most of the men returning home were invalids, and included in his responsibilities were many deserters and Federal prisoners traveling under a weak guard. This forced him to move very slowly. Armstrong, like Captain Carrington, refused to put his men at risk, and informed Thompson he, too, would surrender him if the authorities requested it. He did favor Thompson with information about another party of Confederate soldiers nearby. It consisted of a small train of artillery lead by Captain Robert Gardner[36] and if Thompson moved fast enough, he might catch up to them and find safety. Rejecting the offer of a fresh horse, Ben mounted his mule and even though the dog bites gave him a great deal of pain he explained, "I am stoic in great measure, and endure bodily ills without murmur." At 3:00 a.m. he set off using the southern constellations as his guide.

At about daybreak, the mule suddenly stopped, lifted his ears to listen and refused to move. Thompson dismounted, laid flat down on the ground and placed his ear against the earth. He could hear the pounding of many rapidly moving hoof beats and he listened intently until he learned the sound was growing fainter. Relieved that the horsemen were riding away from his position, Thompson mumbled, "a Daniel come to judgment,"[37] remounted and gave his mule a gentle spurring. Then and there, he christened his remarkably intelligent mule "Dan" and without hesitation little "Dan" moved off, maintaining a gait of six to eight miles an hour.

Convinced the horsemen could only be a Mexican posse searching for him, Thompson determined to cover a full sixty miles that day until he reached the road Captain Gardner was on. Finally, that night, he found the road, and upon examining the ground, he was relieved to learn he was close behind the artillery train. Exhausted and with his wounds reopened and bleeding from hours in the saddle, Thompson moved off the road to rest. Dan began to munch on the rough, stunted grass and slake his thirst chewing into a cactus plant. Suffering from thirst more so than hunger, Thompson took a cue from his mule and carefully peeled a cactus apple, removing the thorns, before sucking the moisture from it. Thompson stated this "gave him the sweetest relief." He then tended to the dog bites by removing the thorns and rind from some of the broad cactus leaves and crushing them into a pulp he applied them to his wounds. Again, after finding comfort and relief he fell into a deep sleep and did not wake until morning when the sun was full up. Hastening after the slowly moving artillery train, Thompson caught up to Captain Gardner at about 10 a.m.

Thompson explained to the officer what had happened in Laredo, and concealing nothing, informed Gardner he feared pursuit was not too far off. Pulling six light cannon, Gardner's artillery train had an abundance of firepower. However, his command was a woefully small party consisting of only four soldiers and three freedmen. Still, Gardner welcomed Thompson to join him, and they traveled slowly out of necessity. They stopped at a well to rest during the heat of the afternoon. Later in the evening Thompson saw a ranch house and set off to try and purchase some food. The rancher was a gossip and revealed that a body of Mexican-Confederate cavalry was a short distance away seeking a man who had killed some of their number in Laredo. Rejoining Gardner, Thompson shared the information. "Oh, well," said Gardner nonchalantly, "I reckon we can stand them off. If they come they will not approach before night. We will travel on leisurely, find the best point to receive an attack, and then bivouac, and see what we will see."

Captain Gardner and his small command continued until they came upon a most favorable piece of land, a salt marsh that protected their rear and flanks. They stopped and unlimbered the six cannons, loading and aiming them at the only approach to their camp. Hours passed quietly. The stillness was suddenly ended when a single pistol shot rang out. A solitary rider, a flagman from the Mexicans, rode up and demanded the surrender of Thompson, announcing that all who protected him would be put to death. Captain Gardner refused to speak to anyone besides the officer in charge, and when the officer approached, Thompson's protector turned black with anger and said, "If you want this man—murderer, as you call him, charge and take him! He is here, and here he will stay until I and my men are dead."

The Mexicans charged only once. The six cannons rang out, two of them fired by Thompson, who observed,

> Of all the races ever seen made to the rear, I do believe those Mexicans made the best. They fled, and as there is hope within me, I do not believe they halted for rest or food until they were on the banks of the muddy, angry Rio Grande ... None were killed, or even hit, so far as I know [as] the sound of the ... guns were enough. From that day I was not disturbed. No man followed, and no further effort was made to arrest or molest me.

In summation of the gambling hall gunfight, Ben himself wondered how it all happened.

> I have never known why Zertuche did not kill me; whether ... something ... turned the bullet I cannot say, but ... I was not even slightly wounded by gun-shot ... Of Gonzales and Zertuche, both of whom, died that night, as I was afterwards informed, and also Juan Rodriquez [*sic*], another Mexican, who was shot on the same occasion, but by whom I do not know. I shot three times, but whether Rodriquez [*sic*] was

> killed by me or his friends in firing at me, no one perhaps will ever know.

Nonetheless, the soldiers exposed the bloody clothing hanging on lines along the streets in Laredo in an effort to incite their fellow Mexicans. This was part of their quest to punish Ben Thompson, and it also provides grim evidence of the wounded and dead bodies he left behind in Dick Miller's Saloon.[38]

On the back of his mule, Dan, Thompson thanked Captain Gardner and his men and went on to Austin to rejoin his wife and mother.

In Austin, on July 22, 1864, a tragedy unfolded that may have involved Ben Thompson. Three brothers named Willis were lynched in broad daylight. Captured only the day before about fifteen miles northwest of Austin, they were brought into the city. A mob did not take long to assemble. The three prisoners were openly taken from Confederate military custody by approximately fifty undisguised men who had calmly gathered at the Leander Brown building, where the upstairs was being used as a guardhouse. Depending on who relates the story, the Willis boys were suspected of many crimes including recruiting Federal sympathizers to join their group of bushwhackers. Rumors said they had incited slaves and assisted them to flee the country. It was also claimed they were living as renegades, murdering settlers and stealing livestock. In Texas, any one of these actions would bring swift retribution.

The Willis brothers were taken to an open stretch of land on east Pecan Street (now 6th Street), securely tied and stood under a tree. Ropes were then adjusted around their necks, and a portion of the mob grabbed hold and pulled them up to strangle to death. The bodies were left hanging for close to three hours before they were cut down and buried in unmarked graves in an undisclosed location.[39] Many years later it was reported Ben Thompson had a hand in the affair. "It was during the war that he assisted in lynching the Willis boys who had been arrested by military authority and confined in the guard house," said the *Statesman* decades later. "Thompson and those with him took them to a tree still standing near the pecan elevator, and strung them up and left them to strangle to death."[40]

In August, Ben Thompson was serving in the quartermaster department.[41] Colonel Ford soon reassigned him, and Ben began recruiting a new company to join an existing regiment serving on the northwest frontier. Thompson's long-time friend John Rapp joined Ben in signing up men. During the course of the war, Texas provided more than 60,000 men to the Confederate armed forces and Travis County, was well represented in that total. Finding recruits proved to be difficult, but Thompson and Rapp had some success attracting men who had been previously wounded and recovered or were on furlough and unable to cross the Mississippi River in order to return to their units fighting in the east. They also approached a second source of possible recruits, which was the local militia unit commonly called the Home Guards. Among their ranks were good men. Still, many of these were old men and invalids unable to serve in the field. The Home Guard was also comprised of others Walton denounced as "dodgers, shirks, cowards, and dead beats," exempt from active service due to some pretense or another. According to Walton, among the latter was John Coombs (Combs), who exhibited a personality described as "desperate and fearless, insulting and aggressive." Coombs had a special animosity toward one of Rapp's friends, the former commander of the Home Guards, Captain L. D. Carrington.[42]

On the night of August 22, at Old Dutch John Wahrenberger's beer hall and bakery, standing at the north end of Congress Avenue near Hickory (present day 8th street), John Rapp, accompanied by a handful of friends, was having a drink when John Coombs, "more or less under the influence of drink," entered the beer hall. Rapp, reputedly a hot-tempered man himself, ignored Coombs's insulting comments and tried to leave the hall without an incident. Angry that he couldn't bait Rapp, Coombs stepped up to within a few feet of him and pulled one of the two pistols he was wearing and cocked it. Rapp grabbed at the weapon and the hammer fell on the skin between his thumb and forefinger preventing it from firing. Coombs wrenched the pistol from Rapp's grasp tearing out a chunk of flesh. He then pulled a knife, striking with it as patrons moved to stop the attack. Coombs's knife sliced into Rapp's right hand, causing a defensive wound at almost the same point where his left hand was injured, rendering him almost defenseless. Coombs was dragged away and Rapp, bleeding freely from both hands, was taken to Dr. J. M. Litten,[43] the surgeon who dressed and bandaged his wounds.

Several hours later in the evening, John Rapp showed up at Thompson's home with bandaged hands and related to him what had happened. He asked Thompson to accompany him to Leander Brown's building, located two short blocks southeast of Wahrenberger's Beer Hall, where he could purchase clothes to replace the bloody ones he was wearing. Against the pleadings of his wife and mother who begged him to stay home and avoid any possible trouble, Thompson retrieved his pistol and agreed to accompany his friend.

On the way, they met a young boy, a former slave, who told them Coombs and "about twenty more men with him" were in the alley behind Miller's livery stable a mere half block away.[44] Within moments, John Coombs on foot with others on horseback emerged from the alley firing weapons. With only the light created by the flashes of gunfire, Thompson "saw a man quite near him, behind a post, shooting as fast as he could revolve his pistol." Holding his fire, Thompson rushed up to this man, shot him, wheeled and fired a round at another man on horseback knocking him to the ground. Quickly losing their desire to continue the fight, Coombs's followers started fleeing in all directions. Thompson walked across Congress Avenue to the southwest corner near the Sampson & Henricks mercantile. There he met R.R. Robertson, a well-known and respectable gentleman who was not involved in the fight. Robertson demanded to know who was doing all of this shooting. Stating he had defended himself, Thompson thought he had killed one man, possibly two. Checking his pistol, he called out a challenge that did not draw a response. John Rapp was no longer within sight and Ben thought it best to return home. A little later, Ben Miller, a man identified as a "yellow Negro," came running up to Thompson's door yelling loudly. He warned Thompson that a mob was being formed to find and hang him. Thompson asked Miller what the results of the fight were, and learned that Coombs and the other unnamed man were both seriously wounded. According to Walton, Ben "was inclined to stand his ground and try the game of death with those who might come." However, with his wife and mother frantic and frightened, he finally relented and followed their advice. He went to the home of Mrs. Sterzing, a family friend (and mother of the future city assessor and collector, Fred Sterzing), where he quietly spent the night in safety.

The next morning, Thompson appeared on the street. He first spoke with the military provost marshal. After he left that official's office, he was approached by the forty-seven-year-old city marshal, W. H. Sharp.[45] Sharp informed Ben that he had a warrant for his arrest issued by Travis County Justice of the Peace, E. McLaughlin, charging him with "assault and battery with intent to kill and murder John Coombs." According to Walton, Thompson refused to be disarmed or placed in jail where he felt he would be easy prey for a mob. He promised Marshal Sharp he would appear at any time or place for an examining trial. John Coombs was not a man without friends, and since mob justice had taken the lives of the Willis brothers only a month prior, the tightening of a lynch mob's rope around Ben Thompson's neck was a real possibility. Thompson's bond was set at $15,000, a huge sum for the times, but Ben was released when L. D. Carrington and William H. Roberts pledged to be his sureties. Rapp retained Attorney Charles L. Robards as his defense counsel, and after an examination of the facts surrounding the case by Justice McLaughlin, Rapp was released after posting a $2,000 bond. By now, word had spread that the fatal shooting of John Coombs was an act of self-defense, and the threat of mob violence ebbed. Lingering for more than a month, Coombs's wounds would finally prove to be fatal. He died on October 1. On the same day he succumbed, Rapp and Thompson were subsequently indicted by the Travis County Grand Jury, and charged with murder.[46]

Ben Thompson's trial for the killing of John Coombs was delayed through the winter and spring of 1865 and was not held until after the Civil War ended but as one San Antonio newspaper later noted, the killing provided young Ben with an "abundance of notoriety."[47]

On October 10, 1864, Ben Thompson was again placed on detached service from his regiment and ordered to help drive a mule herd to Bolivar Point, near Galveston Bay.[48] By November, he returned to Austin but Ben being Ben, he could not remain out of trouble for long, and was indicted in March by the Spring Grand Jury for gambling at euchre on February 15 in a room attached to James R. Jackson and R. H. Clement's public house. Ben's arrest did not deter him from publicly gambling. On the night of March 18, Ben and three other men were seen playing cards at the same location. At the table were fifty-seven-year-old, former City Marshal, James R. Jackson (1859-1860) and Hugh Robinson, a man prone to sudden violence. Without any noticeable provocation, Robinson drew his knife and fatally stabbed Jackson in the chest multiple times. The other players, including Ben, must have been so stunned they did not react in time to hinder the fatal attack. Then drawing

Austin attorney and United States Congressman John Hancock. In 1866, Hancock purchased from Elizabeth Moore, Thompson's mother-in-law, her farm as an investment. With his law partner, C.S. West, Hancock successfully defended Thompson on the charge of murder in the John Coombs killing.

Courtesy the Austin History Center. Image # PICB 03432.

his revolver, Robinson ran from the room and escaped, fleeing to San Antonio. Before he could continue his flight to Old Mexico, he was shot dead by an unidentified assailant, probably a relative or friend of Jackson.[49]

As the Civil War raged to a climax in the Eastern Theater through the remainder of the year and into the spring of 1865, the war in Texas continued to slumber. Lee surrendered the Army of Northern Virginia on April 9 and seventeen days later, Johnston capitulated to Sherman in North Carolina. Ironically, the last fight of the war was a Confederate victory. On May 13, 1865, outside of Brownsville at Palmetto Ranch, Colonel Ford whipped an advancing Union force. Accepting the inevitable, on May 26, Confederate General Edmund Kirby Smith agreed to terms and on June 2, he formally signed the document surrendering all troops and military posts in the Trans-Mississippi Department, which included Texas. With this act, the last significant Confederate army officially laid down their arms, and the American Civil War had finally ended.

Thompson was near the town of Waco when the Confederacy's life slowly came to an end. When his regiment disbanded, he returned to Austin and his pregnant wife, Kate. According to Walton, Thompson remained peaceful and quietly lived with his family attending to his own business and molesting no one.[50] However, court documents show Ben was taken into custody during the final week of 1865 and charged with the theft of almost four dozen bags of coffee beans from an Austin businessman. It is unknown what the legal result was from this charge, however if he was convicted of any crime, the punishment must have been trivial.[51]

Walton's short description of Thompson's peaceful homecoming omitted mention of a fatal shooting scrape. At a time and place when the saying "buckshot means burying" indicated the intense fear most westerners felt towards fighting a man armed with a shotgun, Ben Thompson was one of the very few who possessed the self-confidence in his own quickness and unerring accuracy with a pistol to face a man so armed.

An Italian teamster named Alberto Algerio was driving a wagon pulled by a six-horse team through Austin. Ben Thompson, accompanied by an unidentified Confederate soldier, spotted the C. S. A. brand on one of Algerio's horses. They decided to follow him and recover the stock. Algerio headed north, out of town toward the spot where the state's lunatic asylum was later located. There they finally overtook Algerio, forcing him to stop. The two soldiers began to unhitch the animal with the C. S. A. brand, declaring him property of the Confederate government and stated they were taking possession of the horse. Algerio was confused as to what was happening. He did not speak English, and a short, angry verbal exchange began in which none of the parties could understand each other. Frustrated, angry, and determined to keep what he perceived as his property, Algerio drew a shotgun and leveled it at the two soldiers. Before he could squeeze the trigger, Thompson drew his pistol and shot the Italian dead. He was buried in the Austin City Cemetery on May 27. As to the cause of death, the sexton simply recorded, "Alberto Algerio Italian Kild [*sic*] by Thompson."[52]

Chapter 3

A Guerrilla Chieftain South of the Border

"My heart longed for home."

—Ben Thompson, 1867

U.S. Army General Gordon Granger was given command of the Department of Texas on June 10, 1865. Upon his arrival in Galveston nine days later, he read the proclamation that the institution of slavery had been abolished and all slaves were now free. In addition, Granger declared all laws passed by the Confederacy were void. The now former slaves joyfully celebrated the news. This was the start of the unofficial holiday known as "Juneteenth," which continues to be celebrated every year on June 19. Following the end of the war, the functions of civil government had all but collapsed in Texas. Only in the towns where Union troops were garrisoned was there any semblance of order. General Granger declared that those committing acts of violence or theft were outlaws and enemies of the human race, and promised they would be dealt with accordingly.

Another historic event took place only days before Juneteenth. During the night of June 11, approximately fifteen to twenty men broke into the state treasury in Austin and absconded with about $17,000 in coin, the equivalent of over $3 million in modern terms. The group struck after 9 p.m., but made so much noise breaking into the safes that they aroused the neighborhood. Prior to the heist, George R. Freeman, a former Confederate cavalry captain, took it upon himself to organize a thirty-man militia to act as peacekeepers until the Union could send troops to preserve order. When he called for the militia to gather by ringing the bells of the First Baptist Church, nineteen responded. Captain Freeman led his band to the state house, then to the building next door, which housed the treasury. They fired a ragged volley sending the robbers fleeing on horseback. Freeman entered the building with three men, a small group consisting of Freeman's brother, Friedrich "Fred" Sterzing, and Albert Musgrove. Once inside they challenged the sole remaining robber who chose to draw down on them. The young outlaw, Alex Campbell, was mortally wounded in the gut during the brief gunfight. Blood and the strong smell of whiskey oozed in equal measure from his fatal stomach wound. Despite this, Campbell upheld a measure of honor by refusing to divulge the names of his partners, though he did curse them as cowards who ran at the first shot. Captain Freeman received a minor shoulder wound in the melee but soon recovered.[1]

Although never formally charged, John Rapp, Campbell's former company commander, was accused of being the ring leader and Ben Thompson, being a close friend of Rapp, was suspected of being a participant through guilt by association. No proof of Ben's culpability has ever been presented, though the same cannot be said of John Rapp. Lafayette Rogers, a citizen of Austin from 1852 to 1866, later stated he met John Rapp many years later in New Mexico. There, Rapp freely confessed to his involvement in the robbery. Historian Mike Cox has suggested that Rapp "may have felt such a strong sense of entitlement that he and his comrades helped themselves to some hard currency."[2] Officially, the robbery has never been solved.

At first, the Federal occupation moved slowly into the interior of the state due to inadequate roads and the lack of extensive railroad lines. The eventual arrival of the blue-coated occupation troops heightened the hatred many Texans already felt for all those who were forcibly changing southern society and the southern way of life. This hatred was returned, resulting in many criminal acts between soldiers and citizens. Not surprisingly, many of the Texans whose inner nature drew them to acts of violence did not often find themselves treated as outcasts. Instead, hard men like Cullen Baker, John Wesley Hardin, William Longley, and Joe Horner, to name the best-known, found help from a multitude of supporters and apologists, and Texas remained in turmoil for many years to come.

Per Walton, Thompson wisely remained at home and attended to his own business. He had a joyous reason to behave, because on Friday, July 14, 1865, his wife, Kate, gave birth to their first child, a daughter. They named the newborn Mary Elizabeth after the child's grandmothers.[3]

On the morning of July 25, a small infantry unit comprised of two hundred Federal soldiers finally arrived in Austin and occupied the state's seat of government. One week later, on August 1, the United States First Louisiana Cavalry Regiment, commanded by Colonel Algernon Sidney Badger, was sent to bolster the meager force.[4] The new and federally appointed provisional Governor of Texas, Andrew J. Hamilton, took control of the state government the following day. Hamilton was a Texas politician prior to the war, and as a leader of the unionists, he opposed secession.

On August 28, 1865, Ben Thompson was officially released on parole by the Federal provost marshal.[5] This act was probably a paperwork shuffle in which he was merely part of a mass parole. Instead of remaining free, he was arrested again and placed in the Travis County jail by the order of Colonel Badger. Walton stated the arrest order did not mention any crime or offense.[6] Maybe Thompson was incarcerated because of the Algerio killing, or perhaps for the earlier killing of John Coombs. The records are inconclusive. A former comrade-in-arms later complained of the ill treatment Ben Thompson received from Colonel Badger, and declared unconvincingly that it was the cause, at least in part, of Thompson's subsequent wild and desperate career.[7] This declaration defies the facts, because Ben was already on his way to a life seeped in violence.

With the help of his family, Ben Thompson appealed to the most influential pro-union citizens of Austin, including Governor Hamilton. These men proved to be unable to secure his release.[8] His wife, baby, and mother visited the jail daily. They brought him food, clean clothing, and more importantly, information about the dramatic events occurring south of the Rio Grande. Frustrated with his seemingly endless confinement, Ben Thompson began to plan his escape. He learned that Imperial agents had moved into Texas seeking to recruit men to fight in Mexico for the Emperor Maximilian.[9]

Many former Confederate soldiers of all ranks were welcomed by Maximilian, and in fact, were invited by him. These former soldiers chose to move south of the border rather than live under Federal rule. The emperor set land aside to be used as colonies specifically for the ex-Confederates and thousands resettled in Mexico.[10] There, many joined the ranks of Maximilian's Imperial army.

In the early 1860s, the American Civil War was not the only conflict raging on the North American Continent. By 1863, Benito Juarez, the duly elected President of Mexico, along with his Liberal party was in full retreat from almost 50,000 French soldiers. The instability of the Juarez government, alongside the inability of the United States to enforce the Monroe Doctrine, allowed France to intervene in the internal affairs of Mexico through both political and military means. President Juarez and the Liberal-controlled Mexican legislature sowed the seeds of the French intrusion by suspending the repayment of loans made to Mexico by French, English, and Spanish bankers. The bankers appealed to their various governments, but only Napoleon the Third, the Emperor of France, was bold enough to defy the United States and send troops into Mexico.

Napoleon and Conservative Mexican leaders scoured the royal courts of Europe for a man to rule over Mexico on their behalf. They approached a Hapsburg prince, the younger brother of the Emperor of Austria, the idle Archduke Ferdinand Maximilian. Deceived of the true political situation and believing that a huge majority of the Mexican people would accept him as their regent, Maximilian unwisely accepted Napoleon's offer to become the Emperor of Mexico.

In the spring of 1864, Maximilian's party disembarked at Vera Cruz. He was shocked to learn the actual condition of the country and immediately set to work to establish an effective, honest government and invigorate the impoverished Mexican economy. Maximilian was eager to abolish injustices and to help the oppressed. One focus was a Liberal law commonly known as the *Ley Lerdo*, which was enacted in 1857 with the well-intentioned aim of helping peasants farm their own land. In actuality, *Ley Lerdo* restricted property ownership to the individual, and many Indian tribes were inadvertently stripped of their communal lands. The vast majority of Indians were unfamiliar with the concept of individual ownership, and consequently sold their lands for trifling sums.

In response to *Ley Lerdo*, Maximilian pronounced decrees that returned the land to the natives. From that time on, many Indians showed a fanatical enthusiasm and fierce loyalty to the Emperor, but none more so than a chieftain named Tomas Mejia. From his home located deep in the mountains surrounding the town of Queretaro, Mejia had led his tribe against the rule of the Liberal party. Maximilian rewarded Mejia with a general's commission.

Major General Mejia was universally respected. In an extremely brutal war, he was renowned for the kindness and mercy he showed to his enemies. In a struggle where betrayal was commonplace, he made no attempt at duplicity and never concealed his true sentiments. As a leader, few generals south of the Rio Grande could equal his military skills and fewer still matched the personal fearlessness he demonstrated in the heat of battle.

At first, the powerful French armed forces faced moderate opposition, and captured the principal gulf port town of Vera Cruz as well as the country's capital, Mexico City. The city of Matamoros, located across the Rio Grande from Brownsville, Texas, was likewise overrun by French troops.

When its own civil war ended, the United States was able to send munitions, arms, medical supplies, and money across the Rio Grande to help President Juarez in his efforts to drive out the French. The Liberal forces were propped up by all of this aid, and they started to show a remarkable ability to recuperate after a defeat. Correspondingly, a victory swelled their ranks with thousands of new, eager volunteers. General Mejia, without French troops, successfully defended Matamoros for a year from a series of Liberal attacks on the city. In early September of 1865, the Liberals again moved on Matamoros. A former mule contractor with no mili-

José Tomas de la Luz Mejia (1820-1867), rose from poverty to become a general under Emperor Maximilian, only to be executed with him on June 9, 1867. He was Ben Thompson's commander at Matamoros, Mexico. *Courtesy the Library of Congress.*

tary experience led the Juarista attack[11], and in Mariano Escobedo, President Juarez had finally found his general.

General Mejia desperately needed more seasoned fighters to bolster his army. Ex-Confederate veterans like Ben Thompson were ideal targets for recruitment. With no foreseeable hope of being released, Thompson cautiously approached the guards who had charge of him. Two sergeants named Benito Gomez and Jack Brickhouse agreed to a bribe. Once freed, Thompson planned to join General Mejia's garrison at Matamoros where a commission as a lieutenant had already been prepared for him and was in the possession of one of Mejia's adjutants, Captain W.J. Gilly (Gilley), an American.[12] On more than one occasion, Thompson was allowed to slip secretly from the jail to visit with his family late at night, and to prepare for a prolonged stay south of the border. The two bribed guards decided to accompany Thompson and enlist in Mejia's command. They also convinced five others to join them in their search for fortune in Mexico.[13]

On the evening of Sunday, September 17,[14] Ben Thompson disguised himself as a Federal soldier and was released from his jail cell for the final time. Using side streets and alleys, Thompson and the seven deserters easily avoided the sentries stationed throughout the city. Ben slipped out of Austin on the back of his mule, Dan, and the fast and unrelenting gait of the little mule almost ruined the other men's horses. They separated but planned to rendezvous sixty miles southwest of San Antonio. Gomez and Brickhouse chose to accompany Thompson. The three men were first to arrive at the rendezvous point where they waited for more than a full day, but the others failed to appear. Deciding it was foolish to remain in Texas any longer, they pressed on and crossed the Rio Grande. While massing Liberal companies had laid siege lines surrounding Matamoros, Thompson and his companions were still able to slip into the city where he reported to Captain Gilly.[15] As promised, Gilly presented Ben Thompson with his commission as a lieutenant in an independent company of contra-guerrilla cavalry. The company was comprised of a total of 153 men including Gomez and Brickhouse.

General Mejia had readied the defenses of Matamoros and the nearby port of Bagdad to withstand an assault. His regular Imperial Army troops were standing on full alert, while the citizen volunteer companies were called to muster. At dawn, the contra-guerrillas and other Imperial troops went into battle with Ben Thompson among their ranks.[16]

At 5 a.m. on the morning of Thursday, October 26, the fortifications protecting Matamoros were attacked at several points, some as a feint. Over one thousand men charged against the upper forts, but the breastworks proved too strong and the attack failed. General Mejia, upon seeing the situation, led his Imperial cavalry force out of the city and put the Liberals to flight. The slaughter of the Liberal soldiers left some five hundred dead and wounded men littering the battlefield. During the battle, General Mejia noticed and admired the actions of his new lieutenant, Ben Thompson. Mejia acknowledged his fighting ability with an immediate field promotion to the rank of captain.[17]

Ben Thompson gave his biographer Walton lengthy descriptions of his actions. He described how, when the battle was over, the "ambulance corps with flags" went out to recover the wounded. "I went along," Thompson recalled, "to give my personal attention to the men of my company who had been wounded, and more than twenty of them were missing." Although he had been with these men but a short time, he had become acquainted with everyone and had already developed a strong attachment with some. Thompson searched the battlefield, and there found all his missing men. Among them were Sergeant Gomez, mortally wounded, and Jack Brickhouse, who had been hit on the head and was not sensible, but he survived the injury. Brickhouse did not survive the war, however. He was killed later in a fight near the town of Camargo.[18]

General Mejia's victory did not completely drive the attackers away, and many scattered Liberal companies still harassed the

Imperial positions. To secure the surrounding area, Mejia ordered out patrols to find and punish any enemy troops still lingering near Matamoros. Thompson claimed that sorties were frequent for several weeks and he was engaged in every one. On one occasion, he requested permission to go out into the country with about fifty men, all well-armed and mounted. At this point, Ben Thompson was not only a soldier and mercenary, but also a chieftain of guerrilla fighters.

Ben had no particular objective in mind other than crossing the river and moving west into a region where there were enemies. After some fifteen miles, Ben observed about fifty wagons, which proved to contain commissary stores for the enemy. Knowing the besieging army was short of provisions, Thompson resolved to destroy this train. In so doing, Thompson believed, "we would do great service to General Mejia." The train's guard was made up of ninety men, but they had weapons of a lesser quality than Thompson's company. "We opened up on them with our rifles at about two hundred yards, and so rapid and effective was our fire that confusion among them ensued very quickly." After a few more volleys, Thompson ordered a charge, believing the wagon train guard would not stand up to their onslaught. His men answered with a shout and the attack forced the enemy to break up and flee for their lives. After following the fleeing enemy for a few hundred yards, the fight was over and Thompson's command was victorious. The mules were cut loose, and the contents of the wagons were set on fire. Thompson forced the captured teamsters to drive the mules to the river and cross over where they were given to one James Mason, a ranchero. Thompson made a deal with Mason. Ben claimed, "with the injunction to turn … the mules … into money and deposit two thousand dollars of it with Mr. Twohig, banker, at San Antonio, payable to the order of my wife, and do what he pleased with the balance."[19] Thompson observed, "Some men are ungrateful rascals." He never again heard from Mason, the mules, or the money from the sale. In light of the results of his raid, Thompson was offered another promotion but he declined, stating that he "could do better service in the position I occupied, besides I was not capable of managing a battalion."[20]

On November 25, in a formal ceremony honoring their efforts, the volunteer citizen companies were permitted to stand down and Matamoros returned to relative calm.[21] With the city now considered safe, many of the soldiers, including Thompson and his friend Captain Gilly, started to seek out some fun. Once, they began an evening at one of the city's many gambling halls. There they lost their watches, almost all of their money, and Thompson lost a diamond ring. Due to their earning good wages, this did not bother Thompson so much, but it was different for Gilly. He drank heavily before they quit the game, and at this point "he was three sheets to the wind." In spite of Ben's efforts to leave the house, Gilly insisted on having more drinks. Finally, an inebriated Gilly agreed to leave the hall and as he exited, he decided to end the evening by shooting off his pistols. Thompson recalled that, although numerous, the Matamoros police were both "inefficient and unpopular." Well aware of the animosity between soldiers and the police, Ben was concerned that on their way back to quarters there might be trouble.

Soon the police appeared. "As if by a pre-concerted signal," Ben related to biographer Walton, "the guardians of the night presented their pistols right in our faces and thus held us still until we were disarmed; then began the march to the city jail; it was quite a distance to the lock-up. On the way we met one of my men. I said in a low tone to him in English; 'Go to the camp and tell the men to arm and meet me at the market house instantly, you see the police have me and Gilly.'"

Ben believed a show of force by his comrades would secure their release. Even though he had spoken quietly in English, one of the policemen understood very well what he had said. The policeman accused Ben, "You will send for your soldiers to shoot us, will you, you gringos" and with that, jabbed Thompson several times hard in the throat with the barrel of his pistol. Ben admittedly became "so mad I almost took a fit." However, he instinctively knew if he resisted both Gilly and himself could be shot down in a matter of moments. Fortunately, a distraction occurred and in the near distance, the rapid firing of guns and pistols could be heard. The fellow soldier Ben had spoken to blundered miserably, and mixed up the message. His comrades believed the police had already killed him and Gilly. Surging out onto the street, they began shooting at every policeman in sight and many fell dead or wounded. In the confusion, Ben's "punching friend" managed to sneak away, but Ben had "photographed this man in my mind so that I should remember him," perhaps believing he might someday even the score.

General Mejia sent for Thompson the next morning. He wanted an explanation of the previous night's disturbance. Ben gave a truthful account as to his connection with it. Mejia was not too concerned, only advising with emphasis that it should not happen again. Ben's final comment on the incident was, "the life of a Mexican policeman was not valued very highly."[22]

Throughout the fall of 1865, General Mejia sent many reports to his superiors imploring them to provide more men and material assistance. Except for a small reinforcement, his pleas for additional help were rejected. The New Year brought more evidence of General Mejia's slowly deteriorating position.

At 4 a.m. on January 5, about sixty-five former United States soldiers, who were also mostly former slaves, and Mexican adventurers crossed over the border from Texas. It was a private venture without allegiance to either of the fighting political factions in Mexico. Their sole purpose was to surprise and loot the port town of nearby Bagdad. This small band easily captured the slumbering Imperial garrison posted there. When given a choice, much of the garrison gleefully joined in the looting. Ultimately, a detachment of United States soldiers had to cross over from Brownsville to establish order, and to protect the lives of American citizens. Loyal Imperial soldiers did not enter Bagdad until three weeks later, and that was only after the looters had abandoned the town because there was nothing else worth stealing.

Throughout Mexico, the tide of war was beginning to turn against Maximilian. The Imperial garrison of Chihuahua City surrendered after a Juarista assault. Mazatlán fell, and the entire eight-hundred man Imperial garrison there was put to death after surrendering. At San Luis Potosi, two hundred captured Imperials were executed by firing squad. Outside of Matamoros, the Juarista partisans controlled the countryside all the way to the port town of Tampico, which they had under siege.

All merchandise trains moving through the interior of the country required the protection of Imperial soldiers. In early April, Juarista troops attacked a large wagon train transporting vital goods and more importantly, half a million dollars' worth of gold specie to Matamoros. In response, General Mejia personally commanded the relief of the convoy, scattering the ambushers after a brief but bloody fight. The businessmen of Matamoros were encouraged by this success. With the desire to see open traffic and commerce, they convinced Mejia to provide a strong military escort for another wagon train of even greater value. Its destination was to be the interior city of Monterrey, two hundred miles away.

General Mejia decided to remain at Matamoros. He retained nine hundred soldiers to guard the city and assigned a subordinate, Brigadier General Rafael Olvera, to command the column. Capt. Ben Thompson and his company were selected to ride point on the wagon train. The convoy set out on Thursday June 7, 1866. Ben

Thompson left a vivid description of events and the fate of what he called the "treasure train." It had an estimated value of several million dollars.

> We went out in fine style, all dressed in the ... finest Mexican clothes ... laughing, singing, anticipating a pleasant journey. Quite a number of the ladies, accomplished and beautiful, accompanied their friends for a few miles, and were escorted on the return by a squadron of cavalry. My company was the advance guard on the march. No danger was looked for. [Juarista General] Escobedo was thought to be many miles in the interior, and no other enemy in force had been reported; nevertheless I kept as vigilant a watch as if I had known an attack would be made.

For two days the train traveled undisturbed. Suddenly, Thompson and his men were ordered to join the main body as an attack was threatened from the rear.

> I hastened to obey ... but by the time I reached the command the attack had been made, and the fight became general. I obeyed orders, and fought as I never fought before or since. Our men fought for the train, over it, under it, around it ... it was no use, the attack was too strong to resist ... out of my fifty-eight [contra-guerillas], I now had but seventeen, and eight of them were seriously wounded, and the others were all dead ... We were terribly whipped and the treasure lost ... It was suicidal to fight longer ... in darkness and silence we left our dead comrades to the mercy of the jackals and crows.[23]

The unorganized retreat staggered north to the Rio Grande, mostly with the intent of traveling east towards General Mejia and what was left of his command at Matamoros. Deciding to desert, some of the Imperial soldiers turned to cowardice and began to swim to the safety of the Texas side. As they rushed down to the riverbank, they found themselves being fired upon by the companions they chose to forsake. Ben Thompson was exceptionally loyal and felt nothing but disdain for any and all who were not cut from the same cloth. Pulling his revolver, he emptied it into the swirling shallow waters of the Rio Grande. Thompson himself would later tell how he killed six men floundering in the water. Some who later heard his tale believed he exaggerated, however companions of his at the time verified that he carried out what he claimed.[24]

The disaster became known as the Battle of Camargo, and Ben Thompson's account of the magnitude of the defeat was no exaggeration. Twenty-five hundred well-armed Juarista soldiers ambushed the wagon train; however the result of the battle was only assured when an Imperial battalion refused to obey General Olvera's orders, preferring instead to mutiny and fight for the other side. Panic ensued at Matamoros and thousands of residents evacuated to safety by crossing the river into Texas. With his position untenable, General Mejia entered into negotiations to peacefully extract the remainder of his army and surrender the city. Eager to occupy Matamoros intact, the Juarista commanding officer allowed the Imperial troops to keep their small-arms and withdraw through Bagdad, where they boarded French ships without molestation.

On Saturday, June 22, the night before the surrender ceremony, a chance encounter at a dance hall provided Ben Thompson an opportunity to permanently settle a personal matter. Thompson entered a fandango and was soon dancing. He would remember his dancing partner as "the handsomest and most graceful senorita" he had ever seen. As they passed another couple, Ben's eyes, "encountered those of the [policeman]" who earlier struck him repeatedly in the throat with his pistol. Recognition was instantly mutual. Ben decided that the dance was neither the time nor the place to demand satisfaction, but he did pay close attention to the policeman, and recalled what subsequently happened.

> After a time the dance ended. My partner was seated, and, as is customary, I asked her what wine, confection or ices I should bring her. Before she answered, this man touched me

> on the shoulder and asked me to step outside the door with him. I excused myself on the plea of the lady. The devil was already jumping out of him through his eyes. He insisted, but had stepped back a pace or two, as if he expected me to comply with his request. I again said 'No, you will excuse me.' He then had his hand on his knife. He seemed to hesitate a moment, but only a moment, drew quickly and dashed at me. I was just in time: a step sideways and backward avoided the blow. I struck him on the head with my pistol, and then, as rapidly as thought, shot him four times. I don't think he even moved after he fell—and he commenced falling on the first shot—nor did I shoot after he touched the floor. The sound of the report had not ceased before I was out at the door and in the dark.

The dead policeman's friends pursued him, but Ben outran the danger and arrived at the quarters of General Mejia safely. There he explained what had happened, but the general was not concerned. Mejia handed over $2,000 in gold to Ben, remarking that "Every man must be his own commissary." At this point Ben wrote to his wife in Austin, and also dispatched a note to a friend on the Texas side of the river asking him to send over "and get my mule Dan and keep him for me. I was then ready [to follow Mejia] ... let it end where or how it might."[25]

Early the following morning, the garrison started moving toward the levee taking with them their flags, baggage, side arms, ammunition and two small artillery pieces. Of all the members of the contra-guerrilla companies, only forty men remained. By 11 a.m., all the troops were gathered together on board three steamships, and after the formal surrender ceremony Major General Mejia and his staff joined their men for the start down river to the Gulf of Mexico. The ultimate destination of Mejia's command was Vera Cruz, and with this withdrawal the reign of the Empire passed forever from Northern Mexico.[26]

The losses of Matamoros and Bagdad were just two of many blows that fell against Maximilian's empire in the summer of 1866.

However, the most serious misfortune was the lack of resolve from Maximilian's chief benefactor, Napoleon the Third, who had decided to abandon him. Facing diplomatic pressure from America, and the unending cost of this foreign venture, Napoleon agreed to withdraw his army from Mexico. It was decided that the entire contingent would be out of the country by April 1867. French soldiers were also ordered not to take part in any further military campaigns. The troops would only be permitted to defend themselves. On February 5, 1867, the French army evacuated the City of Mexico and began their long retreat to the troop ships anchored at Vera Cruz.

On February 12, at San Luis Potosi, Mejia outmaneuvered and defeated a Juarista force more than twice his size before he and his men withdrew into the interior. For a time, General Mejia and his command faded from the newspapers reporting on the war. The outside world could only speculate on his location and future plans.

Ben Thompson related Mejia's continued loyalty to the Emperor and his own decision to fight to the end.

> Maximilian had met with the most serious reverses, his armies defeated, the fickle people rising, and some of his own generals pronouncing against him. He was on the retreat from the City of Mexico. Mejia was ordered to join Maximilian at Queretaro by rapid marches. Mejia, ... faithful to the Emperor, one of the few Mexicans who did not turn traitor when the crisis came ... Volunteers were called for; [Mejia] well knew that only such as would volunteer would remain faithful even to him in this hour of adversity; besides, a slow march could serve no purpose, and would only expose him in the open field to attack and destruction by the enemy. Seven-hundred and sixty-one men volunteered, I among the number ... The Mexican is fickle, ungrateful and treacherous. They saw the certain downfall of Maximilian; no power on earth within reach could save him. Ever ready to espouse the stronger side, the soldiers who did not volunteer, joined by the citizens, were ready to declare for Juarez and massacre those who adhered to the

> Emperor. They were particularly malignant towards the alien mercenaries, and I fell within that class … I have been on a great many rides, but this was the most energetic, determined, constant and compact I have ever participated in … but twenty-three of the men fell by the way—they from exhaustion, and not from want of will to do or attachment to our glorious leader. We entered Queretaro on the fourth night, a little after twelve o'clock.[27]

On February 13, 1867, at the head of six thousand men, Maximilian abandoned Mexico City. The valley town of Queretaro was selected as the point of concentration for the remaining Imperial armies for two reasons. First, it blocked Juarista General Escobedo and his Army of the North from the capital city. Secondly, Queretaro had long been a bastion of support for Maximilian. Mejia had recruited thousands of Indians for the Imperial army from the tribes living in the Sierra Corda mountain range northeast of the city. Strategically, Queretaro may have been an excellent choice, but tactically, the town was impossible to defend. Every building was within the range of artillery fire from the surrounding hills, and with only a combined total of fourteen thousand soldiers, the Imperial army no longer had the manpower to successfully hold the high ground.

By March 5, Queretaro was firmly surrounded by General Escobedo and a combined Juarista army of forty thousand well-armed soldiers. In desperation, Maximilian personally led a breakout attempt on April 22. After hours of fighting, the road to return to Mexico City was laid open, but the Imperials were too exhausted to exploit the opportunity. Instead, they stumbled back into their own fortifications. The water supply was cut off on May 10, and food was becoming more and more scarce. General Mejia was ordered to plan another breakout attempt for the night of May 14-15. Three thousand of his Indian tribesmen were to spearhead the attack. The night before the scheduled assault, Mejia met with

Maximilian. Ben accompanied Mejia, and later remembered his meeting with the Emperor: "I am no admirer of emperors or kings, as such," he began, "but Mejia was entitled to see and speak to his chief, whom he idolized. I could go where Mejia went. I was his close follower and humble friend ... I am not able to forget the impression Emperor Maximilian made on me. His presence was the magnificence of human appearance." All present certainly knew that within a few hours, Maximilian's fate would be decided. However, before morning arrived, Maximilian was betrayed when one of his officers sold passage through the section of the line he commanded. General Escobedo's soldiers poured into the city, and within hours Maximilian and Mejia were prisoners.[28]

On May 15, Queretaro fell after a siege of seventy-two days. The Emperor and his top generals, Mejia and Miramon, found escape impossible, but not the lesser officers and enlisted men of the Imperial army. A "confused rejoicing" took hold of the Juarista army. Ben Thompson and his comrade, who he identified as Jean Lefebre, seized this opportunity to flee by heading in the direction of the gulf port of Vera Cruz, which was almost three hundred miles away. They had hoped to reach the French lines, but were ignorant of the fact that the last French troopship had long since departed.[29]

The trial of Maximilian, Mejia, and former President of Mexico, General Miguel Miramon for treason began on June 12. The Emperor steadfastly refused to attend the proceedings, and rather than dragging him bound and gagged into the courtroom, he was tried in absentia.[30] Despite protests from the United States government, the court unanimously condemned the three defendants to death by firing squad. In defiance of a global consensus, President Juarez approved the executions.

Maximilian stood before a firing squad on the Hill of the Bells in Queretaro on the morning of Wednesday, June 19, 1867. Five rifle balls tore into his chest. As he lay stretched out on the ground, his

Emperor Maximilian of Mexico and Archduke of Austria (1832-1867). He accepted the offer of the Mexican throne. His efforts in dealing with the politics of Mexico were unsuccessful and he was executed on June 9, 1867. *Courtesy the Library of Congress.*

body continued to quiver. Two soldiers were called up and, in respect of the Emperor's request not to be shot in the head, they were ordered to fire their muskets into his body. Mejia and Miramon were then placed before the firing squad. During the first volley, each man received four balls in the breast, which instantly killed both of them. Afterward, President Juarez returned Maximilian's bullet ridden corpse to his native Austria as a warning to all those who would consider meddling in Mexico's domestic affairs.

Leaving Queretaro behind, Thompson and Lefebre changed horses as needed. Ben acknowledged that these changes were "by force or fraud." Announcing, "the country [was] aroused; every Mexican an enemy, and none but Mexicans on the line of flight," Thompson knew their chances of seeing Vera Cruz were slim, but somehow, they reached the city. It didn't matter if the French were gone, no one was interested in the two Americans. After escaping the bullet and the knife, Ben almost succumbed to another fate. He gave in to "the most malignant type of the yellow fever."

> The conviction fastened itself upon me that this sickness would end in death. I had seen [many] die; so few recover in sickness so deadly as mine. But I did not die; the sickness was long, and I rose a skeleton. Months had elapsed. The French were gone, and I, indebted for my life to the noble Sisters of Charity, Sister Josefa having had special charge of me ... When I was sufficiently recovered to think and to look about me, I found my money greatly decreased, though I know as I live that all the missing coins had been expended on me in my sickness and invalidism; besides, a stray newspaper, the New York Herald, found its way to me, and from it I learned that civil government had been established in Texas, J. W. Throckmorton elected governor. My heart longed for home. There was no barrier to my return; no reason why I should longer expatriate myself. I had done nothing for which I was afraid to meet the gaze of twelve jurors and hear the charge of any honest judge. I returned, and was again clasped in the arms of my wife and to the heart of my mother.[31]

Prior to the fall of Maximilian's empire, former Confederate officer James Webb Throckmorton was elected in a landslide to be governor of Texas. Also elected to fill the executive arm of Throckmorton's administration were many ex-Confederate officers and politicians. Yet, Governor Throckmorton was a moderate. As a member of the 1861 secession convention, he was one of only eight who voted against leaving the Union. From the moment he took office, Throckmorton insisted on the supremacy of the civil government over military authority. Upset with this insistence and deciding Throckmorton was an impediment to Reconstruction, General Philip Sheridan used his power to intervene. Sheridan, on July 1, 1867, ordered Throckmorton removed from office. Before August ended, all of the important statewide officials—attorney general, treasurer, comptroller, and commissioner of general land office—were also removed and replaced.[32]

As Ben lay sick at Vera Cruz, his infant daughter Mary Elizabeth was also seriously ill. On May 25, Ben's wife and mother hurriedly baptized little Mary in anticipation of the tragedy that would soon follow. The child died less than two weeks later. She was buried on June 6, and her death was recorded at Saint David's Episcopal Church.[33] While the exact date of Ben Thompson's return to his hometown of Austin is unknown, evidence exists that he was back in Austin no later than the second week of July 1867.[34] Ben kept a worthless bank draft from Maximilian's government in the amount of $10,000 for the rest of his life as a memento for his services to the fallen emperor. In reality, Ben Thompson's adventure south of the border, his "valiant service" for General Mejia and the Emperor Maximilian, rewarded him with nothing but a series of close brushes with death.[35]

With the recent removal of Throckmorton's administration and having already felt the heavy hand of Federal rule, Ben moved carefully around Austin, preferring to stay with relatives outside of town. Thompson remained under indictment for the charge of murder in the death of John Coombs, so he would often slip into Austin at night to confer with his attorneys. Once, he went into town to have his horse shod dressed in the fancy garb of a Mexican. Soldiers learned he was in the city, and he was only able to retrieve his horse at gunpoint. Two patrols rode in close pursuit, firing at him as he fled but he managed to escape unharmed. The close call and the continued efforts of the Federal military to push aside civil authority convinced Thompson to face the murder indictment, be tried and finally settle the issue. Since the principal witnesses were readily available and civil court was currently in session, his legal counsel agreed he should submit for trial and the representation he chose was notable. Thompson retained the law partners John Hancock and Charles S. West for his defense.[36]

The partnership of Hancock and West was one of Austin's finest law firms. Prior to the Civil War, John Hancock was elected to the judgeship of the Second Judicial District, and afterward to the Texas legislature. A loyal unionist, Hancock was a prominent member of the Constitutional Convention of 1866, where he stood in favor of restoring the southern states into the Union. That same year, he purchased from Ben Thompson's mother-in-law, Elizabeth Moore, her 521-acre property outside of Austin. Hancock placed his former slaves there to live and work the land. Charles West had also served in the Texas Legislature. In 1859, West was Governor Francis R. Lubbock's secretary of state, and in 1861, he entered the Confederate army with the rank of captain. Two years later, he was promoted to major for gallantry on the battlefield. Eventually, West would rise to great distinction as an associate judge of the Texas Supreme Court.

The prominence of his attorneys and the skill and eloquence they used in presenting the facts of the case brought in a jury verdict of not guilty. Free of the Coombs murder charge and not facing any other indictments, Thompson returned to his profession as a gambler. At the close of the Civil War, Thompson's old friend, Phil Coe, arrived in Austin and in partnership with a young local sporting man by the name of Tom Bowles, purchased a barroom reportedly named the Rawhide saloon. Thompson was approached by Coe and Bowles, and was granted the gambling concession at their establishment.[37]

As 1867 was coming to a close, Ben and Billy Thompson's younger sister, nineteen-year-old Mary Jane, became engaged to Robert Gill, a young Confederate veteran who had served in the army during all four years of the war. Born in Tennessee in 1844, Gill came to Texas early in life with his parents, five brothers and sister. The Gill family settled in the town of Bastrop, located some thirty miles southeast of Austin. Gill's father, also named Robert, would serve Bastrop County as its sheriff. Young Robert Gill did not emulate his father, but instead followed his older brother into the butcher trade, before becoming a dairy farmer, and over the years, eventually a Bastrop businessman owning a dry goods store. On December 18, Mary Jane Thompson and Robert Gill were married, and they made their home in the town of Bastrop.[38]

An announcement of political opinion in Texas at this time often resulted in violence. Such was the case in Austin when thirty-two-year-old Julius Schuetze, a speech and music teacher as well as a prominent leader of the German community, pushed his Republican-based political views too far. Five enraged men drew knives and advanced on the mild mannered Schuetze, and his well-being, perhaps, his life appeared in jeopardy until Thompson intervened. Drawing his revolver, Ben drove off the attackers. The young German went on to a long career of public service. He was elected to the bench, becoming a county judge in Bastrop, a Texas legislator, and publisher of the *Vorwaerts*, a prominent German-language newspaper. For many years after, Ben received much credit for intervening and saving Schuetze's life.[39]

Chapter 4

A PRESIDENTIAL PARDON

"If I ever see you playing officer again I will kill you, [even] if I hang for it!"

—Ben Thompson to Justice of the Peace W. D. Scott

In the early spring of 1868, Ben Thompson traveled eighty-five miles northeast to Bryan, the rough and tumble county seat of Brazos County. The Civil War prevented most of the railroads in Texas from laying track, and the Houston and Central Texas Railroad was no exception. During the first two years following the war, the H. & C. T. crept slowly northward through the center of the state until it finally reached Bryan. As a terminus town, it attracted attention from all kinds of opportunists, particularly saloon owners and professional gamblers.

"Big King" reached a place of prominence among these sporting men. He was a physically large man, and he was the owner of the Blue Wing Saloon, which was renowned for attracting a wide spectrum of desperate characters. Now only remembered by his nickname, Big King was an inveterate gambler.[1] In an all-night *monte* game, with Ben Thompson as the dealer, Ben won all of Big King's ready cash. Exhausted, Ben gathered in the last pot and voiced his desire to get some sleep. Big King asked him to hold on, and stated he wanted to continue the game by offering his sole-ownership of the Blue Wing Saloon, including the property, fixtures and stock as collateral for one thousand dollars' worth of credit. Thompson wearily agreed, and called upon Henry Coffield, a young lawyer who was hanging about the saloon, to formally set the terms down on paper. Later in his life, Coffield would rise to prominence, and became mayor of the town of San Marcos in Hays County. Among the witnesses to the game was a gambler and longtime friend of Thompson's, Bill Johnson. Also witnessing the card game was the notorious John Watson, a suspected horse thief who ended up in prison for the Austin killing of John Eikel, and the unfortunate Dan Gallagher, an eventual victim of a lynch mob. The *monte* game seesawed back and forth in the dark smoke-filled room, through all of the next day and the following night. The two men played as though "they had not seen cards for a week." As the game continued on, neither man would risk their concentration and would not touch a drink. With another dawn upon them, Big King turned over his last card and was finally cleaned out. He calmly stood up, and without uttering a word, handed over the keys to his business. As the new proprietor, Ben Thompson called for a celebration and popped open all of the bottles of champagne in the house for everyone to enjoy.[2]

As the new owner and operator of the Blue Wing Saloon, Thompson promptly set up a backroom as a gambling den. For several nights, his business was very successful. But it wasn't long before sore losers threatened his friend Bill Johnson, who was now one of Thompson's dealers. Thompson's biographer knew Johnson and obviously liked him. Walton described him as "a reckless, brave, open-hearted, loud-talking, generous gambler." Only the timely arrival of Thompson and two of his friends kept Johnson from harm. Later that night, vandals entered the saloon after closing and trashed the place. They wrecked furniture, smashed open liquor barrels and destroyed everything of value. Thompson's concern over the damage to his establishment was instantly forgotten, however, when word reached him that his younger brother had shot and killed a man in Austin, the first known victim of Billy Thompson. Ben's concern was not only that Billy had killed a man, but also that Billy's victim was a Federal soldier.[3]

While Ben had continued his career as a gambler in both Austin and Bryan, Billy had lived in San Antonio pursuing the same occupation until the Alamo City's administration ran him out of town.[4] On Tuesday evening, March 31, Billy Thompson was back in Austin and visiting a bordello when he fired three slugs at Sergeant William Burke. The first bullet tore into Burke's bowels, then passed through his body. The second shot glanced across his right breast and the third grazed Burke's head. The latter two wounds, while painful, probably would not have been fatal. The first shot proved to be the lethal one. Burke lingered through the night under the care of two physicians, and he died in the early afternoon of the next day.[5] Different versions of the events that led to the shooting death of Sergeant Burke do exist, as is so often the case.

The first reports of his death appeared on the day of Burke's violent end. Austin's *Tri-Weekly State Gazette* reported the incident as, "Shooting Affray." The cautious editor of the *Gazette* admitted that he did not have the "particulars," and even refused to mention the names of those involved fearing he "might make some mistake, which might do an injustice." He did print that the fatally wounded soldier was a clerk employed at headquarters, and the young man accused of shooting him had been "raised in this city."

The April 1 edition of the *Weekly Austin Republican* did not hesitate to name the killer as "Wm. Thompson of this city," and termed the affair as a "cold-blooded murder," and acknowledged that "Thompson is still at large." The *Republican's* editor called upon the people of Austin to "assist the authorities by every means in their power to bring the murderer to justice."

William Burke (also spelled Burk) was born in Germany and as a child, emigrated to America with his parents, who eventually settled in Richmond, Virginia. When the war ended, Burke joined the army and rose to the rank of Lance Sergeant in the 6th Cavalry. In October 1867, Brevet Major General Joseph J. Reynolds signed an order commanding the young Burke to take charge of all the clerks and records of the office of the Acting Assistant Adjutant General, District of Texas. The records were housed in Galveston and Burke was to convey them to the state's capital city. He would remain in charge of the office and its records, eventually becoming the Chief Clerk of the department in Austin.[6]

The clerks in Burke's department believed he was shot and killed without any apparent provocation.[7] A single line in the Adjutant General Records clearly voices their opinion, "Burke was most foully murdered because he was a soldier."[8] Extremely bitter over the death of their companion and upset over their poor treatment by many Texans, the clerks authored a long, rambling statement written for publication in the newspapers of central Texas.

The Federal soldier's letter insisted "it is, at the present time, impossible for a person with the ... uniform of the United States to go into the streets of your city without being subject of an insult from the citizen population," the soldiers angrily questioned, "does the prerogative of citizen-ship in Texas necessarily consist in being a cut-throat and murderer, desperado, [or] an outcast from civilized society?" The soldiers then issued a warning. "You have forced us to defend ourselves, and we shall. Let one more soldier be shot in the streets of Austin—let one more man be insulted without provocation, and we will show you what we have forgotten since 'Lee's surrender.'"[9]

Billy was in an ugly mood the night he shot Burke. Earlier that evening, at a saloon and billiard hall, he had made up his mind to shoot William M. Walton. What occurred between them is now unknown. Billy was prevented from using the pistol he carried through the timely intervention of friends and others present.[10] Walton, commonly called "Buck," was an articulate, educated man of strong intellect, and as his nickname indicates, he was a proven man of action. As a Confederate officer, he fought in the backwoods war that consumed Missouri and Arkansas, leading many mounted patrols deep behind enemy lines. If a revolver was within Walton's easy reach, the result of a shootout with Billy Thompson would have certainly been open to speculation.

Continuing on with at least one friend in tow, Billy arrived at the house where Burke was sitting in the front parlor. Outside, three or four soldiers were scattered about the yard, passed out and sleeping off a drunken spree. Billy and his friend wanted to strip the uniforms off those "damned Yankee sons of bitches." They planned to burn the uniforms, leaving the soldiers in a humiliating state. Overhearing the conversation, Sergeant Burke spoke up and warned the two men not to do it, since the soldiers weren't bothering anyone. As soon as these words came out of Burke's mouth, Billy pulled his pistol and commenced firing. He easily made his escape from the scene amidst the subsequent chaos.[11]

A second, more detailed, version of the shooting, and one very sympathetic to Billy Thompson is provided by William Walton. In his rendering, Walton made no mention of having any kind of a problem or altercation with Billy that night. Instead, Walton asserted it was Sergeant Burke who was in an ugly mood on the day he died. One or two days earlier, he had met Billy for the first time when they both stopped to watch a fistfight between a black citizen and a white soldier. A group of townspeople who were watching favored the black man over the hated blue-belly, and from the pack, one loudly called out encouragement. Burke accused Billy Thompson of cheering the black man and was ready to fight over the issue until another Texan confessed to the deed. Burke then apologized and offered to make amends to Billy by treating him to a drink. They parted that day amiably.

On that fatal night, Burke and Billy spent hours drinking together before deciding to visit a nearby house of ill-repute. As they approached the place, they discovered some drunken soldiers sleeping in the yard. Billy wanted to play a trick and strip the soldiers of their uniforms. The idea angered Burke who stopped Billy's mischief and threatened him again. Once inside, they separated, and Billy retired to an upstairs room. When Burke realized Billy was gone, his temper flared for the last time. Incensed, he hunted for Thompson, rampaging through the house screaming threats. Finding the room where Thompson was sleeping, Burke kicked in the door and drew his revolver. Shots rang out, and the small room filled with gunsmoke. Hastily pulling on his clothes, Billy stepped over the dying Burke and fled before the authorities arrived. He went into hiding, and for the first of what would be many times in his life, called upon his older brother for help. Through a messenger he sent word to Bryan that he was in trouble and Ben rushed back to Austin without delay.[12]

Billy Thompson managed to get out of the city but he was unable to go very far. He hid at a secluded spot called Bee Springs less than three miles west of town, where the Colorado River began to swing northward. The spring was immersed in a section of rough, wild country, where it sat at the bottom of a deep gully. In this isolated space, Billy was temporarily safe, but he lacked money and the strong mount necessary to continue his escape. In Austin, soldiers followed Ben Thompson everywhere he went, and watched both his house and his mother's home. Suspecting Billy was hiding there, the soldiers set fire to his mother's house in an effort to smoke him out. Unable to see his brother, Ben left Austin and went to the neighboring county of Bastrop where he visited with his younger sister, Mary Jane, and her husband Robert Gill. Soldiers, dressed as civilians, relentlessly shadowed his every movement there as well. Over the next several weeks, a deadly game of cat and mouse ensued with Ben calling upon trusted friends to relay messages to his brother. Somehow, probably through a betrayal, the soldiers learned about Billy's hideout at Bee Springs. Ben was forced to make a desperate ride to warn his brother and move him to another safe place. Again, Billy was unable to flee far. He traveled ten miles to the home of some cousins living in northern Travis County. Within a few days, the soldiers learned of this hideout too, and in the middle of the night, they rode out to raid the house. At this point, the final arrangements had been made and it was decided that Billy should flee to the relative safety north of the Red River in the Indian Territory. Fortune now rode with Billy Thompson, a long streak of good luck began to unfold for him. Billy rode north, unbeknownst to the soldiers who were on their way to raid the now-vacant safe house. He made his escape unmolested through the Hill Country, not realizing he was leaving a wrathful posse behind.[13]

Billy Thompson did not stay in the Indian Territory long. He had returned to Texas by that May, and was lingering in the bustling gulf-port town of Rockport, which was part of Refugio County at the time. Local cattlemen used the town's stone wharf and shipped their herds to the beef-hungry market of New Orleans. The presence of hard currency naturally attracted the usual riff-raff. Indeed, besides the free-flowing money, Rockport offered an important reason to entice a wanted man like Billy Thompson: it lacked lawmen. The growing community was thirty miles north of

Corpus Christi, Union soldiers were not even stationed there, and formal law enforcement did not exist in Rockport.

Exactly two months to the day after Sergeant Burke died, Billy once again held a smoking pistol in his hand while a dying man lay at his feet. Few details were immediately known, but *Flake's Daily Bulletin* of Galveston printed a letter it had received from Refugio declaring the killer was "a man named Thompson, a well known desperado hailing from Austin." Perhaps, quite understandably, the letter writer confused Billy with his better-known older brother. The letter alleged that, "The murder is said to have been committed in mere wantonness, and was entirely unprovoked. The man Thompson, shortly after committing the murder, quietly ate his supper and then mounted his horse and rode away." Depicted in the newspapers as such a careless, arrogant killer, Billy's reputation as a gunman began to emerge.[14]

One of the first respectable establishments to open for business in Rockport was a retail grocery. The proprietor, D. D. Scrivner, was a man of fifty years with small children and a pregnant wife twenty-four years his junior.[15] Hampered by his growing family, Scrivner needed help to run his store. He chose to employ a strong, young man, probably around eighteen-years-old, by the name of Remus Smith. Because Smith was an orphan, his age could only be approximated. On Monday, the first of June, a lull in daily business allowed Scrivner to briefly leave the store. He left Smith in charge. Stepping outdoors, Smith took a moment to feed his horse. Billy Thompson's horse then came up and started bothering Smith for feed. Smith unwisely picked up a handful of stones and threw them at Thompson's horse, driving it off. Seeing what had just transpired, a furious Billy Thompson came up and shouted at Smith, "God Damn You! What did you chunk my horse for? Damn you, I've a notion to whip you!" Smith calmly looked at Billy and told him, "Lay off your six-shooter and come ahead." Realizing he was armed and young Smith wasn't, Billy drew his revolver and squeezed the trigger twice. The bullets were well placed with both shots striking Smith. Either of the two wounds would have proven fatal, and when Scrivner returned he found his young employee on the ground, gasping his last breaths. Moments before he died, Smith told Scrivner it was William Thompson who had shot him, and described how it had occurred.[16]

The letter published in the *Bulletin* claimed Billy Thompson shot Smith and then took the time to enjoy dinner before mounting his horse and calmly riding away. This was an unrealistic characterization. Billy was known to move very fast when in trouble, and even without lawmen nearby, it is doubtful he chose to delay before making his escape. Instead of fleeing on horseback, deeper into Texas where he was now wanted for two murders, existing evidence speaks to the fact that he wisely picked a simpler way to avoid the law: the younger Thompson brother slipped aboard one of the cattle-loaded steamships bound for New Orleans.[17]

Remus Smith was interred in Rockport's original cemetery, which was a small area set off behind a ridge next to Water Street. If his grave was marked at the time of his tragic death, the marker has long since been lost. He died young. without family, money, position or influence. Nonetheless, the government officials chose to remember Smith. Three years later, in September 1871, the coastal portion of Refugio County was detached and formed into a new county, which was named Aransas. Rockport became the county seat and on October 21, 1872, an Aransas County grand jury formally approved an indictment charging Billy Thompson with murder.[18] For more than fifteen years, Billy would remain a fugitive and on the dodge from that murder charge.

On the day Remus Smith died, ninety delegates gathered at Austin to begin writing a new State Constitution. Only the overwhelming support by ex-slaves, now called Freedmen, provided the votes necessary for the Convention to be approved. An investigation into the lawlessness raging across Texas became one of the focal points of the Convention's efforts. Delegates learned that from June 1, 1865, to June 1, 1868, Texas had been plagued by at least 939 homicides. More people had been killed in Texas after the war than the total number of combat fatalities the state suffered during the war. And the investigating committee sadly admitted the number was undoubtedly low due to inadequate record keeping. It confessed that it was simply impossible to chronicle lesser, but still serious crimes, such as assault with intent to kill, rape, and robbery.

Conscientious judges and officers of the court faced intimidation and violent reprisals while trying to provide law and order. In many sections of the state, Freedmen were prevented from serving as jurors. Many citizens observed that a fair trial in a criminal court was becoming a rarity. In many counties, officials could not even hold court. In Refugio County, a judge complained that the confusion and disorganization rampant in his jurisdiction was so widespread that he was unable to seat juries and conduct trials. He sent out an appeal calling for help from any source. Often those accused of violent crimes were forcibly released by friends and relatives. Jailbreaks were common, and shootouts even occurred in courtrooms. In an already harsh land where violence was always a potential companion, the State Convention's report gave grim evidence that the lawlessness and bloodshed splashing across Texas had not begun to wane.

Many law-abiding Texans demanded action, and if civil authorities such as county sheriffs and town marshals were unable or unwilling to quell the lawlessness, they called for Federal troops to be used to fight crime and protect judges and courtrooms. Major General Joseph J. Reynolds agreed and decided to act. Disgusted with many local officials, General Reynolds wielded the power he possessed as commander of the Fifth Military District and began to enforce the law by having soldiers arrest offending civilians. He decreed that any law enforcement officials who appeared lax in performing their duties be removed from office. Removal was the easy part. Finding willing and competent men to serve as their replacements, however, became an even bigger problem. Squads of soldiers had to be assigned as bodyguards to protect incorruptible judges from assault, and sometimes assassination attempts. They often had to be stationed in courthouses, and when requested, they provided escort to judges as they traveled around their circuit holding court.

In an effort to see justice served in such turbulent times, General Reynolds decided to intervene even further by ordering many criminal cases to be tried by military tribunals rather than civil courts. In central Texas, the accused were often jailed in the stockade at the Austin military encampment, commonly called the bullpen. The Republican-minded newspapers across the state applauded Reynolds's efforts. Others took a dimmer view of his zealous actions, and many Texans criticized him harshly for circumventing civil trials. None more so than Thompson's first biographer, William Walton, a Southern firebrand of the first order who would later complain angrily and bitterly about how civilians were incarcerated and tried by the Federal military.

Walton described the bull pen "as [a] space of ground ... measured off and securely enclosed with high plank or rock walls." From an elevated lookout, armed guards were always at the ready to shoot down any citizen who might try to escape. Prisoners "accused ... of [a] crime, great or small ... were thrown" into this pit to await their trial before a military commission. Walton's rage continued, "when all the machinery of civil government was in full operation" in Austin, he said that "there were judges of the District and Supreme Courts, sheriffs and clerks, courthouse and jails" ready to protect a man's right to a fair trial. Yet, he lamented, "men were convicted by the military commissions and actually sent to the penitentiary, and there made to serve out long terms of imprisonment."[19]

In mid-August 1868, soldiers began to sweep through the capital city and the surrounding countryside making arrests. Authorities were still hopeful they might find Billy Thompson. Within a few days, at least ten desperadoes were confined in the bullpen.[20] On Saturday night, August 22, five miles northwest of Austin near Spicewood Springs, a small patrol led by Lieutenant Howe of the United States 6th Cavalry dismounted and approached a farmhouse, which was the home of a husband and wife. The man was John McGuire, nicknamed "Old Man" McGuire, he was an Irishman with a reputation for being quiet and peaceable. It was an hour past midnight and there was very little light as the soldiers approached the house. McGuire was alerted to their presence and he called out, warning them to stay away. Lieutenant Howe refused to leave and after hailing the house and identifying himself, Howe demanded to be allowed into the farmhouse. McGuire hollered back that he would not come out, nor would he let anyone in. He just wanted the strangers to go away and leave him alone. Lieutenant Howe then threatened to force the door. McGuire had already been robbed at least once before, so fearing they were thieves, he pushed his double-barrel shotgun through a loophole and fired a barrel. The spread of slugs ripped into two soldiers. With two men down, Howe ordered a messenger calling for reinforcements. Instead of continuing the effort to force an entry he decided to surround the house until daylight.

When the messenger reached Austin, somehow a rumor started that one or both of the Thompson brothers had fired upon the patrol. Ben Thompson's house was surrounded, and he was arrested while sleeping next to his wife in their bed.

In the morning light, McGuire realized the terrible mistake he had made. Trying to escape, he slipped out of his house and into a nearby cornfield. There he threatened Captain Clarence Mauck, 4th United States Cavalry, with his shotgun before McGuire allowed himself to be taken into custody.

The morning also brought death to the two wounded men. Daniel O'Connor took his last breath at 9:45 a.m. and fifteen minutes later, Bernard Curry succumbed to his wounds as well. Pvt. O'Connor received most of the blast. He was struck in the left arm and breast, which caused damage to his left lung, stomach, and abdomen—shotgun pellets pierced the large intestines, liver, spleen and kidney. Only one pellet hit Pvt. Curry. It caused a wound one inch in diameter, but it entered six-inches-deep, ripping through his abdomen and lacerating layers of his intestines. Before they left, the soldiers angrily burned down McGuire's house and everything inside of it as retribution.

McGuire was then conveyed to Austin and thrown into the bullpen. Ben Thompson was released because everyone now knew his involvement in the shooting at McGuire's homestead was a preposterous misunderstanding.[21]

It was at this time that James Moore, the brother-in-law Ben Thompson chased out of Austin during the war, started to commit petty acts, which Thompson and his family found to be a nuisance. On September 2, Ben went to see W. D. Scott, a Justice of the Peace,[22] and asked this officer to write a warrant of protection with the hope the document might constrain his brother-in-law's troublesome behavior. Justice Scott refused, explaining he did not know how to draw up the proper papers. While talking to a second magistrate, Thompson was interrupted, and what he was told made him forget about legalities. He rushed home to see his wife Kate, who was pregnant. Upon arriving, he received confirmation that James Moore had struck Kate with a gun knocking her to the ground.[23] His brother-in-law had gone too far. Ben did not seek any explanations, and this time, he did not place his pistol shots high over Moore's head. Instead he hunted Moore down and shot him in the side causing a painful, nonlife-threatening wound. Walton noted, "the ball cut into the meat of the man but made no dangerous wound," and he insisted that Thompson fired not to kill, but to frighten and intimidate Moore.

Ben returned to Justice of the Peace Scott, and requested he be put under bond to appear in civil court to answer any indictment that might be drawn against him for this assault. Scott again frustrated Thompson. He refused to bind Thompson to the civil court, once again claiming ignorance. Thompson left his office, piqued by Scott's lack of utility. Later in the day, and under the insistence of General Reynolds, W. D. Scott started to draw up an affidavit charging Ben Thompson with assault with intent to kill. Word of this reached Thompson, who stormed into Scott's office and angrily drove the officer out onto the street threatening, "If I ever see you playing officer again I will kill you, [even] if I hang for it!" and "You God damned old ____, if you attempt to have me arrested again, I will kill you and every one who has anything to do with it." Within the hour, Thompson was taken in by Federal soldiers and incarcerated in the bullpen.[24]

Ben Thompson was locked into the same pen as Old Man McGuire and a hodge-podge of other prisoners including soldiers locked up for disciplinary reasons. Even at sixty years of age,[25] McGuire's incarceration did not take the edge off his combativeness. He was still a "testy old Irishman ... [with] ... a long tongue, hot head and bitter heart." Having previously been held by the military, Thompson realized the value of making friends of the other inmates, and of course, the guards. McGuire's unending anger for his situation prevented him from following Thompson's advice. When harassed, he continually scrapped with anyone and everyone who bothered him. He took many beatings, but always fought as best he could. Finally, the guards decided to shackle McGuire to a forty-two-pound iron ball. Although weighted down, he still did his best to defend himself, and in one instance broke another inmate's leg below the knee by swinging the iron ball as a weapon. As time went by, Thompson and the old Irishman befriended each other. When two soldiers were thrown into the pen for being drunk and disorderly, they passed their hostility onto McGuire and immediately pitched into him. Again, he started to take a beating until Thompson hurriedly helped him by pulling a hidden weapon, and "impulsively jabbed his knife in the face of the more brutal of the two [soldiers]; the knife happened to be closed, but the end of the handle entered the left eye, and penetrated fully an inch" blinding the soldier in that eye.[26]

To punish him the authorities shackled Thompson to an iron ball similar to what his friend McGuire was forced to wear. For weeks, the two men remained shackled as they waited for their trials. Ben Thompson was called to have his day in court first, and on Tuesday, October 20, the military commission found him guilty of assault with intent to kill, and threatening to kill. During his trial, Thompson was compelled to walk everyday carrying his iron ball from the bullpen to the courtroom, a distance of over one mile. As he trudged through Texas dirt, the iron shackles lacerated his ankles, which oozed so much blood his socks became saturated.

Walton insisted that Ben Thompson was tried without legal representation. His sentence was read at a dress parade, and it was announced that he was to serve four years of hard labor at the prison in Huntsville, Walker County. Four days later, Old Man McGuire was found guilty of murder and initially received a sentence of ten years, but in consideration of his age and the "peculiar circumstances of the case," his sentence was mitigated. His time to be served was cut in half, since five years was the lightest sentence that could be assessed according to the laws of the State. On Sunday, October 25, without being able to say goodbye to their wives and families, Ben Thompson and John McGuire left for Huntsville.[27]

The following day, the *Daily Austin Republican* commented on Ben's departure. "Somewhat notorious for murders and assaults," Thompson, "left for Huntsville under a strong cavalry escort." Respecting the rumor "of a rescue," the authorities "have honored him with this special attention. He goes up for … shooting and wounding his brother-in-law … [he] slipped through the meshes of civil authority, as no one dared appear against him." Thompson still, "saw fit to inform the magistrate who issued process against him that he intended to kill him at his earliest convenience. Ben goes to Penitentiary duty endorsed by the finding of a military commission."

On Sunday morning, precisely one week after leaving Austin, Ben Thompson and John McGuire were formally placed into the custody of the Huntsville prison authorities. The following day, Thompson celebrated his twenty-fifth birthday. Records indicate that when incarcerated, neither man carried any money on his person. Thompson was described as five feet eight inches tall, weighing a lean 117 pounds with blue eyes, brown hair, and a fair complexion. Prison officials did not bother to list any marks or scars on his body, and no identifying photograph was made. It was recorded that he was married, used tobacco, his habits were considered temperate, and his education limited. His occupation was that of a printer, and his sentence was scheduled to expire exactly four years hence on November 1, 1872.[28]

When Thompson and McGuire joined the inmate population, they became part of an overcrowding problem, which seems to plague every prison during every period of time. The State Constitutional Convention concluded that, after examining conditions at Huntsville, the four hundred convicts being held there created a serious problem of overcapacity, but officials never sought the funds for expansion to alleviate the excess numbers. Because of the injuries caused by the leg irons, the prison officials excused Thompson from the hard labor portion of his sentence until he healed and was strong enough to work. During this time, Thompson was obedient and behaved himself. As soon as he was able to perform a job, he got to leave his congested cell and avoid heavy labor when he was assigned to the hair department, where he learned to become an expert at "plaiting, twisting and weaving hair into any shape, and could fashion the most beautiful articles."[29] It was also during the year of 1869 that Ben Thompson again became a father. His wife, Kate, and the baby she carried were not seriously injured when her brother struck her, and she named their infant son Benjamin. The exact date of the boy's birth is not known.[30]

During April 1869, Billy Thompson and another accused killer by the name of Bate Bell were detained and questioned intently by a makeshift posse. The two wanted men were encamped in a thicket seven miles north of the town of Bastrop, where Billy's sister, Mary Jane, and her husband, Robert Gill, resided. The men who came upon Billy and Bell were a group of Freedmen and white stock owners led by an Indian tracker named Tom Hodge. These men were in hot pursuit of thieves who had taken a valuable string of horses. At first, Billy and Bell held their heads down, refusing to speak. Eventually, they vowed they knew nothing about the missing horses. Billy Thompson was recognized and, being under the firm authority of the posse's guns, could have been dragged back to Federal authorities but his streak of good luck had not yet run out. The posse was so keen on regaining its lost stock that they left the accused murderer at his campfire in peace.

At that time, stock thieves, robbers, and murderers had the run of Bastrop County. A local judge, William T. Allen, kept Federal military officers apprised of their depredations. Among the many outlaws, Judge Allen listed, "Bill Thompson, brother to the one sent to the penitentiary for assaulting an officer in Austin." Other suspects and outlaws included the above mentioned Bate Bell, noted desperado and knife fighter Ben Hinds, along with Cornelius Lane, Henry Alexander, the brothers William and Robert Glass, young Parkinson, and a two-gun man known only as Hamilton, said to have killed several persons including a soldier. According to Judge Allen, the Gill family were related to the Glass brothers[31] and were also in-laws to Cornelius Lane, an occasional stock raiser and probably a full-time rustler.

In November 1869, the Federal military assigned a new officer to be the prison superintendent at Huntsville. His name was Nathan Augustus Monroe Dudley, and he would play a future, controversial role as the commander of the United States 9th Cavalry stationed at Fort Stanton, New Mexico during the bloody Lincoln County War. Colonel Dudley briefly supported the Murphy-Dolan-Riley faction against Alexander McSween, Billy the Kid, and other Regulators. In 1869, Colonel Dudley found the Huntsville prison facility to be in a wretched, filthy condition. He informed the governor of Texas that nine out of ten of the prisoners were kept locked in their poorly ventilated cells because there was no work for them to perform. Sick prisoners, of which there were many, were treated in their cells for want of a prison infirmary. To his credit, Dudley recommended both a hospital and chapel should be built, and that work should be provided to teach the inmates a trade or at least keep them occupied and productive. His recommendations brought no meaningful changes, and after a five-week tenure, a civilian official replaced the colonel.

In the spring of 1870, an Act of Congress finally brought Reconstruction and Federal military rule to an end in Texas. The Lone Star State was the last to be accepted back into the Union.

On April 16, in Austin, General J. J. Reynolds issued order Number 74, which returned the full reins of government to the civil authorities. In June, Federal census takers were scattered across Travis County, and in the city of Austin, enumerator Otto T. Zink found Ben's wife, Kate Thompson living with her one-year-old son Benjamin, her mother Elizabeth Moore, her two teenage sisters Molly and Sarah, and her twenty-one-year-old, previously abusive brother James. The family was financially secure. Elizabeth stated she owned real estate valued at $6,000. No one in the household worked outside the home or had a job, and the enumerator noted that Jim Moore was "without any occupation." He was well on his way to living the life of a sporting man, and it is highly probable that at this time he was already addicted to cocaine.[32] The living arrangement must have been harmonious, because after being shot, there is no formal record of Moore ever bothering any family member again. Later that month, census takers were in Walker County, and on June 28, an almost twenty-seven-year-old Ben Thompson was counted among the prison population in Huntsville.[33]

After his brush with the posse, Billy Thompson left Bastrop County heading south, where he slipped across the border to help move a drove of beeves belonging to a William English. Charles S. Bell, a special officer working for the secretary for Civil Affairs in Austin, learned of Billy's presence in Monterrey. He was searching for a number of wanted Texans hiding out in Mexico. However, Officer Bell did not apprehend Billy.[34] It is unknown when Billy returned to Texas, but as a fugitive running from two murder charges, it is doubtful that Billy Thompson allowed a census taker to enumerate him.

During the year of 1870, Huntsville prison records reveal the names of eleven men pardoned and released early. Surprisingly, these convicts were not pardoned by the governor of Texas but by President Ulysses S. Grant. Among those eleven names were both Old Man McGuire and Ben Thompson. The convict record ledger concerning the pardons of the two men is but one slim line: "Pardoned by President Grant 1870" without a hint of an explanation as to how or why the President of the United States would intervene with their punishment, and order their release. The Huntsville records do not even establish a firm date as to when their incarceration officially ended, but it is believed that Thompson and McGuire were freed from their imprisonment sometime during the fall.[35]

Grant's presidential papers also fail to solve the mystery as to who had pushed for clemency all the way to the door of the White House.[36] The only hint of an answer comes from Ben Thompson who declared years after the fact, "I was tried … in 1868 by a military court for shooting a man … and sentenced for four years … but was confined [only] two years in prison and was afterwards released on the grounds of the unconstitutionality of the law under which I was tried."[37]

Thompson stepped through the gate at Huntsville and returned to Austin, his family, and to gambling for a living.[38] For the first time, he hugged, kissed and played with the son named after him. His gambling friends, Phil Coe and Tom Bowles, informed Thompson about a lucrative opportunity developing outside of Texas, from which they planned to benefit. Cash poor, and with an untold number of wild longhorns roaming the open range, Texas ranchers continually searched for a ready cash market for their beef. During the spring and summer of 1871, Texas cowboys pointed their herds north and prodded them towards Kansas.

Chapter 5

ON TO ABILENE

"There's no bravery in carrying revolvers in a civilized community."

—Vear P. Wilson, Editor, *Abilene Chronicle*, June 8, 1871

Baxter Springs, a town tucked into the southeastern corner of the state, was the first place in Kansas to attract the Texas cattle trade. John Baxter, with his wife and children, built a cabin there near the Old Texas Road in the spring of 1849. They set up a trading post and dram shop with the idea of attracting business from the passing traffic. For years, the road was used to move settlers from the Midwest south into Texas and livestock, primarily horses, north to Kansas and Missouri. At the close of the Civil War, the road became known as the Shawnee Trail and Texas cattlemen began in earnest to move their herds northward, looking for a suitable market in which to sell their beef cattle.

By 1869, Baxter Springs was approaching the end of its time as the leading cattle market in Kansas. Cattle buyer Joseph G. McCoy was then looking for a perfect spot to build a railhead for shipping beef on the hoof to eastern cities. He found what he was looking for in the village of Abilene, a small community set in an endless sea of rich grass with plenty of fresh water nearby, free from marauding rustlers and angry farmers. Soon, more and more herds were being driven to the Dickinson County village. McCoy had first purchased extensive acreage adjacent to Abilene and started building facilities to handle the anticipated herds. Next, he convinced officers of the Union Pacific Eastern Division to build an extension of track into the town. He then lobbied state representatives to ignore their Texas fever quarantine laws and allow for cattle to be moved through this relatively unsettled area of their state. In his home state of Illinois, he was able to sway officials there to revise their quarantine restrictions and allow carloads of Texas cattle to be shipped to the emerging Union Stockyards of Chicago. This in itself was a major accomplishment, because the tick carried by the Texas cattle could infect and kill any local cows, much to the anger and disgust of their owners.

To complete his business plan, McCoy purchased advertisements and sent agents armed with handbills to Texas informing the ranchers that a Kansas town existed purely for them, their herds and the business they would bring. At first, the droves trickled in but then Abilene started to grow as satisfied cattlemen returned home with cash bulging in their pockets. Word of mouth did the rest, and by 1871, countless herds began pouring up a new trail laid out by Jesse Chisholm, a trail which ran further west than the Old Shawnee Trail. Ben never drove cattle, but his brother Billy may have went up with a herd to Abilene.[1] If Billy did visit Kansas in the summer of 1871, he didn't linger there or cause enough trouble to be remembered.

Abilene was rapidly becoming the destination for the majority of Texas cattlemen. With the town's rapid growth came the usual entertainments and haunts, which followed any economic boomtown in the Old West. Saloons, dance halls, gambling dens, and brothels began sprouting up on the once bare streets of Abilene.

Among such businesses was the Bull's Head Saloon, owned and operated by Phil Coe with his partners, thirty-two-year-old Tom Bowles and Ben Thompson.[2]

Walton declared Ben "slowly accumulated money enough to leave his family, while he tried his fortune in the Northwestern States and territories, where Texans yearly drove herds of beef cattle." Walton explained how Thompson, with the usual ups and downs any gambler faced, pushed fate to the limit when "more than once [he] had to pawn his pistol ... once, twice, thrice: but at last, however, fortune sprung from the pawn money ... he quit with twenty-five hundred and eighty-three dollars."[3]

Pawn money may have occasionally kept Ben Thompson afloat, but the seed money to invest in a business enterprise and care for his family while he was gone apparently came from the sale of three Austin properties that he jointly owned with his wife. Official records show that the couple sold two parcels of land in January 1871. The first was sold to a butcher named Albert Budington for $250 and the second for $600 in gold to John Hancock (one of Thompson's lawyers in the Coombs affair and past purchaser of the Moore homestead). In March, Kate and Ben sold a third lot acquiring another $600. This time the purchaser was John Hickey, a stonemason.[4] However, he secured the necessary funds and in the spring of 1871 (most likely in early April), Ben Thompson was flush enough to travel to Abilene with his partners and go into the saloon and gambling business.

On April 3, 1871, Abilene citizens elected Joseph McCoy as their mayor. With the arrival of the Texas herds and the countless drovers only a few weeks away, the new mayor needed to find a man tough enough to serve and protect the town as city marshal. Following the advice of a friend, McCoy contacted a well-known frontiersman by the name of James Butler Hickok, better known in both life and death as "Wild Bill." Within days, Hickok arrived and sized up the town and the job. He agreed to McCoy's terms and began his duties on April 8. After the formality of being confirmed by the city council, he was officially sworn in on April 15. Word soon traveled down the trail to Texas that the legendary Wild Bill Hickok was in charge in Abilene, and he became one of the sights the cowboys looked forward to seeing when they hit town.[5]

A Texas drover named Paschal Brown left behind his first impression of Wild Bill. Brown watched as Hickok "came out of Ben Thompson's Bull's Head Saloon [wearing] a low-crowned, wide black hat and a frock coat." As he slowly walked up the street he kept an eye on Wild Bill and observed, "He was standing there with his back to the wall and his thumbs hooked in his red sash. He stood there and rolled his head from side to side looking at everything and everybody from under his eyebrows—just like a mad old bull." Wisely the young cowboy "decided then and there I didn't want any part of him."[6]

The intuitive Brown recognized a man-killer when he saw one. Wild Bill Hickok became nationally famous when *Harper's New Monthly* magazine published an article greatly exaggerating his adventures to date. A few months after *Harper's* write-up, in April 1867, Englishman Henry R. Stanley,[7] added to Hickok's luster with a fanciful interview that appeared in the St. Louis *Missouri Democrat.* Other newspapers repeated or refuted the tales, only adding to his celebrity.

In truth, Wild Bill was a natural-born plainsman. He was thirty-four-years-old and still in his prime. In the previous decade, he served as an army scout during and after the Civil War, campaigning against Indians and Confederates with equal vigor, and allegedly killing many. As a Kansas lawman he had a checkered career. Sometimes he won election to office, but more often than not, voters rejected his candidacy. In the five years before his arrival in Abilene, he served as the sheriff of Ellis County, as a policeman in

Hays City, and as a deputy United States marshal. In pistol fights he killed a number of men both during personal squabbles and as an officer performing his lawful duties. Hickok's life didn't quite match the unrealistic published accounts, but his exceptional ability to pull his pistol and shoot down an opponent was sufficient enough to instill plenty of fear into potential troublemakers. It was the same fear that Paschal Brown felt when he first caught a glimpse of Wild Bill.

The first herd reached Abilene during the second week of May. Columbus Carol was the boss of the outfit, and the herd numbered a substantial 1,600 head. Prominent among Carol's young drovers was John Wesley Hardin, a teenager who was just starting to blossom into his own blood-stained career. The speed in which the young psychopath would kill was terrifying to behold, but while he was your friend he was a fun-loving and dependable companion. He joined the cattle drive to avoid the Texas authorities, who relentlessly searched for him. While in Abilene, Hardin celebrated his eighteenth birthday. On the trail up to Kansas, he shot down a handful of *vaqueros* who were foolish enough to quarrel with him and his companions. Hardin bragged about what his friends would corroborate, that he accounted for five out of the six slain Mexicans.

A little more than a year prior to his arrival in Abilene, John Wesley Hardin had fled to Brenham, Texas, to hide out at his uncle's farm after another killing. In Brenham, he claimed he met Phil Coe, and for reasons unexplained he described the normally good-natured Coe as "notorious." He also stated that he met Ben Thompson back in Texas, but did not provide an explanation as to when, where or in what circumstances they became acquainted.

Hardin boasted he had seen many fast towns, but Abilene beat them all. Upon his appearance there, he found Coe and Thompson already running the Bull's Head saloon and gambling hall and he renewed his acquaintance with the two gamblers. William Walton explained that the saloon and its games of chance were a favorite of the Texas cowboys, and Thompson, along with Bowles and Coe, were very "successful and had a great run [making] money rapidly."[8]

The Bull's Head Saloon sat on busy Texas Street, between Cedar on the east and Mulberry Street to the west. It was a common, slapped-together wooden structure large enough for a bar and a handful of gaming tables. Its front entrance looked north towards the railroad tracks, and directly across the street from its front door stood a small stone building, which served as the city jail. Around the corner, going north about one hundred feet on Cedar was the Alamo Saloon. It was sandwiched in-between Jake Karatofsky's Great Western Store and the Novelty Theatre on "A" or Railroad Street. The Alamo, with a forty-foot wide street frontage and several entrances, was a larger and more elaborate competitor to the Bull's Head. The Alamo, unmistakably named thus to attract the Texas trade, served as Wild Bill's unofficial headquarters. He enjoyed spending much of his on-duty and leisure time there.

Vear P. Wilson edited the town's only newspaper, the *Abilene Chronicle*. He rightfully considered the professional card-turners like Coe, Bowles, and Ben Thompson, along with the other saloon men, pimps, and harlots who were feeding off the cattle trade, to be the bane of the town. Wilson, a former newspaperman and Universal preacher from Ohio, founded the *Chronicle*, and used virtually every issue of his newspaper to launch attacks against Mayor McCoy and his lax attitude about the surrounding vice. In the middle of the season, as the Texas drovers arrived, Wilson published extensive articles calling gambling one of the worst vices of the West, and deplored its existence. He warned the cattlemen and drovers how gamblers eagerly fleece them, explaining in detail the crooked ins-and-outs of games like Chuck-a-Luck, Faro, Rouge et Noir, Poker, Vingt et Un, and Roulette. His exhortations were

Professional gambler Phillip Haddox Coe, who operated the Bull's Head Saloon in Abilene, Kansas, with fellow gamblers Tom Bowles and Ben Thompson. Coe became the last known victim of City Marshal James Butler "Wild Bill" Hickok. The cause of their trouble has never been fully established.

Courtesy the Chuck Parsons Collection.

in vain. The saloons and gambling dens swarmed with countless customers ready for fun and a little excitement, no matter the cost.

The previous spring, with the laudable desire to prevent bloodshed, the city elders did what most frontier towns attempted to do. They passed an unenforceable ordinance making it against the law to carry a weapon in town. In 1871, they endeavored again to keep violence to a minimum by resurrecting the old law. On June 8, Editor Wilson gladly heralded in the *Chronicle* the posting of signs by City Marshal Hickok forbidding the carrying of firearms or other weapons while in Abilene. Wilson commented that the ordinance would be enforced as there was "no bravery in carrying revolvers in a civilized community."

In the middle of June, Ben Thompson's short amount of time in Abilene came to an abrupt end. Longing to see his family, he left to meet his wife, who was three months pregnant, and their two-year-old son. Thompson had earlier telegraphed Kate to bring little Benny and travel by railroad to Kansas City, Missouri.[9] On Sunday, June 18, they gathered together and that evening decided to go out and enjoy a buggy ride. It ended in disaster. The buggy overturned, crushing and injuring all three of them. Ben's leg was broken and little Benjamin's foot was broken, but Kate Thompson was the most seriously injured with a broken arm. With the fear of gangrene setting in, the doctors were forced to put Kate through the horror of amputating her arm above the elbow. The operation saved her life and the life of her unborn child. Ben Thompson was also bed-ridden because of his fractured leg (the same limb broken in San Antonio during the Civil War). The break was so severe it was predicted he would be unable to stand on it for at least a month.[10]

Back in Abilene, much sympathy was expressed over the accident and resulting injuries, with a Kansas City newspaper stating Ben Thompson "is a great favorite among the Texans."[11] Financially strapped, Thompson turned to Phil Coe for help, who generously provided him with a large sum of money. Walton reported it was $3,000. The Thompson family would spend many weeks convalescing at Kansas City's fashionable Lindell Hotel, situated at 5th

Street and Wyandotte, before they could manage the long return journey to their home in Austin.[12]

Before Thompson left for his ill-fated family reunion, everyone in Abilene expected trouble between Marshal Hickok and Ben Thompson. Wes Hardin wrote, years later, that the source of the bitterness between Hickok and Thompson stemmed from the sign on the false front of the Bull's Head Saloon. Under instructions from Coe and Thompson, a painter had depicted an anatomically embellished bull. Many townspeople found it offensive. Parents were especially upset because their children walked by it daily on their way to school. Marshal Hickok, with a shotgun cradled in his arms, watched as his own painter washed over the objectionable portion of the sign. Coe accepted the city marshal's actions, but Hardin alleged that Ben Thompson was infuriated, and tried to persuade the young desperado into killing Hickok. Hardin declined and replied to Thompson, that if the marshal needed killing, then he should do it himself.

Although the young gunman refused to yield to Thompson's urging to kill Hickok, he did admit to willingly seeking a confrontation with the famous lawman. In his self-serving autobiography, Hardin noticeably wanted to impress his readers and much of what he wrote is suspect. He recalled how during his time in Abilene, he "really wished for a chance to have a set-to with him [Wild Bill Hickok] just to try his luck."[13] So despite the city ordinance against carrying pistols, or perhaps because of it, Hardin continued to openly wear a brace of holstered six-shooters as he toured the town's saloons, restaurants, and gambling dens. When confronted by Marshal Hickok, Hardin claimed to have tricked the marshal by pretending to hand over his two revolvers but instead, by turning his pistols in his hands, he brought them back to firing position forcing Hickok to relent and not enforce the city ordinance. Of course by the time Hardin wrote this, Hickok was long dead.

Why Hardin, when he had the drop, didn't shoot Hickok was answered by Old West author, historian and Hardin biographer Leon Metz: "Hardin didn't want to kill Wild Bill, he wanted to impress him."[14] The fact is only one man in Abilene resorted to firing his six shooter when facing Wild Bill Hickok and he died because of it.

Looking back, it is difficult to determine exactly why there was trouble between Abilene's City Marshal Hickok and Texas gambler Phil Coe. Many years later, several authors presented different reasons for their animosity toward each other. Walton explained that bad blood existed because of a fallen woman by the name of Jessie Hazel. He wrote, "About her there was a rivalry between Phil Coe and Wild Bill. In such a contest there could be but one result."[15] In his memoir, *A Son of the Border*, Edward C. Little points at Coe's crooked faro box as the cause. Little contended that the city marshal forced Coe to move his faro game out of the back room of the Bull's Head Saloon and out into the open where the drovers now faced a square game. A bad run broke Phil Coe's bank and naturally Coe held Hickok responsible.[16]

Neither explanation holds up under scrutiny. Perhaps a prostitute named Jessie Hazel existed; however, Walton's tale of Coe beating Hickok bloody with his fists over the woman's treatment is pure fantasy. Hickok fought with his guns and would never submit to a beating without pulling out his ever-present pistols and permanently settling the matter. Little's story also dissolves under the facts. The City Council, on July 25, ordered Marshal Hickok "to close up all dead and Brace gambling Games and to arrest all cappers for the aforesaid games."[17] Gambling was being closed down, not just moved out into the open. Seeing the end to the easy profits, though certainly not broke, Coe sold the Bull's Head Saloon license for $50 on Wednesday, August 2, to an Irishman named Thomas Shearan, a former town official, who normally earned his living as a grocer.[18]

The cattle season was quickly coming to an end. Seventy-eight carloads of Texas cattle were shipped out to Chicago during the week preceding September 13, but the market was considered dull with buyers and sellers unable to come to terms. Top price was now $18 per head. Editor Wilson gleefully announced in the September 14 issue of the *Chronicle,* "For the last ten or twelve days almost every train eastward bound has carried away and relieved this community of vast numbers of sinful humanity." The dregs of Abilene, "[p]rostitutes, 'pimps,' gamblers, 'cappers' and others of like ilk," were returning to places such as Newton, Kansas City and St. Louis. The *Chronicle* also pointed out that during the last two weeks, most of the gambling "hells" had closed mostly for want of business.[19] With the end of gambling profit, Thomas Bowles chose to return to Austin while Phil Coe curiously decided to stay on in Abilene. It is possible that Coe's desire to stay was due to Jessie Hazel's charms.[20]

On Wednesday, October 4, the long-awaited Dickinson County Fair was in full swing. A rainstorm passed through the following day and kept many people away. The remaining Texans probably avoided the gales by staying indoors and enjoying a drink or two while waiting for the harsh weather to move on. By early evening, with the sunlight fading and the rain ending, the Texans went outside and began a good-natured, impromptu celebration. Their innocent unruliness ended in tragedy and word of what happened swiftly traveled south, down into Texas. A telegram addressed to Thomas Bowles was sent from Abilene to Austin informing him of the death of his friend, Phil Coe, at the hands of Wild Bill.[21]

When Phil Coe stepped into the street that fateful evening, he was wearing a large, flowing, dark blue cape ornamented with gold buttons and gold braid around the collar to help keep warm. Going against his customary behavior of being unarmed, Coe decided to carry a pistol under his cape.[22] As the crowd of celebrating Texans moved up Cedar Street and reached the front of the Alamo Saloon, Coe took his pistol out and discharged it, which immediately brought City Marshal Hickok out of the saloon. Hickok and Coe exchanged a few words before pointing their pistols and shooting at each other. In the gathering darkness, fear, nervousness, and stress may have caused them to raise their pistols and shoot. Certainly, Coe knew who he was up against when he decided to use his revolver and fire at the marshal. Simply stated, the minute difference between life and death was that Phil Coe was the professional gambler and Hickok the professional gunman. The Junction City, Kansas, *Union* of October 7 was the first newspaper to report the shootout, stating that Hickok was in the Alamo Saloon, described as "a gambling hell" when he heard shots and went to investigate. He recognized one of the men, Coe, who had threatened to kill him "before frost." Hickok yelled at the crowd of men on the street to preserve order when someone fired at him. Wild Bill drew and "fired with marvelous rapidity and characteristic accuracy." The bullets struck Coe in the abdomen.

Editor Wilson reported more details about the death of Thompson's good friend. The crowd of cowboys numbered around fifty men, and Wilson felt they did not intend to do anyone harm but nevertheless became rowdy. The Texans compelled several citizens to "stand treat" by carrying them into a saloon and then insisted they buy drinks. Supposedly Hickok was treated in this manner and apparently did not object. The good-natured rowdiness may have continued uneventfully but the situation changed when someone fired off a shot, the offender being Phil Coe. Hickok confronted Coe in front of the Alamo Saloon. Coe explained that he had only shot at a dog which attempted to bite him. Their tense discussion ended when Hickok drew his two pistols and fired as Coe raised his revolver and pulled off a shot. Mike Williams, a friend of Hickok, came running around the corner and ran into the marshal's gunfire. Fearing it was another Texan about to enter the fight he failed to recognize Williams until it was too late. The last man J.B. Hickok would shoot in his career was his friend Williams, who died within minutes. His antagonist, Phil Coe, lingered until early Monday morning when he died in agony.[23]

Even though Coe was a gambler, Editor Wilson still found a few kind words to say about the deceased Texan, describing him as, "a man of natural good impulses in his better moments. It is said that he had a spite at Wild Bill and had threatened to kill him—which Bill believed he would do if he gave him the opportunity. ... The fact is Wild Bill's escape was truly marvelous. The two men were not over eight feet apart, and both of them large, stout men." Wilson had hoped that "the season would pass without any row. The Marshal has, with his assistants, maintained quietness and good order—and this in face of the fact that at one time during the season there was a larger number of cut-throats and desperadoes in Abilene than in any other town of its size on the continent. Most of them were from Kansas City, St. Louis, New Orleans, Chicago, and from the Mountains. ... We hope that all strangers as well as citizens, will aid by word and deed in maintaining peace and quietness."[24]

Phil Coe's body was placed in the care of Austin resident and fellow gambler, Frank "Bud" Cotton, who agreed to accompany Coe's remains on the sad trip back to Texas.[25] The most convenient and direct route was by rail to Houston, switching there to the Houston & Texas Central line running northwest through Hempstead until it reached the town of Brenham, the county seat of Washington County. The tracks heading into Austin, about eighty miles away, were moving forward but would not be completed for another two-and-a-half months. Walton, in his Thompson biography, wrote how somewhere along the way, Bud Cotton caught up to Ben Thompson and his family traveling by easy phases back to their home in Austin. Their chance meeting was the first Thompson knew of Coe's sudden death. Overcome by grief, Ben rested his head on Coe's coffin and wept.[26]

There is no reason to doubt that Bud Cotton did accompany Coe during his body's return to Texas, but a chance convergence with Ben Thompson seems highly unlikely. Walton did not identify where the meeting was supposed to have occurred, and while he certainly mourned the loss of his friend, the fiction of Ben Thompson resting his head on Coe's coffin, weeping, is hardly believable.

Phil Coe's younger sister, Delilah Coe Portis and her husband Samuel, made their home in Brenham. Possibly due to the deteriorating condition of his body, the decision was made to bury Coe in the town's cemetery. However, what the family truly desired was to have his body shipped to Gonzales where the Coe family cemetery was located.[27]

The local newspaper, the *Brenham Banner* took notice, and commented in its edition of October 19, "The remains of Mr. Phil. Coe, who was murdered at Abilene, Kansas, by a notorious character, known as 'Wild Bill,' arrived on Monday evening last, and was intered [*sic*] at our city cemetery on Tuesday morning, by relatives and friends with whom we deeply, sympathise [*sic*]."[28] Relatives of Phil Coe and their descendants maintain to this day that he was unarmed when he was shot and killed by Hickok. The reason the family gives for the murder was the animosity Hickok held for Coe because of their rivalry for the affections of Jessie Hazel. Many Texans, both then and now, believe that Coe was not killed in a fair fight.

One Kansas newspaper commented, "Coe is said to have been a kind and generous hearted man, well thought of by all who knew him. He had many friends among the Texans and cattle dealers about Abilene. It is darkly hinted that avengers are on the trail, and we will probably soon hear of another tragedy in Abilene."[29]

Revenge, or the fear of it, appears to have been on the mind of a lot of people, especially Wild Bill Hickok. Traveling to Topeka by rail in late November, he faced down five Texans, convinced that they were hounding him and looking for an opportune moment to take his life. At gunpoint, he forced them to remain on the train and continue on to Kansas City as he exited.[30]

Many substantial citizens of Abilene grew tired of the Texas cattle trade and the challenges that trailed behind it. A tick carrying Texas fever had already overcome so many of their domesticated cattle, and the citizens were sickened by all the death. They envisioned wheat farming to be the true long-term future of Dickinson County. By early December, the cattle trade was fizzling out and they managed to persuade a majority of city officials to ban it. Several months later, they sent notices to Texas asking cattlemen to drive their herds to other shipping points. The town no longer felt the need to cater to the Texas cattle trade and therefore did not require a lawman like Wild Bill Hickok. He was officially discharged along with his deputies on December 13, 1871.[31] After a visit to Colorado and Kansas City, he decided to go east. By January 1872, he was reported to be in Boston, Massachusetts. Later that year, he entered into show business where he unhappily performed on the stage for a brief period. He wisely avoided the Kansas cattle towns for the remainder of his life.

Catherine Thompson's pregnancy progressed normally as fall turned to winter. The Thompson family struggled through such a difficult and trying year, but it ended in joy. On December 8, 1871, Catherine gave birth to a healthy baby girl. They named her Kathryn Florence, but like her mother she was always called Katie throughout her life.

At Christmas time, Ben and his family came together with the extended Thompson family to celebrate the holiday. They stayed in Bastrop at the home of Ben's sister Mary Jane, her husband Robert

Gill, and their three-year-old daughter Edna. The family matriarch, Mary Ann Thompson, was there along with her youngest daughter, thirteen-year-old Fannie. Billy may have been in attendance because of the security afforded by so many friends and relatives living in the area. Three days after Christmas, Ben Thompson looked back at the year of 1871 and penned the following poem:

> "O give not way to dark despair
> Within this world of ours
> For still some sweetness is contained
> In life's fair blooming flowers
> And though upon the sea of doubt
> You may be tempest tossed
> Believe that in the heart of man
> All virtue is not lost."[32]

CHAPTER 6

TRAGEDY IN ELLSWORTH

"Get your guns you Texas sons of bitches and fight."

—JOHN "HAPPY JACK" MORCO TO THE CROWD, AUGUST 15, 1873

The winter months at the start of 1872 were uncommonly cold, and sheets of ice three inches thick covered the ponds in and around Austin, Texas.[1] Ben Thompson's anger was not cooled by this unusual drop in temperature, however. The animosity he held toward those who did not do enough to prevent his earlier conviction and imprisonment by Federal military authorities led to a liquored up display of Thompson's displeasure.

On Thursday, January 25, one of Austin's most prominent and respected jurists, James Hall Bell stood on the town's main boulevard, Congress Avenue and was "suddenly assaulted by the well-known Ben Thompson, who, with foul words and much abuse, threatened his life and struck him with his riding whip, accusing him of being instrumental in his imprisonment."[2]

Bell, forty-seven-years-old and a married father of five, was a former district judge who had been elected to the Texas Supreme Court in 1858, where he served for six years as an associate justice. Judge Bell was a political leader of the Republican Party, and during the years which immediately followed the end of the Civil War, Bell served as the Secretary of State under Governor Andrew J. Hamilton. While in that powerful position, Bell contended with the issue of civilian arrests made by the Federal mili-

Judge James Hall Bell (1825-1892) was born in Brazoria County, Texas and received a superior education in Kentucky and then at Harvard. He was a district judge by the 1850s and was elected to the Texas Supreme Court as an Associate Justice in 1858. On January 25, 1872, Ben Thompson assaulted Judge Bell with a riding whip. Thompson threatened Bell's life during the drunken attack before being arrested.
Courtesy the Austin History Center. Image # CO 8434.

tary. He was a forceful advocate for trials under the jurisdiction of civilian courts. As one of Austin's pro-Union men, Judge Bell was approached by Thompson's wife and mother, who sought his help when Ben Thompson was held in Federal custody after wounding his brother-in-law and threatening the magistrate. Obviously, Thompson felt Judge Bell could have been more helpful. "After his liberation [from Huntsville] he harbored an ill will against ... Bell ... for some remark made about him while in prison, and thus administered a dose of cowhide to him on the streets of Austin." According to Austin's *Daily State Journal*, an unarmed Judge Bell "acted with great coolness, until Judge [Julius] Schuetze and policeman [William] Fletcher interfered and led Thompson off." Both the mayor, John W. Glenn, and the city marshal, W.E. Evans, were out of town, so Officer Fletcher released his prisoner on the condition that Ben Thompson went home, kept the peace, and appeared that next Saturday to post bond for good behavior. However, Thompson remained in town and continued his drunken tirade "riding up and down the Avenue, loudly threatening the lives of those who had, as he supposed, been active in his imprisonment." It was an unseemly and dangerous display of ill-temper on the city's main thoroughfare. City Marshal Evans, who had just returned from Houston, showed Thompson the same leniency and Ben was again released on the condition that he appear on Saturday. The *Statesman* concluded that every Austin citizen was "capable of making his own comments on such proceedings."[3]

Three days later, the Sunday edition of the *Daily State Journal* reported the result of Ben's misbehavior: for the assault, a $1,000 bond, for threatening Judge Bell's life, another $1,000 bond. That was not all, as the mayor insisted on an additional $3,000 bond to keep the peace. Faced with having to provide a total of $5,000 in bail, and most likely unable to raise that large amount of money, Ben Thompson "declined to give the required bonds and was committed to jail." Thompson was scheduled to face justice on Monday, February 5, but the results of the trial remain unknown. If he was punished, it could not have been very severe because the newspapers failed to take notice of it.

Meanwhile, Billy Thompson remained in the shadows during the early 1870s. He spent some time in Galveston. In early February 1872, as his brother lingered in an Austin jail cell, Billy and a companion received a small mention in the press. Dennis Crowley was arrested and fined $10 for being "drunk and down" and $10 for resisting arrest. William Thompson was fined $20 for interfering with the police on Crowley's behalf.[4]

On February 8, 1872, the *Abilene Chronicle* published a notice that the newspaper would continue to reprint in its three subsequent issues. With each printing, a longer list of names were added to the notice. Members of the Farmer's Protective Association and Officers of Dickinson County, along with many local residents, respectfully asked "all who have contemplated driving Texas cattle to Abilene the coming season to seek some other point for shipment, as the inhabitants of Dickinson will no longer submit to the evils of the trade."

Rejected by Abilene, the Texas drovers had little trouble finding other eager shipping points for their herds. Many Kansas towns clamored for the economic boom the Texas cattle drives would bring to their town. For years, Ellsworth had invited the herds and like a few other towns had enjoyed a small portion of the business. The Kansas Pacific Railroad began making improvements on its line in anticipation of Ellsworth becoming the next major shipping point of Texas cattle. Ellsworth apparently was not concerned with "the evils of the trade."

Five years earlier, a corporation was established to create the Ellsworth Town Company. On May 4, 1867, a town plat for Ellsworth was recorded in Salina, Kansas at the Register of Deeds of-

A panoramic view of the main plaza of Ellsworth, Kansas, looking west. This image shows both North Main Street and South Main Street. The Grand Central Hotel, headquarters for many of the Texas cattlemen, stands at the far right. The

fice. Located on the north bank of the Smokey Hill River, Ellsworth soon flooded and cholera quickly followed. Early residents pitched their tents on a nearby hill in response. Indian war parties harassed would-be settlers and railroad construction crews alike, but with the additional military protection that was provided to them, the first railroad tracks reached Ellsworth on July 5. A United States post office was established in Ellsworth less than two weeks later, and in an effort to avoid future floods, a new town site on higher ground was selected, laid out and officially filed. The editor of the *Leavenworth Daily Conservative* let his acerbic pen loose when he commented on the types of people attracted to the fledging town of Ellsworth: No "fouler birds ever congregated around a putrid carcass of a departed ox than those which frequent and tenant the brimstone scented dens of this modern Sodom." The few lawmen serving Ellsworth were about to have their hands full.

At nearby Fort Harker, William F. "Buffalo Bill" Cody was employed as a courier for the army and two of the best-known army scouts were James B. Hickok and his partner Jack Harvey. On August 10, 1867, Ellsworth County held its first election, and Hickok announced his candidacy for sheriff. In spite of his notori-

altercation between Billy Thompson and Sheriff C.B. Whitney occurred on "Snake Row," which is at the far left.

Courtesy the Ellsworth County Historical Society.

ety, he lost the election to the man who had put up the first permanent building in Ellsworth, a former captain in the United States Cavalry, Ezra W. Kingsbury. For undersheriff, the voters elected Chauncey Belden Whitney. Shortly thereafter, he was also appointed a township constable. During the early years of Ellsworth's history, Chauncey B. Whitney served the town as a peace officer far more effectively than any other lawman.[5]

Often called "Sandy" or "Cap," Whitney was born and raised in Michigan and fought for the Union. He saw combat in the 1864 Arkansas Campaign. Twice a widower, he was engaged to a third lady after the war ended when he decided to seek opportunity on the Kansas frontier.[6] In August 1867, Whitney first accepted a leadership position as one of the lieutenants of the First Independent Kansas State Militia before subsequently enlisting into Major George A. Forsyth's special battalion of fifty frontiersmen. With Whitney among them, Forsyth's command fought an epic battle-turned-siege against Cheyenne Dog Soldiers from September 16 through September 25.[7]

The harshness of the Kansas frontier may have taken its toll, or, perhaps thoughts of his fiancée in Michigan were foremost on his

Ellsworth County Sheriff Chauncey Belden Whitney. Billy Thompson, holding brother Ben's shotgun, narrowly avoided shooting cattlemen Seth Mabry and Eugene Millett before discharging the shotgun into Whitney, fatally wounding him. Both Mabry and Millett were friends of the Thompson brothers.
Courtesy the Kansas State Historical Society.

mind when Whitney announced his intention to leave Ellsworth. The people of Ellsworth were surprised and saddened by their under-sheriff and town constable's decision to return to Michigan. Prior to his departure, he stopped by a friend's house, Marius H. Henry, who also hailed from Michigan. Mr. Henry, his wife, and their daughter, Nellie, had become very close to Whitney, and on this last visit before returning east, he bid the Henry family goodbye. Whitney made it as far as Kansas City when he stopped and wrote a letter to his fiancée. Miss Nellie Henry later recalled that "the thought of leaving me, only a child perhaps fourteen or less—was more than he could do. So he wrote to her breaking the engagement and in a week was back in Ellsworth."[8] Patiently, Chauncey Whitney stepped back and waited until little Nellie became a woman.

Ellsworth County Sheriff, E.W. Kingsbury, unexpectedly left the state and on February 11, 1869, undersheriff Chauncey Whitney became acting sheriff. The law dictated that the governor approve Whitney as sheriff, since the position was an elected one and the election was nine months away. Prominent citizens began taking sides. Several wrote to the governor expressing Whitney's qualifications for the position, but not everyone issued an endorsement. Among the opposition was former probate judge James B. Miller. He wrote asking the governor to withhold the commission from Whitney. Subsequently, support for Whitney collapsed and another candidate was awarded the job. Edgar A. Kesler, a wounded Civil War veteran from Michigan, was issued the commission for Sheriff of Ellsworth County on March 1, 1869. Whitney continued on as undersheriff and township constable.[9]

In its eager pursuit of the cattle trade, Ellsworth sent trail guides, printed posters, and circulars to Texas in order to lure the herds. Optimism ran high with the construction of a new stockyard in May. In an effort to present Abilene with competition, Kansas Pacific railroad officials built a siding for cattle loading. Even with these efforts, the Texas cattlemen largely ignored the overtures and the 1869 summer season was another disappointment for Ellsworth. Even without the boom of the cattle trade, optimism continued to mount. Ellsworth erected four hotels, an Episcopal church, a school, a drugstore, two general merchandising firms and more saloons than all of the other businesses combined.[10] One of those hotels—and certainly the most impressive for a frontier town—was the Grand Central, owned and operated by businessman Arthur Larkin. Larkin was proud of the hotel's two-story, handsome red brick edifice, and he underlined its significance by installing a sidewalk of magnesia limestone twelve-feet wide along its front.[11]

On July 5, 1869, forty-two citizens of Ellsworth realized their limited local law enforcement was unable to control all of the violence and lawlessness in their frontier town. They prepared a vigilante manifesto stating, in part, "that the law abiding Citizens shall rule the Town, the Vagrants and roughs must leave, the innocent be protected—the guilty to have justice meted out to them, at all hazards the law first—when that falls Judge Lynch to finish up the work." This dire warning would prove to be more bark than bite.

Roaming Cheyenne Dog soldiers again heightened settlers's fears, and four companies of militia were formed to man an equal number of blockhouses in the Solomon Valley north of Ellsworth. Once again, Chauncey Whitney answered the call and became the 1st Lieutenant of Company A. He would not return to Ellsworth until late November. While he was away, newly sworn-in Ellsworth Constable, "Apache Bill" Seamans, died in a hail of gunfire attempting to quell a saloon row. United States Deputy Marshal Jack Bridges tracked a gang of four horse thieves to Ellsworth. Bridges unexpectedly came face-to-face with his quarry in a saloon, and during the ensuing fight, he was almost beaten to death. Bridges left the saloon with a fractured skull and many broken ribs. The unstoppable violence accentuated the need for a strong city police force, and in the spring of 1870, Ellsworth was incorporated under the laws of the State of Kansas as a village. Chauncey Whitney was selected for chief of police and he chose two men to make up his small staff of policemen.[12]

The Kansas Pacific Railroad purchased the stockyards at Ellsworth and expanded them. Large herds began to arrive into Ellsworth County and on July 14, 1871, it was estimated that thirty thousand head were grazing in the surrounding countryside. At this time, the current county sheriff, J. Charles Seiber, followed in the footsteps of what the first sheriff of Ellsworth County did: he vacated his office, abandoned his bonds, and left the county suddenly. The Ellsworth County Commissioners turned to their most experienced lawman and on July 21, 1871, approved Chauncey Whitney as the county sheriff without opposition. Two days later, he married sixteen-year-old Nellie Henry. She later recalled how her new husband supplemented their income from law enforcement by working as a carpenter: "We bought a lot—but did not pay for it. We also put up a one room house but the lumber was not paid for."[13]

As 1871 unfolded, Ellsworth and other Kansas towns kept trying to attract the Texas drovers. Meanwhile, a larger and larger portion of the citizens of Abilene and Dickinson County wanted the Texans to move on. They formed a Farmers Protective Association to help them on their way. Major Seth Mabry and Abel Head "Shanghai" Pierce, along with the one-armed Capt. James D. Reed, decided to move their cattle operations to Ellsworth. This decision opened up a steady flow of herds toward Ellsworth County and the prime grazing tracts around the town. At the state capital, the *Topeka State News* editor commented on the rapid influx of drovers and the unsavory element drawn to the trade with a single simple sentence. "As we go to press, Hell is still in session at Ellsworth." On December 8, 1871, the first issue of the *Ellsworth Reporter* appeared. It was a four-page paper declaring on its mast head. "For the Future in the distance, and the Good that we can do." The *Reporter's* first printer was a young man named

John Montgomery. Born in Fairfield, Iowa in 1850, Montgomery was a veteran of the newspaper business, having apprenticed as a printer's mechanic during the Civil War. In 1871, he was the foreman of the newspaper in Moulton, Iowa. Montgomery came highly recommended by the owner of the newspaper in Moulton. As he traveled to his new position in Ellsworth, Montgomery stopped in Kansas City, Kansas, and Fort Leavenworth where he picked up a Washington Hand Press, type, and an inking stone. By 1873, after serving as printer for the first three editors, Montgomery became co-owner of the *Reporter*, a name he had selected. In a few short years he would marry Abbie M. Henry, the sister of Mrs. Nellie (Henry) Whitney.[14]

Halfway through 1871, Ellsworth reorganized itself from village to third-class city, and enacted a series of law and order ordinances. The city council ordered chief of Police, Chauncey Whitney, to "instruct all 'soiled doves' that they will not be permitted to live in or carry on their business within the limits of the city of Ellsworth." The busy purveyors of immorality decided to move just outside the city limits, which was located slightly more than one city block away from the business district on South Main Street. This sliver of an area southeast of town, near the banks of the Smokey Hill River, was filled with brothels and dance houses and was commonly called "The Bottoms," "The Nauch," or "Nauchville." "Nauch" was a term for dance during the nineteenth century throughout the British-Indian Empire. Not surprisingly, saloons and gambling dens appeared alongside the dance houses run by the demimonde.

For a few short weeks during the early days of 1872, Chauncey Whitney held three different offices simultaneously: Ellsworth Township Constable, Ellsworth City Marshal and Sheriff of Ellsworth County. This feat was probably unequaled by any other lawman of the Wild West at the time, and when Ellsworth city authorities finally delivered six months of back pay totaling $450, he was not satisfied. Whitney would relinquish his role as city marshal by resigning on April 3, 1872. To supplement his income and to take advantage of the anticipated growth of Ellsworth, Whitney began a partnership with George Kendall on May 1, 1872. They operated a furniture store and undertaking business on South Main Street, near the start of Bayers Street, the one short road running through the unincorporated Nauchville. A few short months later on July 3, Chauncey Whitney acquired his greatest responsibility when his wife Nellie gave birth to their first and only child, a healthy baby girl; a job he was not destined to fulfill. They named her Mary Elizabeth but affectionately called her Bessie.[15]

During June of 1872, Ellsworth finally began to realize its goal of becoming one of the principal cattle markets of the great American West. Before the shipping season ended in the late autumn, over forty thousand head of cattle had moved through the Kansas Pacific improved stockyards and rail line.[16] The *Reporter* informed its readers, "cattle men find that as they come farther west they are less troubled with settlers, and that the grass growing is better adapted to fatten [the cattle]."Also many professional gamblers arrived early in anticipation of a busy time fleecing the Texas drovers.[17]

Early in the cattle season, Ben Thompson ignored Ellsworth and decided to travel, paying a brief visit to another cattle shipping point, Wichita, Kansas.[18] Given the absence of official records bearing his name, Ben had no trouble during his time in Wichita.

The remainder of 1872 was a quiet one for Ben Thompson and an even quieter year for his younger brother Billy. Records indicate Ben was arrested only twice and details are sketchy. A Travis County deputy sheriff and Austin policeman named John F. Stokes hauled Ben in, but the charge and date of said arrest are unknown. On September 20, Ben was arrested in Hopkins County, located in northeast Texas, but the offense was not recorded. Throughout the entire year, Billy Thompson stayed out of trouble, old troubles still haunted him. On October 25, Aransas County formally indicted him for murder stemming from the 1868 shooting death of Remus Smith.[19]

As the year came to a close, Chauncey Belden Whitney won a court case to remain the sheriff of Ellsworth County against a man named E. Lynch. Whitney was represented by the County Attorney, Phillip T. Pendleton. Lynch failed to appear and was not represented so the case was decided in favor of sheriff Whitney by default.[20]

By March of 1873, a small portion of the expected cattle buyers began arriving in Ellsworth. Many herds around Ellsworth were suffering because of the lack of spring grass. In its effort to prevent the cattlemen from moving to rival cities like Wichita, Ellsworth promoted the Kansas Pacific guide map directing the Texans to turn west and take Cox's Trail. Aside from avoiding Wichita, Cox's Trail also moved the herds further away from potential trouble with settlers.[21] An Austin, Texas item received wide coverage in the press when the *Daily Journal* informed its readers how "Several herds of cattle have crossed the Colorado [River] below this city en route [*sic*] for Ellsworth, Ks., which seems to be the market now instead of Abilene." A Travis county rancher named Cad Pierce, known to be a good friend of the Thompson brothers, "has gathered a herd of 1800 head," which he sent up to Kansas. A second herd, he himself bossed up in May.[22]

It would prove to be the peak year of the Texas cattle trade. More than four hundred thousand cattle, an enormous amount, would splash across the Red River in 1873 on their way to the Kansas railheads.

In Austin, on the evening of March 26, 1873, Ben Thompson was enjoying himself in the Woodlief & Wilson Saloon on Congress Avenue when he was forced to pull his pistol and kill an unexpected four-legged adversary. Napoleon B. Mitchell,[23] a bartender at the nearby Iron Front Saloon, owned a dog described as "a very fine one but very dangerous, as he had the very unpleasant habit of biting any one that came his way." The dog entered the saloon and "endeavored to jump over the counter and attack the bartender, who succeeded in driving him off, when he turned and flew at Mr. Ben Thompson, who shot and killed him."[24]

On April 18, three weeks after Ben's unfortunate canine encounter, Billy Thompson stepped out of the shadows and signed his name to the register at Ellsworth's Grand Central Hotel. Billy had come up with one of the herds, and evidently being in Kansas and surrounded by friends made him think he had little to fear from Texas authorities. When not engaged with stock work, he turned to his usual vices: socializing with the *nymphs du pavé*, drinking to excess, and gambling. L.B. Anderson, an experienced trail boss who worked for the Millet Brothers, stated that Billy Thompson "was one of the men he made the trail north with." The Millet crew were rough and able to shoot their way out of tight situations. Needless to say, Billy easily fit in.[25]

It wasn't long before the Grand Central Hotel greeted Ben Thompson as well. On May 23, he signed the hotel register, easily making friends with proprietor Arthur Larkin and his family. Many years later, Mrs. Larkin fondly remembered Ben Thompson, describing him as a gentleman and a good boarder.[26] The Thompsons found themselves among many friends and acquaintances from the Lone Star State, as many Texans made the Grand Central their headquarters during their stay in Ellsworth. At first, Ben wanted to open his own establishment to cater to the Texas drovers. The *Reporter* announced that eight saloons were open, and the number would soon double. Because of this, Ben decided against opening his own house.[27] Instead, he made an arrangement with Irishman Joe Brennan to set up a gaming table in the back room at Brennan's saloon, located south of the tracks on South Main Street diagonally across the wide railroad plaza from the Grand Central Hotel. On account of its somewhat unsavory clientele, this strip of businesses on South Main Street became known as "Snake Row." Dick Clark, one of the most famous gamblers of his day, also dealt cards at Brennan's saloon and he drew a good crowd due to his reputation as a big-hearted, clever poker player. Another celebrity gambler working the Ellsworth card tables was one-legged Jim Goodwyn (also spelled Goodwin). Similar to Ben Thompson, these men ran a square game which helped to attract the sporting crowd. Brennan's saloon was soon being called the "Gambler's Roost."[28]

In the June 5 issue of the *Reporter*, Editor John Montgomery listed the names of sixty-three Texas cattlemen whose herds swarmed the open range surrounding the town of Ellsworth. Among them were good friends of the Thompson brothers, such as J.C. "Cad" Pierce, his twenty-three-year-old partner Frank H. McGehee, Major Seth Mabry, Neil Cain, Eugene Millett, and his brother Alonzo. The newspaper bragged that the well-watered grassy prairie of Ellsworth County was the best stock country in the United States and the number of longhorns outside of town totaled at least 125,000 head. A few weeks later, the number exceeded 170,000. With an estimated one thousand people sleeping overnight in Ellsworth and with an uncounted number sleeping in their bedrolls out at the cow camps, John Montgomery could justly print in the *Reporter,* "the spurs of the Texas cattlery jingle in Ellsworth" and "everything is decidedly Texan."[29]

The only element lacking was enough buyers for all of the available longhorns and without buyers, the cattlemen and their many drovers found their time in Kansas extended indefinitely. The majority of trail bosses were heavily in debt for notes taken out to purchase cattle, pay their hands, and for other expenses. Some chose to sell their herds at a huge discount. One observer remarked "cattle men, as well as cattle, are slaughtered every day." Before the season ended it was estimated that the longhorn owning Texans who decided not to sell were "collectively some $1,500,000 in debt." They never anticipated the coming banking collapse causing the Financial Panic of 1873 and the end of any substantial market for their herds.[30]

As soon as summer started, Ellsworth was insufferably hot. Day after day, the temperature went above 90 degrees. Per historian Robert Dykstra, "The heat, the general economic anxiety, the transients' aimlessness, all added up to trouble. In Ellsworth it also turned out to be one of the two most fatal cattle town seasons on record."[31]

City officials beefed up the number of policemen in an attempt to control the sometimes-unruly Texas visitors. The police force consisted of a city marshal and four assistants. The *Reporter* printed, perhaps with a figurative smile on its editorial face, "Brocky Jack, Happy Jack, Long Jack, High Low Jack and Ed Hogue are the names of our excellent policemen." Historically these lawmen became known as "Four Jacks and a Joker."[32]

The current City Marshal, John W. "Brocky Jack" Norton, whose pock-marked face inspired his nickname, was formerly a deputy of Wild Bill Hickok in Abilene along with Tom Carson, who was reputed to be a nephew of Christopher "Kit" Carson. One day in late January 1872, the two former deputies had a falling out and quarreled. Carson responded to Brocky Jack "the way he knew best with pistols blazing." Brocky Jack was wounded, but he survived and upon recovering, moved on to Ellsworth. He was added to the city's police force initially as the assistant city marshal.[33] When John "Happy Jack" Morco arrived in Ellsworth, he was charged and tried for vagrancy in the Ellsworth Police Court by Judge Vincent B. Osborn. He had come from California to Ellsworth. Surprisingly, "Happy Jack" was chosen to join the city police force. It was an ultimately unwise decision, given Morco's illiteracy, swaggering braggadocio, and dubious claims that he had been an Indian fighter in the Pacific Northwest. He also claimed to have shot and killed twelve men in Oregon in self-defense, of course. His wife told a different tale however, "that he used to get drunk and abused her … one time she called for help while they were living in Portland and that Jack shot four good citizens who came to her relief. He was put in jail but managed to escape." Happy Jack preferred to carry a brace of holstered revolvers.[34]

Police officers "Long Jack" and "High Low Jack" were John DeLong and John S. Branham. Their service as Ellsworth lawmen had little effect on the events unfolding during the summer

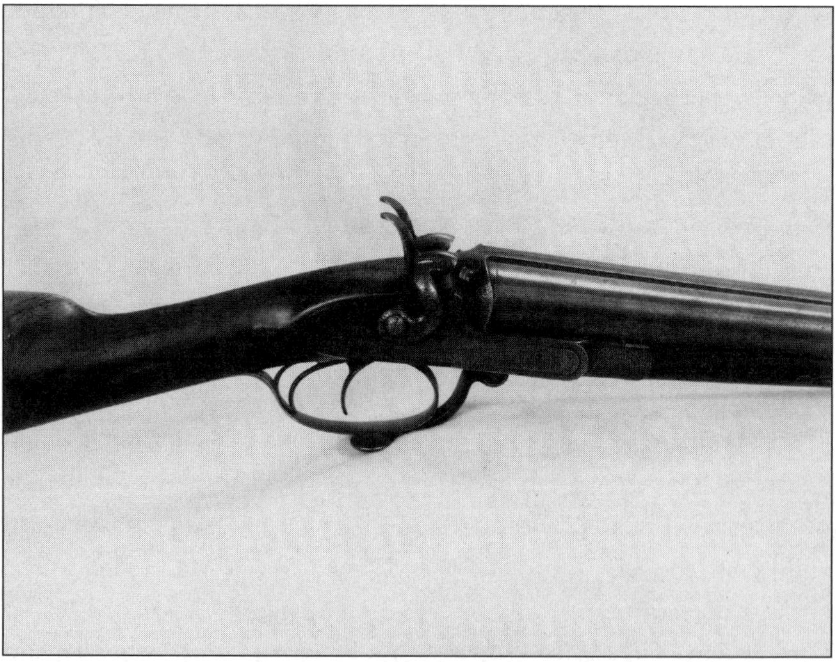

Ben Thompson's English-made shotgun held by brother Billy when they prepared to battle deputy "Happy Jack" Morco and gambler John Sterling on August 15, 1873, in Ellsworth, Kansas. Today it is in the Boot Hill Museum in Dodge City, Kansas.
Courtesy the Boot Hill Museum, Dodge City, Kansas.

of 1873. Edward O. Hogue was of French ancestry, and may have been born in France or possibly at sea. On February 21, 1870, at the age of twenty-two, he was in Hays, Kansas where he killed Peter Murth in a saloon brawl while serving as a bartender. He arrived in Ellsworth in the summer of 1872, and served alternately as chief of police and city marshal. In June of 1873, Hogue was placed on the city police force, and as a deputy served under Ellsworth County Sheriff Whitney.[35]

Kansas historian Floyd Benjamin Streeter developed an understanding of these Ellsworth peace officers during his research on the Kansas cattle towns. "While none of these men then had, or afterward gained, reputations as outstanding frontier marshals … they were capable men and would rate with the average run of cow town police."[36] They were paid accordingly. A self-described "tender-foot," twenty-two-year-old attorney Ira E. Lloyd was drawn to Ellsworth during the mid-summer of 1873, and decided to practice law there. As an attorney defending the many practitioners of wicked trades, Ira Lloyd's relationship with the town's authorities was an adversarial one, especially with Assistant Marshal John "Happy Jack' Morco. Once, Morco drew his revolver as Lloyd was arguing a case and "portraying the villainies" of "Happy Jack" and "Brocky Jack," but several spectators in the courtroom calmed Morco and a shooting was prevented. After the heated session ended, "Happy Jack" Morco was waiting for Lloyd with his revolver in hand. Warned of the danger, Lloyd returned to his office and spent the night behind a barricaded door. Twice during the night, he woke to loud voices on the street below and heard "the drunken and profane voice of 'Happy Jack' telling those who held him, to let him go and kill the s-o-b."

Lloyd later left a vivid, if harsh assessment of Ellsworth's police force. He recalled that every man on the force was "a bribe-taker and a villain. Every man on the force would kill on the slightest provocation, if he felt his hide was safe in doing so. Every man on the force in those days would not hesitate to commit any crime, in order to satisfy his passions or his revenge." Lloyd also provided a brief appraisal for each of the policemen. "Brocky Jack [was] a tall man killer ... a cold blooded, calculating villain, with several notches on his pistol, but none, in my opinion, gained in a fair fight. At heart he was a coward. Brave when he had the drop on another. Under a mask of silence he posed as deep and wise. His few words were esteemed oracles."

"Ed Hogue" was, as Lloyd recalled, "brave when well backed—quick to make terms, if odds were even or greater. He was the stabilizer to the force." The remaining two deputies, John "Long Jack" DeLong and John "High Low Jack" Branham, were cursorily dismissed by Lloyd. "The other members of the police force were just ordinary scoundrels." Many felt that, out of all of the policemen, "Long John" DeLong was the friendliest and had the best rapport with the Texans. Ira Lloyd truly despised "Happy Jack" Morco. "He was 5 feet, ten inches and weighed about 200 pounds," and wore a slouch light colored hat. Lloyd declared Morco "was a born criminal and fled from a western territory for an un-named crime." Listing Morco's many vices, Ira Lloyd asserted, "Happy Jack was a drunkard, a brawler, and brave where there was no danger. Assassination to him was a trade." Grudgingly Lloyd admitted, "He had a certain amount of courage" but only "when drunk and when he thought the fear of him made it safe to bluster and brag."[37]

Ira Lloyd's caustic criticisms of Ellsworth lawmen did not include the county sheriff, Chauncey Whitney. At the newly opened Ellsworth Theatre, Sheriff Whitney was hired to keep order. Editor John Montgomery, exhibiting his confidence in Whitney's peacekeeping skills, wrote in the *Reporter*, "No danger of any disturbance there."[38]

The theatre was proclaimed an instant success, and was set inside a "low one-story building, seventy-five by twenty feet." The interior "was unplastered [*sic*] and unpainted ... plain pine benches afforded a seating capacity for one hundred fifty patrons." Typical of a town on the frontier it was a raw-boned establishment serving more functions than merely that of a performance venue. The building also contained a bar, a gambling table featuring *monte,* and if you could afford it, a "green room back of stage" where you could enjoy "a bottle of wine with the girls." The Ellsworth Theatre was officially not in Ellsworth but on Bayers Street in Nauchville, among the many other businesses catering to the baser desires of the Texas drovers. The few houses included Lizzie Palmer's dance house with inmates Annie Lee, Alice Chambers and Suzie Hart. Benson's restaurant was also a popular dance house and saloon, and Molly Brennan's place was among the other brothels operating under the guise of being a dance house. There is evidence to suggest that Molly was not the wife of the saloon owner, Joe Brennan, but rather she was his sister and partner in vice.[39]

Ben and Billy Thompson checked in and out of the Grand Central during the summer of 1873. When away from the hotel, the brothers stayed with known members of the *demimonde.* Molly Brennan, a beautiful and prominent member, became closer to Billy Thompson than any of her usual clientele. Ben Thompson, having left his wife and children behind in Austin, was unencumbered and free to move from prostitute to prostitute. His favorite, from among all the others, was a woman named Jennie Fields.[40]

On Tuesday, June 10, the Thompson brothers were drinking heavily into the evening with several friends. Word of their carousing reached City Marshal "Brocky Jack" Norton. The marshal stayed ahead of the partying Texans and positioned himself in a Nauchville dance house, where, in reality, he had no legal authority. The Texans tried to gain admittance, but Marshal Norton turned them away at the door. Denied access, they turned around and walked the short block back to Ellsworth. Ben and Billy Thompson, in company with S.A. Fine and J.W. Ford, resorted to their side-arms to keep the fun going. They staggered down the streets of Ellsworth, pulling their revolvers and firing at improvised targets. To avoid a violent confrontation, Norton decided to leave the Thompson brothers and their friends alone and simply wait for them to tire and go to bed. The next issue of the *Reporter* lectured the city authorities. Montgomery wrote, "It sounded very much like the 4 of July yesterday morning ... Firing shots at sign boards had better be suspended. The authorities should enforce the ordinance prohibiting any shooting in the city limits. In order to have good government it is necessary to commence right."[41]

Before the morning newspaper was in print, City Marshal Norton roused Billy Thompson from his bed at the Grand Central and hauled him off to face Police Judge Vincent Osborn. Edward Hogue simultaneously arrested Thompson's friends, Fine and Ford, and together were charged $20 for their evening's pleasure. Both promptly paid the court and went free. As the leading perpetrator, Billy Thompson's pocketbook was hit slightly harder. He was fined $25 plus costs, but Billy was unable to pay and consequently jailed. The following day, his brother Ben went to the police court on his own volition, pled guilty, and paid his $10 fine. The Thompson brothers must have run out of money, because Billy was left behind to sit in jail for a week before Ben returned on June 18 with the necessary cash to finally release Billy.[42]

For reasons now unknown, the mayor vacated his office in a similar fashion as the two county sheriffs previous to Whitney. A special election took place on Saturday, June 21 and two prominent men contested for the office of mayor. One was sixty-three-year-old former probate judge, James B. Miller, and the second was Major James W. Gore, a current member of the city council and manager of the Drovers' Cottage Hotel. Both Gore and his wife Louisa were very popular with the visiting Texans. With regard to the pressing issue of visiting drovers, the candidates offered the voters a clear choice between law and order or moderation. Law and order proved to be slightly more desirable amongst the citizens of Ellsworth when Miller secured a total of ninety-four ballots, defeating Gore by a narrow margin of eight votes.[43]

James B. Miller was born in Rochester, New York on August 2, 1811. Prior to the start of the Civil War, Miller, his wife Delia Francis (Ross), and their two children moved to Chicago where he practiced law. Politically, Miller identified as a Republican. In 1868, he moved to Kansas to work for the railroad as both a land and ticket agent. As a religious man, Miller was instrumental in building a church in Ellsworth and after only a year as a resident, he became the county's probate judge.[44]

It was Tuesday evening, June 31, and as usual Billy Thompson was drunk, armed, and enjoying a night of it when he ran into Policeman "Happy Jack" Morco. Billy decided not to go easily, and resisted Morco's attempt to arrest him. Billy made another unwilling visit to Judge Osborn's courtroom after he was eventually thrown in jail to sleep it off. He was charged with breaking three local ordinances: unlawfully carrying a revolver, disturbing the peace, and assaulting Policeman Morco. Billy confessed he was drunk and pled guilty. Sheriff Whitney appeared as one of six witnesses for the prosecution. This time he was able to pay the court a fine of $10, plus costs of $15. Billy was immediately released, and the friction between Policeman Morco and the Thompson brothers would only continue.[45]

The city council and Mayor Miller had their first meeting on the same day Billy was in court. Miller emphasized the necessity of preserving good order. Many of the town's businessmen took exception to Miller's assertion, especially the saloon crowd, who wanted to curtail the police and take a more lenient attitude toward the behavior of the Texas cowboys. Two policemen were subsequently fired, one of them being the domineering and tyrannical Morco, an action which was warmly welcomed by the Texans. Ten days later, feeling Morco had been acting with commendable zeal, a citizen's petition on his behalf forced the city council to rehire him and with this public backing, he became even more aggressive in making arrests.[46]

"Nobody Killed Yet," John Montgomery proclaimed at the top of his "Local News" column in the July 3 issue of the *Reporter*. What did he mean by that proclamation? Were these three simple words a mere reporting of fact or an expression of cynical surprise? Perhaps they were boastful words, or maybe an utterance of nervous apprehension. Whatever the intention, Montgomery's headline did not ring true for long.

The issue on Thursday, August 14, protested that "these are not the days of '67 and all people know it," the *Reporter* conceded that the city marshal and his assistants needed to go armed, but "one pistol is enough and that should be concealed as much as possible." The *Reporter* had had enough. With an obvious reference to two-gun "Happy Jack" Morco, "It is too much to see double armed men walking our peaceful streets."

Friday, August 15, 1873, was another day of oppressive heat in Ellsworth, Kansas. The temperature was again over 90 degrees and the Whitney family planned a picnic with a group of their friends at a grove owned by J. C. Howard on the banks of the Smokey Hill River, about six miles out of town. It was to be a day of recreation, perhaps mixed with some political overtones. J. C. Howard was a cattleman and an Ellsworth County commissioner who favored the Texas cattle trade. John Montgomery recalled it was before noon when he was approached by Sheriff Whitney and invited to join them, however previous commitments made it impossible for

"Texas Billy" Thompson from an image probably made in Wichita, Kansas, in 1872. *Courtesy the Western History Collection, University of Oklahoma. Image # 2145.*

Montgomery to leave town. In passing, Montgomery mentioned Billy Thompson was on another drunken spree. Learning this, Whitney sent his wife and daughter to the picnic but he decided to stay in town. He knew that when one or both of the Thompson brothers were drinking hard, trouble often followed.[47] Based on his friendly acquaintance with them for the previous two months, it appears Sheriff Whitney was confident he could influence the Thompsons's behavior in a positive manner. "There was no difficulty or grudges or animosity" between the Thompson brothers and Whitney. They were "fast friends."[48]

Billy Thompson was up early that morning or more likely, he had never gone to bed from the night before. He was drunk and on horseback riding up and down the plaza firing off his pistol. Seventeen-year-old Ernest Cunningham, who was in town to see a butcher about fresh meat for his family, was almost shot by one of Billy's wayward bullets. Before any lawman arrived, Ben Thompson quieted his brother and convinced him to return to his room and get some sleep.[49]

The police court had a special case scheduled on August 15. The town's city marshal was being tried before Judge Osborn, and was charged with being unlawfully drunk, disturbing the peace, and discharging his pistol. Attorney Ira Lloyd, as part of his continuing feud with law enforcement, wanted to demonstrate to all that the police officers were not above the law. He convinced a witness to file a complaint against "Brocky Jack" Norton for his behavior on August 10. Norton didn't argue about being drunk and disturbing the peace, but did lamely allege his pistol accidentally discharged. The court costs were remitted, but he was fined for his behavior.[50]

In Joe Brennan's saloon, a card game had been going on for hours. Although Ben Thompson was not playing, two of his best friends were going up against each other. Neil Cain was dealing *monte* and fellow cattleman Cad Pierce, flush with cash, was betting more than Cain wanted to handle. Pierce asked Ben to find another gambler who would cover any extra amount Cain was unwilling to accept. Thompson looked around the room and made the offer to enter the game to John T. Sterling, who at once agreed to cover Cad Pierce's over-bets. For inviting him into the game, Sterling promised Ben that he would split any winnings.

John Sterling, born in Illinois, had served during the Civil War with the 11th Indiana Infantry. At the third battle of Winchester, Virginia, on September 19, 1864, Sterling captured fourteen Confederate soldiers with the help of one companion at the height of the action. For this act of bravery, he was awarded the Congressional Medal of Honor. As a gambler, Sterling was said to be "a good natured, warm-hearted man and always ready to help the needy or skin a sucker."[51]

Sterling joined the game and while handling the over-bets, he started to win. He began to drink and before long, the liquor had its effect. But he was lucky, and when the game ended in the middle of the afternoon, the amount of cash he'd taken off of Cad Pierce was in the neighborhood of one thousand dollars. Sterling forgot about sharing with Ben Thompson, or perhaps didn't care to split his winnings and left Brennan's place. Thompson certainly cared about his split, and he searched for Sterling, determined to collect. Ben found him in Nick Lentz's Saloon. Thompson asked Sterling for a settlement, which infuriated Sterling. He lashed out, striking Ben in the face. "Happy Jack" Morco, a friend of Sterling, was lounging nearby. Morco intervened and drew down on Thompson, forcing him to back away. Ben Thompson, unarmed and furious, yelled at Morco not to interfere, and to take the drunken Sterling away. They left Lentz's Saloon and went up the street heading west. Thompson headed in the other direction toward Brennan's Saloon. He found Cad Pierce in the back of the barroom and the two friends began talking about what had transpired. Sterling, now armed with a shotgun, and Morco, with a revolver in each hand, stood outside the saloon's front door. They called out a challenge, yelling through the door, "Get your guns you Texas sons of bitches and fight!" Ben Thompson later understated it, saying, "It caused considerable excitement at the time."[52]

The men inside Brennan's saloon tried to calm Thompson, and in an effort to avoid bloodshed, refused Ben the loan of a pistol or any other type of their checked firearms. Frustrated, Ben ran out the back door and down the alley to Jake New's billiard hall, where he had earlier checked his weapons. There he stuffed a six-shooter into his waist belt and checked his Winchester rifle. Satisfied, he walked out the front door and headed to the middle of the railroad plaza. He would later claim he wanted to be on open ground so if a difficulty occurred innocent people would not be hurt.[53] As an experienced gunman, Ben Thompson was well aware how a Winchester in the wide expanse of the plaza would provide him a distinct advantage over the limited effective range of Sterling's shotgun and Morco's pistols.

Before Ben had gone far from New's billiard hall, his brother Billy approached him, obviously still under the influence. Billy was holding Ben's double-barreled shotgun with both hammers cocked.[54] Billy refused Ben's advice when he "entreated" his drunken brother to go back into the billiard hall "and put up his gun." Ben told his brother he was too drunk to be of help and feared "he would end up killing some of his best friends if he was not careful how he handled his gun." No sooner said than done, Billy accidentally caused one barrel to discharge. The buckshot tore into the sidewalk in front of the billiard hall, barely missing two close friends of the Thompson brothers, cattlemen and partners Seth Mabry and Eugene Millett. Ben grabbed the shotgun out of Billy's hands and attempted the additional precaution of unloading the second barrel, but found the brass cartridge swollen. Unable to extract it, Ben handed the shotgun off to another bystander and continued to walk toward the railroad depot. Only a few moments went by before Billy staggered up to his brother again with the cocked shotgun in hand. Ben looked back at Snake Row, and then hollered at the crowd of men standing in front of the barrooms along South Main Street, "If you damn sons of bitches want to fight [,] here we are!"[55]

The noise of the impending gun battle reached beyond Snake Row. John Montgomery was working in the newspaper office adjacent to the Grand Central Hotel, and even though he was across the railroad tracks and a city block away, he heard the threats and the shot.[56] The discharge of the shotgun also reached the ears of Sheriff Whitney and former policeman John "Long Jack" DeLong, who had been let go from the force a few days prior. They were on the north side of the tracks at J. C. Veatch's combination hotel and restaurant. Whitney could see the Thompson brothers standing a little west of the railroad depot armed and ready to fight.[57] City Marshal "Brocky Jack" Norton started to walk out onto the plaza to confront the Thompsons but Sheriff Whitney intervened and warned him, "They will shoot you. I will go; they will not harm me." Norton gave no argument and he retreated to the safety of Nick Lentz's saloon.[58]

With DeLong, an unarmed Sheriff Whitney hurried to where the brothers were standing and called out, "boys, don't have any row, I will do all I can to protect you, you know that John and I are your friends." Ben replied, "We don't want to make a fight on anybody if they will let us alone, we will let them alone. They commenced this quarrel and not us, but if they do so for us we propose to defend ourselves." Whitney then made an offer, "come on let us go over to Brennan's and take a drink." Ben Thompson said, "All right I will do so and get Billy to put up his gun." Whitney observed, "Billy is drunk and you are sober, and he will shoot someone accidentally." Both men then asked Billy to let down the hammers of the shotgun. At first, Billy ignored them but he finally agreed to leave the gun when they got to the safety of the saloon. He did declare that, "he was not going to let those damn sons of bitches get the best of Ben." The four men headed to Joe Brennan's saloon, walking south across the plaza in friendly conversation. There were many spectators in front and inside of the saloon, and a handful of these onlookers would later testify as to what they witnessed.[59]

DeLong entered the saloon first; Billy Thompson and Whitney followed him. Ben was hanging back to ensure the safety of the party. As he was entering the saloon, Ben heard a warning yell, "Look out Ben!" Ben stepped away from Brennan's saloon door and watched Happy Jack run down the street with a six-shooter in each hand. Sterling followed with his shotgun. Upon hearing the warning, Morco ran into Beebe's hardware store, while Sterling ducked into Nick Lentz's saloon.[60] Ben instantly whirled and drew his Winchester down on him and fired, but Morco was moving quickly and had safely dodged into Beebe's store. Enraged, Ben "concluded to have it out with 'Happy Jack' then and there." For that reason Ben started in a rapid walk westward toward Beebe's store.[61]

The gunfire drew Sheriff Whitney outside of the saloon, followed closely by Billy Thompson, cocked shotgun still in his hands. With his pair of revolvers presented, Morco reappeared. As Ben Thompson, again, moved in the direction of Morco, a shotgun blast roared behind him. Turning, he saw Sheriff Whitney "standing up, but seemed badly wounded, he had a faintish look."[62] Whitney moaned, "My God, Billy you have shot me!" Instantaneously, Ben Thompson screamed at his brother, "My God you have shot our best friend!" Billy mumbled a remark which Ben did not understand. John Montgomery would write a different tale in his next issue of the *Reporter* claiming Billy "replied that he did not give a d--! That he would have shot if it had been Jesus Christ!" And Ben would forever deny Billy spoke those words. Montgomery explained to his readers how, "Mr. Whitney who made two attempts to get out of the way before he shot and said 'don't shoot'—Thompson fired and Whitney received the charge." The wounded Whitney whirled around twice, screamed out that he was shot and called for his wife. Spectators rushed to Whitney's side and began to help him as best they could and began to carry him to his home, a few blocks away.[63] In the first few moments of confusion, Ben lost sight of his brother and started to walk across the railroad tracks to the north side of the plaza and the Grand Central Hotel. Billy Thompson staggered in the opposite direction of his brother, re-entered Brennan's Saloon, went through the barroom, and out the back door. He traced his brother's earlier steps, turned westward, and ran down the alley behind Snake Row to Jake New's billiard hall.[64]

A few minutes after the shooting, Ben Thompson was standing on the stone pavement in front of the Grand Central when Billy, empty shotgun in-hand, rode up to him. "The common story is that he appropriated some fellow's cowpony." However, Montgomery stated it was Billy's horse brought to him from Sam John's livery stable in the rear of the Grand Central Hotel by some quick-thinking friend.[65] It may have been cattleman Eugene Millett, while others thought it was Neil Cain. Ben took the shotgun from his brother, and someone gave Billy a six-shooter. Cad Pierce shoved $100 into Billy's hands.[66] Ben "knew the mob would be present in a moment" and he "urged Billy to fly." Ben felt, "the misfortune seemed to have confused him worse, instead of shocking him into a sober state of mind."[67] Billy asked his brother what he had done, and after learning what had happened, he asked if Whitney was dead. Upon Ben telling him Whitney was yet alive, he stated his desire to "go and see him for you know I never intended it." Ben pleaded with his brother to flee to the cattle camps outside of town, promising him he would visit Sheriff Whitney since he believed Whitney was not fatally hurt. Billy refused to flee and was not sensible to the imminent danger. He chose to foolishly ride about shooting his pistol off in the air. Billy's continued drunken antics made Ben crazed. He made up his mind that, if a mob were to lay hands on his brother, he would shoot and kill him and then empty his weapons until the moment he fell dead. In preparation, Ben reloaded the shotgun. Finally, Billy began to calm down, but still defiantly rode slowly out of town cursing and inviting a fight. He trotted off in the direction of Nauchville, heading to Molly Brennan's house.[68]

In the meantime, Sheriff Whitney was suffering intensely but people held hope he would survive. Two Ellsworth doctors, A. Gregg and William Fox, addressed the wounds created by the buckshot pellets in an attempt to stop the bleeding and comfort the patient. Major James Gore, failed mayoral candidate and proprietor of the Drovers Cottage hotel, provided fifty dollars plus expenses to bring in Dr. William Finlaw, the post surgeon at Fort Riley. An urgent telegraph was sent asking Dr. Finlaw to hurry to Ellsworth.[69]

Ben Thompson kept his guns for a full hour after Billy rode out of town. The street filled with armed Texans ready to defy anyone who might attempt to arrest Ben. Mayor Miller was at his residence during the shooting. He was notified of the disturbance and hurriedly arrived at the town's railroad plaza. The mayor was shocked to learn of the inaction of City Marshal Norton and his policemen. Mayor Miller immediately fired them all and went to the front of the Grand Central Hotel himself, intending to disarm Ben Thompson and personally take him into custody. He fearlessly passed all of the armed Texans and demanded Ben Thompson surrender. Ben admitted Mayor Miller was "a man of great decision of character, and brave, too." He explained to the mayor, "I respect you, and am inclined to surrender to you but before doing so, must have your word of honor that no mob shall in any way interfere with me, and besides Happy Jack and Hogue must be disarmed." The mayor agreed to the terms and with the proprietor of the Grand Central, Arthur Larkin, went off and found Happy

Jack. He returned with the unarmed Morco to the hotel. As the only official lawman left, Ellsworth County Deputy Sheriff Edward Hogue "received the arms of Ben Thompson." John Montgomery's opinion was that the mayor had made a "bad move" by firing the entire police force. However, he also acknowledged the decisions Mayor Miller made under great pressure, as well as the subsequent actions he personally took, prevented further blood from spilling on the streets of Ellsworth.[70]

A posse of Ellsworth citizens finally formed and began to search for Billy Thompson. It must have been a half-hearted attempt, because they gave up and returned to town after riding for about ten miles. Cad Pierce openly mocked the attempt loudly offering a thousand dollars to anyone who would arrest the posse.[71]

Ben Thompson was charged with firing his rifle at Morco. At the mayor's office, Ben offered to give bond to ensure his later appearance in an Ellsworth court room. The mayor hesitated, but at last concluded to demand a $10,000 bond. The stated amount was so high it must have been the mayor's intention to keep Ben Thompson incarcerated until the hearing took place. Ben's wealthier friends came forward to help with covering the high bond amount. Seth Mabry and Eugene Millett provided the money, the deposit was made and Ben was released from custody.[72]

Mayor Miller continued to demonstrate leadership. He called the five members of the city council together to select a new police force. Voting three to two, the council reluctantly approved the mayor's earlier action of dismissing the city marshal and all of his staff. The mayor wanted John DeLong, a noted friend of the Texans, to be the new city marshal but his motion failed to win a majority. Deputy Sheriff Edward Hogue was acceptable to all, and was duly sworn in as city marshal. DeLong was rehired as a policeman, and shockingly, John Morco was reinstated after his checkered tenure and the sad role he played on that fateful day

Arthur Larkin, Ellsworth entrepreneur and operator of the Grand Central Hotel. He helped resolve the differences between the Texans and Ellsworth townspeople after the accidental killing of Sheriff Whitney. Larkin accompanied Mayor James Miller and helped disarm "Happy Jack" Morco, as part of Ben Thompson's terms of surrender. *Courtesy the Ellsworth County Historical Society.*

with the Thompson brothers. A new man, Edward Crawford, was then added to complete the four-man force. Crawford was a hothead who was quick to pull his pistol, and he would prove to be a disastrous choice. Later that evening, Mayor Miller went back to Snake Row, found John Norton and removed the city marshal badge from his chest.[73]

Ben Thompson learned that Billy had not followed his advice and had yet to hide out at one of the cow camps. He was still down by the river bottom in Nauchville enjoying Molly Brennan's well-worn charms. Ben approached a trusted friend of his, a man named Nat Good, and asked Nat to go and get Billy to one of the cattle camps and stay with him until he sobered up.[74] Eventually, a drunken Billy left Molly and rode off onto the prairie. He didn't go far before he stepped down from his horse and went to sleep. Billy woke up around 9 p.m. with no money and no idea as to how he ended up in the middle of a prairie. Perhaps Molly Brennan absconded with his get-away money. Billy had also lost the pistol he was carrying. He wandered around for more than an hour until he saw the lights of the town and thought it would be best to return to Ellsworth. Fortunately he had sense enough to slip into town unnoticed. Billy trusted a friend to pass word to his brother that he had returned and was hiding near the Grand Central Hotel.[75]

Once he was released from the mayor's office, Ben Thompson went into Nauchville and eventually took a seat at the theatre there. As he was watching the entertainment, Billy's emissary tapped Ben on the shoulder and whispered Billy was in town. Ben admitted his utter astonishment, "If a streak of lightning on a clear day had struck me I should not have been more surprised. I sat still for a few moments, in order not to attract attention by a sudden leaving, and then departed." He took a round-about way to throw off anyone who might have been watching his movements. When he reached his brother, he saw that Billy had sobered up after his nap and evening stroll about the prairie, but he was feeling the intense effects of his whiskey hangover, and he was beginning to become aware of what had happened. "What in the name of God, Billy, are you doing here, you ought to be at least thirty or forty miles away," Ben exclaimed. Billy thought that the authorities had certainly telegraphed in all directions, and to try and run now would only result in his arrest. He concluded his best option was to return to Ellsworth. Both brothers knew that if Billy was to try to stay in town, it would only bring more trouble. They agreed to the original plan of action: that Billy must hide at one of the cattle camps. To be successful, he would have to change his appearance so as to be unrecognizable. He took on a disguise with Ben's help. Ben explained.

> [Billy's] hair was very long, hanging down on his shoulders. I first cut that as best I could by shingling it, then made him strip, and covered him to the hue of a Mexican, from head to foot, even between the toes, and then, with yellowish paint, stained his milk white teeth to the color that is given by tobacco juice; changed his shoes for boots, not new ones, then replaced his Mexican hat with a cap, and his black clothes with second-hand army blue blouse and brownish pants, and he was ready for the road. His most intimate friend would not have known him—should not have known him myself, had I met him accidentally. I instructed him to speak nothing but Spanish, which he could do fluently.

Ben told his brother he did not think Sheriff Whitney had been badly hurt, and as soon as he could, he would visit Whitney and try to square things. Billy left town accompanied by a young man named Jack, who drove cattle for Cad Pierce's partner, Frank McGehee. In the morning, Ben appeared in court in accordance with the conditions of his bond. For reasons unknown, Morco failed to show. Since no other witness appeared and no other charges were pressed against him, Ben Thompson was released. He then approached several of Sheriff Whitney's friends expressing his desire to call upon Whitney. When no one returned with an invitation to Whitney's home, he decided it was best not to go. Two days after the shooting, Billy proposed to Ben a subscription drive be promoted among the Texans in an effort to raise money for the benefit of Sheriff Whitney and his wife and child. The brothers started the drive with a donation of $25 from each of them. Texans generously participated and soon the total reached $400.[76]

Doctor William Finlaw arrived from Junction City by train and immediately examined Sheriff Whitney's wounds. Friends and family hoped the surgeon could do what the other doctors were unable to accomplish. Dr. Finlaw discovered several of the buckshot had entered the chest, cut through the lungs and lodged in Whitney's backbone. It was an inoperable wound. After almost three days of suffering, Chauncey Whitney mercifully succumbed late Sunday night or very early in the morning on Monday, August 18. He was comforted by his close friends, his family, and his doctors. The community was devastated, and they planned an elaborate funeral. "One coffin for Sandy" was ordered at a cost of thirty-three dollars—ironically from the firm of Whitney & Kendall Furniture & Undertaking—the late Whitney's place of business. His brother members of the Masonic Order took charge of his body. Dr. Levi Sternberg conducted the funeral service and elegantly delivered Sheriff Whitney's eulogy to a large concourse of mourners. He was laid to rest in an impressive graveside service. His young widow, Nellie (Henry) Whitney, her father, and her family members graciously thanked the people of Ellsworth for their many favors and kindness during their "great trouble" through a published note in the town's newspaper. John Montgomery expressed the cares of many in the *Reporter*, "Dust was rendered to dust; safe from the storms, free from cares, in the bosom of mother earth, rests the body of our late Sheriff C.B. Whitney."[77] His six years of loyal service to the town and county of Ellsworth had come to an end.

Chapter 7

WHITE AFFIDAVITS

"We are glad to have you with us!"

—The Ellsworth's *Reporter* to the Texas cattlemen, August 28, 1873

After Sheriff Whitney drew his last breath on Monday, August 18, 1873, Ellsworth County Coroner Dr. William Masterson Duck held an official inquest. Six witnesses were called to testify. However only three of the six can now be identified: newspaper editor John Montgomery, German-born bathhouse and saloon owner Nick Lentz, and Ben Thompson.[1]

Regrettably, Montgomery chose not to publish the testimony given during the coroner's inquest. In his article appearing in the August 21 issue of the *Reporter* entitled, "Cold Blooded Murder/ Sheriff C.B. Whitney Shot and Killed by a Drunken Desperado," he explained, "We will give the particulars of the unfortunate affair as correctly and as briefly as possible. Coroner Duck held an inquest Monday, but we are not at liberty to publish the testimony; the important points will probably agree with the following particulars." It was clear that he believed Billy Thompson intentionally aimed, pulled the trigger, and unloaded a fatal barrel of buckshot into Sheriff Whitney.[2]

Nick Lentz's testimony explained a little of what transpired. The bystanders lining Snake Row, including the crowd in front of his bathhouse and saloon, "melted away" as soon as Ben and Billy Thompson walked out onto the plaza and called out their challenge. The Thompson brothers were reputed man-killers. This fact was both established and well-known to all. The only people left in Lentz's establishment after Ben Thompson fired his errant rifle shot at "Happy Jack" Morco were City Marshal Norton, gambler Jack Sterling, and Lentz. When he saw Ben Thompson shoulder his rifle, Lentz locked his establishment. He testified that he did not see any shooting, but heard some.[3]

In the days following the shooting, the townspeople's anger and bitterness toward undesirables, and particular Texans, reignited their vigilante tendencies. Ben Thompson learned that a vigilance committee was forming and he advised his friends, especially Cad Pierce and Neil Cain, that it was time to leave Ellsworth. After Ben provided his testimony at the coroner's inquest, he went to the plaza railroad depot, stepped aboard an eastbound train, and didn't get off until he reached Kansas City. Pierce and Cain chose to remain in town, even though Pierce was considering driving his unsold cattle north and making Nebraska City, Nebraska, his new headquarters.

The vigilantes decided on a method to order people out of town, and a short note informing the undesirables to leave immediately or face the consequences was usually delivered by one or more of the town's policemen. This slip of paper was called a "White Affidavit," and if obeyed promptly, no harm would come to the recipient.[4]

One of the first to be warned out of town was Ira E. Lloyd, the young attorney who filed charges against then City Marshal

Norton, and who insulted Policeman Morco in open court. Afraid he would continue "to concoct mischief against the police," City Marshal Edward Hogue appeared at Lloyd's office and handed the lawyer a white affidavit. Lloyd was no coward who ran at the first hint of trouble, so he sought out Mayor Miller, several of the coun-

Ellsworth's Ira E. Lloyd began his legal career as a defense attorney antagonizing members of the town's police force. Lloyd unsuccessfully prosecuted Billy Thompson for the shooting death of Sheriff Whitney. This photograph was made by Henry T. Martin. *Courtesy the Ellsworth County Historical Society.*

cilmen, and saloon owners friendly to him. With the backing of these prominent men, "it became apparent to the police—the order could not be executed."[5]

At 4 p.m. on Wednesday afternoon, August 20, Cad Pierce, John Good, and Neil Cain appeared on Snake Row. Earlier, the three Texans had heard the rumor that the new City Marshal Hogue had given white affidavits to Policeman Morco to deliver, and that the trio was about to be ordered out of town. With Pierce in the lead, they approached the marshal in front of Jerome Beebe's hardware store demanding to know if the rumor was true. Hogue "told Cad Pierce that it was no such thing, that he ought to know better." Pierce wanted Hogue to accompany him in finding "Happy Jack," and to give him a talking-to. Hogue refused to go, claiming that "there had been too much talk already." Policeman Edward Crawford was standing among the crowd and watching the confrontation. He stepped forward, toward Pierce and stated, "Yes, a damn sight too much talk ... and bad talk on your side." Crawford then asked Pierce, "what did you say yesterday when you had that shot gun in your hands? You said this gun killed one short horn son of a bitch, and that it cost $100 and you would not take $200 better for it." Hogue tried to intervene and get Crawford to "come away." Pierce said something Hogue did not understand, then Crawford demanded, "What is that you say? If you want a fight here is the place for it—as good as any!" Crawford then took a step backward and placed his hand on his holstered revolver. When Pierce supposedly put his hand behind his back, Crawford drew his weapon and fired. Pierce turned and ran through Beebe's front door. Crawford followed and fired off a second round in Pierce's direction. Pierce fell to the floor severely wounded, as Crawford rushed up and beat him over the head with his revolver until Pierce's brains spilled out onto the floor. He "lived but a few minutes."[6]

The pistol shots brought Morco running to the scene. Drawing both of his six-shooters, he pointed them at Neil Cain, who begged for mercy. City Marshal Hogue's intervention was successful this time, and Cain's life was saved. Cain ran off to find his horse, then raced out of town toward the safety of the cattle camps. A crowd gathered around Pierce and a search of his body found him to be unarmed. Still, Policeman Crawford bragged to the *Reporter,* "Pierce wanted a fight and he reached for his revolver but I was too quick for him."[7]

James C. Pierce was well-known and well-liked among almost all associated with the Texas cattle trade. The *Nebraska City Press* published a notice of his passing, pointing out that although the Thompson brothers were "not known" there, but of "Capt. Cad Pierce" the *Press* proclaimed "we can truly say a more perfect gentleman, since we have been acquainted with him, would be hard to find in any city or state." Although some other newspapers described Pierce as "a gambler and that he was a 'rough,'" the *Nebraska City Press* refuted that description and wrote, "and right here we wish to stamp the whole thing as false. It is true he played cards when not on the road [however] in our city he gained many friends. He was a quiet, unassuming gentleman, never intoxicated, and always a gentleman in every respect. He was very wealthy and rather free with his money." The editor may have known Pierce well, because he pointed out there was "a young wife to mourn his death, besides his many friends."[8]

His many friends and other angry Texans in Ellsworth were "breathing vengeance and threatening to burn the town."[9] The remaining cow camps emptied, and a group of drovers went into Ellsworth riding around for almost twenty minutes telling everyone within earshot of their deadly intentions. In reaction to the threat, many citizens armed themselves and went to the mayor's office offering their services to protect their town. Miller selected twenty Ellsworth men to patrol the town at night to watch for fires and to stop any disturbances. Other citizens ransacked the rooms of the Grand Central Hotel and seized the weapons the Texans had checked in there.[10] Under the heated circumstances, these citizens determined their actions were necessary for the safety of the town.

As word of the death of his friend, Cad Pierce, spread, some believed Ben Thompson would return to Ellsworth with guns and ammunition to help rearm his friends and supporters. People began looking for Thompson, and westbound trains in Salina were searched. Seeing no useful purpose in continuing the violence, Ben Thompson remained in Kansas City for a few days before he traveled to St. Louis by rail. Boarding a steamboat there, his trip downriver passed by Cairo, Illinois, which was situated at the confluence of the Mississippi and Ohio Rivers. He continued down the Mississippi to New Orleans and finally headed home to Austin, Texas.

The search to bring Billy Thompson back to Ellsworth to answer to his crimes was very short-lived. Without fear, he safely rode back down the cattle trail to Texas in the company of other returning drovers. About the time the Thompson brothers would have arrived back in their hometown of Austin, James K. Farrell, a bartender at Stuart's Saloon on Congress Avenue, married Ben Thompson's sister-in-law, Sarah Isabella Moore. If he had returned to Austin by this time, Ben would have attended the wedding with his wife Kate. However, Billy Thompson, on the run from two murder charges, was certainly not expected to be there.[11]

Many of the professional gamblers, roughs, unsavory transients, Texas cattlemen, and drovers boarded the eastbound trains and left Ellsworth behind. The *Commonwealth*, a leading newspaper in Topeka, commented, "that class of persons commenced looking after their carpet bags, and the next train east on the K.P. [Kansas Pacific] was freighted with more infamy than is usually transported in one day. The 21st of August will be remembered in Ellsworth for the exodus of the roughs and gamblers."[12] The casket holding the remains of Cad Pierce was also aboard one of the eastbound trains. It was attended by approximately fifty Texans on its way to Pierce's hometown of Webberville, a small community a few miles southwest of Austin, Texas. Upon the casket's arrival, it is believed his family laid Cad to rest in the Pierce Family Cemetery.[13]

The Governor of Kansas, Thomas A. Osborn, learned of Ellsworth's violent troubles and sent a telegram to Mayor James Miller that was both an order for him to keep the peace and an offer of help from the state if needed. Governor Osborn assigned his Attorney General, Archibald L. Williams, to investigate the situation. In an attempt to bring Billy Thompson back to face an Ellsworth jury, Osborn issued a proclamation on August 22, 1873, offering a $500 reward for Billy Thompson's arrest and conviction.[14] The proclamation's description spoke of Billy as "about six feet in height, 26 years of age, dark complexion, brown hair, gray eyes and erect form."[15] Soon a different version of Billy Thompson's actions concerning the shooting of Sheriff Whitney began to form and take hold. The August 25, 1873 issue of the *Nebraska City Press* was the first to publish the following explanation, "Ben Thompson had been quarreling ... when brother (Billy) came down the street with a shot gun on his shoulder, and shot Sheriff Whitney accidentally."

Ellsworth's *Reporter* of Thursday, August 28, addressed the Texas cattlemen on its front page. "We are glad to have you with us! You were invited to our county; we sent out men to guide you here, with your cattle, and when you arrived you were warmly welcomed. Every facility that the town and county could offer, was and is yours." The newspaper explained, "It is then, foolish to imagine that there could be any hard feeling towards Texas men by our people. After having been invited and conducted here we wished for your good will, as you had ours; and we believe there is a good feeling between us and that it will continue. This splendid country is open to you; our markets, our stock yard, cattle buyers, all make Ellsworth the best point for drovers. Probably there is not a man in this city, and but two or three farmers in the county who are not in favor of you staying." However, the newspaper asserted, "But there are more important things than money making. Self respect, honor, reputation, are of more account than dollars, and if we cannot have both [,] we will have the best." Asking for their cooperation the article also let the Texans know the law will be upheld. "Do not let the unfortunate events of last week make any trouble or break in the amity of old. We trust that there will be no more scenes of violence in Ellsworth; that none of us will defend or excuse crime, but stand up for the dignity of law and order, and for our common humanity."

The Ellsworth city council met with Mayor Miller per his request on August 27, and a majority felt it was again time to make another wholesale change in the city's police force. In addition to being fired, Morco and Edward Crawford were so disliked by both the remaining Texans and the citizens of Ellsworth that they were ordered out of town. After a long discussion, the council agreed with the mayor's recommendation and Richard Freeborn was chosen to be the new city marshal. He was authorized to select two officers to serve as his police force. Having been a bartender, Freeborn was popular with the Texans. He was also a clerk at the American Hotel and Saloon. City Marshal Freeborn retained John DeLong and J. Charles Brown, a novice to police work. DeLong always had a good rapport with the visiting Texans, and was well liked by them. Brown, using his middle name "Charles," hailed from Illinois and supposedly grew up on a farm. All three officers were acceptable to the Texans.[16]

In his memoirs, Attorney Ira E. Lloyd, recalled that Freeborn was "a good hearted man as ever mixed a drink, but he was too good to injure a fly." Charles Brown was "a friend of mine, and a man who saved my life after the council meeting [when Morco laid in wait to shoot Lloyd]. Brown was a tall, black-haired, slender person, who had many years been a [house] painter and lived much in frontier towns. He was a good pistol shot, brave, and I always felt with a strong desire, if justifiable, to have a notch on his pistol." Lloyd felt that Brown, "if called upon to make an arrest," would "prefer to perform the duty by arresting with a well directed bullet."[17]

When John Morco was dismissed from his duties as a police officer, he left the following day on an eastbound train. When the train stopped in Salina, Morco was arrested. The arrest was based on a telegram from Ellsworth asking for him to be jailed for carrying off a brace of revolvers worth $100. The pistols were owned by John Good, who was a close friend of Ben Thompson, and had shared a room with him at the Grand Central Hotel.[18] Policeman Brown and John Good traveled by train to Salina. Brown had requested a warrant but Mayor Miller told him one would not be necessary.

In Salina, Happy Jack insisted the revolvers belonged to him. He claimed that to surrender them would put him at an insurmountable disadvantage when faced with any of the Texans holding a grudge against him. The officials in Salina chose not to try Morco, and he was released after one night in jail. Curiously, John Good did not press his claim. Perhaps he feared Morco. Whatever the reason, he left on the next train to Ellsworth. Staying to have a word with Happy Jack, Policeman Brown asked him not to return to Ellsworth, that he would send Jack his things and anything else he needed or wanted. Upon reaching Ellsworth, Brown followed through and sent Morco his few belongings by express. However, Morco was determined to go against all well-intended advice, even if it came from his sympathetic friends in Salina or in Brookville where he was warned again as he purchased ammunition. Morco retorted, "He was good for all his enemies up there" in Ellsworth.[19]

On the night of Wednesday, September 3, Happy Jack rolled into Ellsworth riding a freight train. The next morning, he openly walked the streets of the town wearing the disputed revolvers without causing a disturbance. All day long, people asked him to obey the ordinance, disarm, and check his revolvers. He refused, and with an oath, he threatened to "make way" with someone before morning. Policeman Brown came upon Morco and demanded he finally give up the revolvers. Refusing for the last time, Morco attempted to draw a revolver. Brown proved how well he could handle a six-shooter. His first shot hit Morco in the heart, and as he was falling, Brown triggered a second shot which struck Morco in the head. He fell in the street and died without struggle. Montgomery commented in the *Reporter*, "Thus ended a career that is sure to come to all who live such lives ... We are sorry for the unfortunate event. Jack was a man, and not without good qualities. But he invited his fate: it came quickly and he is at rest."[20] Morco was hastily buried without ceremony in Ellsworth's original cemetery on the hillside east of town. Not a single person appeared to mourn him.[21]

Policeman Charles Brown most emphatically denied he was "hired or asked to kill Happy Jack," and he insisted that an attempt to arrest Morco would have cost him his life. Doctor W. M. Duck held a coroner's inquest over the body of John Morco. It was determined he died from the effects of two bullet wounds, fired by Policeman Charles Brown "in self defense, while in discharge of his duty, and was justified in the act."[22]

Ira Lloyd has the last word on his nemesis John "Happy Jack" Morco, "Some years later the cemetery, where he was buried was abandoned as a burying place and Happy Jack's remains were removed to [an unmarked grave in] the new cemetery [on West Douglas Avenue]. A man named Al Prime, who knew the trouble between myself and Happy Jack, when he dug up Happy Jack's remains, took his skull and gave it to me. I caused it to be cleaned and sawed in two and placed it over a bookshelf in my office."[23]

Added to the violent passing of Whitney and Pierce, this death brought much criticism to the town and citizens of Ellsworth from newspapers across the state. Often, the out-of-town editorial accounts of events in Ellsworth were greatly exaggerated and ripe with errors. One stands out. The article below first appeared in the columns of the *Press*, a newspaper published in Wellington, Kansas, a town south of Wichita, and it was reprinted on September 11, 1873, by the *Courier* of nearby Winfield, Kansas. Its sensationally false headline guaranteed high readership, "Seven Men Killed in Ellsworth." The older brother of Wyatt Earp provided some true information and some inaccurate information for the article, "From Mr. J. C. Earp, who left Ellsworth a week ago, we learn that the excitement following the murder of Sheriff Whitney, and the shooting of Cad Pearce [*sic*], by policeman Crawford, was unabated, and that the bad blood ... between roughs and city authorities had culminated last Thursday [September 4th] in a general fight, in which seven men were killed outright, and thirteen others more or less wounded." According to this report, "Mr. Earp was present and witnessed the shooting of Whitney and Pearce [*sic*], and was not surprised when news reached Wichita on Sunday that more blood had been spilt. A reign of terror is said to exist in Ellsworth, and the unhappy people are in constant fear of outbreaks of lawlessness and violence. Among those reported killed in last Thursdays fight are policeman Crawford and Happy Jack."

James C. Earp made no mention of any heroics performed by his younger brother, twenty-five-year-old Wyatt, after Sheriff Whitney was fatally wounded. An account written almost fifty years after the fact tells the tale of how Wyatt Earp borrowed a pair of six-shooters, pinned on the city marshal's badge, disregarded a mob of armed Texans and arrested a shotgun wielding Ben Thompson[24]

James Cooksey Earp, older brother of the legendary Wyatt of the fighting Earp brothers. An article in the Winfield, Kansas, *Courier* of September 11, 1873, stated that James Earp was "present and witnessed the shooting" of Sheriff Whitney in Ellsworth. In the *Courier* article, he made no mention of Wyatt being there. Through his biographer, Stuart N. Lake, Wyatt claimed he had made the arrest of Ben Thompson. *Courtesy the Robert G. McCubbin Collection.*

(see Appendix A). If Wyatt Earp did make this arrest, certainly his older brother James would have made some mention of it in his report to the *Courier*. No contemporary record is known to exist which places the famous frontier lawman Wyatt Earp in Ellsworth, Kansas on that fateful day. The story that he arrested Thompson is simply not true. The man who walked across the wide expanse of the town's plaza and faced Ben Thompson and the many heavily armed Texans backing him up was not Wyatt Earp. It was sixty-three-year-old Ellsworth Mayor James Miller. Only through the mayor's bravery and efforts was Ben Thompson disarmed, the standoff ended and any further bloodshed prevented.[25]

Performing the promise stated on its masthead, "For the Future in the Distance, and the Good that We Can Do," the *Ellsworth Reporter* defended the town's reputation in the days and weeks after Sheriff Whitney and Morco were fatally shot. "Everything is quiet, revolvers hang high, you cannot see an armed man on the street." And "We affirm that life and property is just as safe here as in any city in the Union ... The roughs, if there were any here, have left the city and will not return." Further, "Ellsworth is said to have a hard name over the country. This is not as it should be. The citizens of Ellsworth are orderly, intelligent, worthy people, such as would give a good character to any town. Ellsworth being a commercial city during six months of the year, a number of desperate men meet here to remain a few days or weeks, and sometimes their revolvers go off and some one [*sic*] gets hurt—but we protest, such non-residents should not give Ellsworth [its] reputation." And in case the newspaper's readers had doubts, the *Reporter* assured all. "From this time on it is very certain that our city will be as orderly and quiet as any other equally large place in the West."[26]

Reporter Editor John Montgomery's assertion was shortly thereafter proved wrong. The evils of the Texas trade which had caused Abilene to oust the cattle business had not yet let go of Ellsworth.

On Sunday, November 3, Edward Crawford arrived back in Ellsworth to the surprise of all who recognized him, since it was common knowledge that his life would be in danger on account of his shooting Cad Pierce. He ignored all entreaties to leave town and flatly stated he was not afraid. He remained in Ellsworth, and on Thursday he began drinking heavily. On Friday evening, Policeman John DeLong and Ed Crawford were seen drinking together at the American House Hotel and Saloon on Snake Row and both men were judged to be considerably under the influence. Crawford was heard to say to DeLong, "I will fight my own fights. I do not want to fight any body [*sic*] else's." Policeman Charles Brown joined them and asked them to say no more and take a drink with him. Earlier in the day, Crawford told Brown he did not want any fight with anybody. Downing his drink, Crawford left the American House with J. W. Nall and Charles Seward, who both lived in Ellsworth.[27]

The three men walked east down Snake Row turning on to Bayer's Street and going toward Nauchville. It was a few minutes before 8 p.m. and Crawford was seen openly wearing a revolver. They went to house number 31, Mollie Brennan's place. After they had been there for a few minutes, George Harris, an Ellsworth drayman, asked Crawford to go with him to Benson's Saloon, dance hall, and restaurant to have a drink. Strangely, picking up a nearby chair, Crawford's response was to go after Harris, who quickly left and ran over to Lizzie Palmer's house. Calming down, Crawford, accompanied by Nall and Seward, decided to go have a drink at Benson's Saloon after all. Crawford walked into Benson's with ten cents in his pocket and continued to be the worse for wear. He swallowed down another drink and said he was going to one of the whorehouses to stay awhile. That night there were a lot of men down in Nauchville, most of them drunk, and many of them Texans.[28]

Nall and Seward remained with Crawford until he reached Lizzie Palmer's house. Seward left Crawford there and walked back to Benson's Saloon. Crawford asked Nall to stay and told him, "I have plenty of sugar," and that he wanted to sleep with one of the girls. Nall declined, left the house, and started back to Ellsworth on foot. It is unknown who provided Crawford with "the sugar" necessary to enjoy one of Lizzie's girls. Lizzie knew none of her girls would accommodate Crawford for any price and she needed help to get rid of him. She acknowledged a great number of men were in her front room, mostly Texans, along with three of her girls, Suzie Hart, Alice Chambers, and Annie Lee. When she left her house for Benson's Saloon, Lizzie heard two or three men come in through the back door and into the hallway leading to Suzie Hart's room. Everyone later agreed Crawford was very quiet and peaceable in Lizzie's house and did not have a harsh word for anyone. No one threatened him. Suzie Hart, alone, walked down the hallway to her bedroom situated in the back of the house. Moments later, Crawford followed Suzie, and upon reaching her room, found her seated in a chair having a conversation with a man sitting on her bed. As Crawford loomed in the bedroom doorway, the other man ordered him away. Crawford did not move; Suzie Hart admitted she became frightened, left her room, and ran out of the house by the front door going toward Mollie Brennan's place. Alice Chambers who heard a noise from Hart's room also became frightened and ran from the house. The sound of breaking furniture was soon followed by five or six shots ringing out in rapid succession, then three men came up the hall from Hart's room toward the front parlor. In response, the men in the parlor rushed past them to the back of the house in order to discover what had happened.[29]

Isaac Ziegler, an employee of Benson's Saloon, ran to Lizzie Palmer's house. On his way Ziegler overheard someone say, "Crawford had drawn a pistol on me." He was one of the first to enter Suzie Hart's room and find Crawford on the floor. J. W. Nall was half way to town when he heard the gunshots and shortly "saw two men on horseback riding very fast" as they passed him. Policeman Brown also heard shooting and hurried there as fast as he could. Brown said Crawford died immediately upon his arrival. Brown proceeded to take control of the situation by locking the room and sending for Coroner Duck. Brown heard several in the crowd of spectators remark that Putman had shot Crawford. It was known earlier in the day Putman was armed with a Navy pistol. Seward stated he "heard someone in the [front] room say that Putmam had been shot in the hand."[30]

Coroner Duck began an inquest; however the testimonies given by the key witnesses were of a common theme, which hindered the investigation. Suzie Hart claimed, "I should not know the man that was in my room again if I saw him." Charles Seward also stated he would not recognize any of the men if he saw them again. Lizzie Palmer did "not know the names of any of the men that was in the [front] room," she added, "I did see 'Put' or 'Putman' in the afternoon talking to Annie Lee, he was a friend of hers," but stated she did not remember seeing him there after that. J. W. Nall turned around, returned to Palmer's establishment and overheard that Crawford was shot, then "saw a big crowd, but do not know any of the men." Annie Lee heard Suzie Hart talking to someone in her room, but didn't know who it was she was speaking with. She testified "I heard a noise in Hart's room, I was afraid and run out of the house, I do not know any of the men that was in the room at the time."

No one seemed to be willing to say anything pertinent about the shooting. Policeman Brown was the only person who seemed able to identify anyone who could help solve the mystery of who killed Crawford. "I noticed a man there called Monte Price & a man the name of Barney who works in Kelly's Livery stable. I know several men I think would make important witnesses."[31]

The coroner's inquest reconvened on Monday, November 10, at 10 a.m. An examination of the body revealed Crawford was hit by two pistol balls, the first passed through his head and the second plowed into his torso. Policeman Brown completed his testimony and admitted his investigation had stalled, and that he had learned nothing further about the fatal shooting. The eleventh and final witness called by Coroner Duck was Mark Lambert Hopkins, an Ellsworth resident, who admitted he was "down in the bottom [Nauchville] when the shooting of Crawford took place but I did not see or hear who it was that did the shooting." He continued, "I was in company with Putman down there about half an hour before the shooting. We came up into town [Ellsworth] together and I immediately returned to the bottom but did not again see Putman there, I do not know where Putman is now."[32]

Within twelve hours of being killed, Edward Crawford was under the sod in an unmarked grave in the same hilltop cemetery where Happy Jack was interred. No one was ever charged with his murder.[33]

In its November 13 issue, the *Reporter* observed, "Most of the Texans have returned home." Mollie Brennan decided to quit Ellsworth, probably because most of her customers had departed. She sold her house in Nauchville and all of the fixtures and furniture in it before she left. Mollie Brennan would never return to Ellsworth.[34] When the manager of the Ellsworth stockyards, Robert D. Hunter, left town he heralded the close of the shipping season. The stockyards shipped almost 2,000 railroad cars of longhorns, a respectable number considering the financial panic of 1873 greatly slowed sales and left a surplus of Texas cattle available for sale at rock bottom prices. Many in Ellsworth wished the Texas cattlemen and their herds would return the next summer. The *Reporter* printed, "We would like to see the cattle trade here again next year. The trade ... makes money plenty. One thing is certain: gambling must not be allowed and the number of saloons licensed must be limited and licenses issued to none but responsible men."[35]

The year of 1873 ended with law enforcement officers in Texas and Kansas interested in arresting and prosecuting Billy Thompson. Suspecting Billy might be found in one of his favorite haunts, E. S. Windsor, the Clerk of the District Court of Aransas County, Texas, issued arrest warrants on December 20 for Billy Thompson, who they charged with the murder of Remus Smith. Windsor sent the warrants to the sheriff and any constable of Travis and Galveston Counties to execute.[36] Less than two weeks later, Philip T. Pendleton, the Ellsworth County Attorney, filed papers with the Fourteenth District Court of Kansas in order to have extradition papers ready for any request required by out-of-state officials. The information was duly authenticated by five witnesses in the indictment papers of The State of Kansas v. William Thompson, murder in the first degree.[37]

In February and March of 1874, officials in Travis and Galveston counties replied to E. S. Windsor's request but they failed to find and arrest him, attesting that Billy Thompson was not to be found within their jurisdiction.[38]

By late spring, a rumor had traveled sixty miles from Belton, Bell County, Texas, to Austin stating that a man named Baker had killed Billy Thompson. The report was generally not believed and was quickly dispelled.[39]

But Billy couldn't stay away from his hometown forever. Not surprisingly, one night he turned up in an Austin barroom, and he was creating trouble. At 1:00 a.m. on Tuesday, June 2, Billy called for a drink at the Office Saloon. Dissatisfied with the level of service when the bartender merely handed him the bottle, Billy threw his shot glass at the bartender's head and ran for the door. The unidentified and very angry bartender escalated the incident by picking up a six-shooter and firing twice at the fleeing Thompson.

Luckily for Billy, the shots went wide of their mark. Hurrying to the horse he had left in a nearby alley, Billy came upon an Austin policeman on night patrol who thought it suspicious a horse would be left there at such a late hour. Billy charmed the officer, convinced him the horse was his and invited Officer Johnson to take a drink with him. Johnson was still suspicious, however he had not recognized Thompson so he consented to go, if only to satisfy his need to learn the man's identity. At that late hour, the saloons along Congress Avenue were closing. Billy was still mounted when he neared the Office Saloon. Refusing to enter, he placed his hand on his revolver, spurred his horse, and galloped off shouting a warning to Johnson not to follow. Billy was known to move fast when he had to and pursuit was deemed impossible. The newspaper described him as "a well-known desperado, ... who is reported to have killed a Federal officer some four years ago, also a county sheriff, and is credited with a large number of red-handed outrages ... and is decidedly a dangerous man."[40]

Demonstrating a lifelong trait of fearlessness and determination to would go wherever he pleased, Ben Thompson returned to Ellsworth in the summer of 1874. He again stayed at the Grand Central Hotel, but upon finding that the play had moved, he traveled south to Wichita where he occasionally lodged at the Douglas Avenue Hotel or boarded at private homes. While in Wichita, he operated a faro bank and dealt *monte* at the two-story Keno House located in the center of the town's business district at the intersection of Main Street and Douglas Avenue. The Keno House was owned by William W. "Whitey" Rupp, a one-time farmer from Pennsylvania who learned the gambling trade in Kansas City.[41] Ben behaved himself, avoided trouble and was a popular dealer while earning a living in Kansas. Thompson spent several months there during the height of the Texas cattle-trade, but after the 1874 season, it would be a number of years before he returned to the gambling houses of Kansas.[42]

In July, Billy proved once again to be very slippery while in the hands of legal authorities. Details are sketchy, but a report in San Antonio's *Daily Herald* explained, "About a month ago a young man named Billy Thompson, while en route [*sic*] to Austin, (where there are several indictments against him) under guard, made his escape at Mountain City from the deputy sheriff."[43]

While Ben was behaving in Kansas, Billy was again causing a disturbance. This time it was at the Long House, a popular whorehouse in San Antonio. While there with Burdet Sublet, one of his Austin pals, Billy turned nasty and struck one of the prostitutes across the face with his riding quirt. The proprietors of the Long House took offence at the ill-treatment of one of their women and summoned the police. Officers Cooley and Coy arrived and attempted to arrest Billy and his companion. Instead of submitting, the pair drew their revolvers and made good their escape on horseback. Later, the policemen explained to a newspaperman they withheld from firing their weapons due to the number of innocent people on the street who may have been mistakenly killed or injured.[44]

During the fall, in Ellsworth, County Attorney Philip T. Pendleton and C. C. Sprigg, Clerk of the District Court, certified to Kansas Governor Osborn a "true, full, and complete copy" of information against William Thompson. By October 30, the governor issued both a requisition and an arrest warrant which were sent to Texas Governor Richard Coke in what would be a long running effort to return Billy Thompson back to Kansas, to stand trial for the murder of Sheriff C. B. Whitney.[45]

Chapter 8

BEN THOMPSON ON BEN THOMPSON

"When will I meet my fate?"

—Ben Thompson to Clara Baldwin, clairvoyant extraordinaire

By 1875, Ben Thompson's reputation placed him among the most dangerous gunfighters in Texas. The editor of the *New York Sun* was one of many eastern newspapermen who knew their readers found such men fascinating. Eager to capitalize on this appeal, the *Sun* assigned a reporter to interview Thompson about his strategy in a gunfight. The gunfighter did not disappoint. He provided a clear understanding of how best to survive a shoot-out and any possible legal consequences. In an article headlined "Ben Thompson on Ben Thompson," he explained, "I always make it a rule to let the other fellow fire first. If he wants to fight, I argue the question with him and try to show him how foolish it would be. If he can't be dissuaded, why, then the fun begins but I always let him have first crack. Then when I fire, you see, I have the verdict of self-defense on my side. I know that he is pretty certain in his hurry, to miss. I never do."[1]

The City of Austin decided to take an official count of its inhabitants in February 1875. As expected, the census failed to find Billy Thompson. Ben and his family were counted, however, and the head of household was listed as age thirty. Ben's wife Kate, age twenty-eight, and their two children Bennie, age five, and Kate, age three were also listed. They lived with Kate's recently married sister, Sarah Moore Farrell, age seventeen, and her husband James K. Farrell, age thirty-eight. Mr. Farrell had left the bartending trade behind and was now serving the citizens of Austin as one of their policemen.[2]

Throughout all of 1875, Billy Thompson remained in hiding, apparently staying out of any serious trouble. Ben Thompson traveled around central Texas earning his living as a professional gambler while having a little fun. He was arrested for both betting at a gaming bank and exhibiting a *monte* bank of his own. In Caldwell County, just south of Travis, his attorney twice pled guilty on his behalf. The first was for gambling and the second for simple assault. Both offenses cost Ben $10 plus court costs. However Ben was not the only lawbreaker in the vicinity of Austin: other notable sporting men were also arrested for gambling. Men like saloon owner and killer, Dr. Matt Woodlief,[3] Mannen Clements, a cousin of John Wesley Hardin, Jacob C. Johnson, who would later become closely allied with professional gambler and gunfighter, Luke Short; Joel Collins, who would gain notoriety as a companion of train robber Sam Bass; "Rowdy Joe" Lowe, a hard case from Kansas, and possibly, Ben's brother Billy. The name William Thompson appears in the docket records, but as that name was so common it may have been another man. Ben Thompson was also arrested much farther south in Bee County for exhibiting a *monte* bank. He failed to appear at his scheduled June 22 hearing, and surviving records do not indicate how that case was settled.[4]

Even with his notorious reputation as a gunman and professional gambler, many good citizens still respected Ben for his honesty and courage. That encouragement caused him to consider becoming a lawman. In late August of 1875, his name was one of seven Travis County men who announced for the office of Austin city marshal. The announcement appeared among other items in the popular "Local Matters" column in Austin's principal newspaper. The list of the candidates on that date is as follows: Murchison, Cotton, Creary, Jeff Johnson, Thompson, Ziller and P. L. Hopkins. Like many of the other candidates for office, the voting public chose Edward Creary, a saloon man, to be in charge of law and order in the capital city.[5]

September and November newspapers report stagecoach passengers coming and going, that Ben Thompson traveled to and from San Antonio. While staying in the Alamo City, he seemed to prefer either the Vance Hotel or the Central Hotel. On November 18, Ben Thompson was registered at the Central Hotel and was certainly enjoying the nightlife of the town's three most famous plazas: Military, Main and Alamo. Frontiersmen-turned-entertainers, William Frederick "Buffalo Bill" Cody and John Burwell "Texas Jack" Omohundro arrived in San Antonio during the final week of November to perform their popular melodrama *Life on the Border.*[6] Thompson and Cody eventually became friends, and perhaps this is when they first met.

William B. "Bat" Masterson would become fast friends with Ben Thompson, and similar to Cody, it is difficult to pinpoint when Masterson and Thompson first became acquainted. In early 1875, twenty-two-year-old Masterson was already a tough, experienced buffalo hunter, Indian fighter, teamster, and army scout. In 1874, Masterson was a member of a small party of buffalo hunters who fought off a determined attack and subsequent siege by Comanche Chief Quanah Parker's war party at the Battle of Adobe Walls. About a month after the fight, he signed on as second in command of a company of eighteen civilian scouts to help U.S. Army General

Nelson A. Miles in his campaign against the hostile Comanche. In late January 1876, Masterson was serving as a scout and teamster at an army post named Cantonment on the Sweetwater in the Texas Panhandle. A small trading post set itself near the fort to cater to buffalo hunters and soldiers. Bat comfortably fit in.[7]

Despite his popular reputation as a deadly gunfighter who had many notches on his six-shooter, Masterson was never a wanton killer. The first, and probably only man he killed in a gunfight was late one winter night in January 1876.[8]

With information from Wyatt Earp, author Stuart Lake published the following suspect account in 1931. It placed Ben Thompson with Bat Masterson in a saloon called the Lady Gay on the Sweetwater. "[Sergeant King] shot it out with Bat Masterson at old Sweetwater ... near Fort Elliott, Texas ... King, entering the combination dance hall, gambling house, and saloon which the soldiers patronized, found Bat dancing with a girl whom the soldier regarded as his special property." He pulled out his revolver, fatally shot the woman and fired a slug into Bat's leg. At first, Bat was stunned, however, "as he hit the floor, Bat jerked a Colt's and shot King through the heart. When King's fellow troopers would have taken up the sergeant's battle with Bat, as the latter lay on the floor, it was none other than Ben Thompson who leaped to the top of a faro layout with a gun in either hand." Ben held off the soldiers until Bat was moved to a place of safety.[9]

In actuality, Sergeant King was a longtime soldier whose real name was Anthony Cook, but at the time of the fight with Masterson, he was a corporal serving under the alias of Melvin A. King. The dead woman was none other than Mollie Brennan, Billy Thompson's paramour from his Ellsworth, Kansas, days. Mollie died from the gunshot wound before a doctor could arrive. Corporal King lingered until morning with medical care, before he too suc-

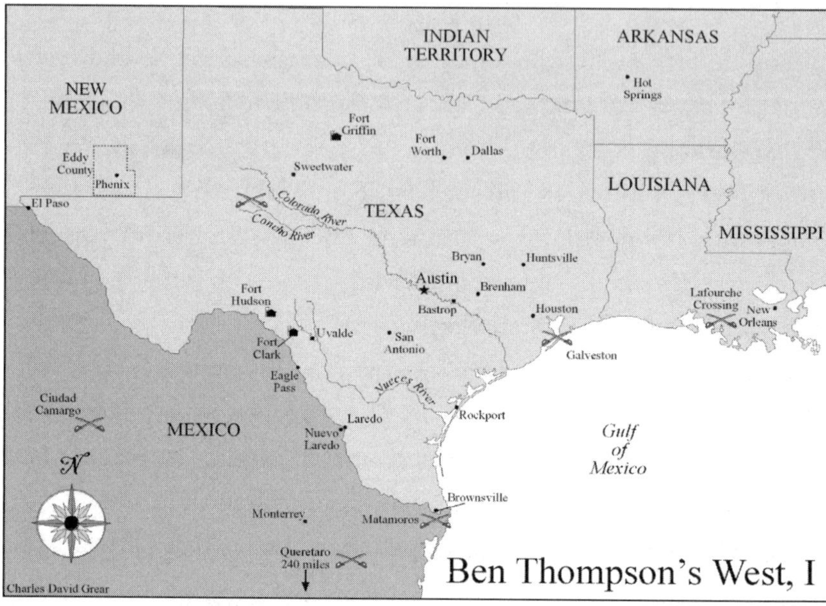

The West of Ben Thompson – 1. *Map by Charles David Grear.*

cumbed to his wounds. Of course, Masterson eventually recovered from his bullet wound.[10]

Other than Lake's version, there appears to be no evidence that Ben was at Sweetwater that night. In fact, one week after the shootout between King and Masterson, Ben Thompson was almost four hundred miles away in his hometown of Austin, Texas. The *Statesman* reported that on Monday night, January 31, "at the raffle for the fine Mexican saddle, valued at $150, Mr. Ben Thompson was the winner on a throw of 41."[11] It is difficult to imagine that Ben, a man renowned for his loyalty, would leave a badly wounded friend to hurry back to his hometown. Perhaps it was not Ben Thompson at the Sweetwater. More likely, it was his troublesome younger brother Billy.

There is considerable logic in Billy Thompson being at the Sweetwater at that time. Due to the lack of civilian law enforcement in the area, he would have been safe from arrest, and with one of his favorite girls on hand, Billy could not have found a more perfect hideaway than this remote place in the Panhandle of Texas. Gambling alone may not have provided a living, but there is evidence he had invested in a dance hall there, partnering with Dodge City businessman Colonel Charlie Norton. Throughout his long life, Masterson had ample opportunities to fully explain what happened that night on the Sweetwater, but he remained as quiet as possible about the incident. When questioned by a reporter from the *Kansas City Journal* in 1881, Masterson—obviously upset at being asked—answered, "I had a little difficulty with some soldiers down there, but never mind, I dislike to talk about it." Masterson held Ben Thompson in high regard, however he also liked Billy. Years later, he wrote that Billy was a "close personal friend of mine." If the legend is true that a Thompson brother did protect Bat Masterson after he was badly wounded and sprawled bleeding on the saloon floor, that Thompson must have been Billy.[12]

Meanwhile in Austin on Friday, February 4, three or four men claiming to be in town from Llano stood on Congress Avenue in front of Mitchell's Saloon in the middle of the afternoon. The out-of-towners were on a spree, they were rowdy, boisterous, and they had already insulted the saloon's barkeeper. He protested their behavior, but it was useless. They continued to curse and play recklessly with their six-shooters. At a previous saloon earlier in the day, they pulled out their revolvers saying they wanted to show the Austin fighters the Llano style of fighting. They especially wanted to test someone in Austin who had a reputation as a fighter. Mitchell's Saloon offered billiards, the finest liquor, plus a number of gaming tables separately owned and operated by Ben Thompson. The men from Llano gambled heavily and with luck, won a considerable amount of money, which only added to their drinking and recklessness.

Ben Thompson was dressed in his gambling finest. He carried a cane and wore an expensive diamond stick pin. He also wore a tall top hat, which exuded a type of style rarely seen in rural Texas. He walked up the Avenue intent on entering Mitchell's establishment to look after his interests there. Thompson was unaware of the losses his gaming tables had recently experienced. William Hannah, the leader of the Llano men, spotted Thompson. Hannah felt he had found someone with whom he could have fun, called out a hello, and asked Thompson where he was from. Ben, playing a role, replied that he hailed from Boston and had traveled to Austin for his health, seeking benefits from the dry air. Hannah expressed how tough Llano men were in a fight and invited his new acquaintance to visit the town. In response, Ben said he didn't see how men from Llano could fight better than any other Texan. Then Thompson stepped close to Hannah, and in a slow taunting manner intended to intimidate, announced who he was, and gently drew the back of his hand down Hannah's face calmly stating, "If I should go up there I would serve the boys just so." Enraged, Hannah struck out with his fist knocking off Thompson's top hat as the pistols came out and the firing commenced.

Many of the witnesses said William Hannah fired first and missed while his friends took to their heels down the avenue, abandoning him. Others said he tried to fire, but his revolver malfunctioned. Hannah stepped down from the sidewalk into the street gutter, hid behind a post, and tried to unjam his six-shooter by revolving the cylinder. Thompson adhered to his code and allowed his opponent to fire first, then he called for Hannah to come out. Ben raised his pistol arm and said, 'Well, I will mark you anyway." Thompson's shot struck Hannah in the ear and grazed a portion of his neck. Retreating farther into the street, the bloodied Hannah kept trying to get his revolver to work. He unwisely stopped in the middle of Congress Avenue. There he received a more severe wound when Thompson fired a second shot, which placed a pistol ball through Hannah's right side. Finally having enough, Hannah quit the fight and ran onto the opposite sidewalk. To Thompson's credit, he did not continue to shoot at the fleeing man, although Hannah had instigated the fracas. Officer John Chenneville arrived at the scene, and arrested Thompson. Both men were taken to Mayor Thomas Wheeler's office, where Ben was put under bond to assure his appearance at trial. Hannah's two wounds, not considered life-threatening, were dressed and he was also released from custody. The *Statesman* admonished the two combatants writing, "Shooting in the streets of the city is at all times entitled to the severest censure," but the newspaper admitted, "in this instance it fortunately happened that no one was injured except the Llano man who was spoiling for a fight." The writer of the article concluded his report of the affair by commenting humorously, "No doubt frontier 'bad ones' will hereafter be a little shy of Boston invalids who are down in Texas to restore weak lungs."[13]

The *Statesman's* account of the Congress Avenue shooting was picked up, embellished for their readership, and reprinted with relish in several newspapers in the East, which only added to Ben Thompson's growing national reputation. One eastern editor, drawing the measure of the man, pointed out that Thompson, "is one of your quiet inoffensive citizens when let alone, but able to take care of himself upon occasion." However, the editor had to admit that this time Ben Thompson simply could not resist involving himself in the potentially "dangerous situation."[14]

John Cardwell, the first editor of the *Statesman*, warned against further violence in the streets in a lengthy editorial entitled, "The Reign of Law or of the Pistol," published a few days after Ben Thompson's bullets flew on Congress Avenue. Cardwell forcefully attacked the behavior of the street-fighter and the dram-shop bullies stressing, "this shooting and fighting, which now and then disgraces Texas towns ... is senseless and ruinous to communities that suffer it done" and it "should be suppressed by public opinion." He further exclaimed, after the murder of two prominent men in nearby Bastrop County, that "public opinion in Austin will wreak fearful vengeance whenever a bloody deed is done in this city. Popular patience is exhausted and violence must be still."[15]

Ben Thompson was charged with assault with intent to kill, and was called before a judge of the District Court. Since the men from Llano were viewed as instigators of the affair, Ben's case was officially dismissed without being argued by his attorney. Editor Cardwell certainly had thoughts about this result, but chose not to express them further in the columns of the *Statesman*.[16]

While on tour throughout the state, a self-proclaimed entertainment sensation arrived in the capital city of Texas with great fanfare in March of 1876. Twenty-eight-year-old Professor Samri S. Baldwin was a master conjurer, medium, magician, illusionist, and "exposer of spiritualism," with his wife, Clara Baldwin, who was a clairvoyant extraordinaire. The town's newspapers were plastered with their advertisements. They were booked for a two-night engagement at Austin's opera house, where they performed for an overflowing crowd eager to see what mysterious talents and miracles the conjurer and clairvoyant had to demonstrate. Both of Mr. and Mrs. Baldwin's two appearances were virtually assured to sell out. They would put on their amazing exposition during their opening night's act. In order to entice the crowd to attend the following evening's performance, the couple promised to reveal the secrets of their abilities to the audience and, in addition, perform many more tricks and manifestations.

Professor Baldwin opened the act by performing many astonishing feats, like escaping from handcuffs supplied and placed on his wrists by Ben Thompson's brother-in-law, police officer James K. Farrell, within a matter of seconds. Next he turned water into wine and wine into water right in front of a committee of four prominent citizens, who were invited onstage from the audience. Then he created the "famous Katy King Apparition," by conjuring the faces of spirits who were instantly recognized by the people in the theatre.

Clara Baldwin took the stage next, and in a trance-like state, performed clairvoyant tests unsurpassed by any medium of the time. She revealed the past, the present, and the future. During her performance, Ben Thompson stepped onstage from the audience and became part of her act. He had previously written a question on a small piece of paper, which was then carefully folded and kept secret from Clara. While in a trance, she held the paper up in her hand and loudly proclaimed that, "in two years and nine months from today you will be murdered!" The paper was unfolded and Ben's inquiry was revealed, "When will I meet my fate?" Ben good-naturedly joined in on the laughter and amazement of the applauding audience.

On the second night, the hall was packed with patrons from the first performance. The Baldwins showed the audience exactly how each feat was performed, which meant revealing the secrets of their "acts of wonder." They offered a $500 reward to anyone who could perform a feat they could not duplicate or explain. The couple's act highly offended many people of the time who believed in Spiritualism. The *Statesman* stated, "The different spiritualist papers published in the United States have been fighting and denouncing him for a number of years, and they seem to fear the man; many professed spiritualists believe Baldwin to be a genuine medium who is controlled and does his wonderful feats through the agency of evil spirits."[17]

During the third week of April, Texas newspapers reported how "the spring fights have commenced, and that a prominent San Antonian was badly used up." The trouble occurred between Luciano Navarro, the Bexar County Surveyor, and Ben Thompson. Details were not reported, and the cause is unknown. It appears that no shots were fired during the altercation. At first, it was believed Navarro's life hung in the balance after being struck on the head by Thompson. However the injury proved to be exaggerated, because Navarro fully recovered. Perhaps in adherence to his code, Ben allowed the first blow to be struck and then tore into Navarro. He was arrested and after many months of extended court dates, Ben finally agreed to enter a plea of guilty. He paid Bexar County the court costs as well as a twenty-five-dollar fine.[18]

Billy Thompson must have remained peaceful and in hiding during the summer of 1876, since his whereabouts remain a mystery. L. Ballou, Clerk of the District Court of Aransas County, issued an arrest warrant on August 22, and sent it off to Atascosa County, probably because he'd received a tip about Billy's whereabouts. At this time, the area was mostly rural with a few small towns, with Bexar County and the city of San Antonio touching the northern border of Atascosa County. Two weeks later, the local sheriff returned the warrant to Ballou, stating the arrest warrant was not executed because Billy Thompson was not to be found within his jurisdiction.[19] Evidence exists that Billy may have skipped into Mexico.

In his book, *A Texas Ranger*, Napoleon Augustus Jennings provided a lively, if perhaps embellished, portrayal of Billy Thompson as a desperado south of the border. Before Jennings joined up with Captain Leander H. McNelly's command, a Mexican gang was attempting to run Jennings down. Fortunately, he received some unexpected help from Billy Thompson. Jennings called Billy "a superb looking fellow. He was over six feet in height, and built like an athlete. His handsome manly face was smiling good-naturedly. His mouth was hidden by an enormous drooping light moustache, but his blue eyes twinkled in evident enjoyment of my discomfiture." Dressed extravagantly, Billy "wore a big, wide-brimmed white hat and a richly embroidered buckskin Mexican jacket, and he was puffing a *cigarillo* … 'here, take this gun, an' use it.' My new friend whipped out the mate to the revolver he had given me, and fired straight at the rapidly approaching men. They turned, instantly, and ran the other way. I think they went a little faster than they had come." Then Billy, "who had so strangely come to my rescue, smiled again, in his quiet way, and putting up his six-shooters, said: 'Come in and have a drink; it'll do you good.'" Jennings was eager to put some distance between himself and his pursuers, so he asked, "Hadn't I better get over to Texas? Those Mexicans may come back here at any moment." Billy gave an unconcerned reply, "Oh, I guess they ain't in any hurry to come back for a while … If they do, we can have some more fun with 'em." Jennings resigned himself and followed Billy into a saloon, and admittedly "took a drink of the vilest whiskey that ever passed my lips. I got away as soon as I could, and reached the ferry and the Texas side of the river without any further adventure. The name of my friend [was] Bill Thompson. He was the brother of the notorious Ben Thompson, the desperado marshal of Austin. Bill Thompson, at the time he helped me, was a fugitive from justice, charged with killing a man in Kansas. There was a $500 reward on his head."[20]

Shortly thereafter, as a Texas Ranger, the young Jennings found an opportunity to repay Billy. It was during the summer of 1876, when Captain McNelly was searching for outlaw John King Fisher and his cohorts. Jennings walked into a saloon in Eagle Pass and spotted Billy Thompson leaning up against the bar. Jennings was the only ranger to recognize Billy, so he quietly warned him that his description was on their wanted list and he should cross over into Mexico. Billy thanked him and slipped out of the barroom.[21]

On August 29, 1876, the day after Billy Thompson's thirty-first birthday, Ben most likely read in an item in Austin's *Daily Gazette* from which he may have gained a small sum of grim satisfaction. The article reported the death of a man in Deadwood,

Dakota Territory. The man who killed his friend, Phil Coe, had finally met his fate. Per the newspaper, "a friend in this city [Austin] received a funeral notice of J. B. Hickok, familiarly known as Wild Bill, who was killed from a shot in the back of the head, by Jack McCall, at Deadwood, Black Hills, on the 2nd inst." The *Gazette* recalled how "Wild Bill, it will be remembered killed Phil Cole [*sic*], well known in this city, about five years ago ... McCall shot Wild Bill under a belief that he had killed his brother, some years before, at Fort Hayes [*sic*], Kansas. McCall was tried by a jury, and as a matter of course acquitted. Wild Bill was a desperate character, who had, like all others of his cast, redeeming traits of fidelity to friends." The *Gazette* correctly predicted how some would yet profit by Hickok's death. "He appears to have had the sympathy of the eastern press, and they will probably write up the thrilling incidents of his history for some dime novel."[22]

Billy Thompson didn't remain in Mexico for more than a few months. He headed north toward his family and friends.[23] Both of the Thompson brothers were in Austin during October 1876. On October 23, a Monday night, Billy was out on the town enjoying a spree. The press reported that an Austin policeman drove him around in a hack and provided him with protection. The press did not identify the officer, but most likely it was Ben's brother-in-law, James Farrell. Somewhat surprisingly, both brothers remained peaceful that evening. One wonders if Farrell was able to temper their usually rowdy behavior.

A couple of days later, Billy was found hiding out at the ranch owned by Neil Cain's father, some twelve to thirteen miles northeast of Austin. Thompson had successfully evaded the Ellsworth, Kansas, murder charge for three years, but he was about to face a serious challenge.

On Wednesday, October 25, John C. Sparks, who was only recently mustered in as Captain of Company C of the Frontier

Battalion, left Llano with a squad of nine Texas Rangers in search of a stolen herd of cattle and the rustlers who currently possessed them. Sparks and his Rangers arrived in Austin the following day, where Travis County Deputy Sheriff Carrington told them there was a small herd of cattle grazing about thirteen miles northeast of the city. Suspecting that this herd was the object of their pursuit,

Ben Thompson in the prime of life, *circa* 1879.

Courtesy the Robert G. McCubbin Collection.

Captain Sparks and his men hurried to the location. Once there, they found the herd, which had been inspected on the thirteenth of October in Llano. They also found a second, larger herd of eighty-five head that had been stolen from Llano, Mason, Gillespie, and Blanco Counties. The thieves were penning the cattle for the night with the ultimate intention of driving the beef to Rockdale, Texas, for shipment on the International & Great Northern Railroad when the Rangers rushed upon them. There were several wanted men in charge of the herd, including Neil Cain, a longtime suspected rustler. Cain managed to make his escape, but Eb. Stewart, wanted in Travis County, and Billy Thompson, the man with a $500 reward on his head were not so fortunate.

Billy had had nothing to do with the stolen cattle. He was only staying at the Cain ranch, and wisely made no effort to run or resist. Stewart, however, first chose to evade arrest, but then quickly decided to surrender once a few shots were fired in his direction. Curiously, neither Stewart nor Thompson was armed at the time. The prisoners and the cattle were delivered to Austin, where the prisoners were locked up in the county jail at about 1 o'clock in the morning.[24]

Friday, October 27, 1876, became a very long but exciting day in Austin. As soon as the telegraph office opened, Captain Sparks sent a message to the Ellsworth County sheriff inquiring if a warrant was still in force for Billy Thompson. Receiving a positive reply, Sparks telegraphed back asking for a requisition at once.

Sparks had carried a handful of warrants on the way to Cain's ranch. Among them were papers for George Gladden, John Ringo, and Billy Thompson. A *Statesman* reporter was aware of this important story and interviewed the captain. Sparks explained how they were disappointed that two notorious desperadoes, Gladden and Frank Enox, were not to be found at the ranch and that they only arrested Billy Thompson in the hope of collecting the reward outstanding for him. Sparks admitted he knew Billy had taken no part in stealing the cattle.[25]

Captain Sparks was born in Alabama and came to Texas as a boy. During the late war, he enlisted in the Confederate army and later served as a first lieutenant in a volunteer company he helped raise. At this point in his career, Sparks was thirty-five-years-old. He had black hair and dark eyes. He was tall and lean, standing several inches over six feet. The reporter was noticeably impressed with the man's physicality and described how Sparks moved with "an ease and deliberation" that indicated "great coolness in times of excitement." This apparently tough man appeared to be "a thoroughbred Texan" and was "without fear, and of indomitable will."[26] Sparks was about to be relentlessly tested over the next twenty-nine days, and he would have to call on all of those attributes to successfully deliver Billy Thompson to Kansas.

As Sparks waited for the requisition to arrive from Kansas, Ward and Pendexter, attorneys hired by Ben Thompson, served Travis County Sheriff Dennis Corwin with a writ of habeas corpus. Before Billy was brought before County Court Judge James W. Smith Jr., a reporter for the *Statesman* called at the judge's chambers asking for permission to interview Billy Thompson. The request was granted and after Ben Thompson introduced the reporter to his younger brother, the following was revealed.[27] "The prisoner conversed freely and seemed to have a social turn of mind much like his brother, to whom he bears a resemblance, save that he is [a] trifle taller and his complexion is browned by the sun, which gives him a hardy, pioneer appearance." Answering the reporter's "question as to whether he felt any concern over his arrest he said no; that he was not charged with any violation of the law, and had no fear of the result of the examination." Billy went on and "stated that he had no connection with the men who were suspected of driving stolen cattle out of the country. He had, he said, been stopping at Neal Cain's for some weeks past, but that he had nothing to do with his cattle drives." Asked "if he was aware that dispatches had been sent to the State authorities of Kansas, asking if a reward had been offered by that State for his arrest," Billy acknowledged, "that he was, but seemed to attach little importance to the matter." Billy finished the interview by stating "he was sitting on the fence at old man Cain's when the rangers dashed in to arrest the parties in charge of the cattle, Neal Cain and others, and that he made no effort at resistance or escape because he did not feel that he was one of the men wanted."[28]

Judge Smith's courtroom was packed with people, quite a number of them being friends of the Thompson brothers, although many in the audience were present out of mere curiosity. Judge Smith briefly examined the facts of the case, during which he learned from Sheriff Corwin that Billy Thompson was in his jail only to be held, and that no official complaint had been made. Judge Smith discharged the prisoner and ordered him released.[29]

As he walked out of Judge Smith's courtroom, Captain Sparks appeared. Stalling for time until Kansas responded to his latest telegram for a requisition, he arrested Billy a second time. With a Travis County warrant sworn out for theft of cattle, Thompson was led back to the Travis County jail where he was again incarcerated. A hearing took place before Justice Fritz Tegener on the theft of cattle charge, but since no evidence could be produced against Billy, Judge Tegener, too, ordered him released from custody. This time, Thompson made it as far as the bottom of the courthouse steps before Captain Sparks and his Rangers arrested him for a third time. Sparks had received a telegraphic dispatch from the Ellsworth County Sheriff stating a requisition would arrive shortly. This was enough, along with Sparks's affidavit stating Billy Thompson was a fugitive from justice for the murder of a Kansas county sheriff, for 16th Judicial District Court Judge Ezekiel B. Turner to approve a bench warrant. Four Rangers were assigned to bring Billy back to the county jail where they were met by Sheriff Corwin, who refused to place him in his jail upon a warrant based solely on a telegraphic dispatch. Baffled and unwilling to have a conflict with the Sheriff of Travis County, the Ranger in charge of the small detachment surprisingly uncuffed his prisoner and set Billy free. Within minutes, Captain Sparks and Sgt. Joseph L. Leverett[30] rode up to the front of the jailhouse and were dismayed to learn Billy had again been set free only minutes before. Leverett, on the faster horse, caught up to Billy Thompson as he was preparing to flee on a mount furnished by his friend James Burditt. Billy was arrested for a fourth time and taken by the heavily armed Rangers, who rode rapidly through the streets of Austin while excited citizens followed along or gathered in groups to discuss the latest phase of this unfolding drama. Unsure of the security the county jail provided, Billy Thompson was surprisingly taken to the State Capitol Building and lodged in the adjutant general's office, while Captain Sparks went to ask Gov. Richard Coke for his help. The Rangers closely guarded their prisoner and were seen patrolling the corridors of the State House fully armed and prepared for trouble. A rumor spread through the town that many of the men who shared a strong friendship with the Thompson brothers were willing to fight to secure Billy's release. Governor Coke agreed to back up Captain Sparks, and with this important support, Sparks drew up an arrest warrant charging Billy Thompson with the murder of Sheriff Whitney. After an exhausting, unbelievable day, Billy Thompson was finally accepted by Sheriff Corwin into his custody and placed once again into the Travis County jail.[31] With his freedom permanently at stake, Billy probably spent the weekend behind bars thinking long and hard about his situation and how to get out of it.

In Kansas, Ira E. Lloyd, the young lawyer who had been a thorn in the side of the Ellsworth police force during the summer of 1873, was now the Ellsworth County attorney. He contacted Kansas Governor Thomas Osborn, informing him that he had examined the case and information against William Thompson for the crime of murder and was convinced of his guilt. Based on this, he asked that a requisition be sent to Texas Governor Richard Coke. Lloyd recommended that Captain Sparks serve as the agent for the State of Kansas and to arrest William Thompson and convey him to Samuel Hamilton, Sheriff of Ellsworth County.

On Monday, October 30, Governor Osborn sent out two requisitions to Texas for Billy Thompson, a specific one to Governor Coke and the second a general call "to all to whom these presents shall come." Both requisitions asked for "William Thompson [to] be apprehended and delivered to John C. Sparks."[32]

As Billy Thompson lingered in jail over the weekend, his brother Ben and the attorneys they hired were hard at work.[33] In a desperate and dangerous ploy to prevent Billy from being placed in the hands of Texas Ranger Captain Sparks and taken to Kansas, Ben tipped off law enforcement officials in Aransas County about his brother's incarceration in the Travis County jail.[34]

On Tuesday, Billy was taken back to the 16th District Court. Before the proceedings were ready to convene, Sheriff Corwin served a *capias* warrant on him and he was returned to jail. In an effort to detain Billy Thompson and guarantee his appearance in their courtroom, Aransas county officials had telegraphed Sheriff Corwin requesting that he keep Billy in custody.[35] Early in the morning on Friday, November 3, Captain Sparks and his Ranger detachment served Sheriff Corwin with an executive order issued by Governor Coke. This order commanded the execution of the Kansas requisition and clearly instructed all Texas sheriffs and officers to turn Billy Thompson over to John C. Sparks, the Governor of Kansas's assigned agent. Sheriff Corwin disregarded his governor's executive order and flatly refused to comply. Corwin clearly favored Billy Thompson, as evidenced by his unwillingness to accept a telegraphed document from Kansas, and his decision to honor the telegraphed warrant from Aransas County charging Billy with the 1868 murder of Remus Smith.[36]

Expecting Billy Thompson to be sent off beyond his reach to Aransas County, Sparks countered with dogged determination by serving Billy Thompson with a court order detaining him in Austin until the question of priority of custody could be decided by Judge Ezekiel B. Turner of the District Court.[37]

Billy Thompson's hearing took place before the district court on Tuesday, November 14. The following day, Judge Turner announced his judgment in favor of the Kansas requisition, stating that it had precedence over any state warrants. Still fighting for his release, Billy's attorneys filed a writ of habeas corpus with the Court of Appeals. Wanting to have the prisoner out of the court's jurisdiction before it held a hearing, Captain Sparks sent his men for Billy Thompson. On the morning of Thursday, November 16, Captain Sparks detailed Sergeant Robinson and two men to bring the prisoner out of his jail cell to begin his trip to Kansas. The three Rangers were stymied, perhaps intentionally, when they found no one in charge. Coincidentally, both Sheriff Dennis Corwin and the jailor were absent, and the keys to the cells were nowhere to be found on the premises. One of the Rangers, Private David Ligon, once a former guard at the Travis County jail, proceeded to the sheriff's private residence attached to the jailhouse where Mrs. Corwin answered the door. Ligon entered the premises in search of an extra set of cell keys. He found them, and Billy Thompson was finally removed from his cell and taken to the train depot. Ben Thompson viewed the Ranger's actions as a quasi-kidnapping when they took his brother from the custody of Sheriff Corwin[38] but Billy was on his way to Kansas with a strong guard watching over him.

Billy may have been headed north, but he wasn't in Kansas yet. His brother Ben embarked on a legal strategy to at least delay Billy's arrival in Ellsworth, and give the Texas Court of Appeals the time necessary to hear the case and issue an order that would overrule Judge Turner's decision. He telegraphed ahead to several major railroad towns on the route, charging Captain Sparks with the kidnapping of his brother. He also had writs of habeas corpus waiting upon arrival. Ben was using all of his influence to save his brother and a large portion of the income provided by his Austin gambling house to cover the very substantial legal fees.[39]

Ben Thompson had a writ of habeas corpus waiting for Captain Sparks to answer in Corsicana, Dallas, and Denison.[40] The writs claimed Billy was being illegally held and transported against his will. But the legal roadblocks Ben attempted proved to be mere hindrances. Each time local judges honored Captain Sparks's legal right to take Billy to Kansas. South of Corsicana, friends of the Thompson brothers shadowed Sparks and his small command. Captain Sparks suspected a rescue attempt was being formulated and leveled his Winchester on a man and ordered him to jump from the moving train. Upon their arrival in Dallas, Sparks called on the local sheriff to add manpower to Billy's guard detail. The sheriff called up his own deputies, members of the city police, and the Lamar Rifles militia company in a show of overwhelming force, which quashed any thought of rescue. On Thursday, November 23, Billy finally rolled into Ellsworth on the evening train, closely watched by all of his guards. A large concourse of men awaited his arrival. Ellsworth County Sheriff Samuel Hamilton also greeted the train. As the lawmen and their prisoner started up the street towards the county jail, someone in the crowd called out loudly, "Get a rope boys!"[41] The heavily armed Texas Rangers and the determination of Sheriff Hamilton quashed any desire from the crowd to attempt a lynching. A few minutes later, Billy was safely locked up and the almost month-long physical and legal odyssey of Captain Sparks and his nine Rangers finally came to an end. Sparks would spend a few days in Ellsworth before going to Topeka to meet with Governor Osborn and claim the $500 reward. Billy would spend a single night in the Ellsworth jail. Fearing a rescue attempt by Thompson's many supporters or a lynching brought on by his fellow citizens, Sheriff Hamilton deemed the two-story stone jail not secure enough to hold his prisoner without incurring great expense to the county. He would have to place numerous guards on constant duty until the next district court session which would not take place until March, nearly four months away. Early the following morning, Sheriff Hamilton was on an eastbound train headed to Salina with his prisoner and a handful of heavily armed guards, hoping to locate a more suitable jail for the housing of Billy Thompson.[42]

Threats of a rescue attempt motivated Sheriff Hamilton to move Billy Thompson to Salina, but Thompson's friends followed them there, too. It made the situation so serious that it was necessary to deliver Thompson to the state penitentiary at Leavenworth. John Prescott, Judge of the 16th Judicial District Court, signed the order on December 1, officially approving Billy's transfer. Calling him the "notorious Bill Thompson," the editor of the *Leavenworth Daily Times* welcomed him to his city in an article headlined, "A Distinguished Arrival." The guards, "while conveying him to the prison, not only had him heavily ironed, but kept him constantly covered with well-loaded double-barreled shot-guns." The editor estimated that the capture and subsequent movement and safe keeping had cost "a trifle over $900, including the reward." Billy Thompson was described as "a powerful man and a willing slave to the worst passions."[43] Ben Thompson failed in preventing his brother's arrival in Kansas; however he had not given up. He was already plotting a legal strategy to keep Billy's neck from being encircled by a rope.

Chapter 9

A LITTLE CHRISTMAS FROLIC

"A Bloody Fight at Austin"

—*San Antonio Daily Express*, December 27, 1876

A large commercial building sat one block south of the State Capitol on the northwest corner of Congress Avenue and Mulberry Street (10th Street). It was named after its owner, Carl Krohn, and in the fall of 1876, it sat empty except for one small store, O'Neal's Ice Cream Depot. Krohn Hall formerly housed the United States Courthouse and its offices. Alf Gardner and Mark Wilson, the owners of Austin's Bank Saloon on Congress Avenue, approached Mr. Krohn with the idea of operating a variety theatre in this building. On October 1, a two-year lease was signed, and a considerable investment was made that employed carpenters who created a large, open auditorium with a stage and scenery. The name they chose was the Capital Theatre.[1]

Gardner and Wilson planned on running a first-class entertainment hall, booking popular acts that incorporated actors, comedians, song and dance men, singers, magicians, and minstrel players. Wilson would run the day-to-day operation and a long, well-stocked bar would sell liquor, beer, and other refreshments. The theatre would not be used as a common dance-house, and it wouldn't have any gambling rooms.

Mark Wilson was a popular Irishman. Earlier in the year he was elected Sergeant-at-Arms of Austin's Hibernian Benevolent Society.[2] He was also a member of the Volunteer Hope Hook and Ladder No. 1 Fire Company.[3] His history was spotless. He had never been arrested or charged with any crime.[4] He was active in politics and supported the Radical Republican party, and while the renovations were going on at the Krohn Building, he was chosen to serve as a Travis County delegate at the party's convention at Bryan.[5] Wilson was a thirty-two-year-old single man who supported his widowed mother, Kate, and two teenage sisters, Lucy, age eighteen and Matilda, age sixteen.[6] Walton described Mark Wilson as "a stout, red complexion, ruddy face, fearless, impulsive Irishman [who] was an athlete, and could overcome the resistance of almost any ordinary man."[7]

The city was eager for the Capital Theatre to open. The *Statesman* announced that on Saturday, November 4, "a first rate variety show will be given [tonight]. Messrs. Gardner & Wilson have employed as their first engagement fifteen professionals, several of whom enjoy enviable stage reputations. Go and see the show at the new hall tonight." Two hundred and fifty patrons heeded the call and packed the Capital Theatre's inaugural show. A handful of private boxes were available at a rate of only four dollars for the evening, a single seat cost one dollar, and main floor general admission went for fifty cents. The *Statesman* reviewed the show and reported, "The performance was varied, and a portion of it was very good." Among the many acts was a man named Martin, who danced "on one leg and a crutch."[8]

For its first six weeks, financially, the Capital Theatre was proving to be a wise business venture for Gardner and Wilson. It was a popular, inexpensive place of amusement for the average working man, however a few patrons in the crowds pouring into the theatre started to become more and more unruly. Wilson took precautions in case of serious trouble by strategically placing a double-barrel shotgun, Winchester rifle, and several pistols behind the long wooden bar. Several nights before Christmas, nineteen-year-old James Burditt, a well-known local troublemaker[9] and friend of the Thompson brothers, caused a minor disturbance while attending a performance. He was knocked to the ground by Mark Wilson and thrown out of the establishment. Burditt stood outside of the theatre inviting Wilson to come out and fight. Frustrated by Wilson's refusal, Burditt threatened to tell his friend Ben Thompson about how the theatre man had treated him. James's brother, Newell Burditt, was overheard to exclaim that it was a good thing "I was not there, but a time will come. The damn shebang must be busted up or the damn son-of-a-bitch must be killed." Anticipating more disturbances, and determined to keep strict order, Wilson sought out Mayor T. B. Wheeler and was sworn in by the mayor as a special policeman. In addition, City Marshal Edward Creary assigned two of his officers, James W. LaRew and William P. Allen, to the theatre to keep order.[10]

A handful of Burditt's and Ben Thompson's mutual friends later testified they planned on attending the Christmas night performances at the Capital Theatre to have "fun." A black man named McHorst, at James Burditt's request, purchased lampblack from Tobin's drug store on Pecan Street near Congress Avenue prior to show-time on Monday, December 25. Thompson was repeatedly asked to visit the theatre with Burditt and friends, and he at first declined to go but later relented.[11] As a large audience was enjoying the show, Mark Wilson and bartender Charles Mathews were working the bar. Alice Kesler, one of the actresses, was helping to serve drinks to the seated customers. At about 11:30 p.m., as the variety troupe was concluding the night's entertainment, someone threw a pack of firecrackers that popped harmlessly on the floor, near where Burditt and Thompson were sitting. Mark Wilson came from behind the bar and accused Burditt of lighting the firecrackers. Burditt threw lampblack in Wilson's face in response. Wilson called out to Policeman Allen to arrest Burditt and remove him from the theatre. Bartender Charles Mathews moved towards the Winchester secreted behind the bar. Hot words ensued as Allen was in the act of making the arrest. Burditt attempted to strike Wilson as Thompson came forward and said he would stand good for Burditt. Wilson's response was, "I am running this thing." Thompson reached over Policeman Allen's shoulder, swinging his fist at Wilson. Allen managed to take the "lick off" Thompson's blow. However a heavy ring on Thompson's hand cut into Wilson's face, causing it to bleed. Allen told Thompson to be quiet and Ben stepped back believing the trouble had ended. Pulling out a handkerchief, Wilson began to wipe off both the lampblack and blood on his face. Officer LaRew was not near enough to the trouble to help control the escalating fracas. Wilson was known as a hot-tempered man, and he became furious. Instead of leaving it to the police or settling the matter physically, which he was eminently able to do, he decided to resort to firearms. He turned, reached around the bar, and picked up his double-barrel shotgun. That act proved to be a mistake.[12]

Raising his shotgun, Wilson stepped out in front of the bar yelling, "Clear the way there." He aimed it at Thompson who stood only ten feet away. Thompson's eyes were turned. As Wilson squeezed the trigger, Policeman Allen knocked the barrel off target and changed the direction of the load of buckshot, which harmlessly struck the north wall. Thompson stepped into the aisle, instantly drawing his revolver, and before Wilson could fire a second time, Thompson repeatedly shot at Wilson until he was struck in the head, neck, chest, and stomach. He fell forward toward Thompson, dead. Bartender Mathews fired several shots at close range from the Winchester as Thompson was firing at Wilson. One of Mathews's bullets tore through Thompson's coat and creased his hip. Thompson immediately turned his pistol on the bartender and fired once. He sent the ball through Mathews's jaw, knocked out a tooth in the corner of his mouth. The ball passed under his tongue and lodged in his neck. Mathews's face was so bloody, witnesses were sure he could not survive.[13] The fight was over, and the floor was drenched with the blood of two men.

Only five seconds had expired from the moment Wilson raised his shotgun until Mathews lay severely wounded on the floor. For the second time in Ben Thompson's career, a man who relied upon a shotgun to face him lay dead at his feet.

Panic reigned in the theatre. "A scene of perfect uproar, confusion and screams ensued; the room was filled with smoke, and the floor was covered with blood and lampblack," the *Statesman* reported. One man lay dead and a second perhaps mortally wounded. The crowd made a hasty exit, going out the front and rear of the auditorium. Some burst out the front window, while others ran through the scenery on the stage. James Burditt fled the theatre as well. Ben Thompson was not held or arrested by either policeman, Allen or LaRew. Within the hour, he surrendered to Travis County Sheriff Dennis Corwin, and expressed the desire for a full investigation. He was safely placed in the county lockup. A coroner's hearing was held the following morning, and doctors for both the coroner and the defense performed an autopsy on Wilson's body. The jury listened to witness testimony and easily concluded: "Wilson came to his death by being shot by a pistol in the hands of Ben Thompson." Sheriff Corwin remanded Thompson to the county jail, and it was expected an examination of the case would take place within a day or two. On the streets of Austin, whispers began expressing a need to form a vigilance committee and extract immediate justice for the dead Mark Wilson. Editor John Cardwell forcefully expressed his view in the *Statesman*: "We repeat, let us have no organization to stop violence by violence, but let every man exert his influence in favor of moderation, law and order."[14]

The fatal shooting at the Capital Theatre became front page news throughout Texas. On December 27, the *Daily Express* of San Antonio described the tragedy, calling it, "A Bloody Fight At Austin." In another article two days later, the *Express* commented, "Ben Thompson has killed quite a number of men, but always under such circumstances as on this occasion—that is self-defense. He is cool and brave, but does not bear the name of a desperado, as he has so far been justified by the courts for his acts." The *Galveston Daily News* added to the gunfighter's reputation, and gave him justification as well: "Thompson who is known and feared because he has eminent courage, is a crack shot, and is a man of sudden passion, but [maintains] great coolness in conflict, always victor in his personal rencontres, [he] had to kill Wilson or be killed himself." The *Express* editor went on to lay the lion's share of the blame at the theatre proprietor's doorstep. "Had Wilson ... called a policeman to stop any misconduct on the part of Thompson, the serious affair we have recorded would not have occurred."[15]

A complaint charging Thompson and Burditt with murder was made on Wednesday, December 27. One of the finest law firms in the city of Austin, Walton, Green and Hill,[16] was selected by Thompson to represent him. Initially, there was a great deal of feeling against Thompson, Burditt and his brothers, and other close associates from the gambling fraternity. His lawyers advised Ben to quietly remain in the Travis County jail, as their strategy was to postpone the examining trial until the excitement died down. "Thompson is an excellent client, the directions of his attorneys are obeyed implicitly," Walton later wrote, "without hesitation or murmur."[17]

Many friends of the late Mark Wilson believed that the killing was premeditated, brought on by a number of professional gamblers. Speculation said the Capital Theatre was broken up because it was interfering with many of the gambling halls in Austin, and Ben Thompson was not the only one responsible. James Burditt was out of reach of the Austin authorities as he was headed towards the Rio Grande valley where lawmen were few. The public began to expect other arrests to be made, and soon Newell Burditt and "Red" Mitchell found themselves in the Travis County jail with Thompson.[18]

English-born bartender Henry Naphtali "Charles" Mathews, a brave and forgiving man with a healthy sense of humor, was also officially arrested for his role in the shooting affair. He was charged with resisting an officer of the law, but was later acquitted of the offense. At 5 p.m. the day after the shooting, Dr. John W. Stalnaker, one of the doctors who performed the postmortem on Mark Wilson, operated on Charles Mathews and successfully removed Thompson's bullet lodged in his neck. Dr. Stalnaker felt that Mathews stood a good chance of complete recovery. Mathews did eventually recover, but he retained several deep scars on both sides of his jaw for the remainder of his life. Newspaper readers in San Antonio took a particular interest in the shooting scrape and its aftermath, since Charles Mathews was well known in the Alamo City. For a time, he served as a clerk in the post office, and he had also been a popular bartender at Jim Trainer's Saloon.[19]

Mark Wilson's funeral mass was postponed until 11 o'clock, Wednesday, December 27, to allow for two Roman Catholic nuns close to the family to travel from Galveston and be in attendance. With rain falling, the members of the volunteer fire company paid their respects in full uniform along with a large concourse of his many friends and mourners. Prominent among the funeral procession was City Marshal Edward Creary. Wilson was laid to rest in Oakwood Cemetery and his headstone read: "In memory of my

A young William M. "Buck" Walton (1832-1915) as he appeared during his days as a companion and attorney for Ben Thompson. As a highly regarded attorney, Walton successfully defended Thompson in two first degree murder trials. He began working with Thompson to compose his autobiography, but had to complete it shortly after his death. *Courtesy the Austin History Center. Image # PICA 09534.*

only beloved son—Mark Wilson—born in Dublin, Ireland Feb. 19, 1844 murdered in Austin Dec. 25, 1876—May the Lord have mercy on his soul and the joy and the perpetual light of Heaven shine on him." The Hibernian Benevolent Society appointed a committee to call on his grieving mother and sisters to ascertain if they were in need of any financial aid.[20]

At first, the finger of blame for the Christmas night tragedy was pointed at the two policemen, Allen and LaRew. Criticism of their conduct—at least in the newspapers—was fierce. The opinion of Wilson's friends was that Allen, "by his conduct, is somewhat responsible for Wilson's death, and that he either favored or feared Thompson." People wanted to know how Officer LaRew, "amused himself all the time the fight was progressing and what disposition he made of his darling self afterwards." The police committee of the city council examined the two officers, suspended them, and the city council subsequently voted to remove them from the police force. Within days, the ultimate blame began to be pointed at higher officials. The *Statesman* felt the poor policing of the City of Austin might call for a complete change in the city administration.[21] The city marshal received a lecture in the *Statesman* as well. "Marshal Ed Creary was yesterday improving muddy street crossings by a liberal distribution of gravel. In many respects Ed is attentive to the people, and his genial, accommodating nature has made for him many friends, and they regret that he does not devote himself more zealously to the arrest and punishment of lawless characters." Telling the city marshal to toughen up, the *Statesman* explained how Creary should be doing his job. "A city marshal should know every bad, dangerous character, and he and his police force should ever be on the alert to 'take in' that class of people. A mild way of dealing with rough characters won't do at all, and especially in Texas."[22]

Sensing the need to get his version out to the public, Ben Thompson agreed to be interviewed by the *Statesman* on Friday, December 29. A reporter visited the county jail where he failed to find Thompson behind bars with the general population of prisoners, but instead he was "comfortably situated in a private room in Sheriff Corwin's residence, and surrounded by friends." Newell Burditt and "Red" Mitchell, who were being held as accessories in the killing, were with Thompson. Both men would soon change roles from accused accessories to that of witnesses for the defense. Deputy Sheriffs John P. Kirk and H. Grooms Lee were also relaxing in the room. The reporter found Thompson to be "cheerful and conversational" and "his manner was calm and gentlemanly, and he talks entertainingly and expresses himself with ease and clearness, and he seems to be conscientious and free from malice." Ever courteous, Thompson extended an invitation to the reporter to be seated. In a "kindly" manner Thompson said, "I have just been cursing you because of the articles that have appeared in the *Statesman*." The newspaperman invited him to explain. Thompson "thought the tone of the paper might be somewhat detrimental to his side of the case," and took exception to the newspaper's editing out a portion of Policeman William P. Allen's coroner's inquest testimony, which was favorable to him. Thompson complained that his mother, who was unwell, was very much upset by how the *Statesman* was reporting the affair. "Regarding the difficulty, he said that he felt clearly justifiable in killing Wilson and in shooting Mathews, and that he had no doubt of his acquittal." Thompson claimed his presence at the Capital Theatre that night was accidental and also stated that "he had no idea there was going to be any trouble." He explained that what happened before Wilson ordered Burditt's arrest was only a "little Christmas frolic." When questioned about the possibility of a vigilance committee being formed, Thompson replied that,

> He paid no attention to that whatever, and that so soon as he was released he would conduct himself as heretofore in his intercourse with people about the city, and that if any man or any set of men interfered with him he would interest him or them to the best of his ability, and be content with his fate, whatever it might be.

Thompson inherently understood how any man who is not afraid, in turn, makes others afraid of him.

William H. Simms, who was better known as Billy, was a young protégé of Ben Thompson, and he often visited Thompson at the county jail, bringing him newspapers and informing him of the rumors circulating around the Capital Theatre affray. As a youngster, he lived with his family in Austin's First Ward, where he received little formal education. As Simms grew up, the First Ward was filled with dance houses, barrooms, brothels, and gambling dens and it grew into Austin's primary vice district,. Like Thompson before him, Simms began working as a printer, but Simms left the printing trade at a very young age and began the lifestyle of a sporting man. In September 1874, at the age of eighteen, he fought with Giles Burditt Jr. in a brawl at Woodlief and Wilson's Saloon. Simms was critically wounded, and lucky to survive two very serious stab wounds, one in his side below his rib cage and another in his stomach. Charges for gambling were precursors for Simms's future behavior, and in July 1876, Policeman John Chenneville arrested Simms for disturbing the peace. Nearly a decade later, Ben Thompson and Billy Simms would be linked together in life and finally in death.[23]

Statesman editor Cardwell composed two long and powerfully written editorials, "No Lynch Law" and "The Vigilance Committee Not Yet Needed." Cardwell lectured his readers saying, "The courts are open. The Judge is learned and upright and if a jury cannot be organized here, one may be in an adjacent county. Enough harm has resulted from the calamity that befell us." That was certainly true, but he had more, "No good, but infinite evil, may come of the organization of which we tell and of which people are talking on the street."[24] In the case of Thompson and Burditt, those who would have preferred a lynching grudgingly accepted Cardwell's advice.

It was believed that Justice of the Peace James Neil, advised by Judge Ezekiel B. Turner of the 16th Judicial District Court, would preside over Ben Thompson's examination trial and decide whether or not he was fit for bail. However, the case was transferred over to thirty-three-year-old Justice of the Peace Fritz Tegener. The examination began at 9 a.m. on Friday, January 5, 1877. The new courthouse was packed with onlookers, and conspicuous among them, all dressed in mourning, were the late Mark Wilson's ailing mother and his sisters. Also noted in attendance was the recovering and heavily bandaged Charles Mathews. Maj. William M. Walton, attorney for the defense, argued for a severance of the defendants, wanting to proceed with evidence solely relating to Ben Thompson. Co-defendant James Burditt was not yet in custody. Justice Tegener rejected Walton's motion, deciding the law of severance applied specifically to jury trials and not to a bench examination. The state spent the next two weekdays, Friday and Monday, presenting its evidence and witnesses.[25]

On Tuesday, the defense put forth its case. Ex-policeman James LaRew stated that "he did not know that Mark Wilson was a special policeman," obviously inferring that neither Burditt nor Thompson would have known this when they resisted Wilson's orders and actions. The testimony of Drs. Wooten and Hadra was of the most importance. They confirmed Dr. Stalnaker's findings, and emphasized the wound on Wilson's neck was caused by a gunshot and not by a knife cut as many people previously speculated. This was an important determination, because a knife wound would justify Wilson's use of a firearm in defense of himself. In the late afternoon, the defense rested and the court adjourned until the next morning when the attorney's arguments were expected to commence.[26]

Attorney Walton spoke for Thompson's right to be released on bail, which brought forth this comment from the *Statesman*: "The Major has quite a reputation as a criminal lawyer, and he sustained that reputation with his usual force, logic and eloquence." All of the evidence, testimony and legal arguments were considered by Justice Tegener and on Thursday, January 11, defying any thought of retribution for his decision against the defendant from any lawless, reckless elements of society, he denied granting bail. Instead he consigned Thompson back to the Travis County jail.[27] With Ben and his brother Billy both being held and awaiting trials for the charge of murder and unable to come to the aid of each other, many must have murmured that this could be the end of the Thompson brothers.

Later, Major Walton expressed his opinion of Tegener's personality and his legal talent, describing him as "a fat, good-natured German and capital beer drinker, who, perhaps had never seen the inside of a law book until judicial robes were thrown across his broad shoulders by votes of radicals and negroes [*sic*], but withal, honest, generous and a good fellow, as the world goes."[28] Editor Cardwell, an attorney prior to running a newspaper, lauded Tegener's decision. Conceding Justice Tegener's ruling may not have been in conformity with evidence and law, and admitting there was doubt of premeditated guilt on Thompson's part, Cardwell congratulated him for his moral courage and devotion to law and order and, to the fact, "Tegener did not consider any threat to his well-being and discharged his public duty with an honest fearlessness that should receive the approval and admiration of the citizens of Austin." In response, Thompson's attorneys filed a writ of *habeas corpus* at the Court of Appeals for the State of Texas in session at Galveston.[29]

The Capital Theatre reopened in mid-January and Mayor Wheeler immediately ordered City Marshal Creary to shut it

William Penn DeNormandie. A neighbor of the Thompson family, he served Austin as its mayor in 1853 and later became a law partner of William M. Walton. Perhaps it was DeNormandie who introduced Thompson to Walton.

Courtesy the Austin History Center. Image # PICA 16380.

down. Once greeted as a welcomed addition to Austin, in less than two months, the Capital Theatre was described as "a shame to our fair city" and "a rendezvous for debauchery and crime." A legal battle ensued between the city administration and the surviving theatre man, Alf Gardner, with the theatre permanently closing after a five-month legal fight. Either Gardner or one of his supporters in defense of the theatre sent an unsigned letter to the editor of the *Statesman*. The letter writer declared the newspaper was prejudicial to the theatre's case by incorrectly calling it a dance house and wrongfully stating lewd women plied their trade in the private boxes. The writer alleged the legal proceedings coming from the city council to close the theatre were led by Alderman John H. Robinson, part-owner of Jobe and Robinson's Iron Front Saloon on Congress Avenue. This was only another attempt supported by the professional gamblers of the city to shut down the Capital Theatre. It is not known exactly when Ben Thompson became an owner of the gambling concession above the Iron Front Saloon, but eventually he was deeply involved in its operation. The letter writer felt the killing of Mark Wilson was the first blow struck against the theatre. Its closing by order of the city council was the second. In frustration, the writer stated how every major city in the United States, Canada, England, and Germany has a variety theatre. Austin, as the capital of Texas, had a population large enough to support a theatre and was certain to eventually have one. That prediction was correct. In October 1877, five months after the Capital Theatre had to close its doors forever, the Casino Theatre opened on Pecan Street. Over the coming years, more variety theaters would follow.[30]

Sheriff Corwin and his prisoner traveled via rail and arrived in Galveston mid-day on Monday, January 22. Ben Thompson was not incarcerated in the county jail, even though he was in custody. Instead, he registered with Corwin at the Girardin House, one of the finest hotels and eating establishments in Galveston. The *Galveston Daily News* acknowledged how Thompson was recognized in the Island City, due to its many citizens who served in the same regiment with him when it was stationed there during the Civil War. "Judge" Joseph Lee of Austin, an attorney representing Thompson, joined his client in enjoying the fine accommodations of the Girardin House. For an unknown reason, Attorney Walton chose to remain in Austin. Thompson retained Major F. C. Hume, an eminent local attorney familiar with all of the courts in Galveston, for his lead counsel instead. Ex parte Ben Thompson's habeas corpus case was scheduled to begin at the Court of Appeals at 10 a.m. Tuesday morning. The three jurists who comprised the appeals court, Presiding Judge Mathew D. Ector, John Preston White, and Clinton McKamy Winkler would decide if Thompson should continue to be held in custody or released on bail. Two attorneys traveled from Austin to represent the people, the Travis County Attorney Colonel Whitehead and, denoting the importance of this case, the Honorable George McCormick, Assistant Attorney General of the State of Texas.[31]

The court moved through its order of business, speedily arriving at Thompson's petition. Major Hume stated it had been agreed between the prosecution and defense in Austin that witnesses did not need to be present, that the written testimony given before Justice of the Peace Tegener would be sufficient, and that the defendant was ready to go to trial. Assistant Attorney General McCormick disagreed, insisting he had not bound himself or the State to any such agreement. The written testimony filled a full seventy-five pages. Most of it was given by witnesses for the prosecution with Thompson's defense attorneys making a strong cross examination and introducing their witnesses in rebuttal. McCormick insisted he must acquaint himself with the contents before agreeing not to call witnesses to appear in the courtroom. The three judges decided they wanted to hear witness testimony, and they adjourned until Thursday morning to provide witnesses with time to travel down from Austin. Presiding Judge Ector promised the defendant he would have every opportunity to obtain the witness testimony necessary to present his case. The court ordered Ben Thompson released from Sheriff Corwin's custody, and he was turned over to the Sheriff of Galveston County. His comfortable room at the Girardin House was changed to a simple cell at the county jail.[32]

Presiding Judge Ector issued several court orders commanding Travis County Sheriff Corwin to attach sixteen witnesses to appear on behalf of the State and twenty defense witnesses to testify on behalf of the prisoner. The orders specified that the witnesses must be in attendance in the courtroom, and Sheriff Corwin was to "detain them in custody until discharged by the court."[33] This proved to be an impossible task. All expenses related to travel, food, and housing was to be covered out of pocket by the witnesses. Only two are known to have actually arrived in Galveston, and one was an important participant in the affair, former policeman William P. Allen. His testimony before the appeals court was aided by the use of an illustrating diagram of the theatre's floorplan showing where he stood during the affray. However, due to the lack of attending witnesses, no new testimony of any importance was introduced into the record. The court was forced to use a considerable amount of time reading the written testimony from the two previous hearings during the three days it listened to the case.[34]

Throughout the proceedings, Mark Wilson's mother and one of his sisters were in the courtroom daily, showing the greatest interest in the proceedings. On Tuesday, January 30, in front of a large, curious audience, the three judges announced their decision. Abiding by the rules of the Court, no opinion was offered pertaining to the charge of murder, and the judges made no comment upon the evidence in order to not prejudice the case either way when it would be presented in the district court. They did, however, grant Ben Thompson bail in the amount of $5,000. Mrs. Wilson exhibited a great deal of nervousness when the decision was being read. When she learned her son's killer was to be set fee, Mrs. Wilson surrendered to her feelings. Between sobs, she loudly reproached the judge's action, and for some time she refused to be quieted.[35]

J. H. F. Chapman, John G. Duffield, and Henry James, three friends of Thompson and residents of Galveston, came forward and rendered the surety for Ben's bail money. Chapman and Duffield, together with others, owned the Bank Exchange Saloon at 112-114 East Market Street. Henry James was a retailer of dry goods, principally offering clothing, boots, and shoes.[36] Once released from the Galveston County jail, Thompson promptly boarded a train bound for Austin.[37] With all of the expensive and escalating legal fees for both himself and his brother, he had to return at once to running his gaming tables.

In an editorial entitled, "The Cost of Blood," and in several subsequent articles John Cardwell explained to his readers how they had to pay the intolerable financial costs of the drunkenness, fighting, and killing that took place in Austin. Calculating that it cost $6,000 per year to confine the forty inmates per day, on average, residing in the Travis County jail, Cardwell blamed ninety percent of these costs on the saloons and on the whiskey they served. He preached how whiskey brought out the Bowie knives and pistols, and told how law-abiding men would not purchase homes nor labor and pay taxes in a town degraded by violence and brutality. Citing the upcoming murder trial talked about by all, Cardwell detailed a total cost to the government for Thompson's ongoing case at a minimum of $10,000, all paid for by the hard-working people of the county. Depending on appeals, it could rise to double that amount. Cardwell called upon the Temperance people and the married women's association. He even pointed out what he felt could be an even more potent voice than those two organizations. He instructed the "pretty girls of the city" to reject a future in which their married home would be made intolerable by their husband's enslavement to dram shops brought on by their youthful habits. He even called upon the professional gamblers to better police their businesses and help end the violence. Cardwell went on to explain how, "All the whisky [*sic*] licenses and taxes collected in the county will not foot all the bills in this case, to say nothing of the value of a man's life that money can't buy."[38]

With Wilson dead, Mathews severely injured and scarred for life, fate had yet another tragedy awaiting one of the main participants in the Capital Shooting. Ex-policeman William P. Allen had been hired to bring a suspected horse thief back to Austin and was thrown from a stagecoach bound for San Antonio. He had been riding on the top seat outside of the coach when a wheel broke. Allen was thrown to the ground and his leg was crushed by the stage causing an extremely serious injury. No one else was hurt in the unfortunate accident, which occurred about three miles east of the town of San Marcos. Two doctors were sent for and they reset his leg, which was broken in two places below the knee. An ambulance returned Allen to his home in Austin where, on Saturday evening, February 10, three days after the accident, he succumbed to his injury. His end was not unexpected and a Reverend Wright was by his side, as was his family and several of his closest friends. William Allen, who was thirty-three years old, was survived by his wife, three small children, and aged parents, all of who were entirely dependent upon his support.[39]

In Ellsworth, Kansas, the spring session of the District Court was set to begin, and Case Number 286 was on the schedule, *The State of Kansas v. William Thompson*, the charge of murder in the first degree. This was declared a nonbailable offense. Ellsworth County Sheriff Hamilton traveled to Leavenworth and returned with Billy Thompson, delivering him to the district courtroom on March 16. In a brilliant public relations move, Philip T. Pendleton, the former county attorney who first authored the indictment papers charging Billy Thompson with the murder of Sheriff C. B. Whitney, was retained and he joined A.H. Case as a member of Billy's defense counsel. On March 19, Pendleton and Case filed a motion petitioning the court for a continuance until the next term. After due consideration, the motion was granted and the court again ordered Sheriff Hamilton to return and recommit Thompson to the Leavenworth County jail where he would remain incarcerated until the fall term in September.[40]

In a subsequent letter, Texas Adj. Gen. William Steele continued his interest in Billy Thompson's legal situation, most likely on the behalf of Aransas County where Billy was still wanted for murder. Unaware of the continuance, Steele inquired of attorney Ira Lloyd for the results of the trial previously scheduled for the spring term. In Lloyd's response, he announced he had little apprehension that Billy Thompson's friends would interfere in any way with the pending trial.[41]

During the spring of 1877, five stagecoaches in central Texas were robbed over a nineteen day period by a single highwayman. Most of the robberies took place in Bastrop County, south of Austin, and it turned out Bastrop was the hometown of the daring highwayman, Ham White. On March 26 at half past 10 a.m., White committed the first of two robberies that day. He stopped the stage bound from Austin to Lockhart on open prairie at Willow Spring, about thirteen miles west of Austin. The driver and three passengers offered no resistance as White took $96 in cash before rifling through the contents of the mail pouch, where he found an additional $12. He then leisurely rode off toward the Austin and San Antonio Road, and the stage was allowed to continue on its journey. Returning from a hunting trip near Luling, Ben Thompson and his friend and fellow sporting man, Augustus "Gus" Lorraine, came upon the opened letters. Gathering the remnants of the mail, the two men rode on to Austin and reported the robbery. The *Statesman* commented, "Ben says if the robber had come upon them he would have afforded him an interesting time, and we believe it."[42]

Before the month ended, Ham White was captured in a Luling livery stable by Texas Ranger Lt. Jesse "Lee" Hall and three other rangers. White was taken to Austin. During his April 13 preliminary examination, William M. Walton represented him temporarily. Walton withdrew as one of White's legal counsels in short order as his time, attention, and all of his legal skills were soon to be focused on defending the life and freedom of Ben Thompson.[43]

In Travis County, a grand jury was duly sworn and began its spring session in April 1877. A formal indictment was issued on May 10, charging Ben Thompson and James Burditt with the murder of Mark Wilson. The few surviving records show it was listed as Cause Number 5005. The trial was assigned to the 16th Judicial District Court of Judge Ezekiel B. Turner, the same jurist who ruled in favor of extradition and sent Billy Thompson off to Kansas. Ben's trial was scheduled to start on Wednesday, May 30, 1877.[44]

A well-led sweep through the counties west of San Antonio by a company of Texas Rangers commanded by Lieutenant Hall resulted in the arrest of as many as thirty-three wanted lawbreakers. Caught up in the net was young desperado, John King Fisher, wanted on a charge of murder and six other indictments for cattle rustling. None of these numerous charges would ultimately stick with a conviction. James Burditt was found hiding out at Fisher's ranch. Lieutenant Hall telegraphed Adjutant General Steele in Austin from the border town of Eagle Pass on May 16, "Made three arrests last night among them King Fisher for murder [.] Also Jim Burdett [*sic*] charged with Ben Thompson for killing Wilson in Austin[.] see if they want him." Steele answered Hall the next day replying that "Burdett [*sic*] wanted here." The Rangers returned Burditt to Austin, where he was placed in the Travis County jail.[45]

The Thompson murder trial was called before the district court on its scheduled date. Between the prosecution and defense, the witness list consisted of fifty-one people, yet the taking of testimony was concluded in only one day. Walton later wrote, "By this time, however, the true facts and circumstances and surroundings connected with the killing had become public and well known to most people; prejudice and passion had subsided and cooled down. The trial was orderly and quiet."[46]

The lawyers concluded their arguments the following day on Thursday, May 31. Before the jury began its deliberations, Judge Turner prepared a detailed charge to the jury reaching almost six pages long. Walton wanted to introduce a motion asking for additional language to be added to the jury instructions stating, "There is no testimony before you to prove or which tends to prove any connection between Thompson and Burditt and whichever acts may have been committed by Burditt, such acts are not to be considered by you to the prejudice of Thompson." Judge Turner refused Walton's motion. However, he did tell the jury that Thompson's presence at the theatre could not be viewed as unfavorable to him since it was a place of public amusement and everyone was invited. The judge did caution the jury, making the powerful point that if Thompson, "did voluntarily take part in a quarrel with Mr. Wilson and by aiding in an attack upon him did provoke Wilson to anger and cause him to shoot at defendant and that shooting presented the opportunity sought for by defendant in order to prepare the way for killing Wilson, then the fact that Wilson shot first would not justify or excuse defendant for killing him but such killing on the part of the defendant would be murder." The judge ended his charge making the opposite point that if Thompson did not provoke a difficulty with intent to kill Wilson, since self-preservation is the first law of nature, Thompson was justified in taking Mark Wilson's life. The jury deliberated for only a few minutes before they reached their decision.[47]

After so many months of excitement and drama swirling around the fatal shooting of Mark Wilson, John Cardwell, in his one sentence reporting of the verdict, brought to the readers of the *Statesman* an end to the Capital Theatre tragedy: "The case against Ben Thompson was concluded yesterday in the district court, the jury bringing in a verdict of acquittal.[48]

In San Antonio, Joe Foster, a prominent gambler and turfman, received a telegram from Austin informing him of the Ben Thompson verdict.[49] In a few years, Billy Simms and Joe Foster would soon be the key associates along with Jack Harris at one of San Antonio's best-known amusement venues, the Vaudeville Theatre and Saloon.

On June 6, James Burditt stood before a jury. The charge of murder was dropped and he pled guilty to simple assault, a misdemeanor. For his role in the bloody affair he paid a $12 fine.[50]

Ben Thompson returned to running his gambling house. During the summer of 1877, he was arrested five times for reasons now unknown, but speculation would point to his illegally running games of chance. Four charges were dismissed and he pled guilty on a fifth charge, for which he was fined $25.[51]

In preparation for Billy Thompson's upcoming Ellsworth murder trial, both the prosecution and the defense were eager to get favorable testimony into the official record. In Ellsworth, Kansas, everyone knew Billy fired the fatal shot, so it would be ridiculous for his legal counsel to argue otherwise. The legal strategy of the Thompson brothers was to wisely admit that Billy did fire the fatal buckshot into Sheriff Whitney, but pled it was an unfortunate accident. Since he did so unintentionally, and without malice or motive, he should be found not guilty of the charge of murder.

On June 18, Ellsworth County Sheriff Hamilton received legal correspondence from Thompson's defense attorneys, which he personally served on county attorney Ira E. Lloyd. It consisted of a list of questions (eleven interrogatories) that three witnesses of the fatal shooting of C. B. Whitney had agreed to answer. The witnesses were Ben Thompson, Neil Cain, and W.A. Langford. Interrogatory number five contained the most important word for the defense, "accidental." Doubtful that Ben Thompson would appear in an Ellsworth courtroom, Ira Lloyd probably perceived this as an opportunity to help establish Billy's guilt or at least smear his reputation and that of his older brother. Co-authoring a legal document with C.C. Sprigg, Ellsworth's clerk of the court, Lloyd and Sprigg appointed Osceola Archer, a Travis County Notary Public, to examine Ben Thompson, Neil Cain, and W.A. Langford under oath. Lloyd agreed to the defense's original eleven interrogatories and countered with fifty-four cross interrogatories of his own. These were given to defense attorney Philip T. Pendleton on June 21, and on the day the testimony would begin, A.H. Case officially wrote on the document containing Lloyd's interrogatories, "Each of these are not legitimate or proper cross examinations." Nonetheless, for two days, July 10 and 11, Austin, Texas Notary Public Osceola Archer used those interrogatories to question Ben Thompson and W.A. Langford. Regrettably, if Neil Cain was examined, his answers are no longer part of the court records.

Mr. Archer went through Lloyd's fifty-four cross interrogatories, which verified some embarrassing truths about the Thompson brothers. Ben freely testified he did earn his living as a professional gambler. He was married, yet in Ellsworth, he repeatedly enjoyed the company of one Jennie Fields, a prostitute. In addition, he also slept with a number of other lewd women. He acknowledged he did spend several years in a Texas prison for assault and, lastly, his brother Billy had another murder charge awaiting him in Aransas County, Texas.

In addition, with information screened from the correspondence between the Thompson brothers, Lloyd quoted the contents of a letter from Ben to Billy Thompson in one of his questions, "I always told you Billy, that you would have no show if you were arrested on this charge and I was caught broke. We will do what we can for you and see that you have able counsel but it is a hard case and will take a good deal of money to get you out, keep up good spirits, I will not leave a stone unturned to get you clear." Ben Thompson claimed in his answer to the above quote,

> I did not mean to convey the idea by that letter that my brother had a hard case because of any guilt on his part, but that it would be a hard case because all of his witnesses are here in Texas and it would be almost impossible to get them there because I was without money at the time myself, because he was in a distant state without friends, without counsel and at a place where there was a prejudice against him by those who did not know the facts of the case. These were the causes that induced me to say he had a hard case. I will further state that I will do all I can to get him counsel and with proper counsel and a fair trial I have never had any fears of the result.[52]

The second witness to be sworn in was thirty-six-year-old W. A. Langford, a Williamson County, Texas, farmer and stock raiser. Per Langford's answers: On August 15, 1873, Langford, who at the time was earning his living as a cattle drover, found himself in Ellsworth standing in front of Joe Brennan's saloon watching the unfolding tragedy that would take Sheriff Whitney's life. At that moment, he had known the Thompson brothers for several years and had been acquainted with Sheriff Whitney for about a month. He observed Whitney and the two armed Thompsons walking to Brennan's Saloon from the railroad tracks in the middle of the town's plaza. As Billy Thompson and Whitney entered the saloon, it was Langford who "hollered" out the warning to Ben Thompson to "look out" as John Sterling and "Happy Jack" Morco were advancing with their weapons drawn. Ben whirled, took a few steps towards Beebe's Store, shouldered his rifle and fired one errant shot. Whitney responded by retracing his steps, leaving the saloon, and moving out onto the sidewalk toward Beebe's store. Following closely behind him was a very drunk Billy Thompson. Langford stated he was twenty feet away from Whitney as he watched Billy, and "as he passed through the saloon's front door, he staggered back as a drunken man frequently does and in trying to recover himself, the gun which Billy Thompson had in his hands went off accidentally and shot Whitney." Langford added: "For a moment after being shot he stood up straight and then he seemed to be in a sinking condition." Langford hurried to Whitney and asked him if he was badly hurt and did he think the shot would kill him. "Oh yes" and "yes" were Whitney's reply to both questions. And in response to Langford, Whitney said "that he knew it was accidental but that it had killed him." These were the last words Langford heard Whitney utter. He was suffering so intensely Langford could not bother him any further. Billy Thompson did say something, but Langford could not understand what it was because Billy was "so drunk he did not speak distinctly." In several of his other answers Langford emphasized, "I will further state that Whitney was not murdered" and "Wm. Thompson never [intentionally] fired at C. B. Whitney, but when Thompson's gun went off accidentally he was about 7 or 8 feet from him."[53]

Ben Thompson paid the $17 notary fee charged by Archer out of his pocket. The testimony was received in Ellsworth on July 19, where County Attorney Lloyd issued an official objection to no less than thirty of Thompson and Langford's answers.[54]

The *Statesman* of August 22, under its "Personal and Local Dots" column, reminded its readers, "Billy Thompson, arrested in this county nearly a year ago by Capt. Sparks, is to be tried at the next term of the court in Ellsworth, Kansas. ... Thompson is charged with shooting an officer in Ellsworth four years ago."

As expected, Ben Thompson stayed in Texas to continue to earn the money necessary for Billy's defense. The Thompson brothers enlisted their brother-in-law, Robert Gill, a quiet, well-behaved man and a respected merchant from Bastrop to go to Ellsworth and help Billy in the legal fight for his life. They and Gill selected wisely, and put together an enviable group of advocates to defend Billy. Ira Lloyd complimented Philip T. Pendleton later writing, "He happened to be one of the finest lawyers in Kansas."[55] A.H. Case of Topeka and J. D. Mohler were considered two of the finest trial lawyers in the state, the *Ellsworth Reporter* calling Mohler "a Napoleon among lawyers." The initial tactics of Billy Thompson's legal counsel were to delay the trial, and, if possible, have it thrown out of court.

The fall term of the 16th Judicial District Court of Kansas convened at Ellsworth on Monday, September 3, with Judge John Prescott presiding. The first order of business was to consider two motions filed by Billy's defense attorneys. The first petitioned Judge Prescott to quash the indictment because it "does not contain a statement of the facts of the case as constituting the offense, in plain and concise language without repetition." Prescott refused to free a prisoner on a technicality, especially one who was accused of murdering an officer of the law during the performance of his duty.[56]

The second motion stated the defendant needed more time to gather important witnesses. Billy's lawyers wrote how they had spent most of the month of August unsuccessfully trying to assemble these witnesses. The motion read, "that this application is not made for delay but that justice may be done and applicant further states that he has from about the month of October 1876 up to the present time been under arrest in this case and in close confinement ... mostly ... in the county jail of Leavenworth ...

he therefore prays the court to grant him a continuance of this cause until the said next term of the court." Judge Prescott rejected their argument and denied the application for a continuance stating that the defense had had plenty of time to locate and insure the witnesses were available to testify. Billy Thompson's arraignment took place immediately, he entered a plea of not guilty and the jury selection began.

On Tuesday, both the prosecution and defense took great care in selecting twelve acceptable men from the forty-eight in the jury pool, and the editor of the *Reporter* admitted that "some of the best citizens of Ellsworth County" made up the jury. The *Reporter* also stated, "The jurors on the Thompson case will earn their county scrip." To ensure that no undue influence might affect their decision, they were to be kept under constant surveillance.[57]

With one simple sentence at the very top of its second column, "The lawyers are at it now," the *Reporter* informed its readers that the first-degree murder trial of Billy Thompson had begun.[58] The trial started on Wednesday, September 5, 1877, and it lasted nine grueling days. Ira Lloyd's well-prepared prosecution paraded three dozen witnesses to the stand. That their testimony no longer exists is a loss to history. The defense witness list contained a mere seven names, only one of which resided in Texas. The others were residents of Kansas, and the power of their statements stunned the courtroom. Their testimony remains today in the file records of the district court, and it coincides with Ben Thompson and W. A. Langford's earlier statements in July. The testimony of these witnesses supported the three critical elements of the defense's argument. Sheriff Whitney and the Thompson brothers were on the best of terms, hence no malice, no motive. The Thompson brothers were not the aggressors in the fracas that eventually caused Whitney's death, and, lastly, how Billy Thompson was so intoxicated that he could barely stand, and without raising the shotgun up or aiming it, one barrel went off accidentally striking Whitney. Several of the defense witnesses even quoted the fatally wounded sheriff as saying: "Billy did not intend to do it, it was an accident." Others testified Whitney exclaimed after being shot, "he did not intend to shoot me, send for my wife and child." Prosecutor Ira Lloyd often objected, calling many of these statements "incompetent, irrelevant, immaterial and hearsay." However, most of his objections were overruled by Judge Prescott.

The jury received their charge and instructions from Judge Prescott and finally began their deliberations on Friday, September 14. Surprisingly, with only about one hour of deliberation, the jury reached their decision. John Montgomery, editor of the *Reporter* wrote, "When they came back with their verdict the courtroom was full and everyone but the prisoner seemed intensely interested to learn the result. [Billy] Thompson came in with the Sheriff and Deputies smiling as if *he* was sure that his bonds were about to be loosed. The clerk commenced reading and just as we expected to hear 'guilty' pronounced he read 'not guilty,' when all decorum was forgotten by the friends of the prisoner who congratulated him on his escape … . This was a surprise to most of our citizens, especially to those who were living in the county at the time Thompson shot Whitney. They expected nothing less than twenty years in the penitentiary for him, as until this court met the shooting had not been called 'accidental.'"

At first count, the jury stood with seven for acquittal and five for conviction, but the minority easily relented and agreed to the not guilty verdict. Montgomery astutely complimented Billy's attorneys for their efforts stating, "Messrs. Case and Mohler … are very able men, and they used all their eloquence and ingenuity to save their client … and so this case is settled—all but the $3,500 costs to the county … [and] the old residents walked home feeling that law had not been vindicated [however] on the other hand, we have been informed by unprejudiced persons who attended the trial, that the verdict was such as they expected it would be after listening to all the evidence, *pro* and *con*."[59]

The day following his acquittal, Billy Thompson and Robert Gill boarded a train for Texas, leaving Kansas behind them. Before they left, they published a card in the *Reporter*: "To the citizens of Ellsworth, who so kindly sympathized with us in our recent trouble, we wish, through this medium, to return our heartfelt thanks. Their kindness shall never be forgotten. [Signed] Wm. Thompson [and] Robt. Gill."[60]

Word of Billy Thompson's acquittal spread as several major newspapers printed articles heralding his release. As he traveled south into Texas he stopped in Fort Worth and on Tuesday, September 25 the local newspaper, the *Democrat*, published a write-up entitled: "Bill Thompson Free." The newspaperman reported that Billy "has just been honorably acquitted on the charge of murdering Sheriff Whitney, of Ellsworth County. We had the pleasure of a long call and interview with him last evening and found him to be an entirely different appearing man than that which we had pictured him. Bill is in his thirty-first year. He possesses a pleasant countenance, a sparkling and brilliant eye, an intelligent looking face and the *tout en semble* of the man, to say the least, is not such as one would suppose a person of his notoriety would possess."

Billy Thompson must have liked the look of Fort Worth because he decided to stay there awhile.

Chapter 10

SHOOTING UP AUSTIN

"Ben Thompson probably comes nearer the ideal knight of chivairous [sic] desperadoism than any other man in Texas."

—*St. Louis Globe-Democrat*, October 7, 1877

On Wednesday, October 3, 1877, at 9:00 o'clock in the morning, Texas Ranger Captain John Sparks was before the mayor in Austin's police court having been arrested by Police Officer Dennis Sheehan for disturbing the peace. The cause of his misbehavior is unknown, but the ranger captain decided to fire off his pistol in Burland's Restaurant that previous evening. Sparks pled guilty to discharging a firearm within the city limits, and Mayor Jacob C. DeGress accessed a fine of $25 plus the added court costs of $4.80. Less than an hour and a half later, Ben Thompson slipped up the back stairs and his presence in the courtroom was acknowledged by City Marshal Edward Creary. Thompson was then officially arrested for his own pistol playing antics the evening before by Officer John Chenneville. According to Walton, Ben with his friend and fellow sport Bill Johnson, whose life Thompson saved years ago in the town of Bryan, had decided on spending the previous evening together. At dinner, Thompson enjoyed a bit too much champagne. They started their "tramp" through Austin's sporting houses at Ben's own establishment, called the Golden Rule, on Congress Avenue underneath the offices of the *Statesman.*[1]

At the Golden Rule, they found Ben's friend and gambling partner, forty-seven-year-old Augustus "Gus" Lorraine, dealing faro. Lorraine enjoyed the title "Major," and was originally from South Carolina. Walton explained, "For some reason ... [Ben and Lorraine] ... were not in exactly good humor with one another." Johnson instinctively felt the tension and searched Ben for any firearms. Finding none, he let his guard down and briefly left the gaming room. Moments later, pistol shots rang out in rapid succession and filled the air with gun smoke. At first, Ben directed his fusillade into the stacks of chips on the table and the dealer's box Lorraine was using, stating to all, "I don't think that the set of tools altogether honest, and I want to help Mr. Loraine [*sic*] buy another." Ben graciously informed Lorraine to charge a new set to his account. Remaining remarkably calm, Lorraine did not utter a sound or move a muscle as the patrons of the hall scrambled to exit the building as fast as possible. Thompson then fired up at the chandelier smashing it into a thousand pieces. Bullets tore through the ceiling and up into the quarters of the *Statesman*. Bill Johnson caught hold of Ben and prevented any further promiscuous gunplay. Johnson slipped out through a back door with Thompson in hand in order to avoid the police he expected to arrive at any moment. The sound of gunfire drew a great crowd, though Policeman O'Brien, the officer assigned to Congress Avenue, was off his beat enjoying his supper.

At first, the *Statesman* took a sarcastic view of the incident: "Several fellows told the innocent police that it was the vanguard of the Mexican army that was firing on the *Statesman* office, and the police properly kept away." The newspaper mirthfully acknowledged, "It seems no great harm was done ... [but] ... if this shooting below isn't stopped the ... [printers] will be compelled to have chain armor made for their shins [since they are setting type late into the night for the next day's newspaper]. During the bloodless shooting, a few window panes were broken, drinking glasses smashed, the dealer's box and chips were shot up, and bullet holes had cut into the gaming table."[2]

Ben Thompson exited the empty gambling hall full of his gun smoke and traveled south on Congress Avenue until he reached Pine Street (5th), where he discovered Abram Simon,[3] a "most peaceful, quiet, dreamy-looking Hebrew with a bald head and fair, round belly with good lager swollen, [who] was sitting in front of the Raymond House." The reporter, who knew very well who he was writing about and aware that his readers would know as well, continued his story explaining how "some one, who had taken a little wine and has not the fear of policeman ... moved quietly to the spot where our son of Abraham was reposing and from behind him inserted a great Colt's repeater between the innocent Israelite's legs and fired it." Simon's chair went flying and he went rolling into the gutter screaming murder. He jumped up and ran down the avenue howling. In its entertaining report, the *Statesman* explained that the police could not learn the identity of the revolver firing prankster, however "Ben Thompson has laughed about it till his sides are sore."[4] It seems after shooting up his own place of business, Thompson was enjoying himself so much he simply continued the festivities with his six-shooter.

When this second shooting occurred, Policeman O'Brien had returned to his beat on the avenue, but somehow he was unable to learn who fired the shots in either of the two incidents and he made no arrest.[5]

In the police court, Mayor DeGress expressed how strange it was that everyone else on the Avenue knew who fired the gun shots except the policeman on duty. The mayor reprimanded City Marshal Creary for not having the offender arrested. This started a debate between the two city officials, with the marshal declaring he did all he could do but he would not sacrifice his life or the lives of his officers "for nothing or for fun." The mayor replied, how "such lawlessness on the streets of the capital of Texas was shocking and outrageous," and he declared, that "an officer should do his duty in preserving the peace and order of the city or resign." The marshal did not concur with the mayor's opinion. Mayor DeGress was upset to learn the gun-firing offender had yet to be found and arrested, so he placed an arrest warrant for Ben Thompson into the marshal's hand and, once arrested, the mayor insisted the offender was to be put under a $500 bond to insure he was held until he appeared before him in the police court. Within a half hour, Ben Thompson entered through the backstairs and strolled into the courtroom and faced the mayor while the court was taking a brief recess. Ben pled guilty to the charges of carrying and discharging a deadly weapon in a public place, risking the lives of innocent citizens, and damaging property. The mayor charged him twice as much as he assessed Captain Sparks and fined Ben $50 plus court costs.[6]

City Marshal Creary distanced himself from his derelict officer and let it be known through the columns of the *Statesman* that it was not he, but the city council that selected and placed O'Brien on his staff. In the face of such ridicule from the newspaper, Policeman O'Brien turned in his badge and resigned. The *Statesman* felt, "As a policeman he is certainly out of his element, though possibly he may be a fair average in Austin."[7]

The law, as well as the *Statesman*, had not finished with Captain Sparks, and his misbehavior while in Austin had only just begun. The anger Sparks felt in Burland's Restaurant did not wane throughout the day and a second complaint was made against him. This time the charge was for illegally carrying a concealed weapon.

The case was to be heard before the mayor. A *Statesman* reporter visited Sparks's boss, Adjutant General Steele, who denounced his subordinate's outrageous conduct. In the past, the newspaper lauded Sparks's accomplishments as a lawman, and now in an article aptly entitled, "An Official on the Rampage," the *Statesman* lectured him for his lawlessness. "It would seem that when officers become so forgetful of their relations to the public, and indulge in the reckless amusement of shooting out lamps in restaurants, endangering the lives of men, women and children, that the time has come when they can no longer be useful public guardians of law and order." The restaurant owner, M. G. Burland, made a complaint against Sparks and a hearing was held before Justice James Neil. Much to the shock of all present, Captain Sparks attacked Mr. Burland with his cane as they exited the courtroom. Another complaint was immediately sworn out against Sparks, this time for assault and battery. The captain ended his day of uncontrolled behavior by calling at Mayor DeGress's office. Stunning onlookers, Sparks acted like a "bull-dozer and a bully," and the two strong-willed men came close to having a difficulty.[8] After a night of gunfire and subsequent turbulence by both Sparks and Thompson, the *Statesman* pleaded, "Let us have peace."

During the early fall of 1877, the *St. Louis Globe-Democrat* sent a correspondent to visit Texas, who then filed a report entitled "A Land of Wonder. The Empire of Texas and its Varied Resources." He examined many subjects: from the state's geography to its seaports, major cities, towns, railroads, and school systems as well as its view of law and justice. In the section detailing "Society in Texas," the correspondent explained how for many years past, the most influential example for young Texas boys was the "cowboy," defined as a distinctive breed of men whose livelihood involved caring for and working with the famous Texas longhorns. The cowboy "wears a broad-brimmed hat with a snake for a hatband, long hair, 'bell spurs,' a brace of revolvers and a bowie knife, and who gambles and drinks for entertainment, kills negroes [*sic*] as a matter of accommodation, and shoots white men as a pastime. Of course, the popularity of this style of desperadoism has past [*sic*] away," as the reporter explained, the "worst-class of its devotees are being exterminated with the rope. It is stated that the criminal code of Texas is more severe on thieves than murderers—upon the theory, probably, that property can not protect itself, and that the individual can; be that as it may, it is a demonstrated fact that the present healthy status of public opinion has driven most 'bullies' from Texas or to the gallows or 'pen,' and that law and order prevail."

The correspondent reminded its readers that Bill Longley, by his own words, confessed to years of committing "cowardly assassinations and dastardly murders," but now awaited the hangman's noose. Similar in character to the murderer, Longley, but with probably even more victims, young Wes Hardin was facing a jury and possibly also a death sentence. The St. Louis correspondent placed Ben Thompson among these desperate men but he explained a distinct difference in conduct between the likes of Longley and Hardin and that of Thompson.

Proclaiming, "Ben Thompson probably comes nearer the ideal knight of chivairous [*sic*] desperadoism than any other man in Texas. He is a good-looking, dapper little man, of pleasant address and good manners," the St. Louis newsman acknowledged. "It is said that he gambles for a living and sometimes drinks, but that none of his troubles have ever risen from dissipation." Astonished at how Thompson "has survived" such a "large number of deadly difficulties," The reporter asserted "that he has never committed a theft, robbery or taken an undue advantage, but, on the contrary, prefers to have his antagonist take the first shot. He is an expert horseman and an unerring shot."[9]

With pride in their hometown boy, the portion of the account focusing on Ben Thompson was reprinted in the *Statesman* under its "Texas—Facts and Fancies" column in its October 10 issue.

In the fall of 1877, Ben's wife Kate gave birth to a daughter. Augustua Lorraine Thompson was baptized on October 31 at St. David's Episcopal Church. They clearly named the girl after Ben's business partner and friend, Augustus Lorraine. Gus Lorraine, like Thompson, was a married man with a young family. Ben and Lorraine somehow found a way to patch up their friendship. Thompson was always known to easily make friends, as long as it was under his own terms.

In Aransas County, the Rockport *Transcript* published the status of cases disposed of in the fall term. The case of Billy Thompson and his alleged killing of Remus Smith was continued.[10] In the early days of 1878, Ben traveled to Fort Worth to seek opportunity and to be near his younger brother. Ben Thompson's young protégé, Billy Simms, joined him there for a time.[11] Thompson was armed as usual, and he was arrested for carrying a pistol. For this offense, Grayson County Justice A.G. McClung fined Ben $25 plus costs.[12] Ben made his headquarters at the Occidental Saloon on the west side of Houston Street between Second and Third Streets, about a mile north of the infamous tenderloin section of Fort Worth, forever known as Hell's Half Acre. The Cattle Exchange, on the opposite side of Houston Street from the Occidental, was another popular venue Thompson frequented. At this time in his gambling career, he decided to occasionally set up a sure thing to help fill his pocketbook. Raffles of attractive and expensive items were popular with the saloon crowd and Ben would often sell chances, usually numbered from one to a hundred, which guaranteed a substantial profit for a price. Whatever saloon and gambling hall that held the raffle would put the item on display with the dual purpose of promoting the raffle as well as the business's regular attractions.

During the winter and spring months, Ben Thompson held several raffles at the Occidental Saloon. Once for his "valuable gold watch," and a second for his "very fine saddle" valued at $350. He wasn't shy about purchasing tickets in raffles run by others, and while in Fort Worth he won a hack complete with five prime bay horses to pull it. The value of the set-up was placed at $300. He promptly cashed in and put the entire outfit up for sale.[13]

Billy Thompson separated from his older brother and traveled west to Fort Griffin. Originally just a military post for a portion of the 6th U.S. Cavalry, it became a thriving frontier town due to its location. Though it may have been small, it was still the biggest town on the roads between Fort Worth and El Paso, as well as San Antonio and Dodge City. Fort Griffin was set along the Great Western Cattle Trail moving north to Kansas and the major stage line running east to west. The town was protected by the army, and first became a staging point for buffalo hunters. Unsurprisingly, the usual plague of gamblers, saloon men, and lewd women soon buzzed around the soldiers and hunters. The town grew between the military post on the bluff above and the Clear Fork of the Brazos River on a level marshy area below, and this part of Fort Griffin became known as "The Flats." About two hundred substantial citizens earned a living there surrounded by an uncountable number of undesirables. Many notable characters of the Wild West mixed in with the sporting crowd during this short-lived time of debauchery in Fort Griffin. There was prostitute and gambler Lottie Deno, Doc Holliday and his paramour Kate Fisher, lawmen John Poe and Wyatt Earp, the outlaw Dave Rudabaugh, the horse thief "Hurricane Bill" Martin, Jim and Bat Masterson, lawman-turned-outlaw John Larn, and Pat Garrett, who would later kill Billy the Kid. It was the perfect place for Billy Thompson to blend in. On Friday, February 2, a traveler relating a bloody story returned from Fort Griffin. Word spread through Fort Worth's sporting fraternity that Billy had a "difficulty" in a Fort Griffin dance house and he was shot and killed. The upsetting news swiftly reached Ben Thompson, who anxiously sent a telegram to determine if the rumor was true. He was relieved to learn that there was no such shooting and his brother was alive and well and enjoying his usual good health.[14]

Captain B. B. Paddock, an early Fort Worth newspaperman who began publication of the *Democrat* in the second half of the 1870s, later authored his impression of Ben Thompson which could be considered both complimentary and insulting. He "made frequent visits to Fort Worth, where he often indulged in his favorite pastime of 'shooting up the town.' Ben was 'as mild mannered a man as ever cut a throat or scuttled a ship.' When not engaged in a fracas, he was as quiet and debonair an individual as one would care to meet."[15]

On Sunday, January 6, the *New York World*, perhaps inspired by the feature published in the *St. Louis Globe-Democrat*, printed an extensive article entitled "Shooting Men of Texas: The Mildest-Mannered Murderers that ever emptied a Colt's Navy." Eleven days later, the *Statesman* proudly reprinted the write-up on Ben Thompson's life to date and his many adventures. Killers "Bloody Bill" Longley and John Wesley Hardin received extensive coverage along with Thompson. The spotlight also fell on another young gunman who had earned a deadly reputation for his conflicts on the Texas frontier. Said gunman was none other than Billy Thompson's good buddy, John King Fisher.

The account in the *New York World* held Fisher up as an "equal of Longley and Hardin in cold blooded atrocity." The eastern newspaper sensationalized how Fisher was the leader of a gang on the Mexican border "numbering fully a hundred men." The outlaw band "terrified the authorities and made it a rule to kill all witnesses so that if any of the gang were captured it was a difficult thing to establish their guilt." The *World* reported that Fisher was still under indictment for killing four men.[16]

On Tuesday, February 12, Ben learned through a short telegram from Denison, Texas, that his friend, Billy Simms, "had killed his man." A second telegram was sent to an unnamed lady in Fort Worth telling her, "Your friend J. V. George, was shot through the brain last night. He never knew what hurt him." Due to the late hour of the telegram's arrival, nothing more could be learned beyond those scant two messages. Simms, as a member of the sporting fraternity, and George, who had relatives in the city, were both well-known in Fort Worth. On the Friday before his death, George was in town looking for a suitable location to open a grocery store. The *Democrat* stated George "has always sustained an excellent reputation as a man of integrity and sobriety." His actions on the night he died did not match this high opinion.[17]

In February 1878, Simms was hanging out in the saloons of Denison, Texas in Grayson County about one hundred miles northeast of Fort Worth. Billy Simms and J. V. George had made their acquaintance in Denison where George worked as a grocery clerk.[18] That acquaintance became a friendship, and on Monday evening, February 11, they were on a drinking binge together. As the hour grew late, they separated and Simms went to visit a prostitute named Annie Woods, a particular friend of J. V. George. Upon learning that Simms was alone with Miss Woods in her room at the Brown Front, a combination house of ill-repute and saloon on Skiddy Street, George downed a couple of drinks in the adjacent saloon, pulled a knife and started for Annie's room. George broke down the door and screamed that he was going "to kill the damn son of a bitch," but before he could stab Simms, the pair momentarily grappled. Simms somehow managed to grab hold of his pistol and fired twice. His first shot missed, but his aim was true on the second shot and his bullet hit George in the head, killing him instantly.[19]

Two days later, Grayson County Attorney J. R. Cowles traveled from Sherman, the county seat, to scrupulously examine Billy Simms, Annie Woods, and another male witness only identified as Hewins. Cowles was assisted by Colonel Woods, and attorney A. B. Parson conducted Simms's defense. The proceedings were held before Judge Kirk and lasted throughout the day. After considering all of the testimony, County Attorney Cowles formally entered a decision to not prosecute, releasing Simms from custody and allowing him to leave Denison. Several newspapers erroneously reported Simms had been acquitted by a jury, but in fact, Cowles voluntarily decided not to proceed any further in the prosecution against Simms.[20]

Editor Paddock wanted to unleash his feelings of disgust regarding the amount of violence, brutality, and crime that had flooded Texas since the end of the Civil War, and this latest instance of one gambler killing another in a house of ill-repute provided him with fresh material. No reader could misinterpret his anger. "We envy not the gambler, rough or libertine, who boasts over the success attending the killing of his first man—for of such are the devil's cohorts, and for a certainty will they receive punishment adequate to the enormity of their crimes." Pronouncing, "Bill Sims [*sic*] is the last murderer in Texas. He has ever been a gambler, a quarrelsome, troublesome young man, ambitious to 'shoot somebody'—and his selection of a friend for a victim is only keeping with his character," Paddock went on to also condemn the woman at the center of the killing, Annie Woods. "No friendly hand was thrust from under that bed of prostitution to stay the committal of a crime that consigned George to an unsanctified grave." Paddock saw no end to the violence and advised using the rope to deter future killings. "Texas has already suffered greatly by acts of vandalism and deeds of barbarity. Judge Lynch is a commendable character, as compared to the gambler who, with revolver in hand, deals out death according to his individual fancy or compliance with his harlot's decree."[21]

Three weeks later, the *Fort Worth Democrat* reported that Simms was trying to reform. He had returned to his old trade as a printer and was working in Hot Springs, Arkansas. If this was true, he didn't stay in Arkansas or work at as his old trade for very long. By the middle of June, he was in Austin and back to his troublesome ways. Simms was arrested and charged with two counts of assault and one count of abusive language.[22]

According to the *Democrat*, Ben Thompson, accompanied by a "John Chinaman," boarded the 3:20 train in Fort Worth on March 3 with the intent of traveling to New Orleans for the Mardi Gras celebration.[23] Fat Tuesday fell on March 5 in 1878, which left Thompson little time to enjoy the festivities. The term "John Chinaman" represented the nineteenth century, stereotypical Chinese male caricature. This persona often depicted a man who wore a long queue of hair and a common coolie hat. Perhaps Thompson did hire a Chinese servant while in Fort Worth, however, if he did board a train with such a companion, they did not go far. According to the *Dallas Daily Herald,* Ben moved from the Windsor Hotel to the popular Le Grand Hotel in Dallas instead of traveling nonstop all the way to New Orleans.[24] Billy Thompson was still in Fort Worth later in the week, "making the night hideous around the Southern Hotel" and he was arrested and fined $3 plus court costs for his misbehavior.[25]

Fort Griffin and Fort Worth continued to be a hotbed of rumors for the Thompson brothers. A falsehood stating that Ben Thompson had killed a man traveled south to their hometown of Austin. Ben immediately sent a telegram to his brother-in-law James Moore to make his family aware he was in no such trouble. Moore shared the news with the *Statesman,* who related it to its readers on Thursday, March 21, "Ben has had no trouble." This brought an end to any further speculation or worry.[26]

During the first week of April 1878, Dr. J. W. Stalnaker was caring for little six-month-old Augustua Lorraine Thompson. The baby must have been suffering from severe digestive problems because Dr. Stalnaker listed her cause of death as, "inanition, exhaustion, malnutrition." She was buried on April 8 in the E. Moore family plot at Oakwood Cemetery, Section 1, Lot 71.[27] Her mother Kate, her brother Bennie, her big sister Katie, her Aunt Sarah and Uncle James K. Farrell certainly stood at the baby's graveside to mourn her passing. Two of her aunts from the Thompson side of the family, Fannie and Mary Jane with her husband Robert Gill, and the child's grandmother, Mrs. Mary Ann Thompson traveled from Bastrop to be there. Perhaps other friends and relatives attended, but it is doubtful Augusta's father was with her in her final moments, or that he was there to attend her funeral. He was in Fort Worth enjoying his life as a sporting man.

The Austin Hook and Ladder Company Hope No. 2 sent a letter to Fort Worth addressed to Ben Thompson requesting he act as their representative at the Waco Maifest Competition scheduled for May 8 and 9. The best drilled fire company would be awarded an ornate trumpet made of silver.[28] The Austin volunteer firemen won the competition, earning the title of the Champion Hook and Ladder Company of Texas. In Waco, a champagne supper was held in honor of their victory and on their return to Austin on May 10, they celebrated with a torchlight parade and a second champagne supper in the banquet room over Charles Cortissoz's grocery store and saloon on the northwest corner of Cyprus (3rd Street) and Nueces Streets.[29]

In May of 1878, there was a whisper of Billy Thompson's whereabouts when he had a short visit to Dodge City, Kansas.[30] Perhaps he reacquainted himself with the recently elected Ford County Sheriff Bat Masterson before returning to Fort Worth at the end of the month. The "Judicial" column of the *Fort Worth Democrat* on May 28 confirmed Billy's location and condition, reporting that Billy had been fined $3.00 and costs for being "drunk and down." Another arrest, this time for illegally carrying a six-shooter, would later confirm Billy remained in Fort Worth through much of the summer of 1878.[31]

Ben's time in Fort Worth ended after the fireman's drill competition in Waco and by early June, he was back in his hometown of Austin, where he returned to selling raffle chances to raise cash. The Hope No. 2 fire company elected him again to represent them, this time at the State Fire Association of Texas convention in Galveston from June 12 to June 15. Prior to leaving for the convention, Ben offered a raffle "of a beautiful seven stone diamond pin and an elegant gold watch and chain." These expensive items created a considerable amount of interest and were put on display at Michael's Saloon. Saturday night, June 8, he cashed in on the raffle, and on Monday he was on his way to Galveston with the other elected representatives of his fire company, some of whom were known to be his closest friends: Congress Avenue bookseller J. A. Nagle, livery and stable owner Monroe Miller, and Travis County Sheriff Dennis Corwin.

In Galveston, the city organized a grand reception complete with a brass band and a uniformed honor guard made up of the Washington Militia to honor the fire company delegates arriving from the many participating cities and towns throughout the Lone Star State.[32] The volunteer firemen paraded to the venue of their assembly, the Turner Hall on Avenue I, built by the Turnvere who were German political refugees who settled in Texas in the 1850s. The Turnvere believed in physical education in schools, especially gymnastics. One of their principal purposes was caring for the sick and needy and they built halls throughout Texas to promote culture and to provide locales for dramatic and musical entertainment. Fittingly, they founded several of the very first volunteer fire departments in Texas. The assembly was shocked when two delegates from a San Antonio "Colored" fire company bravely presented their credentials and asked to attend the proceedings. A special committee was formulated to consider their admittance and the committee hurriedly denied their participation at the convention. The decision was the unqualified sentiment of the fire delegates, as the vote was almost unanimous. One delegate spoke to the assembly and explained the rejection was not due to "prejudice, hatred or malice but purely a social one and with expressions of genuine affection" and it was hoped that in the near future the colored fire companies might organize throughout the state in sufficient numbers to justify a convention of their own. The last order of business for the gathering was to select Houston as the host city for the 1879 convention.[33]

It was very desirable for a professional gambler to wear a lawman's badge on America's western frontier. Being armed and having legal authority was usually enough to encourage a disgruntled loser to move along without too much trouble. Following an old and popular custom in Austin, Billy Simms succeeded in getting hold of a badge and the legal right to carry a firearm. He applied to an unidentified Justice of the Peace, informing the officer he knew the whereabouts of a particular wanted man and, if authorized as a special deputy sheriff, he would go forth and make the arrest. The *Statesman* stated the type of man who usually receives a commission, thereafter "claims to be a deputy sheriff or an officer of some sort ... but he never acts ... [instead,] goes howling about with a big six-shooter buckled to him" and accomplishes very little in providing any law and order.[34]

Two friends, Nat Davidson and Tom Dorn, accompanied Simms on the little manhunt and the trio were soon on the road to San Antonio. At the town of Selma, about fifteen miles east of the Alamo City, the wagon the three men were riding in suffered a broken tongue while crossing the Cibolo stream. Simms jumped down, soiling his clothes. All of the men were intoxicated and Nat Davidson began to laugh at him, prompting Simms to pull out his six-shooter and continue the good times by emptying his pistol after his fleeing friend. Dorn handed over his weapon, and Simms sent more slugs after the running Davidson. The gunfire disturbed the good people of Selma who were attending their Sunday church service, and they found the unrestrained gunfire less than amusing. Simms and Dorn were arrested. Dorn was charged with abetting an assault with intent to kill. Simms was bound in the amount of $500 to insure his appearance at the next session of court. The charges were later dropped, when at an examination hearing, it was learned the incident was only a "freak of fun."[35] Travis County Sheriff Dennis Corwin let it be known he had nothing to do with giving Simms a position. The *Statesman* printed on August 4, 1878, that it was "understood that Sheriff Corwin did not commission Billy Sims [*sic*] as a deputy sheriff. The authority was extended by a justice of the peace." This comment published by the *Statesman* gives an indication that a legally armed Billy Simms walking the streets of Austin upset many of the town's citizens. Coincidentally, this was the point that Simms's relationship with Thompson became strained, and Billy Simms faced the crisis of dealing with an upset Ben Thompson for the first time.

Johnny Lunsford, a prominent newspaper reporter on staff at the *San Antonio Light* in the 1880s, later wrote that Simms "was a sort of protégé of Thompson" and that when Thompson embarked on the gambling business in Austin, "he induced Simms to join him and both soon were recognized as expert gamblers of cool nerve and daring wagers."[36] In all likelihood, it was Simms who felt he could do even better on his own and soon broke off his business arrangement with Thompson. In 1878, James B. Gillett returned to his hometown of Austin after serving a tour with the Texas Rangers.

Gillett saw two of his old schoolmates and inquired about Billy Simms. His friends informed him that Simms had been run out of town by Ben Thompson and was now living in San Antonio. They explained that Thompson and Simms had been running rival keno games, and that Simms was getting the better play. Ben's response to this loss of business was to load his revolver and visit Simms's place. When he walked in, he "pulled his pistol and shot up the keno goose all to pieces and broke up the game." Gillett explained, "So to avoid trouble Sims [*sic*] probably thought it best to leave Austin." All accounts agree that Billy Simms decided to move on and he was off to seek his fortune in San Antonio.[37]

The bell tower of the old San Fernando Cathedral still looks down upon the town's Main Plaza. The cathedral is located at the exact center of the Alamo City, and in the second half of the nineteenth century, dozens of less holy structures surrounded this church. The plaza was lined with saloons, gambling dens, and brothels that attracted many adventurous men. This is where Billy Simms headed to when he arrived in town. He sought out and at once found employment with saloonkeepers Hiram Mitchell and Frank Wallace. They hired him to work their club room, which was situated on the southeast corner of Market Street at Main Plaza.[38] Jack Harris's Vaudeville Theatre loomed directly across the unpaved plaza on the northeast corner. It wasn't long before Simms moved across the plaza and allied himself with one of the most powerful behind-the-scenes players in San Antonio politics.[39] Jack Harris had a financial interest in the theatre and the downstairs saloon. Harris also ran the second floor gambling hall with his partner and veteran gambler, Joe Foster. Though never elected to office, the *San Antonio Light* claimed, "it is a well-known fact that Harris controlled the sporting fraternity so far as their influence upon our city and county politics was concerned, and that his liberality, shrewdness, and tact made him the real leader of the

Democratic Party." The *Light* article continued, Harris "held his influence unimpaired for years" and actually "dictated in a very quiet way who should receive the favor of the party. Thus he obtained for his fraternity almost immunity from the law. There is no city officer, and hardly a county officer, that does not owe his office to this man's influence."[40]

On Saturday night, August 10, Ben Thompson was out on the town with his friend Tom Greene, who was visiting from Little Rock, Arkansas. The pair unintentionally provided an amusing memory for many of the people on Congress Avenue. The two sporting men had planned a buggy ride for part of the evening. The ride's dual purpose was to exercise and exhibit "the noble steed which [was] advertised to be raffled." Luckily the horse showed the desirable "quality of behaving himself beautifully" when one of the wheels failed. Otherwise, the two men might have been severely injured if the horse had panicked and gone rampaging down the avenue, but Thompson and Greene were merely tossed out of the vehicle and onto the street. The *State*sman in a mirth-filled comment reported, "They made a bad calculation as to the capacity of the buggy ... they were not injured ... not a bone was broken, nor an eyebrow cut; but beaver hats, hand prints, pint flasks, etc., marked the spot where they rolled upon the ground, and the amount of laughing done by those who witnessed the ground and lofty tumbling, we shall not pretend to describe." The raffle went on uninterrupted and the newspaper concluded that there is "nothing like luck after all."[41]

On Wednesday, November 6, at 8 p.m. at a variety theatre, Ben Thompson returned to his seat only to find John F. Allen occupying it. Surprisingly, Ben received a rude reply from Allen when told to relinquish the seat. Picking up a nearby chair, Ben struck Allen over the head. The police did nothing to intervene and word of the assault reached the ears of Mayor Jacob C. DeGress, who proceeded to the theatre intent on arresting Thompson. Several contemporary accounts state the tough and fearless mayor hit Thompson with his heavy cane, and one account went as far as to write that the mayor struck him on the head. Another newspaper stated that Mayor DeGress knocked a pistol from Thompson's hand.[42] A third more logical version, written years later, described how the mayor successfully disarmed Thompson with only his words and determination: "DeGress marched up to arrest him, Thompson covered him with his revolver saying if he approached he would kill him." Disregarding the threat, the mayor continued up to Thompson, stating, "it is my duty to arrest you and I will do it." DeGress then disarmed him and placed Ben under arrest. "Thompson saw he must kill an officer in the lawful discharge of his duty, or submit to an arrest; he did the latter."[43]

On the evening of November 11, with their six-shooters drawn, three men entered Ben Thompson's well-known Congress Avenue gambling room. Surprising Ben's gambling partner Augustus Lorraine and two patrons, they relieved the three men of their pistols, watches, and the $400 in Lorraine's gaming bank. Ben Thompson stored his revolver engraved with his name in the gambling room, and that was also stolen. The thieves tied Lorraine and his customers up, then quietly stepped out onto the Avenue and easily "skipped" out of town.[44] The robbery was part of an ongoing crime spree which included other armed robberies in Travis County, and neighboring Williamson County. The robbers struck at Wayman's store in Circleville, and at E. P. Robinson's hardware shop in Round Rock. The gang also robbed an affluent Travis County farmer known as "Old Man" Jordan of $500. At least one witness in Austin recognized the trio and informed the authorities of their identity.[45]

Mayor DeGress's arrest of Ben Thompson was only the start of many legal troubles for Ben during November 1878. The Grand

Jury of Travis County indicted Ben Thompson, Cause 5737, and placed a warrant for his arrest in the hands of Sheriff Dennis Corwin charging him with assault with intent to murder. The man he allegedly attacked was John Farrell, one of the few witnesses who traveled to Galveston to testify in the fatal shooting of Mark Wilson at the Capital Theatre. Perhaps Thompson was displeased with Farrell's testimony. Sheriff Corwin arrested Thompson on Saturday, November 23, and bail was posted the same day.[46] He needed to be set free immediately for two special reasons. First, this was his youngest sister's wedding day. Twenty-year-old Francis "Fanny" Thompson married Leo R. Fink in Bastrop, and they would make their home in New Ulm, Austin County.[47] Second, Ben and his wife Kate would be celebrating their fifteenth wedding anniversary with their two children, ten-year-old Benjamin Jr. and almost seven-year-old Katie three days later on November 26.

The robbery of his Congress Avenue gambling room may have brought unwanted attention. In the days following his sister's wedding, Thompson was forced to turn his thoughts to the eight indictments issued earlier by the Travis County Grand Jury. He was subsequently charged with five indictments for "keeping a gambling bank," one for "aggravated assault and battery" and one for "carrying a pistol."[48] Out of necessity, Thompson was becoming quite an expert in dealing with the court system of Travis County and the City of Austin.[49]

Lawmen caught up to the gang of robbers in Houston. John Willis and Sam Johnson were jailed. The third culprit, Henry Darlington, succeeded in drawing his revolver and wounding a Houston police officer before he was fatally wounded. A fourth man named Lockwood, who was with Darlington also resisted, however he was successfully overpowered and placed under arrest. The engraved pistols and watches taken from their victims were in their possession. At the time of their arrest, it was believed they were planning a bank robbery or perhaps another robbery of a gambling hall, this time in Houston. Willis, Darlington, and Lockwood had been raised in Travis County, and John Willis was identified as a son of one of the Willis brothers who were taken from Confederate military custody and lynched in Austin in broad daylight. Sheriff Corwin placed the suspects in the Travis County jail where they were held for trial until the Fall 1879 session of the District Court.[50]

Three weeks after Ben Thompson's indictment for assault with intent to murder, cause 5737, the District Court disclaimed jurisdiction and transferred the case to the County Court. Ben Thompson pled guilty to a lesser charge of "simple assault" for his attack on John Farrell, and decided to serve out the $50 fine rather than pay it. The court committed him to the care of his friend Sheriff Corwin. It seems doubtful Ben Thompson shared a cell with John Willis or any other member of his gang.[51]

John C. Bacon, a former printer turned itinerant newspaper correspondent, found himself in Austin. Bacon was known for writing "spicy" commentaries. He decided to send a letter to the *San Antonio Courier* providing a decidedly different view of Ben as compared to the flattering articles which earlier appeared in the *Globe-Democrat* of St. Louis and the *New York World*. Bacon declared, "The city of Austin, capital of the Great State of Texas, with its admirable corps of efficient police, etc., and troops of law-abiding citizens, is actually terrorized by a desperado of the Hardin-Bass-Longley stripe, who has deliberately assassinated several men, and 'amuses' himself whenever he chooses to fill up with liquor, by shooting out lights at public entertainments and intimidating peaceful citizens on the streets!" Continuing his denunciation, Bacon wrote, "Strange as it may appear—humiliating as it is—this brutal, lawless, drunken fellow, finds his greatest delight in such actions, in defiance of law, and he defies arrest! On one occasion

Mayor DeGress felt impelled to crack him over the head, when Thompson gave vent to the following expression: 'Hoope-ee! Who the h-ell cares? It only costs $1,600 [in legal costs] to kill a man, anyhow." It is well-known how the "Austin's police are afraid of this bold gambolier,[52] simply because he is a dead shot with a pistol." The citizenry, "timid" as can be, "excuse the desperado's acts by pointing to his little acts of kindness to several unfortunate persons of the city. What an excuse for violation of law!" Bacon ended his open letter to the public by pointing out how greased palms allow Thompson to earn his unlawful living. "The fair association, in view of his popularity, graciously accepted five hundred dollars of this desperado for a permit to run his little robbing games in plain view of the racing arena, and in flagrant violation of the law against gaming."

Shortly after the *Courier* published Bacon's letter on Thursday, November 28, it was reprinted in San Antonio's *Daily Express.*[53] Bacon wisely left Austin for San Antonio after the article's publication. A fellow newspaperman's commentary soon followed: "No sooner did Ben Thompson get a copy of the San Antonio sheet containing this diatribe upon his virtues than he concluded to go for John C.'s bacon. Ben sued for libel. It is funny of Ben Thompson to invoke the law to protect his fame, but he is a pious, good citizen now and says he will nevermore strike till stricken, and he intends to make an example of Bacon."[54]

True to his word, he sued Mr. Bacon for libel, and a warrant for Bacon's arrest was sent to Bexar County Sheriff Thomas P. McCall, who took Bacon into custody on Friday, December 13. Attorneys on Bacon's behalf placed an application of *habeas corpus* into the hands of Bexar County Judge Felix Smith. A hearing took place on Monday morning, December 16. The arrest warrant was determined to be defective in form since it was not formally signed by the issuing District Judge of Travis County. Bacon was remanded to jail until the warrant was properly prepared. Notice of appeal was filed by Bacon's attorneys Messrs. Tarleton and Hertz. Conversely, Bacon talked of suing the San Antonio officials for malicious prosecution and false imprisonment. The *San Antonio Express* had its fun, "Bacon is being cured in the county jail," but admitted, "to put a man in jail for a libel is not of daily occurrence, and the result will be closely watched, not only by our people, but by the press all over the country."[55]

Judge Smith found the second warrant from Travis County as defective as the original and ordered John C. Bacon released from jail.[56] Not giving up on bringing Bacon to Austin to answer for libel Ben Thompson issued "a fresh capias" to which the *Statesman* claimed, "San Antonio is in a stew about it."[57] In fact, the *San Antonio Express* reported, "Ben Thompson runs [Austin] to suit himself, and that the police officers of Austin are Ben's agents in this matter."[58] Bacon's legal counsel placed an attachment on Thompson's latest warrant demanding he must travel to San Antonio and appear in court. First indicating he would comply, Ben Thompson and the Austin authorities chose to ignore three subsequent writs from San Antonio. After spending weeks in the Bexar County jail, Bacon was released on Saturday evening, January 11, 1879, on a $150 personal recognizance to answer the charge in Austin's district court.[59] The hearing for libel never took place, once freed, John C. Bacon fled to the safety of Mexico.[60]

As the Bacon case was unfolding on January 6, Austin's volunteer firemen of the Hope Hook and Ladder Company No. 2 voted Ben Thompson to be their president.[61] Other legal matters drew Thompson's attention. On the same day he was elected president of the fire company, he pled guilty to four causes in the county court, and the following day six additional causes were dismissed. Fines totaled $100 plus court costs, and Ben was placed in jail until the fine was paid or time served.[62]

Four months after he left central Texas for Mexico, John C. Bacon sent a letter addressed to his attorney, from the City of Las Aguas Calientes. The *San Antonio Daily Express* published it. "This is written for your information as to my whereabouts, and for that should my particular friends inquire for me." Bacon explained, "I had a very rough time getting through, but finally made it. I crossed the Rio Grande [and] you can imagine with what joy I pressed the soil of Mexico after having been prosecuted and insulted for speaking but the truth, and not all of it, either." Bacon asked, "I want you to write me what has been done in my case, how the whole matter stands, and what is the prevailing public sentiment in regard to my change of base." He despaired of justice in the courts of Texas and that is why he crossed over into Mexico. He ended his letter with a flourish, "Yours, in love, the great dead-despaired busted, but undismayed. BACON."[63]

Chapter 11

HIRED GUN

"Austin will not lose this opportunity to distinguish itself."

—*San Antonio Daily Express*, October 9, 1879

In early February 1879, stories about Leadville's vast mineral wealth began to pique Ben Thompson's interest, and a rumor circulated in Austin that Ben, with his friend Frank Cotton and other members of the sporting crowd, were thinking of making an excursion to this "El Dorado of silver" in Colorado's Rocky Mountains.[1] At this time in the nearby town of Bastrop, thirty miles southeast of Austin, Ben Thompson purchased property across the street from the courthouse with the thought of building a home on the lot.[2] Though Ben and his family lived in a house on College Avenue at the east end of the Austin city limits,[3] he had strong ties to Bastrop. His sister Mary Jane, her husband Robert Gill, and their children made their home there with Ben's mother, Mary Ann Thompson.

Ben continued to put off his talked about trip to Leadville. As president of the Hope Hook and Ladder Company No. 2, Ben promoted and raffled off a horse at Julius P. Michael's Cattle Exchange

Saloon. The proceeds went to the benefit of the fire company. "Throwing a forty-six," Julius Michael won the horse and generously donated the animal back to the very grateful volunteer firemen.[4]

In early March, Ben Thompson and fellow gambler Frank Cotton made their start for Leadville.

East of the Continental Divide, and at the headwaters of the Arkansas River, placer gold was discovered in 1859, and the mining district was named California Gulch. Since the gold deposit was easily recovered, the majority of it was exhausted very quickly. A few small gold claims were still being worked into the middle of the 1870s. Even though silver was usually found to be plentiful around most Colorado gold discoveries, no one was looking for it at California Gulch. Veteran miner Will Stevens realized the potential for the presence of silver to exist there. He tested the seemingly worthless black sand with a geologist named A. B. Wood, who was also his friend and partner. Said sand was really carbonate of lead, and after additional testing, learned it contained $40 worth of silver per ton. This seemed worthy of further investigation, so Stevens and Wood traced the source on their claim and pinpointed a vein ten feet thick. This was an enormous discovery. Word soon leaked out and the rush was on.

The first and highest valley of the Arkansas River stands almost two miles above sea level, and extends ten miles long and three miles wide. This valley sat atop one of the most easily obtainable and valuable deposits of lead and silver on earth. Leadville was officially named in January 1878, and more than five thousand frenzied miners, businessmen, and adventurers arrived in time for the summer mining season. Newspapers around the country promoted the value of the mineral production in 1878. The deposit had already produced a phenomenal $2.5 million, and the big discoveries had yet to be made. The growth of the town and the mining district was only limited by the lack of lumber and how fast the mules hauling the freight wagons full of goods and people could cross over the high mountain passes. By the start of 1879, an estimated two thousand teamsters were hard at work.

Ben Thompson wrote a letter to the editors of the *Statesman* from Denver on March 11, and a second letter from Leadville was published on March 26 (see Appendix B). Ben informed his friends in Austin that he arrived in the boomtown and described the trip in detail. "A day or two after writing ... from Denver we started for this place where we arrived a week ago. ... Our trip out on the Denver and South Park Railroad [was] about seventy miles, and seven dollars fare, was very pleasant." This short-trunk railroad enjoyed a part of Leadville's boom as people and goods rode the narrow-gauge track to the next relay station where freight wagons and stagecoaches took over. Ben Thompson and Frank Cotton went through the Webster relay shipping station. There they boarded a passenger stage and were forced to ship their trunks via a freight wagon. Thompson described how all the trees looked dead and blanketed in snow as if it were mid-winter on one side of the mountain valley, while the other side was full of green pine trees similar to the hills above Austin in the summer time. A snowstorm hit three miles out of Webster, but the stage kept rolling until 11 p.m. when it arrived in the town of Fairplay, which was set on the grassland basin known as South Park. The next morning, more than one hundred passengers paid a $10 fare and boarded the stages bound for Leadville. When the timberline was reached, the stage stopped for a noon dinner. By 2 p.m., it began the final run into Leadville. Ben described his first impression of the town.

> I never want to cross the range again ... as we started down the wagon, horses and all come near going over an embankment several hundred feet high, so we got out and walked about seven miles before the outfit overtook us. About 9 o'clock that evening Leadville was sighted and you bet that Frank Cotton and I was glad of it. Nothing that has been

> written, so far as I can judge, is any exaggeration. The mines around this place must be the richest ever before discovered; that is what all the old California miners and gamblers say about them. ... It is impossible to describe this City fully. It is a City of ten or fifteen thousand inhabitants, of which about twenty-five hundred are ladies.[5]

When Fort Worth's March 29 issue of the *Daily Democrat* quoted Ben's estimate on the number of women in Leadville, the editor quipped, "Ben ought to know."

> Leadville has water works and is soon to have gass [*sic*] and a street railroad. Several churches and schools are already in operation; also two variety establishments and a theatre. One variety man pays for his house seventeen hundred dollars per month rent and at least two thousand a week for performers. He takes in about six or seven hundred a night for drinks at five dollars a bottle in the conversational parlors, where the visitors are entertained by the lady performers. Of gambling houses it is useless to speak as there is so many and all so crowded you cannot pass through them morning till morning as they never close. Houses for sporting and saloon business rent for five to ten hundred per month, which shuts out all chances for legitimate business, as most anything you want is nearly as cheap here as in any frontier town in Texas.[6]

A number of Texans from Galveston were in Leadville attempting to prospect or open a business. Several close friends of the Thompson brothers were among them: Joe Owens, who helped Billy escape Laredo after Ben's Civil War gambling hall shootout, and J. H. F. Chapmen, one of Ben's bondsmen from the Mark Wilson murder trial. Owens planned to open a freighting business.[7]

> It has been snowing all day, and in fact it has snowed every few hours since our arrival, still the sun shines nearly all the time and we don't suffer any from the cold. In fact I never felt better in my life than since my stay here.[8] Men with money or machinery can come here and make all the money they want in six months, and not take many chances, all others had better stay away until some time about the last

> of May or the first of June ... There is at present several thousand brooken [*sic*] men that cannot find work, nor will there be any for them to do until the snow is off the ground, and then there will be work for all. Frank Cotton and I will stick it out ... for a few months. We do not advise any of our friends to come out here under six weeks except those who have plenty of means to go into business.[9]

Thompson did not "stick it out" in Leadville and after a mere ten days, he left for home. One newspaper reported on Ben's time in Leadville, "Ben Thompson, who is well known around Austin as a professional "gam," has been doing Leadville in his old familiar style, but does not seem to have played it quite so successfully as he sometimes did in Texas. Ben never was known to labor very industriously, except with his thumb and forefinger, when pulling cards from the box behind the faro table, or sitting in front wrestling with the 'tiger.'" The article recounted how Ben went broke one night in a Leadville gambling hall forcing him to head for home.[10]

A young man from San Antonio wrote the *Daily Express* offering confirmation in greater detail, or perhaps greater exaggeration, as to why Thompson returned so quickly to Austin. "Ben Thompson, of Austin, lost $2,000, his diamond pin or stud, worth $800, his ring, $500, and his watch and chain, $300, at faro, on the night of March 21st, and borrowed money from a friend to go back home on." The following evening he lost all self-control and "drank his first glass of whiskey here, finally got drunk, turned over all the gambling tables in the saloon, shot out the lights, cleaned out the crowd, knocked down one man with his six-shooter, and then took his Winchester and cleared the street." As for the conclusion of this public tirade, the San Antonian ended his report writing that, Thompson "is under bond" and due to an extreme hangover, "Ben is not very well, either."[11]

On Friday, March 25, Ben sent a dispatch to Austin announcing that he was leaving Colorado.[12] A second man from San Antonio, having been a witness to Thompson's behavior in Leadville, downplayed Ben's troubles there saying they "have been of no particular note."[13] Realizing his friends and acquaintances would be greatly interested in learning about Leadville, he brought back photographs of the town, various samples of the lead carbonate, and a number of books providing information about the Colorado mining districts and mining laws. He placed all of these items on display at the Occidental Saloon, and via the local newspapers, the owner of the saloon, Charles Cortissoz, sent out an open house invitation as a way for the public to talk to Ben about his experiences, and inspect the photos, books and ore samples.[14]

While his big brother Ben was in Leadville, Billy Thompson was in Dodge City, Kansas. Curiously, John Montgomery of the Ellsworth *Reporter* printed an old story he picked up in which a desperado named Ben Gladdon fired three times and killed William Thompson over a woman in a Waco, Texas saloon. Montgomery, not realizing the wrong William Thompson of Austin, Texas was killed, wrote: "Thus died the murderer of Sheriff Whitney, who failed to get his just desserts in this county. He committed many murders; and he finally loses his life in a disgraceful quarrel with a man of his own stamp." In Dodge City, the *Ford County Globe* reprinted the erroneous account on March 11, but published a retraction two weeks later: "Not Dead. Mr. William Thompson, whom we reported as having been killed in Texas some weeks ago, made his appearance in Dodge last week. We do not insist upon his being dead."[15]

The ambitions of two rapidly expanding railroads: the Atchison, Topeka and Santa Fe running east to west and General William J. Palmer's smaller Denver and Rio Grande Railroad running north to south butted heads in Colorado, creating a right-of-way railroad war. The two railroads faced each other at a focal point of contention: the Royal Gorge, which was ten miles long and only thirty feet wide at its narrowest point. It was cut so razor-thin that only one set of tracks could possibly be laid through it. Obviously, the railroad that controlled this gorge would gain access to the booming silver mining district of Leadville. From southeastern Colorado, both railroads raced to build tracks at the mouth of the gorge.

At first they sabotaged each other by cutting telegraph wires and stealing equipment and supplies. They also clogged the courts by filing an overabundance of subpoenas, petitions, and injunctions. Their argument had grown more serious by the winter of 1879 and continued to escalate through the following spring. Armed men set up earthen breastworks holding back rival tracklayers and these men occasionally took pot shots at surveyors, causing them to run for cover.

The Atchison, Topeka and Santa Fe Company's round-house and adjoining buildings and equipment were in South Pueblo. This was the most vital section of the line. The company that held this key to the Royal Gorge would control the riches of Leadville.

Officials of the Atchison, Topeka and Santa Fe Railroad sent a telegram on Thursday, March 25, to Dodge City, Kansas, addressed to twenty-five-year-old Ford County Sheriff Bat Masterson requesting he recruit a posse to guard the railroad's workmen, property, and access to the gorge. The railroad felt it needed a man "said to be cool, decisive and a 'bad man' with a pistol." Sheriff Masterson, who had recently been sworn in as a Deputy United States Marshal, was joined by thirty-three men. By Saturday, all were aboard a special train bound for the mouth of the gorge at Canon City, Colorado.[16] For two weeks, Masterson's heavily armed company "had an easy time of it, nothing to do, plenty of chuck and $3 a day from the railroad company." A decisive legal decision had not yet been made, so taking advantage of the lull and with several other members of his "posse," Sheriff Masterson returned to Dodge City leaving his Deputy John Joshua Webb, who would eventually become an outlaw, in command.[17]

Tragedy struck a close friend of Ben and Billy Thompson back in Taylorsville, Texas, a town south of Austin. After darkness fell, someone snuck up to Neil Cain's bedroom window and fired a shot at him. Cain was sleeping in the same bed as his wife and children, and that single shot caused a fatal wound that he suffered through for two days before succumbing. The killer left no clues, and no one was ever accused of the murder, nor did anyone ever admit to the killing, though his murder was apparently revenge for supplying information that led to the arrest of the robber gang consisting of John Willis, Sam Johnson, and Henry Darlington in Houston. Darlington resisted arrest and was killed. Pointing at Cain's reputation for throwing a long rope, the *Statesman* bitingly commented that with the killing of Cain "the stock business is looking up in this corner of creation."[18]

A handful of Austin's sporting men decided they would travel to Leadville during the first week of May and the *Statesman* predicted, "They will 'shuffle' things up lively when they get to Colorado." Zeno Hemphill and Tom Bowles, who was Ben Thompson's old partner along with Phil Coe in an Austin Saloon following the Civil War, set out for Leadville on May 6. Thompson expected to leave for the mining district the next day with his friend Bill Johnson and his brother-in-law Jim Moore.[19] If Ben Thompson was planning a return to Leadville, he changed his mind and chose instead to go to Dodge City, Kansas.

Eddie Foy, the famed variety and stage performer, his partner Jim Thompson, and their troupe played many engagements in Dodge City, and were well-known there. By his own account, he was in town during the Colorado railroad strife, and he remembered how he was "offered the opportunity to enlist as a hired gun." Foy stated that because the Santa Fe was "our own road,"

Dodge City was sympathetic to their efforts to reach Leadville, and "Doc Holiday [*sic*] suggested that I join them." Foy demurred and told Holliday that he was no fighter. Doc replied it didn't matter, the railroad would not know the difference, it would swell the gang, and he would still be paid. Foy declined to join up, despite Doc's disappointment in him, and remained in Dodge City instead. However he did stay apprised of the events in Colorado. Foy called Ben Thompson "a Texas man and a dangerous character who made his home for a while among us," still, Foy acknowledged him as one of the leaders of the expedition. On May 20, deputy sheriff John Joshua Webb returned to Dodge City accompanied by one of his men suffering from rheumatism, and while in town, he spoke with a reporter from the *Ford County Globe*. Webb stated that "the Dodge City boys doing well and taking their hash regular ... they have done no fighting yet, but the difficulties between the two roads are by no means settled. The Denver & Rio Grande have a force of men stationed on the line of the proposed route, several miles ahead of the A. T. & S. F. workmen, who are gradually nearing the enemy." Before taking the morning train back to Colorado,[20] Webb predicted that when the opposing groups of men met, "then comes the tug of war."

In essence, the legal battle centered on a lease General Palmer signed in 1878 with the A. T. & S. F. Company granting the Denver and Rio Grande the road through the Royal Gorge for thirty years. In March 1879, Palmer began the legal fight anew and he argued in court that the A. T. & S. F. did not live up to the terms of the lease. As a remedy, he asked the court to void the agreement and allow only his Denver & Rio Grande Railroad the exclusive right to use the gorge.[21] The Colorado Springs *Weekly Gazette*, the voice of the Denver & Rio Grande, listed many of the abuses the A. T. & S. F. kept committing: "The Atchison company is assuming all together too much power to itself in this state. Apparently no citizen or other corporation have any rights. It … runs the local road regardless of schedule time and the convenience of the public, it delays mails, sometimes … it runs no trains, it defames the judiciary if it is likely to decide against it. It revises the telegraph messages on the Western Union line and decides which may go through, it keeps a standing army to resist the courts, it hires sheriffs not to do their duty, and performs various other illegal and arbitrary acts. Its whole influence in the state during the past six months has been corrupting and lawless. It is time the state officers did something to relieve the people and vindicate the law."[22]

The case went to the Fourth Judicial District Court of Colorado, with the Honorable Thomas M. Bowen presiding. On Saturday, June 7, the lawyers for the two railroads ended their arguments before Judge Bowen and when asked by attorneys representing the A. T. & S. F. when he would reach a decision, Bowen informed them, "I can't tell. I am going to take my own time … I am going to write a full opinion in the case, so I will not be misunderstood, and it will be some time before I can do it."[23] In anticipation of a negative decision from Judge Bowen, the Atchison, Topeka and Santa Fe Railroad, moved to keep their holdings in Colorado in their physical possession, and to repel a takeover from the Denver & Rio Grande—at least until a higher court ruled on their appeal. Possession was of the utmost importance, since the United States court was not in session and it would be months before an appeal would be called before its docket.[24] In response to another telegram from railroad officials, Sheriff Masterson opened a recruiting office in Dodge City. The promised pay must have been very alluring, because he had signed on enough volunteers within thirty minutes and an A. T. & S. F. engine pulling a single passenger car packed with heavily armed men clipped along at a speed of forty miles an hour westward to Colorado. Ben Thompson was considered the leader of the dozen or so Texans in Masterson's command. At first, he was leery of becoming involved in a quarrel between two corporations when a court of law had already offered a peaceful solution. But Thompson was finally persuaded, and he agreed to the sum of five thousand dollars to defend the railroad's property. He announced he would not become an outlaw, and insisted he would not shed the blood of officers of the law armed with due process.[25]

On Monday, June 9, as Bat Masterson and his five dozen mercenaries were on their way to South Pueblo, Judge Bowen issued an order in favor of the Denver & Rio Grande company. His writ of injunction ordered the Atchison, Topeka and Santa Fe railroad company and its "officers, agents, servants and employees to desist and refrain ... from using, maintaining, or operating ... the railway... of the ... Denver & Rio Grande ... at any city, town, or place in this state." All depots, shops, and offices were included in Judge Bowen's writ.[26]

The Atchison, Topeka and Santa Fe Railroad responded on three fronts: public opinion, the courtroom, and with armed men. As an instrument of the A. T. & S. F., the *Pueblo Chieftain* ceaselessly defamed Judge Bowen in its columns, stating how he "has been corrupted, is an unjust judge, and is no longer worthy to discharge the duties of that high office." The *Chieftain* sensationally asserted that Bowen "is steeped to the lips in corruption," and called for him to resign or for the state legislature to impeach him. The same day Bowen's writ was issued, the railroad's lawyers filed an appeal in Judge Moses Hallett's District Court of the United States for Colorado, Western Division.[27] They also protected the railroad property with armed men in West Denver, South Pueblo, and Canon City. Sheriff Masterson and his men were ordered to guard the train station, telegraph office, and railroad round-house in South Pueblo, the most essential point of the Atchison, Topeka & Santa Fe railway system. From the round-house, the tracks went northward into Denver and westward to Canon City, through the Royal Gorge and beyond to the rich Leadville mining district.[28]

General Palmer moved fast. Fearing a reversal of Judge Bowen's order by the Federal Court, Palmer placed printed copies of Bowen's writ into the hands of all county sheriffs up and down the rail line. They also provided plenty of hired gunmen to back the lawmen up. In Colorado Springs, Company B of the First Colorado Cavalry prepared to aid the local sheriff. On Tuesday, June 10, the Denver and Rio Grande forces moved at 6 a. m., and though blood was spilled wherever they met resistance, they took possession of all strategic points from the A. T. & S. F., including their general offices at West Denver. By 3 p. m., only the telegraph office and round-house in South Pueblo stood against General Palmer's D. & R.G. Railroad.[29]

At 6 a. m., Pueblo Sheriff Henly R. Price and his deputies started serving Bowen's writ of injunction to employees of the A. T. & S. F. and making formal demands for them to peacefully surrender. He granted a short time period for them to comply. Previously, he had sworn in one hundred and fifty citizens as deputy sheriffs. They were all armed with rifles or revolvers and each man identified himself as a deputy by wearing a printed badge on the lapel of his coat. For several hours, Sheriff Price remained patient before making a second demand at 10 a.m., which was met with an abrupt refusal. Attorneys for the A. T. & S. F. advised Masterson and his followers that the injunction issued by Judge Bowen had no validity, did not contain authorization for the use of force and that consequently, Sheriff Price had no authority to dispossess them of the facilities they occupied. In addition, the A. T. & S. F. officials fully expected Judge Moses Hallett to shortly reverse Bowen's writ. This strengthened the resolve of the volunteers, and they openly defied Price in the execution of the writ. Spectators filled the streets and covered the surrounding bluffs to watch what course of action Sheriff Price would choose. At 2:45 p.m., he decided he had to use force. On the way to the roundhouse, he first had to capture the telegraph and train dispatcher's office. A handful of shots were fired as Price's men burst through the front door. One of the Dodge City volunteers, Harry Jenkins, received a bullet wound as he was running out the back door. He was struck in the spine and was given medical assistance, but the two doctors attending him pronounced the wound fatal.[30]

The *Weekly Gazette* of Colorado Springs published an account matching the end result of the conflict at the South Pueblo round-house but varies greatly in details from other contemporary publications: "The telegraph office captured, the sheriff collected his little army and prepared to storm the round-house." The *Gazette* acknowledged, "The captain of the Hessians there, was one Thompson, from Austin, Texas, a very, *very* bad man indeed, one of the class which announces itself as a *terror* ... As the sheriff approached he came out of his citadel and fortifying his words with copious profanity defied the embassadors [*sic*] of the Rio Grande as Goliath defied the hosts of Israel. But even while he vaunted his prowess a couple of men stole conveniently near, and suddenly clapping a revolver in dangerous contiguity to his head assured him that his corpse would grace that campus if he endeavored to practice his belligerent theories." The newspaper gleefully proclaimed that Thompson showed himself a coward. "'For God's sake don't kill me!' whimpered the astute Texan Terror; and when the handcuffs were placed upon him he trembled like a leaf. Seeing the fall of their 'big-injin' chief, all the poorly paid 'little injins' filed out of the roundhouse and surrendered like sensible fellows. 'Thus peace and quiet reigned in Pueblo.'" The property damage was minor, and the unlucky Jenkins was the only fatality. "A few rails were torn up on the various lines out of Pueblo; a few telegraph poles chopped down; considerable money spent and bluster wasted; three or four men in the hospital and one in his coffin; thus ends the first day's record of actual hostilities in the railway war, and victory perches on the banners of the D. & R. G."

Other accounts are less entertaining than the *Gazette's* reporting. After overrunning the telegraph office, Sheriff Price and his deputies found the round-house to be easy prey. Confirming a portion of the *Gazette* article, Ben Thompson stepped outside and was quickly arrested without struggle, and after a short parley, those inside surrendered without firing a shot. Another account called him "Mr. Thomas, the city marshal of Dodge City," and declared that Ben put up somewhat of a fight, "tauntingly exclaimed: 'Come on, if you want a fight you can have it' ... the ball now opened. In an instant, the Dodge City marshal was seized by a dozen strong arms and was taken to the calaboose." Fisticuffs ensued, but the few A. T. & S. F. men outside the round-house were overpowered. The Dodge City men inside the round-house gave up after the capture of their leader. They handed over their weapons and meekly marched outside. Sheriff Price and his deputies celebrated by cheering their leaders, firing their guns into the air, ringing the train engine's bells and blowing its whistles. Their celebration was deafening.[31]

By night fall on Tuesday, June 10, the A. T. & S. F. had lost again when Federal Judge Moses Hallett declared he would not overrule Judge Bowen and his writ of injunction remained "unreversed and unchallenged." Proclaiming "Glorious Victory," the *Colorado Springs Weekly Gazette* called the collision between the two railroads a "the fight between foreign hirelings and Colorado citizens."[32] Two days after their surrender, Sheriff Masterson and his party returned by train from South Pueblo to Dodge City.[33] Vaudevillian Eddy Foy admitted the defeated gunmen's return was, "greatly to the disgust of certain citizens of Dodge who had been hoping that the home boys would be permitted to wipe the D. & R. G. off the map."[34]

Their handful of days in South Pueblo proved to be a very profitable venture for Masterson and Thompson. The amount they were paid varies by account, but Sheriff Masterson purchased a house in Dodge City shortly after his return. In August, Ben Thompson similarly moved to a new home in Austin, but it was believed he also used this cash windfall to open and establish a number of gambling rooms in various Texas towns. As to where the money may have come from, there were accusations of bribery and collusion. The treasurer of the Denver & Rio Grande Railroad Company, R. L. Weitbrec, was in South Pueblo, and he advised Sheriff Henly Price in his use of strategy in overcoming the A. T. & S. F. Railroad's hired guns. Twenty years later, a story was published implying that R. F. Weitbrec bought off Bat Masterson: "Mr. Weitbrec, it would appear, held the belief that a man who could be hired by an entire stranger to go out and slay people for a few dollars a day could be dealt with, and so he went over to the round-house to see Masterson, with the result that the men at the round-house abandoned their position." In reality, a payoff was hardly necessary. Faced with a hundred and fifty armed men, and an officer of the law armed with a judge's lawful writ, Masterson wisely decided not to resist a legal order, and surrendered without firing a shot. In his biography of Ben Thompson, Walton mentions a bribe of $25,000 being offered to Thompson to step aside, and give up the round-house. "It was more money than he ever had at one time and offered a life of independence and comfort for his wife and children [and] he … could abandon his irregular and dangerous life, and engage in some legitimate and reputable pursuit." Per Walton, Thompson's answer to the bribe offer was simple, "I will die here unless the law relieves me." Ben Thompson followed his own earlier stipulation, and offered no resistance when Judge Bowen's writ was served by Sheriff Price.[35] It was later reported in several Texas newspapers that Thompson received $5,000 from the A. T. & S. F.

Other newspapers stated the true amount he was paid was $2,300 along with several diamonds, an item quite popular among sporting men.[36]

In Dodge City, vaudevillians Eddie Foy and his partner Jimmie Thompson, "that unequalled and splendidly matched team," often performed at the Comique, packing the house night after night.[37] One evening, either at the Comique or a similar venue, Eddie Foy was applying his makeup behind some backstage scenery temporarily being used as a makeshift dressing room when Ben Thompson "about two-thirds drunk blundered in." Foy called Thompson, "the Texas scrapper," and said, "Thompson was not highly popular in Dodge, Bat Masterson being one of his few friends." Staggering behind the stage, Ben saw Foy and drew his revolver, demanding that Foy get out of the way because he was going to shoot out an oil lamp on the makeup table. Foy's head was between the lamp and Thompson. Per Foy, "Thompson didn't like me, possibly because he knew I didn't like him." Foy was seized with a sudden flush of obstinacy, and he decided, "he wasn't going to move his head just because a drunken bum like Thompson wanted to shoot out a lamp." With a look of impudence, Foy slowly turned his head to look Thompson squarely in the eyes to show the gunman he was not afraid. Threatening that he would put a bullet through Foy's head, Thompson raised his revolver and aimed. The two men confronted each other for a long moment until Bat Masterson busted in, pushed Thompson's pistol upward, and began pushing and coaxing him until he had Thompson out of the dressing area. When they had gone, Foy noticed his hands were shaking and he could not finish putting on his makeup. He admitted he was "limp for the rest of the evening."[38]

Foy proceeded to analyze why Thompson didn't shoot, "Of course his chief desire was not to kill me but to scare me—to show me up as a tenderfoot and a weakling. But when I chose to play the daredevil, it's a wonder his trigger thumb didn't act out of sheer annoyance. Of course I'd have been, in a way, rather small game for him." Foy wrote that there was little to add to such a deadly reputation, especially for killing "that ... ham actor named Foy who was around here last summer and sorter got on my nerves."[39]

Ben left Dodge City by rail, and passed through Kansas City and St. Louis on his way to his hometown. Billy Thompson returned with his brother from South Pueblo to Dodge City, where they separated. Billy traveled on to Ogallala, Nebraska, a small town on the Platte River. At that time, Ogallala was a rising star in the Texas cattle market because of its Union Pacific Railroad connection to the stockyards of St Louis and Chicago. Texas cattleman James C. Shaw and former Texas Ranger David Ligon ran into Billy Thompson in Ogallala when they entered a saloon and came upon him sitting at a poker table. Billy had a white-handled revolver situated on top of a pile of cash and was less than pleased to look up and see David Ligon. Ligon was one of Captain Sparks's men, and he was the former Travis County jail guard who went to the sheriff's residence and found the extra set of jail keys that allowed for Billy's transfer to Ellsworth, Kansas. Warning Ligon that he would kill him, Billy said, "I'll give you ten minutes to get out of here." Ligon and Shaw proceeded to hastily get out of town.[40]

Billy's friend, John King Fisher, was a thousand miles due south from Ogallala in the Nueces River valley, commonly known as the Nueces Strip. In July 1879, Fisher was again on the prod having been cleared of all earlier murder and cattle rustling charges.[41] In response to an article he was unhappy with, Fisher penned a note to the editors of the *San Antonio Daily Express* and in it he explained himself and his motives: "As for being a desperado, all I can say is that I have never killed a man unless it was in self-defense or in defense of my property, and I have very little respect for anyone who would not do the same."[42]

The house Ben Thompson selected for his family stood at the southwest corner of San Antonio Street and Linden (17th street), about a half a mile northwest of the Texas State Capitol Building. They took possession of their new home during the third week of August 1879.[43] Similar to the other homes they lived in, it was well away from the barrooms along Congress Avenue near Pecan Street (6th) and the city's disreputable First Ward. Thompson was always careful to keep his wife and children far from the haunts he could never stay away from for long. Throughout the end of the summer of 1879, the local newspapers chronicled some of Ben Thompson's activities as a sporting man. By early August, he was back to gambling and was arrested on eight counts of the usual gaming charges. He pled guilty to two charges and paid the fines. The other charges were continued and later dismissed.[44]

At this time, Ben appeared in the newspapers for a number of different reasons. On a hunch, Ben offered $500 to a Mr. M. Brahl for his Louisiana lottery ticket. Brahl owned a tobacco shop located on Congress Avenue at Bois d' Arc (7th). Thompson's offer was adamantly refused, and Brahl's winning ticket turned out to be worth $5,000. On another occasion, Thompson was called before the United States court to testify for a now unknown cause. Ben became upset when a lawyer from Chicago discredited some statements he made in his deposition, so he heaved an inkstand at the astonished lawyer's head. A few weeks later at Oscar Sullivan's Gold Room, he held another raffle. This time the prize was an improved five-acre lot east of Austin with a view of the Colorado River. The property was valued more than $1000. Single tickets sold for $2.50. The raffle was also a benefit for the ten orphan children of Confederate General John Bell Hood, commander of the famous Texas Brigade and Army of the Tennessee. General Hood followed his wife and eldest daughter to the grave that previous August. All three had succumbed to yellow fever. On his deathbed, he called upon the gallant veterans of his Texas Brigade to rally and help care for his surviving children. The newspaper reported that a quarter of the proceeds from Ben Thompson's raffle would go toward their support.[45]

Austin was scheduled to host the Texas State Sheriff's Convention, which started on the second Tuesday of September 1879. Texas newspaper editors were aware of the frailties of many of their lawmen, and asked the sheriffs to attend the convention unarmed and to refrain from drunkenness while visiting the state capital. This meeting of peacekeepers from throughout the state was known to be a harbinger of violence.[46]

On the night before the start of the convention, Hays County Deputy Sheriff Tom Martin, a friend of Ben and Billy Thompson, went on a tour of Austin barrooms with his two brothers James and Lew alongside a fourth man named Bill Good. At 5 a.m. on Tuesday morning, their binge resulted in the pulling out of their revolvers and shooting up the Cattle Exchange Saloon. They fired off six or seven shots in quick succession at various targets about the room, destroying a clock and filling a picture full of holes. Austin Policeman James Farrell, Ben Thompson's brother-in-law, hurried to the saloon and recognized the drunken men. Unarmed, Officer Farrell announced to the four revelers they were under arrest. One of them threw his six-shooter down on Farrell, and attempted to fire his weapon. He pulled the trigger four times, but fortunately the pistol only snapped. Before aid could reach the officer, the lawbreakers ran out the back door, and Farrell wisely decided not to risk his life any further by pursuing the drunkards. Justice of the Peace Joseph Lee issued arrest warrants, and county officers searched for the offenders beyond the city limits. None of the men were apprehended.[47]

Ben Thompson decided to try and change his life in an effort to reach a position of respect in the community and to insure greater financial security for his family.[48] An election for citywide offices was to be held in Austin on Monday, November 3. Ben had officially announced his candidacy for the office of city marshal one month prior. He decided to run as an independent. John Cardwell's *Statesman* printed on October 2: "He is well and favorably known to every one in the city, and is in every way worthy the confidence and support of the people. Mr. Thompson is a formidable competitor for the office, and if elected will serve the people faithfully." These kind words may have been a standard courtesy because the *Statesman* was equally complimentary to Timothy Burns when he announced his desire to run for the same position and for incumbent, City Marshal Edward Creary.[49] For Marshal Creary the *Statesman* added this closing thought, "[Creary] will be a hard one to beat. His opponents will have to do the best day's work of their life to shut him out."

Thompson authored a statement "To the good people of Austin" which was published in the local newspapers. The *Statesman* ran it in its Friday, October 17 issue:

> I have been solicited by a number of old citizens who have known and been kind to me from my boyhood to become a candidate for the office of city marshal. No man, from the highest to the humblest, can successfully charge me with dishonor or dishonesty. I can truthfully say, without boasting, that I have always been the friend of the defenseless, and most of the difficulties attending the independent life I have led were incurred by sensitive love of fair play and an irresistible impulse to protect the timid and weak from the aggressions of the overbearing and strong. I am thoroughly acquainted with the true character of Austin and the magnanimity of her citizenship. I have a family of interesting children growing up under my hands for whose welfare and happiness in society I have an abiding solicitude, and I now beg leave to repeat, in this public manner, the promise I have made to my friends in private, that if honored with the confidence of the people in their selection for the important and responsible post to which I aspire, my whole time and busi-

Daily Democratic Statesman newspaperman John Cardwell. As editor, he authored numerous editorials against the many vices of Austin. He supported Ben Thompson in his successful run as City Marshal. *Courtesy the Chuck Parsons Collection.*

> ness shall be the discharge of official duty, and no good and law-abiding citizen shall have occasion to regret the choice, provided it shall be within the compass of my ability or of fidelity to the high and delicate trust, to prevent it. Upon these terms and conditions I invoke the support and suffrage of all my fellow-citizens. Respectfully, BEN THOMPSON.

Less than a week after Thompson's statement was published, the Democratic party of Austin held a meeting at the courthouse with the intention to select candidates for the important city positions up for election. William Steele, the former adjutant general of the state, was chosen as the mayoral candidate and others were picked to be candidates for city attorney, assessor, and treasurer. However, no one came forward to place his name in consideration to be the candidate for city marshal. Two days into the convention, many attendees expressed a thought that Ben Thompson would be the best man to defeat City Marshal Edward Creary at the polls. They passed a motion calling for all members of the party to openly support and vote for Ben Thompson.[50]

Some out-of-town Texas newspapers also felt Thompson would make a strong run against Marshal Creary.[51] The editors at San Antonio's *Daily Express,* however, mocked his candidacy: "Mr. Thompson is, or has been, we believe, a very popular banker [in games of chance] in Austin and in that capacity was brought into intimate relationship with a large proportion of the male citizens of the capital city. His business associations, as well as his prominence as a peace and order loving citizen have endeared him to all. There can be little doubt of his election. Austin will not lose this opportunity to distinguish itself."[52]

Ben Thompson was officially supported by the Democratic Party as an independent candidate and polled a respectable 744 votes, but he lost the election by a wide margin. Timothy Burns, also an independent, was a non-factor in the race for city marshal, receiving only seventy-five votes. Incumbent Edward Creary was

The offices of the *Daily Democratic Statesman.* For a time, Ben Thompson ran a saloon and gambling hall on the ground floor, and on occasion fired pistol shots into the saloon's ceiling endangering the employees of the *Statesman* working above.
Courtesy the Austin History Center Image # COO 125.

known to be likeable, agreeable, and more professional politician than lawman. He also ran as an independent and with Republican and Greenbacker support, easily stayed in office with his 1,174 votes. In the election for mayor, Jacob DeGress received 1,346 votes and won reelection in a huge landslide over William Steele, who received only 597 votes. DeGress ran as an independent and won many votes from the Republicans and Greenbackers.[53] In Ford County, Kansas on the following day, Ben and Billy Thompson's friend, W. B. Masterson also lost in his bid for a second term as county sheriff. It was later speculated that his friendly association with gunmen like the Thompson Brothers, Doc Holliday, and J. J. Webb helped cost him his reelection.[54]

Thompson was not discouraged by the lost opportunity to change his vocation, and he left Austin on Tuesday, November 18, 1879, to join many of the other Texan sporting men at the horse races in Goliad. Ben experienced "a grand success" at the races and returned to Austin flush with cash. He was away from home for two weeks.[55]

Jacob Carl DeGress, mayor of Austin from 1877 to 1879. While unarmed, he bravely confiscated Ben Thompson's revolver and arrested him when members of the Austin police force failed to act.

Courtesy the Austin History Center. Image # PICB # 00960.

Chapter 12

A HIGH OLD TIME IN SAN ANTONIO

"I reckon I can shoot that son of a bitch standing."

—Jack Harris to M.B. Davis, December 1882

In the late fall and early winter of 1879, "Buffalo Bill and his Mammoth Combination of Artists" began touring the major towns of Texas. On the schedule were stops in Austin, San Antonio, Houston, and Galveston. Four years earlier, W. F. Cody's troupe bypassed performing in Austin. For this tour, however, Cody and his company of twenty-four actors and actresses were booked for three performances on December 9 and 10 at Austin's new, three-story high Millett's Opera House on Ash Street (9th Street). The two evening performances were slated to be "Knight of the Plains, or Buffalo Bill's Best Trail." The matinee was another thrilling drama entitled, "May Cody, or Lost and Won." The opera house was one of the largest performance venues in Texas, seating as many as fifteen hundred patrons. To drum up business, Buffalo Bill Cody led a parade through the streets of Austin. The colorful parade, consisting of his military Brass Band and Orchestra, preceded a handful of Indians on horseback advertised as a "band of genuine Indian Chiefs." To also create interest, Cody invited local people and newsmen to go with him outside of town so he could demonstrate his superb marksmanship with a rifle.[1]

When Cody arrived in Austin, it was only natural for Ben Thompson to call upon him. Both men were renowned for their courtesy, gentlemanly manners, and love of fun. Possessing similar interests in women, firearms, gambling, alcohol, and horses, or the sporting life in general, the two men became fast friends. Prior to the evening performance scheduled for December 9, Cody and Thompson went to the outskirts of Austin and engaged in some competitive target shooting. The following day, the *Statesman* reported, "Buffalo Bill went out of town yesterday with Mr. Ben Thompson and some other gentlemen, and he showed them a little crack shooting. With Mr. Thompson's rifle he struck six half dollars out of seven that were thrown up." Ben entertained the onlookers with a six-gun. The next day Cody and Thompson went out again, and the *Statesman* commented, "Buffalo Bill … again displayed his skill with handling a rifle. He is undoubtedly one of the best marksmen now on the American continent. His shooting was perfectly marvelous."[2]

Thompson accompanied Cody as his acting troupe moved on to performances at San Antonio's Casino Hall. There they again demonstrated their shooting ability for onlookers. A San Antonio newspaperman expressed how Thompson held his own against Cody's rifle at both the demonstration in Austin and outside of the Alamo City, providing evidence that he was one of the finest pistol shots in the United States.[3] A few days later, when the curtain came down on his final performance in San Antonio, Cody traveled on to a scheduled engagement on Wednesday evening, December 17, at Galveston's Tremont Theatre, leaving his new friend behind.[4] It is doubtful that they ever met again.

Remaining in San Antonio for a day or two, Thompson continued his association with stage performers. He presented an autographed photograph of himself to vaudeville performer Eddie Fox, the minstrel violinist. On this same day, twenty-four-year-old Billy Simms, Thompson's former protégé, also presented Fox with a signed portrait.[5] Perhaps Thompson and Simms enjoyed San Antonio's nightlife together and discussed old times. Returning to Austin the next day, Ben again demonstrated his skill with firearms in front of onlookers. This time, however, it came as a surprise, and his pistol firing was unlawful since it was within the city limits of Austin. He was arrested and fined ten dollars for the offense.[6]

Over the Christmas holidays, the New Year's Eve celebration, and throughout the long winter nights of January and most of February, Thompson managed to behave himself. If he didn't, at least, he stayed out of the newspapers. In late February, Ben went to San Antonio. Thompson was very popular in the Alamo City and he was known to sometimes carouse with members of the city's police force. It was said that on at least one occasion, a judge assessed a heavy fine for Thompson's misbehavior, but another judge who favored Ben remitted that fine.[7] While he was there, he "had a high old time in San Antonio ... and made things lively by firing off his pistols upon the streets." The police promptly arrested him and he was fined $50 for the offense.[8] A few days later, he treated the Alamo City to a small mystery. The unmistakable crack of a pistol shot was heard coming from a moving hack. A city policeman immediately stopped the vehicle to investigate, and after a careful examination of both Ben Thompson and the driver, as well as a complete search of the vehicle, he was unable to find any weapon capable of making such a noise. Offering an explanation, the *Statesman* published: "It was a spiritual manifestation—one of those numerous fellows trying to get even with Ben." The newspaper had a little fun with the story, and no doubt many readers enjoyed it as well.[9] Ben continued his spree in San Antonio and decided to try his luck at the gambling room on the second floor of the Vaudeville Theatre. What transpired there sparked a feud, which ultimately cost four men their lives. Each side had a different explanation as to the cause of the difficulty. The following is San Antonio's version: "Ben Thompson was considered a fast friend of the sporting men of this city, always giving and receiving favors when occasion demanded or warranted." The trouble started when "Thompson entered the gambling house" inside the Vaudeville building "kept by Mr. Joe Foster."[10] After playing for a while, Ben decided to quit the game and "drew out ... something in the neighborhood of $300 as his winnings." An evening or two afterward, Thompson returned to Foster's place. "This time he lost $340, which placed him, $40 behind the game. This was all the ready cash he had with him. In order to play more, he 'soaked' a gold watch and some valuable diamonds for one thousand dollars. Of this he lost $360." Ben stopped playing *monte,* and "changed over to the faro table, playing an hour or two, neither winning nor losing. Some friends [arrived] calling for him; he left the house, turning over the chips to Foster, saying, 'keep my watch and diamonds safely.' Three hundred and sixty dollars were due the house on the collateral." At this time, "no unkindly feeling existed" between the two gamblers.[11]

The next night, Thompson again called at the gaming room and asked Foster to give him his watch. Foster freely handed it over along with the jewelry attached to the chain, expecting to be reimbursed. Thompson deliberated a few moments, and then put them all in his pocket. He drew a six-shooter instead of his wallet, stating: "G-d d--m you, you can ----- for them." With his pistol in Foster's face, Thompson "had the drop." Yet, Foster demanded an explanation, telling Ben that if he could show how he was wronged in any manner it would be made right. Without speaking, Thompson, pistol still in hand, backed out of the room and down the stairs leading into the street. The next day Ben and Foster took a drink together at a saloon on Alamo plaza. Foster again asked for an explanation of the previous night. "I was drunk," explained Thompson but, again, made no attempt to reimburse Foster. He then said he was going to the country to sober up and stepped onto a bus, leaving Foster, frustrated and standing in the street. Foster's partner in the large faro room, Jack Harris, was well-known for being "generally quiet and peaceable, [yet] he had a violent temper when aroused" and he "could not brook interference from any source." Certainly, he could not allow Thompson's behavior to pass or others would attempt to take their money back in a similar fashion. As the principal partner of all three of the businesses housed in the Vaudeville building, Jack Harris loudly banned Thompson from ever entering his place of business again.[12]

Walton defended Ben Thompson's version of the event; "What Thompson did not know about cards was hardly worth knowing." He was an accomplished expert and when a run of luck went against him and didn't stop he "wondered and watched—and, watching, he wondered the more. At last he discovered, or thought he discovered, wherein lay the secret of Foster's wonderful luck; whether true or false, Thompson was convinced that the game was not fair." Earlier he used his jewelry as collateral and, now, angry at being cheated, he determined to take advantage of the previous jewelry arrangement by handing in his checks and recovering his jewelry. But he rose to leave still owing the bank several hundred dollars. Foster demanded he be paid. However, all he received from Thompson was a denouncing as a cheat. Indignant, Joe Foster attempted to pull his pistol, but found Thompson's revolver already out and stuck in his face. Covering Foster, Thompson backed to the stairway leading down to Soledad Street and left the building. As Ben would explain to friends, he felt justified in his actions.[13]

During the second week of March 1880, Billy Simms returned to Austin to mourn the death of his younger brother James. It was almost dawn on Monday, March 10, when twenty-year old James Simms and two other Austin undesirables chose the wrong man to try and rob during what was supposed to be a friendly game of euchre. Shot in the lower jaw with the bullet lodging in his spinal column, James died before the sun came up. After his brother's funeral, Billy Simms remained in Austin with his parents and three sisters for at least three months before returning to San Antonio. Even though he was involved in the gambling operation with Joe Foster and Jack Harris at the Vaudeville, it appears he did not incur any trouble with Ben Thompson during his extended stay with his family in Austin.[14]

Trouble and Thompson could not be separated for long. April 1880 was an exciting month for Ben. His troublemaking began at Mattie Farmer's establishment in back of the Raymond House on the corner of Congress Avenue and Pine Street (5th street). At 10 a. m. on Tuesday, April 6, Ben became upset with the piano there, and to make things lively began shooting up the keys. "The cheerful voice of the festive pistol," so early in the day, brought a rush of police officers, but Ben had already left Mattie's place. Since she refused to make an official complaint, the matter was dropped and no arrest was made.[15] Ben's misbehavior had only just begun.

Two weeks later the *Statesman's* April 23 headline enticed its readers with, "Ben Thompson on the Warpath." His warpath started at 2:30 a.m.; the keno goose was being retired for the evening above the Iron Front Saloon near the corner of Congress Avenue and Pecan Street (6th Street) when Ben Thompson walked in. With only a few patrons lingering in the room, he knocked the goose off the table, calmly informed everyone he was closing the game, and assaulted Bob Holman,[16] one of the proprietors. An idea occurred to Ben that he should close the game forever and drew his pistol and fired. This was the only announcement needed, and the keno room emptied in short order. Thompson put his "festive little pistol" away and vacated the building, strolling behind the fleeing patrons.[17]

The April 21 San Jacinto Day's celebration was in full swing the next morning after the incident at the Iron Front Saloon, and Ben Thompson was enjoying it with his many friends from the volunteer fire company. A police officer found Thompson and informed him there were complaints made against him stemming from his antics on the previous night. Ben promised to call and settle up with the fines. From the celebration grounds, Thompson went to the western edge of the city on west Pecan Street (6th) near the Colorado River and visited Paul Pressler's popular German Beer Garden,[18] remaining there until about 9 o'clock that night. When he returned to Austin, he discovered the keno room he believed he had closed the previous evening was again going full blast. Leaving their chips behind at the sight of Ben Thompson, many of the keno players ran out the back door or down the stairs to the street level saloon. Some even went out the front window where they climbed down to safety. Their agility was described as "astonishing." Disappointed because his first attempt had failed, Thompson "cheerfully informed the whole concern that the game had to close, as he was the sole proprietor of the keno business in the city and didn't intend to have any opposition." Standing about ten feet away from Thompson was Isaac Simon, a restaurateur from around the corner on Pecan Street (6th).[19] Simon was also a partner with Bob Holman in the keno operation above the Iron Front. With no apparent provocation, Ben pulled his pistol, pointed it at Simon and snapped off a shot. The *Statesman* reporter would write how Mr. Simon would have been killed if not for the anticipation and action of a bystander, named Hines, who pushed Thompson's arm aside as the shot went off. Believing this final intimidation would finally and completely be understood and his demands adhered to, Thompson left the premises.[20]

Two complaints swore out against Ben by Justice of the Peace Lee, one for assaulting Bob Holman (like Ben, a former printer) and the second for assaulting and attempting to murder Isaac Simon. At Mayor DeGress's office four more complaints awaited Ben's attention, all due to his recent reckless conduct.[21] Thompson sought out Holman and Simon and explained to them how it would be in everyone's best interest to drop the matter, and the two men eagerly and readily agreed. They informed Police Officer Sublette they wanted to withdraw their complaints against Thompson, and Sublette reluctantly followed their instructions. Thompson's shooting up of the keno game points more to a calculated "muscling in" rather than a mere drunken row. Holman eventually became a formal partner with Ben.[22] Unconcerned with Thompson's motivation, but disgusted by his behavior, Mayor DeGress "refused to permit the complaints to be withdrawn" and decided, "Ben will have to answer." Facing an endless amount of legal trouble, Thompson decided it would be a good time to leave Austin.[23]

Dodge City, Kansas, was Ben Thompson's destination, and prior to boarding the train on Saturday April 24, he stopped to purchase "sixteen copies of the *Statesman* containing the account of his dispersion of the valiant keno crew." As soon as word reached the streets that he had left town, the keno players came out of hiding and the games resumed.[24]

The *Statesman* later mocked the Austin police department, publishing how officers learned that Ben Thompson planned to take the morning International train for Kansas, "hurried to the depot at the rear of the Capitol Building to look for him, and continued to search until the train had left." The newspaper's sarcasm obviously implied that the police intentionally avoided Ben. In another issue, the *Statesman's* editor, John Cardwell, enlightened his readers with "Ben Thompson some two or three months ago issued orders to the city police, that in case he became a little playful and used his musical pistol in making things lively, that they, the police, were to let him severely alone, and it seems they carried out the orders to a letter last week. On either of the nights he did the shooting he could have been arrested, and on the night he was riding around the city he was seen by the officers and could have been arrested. A policeman was appointed on that night for the special purpose of arresting Ben, but hearing that he was moving about the city in a carriage and there being danger of his running afoul of him, the officer hurried home and went to bed."[25]

Other newspapers in Texas publicized Ben Thompson's many shooting escapades. The *Galveston Daily News* called Ben, "an Austin desperado and gambler," and stated that he "carries things with a high hand there." The Brenham newspaper wrote, "Nearly

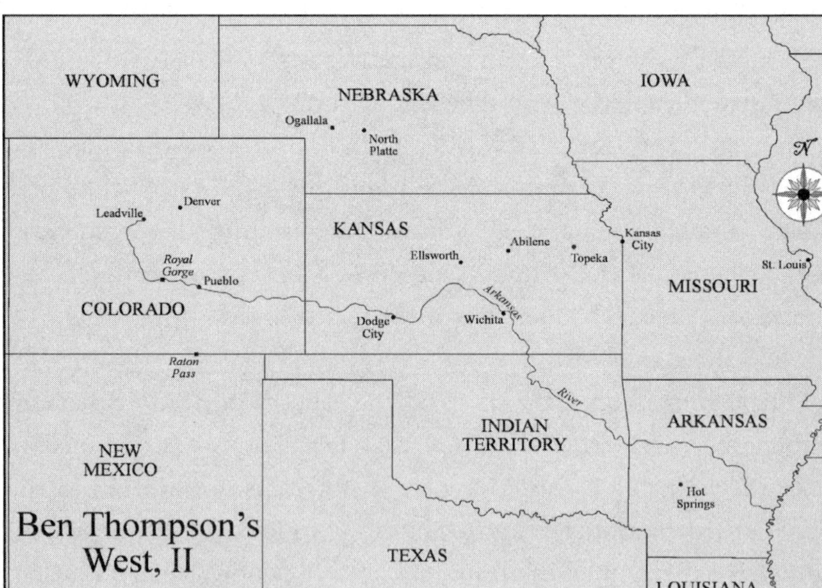

The West of Ben Thompson – 2. *Map by Charles David Grear.*

every town in Texas appears to have its pet desperado," explaining that the officers allowed Ben to do "pretty much as he pleases."[26]

The *Statesman* kept track of Ben Thompson's whereabouts, reporting on May 21, that he was in Dodge City. The newspaper made no mention of his family, although they, too, had traveled to Kansas to be with Ben. The 1880 Ford County Census, enumerated on June 2 and 3, lists his wife Kate, his eleven-year-old son Benjamin, and their nine-year-old daughter Katie. Billy Thompson was counted in Ogallala, Nebraska on June 3. The enumerator listed Billy's profession as a printer, a trade neither brother had followed for many years. Ben's family didn't remain long in Dodge City because they were counted again (less Ben) in the town of Bastrop, Texas on June 12. Ben and Billy's sixty-two-year-old mother, Mary, resided in the same Bastrop household with Ben's wife and children.[27]

Bouncing back and forth between Nebraska and Colorado, Billy Thompson returned to Ogallala in June for the oncoming Texas cattle season. In 1880, Ogallala was a small village on the north bank of the South Platte River, about two hundred and fifty miles northwest of Dodge City. The town was one street, only one block long; however, it was fast becoming a destination for Texas cattlemen.

Only one barroom remained open in Ogallala over the winter. However, when spring arrived so did the saloon men, and during the summer months as many as ten saloons attended to the thirsty needs of the Texas drovers. One of the most prominent of the saloon men was William H. Tucker, who with his twenty-year-old-wife Maggie, older cousin Oscar, and half-brother Thomas, ran the Cowboy's Rest, a combination barroom and gambling house. Tucker had drifted into Ogallala in 1876. In the not too distant past, the early 1870s, Tucker had earned his living as a professional gambler in Rockport, Texas, where Billy Thompson remained under indictment for fatally shooting Remus Smith back during the spring of 1868.[28]

"Tucker," as one newspaper reported, "is the typical border paradox of gentleman and ruffian." Known for his generosity, he would share his money freely with his friends, and whenever cowboys would be physically broken down or financially broke, they would successfully approach him for a few dollars because "no hungry man was ever turned from his door." Bill Tucker was described as a tall, fine-looking man who wore his hair long in the style of Buffalo Bill, and prided himself on his fighting abilities. On horseback riding at full speed, he was credited as being able to break glass balls thrown in the air at up to sixty yards away with his favorite firearm, a shotgun. Onlookers avowed he seldom had to use the second barrel to hit his target. In running his saloon, he would inquire of a troublemaking cowboy whether he would have a "fight or have a drink?" And, mostly, the desire for another drink won out. It was said no man could compete with him in grit, shrewdness, and popularity. However, the latter two traits he must have called on to the utmost when he was accused of rape by fourteen-year-old Miss Flora Rayner. In reporting the attack, the *Omaha Bee* identified Tucker as, "a notorious rowdy" a "sporting man, gambler, [and] brothel proprietor." That he was married with an infant daughter "aggravates the circumstances of this case." Somehow Tucker avoided any serious repercussions from the accusation and continued running his saloon.[29]

Keith County Sheriff Martin DePreist enforced the law in Ogallala. The Alabama-born DePreist came up the Texas cattle trail as a cowboy in 1877 and decided to stay in Ogallala and open a stable. It was common knowledge that he knew how to handle a revolver. As a former drover, he was respected and mostly obeyed, since he was sensible enough not to interfere when the trail hands were only on a boisterous spree and not causing any real trouble.

Bat Masterson's last full day as sheriff of Ford County, Kansas, was January 11, 1880. The next day, Masterson decided to leave

Dodge City and search for new opportunities elsewhere. In the dead of winter, he traveled to Colorado stopping at both Leadville and Gunnison. Throughout the spring, he bounced back and forth between Colorado and Dodge City. Masterson returned to Dodge City in June and was living there with a teenager named Annie Ladue. It was a stroke of good fortune for the Thompson brothers that Masterson was back in Dodge City.[30] He would soon be on his way to Nebraska to perform a difficult errand for Billy Thompson.[31]

Edgar Beecher Bronson, a former New York newspaperman, who several years prior had established a cattle ranch in northwest Nebraska, was in Ogallala on Monday, June 21. He was enjoying the company of two notable Texas cattlemen, Seth Mabry and Dillard R. Fant, when they "were tempted to join the crowd" in Bill Tucker's Cowboys' Rest Saloon. In his *Reminiscences of a Ranchman,* Bronson provides a vivid narrative of the Billy Thompson - Bill Tucker gunfight. "Later we learned that, early in the day, a local celebrity—Bill Thompson by name, a tin horn by trade, and a desperado by pretence [*sic*, pretense]—had proffered some insult to Big Alice, the leading lady of the house," for which Bill Tucker had "called him down good and plenty," but "to resent it then, would have been to court a fairer fight than Bill's kind ever willingly took on." But brooding over Tucker's abuse and "remembering he was brother to Ben Thompson, then the most celebrated man-killer in the State of Texas," Billy began figuring "what Ben would do in like circumstances." With repeated and generous helpings of "red eye," Billy Thompson had readied himself for action.

When Bronson, Mabry, and Fant found themselves belly up to the bar waiting for Bill Tucker to pass them their drinks, "Bill suddenly stepped within the door of the saloon and took a quick snapshot at Tucker, who was directly across the bar from us and in the act of passing Fant a glass of whisky [*sic*] with his left hand." Bill's shot "cut off three of Tucker's fingers and the tip of the fourth, and, the bar being narrow, spattered us with his blood. Tucker fell, momentarily, from the shock." Supposing from Tucker's quick drop, Billy thought, "he had made an instant kill." Sticking his pistol back in his waistband, Bill "started leisurely out the door and down the street." No sooner was Bill out of the house, then the very game Tucker sprang up, "seized a saw[ed]-off ten gauge shotgun, ran to the door, leveled the gun across the stump of his maimed left hand, and emptied into Bill's back a trifle more No. 4 duck shot than his system could assimilate."[32]

Billy Thompson's bloody wounds struck observers as serious, perhaps fatal, and he was carried to his hotel. It was later determined he would survive as long as an infection did not set in. As to Tucker's mutilated left hand, it was hoped that it could provide him at least a reduced level of service.[33]

Ogallala's citizens were naturally "somewhat uneasy about the outcome of this matter, as Thompson's brother is said to be en route to the town, and may on his arrival, decide to wind up the feud by killing Tucker, or at least, making a strong effort in that direction," warned the editor of nearby Sidney, Nebraska's *Telegraph.* Sheriff DePreist took precautionary steps by swearing in additional men to serve as deputies, both to guard Billy Thompson and to help keep the peace in Ogallala should his brother arrive. Billy was under arrest, since he was seen as the instigator of the fight, and as soon as his recovery would permit, he was to be given a full examination by court officials.

The Saturday before Billy Thompson squeezed the trigger on Tucker, a rumor began circulating in Texas, first in Dallas, and as the weekend ended in Austin, stating that Ben Thompson had been shot down and killed in Silver Cliff, Custer County, Colorado. At the time, Silver Cliff was enjoying a fleeting mining boom, and for a moment, was the third largest town in the fast-growing state behind only Denver and Leadville. The *Statesman* shrugged off the story, since the rumor could not be traced to any reliable source.[34] Still, it must have caused considerable worry to his wife, children and mother. Ben calmed their fears in a letter from Dodge City to the editors of the *Statesman*, which was originally printed in its entirety on Saturday, July 3, 1880. A relevant portion follows: "*Dear Sirs-* As the Dallas and other papers reported me killed in Colorado, I am happy to be able to write that it is a mistake. Inclosed [*sic*] you will find two letters from Ogallala, Nebraska, giving an account of a shooting bee that occurred there between my brother Billy and a gentleman by the name of Tucker, of Texas. You are privileged to publish, as a matter of news, such portions of them as you may wish. As there was no serious damage done, we can afford to make light of it."

The previous day, the *Statesman* did publish news about Billy Thompson's "shooting bee," stating how Billy was painfully wounded, having been struck in the back, "from the head to the heels," with "about 200 No. 8 shot" and "three buck shot." Having received good medical attention, it was expected he would get well in about ten days. The case against Billy was to take place as soon as he was sufficiently recovered to be able to attend court. Since his brother Ben was in Dodge City, it was presumed by the *Statesman* that he would go to Ogallala to ensure Billy would receive a fair trial.[35] But Ben Thompson had a better idea than taking the chance of his younger brother standing trial.

On July 6, 1880, the *Ford County Globe* of Dodge City reported that Bat Masterson had traveled to Ogallala, Nebraska. The exact date of his departure remains unknown, and it seems probable he left many days before the newspaper informed its readership. He later wrote that his object "in going to Ogallala at the time, was to straighten out, if possible, a serious difficulty in which a personal friend of mine, by the name of Billy Thompson … had become involved with a local man by the name of Bill Tucker, which resulted in Thompson being severely wounded." Certainly, Ben Thompson and Masterson discussed how best to help Billy, and based on his own words, Masterson did not hesitate to go to Billy's aid without any arm-twisting from Ben.[36]

Arriving in Ogallala, Masterson found his friend in his hotel bed still recovering from Tucker's shotgun blast. One of Sheriff DePreist's deputies was closely watching Billy's hotel room. Billy Thompson discussed with Masterson the situation and how best to bring a favorable conclusion to his predicament. Masterson decided he must visit Tucker and see if he could negotiate an "amicable understanding." Finding Tucker at home in his bed with a heavily bandaged left hand, Masterson immediately learned how bitter he was. He also learned Tucker was willing to make an arrangement "if the proper inducements were offered." The price Tucker required was at the time beyond the Thompson brothers's pocketbook and, as Masterson described, "therefore my conference with the thumbless one was soon at an end." Masterson returned to Billy's hotel room and informed him of Tucker's monetary demand, which precipitated a different course of action.

It was agreed that Billy must pretend to be suffering greatly from his wounds, and whenever he needed to change positions in his bed, he was to call the guard in and request his help. This ruse was to keep Billy out of the town's jail and in his much less secure hotel room. Ingratiating himself with the guarding deputy, who was a young man recently arrived from one of the New England states, was the next element of Masterson's escape plan, a plan he had not yet fully formulated. Escaping on horseback would have been easy to do if Billy Thompson could ride, but the pain and condition of his wounds made hard riding out of the question. Escape by wagon was worthless to attempt, since a posse would easily overtake them. Only by rail could Masterson and Thompson hope to move fast enough and in a manner which Billy's condition could withstand. Every night at midnight, a Union Pacific eastbound train stopped in Ogallala just long enough to replenish its water tank before speeding on to its next stop, the town of North Platte, about forty miles away.

Masterson, as a well-known friend of Ben and Billy Thompson, had been closely watched by many of the townspeople since his arrival in Ogallala. Getting Billy Thompson to the train depot under such scrutiny would be difficult. Highly suspicious of a rescue attempt, Sheriff DePreist ordered his young deputy to never leave Billy Thompson's room, creating another seemingly insurmountable obstacle. A perfect opportunity occurred when the town decided to hold a dance one Sunday night at the building used alternately as a schoolhouse and church. Luckily, it stood about four hundred yards away from the train depot. Everyone was going to attend, most importantly Sheriff DePreist, as he and his fiddle were expected to provide the music. This distraction was a godsend to Masterson's plan. Only the young guard from New England was in the way, and Masterson easily dealt with him. The bartender at Billy's hotel was a Texan named Jim Dunn, and as an artist among mixologists in Dodge City, was a good friend of Bat Masterson. Explaining to the bartender what he needed to accomplish, Dunn told Masterson, "leave it to me." Dunn was well prepared on how to sedate an unwanted or unruly patron.[37]

The night of the dance, Masterson joined Billy Thompson in his hotel room along with his diligent guard. Regretting he was missing the festivities at the dance, the guard agreed to have a drink or two. Masterson called down to Dunn and ordered up a pair of sour whiskeys. For once, Billy Thompson declined a drink. After a second sour whiskey, the deputy was passed out on the floor. The timing was perfect. Billy was hurriedly dressed, and Masterson lifted Thompson up over his shoulder and proceeded to carry him down the stairs and up the empty street to the depot. The train had hardly stopped when Bat and Billy climbed aboard. Within a few minutes, they were rolling along at forty miles an hour leaving Ogallala, Sheriff DePreist, and Bill Tucker behind forever.

Buffalo Bill Cody owned a beautiful Victorian home on the outskirts of North Platte, so the fleeing men exited the train in the belief Cody would aid them in continuing their flight. Masterson inquired from a station hand where they might find Dave Perry's California Exchange Saloon. With Thompson over his shoulder, Masterson walked into the barroom and found who he was looking for. Cody was there holding court with a dozen or so of his friends. Royally welcomed by the showman, the moment he heard their tale he stated, "The Ogallala authorities will not take you from here." The following day, Masterson and Billy Thompson received Cody's promise to provide "a fine big Texas horse, and his wife's phaeton to carry us across country," enabling them to continue their flight to Dodge City. While en route, riding the promised "phaeton" to Dodge City, a heavy rainstorm opened up and accompanied Masterson and Billy during the rest of their trip. They "had nothing but the sky for a roof." Their "appearance can better be imagined than described," Masterson wrote as they tramped into Dodge City, explaining, "about the first thing Thompson did after reaching Dodge was to send a telegram to the Ogallala Sheriff notifying him of his safe arrival and inviting him to come and get him in case he still thought he wanted him. The fiddling Sheriff made no reply to Thompson's message, and there the matter ended."[38]

On July 17, 1880, the *Dodge City Times* published a short news item informing its readers that Masterson was back in Dodge City. Masterson stated that Nebraska was "dry and many people are leaving that state. He came by wagon and was accompanied by Texas Billy Thompson. The latter has recovered from his wounds."[39] This *Times* item is significant as it marks the first time Ben's brother was called "Texas Billy" in print.

The brothers' reunion in Dodge City was short-lived. Billy disappeared, again, not only from searching lawmen but also from later researchers and historians. Ben may have briefly made another stopover in Colorado, but he was back in Austin by the end of July. Returning to his hometown by way of St. Louis, he purportedly was interviewed by a reporter of the *St. Louis Republican*. Full of needless exaggerations, the *San Antonio Daily Express* attempted to correct the *Republican's* article. "It was stated that during his life Thompson had killed twenty-one men, stood trial for each and was cleared. As to the number, this version is probably much overdrawn. Eight or ten dead men would perhaps satisfy his claims. At Leadville Thompson once 'took the town.' ... Some think he bears a charmed life."[40]

In mid-September, Austin City Marshal Edward Creary announced his intent to be a candidate for the office of Travis County sheriff. After serving as sheriff for five years, Dennis Corwin had decided not to seek another re-election, and instead chose to return to his profession as a civil engineer. On November 1, Creary submitted his final yearly report to the Austin city council. Highlights of his report included how the police force was increased from nine to twelve officers. During the previous year, 1,104 persons had been arrested of which 901 were fined, the fines totaling over $6,000. The police officers had recovered and returned to their rightful owners a remarkable $7,195 of an estimated $8,992 of stolen goods. James Moore, Ben Thompson's brother-in-law, started a new arrest count when he was hauled in on the second of November charged with disorderly conduct. For a reason now unknown, Moore assaulted a man named James Schmity. He was fined $5 plus court costs, and due to his inability to pay the fine, he worked off his debt to the city as part of the city marshal's street cleanup crew.[41]

November 2, 1880, was Ben Thompson's birthday. "Now in his thirty-seventh year," Walton described him as "five feet nine inches, rather swarthy complexion, stoutly built, black hair and blue eyes, quick in all his motions, indomitable energy, modest and retiring in demeanor, speaks gently, [and] is a handsome, generous man." Three days after celebrating his birthday, Ben and Kate Thompson purchased from R. R. and Sarah Penn, for $1,500 cash and a promissory note for $1,000, payable in one year, a fine, beautiful home in Hearst's Addition in Austin. Ben was not included as a grantee and, probably for the sake of safety, the property was deeded only to Mrs. Catherine Thompson.[42]

In the county election for sheriff, thirty-nine-year-old Ed Creary, running on the Republican ticket, easily won, and so Ben Thompson again entered the field as a candidate for the vacated office of city marshal. Police Lieutenant John Chenneville was appointed interim city marshal and chief of police until the special election scheduled to take place on Friday, December 17. Ben Thompson's name had been bantered about in early November as a possible candidate, and rumors of him dropping out of the race were denied in the December 12 edition of the *Statesman*. In the same issue, Ben published a card, which commonly amounted to a paid advertisement, expressing his desire to fill the "remnant of the term made vacant by the resignation of Mr. Creary. I respectfully ask my fellow citizens to give me a trial—the only just and fair probation."[43]

In San Antonio, Jack Harris's extreme bitterness toward Ben Thompson was only beginning. Harris visited with Fort Worth resident and former Texas Ranger, M. B. Davis, at Wolfson's Store on Main Plaza located only a block west of his saloon. Davis later recollected it was in December 1880 when, "Harris began the conversation by asking me—how long I had known Ben Thompson and asked me a number of questions about him. Harris then said to me if Ben Thompson ever fusses my corner I will shoot the dammed son of a bitch with a shot gun loaded with buck shot and make a hole in him that a cat can jump through—he said you folks are all superstitious about Ben Thompson—but if he has a charm about him I will break it." Davis claimed he heard Jack Harris say, "I believe it has come his time to die any way I won't give him any more show than a mad dog. The people will sustain a man in killing that son of a bitch. I don't care how he does it." Davis questioned Harris about his handicapped left hand. By using a long stick Harris demonstrated he had dexterity enough to handle a shotgun and remarked how he was "a good shot on the wing." Finishing his exchange with Davis, Harris said, "I reckon I can shoot that son of a bitch standing." Later, M. B. Davis met with Thompson in Austin at Monroe Miller's Livery Stables. Davis informed him of his conversation with Jack Harris and the threatening remarks made by Harris. Only listening to the warning, Thompson made no response.[44]

A couple of Austin's most prominent newspapers commented on Thompson's candidacy. The *Statesman* wrote, "Mr. Thompson is well-known to the people of Austin. [He is] known especially as a man without fear, and there are very many here who regard him as the proper sort of a person to be marshal of a city like this one. They say his life may appear as a reckless one, but that his disposition is and always has been to act honorably to all men and that they would pledge themselves that he would make a model peace officer. Mr. Thompson … expresses a desire to serve the public in an honorable capacity, and says he will do so if elected," and the *Statesman* noted, "it is known that his word is an excellent bond."[45]

The *Texas Capital* of Austin, ignoring Ben's past misbehavior, supported Thompson's candidacy in a December 12 vote of confidence, describing him as "the right man in the right place. He has eminent ability for the position, possesses the hearty good will of this community, where he has lived since childhood, and where his wife and children now reside. He commands the respect of our business community, and is held in wholesome fear by the many hard cases and dangerous classes that infest all cities, and with whom a City Marshal is necessarily often thrown in contact. It is exactly the position in which Ben Thompson can be of most benefit to the city, and we urge all our friends, all who desire a good city government, to vote for Ben Thompson for City Marshal."

At this same time, Ben Thompson's brother-in-law, James K. Farrell, a former Austin policeman, was selected to become the city marshal of Silver City, New Mexico. Farrell traveled to New Mexico and began his term of office in early December 1880.[46] Before the end of the month, Ben would also be wearing a lawman's badge. Of the five men competing for the office, two were thought of as leading contenders—Ben Thompson and well-known, longtime Austin businessman and current manager of the Anheuser beer agency, John W. Kelly.[47]

The morning of the election, hack drivers and express men, employed by the candidates to get their supporters to the polls, hurriedly drove their vehicles through the city's streets. The turnout of voters was very high even through many of Austin's black residents were out of town picking the fall cotton crop. Ben Thompson received 849 of the total 1,516 votes cast; John Kelly, in second place, received 622 votes.

News of his election raced through Austin, and as word reached the rest of the state, various newspaper editors printed their opinions. In the nearby railroad town of Luling, a newspaperman wrote, "Ben Thompson has been elected city marshal of Austin by a handsome majority. Ben was a [visitor] of Luling during its early days and had a reputation of being a pretty wild boy, but when not in his cups, there is not a more polished gentleman to be found anywhere. As for 'grit' he is literally overflowing with it and we will wager a new hat that he keeps things straight in the capital city during his term of office."[48]

From the *Galveston Daily News*: "It has been urged against Thompson that his election will be cited against Austin, he having figured in some desperate encounters, resulting in death to his opponents, but in each case he submitted to the courts and honorably acquitted. He solicited the place, asking the people to give him a chance to serve them faithfully, and they have taken him at his word." The *News* admitted, "For a man having the reputation of a desperado, he is certainly gentlemanly and mild-mannered, so much so that the people who come in contact with him are disposed to be incredulous as to his alleged character, and have given him a good opportunity to retrieve his errors in a very responsible position. All parties admit his capability and good faith, and he will be generally supported in the effort to control the lawless elements that sometimes infest the town."[49]

The editors of the *San Antonio Daily Express* added their thoughts, praising him but at the same time, verbalizing a few lingering doubts, "With all his faults the people of Austin love Ben Thompson still, and they have elected him city marshal." The editor of the *Express* was a bit dismayed and stated, "This displays a most wonderful independence of the opinion of the outside world. The people of Austin may know Ben to be a good man, perfectly trustworthy when he gives his word, and capable and willing to make a good city marshal; but as he has almost a national reputation as a gambler, who has killed a dozen or two men in broils, and whose favorite pastime has been found in organizing himself into a riotous mob and making the police authorities and everybody else take back seats or bite the dust before him." The *Express* felt, "his election as police chief officer of the capital city of a great state that is an empire in itself will astonish if not a little bewilder the people generally. Those who know Thompson say he will make the best city marshal Austin ever had—and that place needs a good one, too, but Austin's misfortune will be found in the fact that such a comparatively few know him in that way, and the people there will consequently be judged by Ben's general reputation throughout the country." Nevertheless, the *Express* admitted, "if the people of Austin can stand it, we presume those of other places will have to stand it also."[50]

Leading a large assembly of citizens on the night Thompson was elected, members of the Hope Hook and Ladder Company, Ben's old volunteer fire company, serenaded him in celebration of his victory. Both the Colored Band and the Manning Rifles Band provided music. The serenade must have started a long night of revelry for Ben. The *Statesman* reported that Ben Thompson, "marshal-elect, is quite ill. As soon as he recovers he will qualify."[51]

Chapter 13

THE BEST CITY MARSHAL IN TEXAS

Thompson "cheerfully kicked open the door, and to the infinite disgust of Mr. Ringo scooped him in."

—*Statesman*, May 3, 1881

When Federal rule and Reconstruction finally ended in Texas and Austin began to govern itself, the city council approved a new charter. In it, the city marshal's new duties were strictly spelled out. The marshal was now required to make at least two rounds of the city daily, and to check on all of the officers walking their beats at least once after midnight. The charter also increased police responsibilities beyond crime prevention. The city marshal was placed in charge of bridges, streets, and alleys, with orders to keep them clean and in good condition. He was also the city's dog catcher. The police were ordered to keep the water cisterns placed throughout the city full in case of fire, and to somehow prevent horses from drinking out of them. It became the duty of the city marshal to enforce all health and sanitary regulations, even though the council had already established a city health physician. Former City Marshal Edward Creary excelled at these appointed duties.

Throughout the 1870s, the Austin city council kept busy passing all kinds of new laws and ordinances to help ensure the public safety. It became unlawful to carry a pistol, bowie knife, dirk, sword-cane, or brass knuckles. The council also prohibited slingshots and spears. Horseracing was banned on Sunday, no parades were allowed, and the playing of baseball was unlawful between the hours of 9:00 a.m. and 4:00 p.m. It was a misdemeanor to beat a drum, harm birds, and participate in prize fighting as a sponsor or contestant. Swimming or bathing in the Colorado River was punishable by a fine, except wherever designated by law. The police were even ordered to arrest anyone who used a net or trap to fish. A pole and line was the only legally acceptable method of fishing. Aside from dogs, a long list of animals were required to be kept under strict control under the leash law, including goats, sheep, mules, and horses. Milk cows, however, were exempt. Cattle droves were no longer permitted on Congress Avenue or the fashionable Pecan Street, unless you had an adequate number of herders to control them.

The consumption of alcohol in Austin was so widespread during its early years that the city council eventually passed a law forbidding police officers from drinking while on duty. There was also a law against running a fandango house. This was a weak attempt by elected officials to pacify a group of homeowners trying to prevent Austin's first ward from becoming a concentrated vice district. Leading the fight was James Simms Sr., a stone mason and builder who also served the city for many years as a policeman. He would lose the battle to save his neighborhood, and he failed in his efforts to prevent his two sons, Billy and James Jr., from becoming members of the sporting crowd. On the eve of the Civil War, Austin did not contain a single brothel. Ten years later, many bawdy houses openly ran a booming business as the demand for easy female companionship was increased. This was due in large part to the Federal garrison stationed in Austin during Reconstruction. Though state legislators, cowboys, and visiting businessmen continued to provide the damsels of the first ward with an eager clientele long after the soldiers had moved on.

Efforts to stop the spread of vice in the first ward never had a chance as several aldermen and even the mayor were renting property in the district to known members of the demimonde. Fanny Kelley, Blanche Dumont, and Sallie Daggatt owned the best-known brothels that employed a good many of the *nymphs du pave* working in Austin.[1] Although fandangos may have been restricted, the city council readily approved many more new liquor licenses. Before long, dozens of new saloons and gambling dens were spreading throughout the first ward and its immediate vicinity. For many years, Austin newspapers reported on the numerous antics that occurred in the vice district, otherwise known as "the jungles" or the "precincts of Mexico," due to the large Black and Hispanic population residing there. After Ben Thompson's time, the vice district eventually became known as "Guytown." Occasionally, city officials took steps to curtail vice, but mostly they condoned the lively side of town. The famous author, O. Henry, was a resident of Austin from as early as 1884, and a man who witnessed the heyday of "Guytown." He left this assessment of the first ward. "Loafing, gambling, fighting and drinking has invaded this Arcadian spot. Let us pass some more laws against this kind of thing, and then let it go on as usual."[2]

Forty-four gas lamps lit up the city's main thoroughfares, and a new company was formed to look into providing electric light. One of the first to enjoy telephone service was the new city marshal, Ben Thompson, whose home was connected to police headquarters. The *Statesman* reported that, counting the city marshal, the city had a grand total of seventeen telephone subscribers, though subscriptions were selling rapidly and fifty to sixty new customers were expected in the near future.[3] A world-class opera house entertained residents, and a city-run hospital cared for the sick. The city budget paid for a board of health comprised of six physicians, and provided money to the county to help fund a welfare system for the indigent.

Like most municipalities of the past and present, officials tended to outspend the city's tax revenue. In 1881, total police department expenses exceeded $12,000, almost double that of fire department expenditures, and represented a full 20% of the entire city budget. The city marshal's annual salary of $1,800 gave credence to the importance of the position. Aside from the mayor's $2,000 per year salary, the marshal made more money than any other city official.

Like Edward Creary before him, Thompson was tasked with more than just patrolling the streets, ferreting out criminals, and making arrests. Ben Thompson found himself managing an important city department struggling to perform within tightening budget constraints. In accordance with local ordinance, he was responsible for holding public sales of unclaimed property, and for renting out the butcher and vegetable vendor stalls at the city-owned market. Offenders convicted of misdemeanors and without the ready cash to pay off their fines, worked them off on the city marshal's street crew, which cleaned and maintained the city's streets and alleyways. The monthly report that Thompson submitted to the city council listed exactly how many arrests his officers made, and each arrest was itemized along with the amount of fines collected or paid for in sweat. This report was frequently published in the *Statesman* for every citizen to scrutinize (see Appendix C).

The city marshal also had a social function to perform. At times, Thompson attended church services with his officers and he was always present at holiday picnics, like those on San Jacinto Day (April 21) and the Fourth of July. He represented Austin as city marshal as part of an official welcoming committee for visiting dignitaries on multiple occasions. When an Irish Member of Parliament visited the Capital City of Texas, Thompson was among the reception committee. He took great care in decorating his city hall office with so many curiosities that the *Statesman* reported it as "a perfect museum and art gallery." Among his collection was an enormous rattlesnake skin stretching sixty-six inches long. He also kept a powerful field glass on hand, and cordially extended an invitation to any and all visitors to stop by to enjoy a view of the surrounding countryside.[4]

This turn in Thompson's life began on Saturday, December 18, 1880, when the Austin City Council and new Mayor Lewis Mason Crocker examined the results of the election in a special meeting, and officially declared Ben Thompson the city marshal. Three days later, after fully recovering from his temporary illness, Thompson donned his city marshal uniform, pinned on his badge of office, and began his service to the city as a lawman. It was on this day, in all probability, that Thompson posed with other city council members for a historic group photograph that included J.W. Howard, Fred Sterzing, City Attorney C.D. Johns, Mayor Crocker, Marshal Thompson, City Physician Dr. R.H. Bibb, and City Clerk E.B. Connell. Photographer Harvey R. Marks also shot a head and shoulders portrait of Ben with his marshal's cap and badge prominently displayed. Twenty-eight year old Officer John Chenneville, who had been in charge of the police department during the interim two weeks, became Thompson's second in command. Throughout his tenure, Thompson was greatly aided by Chenneville, who was lauded as an exceptional and efficient officer.[5]

John Cardwell of the *Statesman* published an open message to the new marshal on what was expected. "This wish of Mr.

Thompson," to be the city marshal, "has been known to many of our citizens for a long time and on the promises he made during the canvass [*sic*] just ended many of the best and most prominent citizens, firmly relying upon his word buried the past and cast their votes for him." Cardwell confessed, "Such confidence in the simple promise of a man who has lived such an eventful life has rarely been equaled in the annals of this country, and very certainly, has never been excelled. It is something that Mr. Thompson can justly be proud of. The people by their vote … indicated that they had confidence in his word and faith in his ability to perform well every duty pertaining to one of the most important offices in this city." The newspaperman explained how promises are not enough and "it remains now for him to show by his actions and attention to duty that this confidence and faith has not been misplaced."[6]

Thompson could bask in this complimentary statement, at least for his first few days in office. Unlike his predecessor, the new city marshal began to personally direct his officers on the street. He sorted out crimes and made a variety of arrests from preventing riders and their wagons from speeding on city streets to hauling in violent felons.[7] Expensive and congratulatory presents were given to the new marshal, despite his having less than a month on the job. Ben Thompson was thought of as lively, vivacious, and good company, as evidenced by his many "boon companions" in places like San Antonio. His friends there congratulated Ben on his election by sending a handsome and costly saddle over to him. Austin citizens presented Ben with an exceedingly beautiful gold badge engraved with his name and new title.[8] Another gift came in the form of a dismissal on the last case generated by Ben's April 1880 keno hall shooting spree. Though to be fair, the state attorney's gracious motion to dismiss the charges against Ben was based on a lack of evidence.[9] Coincidently, Billy Thompson also benefited from a dismissal of charges when the frustrated Harris County court noted in its records without any further explanation, "the prisoner having escaped."[10]

The *Statesman* praised Thompson and the police officers under his command after only two months on the job. "Marshal Thompson and the efficient ... officer Chenneville,"[11] declared the newspaper, "are managing the police of the city well. The department was never better controlled, and officers and men deserve much praise. They are a careful and polite set of officers, and few cities have their equals and none their superiors."[12] John Cardwell, the observant *Statesman* editor, acted as the unofficial watchdog of Thompson and the police. Generally, the reports were positive. Two weeks later the *Statesman* continued its praise, pointing out the police were "having a quiet time. Very few arrests are being made."[13]

There is compelling evidence to suggest that one of the first arrests Thompson made as city marshal was of Sheriff James Madison Brown of Lee County, Texas.[14] Sheriff Brown was a well-known horse trainer, and it was widely accepted throughout the state that he was a man not to be trifled with. His notoriety peaked when he performed the legal execution of the notorious William "Bloody Bill" Longley. Brown wasn't afraid to use his six-gun either, and by this time in his life, he had shot and killed at least four men, some died in an official capacity while others were the casualties of personal matters. And Ben Thompson and Jim Brown would soon cross paths again.[15]

In mid-February, San Antonio officials invited the Texas Legislature to temporarily adjourn their business and plan a visit to their city. The legislators voted for an excursion to the Alamo City at once. On Monday afternoon, February 21, some two hundred people including members of the state legislature, Travis County officials, Austin city officials, members of the press, and prominent citizens all boarded a special excursion train bound for San Antonio with four coaches appointed for their comfort. The

Denison Colored Brass and String Band played as the train pulled out of the depot. The hotels in San Antonio were overflowing, yet, somehow Ben Thompson found a room at the elegant Menger Hotel on Alamo Plaza. While most of the excursionists toured the ruins of the Alamo chapel and the other Spanish missions, Thompson decided to visit Jack Harris's combination Vaudeville Theatre, saloon, and gambling hall despite threats levied against his return.[16]

Thompson dressed in his city marshal uniform and hat for his night out in San Antonio. One newspaperman felt the outfit made Ben "look like a major general on dress parade." It was noted that Ben "seemed to enjoy his visit ... with peculiar zest, and attracted more attention and elicited more comment than any of the [other] visiting statesmen." Accompanying Thompson on his tour "to uncover the wickedness" of the Alamo city were other Austin city officials and his many sporting friends. Ben's party first stopped at the Green Front Saloon on Military Plaza at the corner of Commerce Street and Flores. Later, they went east to the adjunct Main Plaza and the Vaudeville Theatre. Luckily, Jack Harris was not on the premises. Thompson led the way up to Foster's second floor gambling room, the 101 Club, where he found Joe Foster barring the door and denying him admittance. Ben Thompson pulled out his police whistle in response and informed Foster he would blow it. Realizing the sound would empty his gambling hall of customers, Foster reluctantly decided to allow the party to enter.[17] Jack Harris was furious when he later learned of Thompson's forced entry.

That night Leo Tarleton, a prominent San Antonio attorney and law partner of former Judge B.I. Boone, saw Jack Harris coming out of one of the Vaudeville Saloon's front doors cradling a double-barrel shotgun in his arms. Tarleton asked Harris what was the matter, to which Harris replied, "That damn son-of-a-bitch has been in my house in my absence and he should not come in again." Harris further exclaimed, "[He] is a man I want nothing to do with. He came here and robbed me and I want to have nothing to do with him." Tarleton took hold of the shotgun and told Harris to put it up. Harris followed the advice and walked back into his saloon, placing the gun behind the bar. Harris stepped around the counter and ranted on, "by God I want nothing to do with him. I want him to let me alone. I have told him not to come in my house and if he comes in here I intend to kill him." Predicting how the local authorities would react to his killing of Ben Thompson, he stated, "I would have no difficulty about the matter." Harris had sent for police officers, but as yet, Tarleton did not see any. For an hour or two, Tarleton hung around the Vaudeville before tiring and going home.[18]

A.L. Cashell,[19] a newspaper editor who first met Thompson in 1859, also found Jack Harris walking back and forth in front of the Vaudeville with the double-barrel shotgun under his arm. Cashell asked Harris what he was going to do with that "howitzer" to which Harris responded, "I'm going to kill that son of a bitch Ben Thompson." Cashell thought there was a good deal of foolishness in that, and believed they could settle things without any serious difficulty. He told Harris so and received a reply that, "he [Harris] didn't care and, that he had been imposed upon and he did not intend that Thompson should come to this town, [and] he had sent him word to that effect." If Thompson returned to San Antonio, he intended to kill him. Harris also stated "he would not go to Austin to hunt him, but that [Thompson] ... would come to this town once too often." Cashell later admitted in response to Harris's threats, "I have never heard Thompson make any threats [in return]. I have heard Thompson say that he thought the thing would come out all right if people would let it alone."[20]

As the night went on, Jack Harris sent a city policeman to the home of Bexar County Sheriff Thomas P. McCall. The sheriff responded to Harris's request and arrived at the Vaudeville around midnight. He found Harris still holding his shotgun and standing by the saloon's east door. McCall inquired as to what was the matter, and Harris said Ben Thompson was in town, and "there is going to be trouble and I want the officers all here to keep order." The sheriff went off and found city police officer Captain Edward Stevens and on their return, found other police officers on the scene as well. In response to Harris's threat on Ben Thompson's life, Sheriff McCall reminded Harris how "his house was a public house and anybody had a right to go in there if he behaved himself." The lawmen stood around another two hours before realizing Ben Thompson was not going to show. Then they all went home to bed or returned to their assigned posts about the city.[21]

During the second night of the Legislature excursion, both Ben Thompson and Jack Harris were out on the town with friends and they ran into each other at the Green Front Saloon by pure chance. William H. Simms was a witness to the surprise meeting and heard Thompson say, "Look here Harris I heard that you were looking for me with a shotgun last night." Harris responded, "No sir I was not looking for you with a shotgun." "I heard you were," was Thompson's retort and Harris insisted, "No, I was not looking for you [,] I was waiting for you." Ben asked, "do you mean to say I can't come in your house down there [?]" Harris explained, "Ben if you had a house and forbid me to go into it I would not go around it." Ben asked the question again and received the same answer from Harris. Ben added a final challenge. "Well I'm coming to your house and if the doors are closed I'm going to kick them down ... if you think I care a damn for you, you jump out there on the plaza with your shotgun." The argument ended as fast as it started. Both men, with their friends around them, exited the Green Front Saloon simultaneously, and each man, with his friends in tow, walked down the street in different directions without any further trouble.[22] At 7:00 a.m. the next morning, the excursionists boarded their train and departed for home. Ben was on board the train, and upon his arrival in Austin, he returned to his duties as city marshal.[23]

Soon afterward, several Texas newspapers reported that Thompson had "declared war against [San Antonio's] gambling dens, and threatened to have them closed by the legislature. He declares they are robbers' dens" and there was "not an honest card dealt in them, and that he knows where of he speaks, having been a gambler all his life. He also says he is determined to do all he can to have such dens of iniquity as are openly run in [San Antonio] legislated against and closed up."[24] To his friends, "Thompson accused Harris of swindling him out of diamonds and money in his gambling room, adjoining his theatre."[25] Running into Billy Simms in Austin, Thompson told Simms he "intended to take legal steps by appealing to the law of friends [of] the corporation to close up the [Vaudeville]."[26]

The Austin police force made 133 arrests in February, thirty-seven of which were for intoxication; easily the most numerous of the many and varied infractions. Throughout the late winter and spring, Marshal Thompson adjusted his officers's hours, recovered stolen goods, actively patrolled the streets, and made arrests. The city council passed a resolution permanently establishing the position of Sergeant of Police, which was filled by John Chenneville. Thompson's responsibilities included taking off his marshal's uniform for a day and serving as an auctioneer. At auction, Thompson offered three-month leases on the city market stalls to the butchers, grocers, coffee roasters, brewers, and others who competed for the limited number of spaces.[27] By the end of the month, Ben ran an ad in the *Statesman's* popular "Twenty-five Cents" column looking for a cash loan. "I want to borrow $500 for which will be paid 1½ % interest and give real estate security." Apparently his $1,800 per year salary was not covering his expenses.[28] Leonard Eck, a pawn broker who owned a shop on Austin's Pecan Street

(6th Street), knew Ben and Kate Thompson as good, longtime customers who used his services on a regular basis.[29]

In early April, the circus was in Austin, and three cowboys who came to see the show were leaving on horseback at 3:00 a.m. when they decided to have a little fun. They galloped down Congress Avenue whooping and hollering until they met up with City Marshal Ben Thompson and Officer Cary H. Randolph, who attempted to stop them.[30] Randolph mounted a horse and chased two of the men. Thompson hurried down to the bridge over the Colorado River. He gave up further pursuit as he was on foot and was returning to Congress Avenue when he surprisingly met the third horseman. The man was crossing the bridge astride a tired mount with his six-shooter drawn when Thompson ordered him to stop. "Who are you?" the man yelled.

"Marshal Thompson, and if you don't surrender it will be the most unhealthy moment of your life." The cowboy meekly responded, "Think so myself and to save trouble, and prevent anything like a funeral procession, I'll cave." And cave he did. Thompson locked him up, and the next day at the mayor's court, the man was fined $25 plus court costs for unlawfully carrying a six-shooter.[31]

After a short vacation to Galveston to attend a German singing festival and competition called the *Saengerfest*,[32] Thompson put all of his efforts into law enforcement. The *Statesman* bragged that the police equipment and weaponry in Thompson's office was unexcelled by any other city in the state.[33] Even though the legislature was in-session and the town swarmed with people, the month of March was comparatively dull and arrests only numbered ninety-seven, considerably fewer than usual.[34] Austin continued to be relatively quiet throughout the rest of that spring. The *Statesman* reported how the courts were having a quiet time due to very little criminal business.[35] Only 112 arrests were made in May, and of the eighty-two men arrested, only five gave their occupation as "stockman."[36]

In May, "one of the most desperate men in the frontier counties" of Texas stopped in Austin.[37] John Peters Ringo was on his way from Arizona to visit family in Missouri, and his repute as a killer was based on his participation in the bloody Mason County War.

Early on Sunday morning, May 1, after enjoying the amusements of Austin's spirited First Ward, Ringo was recuperating in a room at "a house in the jungles." About 4:00 a.m., he "missed his purse." He stepped out into the hallway and pulled his pistol on three or four local boys, demanding they put their "hands up" while he searched them. He did not find his purse and returned to his room. The affronted boys reported Ringo's actions to the police who promptly informed Marshal Thompson. Not bothering to wait for other officers to accompany him, Thompson went down to the house and demanded entrance into Ringo's room. Ringo steadfastly refused. Consequently, Thompson "cheerfully kicked open the door, and to the infinite disgust of Mr. Ringo scooped him in." The marshal disarmed and arrested Ringo, and then turned him over to Sergeant Chenneville when he arrived. Ringo was then marched down to the police station and jailed. The next day he was fined $25 for carrying a pistol and $5 for disturbing the peace. "He settled with the city and left a wiser if not sadder man." He never returned to Austin.[38]

The noted arrest brought Thompson more laurels. Alexander E. Sweet and John Armoy Knox, longtime Texas newspaperman, published their opinion of Thompson's performance as a lawman in their new Austin publication *Texas Siftings,* "Captain Ben Thompson is the best city marshal in Texas to-day. He knows his duty and is not afraid to do it. We are not personally acquainted with the marshal, but we admire the way he has executed the law since he was elected to office, and we take pleasure in shaking him by the hand, as it were."[39]

Thompson was not known as a church going man. However, the Austin police force led by City Marshal Ben Thompson attended the worship service at the Cumberland Presbyterian Church, on Sunday night, May 22. The church was a leading force against intemperance, and this was likely a show of solidarity.[40]

Down in the Nueces River valley, John King Fisher was living quietly on his ranch with his wife, Sarah Vivian, and their two little daughters. It was said he was "attending to his own business, and taking no more scalps."[41] In late April, King Fisher faced a Uvalde jury on an older charge for murdering two vaqueros. The jury found him not guilty. Three months later, on July 14, 1881, the last of the criminal indictments against Fisher, this time for horse theft, were tried in Webb County. He was promptly acquitted. For the first time in six years, he was free from any and all criminal charges. The authorities failed to obtain a single conviction on any of the twenty-one indictments he was charged with. Remarkably, he was somehow acquitted by six different juries, and the other indictments were never even brought to trial.[42] Free to leave his outlaw days behind, John King Fisher decided to turn away from his old ways and find the excitement he so craved while wearing a badge. Meanwhile, his good friend, Billy Thompson, did not seem to be changing his wild ways. On May 15, the mayor's court in Fort Worth fined him $1 for being drunk.[43]

During the summer months, City Marshal Thompson continued to perform an active role in investigating and reducing crime. He spent a night on a stakeout when a Congress Avenue merchant had reason to suspect his shop might be robbed. Thompson recovered a watch that a visitor from Chicago reported being "lost" when he toured "the jungles" section of the first ward.[44] When a black woman and maid named Susan Billingsley "filled up with whisky" and ... proceeding to drive a wagon on the city streets 'at a fearful rate'" came upon Ben Thompson, "he stopped her mad career, but she refused to tamely submit to an arrest and calmly sailed into the marshal, and they had quite a lively tussle for some minutes. He succeeded, however, in overcoming her." Miss Billingsley was subsequently fined $10 plus court costs. The *Statesman* concluded its report, stating as a matter of fact, that Ben "keeps the city quiet."[45]

Personal difficulties were never more than a moment away from a man with Thompson's temperament, and the *Statesman* took note of one such near-incident. Herman Lunghwitz, a bartender at the Turner Hall, had too much to drink one night and exchanged a few harsh words with the city marshal. He grasped a beer mug and raised his arm to throw it at Ben until he saw Thompson draw his pistol and warn him not to do it. Wisely, Lunghwitz set the glass down and peaceably worked the matter out with the marshal.[46]

When news of Thompson's election reached his friend Buffalo Bill Cody, the showman decided to send an impressive gift to commemorate the occasion. When a package arrived addressed to Ben Thompson on June 14, 1881 the *Statesman* took notice of it. "Yesterday morning Marshal Thompson received a very handsome present from Buffalo Bill. It is a handsome and costly target pistol, manufactured by Stevens & Co., Chicopee Falls, Massachusetts. The mountings are of gold, handle beautifully tinted pearl, while the glittering steel barrel is most artistically and beautifully carved. It is engraved on the handle, 'From Buffalo Bill to Ben Thompson.' It is the only pistol of the kind in the city, and is a marvel of skilled workmanship."

Single shot target pistols like the one Cody commissioned the Joshua Stevens firm to produce for Thompson were in high demand from sport shooters out east. Stevens received an immeasurable amount of complimentary publicity when Cody and Annie Oakley used his line of target pistols during their performances. Cody ordered the pistol sent to Louis Daniel Nimschke of New York City, a freelance metal engraver. Nimschke was internationally renowned

William F. "Buffalo Bill" Cody, who befriended Ben Thompson in Austin and San Antonio. Cody, the showman, and Thompson, the gunman, demonstrated their shooting ability in front of admiring spectators, prominent citizens, and newspaper correspondents. Later, in Nebraska, Cody was able to assist Billy Thompson out of a situation that could have resulted in a lynching or a long prison term.

Courtesy the Buffalo Bill Historical Museum, Cody, Wyoming.

for his adept adornment of firearms in the popular American style with rich, bold scrolling lines. The pistol was chambered to fire .32 caliber, short Colt center-fire cartridges through a ten-inch barrel, and Thompson prized his gift, apparently providing it with excellent care.[47]

In 1998, firearm experts, historians, and authors R. L. Wilson and Greg Martin wrote, "If any one firearm capsules the color, romance, excitement, and life-and-death adventure of the great American West and the supreme significance of firearms on the frontier, it is the Cody-to-Thompson Stevens No. 36 Target pistol."[48]

During the late spring, a family tragedy struck Ben thompson's home. Mary Ann Thompson, mother of Ben and Billy, was suffering from a malignant tumor on her liver under the care of Doctor J. W. Stalnaker. She was beyond any medical help, and she died at her son's home on Saturday night, July 9. She was sixty-six. On Sunday at 6 p.m., she was interred in Oakwood Cemetery after a well-attended funeral service officiated by Bishop Alexander Gregg at St. David's Episcopal Church. A large procession of mourners followed her remains to the grave. The *Statesman* described her as "a lady of more than ordinary intelligence and possessed to a marked degree all the attributes that ever crown the life of a noble woman. She was highly esteemed by all who knew her." Her family published a card of thanks expressing "lasting gratitude" for the kindness shown to their mother. William Thompson's name appeared with the name of his brother, two sisters, and their spouses, and it is reasonable to believe that Billy was by his mother's side during her final days.[49]

On July 12, 1881, Ben Thompson made his most publicized arrest. Several days prior to the incident, Lee County Sheriff Jim Brown had passed through Austin on his way to Louisiana to hunt for a fugitive named George Keith believed to have committed a murder in his county seven years earlier. A woman dressed in male attire with a belted and holstered six-shooter swinging from her hips accompanied the sheriff. The woman, a German lady, once known in Austin as Emelie Sckerls, was in violation of a local ordinance that outlawed the wearing of clothes of the opposite gender. Sheriff Brown's companion was then going by the name of Mrs. Amelia Schooman, and she was notorious in Austin for previously dealing out the ardent for a financial consideration in her own establishment there. Her first husband divorced her for that behavior. Her second husband, known as old man Schooman, having discovered that she had too many lovers, was appalled and left her. When Marshal Thompson learned of the strange couple, he left orders to be immediately notified should they pass through Austin again.

On their return trip, with their prisoner in custody, Sheriff Brown and Mrs. Schooman stopped at the Austin depot to change trains. Informed of their arrival and imminent departure, Thompson hustled down to the depot in time to arrest Mrs. Schooman as she was boarding her train. With Sheriff Brown, Mrs. Schooman, and their prisoner in tow, Marshal Thompson marched the group down to city hall where Schooman readily agreed to change into traditional female attire and was released on her own recognizance. In the morning, news of the arrest spread like wildfire through the town, and the corridors of the city hall were swelled with people who wanted to get a look at the "small woman with such a big six-shooter." She was described as having "sharp blue eyes, a small mouth, retrousse nose and a naiveté manner, which made her quite attractive." She was arraigned before Mayor Crocker, where he fined her $25 plus court costs. Brown promptly appealed the mayor's ruling, and she paid a bond to ensure her appearance before the county court.[50]

Newspapers throughout Texas carried the story of Thompson's arrest. Sheriff Brown was humiliated, both officially and personally, by the incident. He was married at the time, and lamely stated

William B. "Bat" Masterson, who gained recognition as a buffalo hunter, gunfighter, lawman, gambler, newspaper reporter, and author. In 1907, Masterson wrote that Thompson "had killed many men during his career [but] was what could be properly termed a thoroughly game man." *Courtesy the Robert G. McCubbin Collection.*

to the press that Mrs. Schooman was along to help him identify his man and help work up the case. Newspapers continued to sensationalize the story by calling the prostitute a "deputy sheriff of Lee County." The July 13 edition of the *San Antonio Daily Express* editorialized how Sheriff Brown "forgets the dignity of his office" in going about "with a woman masquerading in men's clothing [and he] should be degraded from his place." The article went on to say that those who elected him should "drive him out of the community."[51] Brown would not easily forget the embarrassment Ben Thompson caused him.

New York's *National Police Gazette,* one of the most popular publications of the nineteenth century, printed a short article in late July about Marshal Ben Thompson that repeated what other newspapers often published about his surprisingly gentlemanly manners for a man known to have killed so many men. The account added to his fame throughout the country.[52]

Earlier, Billy Simms returned to San Antonio from Austin, and he noticed that his partner Jack Harris was now keeping a double-barrel shotgun in the Vaudeville Theatre's downstairs ticket office. Neither Thompson nor Harris had forgotten their feud, and Simms certainly must have had some concern for his friend. Harris explained that he had won the gun in a raffle.[53] Though Jack Harris wasn't the only one about the Vaudeville who could become belligerent and threatening. Simms struggled with an uncontrollable temper. On one occasion, Billy Simms beat a young boot-black on the street to the point that a passerby, Judge Wesley Ogden of San Antonio, had to interfere on behalf of the boy. Billy Simms then turned his wrath on Ogden and struck him. The judge beat Simms with his walking cane until the brawl caught the attention of law enforcement and all were arrested. Once things were sorted out, only Simms was hauled into court and fined $5 for his violent outburst.[54]

Austin Mayor L. M. Crocker and City Marshal Thompson were selected to attend the annual state firemen's convention scheduled to take place in the city of Sherman during the second week of August. At the conclusion of the convention, Ben Thompson went on to Fort Worth and perhaps visited with his brother Billy who still spent most of his time there.[55] While Ben Thompson traveled about northern Texas, Jack Harris left for New York City. He went with the purpose of procuring a first-rate group of performers for his variety theatre and was in New York for almost one month.[56] When Thompson returned to Austin, he presented Travis County Sheriff Edward Creary with a beautiful nickel-plated revolver, the handle of which was engraved with, "Ed. Creary, sheriff, from Ben Thompson, city Marshal, Austin, Texas, 1881." What became of this firearm is now unknown.[57]

Lee County Sheriff J. M. Brown, of the "sprightly looking deputy" scandal, was a noted racehorse owner. During the annual Austin fair, he brought along three of his best mounts to participate in the races. He arrived on Tuesday, August 23, and peacefully remained in town for more than a week. A rumor reported that Brown and his friends from Lee County planned to create a disturbance at the races in order to draw Thompson out and kill him. Fortunately, Thompson was notified of the plot. He "met Brown at the fairgrounds, and approaching him informed him of what he had heard, and said, if it was true, [this] was the time to settle the trouble, like men." Brown flatly denied the report, and violence was averted between the two dangerous men.[58]

That October, a substantial candidate came forward to contest the office of city marshal in the following month's regularly scheduled city election. J.P. Kirk officially announced his candidacy in the *Statesman,* and the newspaper obliged him by proclaiming his merits, stating that Kirk was "known to every man in the city as a gentleman of undoubted integrity and sterling worth. As deputy

The richly-engraved, single-shot target pistol was manufactured by Stevens & Company. Master engraver Louis Daniel Nimschke of New York City decorated the weapon. On the handle he inscribed the words, "From Buffalo Bill to Ben Thompson." The grips are iridescent mother-of-pearl. The weapon is chambered to fire a .32-caliber short Colt center-fire cartridge. *Courtesy the Tom Bicknell Collection.*

sheriff of this county for years, he made a most careful and efficient officer, and no man is better qualified in every respect to fill the office he now aspires."

Ben Thompson had to respond, and on October 11, he announced his desire to seek re-election. Two weeks later, he issued the following statement concerning his year in office.

> Fellow Citizens of Austin: I have announced myself as a candidate for re-election to the office of city marshal. As an inducement to your support for the partial term about to expire, I promised you, if elected, to fill the post to the best of my skill and ability. Honored by your suffrages, I entered upon the discharge of my duties without the knowledge and experience since acquired. That some minor, perhaps important, things have escaped adequate diligence and attention, I will not pretend to urge a denial; but I can truthfully affirm that I have been as faithful and vigilant as under all the circumstances I could well be. And, in this connection, I trust you will pardon me in submitting for your consideration the following extract from the official record of police matters, coming under my supervision during the ten months of my time as city marshal and chief of police, dating from the 21st

> of December last to the 17th of October, to-wit: 'Number of arrests, 1,200; Total amount [of] fines and costs [collected], $9,056. Amount of fines worked out on the street, $2,803. Amount of cash collected, $6,252. Total amount of property and money stolen and reported to police, $1,172; amount recovered, $913. [I] believe that the above statement will favorably comport with any like summary of the city's ministerial affairs, and none can successfully charge that I have disgraced the baton, by abusing the unfortunate, the timid and poor. The reflecting citizen will remember at the same time, that the city has been entangled in the toils of financial embarrassment, and that this condition of things affects the sphere of police, as well as of other municipal relations, and that it was right and proper of me to co-operate with my superiors and the council respecting the interests of the people in this regard, and to subordinate the department under my charge to the exigencies of the situation, without limiting or impairing its substantial efficiency and usefulness. In conclusion, I would gratefully acknowledge my obligations to the ... fair minded citizenship of Austin for its kind support and assistance for the official term that has passed, and would confidently express the hope to one and to all that I may not be deemed entirely unworthy to re-solicit a repetition of the same. Respectfully, Ben Thompson.[59]

As the election neared, a series of political meetings were held, and candidates for various city offices were called to the podium to express their views. On Thursday, November 3, a meeting was held in front of the Theissen Brothers Saloon on East Pecan Street (6th Street). After several speakers, the crowd of onlookers formed a parade led by a brass band, and marched to the corner of Congress Avenue and Ash (9th Street) between the Palace and Club House Saloons where more speakers expressed their views. Ben Thompson was the last speaker called to the stand, and the crowd showed a marked degree of attention, which they had not given to any other of the speakers. In a soft, matter-of-fact voice, Thompson made his debut as a stump speaker.

> I am not a public speaker. This is the first speech I have ever made in my life. My opponent, Mr. Kirk, has not assailed ... my record. ... I have tried to do my duty while I have been in office, and, although there were many people who voted against me... I have treated all alike, and if I am elected again, which I expect to be, I intend to act the same toward those who vote against me as to those who vote for me. I have tried during the past to befriend all who were in need of aid, and I intend in the future to help everybody that I can, whether I am elected or not ... but I say to you now, if anyone can justly charge me with having neglected to do my duty at any time, of failing to befriend anyone when it was in my power to do so ... vote against me. ... I want your vote, but if I am not worthy of it don't give it to me. That is all I have to say.

Thompson was met with enthusiastic applause, and when he stepped down from the stand and started up the street, the whole crowd followed him until he managed to elude them.[60]

The following day at another campaign meeting on the east side of town, a difficulty occurred between two black men. One was stabbed, and the row created considerable excitement until Thompson stepped into the room, and by his mere presence, stopped the fight and arrested the knife-wielder.[61]

W. A. Saylor, a resident of the First Ward, was a leading candidate for mayor, and his many friends and supporters were working hard for every vote. At a campaign meeting for Saylor at the Workingman's Hall on Pecan Street (6th street), several of "the colored brethren made speeches, one of whom suggested that it was 'gittin about time for candidates to bring out their hacks as the cullud folks wanted to ride some.'" The *Statesman* thought free lunch stands, a common inducement in Austin to attract votes, would be opening up soon.[62]

Election Day was Monday, November 7, 1881. It brought no serious disturbances, despite the "usual amount of yelling and other boisterous demonstrations ... indulged in by the hired bummers, strikers and rounders, whose brains were enthused by the free drinks ... gurgled down their noisy throats." Thompson carried the majority in seven out of the city's ten wards, and the lively first ward supported him with his largest plurality. Ben won re-election with 1,173 votes to Deputy Sheriff Kirk's 933 votes.

At midnight, the Manning Rifles band led a large enthusiastic crowd to the new mayor's residence and the homes of other successful candidates, including Ben's, where each of the gentlemen were serenaded and impromptu speeches were delivered, "and a hearty good time prevailed." To show their esteem and to congratulate him on his re-election, Ben's friends presented him with a handsome desk and chair constructed of the finest black walnut, elegantly carved.[63] The newly elected mayor, W. A. Saylor, nominated John Chenneville to carry on as sergeant of the police, and the nomination was confirmed by acclimation. The Austin police force presented "a fine gold watch" to Mayor Saylor, and Ben Thompson delivered the presentation speech.[64]

By the 1880s, the Texas legislature was already aware that the old Capitol building, erected less than thirty years before, needed to be replaced. Plans were being drawn up for a new stone structure when, on November 9, 1881, the building was suddenly engulfed in flames. Two of Austin's volunteer fire companies responded, but the nearest fire hydrant was seven hundred feet away and water trickled out of their hoses. The responders were helpless, and the Capitol crumbled. Col. Amos C. Babcock, Billy's friend and benefactor when he went bust a few years before in Buena Vista, Colorado, attempted to become involved in the replacement effort of the Capitol Building but ran into resistance. City Marshal Thompson remembered how Babcock helped his brother when Billy was in need, and Thompson repaid the kindness by smoothing the way for Colonel Babcock to participate in the capitol rebuilding project.[65]

During the San Antonio Fair in November 1881, Hays County Deputy Sheriff Thomas G. Martin, who also owned a saloon in the town of Kyle, came upon Jack Harris one block west of the Vaudeville Theatre in front of Wolfson's Store on the Main Plaza. Martin had known Ben Thompson for more than fifteen years, and he had known Jack Harris since the mid-1870s. At Harris's request, Martin met with him at the Vaudeville later that evening. At the meeting, Harris asked, "If I and [Lee County Sheriff] Brown and Ben Thompson had settled our difficulty." Martin told him that he had had no problem with Thompson. Harris said, "it was currently reported that ... Thompson had made [you and Harris] run away from the [Austin] fair grounds." Martin reiterated "that Brown and Thompson had had some words but not I." Martin did confirm that Thompson frequently had a black man with him armed with a Winchester rifle. Harris went on, "why did [you and Brown] not kill the damned Negro and Thompson too." Harris then admitted "he had it fixed for [Thompson] once here [in San Antonio] but he slipped by mere accident." He asked Martin to warn Sheriff Brown away from Ben Thompson saying, "tell Brown to let him alone [as] he's mine. I found him first [and] sooner or later you bet I'll get my work in." Harris must certainly have realized Martin would warn his longtime friend Ben Thompson of his threats against him.[66]

Thompson's bodyguard was Alexander Mack, who the *Statesman* once called, "a notoriously bad darkey." He had been arrested for a wide variety of offenses, among them, disturbing the peace, attempting to prevent an arrest, intoxication, carrying a pistol, and he once made a jail break with two other prisoners by cutting the bars and climbing down a blanket to make their escape. Before becoming Ben Thompson's attendant and bodyguard, the troublesome Alex Mack earned his living as a laborer, stone cutter and gambler.[67]

The city of Austin officials during Ben Thompson's tenure as the lead law enforcement officer. Standing from left to right: Captain J.W. Howard, Treasurer; C.D. Johns, Attorney; Ben Thompson, City Marshal; E.B. Connell, City Clerk; Seated from left to right: Fred A. Sterzing, Assessor and Tax Collector; L.M. Crocker, Mayor; R.H.I. Bibb, City Physician. Photograph by Harvey R. Marks.
Courtesy the Austin History Center. Image # PICA 00815.

Thompson needed Alex Mack, and this fact was best articulated by the dramatic actor Frederick Warde, who played Iago in Shakespeare's *Othello* during a string of Texas performances in 1881. Warde's troupe traveled from San Antonio to Austin, where a delegation of officials met them upon their arrival. Warde forgot most of the men in the welcoming committee, but he distinctly remembered City Marshal Ben Thompson, a man who seemed to unintentionally impress people at all levels of society. Warde later wrote that he found Thompson "a very agreeable man, quiet and courteous but always alert. He never spoke of his adventures but said he expected to die a sudden and violent death, as he had many enemies who would not hesitate to take his life if the opportunity occurred."[68] With enemies such as Jack Harris and James Brown, and perhaps others, it is easier to understand the persistent presence of a man like Mack to watch Thompson's back.

In late December, sad news arrived from Silver City, New Mexico. Ben's brother-in-law, James K. Farrell, died without warning. A now unknown, fast moving illness burned through Farrell, and only a few close friends were even aware that he had fallen ill. At the time, he was serving as a deputy sheriff and his death occurred almost one year to the day after he had arrived in New Mexico Territory.[69]

William M. Edwardy, the Galveston correspondent for the *Houston Post*, was in San Antonio during the latter part of December and visited the Vaudeville. On Christmas Day, one of the performers introduced Edwardy to Harris who asked Edwardy, "I believe you had some sort of fuss with Ben Thompson." Edwardy replied that he did but, "it was fixed up all right, that neither of us had any feeling against the other, that it was all a misunderstanding." Harris replied "you may think it is settled but you are mistaken—that Ben Thompson is not that kind of a man [that] if Ben Thompson ever got the drop on [you] he would kill [you.]" Harris further warned Edwardy that "if I were in your place, the first time I got Ben Thompson out of Austin I would walk up to him and shoot him down like a dog and nobody would do anything to me … this is what I'm going to do if I ever got the drop on him if he ever comes into my place I'm going to shoot him down without saying a word to him." Harris repeated his intention to mercilessly kill Thompson if given the chance ad nauseum. He also asked Edwardy if he knew when Thompson was likely to leave Austin saying, "if Ben Thompson went to Laredo he did not think he would ever go back to Austin." Edwardy kept the conversation to himself and chose not to mention any of this to Thompson.[70] Clearly, Ben Thompson was becoming more and more of an obsession with Jack Harris.

Before the year ended, the Hope Hook and Ladder Volunteer Company Number 2 elected new officers. Ben Thompson was voted in as president and John Chenneville was chosen as foreman.[71] As December of 1881 came to a close, the *Statesman* observed that "the city appears to be filling up with hoodlums, cranks and tramps" and advised citizens "to keep a sharp lookout about their premises," admitting "the police are having a very quiet time just now, and the chain gang has been seriously reduced."[72]

As 1882 began, the city council and newly elected mayor announced to the public that the municipal government had accumulated a staggering amount of debt. The city charter had set a legal debt ceiling of $100,000, but Austin's total obligations approached $150,000. The council immediately passed ordinances eliminating several minor city positions and cut the salaries of others. The police department was no exception, and Ben Thompson went before the council and pleaded his case that the number of officers now under his command was insufficient to do the duty required. The next day someone fired three shots at "Mexican Charlie" Cortissoz, also known as Cunio, at his establishment in the first ward. None of the shots were effective, but the *Statesman* sourly commented that under the current regulations, the single policeman assigned to patrol "Mexico" was woefully inadequate. The *Statesman* agreed with the council's attempts to bring municipal spending under control, but editorialized "economy is a good thing if not spread on too thick, the police force should be the last branch of the public service attacked when reductions are taking place. Let the economic minds, which govern us find something else to drive the pruning knife through. Increase the police force, protect the people and make them pay for it."[73]

The council passed a debt-restructuring ordinance allowing for a legal increase of the city's obligations. The measure needed to be approved by voters through a referendum. A town meeting was held at Millett's Opera House prior to the vote, and a series of government officials and prominent citizens took the stage to speak both for and against the proposal. Near the end of the affair, loud calls brought Marshal Thompson to the stage, and he delivered a pragmatic and matter-of-fact address. Thompson said:

> [I do] not feel competent to discuss the great question of finances, but thirteen months in office [has] put [me] in possession of information upon subjects ... [I do] feel competent ... to talk [about]. The city owes about $91,000 in bonds, and about $52,000 in warrants and other floating debts. Much of this was for work on the streets ... and must be paid. There [is] no use in talking about repudiation: you can't repudiate. Vote for the extension of the bonded indebtedness, and don't go back on your word. [I do] not see any economy in cutting down the police, the fire department or the water supply. Do either, and the rates on insurance at once run up. The city administration had been elected to do certain things: there was not a dollar in the treasury with which to carry out these requirements. [I] see no other way than accepting and voting for the proposition now before the people. Whether [it carries] or not, we still owe the money, and honesty and good faith say it must and shall be paid.[74]

Voters subsequently decided in favor of the referendum and the city's financial crisis was over, for the time being. Certainly, Thompson's remarks resulted in many citizens voting "yea."

Marshal Thompson's report for the month of January presented the lightest record of arrests for years. With the exception of a fatal shooting at Sallie Daggatt's house, both violence and crime in Austin was at a significant low. Only seventy-seven arrests were made, and that small amount was mainly attributed to the almost unprecedented bad weather that kept many people from coming to town. Even with the dwindling number of transients, the city was still being vexed by pilferers and petty thieves, but because of the trivial nature of their crimes, they often escaped serious punishment. Thompson saw an opportunity to punish offenders and deter crime while aiding in the maintenance of city streets, one of his ancillary responsibilities. He suggested that culprits be made to break up stones at the rock quarry until there was serviceable gravel to fill the many potholes on Austin's main thoroughfares. Thompson and his officers were commended for their efforts, and one police officer received special recognition. Sergeant John Chenneville meticulously worked up a case against a ring of thieves and burglars who had been plaguing Austin throughout the winter months, and as a gesture of gratitude, Marshal Thompson presented his chief deputy with a gold badge etched with the Texas coat of arms.[75]

Lee County Sheriff James M. Brown and an accompanying deputy were in Austin the night of January 18, 1882. Ben Thompson warned the two men not to "raise any row as it would result badly for them." Brown disregarded the warning, but took no overt action until the following day. As the two Lee County lawmen left on the evening train, they contemptuously fired their pistols at signs and other targets as the train rolled out of the city.[76]

In February, Ben Thompson was again in San Antonio. L. E. Edwards, an Austin attorney and friend of Thompson, and owner of a successful land and collecting agency was also in the Alamo City. After attending a gathering at the Grand Lodge of Odd Fellows, Edwards took a drink at the Vaudeville Saloon at about 3:00 p.m., and was then approached by Jack Harris, who said, "I understand … that killing man of yours is in San Antonio." Edwards replied, "to whom do you refer [?]" Harris replied, "Ben Thompson." Edwards told Harris that "it was about time to stop that foolishness, that Ben Thompson had nothing against him." Harris threatened, "I'm going to kill the son of a bitch if he comes anywhere near here. There is no use of your talking to me." A frustrated Edwards left

Photographer Harvey R. Marks made a separate image of Marshal Ben Thompson on the same occasion as the group image. *Courtesy the Western History Collections, University of Oklahoma. Image # 2148.*

and went to his hotel, the Menger, and he met Lieutenant Hickey there at 4 p.m. in the afternoon. As they ordered some champagne, Ben Thompson sent his card upstairs to Edwards's room. Together, Edwards and Hickey managed to convince Thompson to remain in Edwards's hotel room while they returned to the Vaudeville Theatre to "try and keep down the trouble [and] prevent a difficulty." Between 7 and 8 p.m. they sat down with Jack Harris in a private room, Billy Simms joined them for the second interview. Harris's previous threats against Thompson were emphatically reiterated, and Harris added, "there were enough shotguns and enough men here to kill Ben Thompson and any of his friends." Hickey and Edwards returned to the Menger Hotel and met with Thompson, telling him that Harris was sober when he made his threats against his life. Edwards insisted Thompson must spend the night in his hotel room, saying "I do not want you killed." Ben did not reply and he made no threats against Harris. Thompson hadn't been feeling well was taking medicine prescribed by Doctor Maurice, a United States Army surgeon, so he complied with his friend's wishes, turned over, and went to sleep.[77]

In Ogallala, Nebraska, neither the authorities nor Bill Tucker had forgotten Billy Thompson. On February 27, 1882, a formal indictment was filed with the Fifth Judicial District of Nebraska by the district attorney of Keith County, who alleged that Billy Thompson had "feloniously assaulted one William H. Tucker" with the intention of murdering him. The charge amounted to a waste of paper and ink, because Billy Thompson was never prosecuted by any court in Nebraska.[78] While Keith County officials wanted to bring Billy in to face the charge, he was proposing to surrender to the authorities of Aransas County, Texas where he was charged with the murder of Remus Smith. Billy Thompson contended that he had killed in self-defense.[79]

Ben Thompson saw an opportunity to clear the Remus Smith murder indictment against his brother. To determine the strength of the case against Billy, Ben traveled with twenty-nine-year-old attorney George Pendexter to the gulf coast town of Rockport, Texas, where Billy was charged with the murder of Remus Smith in 1868. The *Statesman* reprinted an article from the *Rockport Transcript*, "Ben Thompson, brother to Bill Thompson, for whom the state has an indictment for murder committed in this county some 14 years ago, was here with our old friend, George Pendexter, Esq., of Austin, to look into the case with the understanding that a trial is to be held during the next term of our district court." But a turn of events would prevent the Thompson brothers from pursuing an end to Billy's legal troubles in Aransas County.[80]

While robberies and violent crime were infrequent in Austin during this time, officials were still being criticized about the vice ordinances not being strictly enforced. The *Statesman* ran an editorial while Marshal Thompson was out of town entitled, "About Gambling." The newspaper declared, "The legislature should, at some time in the near or remote future, do one of two things. Either expunge from the statute every law against gambling and the dens of this unconscionable vice, and license the business, or enact some measure to enforce the law." The newspaper frustratedly pointed out, "We admit here that it is a strange anomaly to pass a law to enforce a law. If gambling is to be, as it certainly is, tolerated, let it be made an expensive avocation to these dainty kid glove professional robbers, and a source of revenue for some laudable public service. Something of good might thus be squeezed out of a monstrous evil." The article warned, "The officers of this city, and of Travis County, are not doing their duty, and our citizens know it. On this subject more is likely to be said in a future issue of this paper, and the *Statesman* may become personal."[81]

Criticism also came from a delegation of Austin ladies who called on City Marshal Thompson and "asked him to enforce the law and close the saloons on Sunday." They reminded him that it was "his duty to do so, and asked, in the interest of the good and morality of the city, that he strictly perform such duty." Thompson, no doubt in the tone of a polished diplomat, explained to the ladies "closing the saloons would not stop the consumption of alcohol on Sundays. If the rule could be applied to all chartered society saloons and private entertainment halls, the saloon men of the city would willingly close up on Sunday."[82]

Ben Thompson turned a blind-eye to prostitution in much the same way that he did for alcohol and gambling. The oldest profession received similar treatment from Austin city marshals before Ben Thompson, and prostitution was largely ignored by the marshals after him as well. For decades, police neglected to regularly enforce an 1870 city ordinance that stipulated that owners and keepers of bawdy houses be fined, or face possible imprisonment in the county jail. In one celebrated case, which occurred a few years before Thompson became marshal, an Irish girl named Fanny Kelley appeared in the Mayor's court to answer charges of keeping a house of ill-fame. Police Officer Sheehan was called to the stand to testify. When asked by the city attorney to tell the court where Kelley's house was located, an amazed Sheehan answered, "Now what are you after asking me such a question as that for? Yerself and every man on that jury know as well as meself where Fanny Kelley's is, and yeve all been thar often!"[83]

By the early 1880s, more than one hundred prostitutes lived in Austin, and additional women would be brought in when the state legislature was in-session. The police and Austin's prostitutes usually got along well with each other, and for decades, they never had an adversarial relationship. In fact, madams did not hesitate to call for a policeman when a problem occurred in their establishment.

Major Walton selected an engraved version of H.R. Marks's bust photo of Marshal Thompson to illustrate his biography. Frank Triplett also chose the engraving to illustrate his book, *Romance and Philosophy of Great American Crimes and Criminals*, published in the same year of 1884.

Courtesy the Austin History Center. Image # PICB 19920.

The fraternization was so ingrained that in 1886, the city council finally had to ban on-duty policeman from entering bawdy houses for any reason other than to discharge their official duties. When prostitutes were arrested, more than two-thirds of the time they were charged with offenses unrelated to their livelihood. From 1876 to 1878, the police made prostitution-related arrests about twenty-four times per year on average. Usually, "brides of the multitudes" were taken to jail for disturbing the peace, intoxication, fighting, and for using abusive or vulgar language.[84] City officials viewed prostitution as a common nuisance, and as long as the demimonde remained separate from the world of respectability, there was no sustained public outcry from Austin's newspapers or citizenry, and hence, no call for the police to rigidly enforce the law.

In March, the San Antonio *Daily Express* announced that "the Vaudeville will be resplendent with electric light to-night."[85] The theatre was the first subscriber to the San Antonio electric company, but this decision to modernize would have a fateful consequence for Jack Harris.

Sprawling railroad tracks were beginning to connect every major city and town in Texas; another sign that a new and modern age was fast approaching. The International Railroad completed the track running from Austin through San Antonio to Laredo, and Ben Thompson and friends decided they would enjoy the ease of traveling by train, and look into that border town. During the second week of March, Thompson took a vacation from his duties with two friends, attorney George Pendexter and painting contractor Ben Marshall, and left on a trip to the southwest.[86] Their train passed through the town of Kyle where Thompson met and spoke with Thomas G. Martin, who earnestly alerted him to Harris's intent to kill him. "When Ben went to Laredo in the winter or spring I told him not to go about Harris, and I told him of the threats that Harris had made against him. I knew Harris' general reputation as to being a determined and desperate man from hearsay. He was called a fighting man, a man that would fight. The boys always kept out of his way ... I never heard of Jack being a bad man about raising difficulties ... [but] ... He was known as a brave man and he was not a coward." Ben Thompson didn't heed Martin's warning and he stopped in San Antonio with his friends on their return from Laredo. However, their brief stay there passed without any problem occurring.[87]

The spring and early summer of 1882 may have been the most enjoyable period of Ben Thompson's life. Ben was always in search of fun, and the *Statesman* noted he was "getting to be one of the finest banjo players in the city." He purchased a sailboat, named it after New York newspaper publishing mogul James Gordon Bennett, and offered to give cruises on the Colorado River. To celebrate San Jacinto Day, the six volunteer fire companies of Austin held a picnic at Presser's Beer Garden. The highlights of the day were Governor Oran M. Roberts's speech, the inspection of the fire companies, dancing to music furnished by the Manning Rifles Brass Band, and competitions like the Walking Match, Firemen's Foot Race, Wheelbarrow Race, Fat Man's Race, Second Fat Man's Race, Sack Race, Pole Climbing, Juvenile Race, and the Ladies and Men's Prize Hooting contest. Thompson competed in the Second Fat Man's Race. In a hotly contested foot race that created much merriment among the many spectators, Judge Fritz Tegener narrowly beat out Thompson and the other contestants. For his efforts, Tegener won the prize of "one dozen beers." In April, the Simpson Shooting Gallery held a series of marksmanship contests. As an enviable pistoleer, Ben Thompson again proved his skill with a revolver when he hit ninety-seven swinging glass balls out of one hundred. Thompson was tied for first with Mr. Edward D. Oesch, a druggist working at the Tobin Brothers Drug Store on Congress Avenue. Oesch was a peaceable man and never exchanged shots

John Peters Ringo, a survivor of the Mason County "Hoo Doo" War who later gained great notoriety in the Tombstone, Arizona Territory during the Earp-Clanton Feud. During his career in Texas, he was also arrested by Austin City Marshal Ben Thompson. *Courtesy the Dave Johnson Collection.*

with an adversary, but the man was a truly exceptional target shooter with both rifle and pistol. He had won two other long gun shooting contests that same day and previously, at the San Jacinto Day Celebration, Oesch won the men's "hooting" contest.

In April, The Knights of Pythias established Mount Bonnell Lodge Number 34 in Austin. The Knights were a fraternal organization founded on friendship, benevolence, and charity, and when they started initiating members, many of Austin's most prominent citizens joined. Ben Thompson was among the pledges, and he passed through each level of initiation. At first he was a Page, then he became an Esquire, and then he earned the right to call himself a Knight of Pythias. Subscriptions were solicited to fund and hold a proposed military drill contest at the annual Fair, and Thompson generously donated $100 to the cause. When his old mates from his typesetting days planned a printer's excursion to San Antonio in mid-May, he again ignored Harris's threats and accompanied them. Thompson spent an enjoyable Saturday and Sunday in their company. This trip to the Alamo City was made without any trouble or incident of any kind.[88]

Jack Harris may have been feeling a sense of mounting frustration as Ben Thompson traveled in and out of his hometown without incurring any of the dire consequences Harris had repeatedly promised. Little is known about the enigmatic man named W. L. Ellis, but during the early 1880s, he must have carried a reputation for being a dangerous man, and perhaps a man receptive to the proposition of paid assassination. Ellis claimed he was approached in mid-May by Jack Harris, down the street from the Vaudeville at Wolfson's Store, with an "offer to bribe him ... with the sum of five hundred dollars to kill" Ben Thompson.[89] Ellis never did reveal what his initial answer to Harris's proposal might have been.

In May 1882, Billy Thompson was briefly sitting in a jail cell in the far away border town of El Paso, after being arrested during a three-card *monte* game for "putting up a job" on a mark named Charles Mitchell. Billy's cohorts, "Curly" Yates, Tom Davis, and Dave Melasky helped him take $50 off Mitchell. Texas Rangers under the command of Capt. George W. Baylor made the arrest, and the four culprits admitted they took Mitchell's money while playing cards. Mitchell swore he was robbed, "bulldozed," and threatened by Billy Thompson. The case failed to provide enough evidence to convict Billy, and he was released from custody. Billy failed to turn a profit on the venture, since he was forced to spend $50 on a defense lawyer.[90]

On a ride out to Presser's Beer Garden during the last week of May 1882, a wagon almost ran into Ben Thompson's buggy. Perhaps because he remembered the terrible buggy accident in Kansas City back in 1871 when his wife lost her arm, Ben ordered the arrest of John Hafner, who he believed was the driver of the wagon. He was mistaken however, as it was not Hafner holding the reins. Hafner proceeded to file a return complaint against City Marshal Ben Thompson "for cursing him at the time of the threatened collision." As it was against the law to curse in public, Judge Tegener responded to the complaint by sending Police Officer Krause to perform the unenviable duty of arresting his boss. Thompson refused to be placed under arrest, and sent Officer Krause on his way. However, at his convenience, he eventually went before Judge Tegener in his courtroom and was fined a token $1.00 plus costs.[91]

On June 6, the *Statesman* informed its readers that "Captain Ben Thompson received a letter yesterday, from a man in Uvalde, asking him if he knew where he could purchase a breast or body plate, or whether he [Thompson] would sell his, the writer having heard that he wore one. Captain Thompson replied and advised the gentlemen that, instead of wearing a breast plate, to get into a strong rock house when danger approached." Others may have worn such protection but Thompson never did.

Ben Thompson's strong and effective performance as city marshal put him among the top contenders to challenge Travis County Sheriff Creary for his job. John Cardwell of the *Statesman* speculated that Ben would be a candidate when the election came up in the fall.[92] However, Thompson never attempted to become sheriff. In fact, a personal feud was fated to intervene, and bring an abrupt end to his career as a peace officer.

Jack Harris's anger toward Thompson continued to smolder. At the Vaudeville on the night of June 23-24, Harris, along with his friend H. A. Burbank and a character called "Johnny-Come-Lately" Conville, were drinking when Ben Thompson's name came up in conversation. Harris declared to Burbank that Thompson "was a cur, a son of a bitch and a coward and would not fight." In an at-

The Travis County jail, located in Austin, was considered to be one of the most secure facilities during the 1870s and 1880s, although there were occasional escapes. The sherriff's residence and the county courthouse stood near the county jail. The courthouse was later renamed the Walton Building in honor of Ben Thompson's famous defense attorney.

Courtesy the Austin History Center. Image # PICA 19698.

tempt to calm Harris's anger, Burbank reminded him that he maintained a friendship with Thompson and he suggested they take another drink and say no more about it. However Harris would not relent and continued to make threats, reiterating that he would kill Ben Thompson if he ever came into his establishment.[93]

By July 1882, Harris's ill-will had only grown. The annual reunion of Hood's Texas Brigade took place in San Antonio over the first weekend in July, and W. A. Pitts of Austin attended. Pitts knew Jack Harris as far back as the Civil War, and was also very familiar with Ben Thompson. During the reunion, Pitts stopped by the Vaudeville Theatre along with a dozen or more members of the brigade. Standing on the pavement in front of the building, Harris began speaking to the crowd, and proclaimed, "Ben Thompson could not walk the streets of San Antonio and do as he does in Austin ... he could not go around and break up shops like he does in Austin ... he had tried his little game on here once and got set back." Pitts admitted he didn't know if Harris ever killed anyone, but he thought Harris was the sort of man who "would be likely to carry out any threat he would make." He understood that Harris was a man "jealous of his rights and would not infringe on the rights of others but would always stand up for his own rights."[94]

During the first week of July, Marshal Thompson received a circular offering a reward of $1,000 for the arrest of a bond thief. Thompson suspected he could find the wanted man in San Antonio,[95] and since he had promised to take his two children and a nephew to visit friends in the Alamo City for some months, they boarded the train for San Antonio on Monday, July 10. While stopped in Kyle, Thompson again spoke with Thomas Martin about Jack Harris, and Martin warned that Thompson would "fool around San Antonio" and get killed. Thompson replied that he had his little children with him, and that he was going to San Antonio on business. And anyway, "he could take care of himself." If he had "business in Jack Harris's saloon," he would go in regardless of the possible consequences.[96]

Upon their arrival in the Alamo City, Ben placed his son Ben, his daughter Katie, and his nephew at the home of the friends who were expecting their visit. He telegraphed a reassuring message to his wife Kate—"Arrived safe—all well—children happy—God bless you." With the children safe and in good hands, Ben went about his business. He went to the fast side of town in search of the bond thief. He checked with many of the saloons, billiard halls, and gambling dens on San Antonio's Alamo, Military, and Main plazas. He ran into Billy Simms by chance on the first night he was in town. The next afternoon, Thompson stopped in at the Vaudeville Theatre as part of his relentless search to find the fugitive, capture him, and claim the reward. Jack Harris missed Thompson's search of his establishment due to his habit of returning home in the afternoon to rest before returning in the early evening to attend to his business. When Ben entered the second-floor gambling room, he was warned by a friend that his life was in danger. Taking this warning seriously, he drew his pistol and protected himself as he backed out of the premises. Biographer Walton explained that Ben "had no fear of being shot when his face was to the foe; he was only apprehensive that some coward might shoot him in the back."[97] Thompson again crossed paths with Billy Simms shortly after he left the Vaudeville, this time at a gambling den run by "Bones" Cullimore. Simms would later recall without further explanation, "Knowing Thompson was in town, I did not apprehend any trouble until I saw Thompson in Cullimore's house."[98] On July 11, 1882, Ben Thompson made a return trip to the Vaudeville Theatre a few minutes prior to dusk. This time, Ben would burn powder.

Chapter 14

GUNFIRE AT THE VAUDEVILLE

"No use talking to me Billy there's going to be hell here tonight."

Ben Thompson to Billy Simms, July 11, 1882

It was a warm Tuesday evening and the sunlight ebbed into dusk as the Vaudeville house band began to assemble and prepare to step out onto the small second story balcony. The ensemble blared out a loud welcome, and a warning to potential patrons that they needed to stop by the theatre's first floor ticket office if they planned to see the start of that night's variety show. Out on the Main Plaza, people strolled along the road enjoying the pleasant early evening air, while others hurried home for supper or to their jobs at the many barrooms and other businesses catering to the nighttime trade. In front of the Vaudeville, horses, hacks, and their drivers stood in a queue waiting for fares. Customers and a number of the establishment's various employees were scattered about inside.

The two Mauri Sisters, May and Kate doubled as stage performers; they were serio-comics, singers, and dancers. When they were off-stage, they worked as "chair warmers" enticing the clientele to purchase expensive drinks in the first-floor bar area.[1] There were two boys on duty that worked as glass washers. The lunch counterman, one M. Harris, who shared a common last name with the prominent proprietor but bore no family relationship, was at his station on the west side of the building in front of the bar. Barney Mitchell was serving drinks behind the long bar. Mitchell was a relatively new employee who had only been on board at the Vaudeville Saloon for about two and a half months. Ramon L. Biencourt, an unemployed clerk and sometime bartender, had been a hanger-on at the Vaudeville for the past month or so, was seated on the stairs leading up to the second floor reading the morning copy of the *San Antonio Express*. His natural curiosity would provide him a vantage point like no other when the Thompson / Harris imbroglio reached its culmination. Two other employees of the Vaudeville Saloon, barkeeper Johnny Dyer and John J. McLaughlin, who worked about the barroom, were lounging about waiting to go on duty. Frank Sparrow, the theatre's business and stage manager, was on the second floor preparing the acts for the evening performances. Billy Simms was somewhere on the second floor of the building, probably in the 101 gambling room. However, business partners Joe Foster and Jack Harris were not yet on the premises.

Ben Thompson returned to the Vaudeville Theatre almost four hours after he had backed out of the 101 Club with his pistol drawn. During that long afternoon, Billy Simms acknowledged that he ran into Ben Thompson at the gambling house controlled by "Bones" Cullimore, and paused to shake hands with him and have a few words. Simms would later state he "had no talk with him about any [future] difficulty," yet Simms felt it necessary to bring two revolvers from his home when he went to work at the Vaudeville that night. Between 5 and 6 p.m., Charles Hummel, the owner of a gun shop down the street from the Vaudeville Theatre, watched

Jack Harris, the influential gambler of San Antonio and arch enemy of Ben Thompson. *Courtesy the Western History Collections, University of Oklahoma. Image # 2149.*

as Thompson purchased five Winchester .44 calibre centerfire cartridges from his clerk for ten cents. Hummel would later explain: "There is a pistol made that uses that [*sic,* those] cartridges. That pistol was a Colt's." Hummel, who knew Thompson slightly, left his shop with the notorious gunman and went next door to enjoy a drink with him at George Horner's Saloon. Horner catered to the most wealthy and successful businessmen of the city, and served only the finest liquor in his upscale establishment.[2]

The Vaudeville Theatre had two front doors facing the plaza. Inside the theater, a lattice screen with moveable slats stood a few feet from the doors. It was positioned to help provide a modicum of privacy to the patrons of the saloon from anyone with an urge to peer in. The old gas jets and the new electric lights Jack Harris had installed were burning. The addition of the electric lighting made the interior of the saloon brighter than it ever had been. At around 6:45 p.m., Ben Thompson, walked in the east door alongside two men, Charlie Bennett and Dick Strayhorn. They took cigars as Thompson ordered a whiskey. As he downed his drink, Thompson exchanged sharp words with bartender Barney Mitchell. According to Mitchell, Thompson inquired, "Where are those sons of bitches with the shotguns?" Mitchell said no one was there with a shotgun. "You tell them when they come that I am here and there is going to be trouble. I am going to close this damn whorehouse. You tell Joe Foster and Jack Harris that I say they are a damn lot of thieving sons of bitches and living off of the product of the whores." The gutsy Mitchell maintained he told Thompson, "Why don't you tell them." A piqued Thompson asked Mitchell, "Who the hell are you? I want some of you to tell them." The three men spent at most two or three minutes standing at the bar before they left the premises through the same east door they had entered. Bennett and Strayhorn walked out first. Thompson was starting to follow them out onto the pavement when one of the musicians stepped in the room with a cornet in his hands. Thompson was momentarily startled and stopped, putting his hand behind his back when he saw a man with something in his hands. "I thought that was one of

Professional gambler William H. "Billy" Simms. Born in Austin, he was a protégé of Ben Thompson as a young man. He joined Jack Harris and Joseph Foster as one of the principal owners of the Vaudeville Theatre, Saloon and Gambling Hall. He was instrumental in Thompson's death. *Courtesy the Western History Collections, University of Oklahoma. Image # 2154.*

the damn sons of bitches with the shotgun," he remarked, before following his two friends and exiting out the east door.[3]

Bartender Johnny Dyer was having a drink before going on duty, and saw Thompson with the two other men at the bar. He overheard the brief argument between Barney Mitchell and Ben Thompson. Dyer walked outside moments before Thompson, and he watched closely as Ben spoke with a San Antonio City Policeman named Jacob Ripps in front of Hart's Cigar Store, but a man named Rouvant, who convinced Thompson to go back inside and join him for a drink, interrupted the conversation between Ripps and Thompson.[4]

With only three months of experience, Policeman Ripps was a relatively new appointee to the San Antonio Police Department. Thompson, seeing the officer, called out asking Ripps, "Is this your beat?" Ripps's responsibility extended from the Main Plaza to the adjoining Military Plaza to the west including nearby Market Street. Thompson then asked if anyone else was on duty, and inquired about San Antonio City Marshal Shardein. Ripps told him that he thought all were at supper. Thompson wanted more men on duty, telling Ripps there would be trouble. He then asked Ripps why he didn't close this whorehouse, and if the San Antonio police wouldn't close it, he would take on the responsibility. Ripps explained he was not instructed to do so. Thompson told the officer. "I'm barred out from this house. I'm going in there. I want you to protect me." Policeman Ripps told Thompson he didn't think anyone would refuse him admittance. Thompson declared. "I'm going in there and if you interfere with me I'd just as soon shoot you as anybody else." Ripps ignored the threat and claimed later that Thompson was laughing the entire time he was speaking to him. "He was not boisterous. If he had been it was my duty to have stopped it."[5]

Vaudeville employee John McLaughlin passed in and out of the barroom. He first talked to bartender Barney Mitchell, after Thompson had words with him, then he stepped outside and watched Thompson addressing Ripps. McLaughlin looked back into the barroom. The next person he noticed was Billy Simms walking up the stairs to the gambling room. McLaughlin decided to follow behind him as Simms passed through the gaming area and into a private room with a man named E. A. Hicks, who watched as Simms hid two revolvers under his coat. Together, the two men headed back downstairs to the first floor saloon.[6]

Leon Rouvant, a watchmaker who owned a jewelry store on Main Plaza, walked up to Policeman Ripps and Thompson and said to Ben, "Well, you are making a little noise." "Mr. Rouvant," Ben retorted, "you tend to your own business and I will tend to my business, but I am your friend." Rouvant was unoffended and invited Ben to join him inside for a drink. Thompson agreed, telling Rouvant, "go ahead I will come." Watching Thompson enter the barroom, Policeman Ripps stood outside the east door until he saw Rouvant and Thompson having a friendly drink at the bar. At the very least, this would be the fourth drink Thompson threw down his throat during the late afternoon and early evening. Satisfied that everything appeared fine, Officer Ripps then walked west, past Wolfson's Corner on towards Military Plaza to the main station house before he turned around and headed back toward Main Plaza.[7]

Having skipped his supper that evening, Leon Rouvant decided to go to the Vaudeville Saloon, the nearest place that offered a meal. He went up to the lunch counter and ordered his supper while he was waiting for Thompson to join him for a drink. Thompson came in and Rouvant joined him at the bar, paying for both their drinks. Ben mumbled to him, "something about gentleman not being permitted to come there." He didn't stay at the bar with Rouvant for very long before heading out the east door near Hart's Cigar Store. Rouvant walked away from the bar and went back to the lunch counter to see if his food was ready.[8]

As Thompson and Rouvant were taking their drink together, Billy Simms left the Vaudeville and turned west on Commerce Street. Jack Harris normally returned to work around 9 p.m., but tonight he was arriving several hours earlier than usual. Simms hurried down the street and came upon Jack Harris at Wolfson's Corner. He told Harris that Ben Thompson was in the first-floor bar area of the Vaudeville, then Simms handed Harris one of the two pistols hidden under his coat.

During the walk back to the Vaudeville, Simms paced about fifteen feet in front of Jack Harris. Ramon Biencourt set down the newspaper he was reading, and also left the saloon in search of Jack Harris. Biencourt liked Jack, and wanted to warn him that Ben Thompson was about his place. He brushed past Simms, and as Harris came up to him, Biencourt said, "better look out [,] Thompson is going to raise hell with [you]." Harris brushed by Biencourt without responding.[9] As Thompson re-entered the saloon to have a drink with Leon Rouvant, Dyer also hurried westward towards Wolfson's Corner, and before he had gone more than a few doors down the street, he met Jack Harris walking toward the Vaudeville. Raising his finger to Harris, Dyer told him that Ben Thompson was inside the Vaudeville Saloon. Harris slowed down, turned towards Dyer, and said "what" in a low whisper. Dyer repeated himself. Billy Simms, Ramon Biencourt, and Johnny Dyer all watched as Jack Harris slowed his gait. He paused, hesitated once, maybe twice, but eventually, decided to enter his saloon. Once in the west door, he took two more steps up to the lattice screen. There, he looked through one of the slats into his barroom and saw Ben Thompson with his back to him. The distance from the screen to the counter where Ben Thompson was drinking with Leon Rouvant was a mere twelve feet. Thompson downed his drink, turned, and walked out through the east door, leaving Rouvant at the bar. At the same time as Thompson's departue,

Harris made his way through his barroom to the theatre's ticket office with his usual confident stride.[10]

Ben went out and stood on the pavement with his arms crossed before his chest as if waiting for someone. Rouvant walked to the lunch counter and noticed Jack Harris coming in. Unaware of any tension, Rouvant greeted him and was greeted in turn as Harris went past him toward the small ticket office where he unlocked the door, reached in, and took something out.[11]

That something was the double barrel shotgun Jack Harris kept conveniently stored in the office. He took a position in an offset in the wall a handful of steps from the ticket office. With his left arm resting on the wall's wainscoting, he laid the barrel of the shotgun across his maimed left hand. He placed the butt of the weapon under his right armpit and examined the lock of the gun. Johnny Dyer went into the saloon, and like Harris, used the west door. He walked over to a pile of stacked whiskey barrels in the back of the room, and placed himself so that he was twenty feet away from where Harris was half-concealed and about forty feet from Ben Thompson, who was outside on the pavement talking with Billy Simms. If he moved his head slightly back and forth, Dyer could plainly see both Harris and Thompson.[12]

Billy Simms walked past the west entrance, heading toward the east door moments after Thompson came out. E. A. Hicks exited the west door, turned back to the east, and noticed Thompson and Simms talking to each other as he walked down the pavement. According to Simms, Ben Thompson accosted him saying, "Billy I'm going to close up this god damn whorehouse tonight, Joe Foster is a god damn thief and Jack Harris lives off these whores."

"Ben don't get into any trouble it is not necessary," said Simms.

"No use talking to me Billy there's going to be hell here tonight. I haven't anything against you, you are my friend but these sons of bitches have mistreated me and they have got to come to me." For three or four minutes, Simms agreed with him that there could not be any trouble between the two of them because they were friends, but he also begged Thompson, "for Christs sake don't get into any trouble it is not necessary."

When they spoke, it was past 7:30 p.m. and the sun would set in less than ten minutes. To some observers, the two men seemed to be on friendly terms. Ramon Biencourt stepped out onto the street and watched as Simms tried to calm Thompson until a man named Terry O'Neal interceded and took Ben by the arm and began to speak with him, too. As Thompson and O'Neal moved a few steps further eastward towards the cigar store, Billy Simms went back into the saloon. He walked right past the shotgun wielding Jack Harris and went up the stairs to the second floor. Once Thompson shook off O'Neal, E. A. Hicks stepped in and attempted to get Ben to quiet down. Hicks had always been on friendly terms with Thompson, and he invited Ben to go over to the nearby Revolving Light Saloon, but Thompson said he didn't need any advisors and declined his friend's offer. Instead, Ben walked back to the front of the Vaudeville where he stood on the outer edge of the pavement facing the saloon's east door. He folded his arms across his chest and waited. Biencourt stayed close to Thompson and was only two or three feet to his right as Ben stepped aside and let two ladies pass by on the sidewalk.[13]

Leon Rouvant spotted Harris holding his shotgun as he began to eat his supper. Upon the realization that trouble might occur, Leon left his food and rushed out through the west door. He was back in his jewelry store by the Revolving Light Saloon within a minute or two. In the first floor of the Vaudeville, the bright new electric light and two or three gaslights were burning, and on the outside, the sidewalk was illuminated by a second electric light. Leon Rouvant was not the only person who had realized Harris had armed himself, and other customers in the saloon rushed out of the building, a few of them loudly called out, "Jack has got his gun."[14] One patron, Thomas O'Conner, apprehended the coming trouble, left his drink on the counter, and rushed out the west door calling to his friend, Pat Carney, that Harris had armed himself with a shotgun. Inside, Jack Harris voiced a warning to his two employees, May and Kate Mauri, telling them they ought to stand back and get out of the way. There was a small crowd blocking the pavement, but O'Conner worked his way through, behind, and past Thompson as he went toward the corner cigar store. Thompson's arms stayed folded across his chest until his attention was attracted to the inside of the saloon. He unfolded his arms and placed his hand on his pistol. Thompson needed to see through the lattice screen and into the barroom, so he stooped down and stepped off the edge of the sidewalk, placing himself beyond the glow of the electric light emanating from the saloon.[15]

Policeman Jacob Ripps had reached the far western end of his beat. He had already turned around and was part way back to the Main Plaza when he heard the loud report of two pistol shots coming from the direction of the Vaudeville Theatre.

Thompson stood amidst the gathering twilight and called out to Harris, "What are you doing with that shotgun you damned son of a bitch?" Harris was half-concealed behind the inset of the wall but replied, "You kiss my ass you damned son of a bitch."[16] His shotgun swung out as he spoke those words, and he leaned forward to look for Thompson in the outer dark. As he did this, Ben Thompson was seen to go "for his six-shooter mighty quick."

The sharp explosion of Thompson's revolver sent the people in front of the Vaudeville Theatre fleeing in all directions. He fired through the lattice screen, and the pistol ball scraped the saloon's sidewall before striking Jack Harris in the chest. A witness named W. J. Ryan told a reporter from the *Express*, "the first shot made by Thompson was remarkable for its accuracy, and ... unless

Thompson had stood exactly where he did and been a dead shot, he could not have done his work so thoroughly well."[17] When the first pistol ball struck Jack Harris, he raised himself slightly before falling forward with his maimed left hand almost touching the floor. One or two seconds ticked by as Thompson moved a few feet to his left, and then he fired again. The second bullet marked the wall lower than the first shot. Harris caught himself from falling to the floor and stood straight up, but then reeled violently backward, causing Thompson's second shoot to go wide of its mark.

With his smoking pistol in his hand, Thompson calmly strode off onto the plaza in a westerly direction. As "Thompson walked away," Ramon Biencourt shadowed him at a short distance. One newspaperman commented on the casual ease with which he left the scene unmolested, "no man caring to stop him. He is too deadly a shot for anybody to fool with him."[18]

Harris gathered all of his strength to turn and slowly stumble up the stairway into the theatre's gallery while still carrying

A view of the north side of the Main Plaza in San Antonio in 1882. Jack Harris's Vaudeville Theatre toward the right corner of the street can clearly be seen. Note the twin towers of the Bexar County court house clearly visible on Soledad Street, looming behind the theatre. *Courtesy the University of Oklahoma Libraries, Western History Collections. Image # 222.*

his shotgun. He was overtaken and helped to the top of the stairs where he was laid down on a bench. He asked for Dr. Amos Graves and called out, "Get Herff, too." The two Mauri sisters and Johnny Dyer were among the people who hurried up the stairway after Harris. Upon reaching the gallery, Dyer found two or three women holding Harris. One woman told him that Jack was shot, so he ran to Schasse's Drug Store to look for a physician where he hoped to find either Dr. Chew or Dr. Cupples.[19]

Both ice and water were applied to Harris's forehead to help comfort him, and he asked for a stronger drink (a toddy), which he was given. Frank Sparrow was on the outside balcony when he heard the shots ring out from down below. When he left the balcony, he passed through the gambling room and found Harris lying wounded on a bench with his shotgun lying flat beside him. Sparrow would later testify the weapon was not cocked, and he asked a nearby actress to take it to her dressing room and keep it safe. Harris's blood oozed from an ugly bullet hole about a half-inch in diameter.

Ben Thompson began walking to the middle of the plaza, but he hastened into a slow trot until he reached Wolfson's Corner. Biencourt never took his eyes off the gunman and also moved out onto the plaza, where he saw Ben stop opposite Wolfson's Store before turning around and heading back toward the Vaudeville. As Thompson neared the theatre, he raised his hand up and looked at the band on the outside balcony. Ben still may have had his revolver in his outstretched hand, and this encouraged Frank Sparrow and the musicians to retreat back into the house. Biencourt watched Thompson walk eastward behind the line of hacks queued up in the plaza as he avoided the gathering crowd in front of the Vaudeville's entrances. Biencourt then gave up on tracking Thompson, and returned to the sidewalk in front of the Vaudeville. By the time he saw Dr. Chew reach the scene and go into the Vaudeville Theatre, ten minutes had passed.[20]

Dr. Thomas R. Chew had served San Antonio as a general practitioner and surgeon for the past ten years. He was the first physician to make a cursory assessment of Harris's wound at the Vaudeville Theatre, and he found that the pistol ball struck Harris's breastbone, then passed between the fourth and fifth ribs before exiting the back of the body. Dr. Chew ordered a stretcher and sent Harris home, which was less than two blocks away on Soledad Street.[21]

While a large crowd gathered around the Vaudeville Theatre and discussed the event, another large group of curious spectators and friends of Harris trailed behind the carriage transporting him to his home. The doctor reached Harris's residence first, and the scene rapidly turned into one of confusion. Dr. Chew had Harris placed in his bedroom. He made another, more thorough, examination of the wound there with Dr. Adolph Herff, and tracked the path of Thompson's bullet. The pistol ball had carved through the breastbone and then passed through Harris's right lung, severing major blood vessels before exiting out below his right shoulder blade. He was hemorrhaging severely. Seeming to acknowledge that he knew his wound was fatal, he repeatedly asked his doctors how long he could last. He spoke a little with his friends, and while looking directly at Dr. Chew, without specifically naming Ben Thompson, Harris remarked, "He took advantage of me and shot me from the dark." Joe Foster approached Harris's bedside and Jack recognized his friend and business partner. When Foster asked him if he was suffering, Harris said, "Yes. He has got me."[22] Jack Harris tossed and groaned in great agony before loudly imploring, "Oh! Someone kill me for God's sake and let me die."

Dr. Ferdinand Ludwig von Herff, the father of Dr. Adolph Herff, was recognized as the most brilliant physician practicing medicine in San Antonio. When he finally arrived, he hurried to Harris's side. An *Express* reporter observed, "Jack took some courage after this, and he was told by friends that it would be all right now." The three doctors stepped aside and conferred. All were convinced their patient could not last much longer because of the intensity of the internal bleeding. A fourth doctor, Dr. Amos Graves, arrived at the residence moments before Harris succumbed to his wound. Graves was too late, of course, and with one last bloody gasp, Harris finally stopped tossing about his bed thirty minutes after he was carried to his home. He was surrounded by many of his companions who were unable to restrain their emotions. Many of his friends crowded throughout his home and openly wept.[23] After returning to the Vaudeville, Frank Sparrow wrote in his ledger book, "Jack Harris, proprietor, shot and killed by Ben Thompson ... died as he lived, a true friend and kindhearted, generous gentleman. God have mercy on his soul." Before he left the building, Sparrow retrieved the shotgun from the dressing room and took it home where he examined the weapon and found both barrels fully loaded.[24]

Telegraph operators relayed news of Jack's death to newspapers throughout Texas and beyond within an hour of its occurrence. Justice of the Peace Anton Adam impaneled a coroner's jury to view Jack Harris's corpse on his deathbed, and a hearing was scheduled to convene at 10 a.m. in the morning.[25]

Ben left Main Plaza behind and walked east down Commerce Street toward the Alamo Plaza and his room at the Menger Hotel. Thompson was seen in various places after the shooting, and he was described as taking it very coolly. Reportedly, he coyly asked at one location where he stopped, "What [is]the fuss up at Jack's?"[26]

Thompson returned to George Horner's Saloon on the north side of Commerce Street. Horner recalled he came in the front door not long after the shooting, ordered a drink, and asked Horner to have a drink with him. Thompson told the proprietor not to be uneasy, he was not going to raise a row, and that he wanted to give himself up to the city marshal. A few patrons came in and spoke with Thompson. L. C. Grothaus, accompanied by H. B. Adams, attempted to converse with Ben Thompson, but he was reluctant to speak about the shooting. As Grothaus shook Thompson's hand, Ben asked Horner to call Marshal Shardein into the saloon if he happened to pass by. Thompson openly stated that he never resisted proper authority, and that the only people he was down on were gamblers and whorehouse keepers. Adams took Ben by the arm, and led him to the back door, saying, "come and go with me." The two men took the alleyway, which was a shortcut to Market Street.[27]

Innkeeper C. J. Beck was in charge of the Braden Hotel on Market Street when Thompson walked in, and unloaded the empty shells and reloaded his nickel-plated revolver. In response to Beck's nervous query, he answered, "No, I'm not going to shoot anybody." Thompson introduced himself, and to calm him, informed Beck he was the city marshal of Austin. Beck had not heard the gunfire and was ignorant of that evening's events. By this time, it was about 8 p. m., and as usual, traffic was scarce after dark on Market Street. Ben was only there for a few minutes before leaving the premises.[28] Shortly after departing the Braden Hotel, Thompson returned to his room at the Menger Hotel, and spent the night undisturbed. Before going to bed, he sent word to Sheriff McCall and City Marshal Shardein that he would surrender himself up when the excitement was over.[29]

Telegrams began to arrive in Austin announcing that their city marshal had shot and killed Jack Harris. The news raced through the capital city and caused so much excitement that many of Ben Thompson's friends planned to take the morning train down to San Antonio. It was thought even some prominent city officials would also go.[30]

The editor of the *San Antonio Times* was disgusted by Thompson's self-appointed surrender. "Ben Thompson this morning about half-past nine o'clock sent for Sheriff McCall and Marshal Shardein and surrendered himself, and is now in the custody of the sheriff." The newspaperman felt compelled to add his opinion, writing, "had a desperado of Thompson's reputation visited Austin and killed a man he would not have been allowed to remain undisturbed for a whole night and then to surrender himself at pleasure. Ben Thompson would have taken him dead or alive, and not rested until he had."[31]

The front page of many major newspapers across Texas reported the fatal shooting of Jack Harris. The killing attracted the attention of newspapers outside of the state as well, and the morning after, the July 12 issue of the *Chicago Tribune* reported on the event. The telegraphed message briefly informed readers in the Windy City that, on the previous evening, Austin City Marshal Ben Thompson, while in San Antonio "shot Jack Harris, proprietor of the Vaudeville Theatre and the best known gambler in the state. There was some trouble two years ago in reference to Harris having swindled Thompson, and Harris has since threatened to kill him. On passing Harris' saloon tonight Thompson saw Harris armed with a shotgun behind a screen. He drew his revolver, challenging him to come forward like a man. Harris replied that he was ready for him, on which Thompson fired two shots through the screen." One of the bullets struck Harris, "passing through the lungs. He died within an hour. Thompson made off and has not yet been arrested." In case there was a question as to who Ben Thompson was, the reporter identified Thompson as "the famous Marshal of Austin, is a dead shot and fearless, and has previously killed several men."

In both Austin and San Antonio, almost everyone talked about the tragedy. Justice Adam's office was overflowing with spectators while the witness testimony was being given before the coroner's jury. Three deputy sheriffs while en route guarded Ben Thompson from his jail cell to Adam's office to hear the testimony and back again through an immense crown of curious onlookers. In the absence of Bexar County attorney Fred Cocke, attorney B. I. Boone appeared for the state while the San Antonio law firm of Green and Green represented Ben Thompson. Ben's lead attorney was Colonel John A. Green Sr., the same benefactor who provided funds for young Ben Thompson's education many years ago. The witnesses who testified were predominantly Jack Harris's business partners and employees, and the testimony against Thompson was very damaging. It was established that Harris held a shotgun, but the testimony emphasized that he did not attempt to use it. The coroner's jury determined, "Jack Harris came to his death by a pistol wound from a pistol in the hands of one Ben Thompson." Many who attended the hearing started to believe that Thompson's long, reckless career had finally run its course. Yet, these same spectators remarked how unconcerned Ben Thompson acted during the proceedings as he chatted pleasantly with his attorneys. He seemed to act more like a spectator himself than a prisoner under arrest facing the likelihood of being charged with the crime of murder. A reporter for the *Express* asked Ben for his version of the affray, but he refused to speak except to say he was in the hands of his attorneys, and he would make no statement while his case was in progress. In spite of his reticence, word of a conspiracy between Harris and others to kill Thompson began to circulate. The examination to consider bail was scheduled by Justice Adam for the following morning. It was reported that if the Judge allowed for bail, Ben Thompson's many friends were ready to come forward and provide his bond up to any amount. However, considering the general conversation on the streets of San Antonio, many people held the opinion that Ben Thompson had finally killed one man too many.[32]

City Marshal Philip Shardein learned Billy Thompson was planning to come to San Antonio to aid and support his brother. Shardein telegraphed the authorities in Rockport, Aransas County, to verify if Billy Thompson was still wanted there. They answered in the affirmative, and sent a warrant to Shardein, asking him to arrest Billy upon his arrival in San Antonio. Despite his incarceration, Ben Thompson found out about Billy's impending arrest from his friends. He arranged for a telegraph to his brother warning him to stay away.[33]

In anticipation of even more spectators, the venue for the inquest for bail was moved to the district court's larger courtroom. The larger space still proved to be insufficient and the district court room was mobbed. People of all colors and nationalities crowded the streets anticipating Ben Thompson's examining trial. As the deputy sheriffs conveyed the prisoner from jail to the courthouse, "a swarm of humanity followed close behind and almost blocked up the passage along the streets "through which the group had to pass.[34]

Thompson was taken in the custody of Bexar County Sheriff McCall to the third-floor grand jury room where his counsel awaited. George Pendexter, of the firm of Pendexter & Wooten, had arrived from Austin the previous evening, and joined Colonel John A. Green Sr., his son, and N. O. Green. Thompson also retained the Austin law firm of Walton & Hill; it was acknowledged that he was gathering together the best legal talent in the state. Thompson and his lawyers conferred almost the entire morning before they finally decided on a line of defense. To the surprise of Thompson and his attorneys, Justice Anton Adam ruled the case was not entitled to bail. He remanded Ben Thompson back to the county jail to await the action of the grand jury in September. Justice Adam was widely applauded by the many citizens of San Antonio who considered this to be a fair and righteous decision. Ben Thompson accepted the setback with coolness and composure. However, he had expected to be granted bail, and planned on returning to Austin where he would continue as city marshal until he was called to return and stand trial. Without leaving the building, Thompson's attorneys paid a visit to the office of District Court Judge George H. Noonan, and asked him for a writ of habeas corpus, which was granted. However, because of his busy case schedule, Judge Noonan could not listen to arguments immediately. He placed it onto his calendar for July 25. When asked for temporary bail, Judge Noonan upheld Justice Adam's decision, and he too refused to grant it.[35]

The San Antonio and Austin press loudly voiced their opinions about the sensational shooting and also speculated on Ben Thompson's ultimate fate in a court of law. One prominent San Antonio citizen remarked on how the death of Jack Harris was no loss, and the only pity was that his shotgun did not discharge blasting Ben Thompson to the same place Harris is spending eternity. The *San Antonio Times* agreed, adding, "Harris' death is but little regretted except by the gamblers and prostitutes among whom he was universally popular." Many residents of the Alamo City agreed and viewed Jack Harris's death as a "blessing" to San Antonio. The *Light*, however, found a different mood among its readers, pointing out that the opinion which seemed to "prevail in all quarters is that the killing of Jack Harris by Ben Thompson was a murder as foul as any that has stained the name of our community in the past." The newspaper felt Thompson had no good reason for shooting Harris, and laid blame on both city and county authorities for letting it happen. The editor explained that, after making himself conspicuous on the streets and voicing his intentions to close an establishment in the center of the city, Thompson was not only allowed to assault the business and its proprietor, but then walk away unmolested after killing him. The newspaper was shocked that all of Thompson's actions occurred "within calling distance of the sheriff's office and [the] mayor's office."

District Judge George Henry Noonan, who repeatedly denied Thompson bail in the aftermath of Harris's death. Because of this, Thompson was held in the Bexar County jail until his trial and ultimately had to resign his position as City Marshal of Austin. *Courtesy Special Collections. University of Texas at San Antonio.*

Ben Thompson's friends in Austin felt he would eventually win his freedom when all of the facts came out, and more than a score of the town's best citizens, including Mayor W. A. Saylor, offered to post his bond. An Austin official in the know asserted that Harris offered $1,000 for Thompson's death. The *Statesman* admitted that their city marshal "committed a terrible deed in killing Harris, and only when it is shown before a proper tribunal that he was justifiable in doing so will [the people of San Antonio] believe Mr. Thompson should be at liberty." In addition, there was much talk of a change of venue, since San Antonio's gambling fraternity was as influential as it was numerous. There were good odds that one or more of those gamblers would appear on the jury bench with an unchecked prejudice against Thompson. A young, unnamed San Antonio attorney who was well aware of Ben Thompson's past successes in the courtroom was appalled at the thought of Thompson somehow escaping punishment again. He proposed, "That there should be a state law limiting the number of men a man may kill even in self-defense."[36]

As scheduled, Jack Harris was buried the day after he died. The ceremony began by 5 p. m. and ended prior to sunset, and the weather was described as a "glorious summer evening." His funeral procession was led by the hearse and followed by forty-seven hacks filled with mourners. It silently rolled by his home on Soledad Street, to Commerce Street, and then continued slowly east out of San Antonio to his waiting grave in City Cemetery Number One. Foremost among the mourners was his old dog Skeezicks, followed by the gamblers, actresses, politicians, and darlings of the demimonde who came to show their respect and honor his memory. A correspondent of the *San Antonio Light* expressed how, "Harris was, in the eyes of religious people a wicked man; he died, apparently, an unrepentant man. He was known to hold all Christian faith in open derision; he was a believer in mankind, a non-believer in religious dogmas." The reporter acknowledged how "he might have been fitly called the 'wickedest man' of the town. But his death brought sorrow to many hearts, and while the closest circle of his friendships embraced the outlaw portion of our community," though many who stood before his grave and paid respects to his memory were some of the town's most prominent citizens.

Reverend J. W. Neal (also spelled Neil) did not know Jack Harris in life; still, he readily accepted the invitation to conduct the funeral. He read selected scriptures, led Harris's friends in prayer, and even though Reverend Neal was not well acquainted with the mourners, he knew his audience. He concluded his sermon with advice to all in attendance, "As a minister of the gospel I exhort you to accept the message I bring. It will not be long before someone of this multitude will be called to his or her last account, and another party of friends will gather at an open grave, as you are to-day gathered, and will perform for you the last sad rites for the dead." He quietly ended with the ominous question, "Are you ready?"

Without the benefit of a marker, Jack Harris was ceremoniously put into the ground and the next day the Vaudeville Theatre reopened for business as usual under the management of Billy Simms, Joe Foster, and Johnny Dyer, who were all acting in the interest of Jack Harris's estate. "The old home ain't like it used to be," Sparrow mournfully scrawled in his ledger, but the show had to go on and the ebbing notes of the funeral dirge had barely ended before the earsplitting haughty dance music began anew.[37]

Jack Harris died without a will. With no opposition appearing in court and with the presentation of the appropriate paperwork, Probate Judge Felix Smith appointed William H. Simms the administrator of the Harris estate. The decision did bring its criticism in the press, with the *Times* declaring a "pious, sanctified man ought to be appointed." The *Light* defended the judge, admitting that Simms was not a church going man, but he was Harris's friend and partner and he was intimately familiar with the business operation of the Vaudeville Theatre, gambling hall, and saloon. It would seem he was best prepared to preserve Harris's assets for his estate. Less than ten days after Simms was appointed, he settled the estate. From the sale of Harris's property, he garnered a total of $1,700 for the dead man's mother and sister, who the newspapers reported were living back east.[38]

Many of Thompson's friends visited him in the county jail, as did a correspondent for the *Statesman*. Reportedly, Thompson remained in good spirits, acted cheerful, and insisted that the rumored conspiracy to kill him by Harris and his friends was indeed a fact. Since the Vaudeville was a public place, he said he had as much right to be at the establishment as anyone. Besides, he had come to San Antonio as a peace officer searching for a wanted man, and that all the blame should fall on the San Antonio Police Department for not protecting him as he had asked. Thompson explained to the newspaperman that he was sure he would "come out alright" as he had "acted in self-defense in shooting a man who was waiting to kill him."[39]

In Austin, the mayor and city council promoted the highly qualified Sgt. John Chenneville to be their acting Police Chief during Ben Thompson's absence.[40]

Thompson's habeas corpus trial, and application for bail before George H. Noonan, Judge of the 22nd Judicial District of the State of Texas, was the sensation of the hour, and the excitement over the legal proceedings was as keen as ever.[41] On Tuesday morning July 25, exactly two weeks to the day after Jack Harris was shot, Sheriff McCall was forced to lock his arms with Ben Thompson, and with the aid of deputies, push their way through the crowd thronging the streets from the jail to the Bexar County courthouse as hundreds of people flocked to see the accused murderer. The courtroom was "packed like herring in a barrel, the space reserved for the attorneys being filled by the eager crowd."[42] The *Express* wrote, "Every nook, corner, aisle and doorway of the district courtroom was crowded with spectators, witnesses and lawyers yesterday morning at the habeas corpus trial of Ben Thompson. The pressure to see was so great, that the machinery of the court became clogged for want of room, and the sheriff was called upon to clear the bar several times, which he had no little trouble doing." The crowd was immense and eager to see the famous defendant. With Harris having been declared publicly "a wicked man" and "unrepentant," even several ministers had deemed it necessary to be in attendance, perhaps out of morbid curiosity. Many people were wagering on whether Ben Thompson would be returned to the county jail or receive bail and set free.[43]

The press exclaimed that the Thompson habeas corpus hearing was the most important one to take place in Texas in a great many years, and the public interest was extreme. Judge Noonan saw to it that a comfortable place, with table and chairs, was prepared for the numerous reporters. One newspaperman wrote, "Ben Thompson does not appear depressed in the least, but on the contrary, is rather good humored. We were told by a friend of his, however, that he had expressed regret for the killing of Harris."

It was written that "the best array of legal talent in the State is engaged on [different] sides," and taking the lead role for the prosecution was John King Fisher's former defense attorney, Trevanion Theodore Teel. Though presently in private practice, T. T. Teel was hired to serve the state as a special prosecutor. For the defense, William M. Walton was the lead counsel.[44]

Fifty-four names appeared on the witness list, although only half were in the courtroom ready to testify. The first witness was Anton Adam, thirty-nine years old and Prussian born, he was the justice of the peace who held the coroner's inquest. Billy Simms and two of the Vaudeville's bartenders, Barney Mitchell and Johnny

Bexar County Sheriff Thomas P. McCall (1831-1902). A longtime Texas lawman, he first served as sheriff of Medina County and then served ten years as sheriff of Bexar County. Ben Thompson surrendered to Sheriff McCall and City Marshal Shardein after he fatally shot Jack Harris. *Courtesy the Western History Collections, University of Oklahoma. Image # 1791*

Dyer, followed him. In essence, the testimony of Simms, Mitchell, and Dyer concurred. They all claimed that Jack Harris retrieved his shotgun to protect himself and his property, and at no time did he place his weapon into a firing position or point it at Thompson. When cross-examined, Dyer denied having entered into an agreement with Jack Harris to kill Thompson. The defense hinted that Dyer was prepared to do more than merely watch the affray while he hid among the whiskey barrels waiting for Thompson to enter the building and confront Harris. The next day, more witnesses for the state expressed similar versions of the fatal shooting. The third witness for the state, a San Antonio architect named W. K. Dobson, made, by request, an elaborate diagram of the Vaudeville barroom, presented the position of Thompson and Harris when the latter was killed. Dobson's work showed the path of the two shots, the lattice screens, ticket office, and other objects in the room. It was admitted as exhibit A and explained in detail by the architect. Sixteen witnesses for the state appeared before the court, and the defense countered with eighteen of their own. However, E. A. Hicks offered the most interesting testimony stating something Billy Simms failed to reveal when he was first on the stand. Prior to the shooting, Hicks watched as Simms placed two pistols in his trousers belt before donning a coat to help conceal the weapons.[45]

Defense Attorney Walton paraded witness after witness who all testified of the many threats Jack Harris made against Ben Thompson over the preceding two years. The testimony Walton elicited "caused considerable comment as to the nature" [and] "the depth, of feeling Harris had against Thompson." He also obtained an important addition to Harris's answer when Thompson yelled out, "what are you doing with that shotgun you damned son of a bitch?" Witness Pat Carney testified that he heard Harris answer, "you kiss my ass you damned son of a bitch. I am ready." He was positive Harris said, "I am ready," and he knew Harris's voice.

Thomas O'Conner agreed with Carney. He too heard Harris shout back, "I'm ready."[46]

Walton recalled Billy Simms to the witness stand, and under an intense cross-examination, Simms finally admitted that, on the day of the shooting, he brought two pistols from his home to the Vaudeville, and while he was upstairs with Hicks, he hid the pistols under his coat. Simms maintained that, when he hurried to meet Harris by Wolfson's corner, he "told Harris not to go down to the bar ... that Ben Thompson was there looking for him." Simms insisted he only "gave Harris the pistol to protect himself." Simms tried to refute the testimony of how Harris wished to kill Thompson and pointed out how Harris could have easily shot Thompson down when he peered into the barroom. Thompson was unaware that Harris was behind him, and his back made a perfect target. Simms professed, "If he desired to have used the pistol at the screen while Thompson was at the bar he could have done so." It was an easy pistol shot and the prospect of following through on his many threats and killing Thompson without the slightest notice lay before Harris. Although a man of many faults, Jack Harris was not a back-shooter. For an unknown reason, he chose not to use the weapon Simms had placed in his hand. The opportunity passed away as quickly as it presented itself. Ben put his empty glass down and left Leon Rouvant at the bar. He walked out the east front door as Jack Harris, after a moment of hesitation, continued on to the ticket office and his shotgun.[47]

Jack Cummings, a young black man employed as a bottle washer at the Vaudeville, was the final witness called to testify. Cummings's evidence was a powerful refutation of Frank Sparrow's statement about the position of the hammers on Jack Harris's shotgun. "I have been living with Jack Harris about twelve years," testified Cummings. "Saw him going up the stairs after he was shot. Harris got up to the head of the stairs, and was sitting down with the gun in his hands and the gun was full cocked. I am positive that the gun was cocked."[48]

Defense attorney George Pendexter informed the court that Ben Thompson "is a man of small means outside of his homestead, but he has influential friends and I am satisfied that he can give a reasonable bond. I think he can give bail to the amount of $10,000."[49] However the offer was soon to be of no consequence.

On Friday, July 28, after four days of listening to the sworn statements and cross-examination of almost three dozen witnesses, both the prosecution and the defense counsel reached an agreement that they would not argue a long-winded summation before Judge Noonan. Both were confident they had won their case through the evidence they entered into the court record. Judge Noonan denied Ben Thompson the right to bail without vacillation and remanded him into the custody of Sheriff McCall, instructing the sheriff that the prisoner be securely held to await the action of the Bexar County Grand Jury at the upcoming September Term. In making his decision, the judge explained that he had "scrutinized with more than ordinary care" and "eliminated all irrelevant material" and was now "of the opinion he is not entitled to bail."[50]

This was a moment of surprise to the hundreds who packed the courtroom. All eyes were on Ben Thompson as Noonan spoke his decision and Thompson's expression changed from casual to concerned. He looked at a nearby friend and said, "You guessed right." William Walton stood and gave official notice that his client would take his case to the court of appeals, which was noted in the record. Throughout the hearing, Ben Thompson exhibited no braggadocio, often smiling, and making pleasant conversation and behaving as one who believed he was in the right to take a life in self-defense. As Thompson settled in at the Bexar County jail, he was visited daily by many of his friends and he gave the impression he was "quite well ... having been amply supplied with all necessities."[51]

The day after his hearing, with his legal counsel on hand, Ben Thompson tendered his resignation as marshal of the city of Austin, effective September 1. William M. Walton and George F. Pendexter witnessed his signature. During their next meeting, Austin's city council refused to accept Ben's resignation, and the council members passed a resolution granting Ben a sixty-day leave of absence. Thompson expressed gratitude for the leave, however speaking with a correspondent from the *Statesman,* "he was loud in his protest of those newspapers who described him as killing many men, whereas, as he states, he has only killed the variety men in Austin and here." Thompson's short memory only called upon the killing of Mark Wilson and Jack Harris, and in the former case he had been acquitted, and now "he expects that he will have an equal measure of justice in the present case." Thompson family members in Bastrop were following the legal proceedings closely through the press. One may surmise that they were not disappointed to read in the *Bastrop Advertiser* the opinion the editor offered to his readership. "If he killed a few more men of the variety stripe, the country would be better off. In fact, if the government would outlaw every man who follows this infamous calling, and put a premium upon their heads, it would save an immense amount of heart-aches and many a woman from a life of shame and ruin. We have never heard of any good man that Ben Thompson has killed, and it must be admitted that the world is better off without those he has killed."[52]

Over five hundred miles away in the border town of El Paso, Billy Thompson surely followed his brother's legal proceedings. In early August, Billy moved on to Galveston, and perhaps, this time the brothers' roles were reversed and Billy provided the money to help pay Ben's many legal bills.[53]

Ben Thompson's legal counsel worked tirelessly, searching for favorable evidence through new witnesses who supported his case. Throughout August and early September, William Walton repeatedly traveled to San Antonio to interview John J. McLaughlin, John Lamar, Daniel Morgan, and M. B. Davis to take down their sworn statements and enter them into the court record.

John J. McLaughlin refuted the testimony of the other Vaudeville employees, stating that Harris did make "a distinct change of position and movement of the gun," which placed "the muzzle pointing towards the door where Thompson was standing … immediately preceding the first shot by Thompson."

While enjoying a beer at the Vaudeville bar, hack driver John Lamar watched Jack Harris walk in the west door. Lamar testified he heard Harris say, "I will blow the top of his head off," as Harris walked to the ticket office and soon emerged with a double barrel shotgun. Satisfied a difficulty was about to happen, Lamar hustled out of the barroom to calm his horses in anticipation of the coming gunfire.

Daniel Morgan, another hack driver, had been acquainted with both Jack Harris and Ben Thompson for about ten years, and was in the Vaudeville Saloon observing the unfolding drama. He saw Harris holding a shotgun with "the muzzle little lower than on level but pointing toward where Thompson was standing." Thompson was characteristically standing with his arms folded across his breast "out on the pavement." Wisely, Morgan "stepped back out of the way," as obscenities were exchanged, and seconds later, Thompson fired the fatal shot.

Former Texas Ranger M. B. Davis of Fort Worth, Texas was the last of a long list of witnesses who testified about Jack Harris's many threats against Ben Thompson, but he may have been the first to warn Ben in December 1880.[54]

In response to Judge Noonan's earlier rejection of bail, George Pendexter traveled by train to Dallas in late August where he submitted to Associate Judge James Mann Hurt of the State Court of Appeals an application on behalf of his client for a writ of habeas corpus. Judge Hurt refused the writ and it seemed to be a wasted trip for Pendexter.[55] The next day, however, another associate judge of the State Court of Appeals, Samuel A. Wilson agreed to a new hearing for the application of habeas corpus to be held on Saturday, September 2 in San Antonio. Leo Tarleton, for the state and William Walton, again, for the defense, argued if another habeas corpus hearing should be held. Walton prevailed and later that evening, in an opinion of considerable length, Judge Wilson decided to grant a hearing on the second habeas corpus application. The hearing was scheduled to take place on Monday, September 11. The friends of Ben Thompson were very much elated by the news, and felt he would finally be released on bail.[56]

As Ben Thompson was in the middle of a legal fight to gain his freedom and possibly save his life, his former protégé Billy Simms deftly filled the role Jack Harris once held as the principal business partner and manager of the Vaudeville Theatre, Saloon, and 101 Gambling Club. As administrator of Harris's estate, he promptly disposed of the responsibility, and paid off Harris's heirs. With Joe Foster and Johnny Dyer, Simms began to refurbish and make much-needed improvements to the building, primarily the theatre portion. The walls were freshly painted and new, more comfortable chairs were purchased. In addition, updated machinery was installed to help with scenery changes. Continuing with Harris's fateful desire to use electric lights, a huge electric chandelier was suspended from the ceiling in the center of the auditorium. Simms had a new dress circle, or mezzanine, built in a balcony placed above the level of the orchestra pit and stage. With an eye to establishing a larger clientele, he surprisingly, but astutely, began to schedule matinee performances catering to women and children. To continue to ingratiate and influence local politicians, the theatre held charity performances, and cash donations were even given to Mayor James H. French to dispense to the town's needy. In early

September, Simms traveled to St. Louis to find and procure a new lineup of performers. He hired a large troupe of seventeen stage artists, and was expected back with his new performers about a week prior to the reopening of the renovated theatre, which was scheduled September 18. It was no longer going to be called Jack Harris's Vaudeville, but would be known simply as The Vaudeville.[57]

Before his second habeas corpus hearing could occur, Ben Thompson was taken before the Bexar County Grand Jury on Wednesday, September 6 where a bill of indictment for murder in the first degree was issued. His case was assigned the number 2118, and a pool of sixty men was called to possibly serve as jurors. The case was set for trial to begin on September 12.[58] Because of the grand jury indictment, Judge Wilson acknowledged, "I think the law is plain, that the indictment has the effect to take away from me all further jurisdiction over the case." Newspapers reported that it was a friendly arrangement, and Thompson's counsel abandoned this attempt for bail since the trial for murder was scheduled to take place the next day.[59]

Having a complete understanding of the importance of public opinion, and in an obvious attempt to influence the jury pool two days prior to the start of his murder trial, Ben Thompson issued a statement through his attorneys in which he explained his version of the death of Jack Harris. Of course, there would be no risk of a hostile cross-examination. His statement appeared in newspapers throughout Texas. In brief, Thompson made the following points. First, he believed the evidence when presented at trial would fully vindicate him. Second, he stated that there was a conspiracy among Harris and his friends and business partners to murder him. Third, the Vaudeville Theatre was the cause of ruin for many young men and the debauchery of a greater number of innocent females than all of the other causes in Bexar County combined. Fourth, he stated it was a well-known fact that Harris had threatened numerous times to kill him. Fifth and finally, he did not draw his pistol until Harris had leveled his shotgun at him. The entire statement, prepared in the Bexar County jail on September 10. Although his statement is signed, "Ben Thompson," one suspects that much of the wording was a product of William Walton's advice (see Appendix D).[60]

Ben Thompson entered Judge Noonan's courtroom neatly attired in black with his hair carefully combed. Acknowledging friends and acquaintances with smiles and bows, he seemed to be in good humor. Judge Noonan took his seat on the bench shortly after 9 a. m., and gaveled his courtroom into session. A large crowd pressed forward until there was little room to move. J. P. Fowler, an attorney from Gill's hometown of Bastrop, there accompanied Robert Gill, Thompson's brother-in-law. As Gill was in San Antonio, his wife Mary Jane, Ben's sister, gave birth to a son, and they blessed their newborn boy with the name Walton Thompson Gill. District Attorney Fred Cocke informed the judge that the state was ready to proceed and move forward in its prosecution on the charge of murder. Roll was taken of the defense witnesses, and it was determined about one third were not present in the courtroom. Walton asked the judge for a recess until 3 p. m., which was allowed, and upon return Walton filed a petition stating the defendant could not safely go to trial without the presence of the missing witnesses. This long, very detailed petition contained a litany of the efforts made to bring all of the defense witnesses to court and explained the evidence they would provide. Ben Thompson's petition, similar to his earlier statement, received tremendous publicity and was published in many of the major newspapers in Texas. The most compelling claims in the petition stated that, two months prior to his death, Jack Harris offered a bribe of $500 to W. S. Ellis if he would murder Ben Thompson, and, as the two Mauri sisters comforted the fatally wounded Jack Harris, he asked them, "Is

Thompson killed?" The women answered no, prompting Harris to ask a second question, "Are any of my friends killed?" The defense argued that Harris's dying inquiries indicated he was acting in concert with others in an attempt to murder Ben Thompson. Without the slightest hesitation, Judge Noonan continued Thompson's trial until the December term. Walton then asked for yet another bail hearing, which Judge Noonan agreed to and scheduled for the following day at 3 p. m.[61]

The *San Antonio Express* reported the following unbelievable statement. "One of the attorneys for Ben Thompson remarked to an opposing attorney: 'If you will let Ben out on bond, we will bind ourselves, if he does not appear promptly for trial to forfeit enough money to build Bexar county a magnificent courthouse, jail, poor house and an office apiece for every lawyer in the city."[62] This was an absurd promise, and one must accept it was not credible by anyone, but perhaps an eye-raising, space-filler in the newspaper.

At the bail hearing, Walton introduced his four new witnesses: McLaughlin, Lamar, Morgan, and Davis and led them through their testimony. For the state, special prosecutor, T.T. Teel cross-examined these defense witnesses in a very forceful and aggressive manner. Judge Noonan weighted the testimony and announced he could see no new facts that would change his mind. He reaffirmed his past decision of denying bail, dismissed the writ of habeas corpus, and remanded Thompson back to the care of the sheriff. Again, Walton filed a formal notice he would seek bail at the upcoming term of the court of appeals. This was scheduled in October, and was to be held in the east Texas town of Tyler. Thompson's attorneys freely admitted they did not expect Judge Noonan to rule in their favor, and they only went before him a second time because the law compelled them to do so before they could take their application to a higher court. They felt confident that the justices of the court of appeals would approve their case for freeing Thompson on bail.[63]

In response to Ben's latest legal defeat, the members of the Austin city council, at a specially scheduled meeting, voted to extend his leave of absence until the next regular meeting. This was a minor blessing; because they also decided he was to receive no pay.[64]

The court of appeals was sitting in Tyler during the third week of October, and four attorneys traveled there to plea their side of the Ben Thompson's latest habeas corpus case. On Monday, October 16, Walton and Pendexter argued the case on behalf of Thompson. Speaking for the state was Leo Tarleton and former justice of the Texas Supreme Court Thomas Jefferson Devine. Two days later, the court of appeals affirmed Judge Noonan's past decisions, and bail was, again, denied. The preferential treatment Ben Thompson received in the Travis County facility after the Mark Wilson slaying did not exist for him in Bexar County. Sheriff McCall returned his noted prisoner to the county jail where his accommodations, "an ordinary cage," were the same as any other prisoner.[65]

Far to the west in El Paso County, was the town of Ysleta. It was the county seat, and also the headquarters of Capt. George W. Baylor's Texas Ranger Company. Baylor's heart was in fighting Indians, not law enforcement, but when he was made aware that Billy Thompson, who was indicted for murder in Aransas County, had returned from Galveston and was in El Paso, he ordered Sergeant O. M. Dampier to take two men and make the arrest. On Thursday, October 19, the three Rangers, who then turned him over to the civil authorities, took Billy into custody without incident.[66]

Word of Billy Thompson's arrest reached Paul P. Court, Sheriff of Aransas County, who at once telegraphed the state Adjutant General W. H. King in Austin asking for his help in bringing Billy to trial. Since his county had no jail worthy of the name, Sheriff Court asked that his prisoner be sent to the more secure Nueces County jail at nearby Corpus Christi.[67] The responsibility of transferring Billy Thompson across the state fell to El Paso County Deputy Sheriff Frank Manning (brother of James and "Doc" Manning, who together killed ex-El Paso City Marshal Dallas Stoudemire). The selection of Frank Manning would prove to be a blessing for Billy Thompson.

Deputy Sheriff Manning and his prisoner reached Austin on Thursday night, October 26. Once there, Thompson asked Manning not to place him in the Travis County jail. The two men had been warm friends for the past sixteen years and based on Billy's word of honor that he would report to Manning promptly Saturday morning, Manning gave him his freedom to move about the city. Billy told the naively lenient Manning that he wanted to consult with his attorneys, have a photograph taken, and settle other business before leaving for Corpus Christi. He may have accomplished those things, but on Friday he was also seen enjoying the fair and making the rounds at several saloons. Travis County Sheriff Edward Creary later admitted he saw Billy several times on Friday night, unescorted and at perfect liberty. Creary even shook hands with him, but said he did not arrest Billy Thompson because he did not have a *capias* for him, and hence could not take him into custody.[68]

On Saturday morning, Billy Thompson reneged on his promise and did not appear and surrender himself to Deputy Sheriff Manning. Much to Manning's embarrassment, Billy was nowhere to be found. Instead of seeking out local law enforcement and requesting immediate help, Frank Manning went to the adjutant general's office and sheepishly reported to Henry Orsay, the chief clerk, how he had released his prisoner and now could not locate him. Orsay was dumbfounded, and told Manning that he could not have expected anything else in a place where Thompson had so many friends, and could obtain any amount of help and money. Clerk Orsay advised Manning to "notify the county and city authorities to try and effect [Billy's] arrest." Unbelievably, Manning steadfastly refused to do this. Orsay went to the local lawmen by himself, but Billy had already fled Austin for parts unknown.[69]

Faced with no imminent release for their city marshal, the Austin city council accepted Ben Thompson's resignation in a unanimous vote on October 23. Mayor Saylor ordered a special election to fill the position of city marshal for the unexpired term. They held the election on November 7, and Sergeant John Chenneville was unanimously chosen to serve as acting city marshal until the vacancy was filled.[70] Austin's voters ultimately selected veteran lawman John P. Kirk, Thompson's rival for the office of city marshal in the previous November 1881 election.[71]

A reporter from the *Statesman* received permission to interview the long-incarcerated Ben Thompson to learn how he took the disappointing news from the Court of Appeals in Tyler, and to ascertain Ben's plans for the future. Thompson was allowed to leave the main cage he currently occupied, and to sit on a bench as "he chatted affably and good humoredly for half an hour." According to Bexar County Sheriff Thomas McCall, the disappointing news from Tyler was met by Thompson with level-headedness and composure. Thompson laughed and told the sheriff, "Well that's a joke, three months more free board." Naturally, Ben had a strong hope that he would be granted bail and released, but was wise enough not to plan on it. As to his attorneys's efforts for a change of venue away from Bexar County, he thought, "I shall, of course, use every effort to that end from this time out, and I fully believe that I can establish my right to a trial outside of Bexar County. The prosecution will, of course, labor to prevent it." As far as the eventual outcome of his legal troubles, he said, "I do not believe any jury, even here, will ever bring in a verdict against me. My case is too plain, and I expect to emerge from here a free man." As to his future intentions, provided he is found not guilty, Thompson explained, "I intend to sell out my business, make a clean up and buy a farm just outside Austin, and bid my public career a final farewell, I have had enough both in experience of this world and its profitable results to content me, and I wish to settle down quietly for the remainder of my life." It was known that Leo Tarleton, of the prosecution had paid Ben a recent visit. Thompson thought Tarleton wanted to be sure he was caged properly, and to throw a fear into him because of "some new or increased danger to his position." Thompson proclaimed, "He came to the wrong shop" and to "tell all of my friends that I am as content and satisfied as any man could be under such circumstances." The reporter ended his article writing how Ben "wished to thank his Austin friends for their many kind expressions of sympathy and their efforts in his behalf."[72]

Relentlessly, for the sixth and final time, Ben Thompson's legal counsel filed another motion to have him released on bail. In Tyler on October 31, they filed for another hearing before the court of appeals. Two weeks later, two attorneys representing the State, Thomas J. Devine and Leo Tarleton, left San Antonio for Tyler. Ben Thompson remained behind in the Bexar county jail. On November 22, the court of appeals refused to hold a new hearing, and Thompson was forced to accept the fact that he would linger in jail until his trial. His day in court was placed on the docket list for the second week of January 1883.[73]

As the months following the fatal shooting passed by, the general public continued to find the Thompson-Harris case interesting, and an account of the killing of Jack Harris with illustrations appeared in the *National Police Gazette* on December 12.[74] The reporting is remarkably accurate, in spite of the *Gazette*'s reputation for sensationalizing. With the simple title of, "Ben Thompson, of Austin," the Gazette retold the story of Jack Harris's death and how the Austin lawman was sitting in a San Antonio jail cell. The article ended with a final comment, "Really, a policeman's lot is not a happy one in the cowboy state."[75]

Christmas 1882 found Ben incarcerated and Billy on the run. Ben's friends in Austin ensured he enjoyed his favorite meal for Christmas dinner, baked possum, which he consumed with much enjoyment. For an after-dinner treat, his friends sent over some fine cigars. Billy Thompson, similar to his time in Fort Worth and El Paso, was hiding out in the open. He was now in the resort town of Hot Springs, Arkansas. He arrived in the fall after "escaping" from the custody of his friend Frank Manning. A later newspaper report stated Billy had "established himself in business" and since the only business he ever followed was running games of chance, it can be assumed he made an arrangement to earn his living in one of Hot Springs's many gambling resorts.[76]

On Wednesday, January 3, Austin's chapter of the Knights of Pythias celebrated the installation of new officers at Millet's Opera House. Grand Chancellor E. B. Connell spoke at the close of the ceremonies, and in his remarks, Connell referred to two vacant chairs in the lodge room. One was vacant due to the death of a brother, the other vacant due to another brother's incarceration. Though no names were mentioned all understood that the brothers referred to were Knights R. A. Shirley and Ben Thompson.

In San Antonio, subpoenas were issued to summon witnesses to appear on January 9 at the Bexar County Courthouse on Soledad Street, located behind the Vaudeville Theatre, and placed into the hands of Sheriff T. P. McCall. Among those summoned to appear were Johnny D. Dyer, Joseph C. Foster, Kate and May Mauri, Barney Mitchell, George Horner, and L. C. Grothaus. Friends and relatives of Ben Thompson boarded the train to the Alamo City to attend the trial, including his wife Kate and their two children, his friend Monroe Miller, his brother-in-law Jim Moore, and Police Sergeant John Chenneville.[77]

When Judge Noonan asked Ben how he would plead, he responded in a loud, clear voice, "Not guilty." Moments before, the county clerk had read the indictment charging him with murder in the first degree. Thompson's defense counsel filed an application for a change of venue, stating the trial must take place in another county because, in Bexar County, they "alleged there is a dangerous combination formed against the defendant, and that prejudice is such he cannot get a fair and impartial trial here." Judge Noonan would not agree to a venue change, and ordered the case to proceed. William Walton brought on an eruption of excitement when, after a moment of consultation with his client and fellow members of the defense counsel, agreed with the judge, withdrew the application for a change in venue, and announced his client was ready for trial. The judge adjourned the court until the following morning when jury selection would begin. One San Antonio newspaperman predicted, "Ben Thompson is now on trial for his life, his case will turn upon the breadth of a hair."[78]

It was observed that Ben Thompson's long confinement apparently did not seem to have an adverse effect on him either physically or mentally. People noticed he appeared "hale and hearty, having materially increased in weight since first incarcerated. He is as pleasant and affable with his friends as usual, exhibiting no mental affliction or trouble."[79] He spent a lot of his time playing the banjo and reading the newspaper stories about him. Thompson craved the newspaper notoriety, and he kept a scrapbook, pasting in every mention of him and his exploits.[80]

On Thursday morning, January 11, a venire of sixty jurors was called, and forty-eight responded. The missing prospective jurors each received a $25 fine. All but two of the forty-eight admitted they already formed an opinion as to the verdict, and were excused. The judge ordered a special venire of one hundred and fifty called. In addition, the missing twelve from the original venire were again ordered to appear. Toward the end of the day's proceedings, some felt the argument for a change of venue was well founded. Noonan released the witnesses until Saturday, and scheduled the jury selection to begin again in the morning.[81]

At the end of three days, only eight men qualified to serve on the jury. Through the efforts of Sheriff McCall, who was credited for doing his full duty in securing an impartial jury, twelve men were finally empaneled. To prevent them from being influenced, Judge Noonan ordered the jurors not to read any newspapers during the trial. The proceedings commenced on Monday morning, January 16, and the prosecution spent three days and used twenty-seven witnesses in presenting its case.[82] The defense now took its turn. William Walton rose and addressed the jury. "Thompson did kill Jack Harris, but he did it in self-defense, at a time and place and under facts and circumstances which the law warrants and excuses. This we propose to prove by good and respectable men of Bexar [C]ounty and the state of Texas." Walton declared to the jury, "It is a notorious fact that Jack Harris has for years past made a continuous and well connected chain of threats to take the life of Thompson—not one time, but repeatedly. There are some of Harris' friends, and others who are not, who will swear to these matters in a court of justice, before God. Our witnesses are officers of the peace, good citizens, lawyers, newspaper men, farmers, &c. Harris deliberately, without cause and under no excitement, threatened to take the life of Thompson whenever he should enter San Antonio and attempt to exercise the poor rights of a citizen." Ben Thompson "knew that Harris was a man, judging from his character, who would carry out his threats if he saw an opportunity, and did actually have his shot-gun presented in an effort to carry out the threat at the time he was killed. He deliberately looked through the blinds of the saloon, got his gun, took position behind the wall, and no doubt would have killed Thompson had he not been prevented. The gun was full-cocked when found." To begin discrediting one of State's most important witnesses, Walton claimed, "We will also show that Biencourt made a very different statement on the morning after the shooting than one made [later]." To bolster Thompson's case, Walton professed how "other witnesses will testify that Harris had been seen with a shot-gun in the streets hunting for Thompson, to shoot him down on sight. If we can prove this, even though ... [Thompson's] ... hands may be stained with the blood of a fellow-man, it has been done in a manner fully warranted by the laws of man as well as the laws of God."

Walton presented witnesses to the jury until 10 p. m., when Judge Noonan closed the proceedings and adjourned the court for the night. John Lamar proved to be the most dramatic defense witness, testifying, "Thompson cried to Harris to 'drop that gun' before any shots were fired, with which request Harris did not comply."[83]

On Saturday morning, the courtroom was packed with spectators all eager to listen to the eloquent William Walton's final address to the jury. "It was well delivered, admirably intermixed with pathos, indignation and argument, and was regarded by many lawyers present as a masterpiece of forensic knowledge." Major T. T. Teel replied for the state, and after Judge Noonan delivered a long charge to the jurors, the case was placed into their hands. The deliberation began at 5 p. m. and at midnight the jurors had made their decision. They were served supper and retired for the night.

On the street, the general feeling was that the jurors would not be able to come to a decision. Men were making bets in the many barrooms, wagering thousands of dollars, most for either a hung jury or acquittal. Thompson and his supporters were very positive, and optimistically looked forward to the verdict.[84] At 8 a. m., the jury brought in a verdict of not guilty. When the courtroom learned of Thompson's escape, the cheering and "applause was deafening and long continued."[85]

As is custom, Judge Noonan was informed of the not guilty verdict before it was read, a decision with which he did not concur.

He voiced his fear, which was reported in the newspapers, that sadly because of the jury's decision, many more future personal disputes would also be settled with firearms.

Ben Thompson was released from the sheriff's custody without any delay, and he walked out of the courthouse a free man. While many of Harris's friends felt he deserved either the rope or a long imprisonment, and though the jury's decision was condemned by many others, the general public seemed to be satisfied that Thompson had been punished enough. He had lost the city marshalship of Austin, incurred tremendous legal expenses, and spent six months in a jail cell. In celebration, Ben Thompson treated the jurors and "all hands in the court room" to a drink before lunching with his family, a few friends, and his attorneys at the Maverick Hotel on Houston Street. At noon he boarded the train to Austin and returned home.[86]

Chapter 15

A LAST VISIT TO GALVESTON

"He was fast becoming a terror."

—William M. Walton, 1884

"Ben Thompson has a host of friends who are on the alert to aid him is nothing to his discredit," the *San Antonio Light* acknowledged. It was reported that the prosecution had some valuable friends, too. Billy Simms and Joe Foster reached into their pockets and provided the money necessary to pursue the case against Thompson.[1] Simms remained as proprietor and business manager of the Vaudeville Theatre throughout Ben Thompson's incarceration and trial. Once Ben was acquitted, Simms brought in another experienced theatre manager and left San Antonio to travel to Chicago for an extended stay.[2]

The sporting men of Austin had arranged for a grand reception for Ben, and as he stepped down from the train the Colored Brass Band thumping out a hero's welcome greeted him. A great crowd, comprised mostly of black people, unharnessed the horses from the carriage he and his family were to ride home in and pulled the vehicle up Congress Avenue from the depot to the Capitol. They cheered Ben the entire way singing, "For he's a jolly good fellow, which nobody can deny." John Cardwell of the *Statesman* expressed in his newspaper how such an "ostentatious public demonstration" was in bad taste. Cardwell had no doubts about the jury's verdict being just, believing as the jury did that Thompson acted in self-defense but he felt, "the reception was not a proper example to be set in any community. The spirit which induced it was a sort of hero worship ... but it was indelicate and sadly advised on behalf of a man who had signalized himself in being the first to take life in private matters." The celebration should have been cast in more "smothered tones" and after months of incarceration, Cardwell was sure Thompson would have preferred to spend his first moments of freedom at home with his family and best friends. Cardwell surmised, "We suspect that some of the very parties who cheered the loudest would liked to have seen Thompson convicted, and perhaps he is shrewd enough to know this."[3]

As far as his future was concerned, a rumor floated that Ben was soon to open a gambling operation in Dallas, though no evidence exists that he followed through on this ambition.[4] He did however purchase a large, fine two-story frame home on the southeast corner of University Avenue at 21st Street across the road from the Main Building of the University of Texas for his family.[5] He would often use the wide expanse of the university in front of his home to practice his pistol shooting. The question was often asked in Austin, "How did Ben Thompson succeed in having so much money?" Alexander E. Sweet and John Armoy Knox in their weekly publication *Texas Siftings* offered up an answer. "He was not a successful gambler, but he owned a third interest in all the gambling establishments of Austin. His income from this source often aggregated thousands of dollars a week. In consideration of this third interest in the profits of these establishments he protected them from any possible interference on the part of the police, and also from any outside competition." Sweet and Knox did not openly state that Thompson was operating what amounted to a protection racket, but that is what it certainly was. The revelation continued, "The gambler who desired to establish a new gambling den in Austin was promptly made aware of the fact that if he made any such attempt he would have Ben Thompson to fight, and that usually caused the would-be intruder to prefer some other city. When Thompson was in jail in San Antonio, he received his dividends from the Austin gambling establishments at the end of every week."[6]

Even though he had only been home for a few days after such a long incarceration, Thompson felt the need for recreation and decided on a lengthy trip. His close friend, Austin businessman, Monroe Miller, chose to accompany him. In an act of true bravado typical of the man, their first stop was San Antonio. He demonstrated his contempt for all of Jack Harris's friends and associates by immediately returning to the scene of his past troubles. Other stops included Laredo, Brownsville, Matamoros, Corpus Christi, Galveston, and New Orleans. It was described as a "trip full of pleasure, fun and recreation, nothing happening on the entire travel to mar the object for which it was undertaken." On March 28, his last stop before returning to Austin was to visit his sister Mary Jane and her husband Robert Gill and their children in Bastrop.[7]

Ben Thompson's fame grew exponentially after he killed Jack Harris and won his freedom after a memorable trial. News correspondents throughout Texas sought out the notorious gunman. A reporter from the *San Angelo Standard* was introduced to Thompson in Austin and was surprised by what he discovered. The reporter expected to meet the famous desperado in a saloon or a gambling house and was surprised to visit him in a quiet, orderly ice-cream parlor. "Ben Thompson and his wife were eating strawberry cream

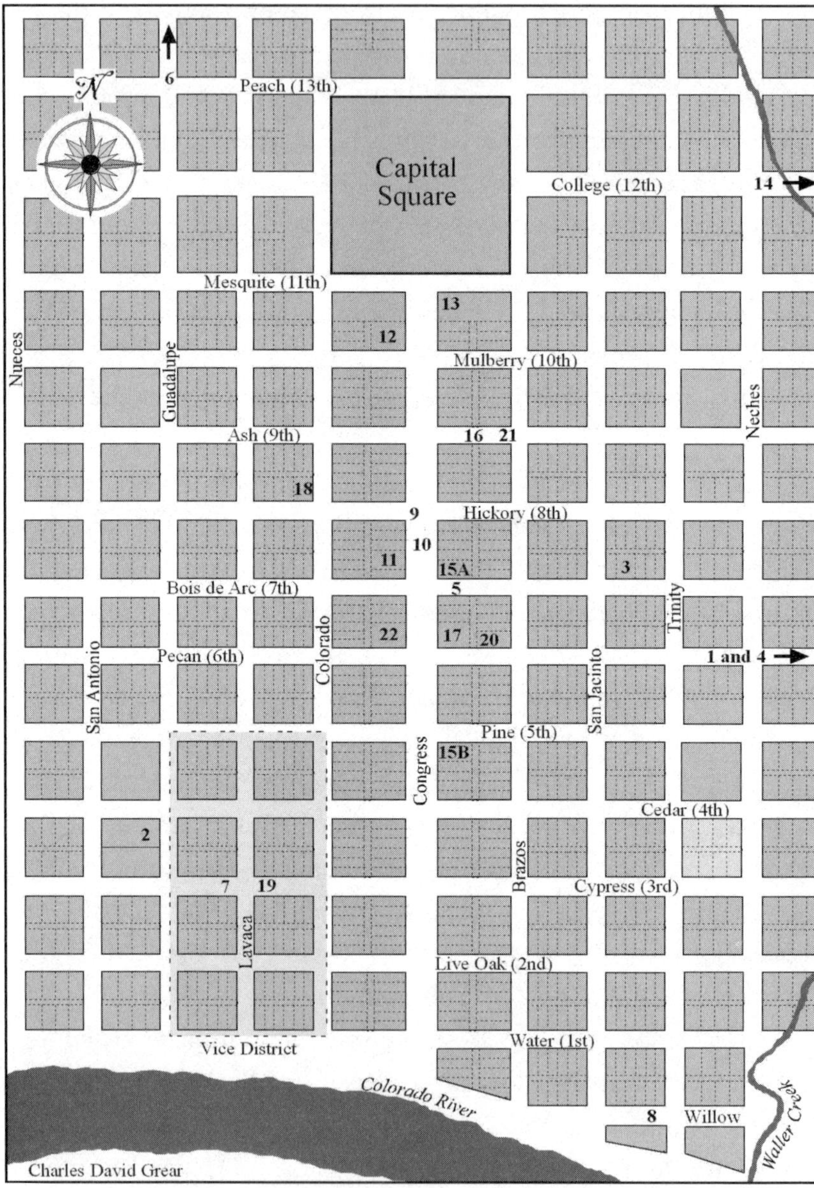

The city of Austin as Ben Thompson knew it. *Map by Charles David Grear.*

1. On October 9, 1858, fourteen-year-old Ben Thompson fires his shotgun and wounds teenager James Smith by Waller Creek near the intersection of Pecan (6th) and Sabine Streets.
2. On March 12, 1859 Governor H. R. Runnels pardoned Ben Thompson for his assault on Smith and Thompson was released from the Travis County Courthouse and Jail at Cedar (4th) and Guadalupe Streets. On the night of September 17, 1865, Ben Thompson slips out of a jail cell here and escapes to Mexico where he joins the command of General Tomas Mejia fighting for the Emperor Maximilian. The aging facility would be replaced in 1876.
3. Ben Thompson marries Kate Moore on November 26, 1863, at Saint David's Episcopal Church on Bois d'Arc (7th) at San Jacinto Street. The original structure built in 1854 stands today.
4. On July 22, 1864, the Willis Brothers are removed from Confederate custody and are lynched on the remote end of east Pecan (6th) Street. Ben Thompson was later reported among the mob.
5. On East Bois d'Arc (7th) near Congress Avenue, Ben Thompson fatally wounds John Combs in a street fight on the night of August 22, 1864.
6. May 27, 1865 Ben Thompson kills teamster Alberto Algerio in an argument over a horse marked with a Confederate military brand. The shooting occurred about three miles north of town near the future site of the State's Lunatic Asylum at Guadalupe and 41st Street.
7. March 31, 1868, in an Austin Bordello, probably in the First Ward, Billy Thompson fatally shoots Union soldier William Burke three times.
8. Per the 1872 Austin City Directory, Ben and Kate Thompson's family home was on Willow Street between San Jacinto and Trinity Streets.
9. January 25, 1872, somewhere on Congress Avenue, a drunken Ben Thompson threatens the life of former Texas Supreme Court Justice James Hall Bell and repeatedly strikes the judge with a riding whip.
10. On the night of June 2, 1874, Billy Thompson becomes involved in an altercation with the bartender of Congress Avenue's Office Saloon. Two shots are fired at Billy without result and he is able to escape on horseback from an investigating Austin policeman.
11. During the afternoon of February 4, 1876, outside of Mitchell's Saloon on Congress Avenue between Bois d' Arc (7th) and Hickory (8th) three out-of-towners confront Ben Thompson. In the ensuing fight, he twice wounds William Hannah.
12. The Capital Theatre, set on the northwest corner of Congress Avenue and Mulberry (10th) Street, is the scene of the 1876 Christmas night gunfight where Ben Thompson kills proprietor Mark Wilson and wounds bartender Charles Mathews.
13. At various times both Ben and Billy Thompson are incarcerated at the Travis County Jail built in 1875-76 on the southeast corner of Congress Avenue and Mesquite (11th) Street. The adjoining courthouse to the south would later be renovated into an office complex for various state agencies and from 1931-1964 it was named the Walton Building after the famous Austin attorney who twice successfully defended Ben Thompson for the charge of murder.
14. The 1877 Austin City Directory places the Thompson home of Ben and Kate on College (12th) Street at the east end of the city's limit.
15. **A:** During the evening of October 2, 1877, in a bloodless shooting Ben Thompson empties his gambling hall beneath the offices of the *Statesman*, with several of bullets sent through the ceiling disturbing the printers setting type above. **15 B:** In a prank later the same night, Thompson fires off his pistol in front of the Raymond House on Congress Avenue near Pine (5th) Street.
16. On December 9 and 10, 1879, "Buffalo Bill [Cody] and his Mammoth Combination of Artists" performed at Millet's Opera House, on Ash (9th) Street east of Congress Avenue.
17. On two successive nights in late April 1880, Ben Thompson "shoots up" the gambling hall above the Iron Front Saloon on Congress Avenue and Pecan (6th) Street. The *Statesman* reported the incidents in an article entitled, "Ben Thompson on the Warpath." Thompson would later become a partner in the saloon's gambling concession.
18. The northeast corner of Colorado and Hickory (8th) Street, originally the location of the Republic of Texas's first capitol building, it later became the town's first firehouse and then Austin's City Hall and Police Station. It was here City Marshal Thompson had his office.
19. On the night of May 1, 1881, City Marshal Thompson kicked in the door to his room and arrested gunman John Ringo in "a house in the jungles," one of the colloquialism for Austin's vice district located in the town's First Ward. The vice district spanned from Colorado Street to Guadalupe and from the river to Pine (5th) Street. Over the years, it was also called "The Precincts of Mexico' and later "Guytown."
20. At Simon's Restaurant on Pecan (6th) Street east of Congress Avenue, Ben Thompson creates a disturbance on January 10, 1884, at the Texas Stockman's convention. No shots are fired.
21. San Antonio *Express* reporter W. A. Bowen was assaulted by Ben Thompson on the evening of February 1, 1884, in front of Millet's Opera House.
22. On February 2, 1884, Ben Thompson twice visited the offices of the *Statesman* upset over what he perceived as inaccuracies in the newspaper's reporting of his lawless antics. He fails in his attempts to intimidate the *Statesman's* staff and management. The 1885-86 Austin City Directory lists the offices of the *Statesman* at 126 West Pecan (6th) Street.

at a table near … a coterie of high-school girls, one of them being a daughter of … Gov. [John] Ireland. Thompson was a small-sized man, yet not slender. He was elegantly, yet not showily dressed; his clothes indicated a correct taste, a diamond stud and thread of gold watch chain comprising all his personal jewelry." To this reporter, Thompson was a handsome man with a small black mustache and hazel eyes, and he continued Ben's reputation that he "was never known to take an unfair advantage of an enemy, a number of his victims having had the first shot at him … and thus with every case of Thompson's numerous killings the preliminaries were always flavored with a dash of dramatic sensationalism."[8] Thompson was credited with being adept at drawing from his waistband, pocket, belted scabbard, or from a relatively new invention, the shoulder holster. One wonders if in this setting the gunman concealed his revolver so well the reporter did not notice it. Perhaps Ben had it secreted in a Texas Pattern shoulder holster he was known to have used, popularized, and may have even invented.[9]

A correspondent of the *Houston Post* wrote a "pen-picture of Capt. Ben Thompson" in which he described him as one of "the most widely-known men of Texas." If one were to hear him tell of his experiences, of his "truly checkered career since reaching manhood" a stranger would never suspect this "unassuming, modest, quiet and gentlemanly narrator" was "Ben Thompson, the killer," the man who is regarded as the worst desperado west of the Mississippi River. To nobody's surprise, the *Post* reporter further described Thompson as "perfectly fearless," and a tough man in a fight, however he "does not deserve the hard name he bears away from home. His life has been a strangely wild and adventurous one, and no doubt he has done many things wrong, but still he has a good heart, as will be attested by those who know him best. True hearted, generous, brave, he never deserted a friend or took advantage of a foe. There are plenty of worse men in the world than Ben Thompson."[10]

Walton quoted an Austin newspaper which correctly predicted Thompson's ultimate fate, "The chances are about ... nine hundred and ninety-nine in a thousand that the man is living to-day who will kill Ben Thompson. He may not know him now; may have never been in a thousand miles of him; but he is wandering somewhere through the world, moving onwards towards the fatal day and deed! The paths of the two men are gradually merging; they will come on, until their paths cross, and then!! Thompson may escape such a fate, but it is hardly within the range of possibility that he will."[11]

The ultimate fate of Billy Thompson's old nemesis, John Sparks, following years as a Texas Ranger, was somewhat ironic. His death occurred as the result of a private matter, one he could have easily left to the authorities. Captain Sparks, after leaving the Ranger service, began ranching and earning his living as a grain dealer south of Dallas near the town of East Corsicana, Navarro County. During the first week of April, Sparks purchased cattle from the Fuller twins, Bigman and Littleman. Once he sorted through the herd, Sparks discovered a yearling calf he had already purchased from another party and had left out on the range. Sparks resented how the Fuller boys threw such a long rope, and had the audacity to sell him his own animal. He went to the magistrate to get an arrest warrant issued but failed to find the officer. Impatient, Sparks along with a few other men, then chose to visit the Fuller twins and make the arrest himself. It was after dark when Sparks arrived at the small town of Purdon, Navarro County and entered the Fuller brothers's house. He found them sleeping and roused them out of their beds. Littleman asked to go into the next room to fetch a candle and returned with one lit candle and his double-barrel shotgun. At the same time, Bigman got hold of his Winchester rifle and as the candle illuminated Sparks, Bigman fired one shot striking Sparks on the left side of his chest above the heart. The bullet went through his body, and the party he came with took the mortally wounded Sparks with them as they left. He died at 7 a.m. as the sun came up, with his brother Thad Sparks by his side. Navarro Deputy Sheriff Cobley took the Fuller brothers into custody, and John Sparks' funeral was held at his home. He was survived by his wife Amazon, their sons Walter and Charles, and their three daughters, Laura, Anne, and Cora.[12]

On May 4, 1883, C. F. Bailey, clerk of the Aransas County District Court, issued an arrest warrant for Billy Thompson under the October 1872 Grand Jury indictment for the June 1, 1868, murder of Remus Smith in Rockport, Texas. Three days later, Gov. John Ireland appointed Aransas County Sheriff Paul P. Court as his agent and authorized him to travel to Hot Springs, Arkansas where he would arrest Billy Thompson and return him to Aransas County. On the same day, Governor Ireland issued a proclamation placing a $200 reward for the arrest and return of Billy Thompson, obviously making it well worth Sheriff Court's while to undertake the enterprise. Billy would tell a *Houston Daily Post* reporter he was "anxious to have the charge against him investigated and disposed of stating he was openly living in Hot Springs and that he negotiated his surrender and even advanced the money to Court to cover the initial expenses for the trip to Arkansas." The only reason he fled from El Paso County deputy sheriff Frank Manning the previous October was because he did not wish to be in custody at the same time his brother Ben was being held in the Bexar County jail. Since Ben had since won his freedom, Billy was now eager to have his day in court.[13]

Sheriff Court arrested the compliant Billy Thompson in Hot Springs on May 10 and delivered him to the sheriff of Galveston County for safekeeping four days later. The jail in Aransas County was deemed insufficient, as was the jail in neighboring Refugio County. On the same day that he arrived in Galveston with his prisoner, Sheriff Court applied to the governor to collect the $200 reward.[14]

As May came to an end, and as Billy sat in his cell in the Galveston County jail, Ben felt the need to pull out his festive six-shooter and fire it into the air in Austin for an unknown reason. He was arrested and fined $10 plus court costs and somehow, the usually sharp eyes of the *Statesman* reporters missed this misbehavior. As the summer of 1883 wore on, Ben traveled to Houston to support, wager on, and become disappointed by the Austin baseball team when they ultimately lost.[15]

On the last day of June, Billy Thompson filed for a writ of habeas corpus with Judge Henry Clay Pleasants of the 23rd District of DeWitt County, who was famous for holding court with a shotgun across his lap during the Sutton-Taylor Feud. Judge Pleasants agreed to hear Billy's plea. It was a wise legal strategy to seek bail in DeWitt County because Aransas was a small county with a long memory, and authorities there thought enough of eighteen-year-old Remus Smith to relentlessly pursue his accused killer for a decade and a half. Though as expected, the DeWitt County District Attorney, Sterling F. Grimes, was unfamiliar with the fifteen-year-old case. Grimes corresponded with Aransas District Clerk C. F. Bailey to learn the facts, but Grimes left Texas for two months before the hearing could take place. A local Cuero attorney named E. C. Jones was chosen to replace Grimes. Naturally, Jones was as unfamiliar with the case as Grimes and on July 24, witnesses gathered in Cuero for the hearing. Prior to the start of the proceedings, someone pointed out attorney George Pendexter and misidentified him as Ben Thompson as a joke, but even Judge Pleasants believed Pendexter was Thompson. When Billy's attorney stood and began to address the court Judge Pleasants sternly addressed Pendexter, "It is against the rules for you to talk in court, sir!" Amazed, Pendexter tried to ask why and the livid judge demanded that he sit down. Pendexter went from amazed to upset, but hesitantly took his seat. One of the other attorneys known to the judge arose and informed the judge the man he was addressing was Mr. Pendexter of Austin. Apologizing, the judge and everyone else in the courtroom had a long laugh. The *Statesman* remarked of the situation, "We'll bet a nickel that if Ben had been there they would have taken him for a Sunday school superintendent or a Presbyterian minister—for he is one of the most gentlemanly men in the state." Pendexter delivered a competent and cogent argument for bail and succeeded. Judge Pleasants ruled in favor of Billy and admitted him to bail in the amount of $5,000. It was thought that he would have no problem raising the sum. However he was still languishing in jail on August 9 waiting for his brother to show up with the necessary money. When Ben finally arrived, Billy was released.[16]

Aside from raising the money for his brother's bail, Ben was willing to pay out any sum required to procure only the most preeminent legal counsel to defend his younger brother. Using the strategy that had been so successful for him in the past, Ben acquired the finest local attorneys. He chose wisely. Politically prominent law partners Kleberg and Crain were not only skilled legal practitioners, but they were also very familiar with the 23rd District Court. Though they were already acclaimed and successful, they were men whose careers were still on the rise. William Henry Crain was a former member of the Texas Senate. He would soon be elected to the United States Congress in service of the Seventh District. He was a longtime resident of Cuero and was renowned as a gifted public speaker. Rudolph Kleberg was a DeWitt County teacher, journalist, attorney, and politician. In the past, he served the county as a prosecutor, and he was serving in the Texas Senate at the time of Billy's trial. His brother Robert, at the request of widowed Mrs. Richard King, assumed the administration of the huge King Ranch, and later married her daughter Alice. In 1885, Rudolph Kleberg was selected by President Grover Cleveland to be the United States Attorney for the Western District of Texas. He would also serve three terms as a United States congressman.

Even with the formidable legal bills, Ben and Billy somehow had money left over for fun. Over the years, the gambling resorts in the town of Saint Mary's of Aransas, located in Refugio County, attracted many professional gamblers including the Thompson brothers, who were known to stop in during Billy's legal troubles. A local legend tells how, once, Ben Thompson brought along another professional gambler named "Gambling Jenny" who excelled at faro. When one of the players insulted her, Thompson pulled out his pistol but was saved when a friend of the offender stepped between the six-shooter and Ben's target. Ben stared at the man, then grimly said, "You're a brave man, now get out of here." Needless to say, the offender and his savior quickly vacated the premises.[17]

During the third week of August, two young, unnamed, men in Galveston enjoyed a lark by spreading a story that a man named McLaughlin had killed Ben Thompson in Laredo. Soon it was the talk on every street corner in the Island City. Even through everyone was repeating the story, one newspaper correspondent expressed skepticism, as the tale could not be verified. The rumor ebbed when it was learned Ben Thompson was alive and well at his home in Austin and had not been out of the capital city for a number of weeks.[18] During that August, Billy Simms was still "absent in the North."[19] If he received false word of Ben Thompson's death in Laredo, he may have been momentarily relieved.

In September, Kleberg and Crain petitioned Judge Pleasants and received his approval without objection from the prosecution to change the venue of Billy Thompson's trial to the judge's DeWitt County jurisdiction.[20] Billy enjoyed himself while out on bail, and traveled freely throughout Texas. He was seen taking in San Antonio during the first week of October in the company of Malcom Hornsby, the Travis County sheriff.[21] Billy wasn't the only one having fun. The water velocipede (a boat propelled by a bicycle-type contraption with paddlewheels), was a fairly new invention and it became the latest craze. Ben Thompson and other gentlemen thought of purchasing one and trying it out on the Colorado River. If successful, others would be bought and a racing club would be organized. Ben ordered one from Galveston at his own expense, and before the year came to a close, he was on the water pedaling up and down the river offering rides to any interested party. However, the plans to form a club never materialized.[22]

Before October ended, Billy Thompson was formally re-indicted by the Aransas County Grand Jury and charged with the murder of Remus Smith. Witnesses were subpoenaed to ensure their attendance at the trial scheduled to take place in DeWitt County during the upcoming December 1883 term.[23]

The year of 1883 was a peaceful one for Ben. In October, James Madison Brown was running his trotter "Glengower" in the mile and a half dash at the State Fair in Austin. He came and went without having any further trouble with Ben Thompson.[24] On November 26, Ben and Kate Thompson celebrated their twentieth wedding anniversary. Of their two surviving children, Benjamin Jr. was now a fifteen-year-old teenager and Kate was almost twelve years old. As far as legal troubles went, he had only been arrested twice throughout the year. Both arrests happened in May, and the newspapers did not mention either one.[25] Perhaps his relatively good behavior was due to his hope of once again becoming the Austin city marshal. On Saturday, December 8, the new mayor, William A. Saylor, and the new city council met to elect the city's officers, including the office of city marshal. The names of eleven citizens were placed in nomination, the most prominent among the candidates being current City Marshal John P. Kirk, who finished serving Thompson's original term, the former city marshal and former Travis County Sheriff Edward Creary, former Texas Ranger and current Travis County Deputy Sheriff H. Grooms Lee and, of course, Ben Thompson. H. Grooms Lee was elected after nine ballots. With the limited support of two aldermen, Ben Thompson was eliminated on the sixth ballot, thus extinguishing the slight chance he had to recapture his former position. This failure to win back the marshalship that provided him with so much acclaim and respect may have caused Ben to return to his lawless ways. He may not have been in the city during the council's proceedings because his brother's trial in Cuero was scheduled to begin in a couple of days on Tuesday, December 11.[26]

Before Judge Pleasants could gavel Billy's trial into session, attorneys Kleberg and Crain, maintaining that it was improperly written, filed a motion to quash the murder indictment. Their motion identified three points. First, the indictment did not properly write up the offense with which the defendant was charged. Second, it failed to allege in what part of the body the wounds were inflicted, and third, the indictment failed to describe said wounds. Not surprisingly, Judge Pleasants ruled against the motion and the trial proceeded. Prosecutor Grimes faced the unenviable task of arguing such an old case. Eight witnesses were called to testify, but the trial lasted one day. Without eyewitnesses, Grimes could not prove that Billy Thompson was the killer. With Ben Thompson and friends watching, the jurors reached their unanimous verdict without even leaving the jury box. A special telegram to the *Statesman* informed their readership of the unsurprising results of the trial. Billy undoubtedly smiled as he once again heard the words, "not guilty."[27]

In western Texas, John King Fisher and his growing family moved to the town of Uvalde, located in the county of the same name. His wife Sarah Vivian Fisher had given birth to their third daughter in November and the family lived in town at 128 W. Mesquite Street. Earlier in the year, Uvalde County Sheriff John Benton "Ben" Boatright convinced Fisher to be one of his depu-

Ben Thompson dressed as the quintessential gambler. He proudly displays his custom made Knights of Pythias watch-fob. Abraham Lincoln said of the Pythians: "The purposes of your organization are most wonderful. It breathes the spirit of friendship, charity and benevolence." This image was made by Austin photographer Harvey R. Marks. *Courtesy the Austin History Center. Image # CO 2505.*

ties. Fisher accepted the opportunity and found a new respectability in wearing a lawman's badge. The robbery of the San Antonio - El Paso stagecoach was the most dramatic and bloody incident to take place during his career as a lawman. Fisher tracked two of the suspects, members of the criminally inclined Hannehan[28] family to their ranch. When they resisted, Fisher killed one and wounded and captured the other in the ensuing shootout. The stagecoach's strongbox was found in their possession, confirming the guilt of the two Hannehans.[29]

A letter from a traveler was published in December 28 edition of San Antonio's *Daily Express* describing how Christmas had passed in Uvalde. "Nobody has been killed and there has been nary [a] fight; not even a drunk and disorderly. However, this quiet status, especially on this occasion—Christmas—I am informed, stands to the credit of Sheriff Boatright and his very efficient deputy King Fisher and [deputy] Kelso.[30] I made the acquaintance of Mr. Fisher (King as he is commonly called), who showed me through the city. The entire town was well lit up, as it were by sparkling fireworks, and the public halls of Churches adorned with beautiful cedar 'trees,' decorated with Santa Claus' headquarters, gave it a holiday appearance. A more hospitable people … here in Uvalde, are not to be found in Texas." The traveler who found Uvalde so peaceful a place to visit signed his letter simply, "Christmas."

As 1883 came to an end, both of the Thompson brothers were free with no charges of murder filed against them for the first time in many, many years. They returned to Austin where relatives and friends advised them to take hold of the great opportunity to shun old vices and begin a new, more respectable life. Their old habits proved to be too deeply rooted however, and instead of changing their lifestyles, Ben and Billy Thompson drank harder and gambled more desperately than ever before. Walton wrote, "When sober [Ben] was polite, affable and as much the gentleman as in all the times past, but when indulging in drink beyond a certain degree he became dictatorial and dogmatic, making it extremely disagreeable to be in his company." Even against those for whom he could entertain no reason for animosity, he became insulting and overbearing.[31] Walton would recollect two Thompson incidents that, surprisingly, went unnoticed by the press if they did, in fact, take place. Once when his gambling room was empty and a nearby variety theatre was full, Ben feigned drunkenness and staggered into a theatre box, and after calling attention to himself by demanding liquor in a loud, intoxicating manner, he pulled out his six-shooter and began firing it off at both the audience below and the performers on stage. He had a hearty laugh "when he saw the people roll, tumble, and mix as they did in their effort to escape ... in less time than it takes to tell it he was the sole occupant of the theatre hall." No one was in any real danger from Ben and his six-shooter because he had loaded it with blank cartridges. When asked why he took such a risk, he answered that his gambling hall needed patrons and it was soon filled. He said he knew how everyone would react because he understood the "natural cowardice of the human heart." Thompson bragged that his antics were a profitable venture because his gaming tables scooped in over two thousand dollars that night.

The second incident strained the social customs of the times. While visiting an Austin saloon, Ben suddenly and without an apparent reason ordered the proprietor to serve a group of black men "at a place at the bar where they were not allowed to stand." The owner was adamant that he would not break his rules. Enraged by the rejection, Thompson slammed his pistol down on the bar top demanding that his wishes be obeyed. Walton felt bloodshed would have ensued if it weren't for the intervention of the other white patrons who restrained Ben and pulled him out of the barroom. It was whiskey, Walton explained, not Thompson. When reason again took over, Ben returned and "humbly apologized for the wrong he had done and the insults offered."[32]

From this moment on, everything Ben Thompson would do was closely chronicled and commented on by the waiting and watching newspapermen of Texas and beyond. With a dark side revealing itself more and more, he entered into the year 1884, and the final ten troublesome weeks of his life.

Ben raised a lot of cash by offering thirty-five chances at $10 each and raffling off a horse he owned at the Iron Front Saloon. On Wednesday night, January 2, two days after the raffle, a perturbed Thompson decided to pull his pistol out at the same locale, and teach the boys how to shoot. The *Statesman* admitted how "no damage [was] done except a few holes in the floor."[33]

A few nights later, City Marshal H. Grooms Lee filed a complaint against Ben Thompson for "discharging a pistol" in the city limits. Ben had been amusing himself by using the city streetlights as targets. The following day, at 3 p. m. on January 7, Police officer Fred Callahan found and arrested Thompson. Ben appeared in court the same day. Knowing his friend, recorder (police judge) Claude Douglas Johns, would slap him with a very large fine, Ben asked for a jury trial and then pled guilty. Recorder Johns had a reputation for being impartial and very rigid in the manner in which he enforced the law. The jury accessed a $10 fine plus court costs as the price for Ben's late night six-gun spree. Thompson paid the court in cash, and the *Statesman* figured Ben's shrewdness saved him at least ninety dollars. Johns normally charged offenders $100 for promiscuously firing off a pistol within the city limits. The next day, Ben visited gunsmith J. C. Petmecky's shop on Congress Avenue where he had his revolver cleaned and he purchased six fresh cartridges. Total cost, sixty-five cents.[34] Before the week ended, Thompson would cause even bigger trouble for himself and the city of Austin. Ben would accomplish the trouble this time without firing a shot.

Isaac S. Simon's restaurant on Pecan Street (6th Street) was known to use the very best ingredients the market could provide. Advertising, "high living at moderate prices," Simon's offered steaks, chops, the choicest Berwick Bay-brand oysters for fifty cents per can, and the freshest of salt water fish. After finishing their meeting, the cattlemen attending their Second Annual Stockman's Convention chose Simon's restaurant as the site for their celebratory banquet. At about midnight on Thursday, January 10, some twenty-five of the state's most prominent cattlemen were busy overindulging with both food and wine. They were loud, drunk, and obnoxious. Many were standing on their chairs clamoring to have their turn to offer up another vulgar toast or speech. In the midst of the chaos, former Texas Ranger Captain Lee Hall and William Henry Crain, Billy Thompson's recent defense counsel, began to have a difficulty with each other. Crain was mad and getting madder. Outside the restaurant, William Lucky, a one-time Austin bartender, told Thompson that his friend Crain was going to get into trouble. Ben hurried into the restaurant and tried to calm Crain down. Thompson got everyone's attention by drawing his pistol and smashing the glassware on a nearby table. Then he pointed his pistol at Hall, who was sitting perched on top of the back of a chair. When the drunken cattlemen finally realized that Thompson had his pistol out, they stampeded out of the restaurant. At that point, James E. Lucy, a close friend of Hall who served under him as a Ranger, pulled out his pistol, cocked it with the same motion, and aimed it at Thompson in an effort to protect his friend. In response, Thompson placed his back against an iron safe and pointed his revolver at Lucy, calling out "Don't crowd me." There the two men stood staring at each other, revolvers in hand. Thompson told Lucy it was not his fight or his concern, but Lucy, not wanting to fire while also wanting to protect his friend, would not lower his weapon. Crain then stepped between Lucy and Thompson saying, "Ben, give me your gun." Without pause, Thompson handed it over. Crain then turned to Lucy and asked, "Will you give me your gun Captain?" Lucy placed his pistol into Crain's hand, and Crain left the building with both weapons. Thompson then called out, "Mack, where are you?" And the large black man employed by

Thompson at his gambling house appeared and handed Thompson a revolver. Lucy quizzically looked at Thompson and remarked, "You have a gun, where do I come in?" Taking a moment to stare at Lucy without a hint of anger, Thompson stated, "There are bad men outside. You must protect me." As he turned the pistol over in his hand, he reached out and gave it to Lucy saying, "Here is my gun." They walked out the main door of the restaurant and down the street past men Lucy described as "four or five as desperate as I knew in Texas. They had no use for Ben Thompson. Regardless of this, they exhibited no signs of hostility." Lucy and Thompson left the scene going down the street together without further incident.

The next morning, Ben Thompson called on Lucy and asked him to accompany him to Bahn's shop, a longtime Congress Avenue jewelry store. He wished to show Lucy his appreciation for preventing both bloodshed and providing him protection as they left Simon's Restaurant. Thompson ordered custom made "sleeve buttons" fastened out of English sovereigns for Lucy. He then insisted that they also visit a clothing store. There he purchased Lucy a "five-gallon hat of the Stetson make and one of the showiest that ever came within ... range of ... [Lucy's] vision." Lucy kept the cuff links as a prized procession, but never wore the Stetson. He admitted that style of hat "never appealed to me."[35]

William A. Bowen, the *San Antonio Daily Express* correspondent in Austin, sent his version of what transpired at the Cattleman's banquet via telegram and he included in his report his low opinion of the Austin police force. "The *Express* correspondent learns that last night as a number of stockmen and friends were enjoying a private banquet at Simon's Restaurant, Ben Thompson walked in with a huge six-shooter and began to knock things from the table. A stampede took place by nearly all who could find strength to go. The scene is described as disgraceful in the extreme. Several policemen stood outside the door and never went nearer, nor dared lift a finger to stop the proceedings. Up to 4 o'clock today no charge had been made against Ben Thompson, as far as your reporter could hear, nor is there likely to be in Austin."[36]

A false report flourished in San Antonio on Sunday, January 13, that Thompson had been killed in Austin that morning, and the editors of the *Daily Express* published that "much disappointment [is] expressed [by their readership] when no confirmation of the report was received." The people of San Antonio had no particular dislike for Thompson as an individual, but "they have some state pride, and would rejoice in almost anything that would relieve the people of the Capital City from the terror they are constantly under through fear that Ben Thompson will get on a spree. The police officers of Austin are impotent and the council have not the nerve or desire to put men on the force who will keep the peace and protect the lives of citizens or strangers at Austin even if Thompson does get on a drunk."[37]

The editors of the *Statesman* voiced similar thoughts, "The police are afraid of Thompson and he knows it, and therefore does as he pleases." The newspaper then put out a call to its readers, "Let the present police be supplanted by men who have some backbone, and who will preserve order at all hazards." Two days later, the newspaper mocked the city police pointing out, "Ben Thompson felt sorry for the chief of police and his chicken-headed subordinates and walked in and gave himself up for trial." City Marshal H. Grooms Lee officially arrested Thompson at 9 a. m. on January 14, and Ben was charged with disturbing the peace. His trial was scheduled for 2 p. m. the following day. The *Statesman* promised to provide its readers "a stenographic report of the trial," and true to their word, the editors did. R. H. Brumby stood as Thompson's defense attorney with Recorder C. D. Johns for the prosecution, and after considerable difficulty in choosing a jury, one was finally empaneled and testimony commenced. Called to the stand to tes-

On the same day Marks photographed Thompson in a standing pose, he made this image in an albumen cabinet card. Thompson appears to be in a more thoughtful mood. Note the cane in both images, probably used more as a fashion statement than a walking-aid, although he had received leg injuries during the war and again in Kansas. *Courtesy the Austin History Center. Image # CO 2506.*

tify for the prosecution were cattleman Seth Mabry, banker James H. Hamilton, and proprietor of the restaurant Isaac S. Simon. When C. D. Johns rested, attorney Brumby brought forth the witnesses for the defense. Those witnesses were businessman and past chancellor of the Knights of Pythias Phil Abrahams, a patron not affiliated with the banquet named Snyder, and William Lucky. The combined testimony as to what exactly transpired was confusing. However, many witnesses agreed that the restaurant emptied in frenzy when Thompson displayed his pistol. It was brought to the jury's attention and amazed most of the people in the courtroom that Thompson was, in fact, an appointed Travis County deputy sheriff and, by law, was allowed to be armed. Confusing or not, the jury heard enough testimony to find against Thompson and they accessed a fine of $25 plus court costs.[38]

The confusion continued when a false rumor reached San Antonio that Ben Thompson was a deputy United States marshal, which was vehemently denied by Hal Gosling, the U. S. Marshal for the Western District of Texas. In truth, Ben was a deputy sheriff for Travis County thanks to a special appointment by Malcom Hornsby, the current sheriff. During an interview with *Daily Express* correspondent, W. A. Bowen, Sheriff Hornsby had to concede that Thompson had yet to make a single arrest. Nonetheless, Sheriff Hornsby stood his ground, defending Thompson's appointment to his staff by stating that Thompson was "ready at all times to assist when called, in putting down lawlessness." Not easily convinced, Bowen persisted, "Do you revoke commissions of deputies for rudely displaying arms, and is not such conduct generally accounted unworthy of an officer?" Hornsby responded, "It has yet to be proven that Ben Thompson did not have good cause to display his revolver." Bowen had one last embarrassing question, "Can the same thing be said in regard to his shooting out lights last week which his jury accounted unlawful by fining him ten dollars and costs?" Hornsby could only feebly respond that Thompson had his commission as a special deputy, and therefore had a right to carry a pistol. The interview ended then, but W. A. Bowen informed his readers, "High legal authority says that neither sheriff nor deputy has a right to carry a pistol unless on an active mission in discharge of duty. If so, Captain Hornsby is in a close place in the opinion of his friends."[39]

In a separate column, Bowen continued his diatribe on how it was disgraceful that one man could trample under his foot the "rights of the whole city." There was blame for all, and Bowen laid it not only on the police, but also on all of the city and county officers. He took the good citizens of Austin to task, "for allowing such things to occur and recur again and again." They did not seem to resent it. Their excuse was a pathetic one at best: that Thompson did not bother anyone except those who were on the streets late at night, and then he did not molest anyone but only damaged property during his drunken fits. Bowen did admit that some of Thompson's warmest friends "were heard to express themselves as thoroughly disgusted." However, they had yet to intercede. Like everyone else, they failed to do anything to remedy Thompson's behavior. "Ben feels like being monarch of the entire universe with unlimited power," Bowen wrote, and stated that he was not alone in feeling thus. Out-of-town visitors, such as the stockmen, stated they would not return to Austin, and in the future would vote to hold their business meetings elsewhere. Prominent and influential people from throughout the state echoed the same sentiments: that as long as Ben Thompson was allowed to rampage without restraint, they would avoid their capital city. In an article the next day, the *Express* admitted, "It transpired at the trial of Ben Thompson that he went into the stockmen's banquet in order to prevent a row, as he was told his friend, Crain, was about to have a fuss. According to this view of the matter Mr. Thompson was playing the role of preserver of the peace and law and order, instead of a disturber of the same."[40]

Thompson was in an ugly mood during the early evening of Friday night, February 1. He was aggravated with proprietor J. C. McIntyre of the Southern Hotel at 402 Congress Avenue over something now long forgotten. After informing McIntyre that he had to close up his establishment, Thompson walked up the Avenue to Ash Street (9th Street) where he came upon newspaperman Bowen on the sidewalk in front of Millet's Opera House. Ben was still seething from Bowen's earlier accounts of his actions at the Stockmen's banquet, and he assaulted Bowen. Thompson struck, then kicked at Bowen twice. He was seen to have his hand on his pistol during the attack, but his efforts to force Bowen to fight were futile. Bowen refused to retaliate because he believed Thompson was prepared to kill him if he did. The newspaperman hurried down the street and made his escape. Ben Thompson then went south on Congress Avenue to Pecan Street (6th Street) and visited Isaac Simon at his restaurant, where he ordered Simon, like McIntyre, to close his business and quit the city.[41]

The morning edition of the *Statesman* reported Thompson's assault on Bowen stating, "The sidewalk was crowded with ladies, and Thompson made use of language that ought not to be tolerated at such a time by any man." Reading this particular aspect of the article upset Thompson so much that he went to the *Statesman* office, and continued his quarrel with freedom of the press. Before 6 a.m. on Saturday morning, eighteen-year-old Rush Debardelebon was alone and at his desk in the Financial Department of the newspaper, which was separated from the main entry by a wire screen. The young Debardelebon had his head down and was hard at work. He was unaware that anyone had entered the building until he heard someone strike the screen. He looked up and saw Thompson brandishing a revolver. Thompson pointed the muzzle at him and

William A. Bowen was the *San Antonio Express* correspondent in Austin. He found Thompson's drunken behavior coupled with frequent brawls especially offensive, and reported on them accordingly. His dissatisfaction with the entire Austin police department was an important part of his negative editorial tirades on Thompson.
Courtesy the Institute of Texan Cultures. Image # 976.4.

demanded to know who had written the article in the morning edition of the newspaper. Debardelebon, remaining composed, replied he had nothing to do with that department. He had no idea who the author was. In the most emphatic language, Thompson again demanded to know the author, and stated that if Debardelebon would not tell him, he would hold the young man responsible. Again, Debardelebon said he did not know who wrote it, but supposed it was the city editor J. Q. Wing. Finally satisfied, Thompson went up the stairway to the second floor. Thompson asserted he only had his pistol out at the onset of his interview with Debardelebon. On the other hand, Debardelebon insisted that the revolver was pointed at him the entire time, but that he did not believe Thompson would have harmed him. The only other personnel on duty were the staff of the mailroom on the second floor, supervised by the chief mailing clerk Mr. Scott. Walking up to Scott, Thompson demanded to know who had written the article. Scott denied knowing who authored it, and when he saw Thompson get excited and reach out to perhaps turn over a burning lamp, he pleaded, "Don't do that, please, you will set the whole place on fire!" Thompson then drew his revolver and loudly threatened the entire editorial staff of the *Statesman*. Afterward, Thompson admitted that he pulled his pistol out, but denied making any threats. Later proclaiming it was an accident, Thompson knocked over "a couple of galleys of type containing the names of subscribers, and dashed them on the floor." The mailroom staff fled, and Thompson left the building, leaving a pile of type scattered behind on the floor.[42]

When the *Statesman's* management learned of the threats and acts of intimidation, they filed multiple criminal complaints before Justice of the Peace William von Rosenberg Jr. and one with Recorder C. D. Johns. Arrest warrants for Ben Thompson were issued on seven complaints. These were for unlawfully carrying a pistol, displaying a pistol in a public place, disorderly conduct and disturbing the peace, committing an assault and battery on the person of Rush Debardelebon, threatening the life of the city editor J. Q. Wing, threatening the life of the proprietor of the *Statesman* and publisher William P. Gaines. There was even a charge of malicious mischief thrown in for good measure. Ben was found, placed under arrest, and taken before Justice von Rosenberg. Thompson was so out of control during the proceedings in von Rosenberg's courtroom that he picked up his chair and went after a man who was aggravating him. Not once, but twice, he attacked the man. Both times, the justice was forced to stop the proceedings and charged Thompson with contempt of court, fining him $25 for each instance. After posting $100 for each of his other charges, Ben was released on bail until his trial scheduled for Monday, February 4.[43]

At last, Travis County Sheriff Malcom Hornsby wisely distanced himself from his unruly special deputy, and revoked Thompson's controversial appointment. With his final status as a peace officer removed, Thompson no longer had the lawful right to go about the city armed. All during the day, excitement raced through Austin as people talked about Ben Thompson's early morning call at the offices of the *Statesman*. But before the day ended, he would return to the *Statesman* and create even more trouble for himself.

Around 7 p. m., J. Q. Wing and John Cardwell were in the newspaper's editorial room when Ben Thompson entered. At the start, he began by addressing both newspapermen; however he turned his attention to Mr. Wing, and began to demand why he filed the charges. Wing told Thompson he did so because he was informed of Thompson's threats. Denying any threat of that nature, Thompson turned the conversation. He stated that he had supper with State Senator Burgess, who was Governor Ireland's law partner. During supper he claimed Burgess told him that the people at the *Statesman* were preparing to shoot him down in the street.

Thompson added, "He had been told he would be killed if he went there [to the offices of the *Statesman*], and that he was ready to attend the killing." John Cardwell then questioned Thompson's statement in regard to the governor's law partner, and Thompson backed away from it replying, "I will not say the governor's law partner. I will take that back. I have no right to say that." Cardwell pressed Thompson: "No, Thompson, take nothing back." But Thompson repeated the retraction of his earlier assertion, "Yes I will. I don't say it was the governor's law partner." As their conversation continued Thompson declared to Wing and Cardwell that he was there acting upon information he received. He then made the absurd statement that he had brought with him ten men, all armed with Winchester rifles, whom he had hired at $100 apiece, and they were outside waiting his call. If the *Statesman* staff were to shoot him down, the hired guns would avenge him. Mr. Wing forcefully responded, "So far as I am concerned Mr. Thompson, I never carried a pistol in my life, do not now and shall not in the future. I expect to do my editorial work faithfully and fearlessly and have no fears of the consequences. I want you to distinctly understand that if you kill me you do it not under the pretext that you are doing it in self-defense." Disclaiming any intention of committing violence, Thompson now denounced the reports that he made any threats of violence. A crowd filed into the editorial room eager to observe Thompson, and soon William Gaines, the publisher of the *Statesman*, arrived and engaged Thompson in a long conversation. For a second time Thompson, "made the statement in regard to his conversation with the law partner of Gov. Ireland, and that he had ten men armed with the Winchester rifles waiting his command." Gaines told Thompson that he was aware of the threats Ben made against his newspaper's editorial staff. He also informed Thompson "a great number of good citizens had volunteered to arm themselves for the protection of the *Statesman's* office." This excited

Thompson, and he professed he could get five hundred men to back him up if necessary. Gaines divulged to Thompson that he did not want to have a personal difficulty with him, but at the same time he declared his newspaper would treat him the same as any other man who violated the law, and that the *Statesman* could not be intimidated. Thompson renounced any such intention, and stated that all he asked was to be correctly reported on. Before leaving, Thompson added he would hold Gaines personally responsible for what appeared about him in the newspaper.[44]

In a long column headlined "The Statesman Verses Terrorism," the newspaper told its readers, "That point in the *Statesman's* history has not yet been reached when it will stand quietly by and allow to go unrebuked any efforts to terrorize any community," the column then stated what everyone knew, that Thompson was "universally, and for good reasons, regarded as a dangerous man, and these displays of his disposition are not only annoying to the community, but they are highly detrimental to its interests. Only a short time ago we have seen public sentiment throughout the state arrayed against Austin, because of the acts of this one man … these conditions must cease or the capital city of Texas will be shunned and abhorred."[45]

Ben Thompson's recklessness was not only making news in Texas, but also around the country. The *New York Times* and the *Chicago Tribune* picked up the stories coming out of Austin, and recounted his dangerous capers to their readers.[46] In San Antonio, the *Daily Express* took the opportunity to criticize its rival city. "Austin has again been placed under a reign of terror by Ben Thompson. We do not believe there is another city or town in the country where the whole population seem to have so little self-respect as to allow a desperado to run rampant over everybody whenever it pleases his own sweet will to do so." The newspaper stated how it was "in favor of stopping work on the capitol and every other public building in Austin until the people there show that they have either a little nerve or some regard for their good name. The people of the state are tired of this Ben Thompson business."[47]

Justice of the Peace von Rosenberg's court opened with the seven cases filed against Ben on Monday morning, February 4. County Attorney Dudley G. Wooten, who had once been part of Ben Thompson's defense counsel during the Jack Harris murder trial, stood for the prosecution. He also became a fellow Knights of Pythias during the same initiation ceremony as Thompson. Colonel Bingham Trigg, a former Travis County prosecutor, stood for Thompson. The proceedings were delayed when a defect was discovered in the original complaints, and they were dismissed. Wooten was made to file new, correctly written substitute complaints. During the course of the legal argument, Colonel Trigg questioned Wooten's presence in the courtroom of a justice of the peace. He asked why the county prosecutor was taking an active role in prosecuting these cases while the county court, normally his responsibility, was in full session. Trigg proclaimed this as evidence of an unusual feeling against Thompson, and a greater than usual attempt to prosecute his client. Wooten confessed that he sacrificed, in some measure, his time and attention from the county court in order to attend to the cases against Ben Thompson. Nonetheless, Wooten would make no apology to anyone for being there as he had sufficient reasons, both personal and official, for prosecuting these cases. Ruling one case dismissed because the charge was to be taken up the next day in Recorder C. D. Johns' court, Justice von Rosenberg rescheduled the hearing on the remaining cases to be heard in two days time on Wednesday, February 6.[48]

At the Recorders Court of C. D. Johns, a jury was easily empaneled. Colonel Trigg again represented Ben Thompson, who was this time charged with disturbing the peace for his Saturday morning disruption at the *Statesman's* office. After listening to the evidence, the jury retired to deliberate, and soon returned with a verdict of guilty. The jurors fined Thompson $25, the most he could be assessed under the city ordinance.[49] Shortly before 9 p.m. that evening, City Marshal H. Grooms Lee arrested Ben Thompson for three past offenses. Jesse McIntyre of the Southern Hotel on Congress Avenue brought a complainant charging him with disturbing the peace. William Gaines had Thompson charged with disturbing the peace, and lastly, in an incident not reported in the press, Thompson was charged with assaulting a man named William Powell. Perhaps this is the gentleman Thompson attacked with a chair in von Rosenberg's courtroom. He was found not guilty under McIntyre's charge, but guilty under Gaines's complaint. Thompson appealed Gaines's ruling, and he only had to pay a small fine for assaulting Mr. Powell. Thompson was scheduled to be in Justice von Rosenberg's courtroom again early that following morning, and his legal problems seemed endless.[50]

Colonel Trigg addressed Justice von Rosenberg, and asked for a postponement due to Ben Thompson being sick. Thompson, in attendance in the courtroom, pleaded for the postponement, explaining he felt so ill he could not remain for the trial. Prosecutor Wooten offered to waive the requirement of Thompson being present. Trigg and Thompson objected to this, preferring to have Thompson available to assist in his own defense. Graciously, Wooten accepted the postponement, stating it was not his desire "to deprive the defendant of any right … by law he was entitled." Von Rosenberg rescheduled the trial for Saturday morning at 9 a.m. Later in the day, Ben Thompson appeared in public on Congress Avenue. The *Statesman* logically felt that if Thompson was as sick as he claimed in court, then he should have been home in his bed. The editors were tired of his defense counsel using every "delay, worry, technical exceptions and in an attempt to impede the course of justice ... every engine of legal ingenuity [has been] resorted to prevent a termination of these cases." Wishing for an end to the episode, the newspaper called on the court and the county attorney to settle the charges against Thompson in a prompt manner and, if found guilty, to suitably punish him.[51]

After all the delays and postponements, Ben Thompson's day in court for his visit at the offices of the *Statesman*, finally arrived. Within minutes of Justice von Rosenberg starting the proceedings, two of the cases against Thompson were dismissed. Publisher William Gaines and City Editor J. Q Wing announced to the court their desire to drop the charges accusing Ben Thompson of threatening their lives.

Thompson's friends had intervened and set up a meeting between the pair of newspapermen and Thompson. Assuring them that he had no remembrance of making any threats, they accepted his word that he held no ill will against them. Prosecutor Wooten decided not to argue against the dismissals, and said he would accept the Justice's ruling, which was to agree with the wishes of the two complainants.

The court moved on to the next charge of unlawfully carrying a pistol. Colonel Trigg and Thompson called for a jury trial, and after considerable difficulty, six citizens were deemed acceptable to serve as jurors. The prosecution placed young Rush Debardelebon on the witness stand. His testimony was confined to one short, simple statement. He said he saw Ben Thompson with a pistol in his hand when he was in the *Statesman's* office. Thompson's defense was not to contradict Debardelebon's statement. Instead, Colonel Trigg pointed out a unique law giving any citizen, including Ben Thompson, the right to carry a weapon. Trigg quoted the applicable exception to the statute making it unlawful to go about armed in Austin. "The preceding article shall not apply to a person who has reasonable ground for fearing an unlawful attack upon his person, and the danger is so imminent and threatening as not to [be able to make the] arrest of the party about to make such an attack." It was common knowledge that Thompson had a large number of deadly enemies who would kill him at the first opportunity. While Ben didn't often need a weapon, when he did need one he would need it very badly. If it became known that Thompson went unarmed, his life would be in danger at all times, and it was foolishness to believe Thompson could hope to protect his person through the use of peace bonds. Three men were called to testify on behalf of Ben Thompson: gunsmith Joseph C. Petmecky, his good friend Monroe Miller, and Grand Chancellor of the Knights of Pythias E. B. Connell, who was also serving Austin as the City Clerk. Their testimonies were essentially similar: that on account of "peculiar facts" connected with Thompson's history, "his life was in constant danger, and that this condition of things was true on the 2nd [of February] the same as any other day." Prosecutor Wooten countered with the argument that the statute was only in effect when there was no opportunity to find and place the threatening party under a lawful bond to keep the peace. Thompson could and should ask the courts to protect him from harm. To follow the defense counsel's logic, prosecutor Wooten explained, "It would license all dangerous characters to carry arms and prevent the good law abiding citizens from so doing." The jury found for the prosecution, and declared Thompson guilty of unlawfully carrying a pistol. They fined him $25, and he made notice of appeal.

The accusation that Ben Thompson assaulted Rush Debardelebon was the final complaint to be tried in Justice von Rosenberg's courtroom. A new jury was empaneled and when the defense presented Debardelebon's earlier statement that he did not believe Ben Thompson intended to harm him, the defense easily won a not guilty verdict.[52]

Recorder C. D. Johns still had a case against Ben Thompson on his docket list. This was the charge of assault on newspaper correspondent William Bowen. The trial took place on Saturday, February 16. The jury found Thompson guilty, but imposed a meager $5 fine as punishment.[53]

Many nineteenth century Texans were not fond of corporate entities and their attempt to control people's lives. Ben Thompson was no exception. The Houston & Texas Railroad prided itself for its punctual record. One evening in late February, as the train slowed near the Austin depot, Ben Thompson pulled his buggy out onto the tracks and forced the train to stop short. Reports vary as to whether or not Ben used his pistol to encourage the train engineer to sit on the brake and remain patient. Apparently, the engineer recognized who was delaying him, because he did not sound his whistle in an effort to frighten the horse out of his way. When Thompson was certain the train would be officially late, he slapped the horse's rump with the reins, and as he slowly rolled past the cab of the train, he brazenly told the engineer, "You needn't think, sir, that any corporation can hurry me!"[54]

Another story about Ben Thompson could be set down as mere legend except that a tombstone was found in "a dark recess" of the old building that housed the Iron Front Saloon. The surprise discovery gives credence to the story's authenticity, and when the Iron Front was razed in late January 1910, it jogged the memory of Jim Long, one of Austin's old-timers, who related the episode to a newspaperman. "That marble slab was won by Ben Thompson in a game of poker more than twenty-five years ago," said Jim Long. "I remember the circumstances very well. In those days, a tombstone peddler named Luke Watts traveled over this part of the country in a one-horse covered wagon."

Watts carried samples of his tombstones, and as he went from town to town, wrote orders and took the corresponding deposits for future delivery. Watts was skilled as a slab sculptor and occasionally accommodated a customer by carving the sentiment the buyer wanted into the stone on the spot. As he moved through the central Texas towns of New Braunfels, San Marcos, and others, Watts did a brisk business and he rolled into Austin with his pockets loaded with cash. Watts was a man who enjoyed gambling, so he headed to the second floor of the Iron Front Saloon to play poker. He was already seated at a table when Ben Thompson walked in and joined the game.

Long explained, "Thompson was feeling good and he jollied Watts about selling tombstones and making a living off dead people." Despite Thompson's reputation, Watts "came back at him good and strong" saying "Ben, you will be took off sudden one of these days and I may not be around just at the time to sell a tombstone to ornament your grave," he said. "You had better order one from me now." Ben laughingly told Watts, "A wooden board is about all I need."

It was about midnight when Watts, after a long losing streak, announced to the table, "Boys, I'm cleaned out." As he stood up to leave, Thompson asked, "Hold on there. How much are them tombstones worth?" Watts sat back down and replied, "It depends on what kind of a stone it is." Ben declared, "I don't want no cheap monument, have you got any made of marble?" Watts bragged, "I have got as fine a marble slab down there in my wagon as you can find south of St. Louis." Thompson wanted to know its value. Watts explained, "Not a cent less than $200, which is cheap, considering it's a long ways from the quarries." At Thompson's request, Watts, with the help from the porters at the saloon, brought the marble slab up from the wagon yard and put it into the pot. Thompson inspected the stone and once he was satisfied, he agreed to the $200 price. The game continued until Thompson cleaned out Watts a second time. Taking the loss with equanimity, Watts suggested to Ben, "Better let me carve the inscription on it now." Ben responded, "No you can wait until I have done something that will give you the subject for a fitting epitaph." The tombstone remained in the center of the gambling hall as a curiosity for a handful of days "attracting much attention," until Thompson ordered that it be removed. It remained tucked away and long forgotten until it was found decades later.[55]

Ben Thompson chose to ignore the court's decision preventing him from going about armed. On Thursday, February 21, he purchased two boxes of cartridges from J. C. Petmecky's gun shop, and on the subsequent day, he returned to purchased two more boxes. He left his revolver to be cleaned and repaired. Perhaps he found a defect while practicing with his pistol. While he was on Congress Avenue, he stopped at the studio of Photographer Harvey R. Marks. In the past, both he and his brother Billy had their likeness taken by Marks, who was widely recognized as one of the finest photographers, not only in Texas, but also throughout the entire south. Thompson dressed conservatively in a tailored suit, and posed with a matching derby hat in his left hand. A custom-made Knight of Pythian watch fob can be seen hanging from his vest pocket. He presented a copy of this photograph, a cabinet card, to his daughter. He signed and dated the back: "To my daughter Katie Ben Thompson Austin Texas Feb. 22nd 1884." The following day he returned to Joe Petmecky's shop for his revolver and, again, purchased another box of cartridges. Well-armed, he went out for his last wild Saturday night on the town in Austin. Ben had only eighteen days left to live.[56]

With friends in tow, including a young deputy sheriff named Theo Hillyer, who was the son of another of Austin's well-known photographers, Hamilton B. Hillyer. Thompson made his way to Denny and Brown's Cosmopolitan Saloon at 1010 Congress Avenue. While Thompson and his friends were enjoying a drink, someone fired a revolver shot into the floor of the barroom. No one dared step forward to interfere with the culprit's fun. Leaving Denny's saloon, Ben with his friends raced around the town in a buggy, and as the night went on, the firing of his pistol seemed to honor every portion of the city. City Marshal Lee investigated the gunfire at the Cosmopolitan Saloon, however, Mr. Denny refused to place a complaint. The frustrated marshal was to later complain to a newspaperman, "That is just the way; when I want to get information parties refuse and then blame me." As the night went on, Ben and his friends came upon an organ grinder named Nicoll Penilla. Penilla was a small, hunchbacked man who was a common sight on the streets of Austin, and he was one who survived on the small coins tossed his way. Thompson decided to appropriate the poor man's music box and wander from place to place, drunkenly serenading his friends and other onlookers. When he returned it, the Italian complained it was broken. To prove otherwise Thompson ordered Penilla to "grind it," and when he was not so inclined, Ben drew his revolver and began to shoot it out of the frightened man's hands. Thompson riddled the instrument with pistol balls, and then agreed with the poor organ grinder that its usefulness was at an end. Police officer Fred Callahan promptly arrested both Thompson and Hillyer. Again, Thompson paid a small fine. Because Hillyer did not fire a shot, and was a Travis County deputy sheriff, his charge was dismissed. The *Statesman* informed its readers that, "Ben Thompson is quite sick today, the result of a carousal Saturday night."[57]

In the evenings after finishing their day at work, members of the Austin Greys drill team were very wary of practicing their drill routine on Congress Avenue. Thompson had spent many a night driving his buggy at a fast pace up and down the Avenue firing off his six-shooter. Many of the drill team members were afraid someone in their group might be injured during one of his drunken sprees. R.P. Smyth, who was a fellow Knight of Pythias, was captain of the Austin Greys, and when members asked to not drill on the Avenue, Smyth reassured his teammates that Thompson would never ride through and hurt them. One night, while they were at ease, Thompson came riding down the Avenue. He stopped his carriage by Mr. Smyth and inquired, "Captain, how are the boys doing?" Smyth answered they were doing fine and that the squad was ready to compete at the upcoming drill contest in Houston. "I am going to Houston," replied Thompson, knowing there were awards given for excellence, "and I will bet on you." However, Smyth later recalled how Thompson's days were numbered, and that he never made it to the Houston competition.[58]

The Austin to Oatmanville Railroad held an excursion to the Oatmanville limestone quarry serving the Capital building contractors. Lunch and desert was planned and Governor Ireland was foremost among the many visiting dignitaries. The quarry was located only eight miles southwest of Austin. Most excursionists traveled by rail while Ben drove out in a coach with three friends. Accompanying Thompson were Recorder C. D. Johns, attorneys Colonel Trigg, and R. H. Brumby. Thompson humorously explained how he brought along a judge and his lawyers, so if he misbehaved, they could hold court right then and there.

Thompson and his three friends decided to enjoy themselves by unleashing their revolvers, and demonstrated their marksmanship by plugging trees and bouncing bullets off of rocks. When it was time to leave, the horses pulling their coach reached a full gallop, and as the buggy rounded a curve at an unmanageable speed, Thompson let loose with his six-shooter in a parting salute, blazing away at the passing trees, though dissipation was taking a toll on Ben. Onlookers noticed that on this day, Recorder Johns was the best pistol shot of the group.[59]

Upon his return to Austin, Thompson resumed his pistol antics, and in the presence of Police Officer Howe, Ben fired off his revolver. Officer Howe made no immediate effort to make an arrest, but he did file a complaint against Thompson. As the night wore on, Ben rode around town in his buggy while still firing off his pistol. His dangerous behavior was beginning to wear down the patience of the good citizens of Austin.[60]

The arrests, court dates, fines, legal fees, and condemnation in the newspapers, along with the well-intentioned good advice from family and friends made no impression on Benjamin Thompson. Night after night, he would still become beastly drunk and roam the saloons, gambling rooms, and streets of Austin. Walton wrote, "For some weeks Thompson had been drinking even more than usual, leading a life irregular and far from commendable. He suffered much from insomnia." Becoming restless, nervous, and impatient with others, Ben's pistol play had developed into an almost nightly occurrence. He was "fast becoming a terror, not only to the people generally, but even to his immediate circle of friends. No night came that there was not nervous apprehension that before the morning came some terrible tragedy would be enacted."[61]

The sentiment in Austin was that City Marshal H. Grooms Lee and his police force must resign due to their failure to preserve the peace, enforce the laws, and arrest wrongdoers. In response, Alderman Bud Driskill offered a resolution at the city council meeting held on Monday night, February 25, demanding the resignation of all of the officers and the city marshal. Afraid to take such a drastic action, only four other aldermen supported Driskill's resolution. Instead the council adopted a milder, if bewildering, resolution. It instructed City Marshal Lee to report, in writing, at the next regularly scheduled council meeting the causes that rendered the police inefficient, and to suggest measures to remedy the situation.[62] Speculation was rampant on the streets of Austin as to what Marshal Lee would put into his report. He had been reluctant to lay blame on the city council, but it was the aldermen who filled the positions of the police force, and Lee had not been allowed any say whatsoever in the selection of officers. Thus, he had had no control over the men.[63]

During the last week of February, many of the major cities and towns along the gulf coast began to celebrate the Mardi Gras season. Mobile, New Orleans, and Galveston welcomed many thousands of visitors to their cities. Ben Thompson chose to take in the Mardi Gras Festival in Galveston where he had many friends. After enjoying the Island City for a handful of days, a correspondent of the *Galveston Daily News* caught up with Ben and was granted an interview.

He found Ben "in a genial and jolly frame of mind, willing to talk, and to talk about himself." It was an unusually long interview, as their talk "occupied fully three hours." The reporter stressed that "it may be remarked that Thompson, in no sense of the word, had the appearance of a desperado; on the contrary, he had the look and bearing of what might be termed a clever fellow." With his close friends and men he was better acquainted with, "he was agreeable and sociable, but he would brook no familiarity from a chance acquaintance. While he was here he slapped the face of a young man who had been running with him, and who, he thought, was traveling too much upon the reputation he had already made" as a part of Ben's extended entourage. The set-down occurred on Market Street, near the Bank Exchange, "and as soon as the job was finished he told the young man not to presume too much on his acquaintance ... [and Ben] ... concluded the lecture by inviting [the young man] to take a drink."

The correspondent for the *News* felt his readership deserved a physical description of Ben Thompson, and he provided a "brief pen picture of the man." Thompson was seen as being "of medium height, square built and square face. He has a clear, keen eye when he is, as the boys say, all right, and his face shows none of the ferociousness or dare deviltry with which he has so long been credited." Thompson had "a pleasant countenance, and is, among his friends, certainly much liked and very popular." Then Ben spoke of himself. "I came to Texas in 1851, and went to Austin direct; and while I have been over the world considerably in my time, I have generally called Austin my home. During the late war I was in Pyron's regiment, and in the after days I was in the service of Emperor Maximilian, in Mexico." The talkative Ben said, with a laugh:

> You newspaper fellows make a target of me, whenever you get short of an item, and magnify my proportions, until actually timid people will cross to the other side of the street rather than meet "that bad man, Ben Thompson." I laugh at all that is said about me in the newspapers, because I know that it is the food that they feed to the public, and of course the public likes it. It is something to make the papers sell. Now, in Austin, while the Statesman is firing at me, I don't mind it. It's bread and meat. They are friendly with me. I am an old printer myself.
>
> Now, since I have been [in Galveston], five days, I don't think anybody can say that I have done anything horrible; do you? The reporter thought not, and asked: "How have you enjoyed yourself, Ben? [Thompson replied] Just as I always do when I come to Galveston. I have lots of friends here and I generally manage to get around and see them and have a good time with them."

It must have surprised the reporter when Thompson "stripped his left leg" to show a fresh bullet wound through the meat of his calf. He had received the wound a few days prior when he and some friends were moving about from place to place enjoying the city. One of the party, "who was partly full [of liquor], got into the hack first and ... [Ben] ... followed, and just as he was in the act of stepping into the vehicle his friend's pistol fell from his pocket, was discharged and made the wound." Ben wanted it kept quiet, as his friend was a Galveston boy and he didn't want to embarrass him. A doctor who "was sensible enough to keep his tongue between his teeth" dressed the injury.

Ben refused to say who had dropped the pistol, but remarked that he ought not to be allowed to handle firearms. Thompson then fixed the bandages on his wound, and pulled down his pant leg. He straightened himself up in his chair and as he did so, he leaned forward and reached his hand behind to his lower back drawing forth a revolver secreted in his waist belt, remarking as he did so, "This d----d thing is in the way."

This, of course, brought up the subject of Thompson's marksmanship. He answered: "I pride myself on my accuracy with gun or pistol, and this has perhaps something to do with my being called a desperado. You have heard it said that I wear a steel mask [breast plate]. Now look at me." Ben bared his chest and back, showing a silk-thread undershirt next to his body and top shirt. Ben continued, "Now I have come down here to have a good time. The newspapers can squirt at me all they want to and when I do wrong I won't blame them for letting into me and doing it strong. I know what's right, and unless I am crowded, or as the saying goes, somebody steps on my corn, I am not going to bother anybody, and I'll walk around a whole block, or two of them if necessary, to keep peace in the family."

The reporter picked up the weapon, which was a handsome silver-plated .44 caliber Colt single action revolver. In answer to the reporter's question, Ben said that the pistol was not his and that he had not carried one since his arrival in town until that night. He would not have had this one if he had not taken it from a friend who was drunk and, as he feared, liable to get into trouble. Ben gave it as his opinion that double-action pistols are untrustworthy. While Thompson was in Galveston, he was upon what might be termed a continued frolic. He came there well supplied with money, but ran short and borrowed money from several parties. Among the number was a personal friend to whom he went and asked for a $100 loan. It was given to him, and in return he offered security. The lender said he did not want it. "All right," said Thompson, "but I don't know what's going to happen to me before I get home, so you take these for me until I send you the cash." With this he placed in the hands of his friend a $50 Mexican gold piece, a $20, $10 and several smaller Maximilian gold pieces, all of which would have been valuable to a coin collector. On his return to Austin, the loan was promptly paid, and the coins were sent back to him. Thompson liked to talk of himself with those whom he knew and liked. He remarked, in the course of conversation with a friend, "I wish I could live like you do; but I have got the name of being a brave man, and of course I have to keep it up. If I didn't every man in town would be hunting after me to kick me." Ben spoke freely and unreservedly about himself, but when the reporter asked him how many difficulties he had been engaged in, he answered pointedly and precisely, "That is my own business." Ben then added that every difficulty he had had was "in defense of myself or my property." Thompson made the statement that Joe Foster was the cause of his difficulty with Jack Harris, and that he had never had anything against Jack. Once he had denounced Foster, Harris took his part, and that is how the trouble grew between them.

The reporter pointed out that Ben had been credited with the killing of thirteen to seventeen men but this was false and that the "most reliable information attainable in this city declares that he is known to have killed five men, with a dispute as to whether he or somebody else 'downed' a sixth." Ben now turned the subject to more pleasant things.

> I have enjoyed Mardi Gras. I went to hear Minnie Hauk [*sic*] sing, and I just think she is immense. If it had been English I would have liked it much more.[64] "What do you think of the Eighteenth legislature?" asked the reporter. "Don't ask

> me, for I have no opinion to express. I am not in politics. I am here now to buy a ranch, and I expect to locate at or near Clear Lake,[65] twenty-four miles from this city, and go into the stock business; and after I settle myself down I hope to be let alone by all the busybodies—the newspapers as well as other people." With this, Ben lit a cigar, called for drinks, and the interview closed.[66]

This talk of purchasing land was not the first time he spoke of stepping away from the limelight. It was, however, the last. If Ben Thompson truly considered leaving his sporting life behind forever, he should have acted without delay on the desire.

In a life so filled with tragedy and sorrow, a glitter of humor occasionally appeared. On Sunday morning, March 2, at the Methodist Episcopal Church of Austin, youngsters were finishing their religious lessons when their teacher began to entertain the class, stumping them with impossible questions such as, "Who was the oldest man? Who was the wisest man? Who was the meekest man?" When the teacher asked, "Who was the greatest warrior?" A ten-year-old girl raised her hand and eagerly called out, "I know." "Well, who was he?" asked the bewildered teacher. The little girl promptly exclaimed, "Ben Thompson!"[67]

Despite his reckless life, some remembered Ben Thompson for his good advice, generosity, sense of justice, and honesty. Longtime friends still invited him to their most important social functions. Captain Edward Creary, Ben Thompson's old rival for the city marshalship was married on Saturday, March 8, to Katie Deats, an esteemed and popular lady. It was a private affair, and only a few close friends and relatives were in attendance. Ben Thompson was among the few guests invited to celebrate the event.[68]

While awaiting his trial for the Harris killing, Ben Thompson received kind attention and care from one of the jailors. When he was acquitted and freed, Ben returned to the jail, and to exhibit his gratitude, he presented the deputy sheriff with a beautiful gold watch and chain.[69]

Called to speak before a citizen's convention, Ben Thompson expressed how he was in favor of all the taxes necessary to provide an education for every child living in Austin. He was glad to pay $100 per year in taxes, and for the greater good, was willing to pay considerably more.[70] For Christmas in 1883, along with six other gentlemen, Ben Thompson generously provided the prisoners incarcerated in the Travis County jail a turkey dinner with all the trimmings, along with fifty cakes, cigarettes, cigars, and a round of whiskey for all, which prompted a large cheer of thanks from the inmates.[71] Perhaps he recalled his time behind bars and wanted to be a light for others in that situation.

Captain of the Austin Greys, R. P. Smyth, later wrote how, when he was twelve years old, his father handed him a few coins and let him pay his way into a sideshow tent on Congress Avenue and Hickory Street (8th Street) where a seven foot giant was being displayed. Smyth explained, "In one corner of the tent there were some men crowded around a small table, and boy like, I wanted to see what they were doing, and I tried to work my way to the table. Ben Thompson took me by the arm and led me away, saying, 'When you get tired looking at the giant, go on out; your father would not like for you to look on what those men are doing.' There was a card game going on." Thompson always showed great respect to Smyth's father, William, who was the Chief Clerk of the Treasury Department of Texas. When Smyth was a young man, Ben Thompson congratulated him on his avoidance of saloons and gambling dens. Thompson explained to Smyth that he wanted him to become an honored citizen, well-liked by everyone, like his father.[72] During Smyth's career, he would rise to become the Special Mail Agent of Texas.

John Talley, an old-time cowboy, would reminisce about Thompson's charity. When the hat was passed for someone who was down and out, and as others tossed in a dime or perhaps as much as twenty-five cents, Ben would always be more generous, and would give at least a silver dollar, but usually it was a five-dollar bill.

Ben Glaser earned a little money for his family washing dishes for a German cook. Glaser was a teenage immigrant from Austria, and the cook, who was often drunk, made life wretched for young Glaser. One evening, the cook threw a frying pan and struck Glaser in the leg. Thompson, a patron of the restaurant, saw the results of the bullying, and crooked his finger at the cook who came running. Taking off his heavy pistol belt, he handed it to Glaser and told him to lie into his tormentor. Glaser admitted, "I whipped that cook until I was exhausted and happy." Of Ben Thompson, Ben Glaser said, "He might have been a gambler, a desperado, a killer to others, but to me he is a hero."[73]

Looking back, Lafayette Rogers, an old-time citizen of the Texas capital who often enjoyed its barrooms and gambling halls, admired Thompson's honesty in running games of chance, In his remembrances, he recalled Ben "as a born gambler [who] never run a croked [*sic*] game in his [gambling] house."[74]

In early March, John Cardwell retired as editor of the *Statesman*, and after having reported on the life of Ben Thompson for so many years, he was about to miss the biggest story of Ben Thompson's life: his sudden and unsurprising death.

During the first week of March, Thompson was in his gambling room above the Iron Front Saloon on Congress Avenue when he received an invitation from Joe Foster asking Ben to visit the Vaudeville Theatre. "They do not catch me in that trap. I know if I were to go into that place it would be my graveyard," Ben prophetically responded.[75]

By 1884, John King Fisher had already served two terms as an Uvalde County deputy sheriff. The current sheriff, Ben Boatright, was under indictment, and would not be a candidate for reelection. Many felt that Fisher's experience, and his excellence in serving the citizens of Uvalde County, qualified him to become the sheriff. He was so highly thought of he probably could have made his election run unopposed.[76] At this time, the entire state of Texas was embroiled in a struggle between the large landowners and the small ranchers. By 1877, over seven thousand tons of barbed wire had been sold in Texas, and in 1883, a severe drought affected both big and small cattle operations, just as the fencing off of almost the entire state had become a matter of fact. The free grass gentry, who owned herds but no land, began to cut down the fences alongside many of the ranchers in desperate attempts to water their dying livestock. The fence cutters formed "clubs" and organized themselves to coordinate the work of destroying the fences they so loathed. In Bexar County, these bands of cutters called themselves respectively, "Knights of the Nippers," "Blue Devils," and the "Order of Javelinas." Many cut the wire because the land had been sold off by the state to corporations. Outlaws and rustlers saw the opportunity to join the tough and desperate ranchers in bringing down the wire so that herds, legitimate or stolen, could be moved as necessary. Fence cutting in Uvalde and neighboring Medina County resulted in huge amounts of damage to properties belonging to large landowners. At first, Governor Ireland set a "shoot and kill" policy with regard to the fence cutters, but he had to promptly backtrack from his position. Public pressure forced him to call a special session of the legislature during the second week of January to enact a law dealing with fence cutting. After weeks of argument and negotiation, the legislature finally passed a law with new penalties and regulations.[77]

John King Fisher and other Uvalde County citizens decided to travel to Austin to make a tax collection report, but also, due to the threats fence cutters were making against Medina County Officials, they intended to clarify the enforcement of the new fence cutting law.[78] By 1883, the Southern Pacific Railroad laid track linking the town of Uvalde to San Antonio, then the road went on to Austin along the International & Great Northern Railway track. Fisher stopped in San Antonio to change trains on his way to the capital, and to visit his friend Joe Foster and Foster's partner, Billy Simms, at the Vaudeville. Over a drink, or perhaps two, Ben Thompson's name probably came up.[79]

Fisher arrived in Austin and completed his business in Austin, and then set out to find Ben Thompson. At some point in the past, the two gunmen had become angry at one another. Ben resented that Major Trevanion T. Teel volunteered to be a special prosecutor during his trial for Jack Harris' murder. For years, Major Teel had been Fisher's attorney and defended him against many charges, including murder.[80] John King Fisher may have also resented the killing of Jack Harris, with whom he had been on cordial terms.[81] However, Billy Thompson was a longtime friend of Fisher, and along with other mutual friends, he intervened before any disagreement between them turned into a confrontation. As a token of their friendship, Thompson presented to Fisher a copy of the most recent picture of himself, a duplicate of the same given to his daughter. The photograph was taken by photographer H. R. Marks. Ben autographed the back writing, "To my friend King Fisher Ben Thompson Austin Texas March 11th 1884."[82]

Thompson and Fisher began their time of visiting Austin's barrooms at W. C. Denny and W. R. Brown's Cosmopolitan Saloon.[83] Having left the Cosmopolitan, Ben paid a pleasant call to the *Statesman's* office with Fisher and three of Fisher's friends, Texas Ranger Capt. Joe Shely [also spelled Sheely], Deputy United States

Marshal Fred Niggli, and John Vance, a merchant and mill owner from the town of Castroville, Medina County. The men made the stop in order to examine newspaper files for a letter concerning Captain Sheely, but their efforts were to no avail as the letter could not be located. The *San Marcos Free Press* expressed disapproval with the actions of officers of the law rhetorically asking, "What are the people to think of State and U. S. officers and others … who were found parading around with drunken desperadoes."[84]

It was true. Thompson and Fisher enjoyed several saloons during the day, but raised no commotion, as Thompson had done so many times before. Fisher, according to Walton, was "anxious that Thompson should accompany him as far as San Antonio. Thompson for some reason, did not wish to go. At last, however he consented to go as far as where the down and up-trains met, some fifteen miles south of Austin."[85]

Many reasons have been offered as to why he made the decision to accompany Fisher. Perhaps he went because his brother Billy was in the Alamo City. The Dallas *Daily Herald* maintained, "He was very fond of a certain beautiful woman … [in San Antonio] … and it was known that he intended visiting her."[86] Others say that Ben was interested in seeing the famous actress, Ada Gray, who was performing that evening at San Antonio's Turner Hall in the play "East Lynne! Or the Elopement." The play was scheduled to show the following two nights in Austin, and Thompson was eager to see the play beforehand and review Miss Gray's performance to his friends in Austin.[87] Many have speculated that John King Fisher offered to mediate reconciliation between Ben and the gang at the Vaudeville Theatre. Some, with more suspicious minds, later asserted, "it was not difficult to allure … Ben … to his death."[88]

Ben Thompson and John King Fisher did not reach the depot in time to board the 4 p.m. International train bound for San Antonio. They rushed to a carriage and raced to a point at the Colorado

River, where the train had to slow as it started to roll onto the bridge. Once there, Ben decided to board the train and continue to San Antonio. Thompson and Fisher jumped from the carriage, easily stepping aboard the slow moving train.[89] It was fitting that Ben Thompson was hurrying to his death, because it was something he had been doing all of his life.

Chapter 16

HELLISH BUSINESS

"The affair was well laid, a coolly prepared plan to murder."

—*Austin Daily Dispatch*, March 13, 1884

"What occurred on the train is of trivial character," Walton wrote in his biography of Thompson, "and will not be noted." Others who witnessed what transpired on the ride to San Antonio did take notice. Evidently Ben made no preparations for the trip. He was unarmed, except for a knife, and in his pockets were only $4 or $5 in cash. While en route, he borrowed $10 from United States Marshal "Hal" Gosling. It was observed both Thompson and Fisher were noticeably intoxicated when they stepped on board the train and one of their first actions was to confiscate a bottle of whisky from another passenger, a man of German descent. Thomas I. Houghton, a resident of Austin known to Thompson, saw that Ben was "considerably under the influence," and "remonstrated with him about drinking, and Thompson replied he knew he had been taking too much liquor and would not drink anymore." He chose not to live up to this promise.[1]

They ordered a porter to bring them water. Apparently, he did not move quick enough to suit Thompson who struck the employee over the head with the German's whiskey bottle, causing blood to flow. A stiff, silk high top hat completed Ben's outfit, and this was splattered with the porter's blood. Disgusted with Ben's behavior, King Fisher intervened, and stopped Thompson from striking the poor man a second time. He warned that if Ben continued the violence, one of them would die. Looking at his ruined plug hat, Thompson offered it to another gentleman on the train named Fred Bader, who refused to wear it. In response, Thompson took out his knife, and cut off the top half leaving only the brim intact. To help prevent any further trouble, Mr. Bader then took the knife away from the drunken Thompson. Family lore places Alden Jackson Thorpe on that train bound for San Antonio. He was then an Austin policeman, and before his career ended, he would rise to be Austin's Chief of Police. Thorpe was related to Thompson by marriage. He was the husband of Ben's first cousin Jane "Jennie" Baker. Before the train made its scheduled stop at the San Marcos station, Thorpe implored Ben to step off the train with him when it pulled into the depot and not continue to San Antonio. But there was no persuading Ben, and A. J. Thorpe exited the train alone. After a ride lasting four hours, the train pulled into San Antonio at 8 p.m.[2]

The International & Great Northern Railroad depot stood on West Houston Street, a little more than a mile west of the town's Main Plaza. Gallagher's Saloon and Restaurant stood directly across the street from the wood frame depot. Thompson and Fisher crossed the street and stepped into Gallagher's place, and while there, downed another drink. As a lark, Ben wore the remains of his cut-up hat, and entertained friends and acquaintances with the story relating how and why he came to remove the crown.[3]

A previously unpublished image of San Antonio's "Fatal Corner" where Ben Thompson killed Vaudeville Theatre owner Jack Harris and was later gunned down alongside John King Fisher. The original image appears as a four by seven-inch stereoscopic view card and is an excellent example of photographer Frank Hardesty's work. *Courtesy the Kurt House Collection.*

San Antonio *Light* reporter, Johnny Lunsford, claimed word that Ben Thompson had boarded the train to San Antonio was telegraphed to the proprietors of the Vaudeville Theatre.[4] Another source also brought news of Thompson's unexpected arrival. When Marshal Gosling exited the train, he promptly went to the Main Plaza and stopped in at the Vaudeville Theatre, where he left word with a clerk that Thompson "had come over on the train, had h—l in his neck," and trouble may be coming with him. Gosling also found and warned forty-four-year-old Jacobo Coy,[5] a house policeman at the Vaudeville. Coy, who was a very large man in stature, went to the police asking for assistance. Coy then told his employer, Billy Simms that San Antonio City Marshal Shardein promised to send six officers to prevent any disturbance.[6] A relative of Simms later stated that it was Simms's intention to leave Texas for good. His presence in the Alamo City was coincidental only because he was delayed there during the early portion of 1884 due to affairs related to the administration of Jack Harris's estate.[7] The *Light* formally announced that during the third week of February, Billy Simms had returned to the Vaudeville Theatre and to his old position as business manager after a brief absence.[8]

After their drink at Gallagher's Saloon, Ben Thompson and John King Fisher separated. A friend of Fisher's, San Antonio attorney Thomas T. Vanderhaven, warned Fisher to stay away from the troublesome Thompson, and even offered the use of his driver and carriage to remove him from any possible danger. Fisher was unconcerned and declined the offer, evidently feeling he could avoid (or handle) any trouble.[9]

When Billy Thompson was told his brother Ben was in town, he was with friends a few doors down from the Vaudeville at the new, and palatial, White Elephant Saloon. Leaving the saloon in search of his brother, Billy spotted Ben in a hired hack, and joined him in it. Still wearing the brim of his former silk hat, Ben asked the driver to take him to a store where he purchased a new one. Ben and Billy next went to a saloon on Commerce Street, and there, unknowingly, took their last drink together. Leaving the bar, Ben voiced the desire to purchase a revolver. Billy persuaded Ben not to buy a pistol, but if he was bound to have one, Billy explained, he would return to the White Elephant where he had earlier checked his revolver, "a large, 45 calibre ivory handled one; engraved and silver mounted." The weapon was a gift from Ben. Agreeing to wait for the revolver, Ben went to a barbershop on Soledad Street to get a haircut. Upon

John King Fisher, who was considered the King Rustler of the Nueces Strip for years, became a deputy of Uvalde County, and was a strong contender to be elected sheriff when he was killed with Ben Thompson. Apparently, he felt it necessary to be armed even for a formal photograph as this image shows. Note: He carries his revolver with the butt forward. Here he poses with his wife-to-be, Sarah Vivian Fisher. *Courtesy the Dovalina Family Collection, Laredo, Texas and Larry Shaver.*

returning to the shop, Billy found his brother gone. However, he learned from a hack driver that Ben had decided to go to the Turner Opera Hall on the northeast corner of Houston and Saint Mary's Street. Encountering his friend John King Fisher by chance, Billy entrusted his revolver to Fisher, begging him to guard his brother against any trouble. Fisher then went on to the Turner Opera Hall to meet Ben. Worried, Billy also asked Texas Ranger Captain Joe Shely, City Marshal Shardein, and others to help keep a watch on his brother. Waiting for Ben and Fisher to return after the show, Billy went back to the White Elephant, where he made the same request of Edward Fowler, one of the proprietors of the saloon.[10]

On the Turner Hall stage, Miss Ada Gray was reprising a role she had performed over five thousand times in the play, "East Lynne! Or the Elopement." Charles A. Watkins' 5th Avenue Combination, her husband's troupe, had crisscrossed the United States for years playing the principal towns and cities. Billed as "the Distinguished Emotional and Tragic Actress," Miss Gray was at the height of her fame, and Ben Thompson was eager to see the play. Somehow, King Fisher arrived at the theater first, and was guided to a seat up front on the left side of the hall. Displaying his pistol conspicuously in a belted scabbard, he attracted considerable attention from both patrons and employees. Soon Thompson paid for his ticket, and took a seat next to Fisher. Newspaperman Lunsford would recall, "The opera house was under the management of Tom Howard, who knew both Thompson and Fisher well and when he saw the condition of Thompson he became uneasy that some untoward incident might occur in his house. But beyond frequent visits to the bar at the Houston Street front of the hall, nothing happened. A few minutes before the final curtain, Thompson and Fisher made another visit to the bar and then made their way to the variety theater at Soledad and Main Plaza."[11] Longtime San Antonio theatre-man Ernest Rische also remembered how Thompson and Fisher both attended Ada Gray's performance at the Turner Opera Hall. During her two-night stay there, Miss Gray was a great hit, and the one thousand-seat hall was packed to standing room only, as the audiences wept over the trials and woes of the heroine. The two gunmen got up and left the hall at the commencement of the last act of the six-act play. Rische claimed, "Thompson was drinking, but not drunk, but slightly affected by the stimulants he had taken. Fisher was strictly sober. He did not drink any intoxicants that night, but each time Thompson drank [Fisher] called for a cigar. He did so at the Turner Hall bar just before he and Thompson left there."[12]

At about 9 p.m., Vaudeville house policeman Jacobo Coy went to a store owned by J. M. Emerson and acquired a single action .44 calibre revolver. Marshal Shardein ordered Policeman John A. Ferris and a second officer, Andres Coy,[13] Jacobo's brother, to the Vaudeville. The marshal followed his officers to the Main Plaza shortly after, and upon his arrival, inquired about Ben Thompson. He was told that Ben was at the Turner Opera Hall, and his brother Billy was sober and trying to take care of Ben and keep him out of trouble. Shardein stayed outside the Vaudeville until about 10 p.m. when another one of his officers, J. B. Chadwell, came up, and Shardein ordered him to be on hand in case of trouble. Strangely, Chadwell positioned himself away from the front of the Vaudeville entrance and across the street on the east side of the Plaza by Solomon Deutsch's Store. It was then that Shardein received a telephone message from his wife asking him to come home and bring a doctor because her mother was very ill. Telephoning for a physician, Marshal Shardein stayed at home until the arrival of the doctor before returning to the plaza. Shardein was standing in front of the White Elephant Saloon when he learned that, during his absence, Ben Thompson and John King Fisher had entered the Vaudeville Theatre. At first "Thompson objected to going there," Walton later explained, "but was over-persuaded, and went." For a reason now unknown, Shardein chose not to enter the establishment and find Thompson.[14]

At almost 11 p.m., the two men who lived their lives by the revolvers they carried took a small step toward eternity when they strolled through the doorway and crossed the threshold of the Vaudeville Theatre. A young black boy, who worked in the Vaudeville Barroom as a glass washer, stated that Thompson and Fisher strode up to the bar, and Ben called for two drinks. Thompson refused to pay, but Fisher handed the money over, and the two men went upstairs to the balcony portion of the theatre. Virtually all of the Vaudeville patrons quickly knew of the presence of these dangerous men, and were familiar with their desperate character. House policeman Coy watched as an unidentified red-faced man walked in with the two gunmen, but chose not to remain with them. Billy Simms, standing next to Coy, asked him if he recognized them. Coy replied he knew Thompson and Fisher. Simms whispered his fear that there might be a difficulty, and warned Coy to be careful. Watching Thompson and Fisher heading upstairs, Coy went to Bexar County Constable Alfredo Casanovas, and asked him to follow them upstairs and keep an eye on them. Coy then went to City Officers Hughes and Karber. He told them that he observed John King Fisher carrying a revolver, and his instructions were to permit only city policemen to be armed while in the theater. Karber and Hughes said Fisher, being a deputy sheriff, had a right to go armed. Coy next went upstairs, and joined Thompson and Fisher, choosing a seat on Fisher's right, close to the pistol he was wearing. After about five, or possibly, ten minutes, Billy Simms arrived upstairs taking a seat at the far end of the hall.[15]

Ben Thompson and King Fisher purchased tickets for the gallery.[16] A new play, or "afterpiece," written by one Charles Frye, was on the Vaudeville's program and was scheduled to close the evening's entertainment. Ironically it was entitled, "Assassination;

or, The Night Owls of the Plaza." Ben Thompson spotted Billy Simms sitting in the gallery and sent a waiter boy over to tell Simms he wished to see him. Simms complied, shook hands with Thompson, and took a seat on Thompson's left. Fisher offered to treat and asked Simms, Coy, and Thompson what they would like. They ordered two cigars, a glass of beer and a whiskey with seltzer. Fisher and Simms smoked the cigars as Coy and Thompson downed their drinks. A few minutes of conversation took place before Thompson noticed Joe Foster sitting nearby in the gallery. At Thompson's request, Simms brought Foster over, and the five men stood during a brief, heated conversation when suddenly gunfire sent the theatre into wild confusion. The "rapid succession" of gunshots, dense smoke, and the screams of women encouraged the Vaudeville's many panic stricken customers to race for the exits. The time was 11:15 p.m.[17]

Prior to the volley of gunfire, Constable Casanovas had seated himself on the left side of the hall. He watched as Billy Simms went up to Thompson, shook hands with him and seated himself on Ben's left side. Simms, Thompson, Fisher, and Coy were seated about six feet from the entrance to the dress circle, which was the first level of seats above the ground floor of the theatre. Thompson put his left arm around Simms, and they spoke together for about five minutes before the whole group stood up and moved towards the door that led to the stairway down. Ben Thompson suddenly stopped and turned around. Casanovás observed that Billy Simms went off to where Joe Foster was seated, spoke to him, and that both men then walked up to Thompson. Unable to hear their voices, Casanovas stared at Thompson as Ben excitedly waved his arms, a silk handkerchief in his left hand while he spoke to Foster for about three minutes. Thompson drew back as Coy said something Casanovas could not hear. The constable could no longer see Thompson's hands as the blasts of gunfire erupted. Unable to see

This cabinet card image of Ben Thompson is the most unique in the photographic history of the Wild West. Ben inscribed the image on the day they both were killed: "To my friend King Fisher – Ben Thompson – Austin Texas March 11, 1884." Officers took this cabinet card off Fisher's dead body and found it dripping with his blood. The blood stains can be clearly seen on the back portion of the card.

Courtesy the Robert G. McCubbin Collection.

who had pistols out, Casanovas ran to the scene with his six-shooter drawn. In the darkened theatre, he could see pistol flashes, but was unable to see who was firing a weapon. The firing had ceased before Casanovas arrived on the bloody scene, and as he hurried there he could finally see well enough to realize it was Coy, with a revolver in his hand, that was rising up by Thompson and Fisher, both of whom were lying flat on the floor. Joe Foster grabbed Billy Simms by the shoulder and called out, "Billy I'm shot all to pieces. Help me down stairs." Foster, like Simms, was holding a pistol, as Constable Casanovas joined in and helped Simms aid Foster down the steps towards the first-floor saloon. As the three men came down the stairway, they met City Marshal Shardein hurrying on his way up.[18]

Hearing what he thought were about eight to ten gunshots coming from inside the Vaudeville, Shardein rushed into the theatre's ground floor saloon just as the patrons were rushing out of the building. Bartender Bob Churchill was pointing a shotgun over the bar top towards the door leading to the stairway. He called out to the marshal that Ben Thompson was upstairs. As Shardein hurried up the stairs, he met Billy Simms and Constable Casanovas supporting the wounded Joe Foster. As soon as he reached the top and entered the gallery, Shardein "saw two men lying in the corner on top of one another." Someone yelled from downstairs, "look out for Bill Thompson, he's coming with a shot gun." Retracing his steps, the marshal again passed Foster and his helpers. He noticed that each man held a pistol in his hand, and as he went by them, Simms cried out, "give us protection." Just after he reached the bottom of the stairs, Billy Thompson was coming in the front door. Shardein heard parties calling "get out of the way" as he covered Billy with his body, shoving him aside and searching him for weapons. He found Billy unarmed and sternly warned him not to go in the building. The marshal ordered the establishment closed

The graves of both Jack Harris and Joe Foster are prominently visible in San Antonio's City Cemetery No. 1. In addition to the photograph adorning Harris's head stone, there is an historical marker explaining his significance to the Alamo City and his eventful life and career. *Courtesy the Chuck Parsons Collection.*

immediately. Jacobo Coy handed the revolver Ben Thompson was carrying over to the city marshal. Examining it without revolving the cylinder, Shardein discovered it had been fired five times with one unfired load remaining in the chamber.[19]

Billy Thompson was at the White Elephant Saloon waiting for the play at the Turner Opera Hall to end when he heard the shooting coming from the nearby Vaudeville Theatre. As Billy ran over to the Vaudeville, he saw everyone was fleeing the building. Forcing his way through the crowd, he made his way to the Vaudeville's front door where he met Police Officer J. B. Chadwell, and asked him if he knew where Ben was. Chadwell replied that he didn't know. Billy continued through the doorway and "was confronted with a number of weapons." City Marshal Shardein came upon Billy, forced him back out the door, and searched him as he told Billy not to enter the building. Policeman Chadwell followed Billy Thompson into the Vaudeville, and rushed to where he heard the sound of gunfire. He hustled up the stairs, and there he found two bodies covered in blood. They were stretched out near a corner of the room with Fisher partially atop Thompson. For a few moments, no one was there except Officer Chadwell and the unnamed theatre's night watchman. Reaching down, Chadwell turned Thompson's body over. He searched for a pistol but found nothing. He removed John King Fisher's revolver from the holster he was wearing, and he found only one chamber empty when he checked it. Later, he handed the weapon over to Officer Hughes. Both of the dead men had severe powder burns about the face. Chadwell noticed that Thompson was shot just above the left eye and Fisher seemed to be shot directly in his left eye.[20]

On his way home from the Vaudeville Theatre, J. M. Emerson heard what he called a "row" coming from the building he had just exited, and he noted the time as "about a quarter after eleven o'clock." He went around the corner to the building's small side

In contrast to his brother Ben who had numerous images made, younger brother Billy had two known photographs. This shows Billy as he was in the latter years of his life. *Courtesy the Tom Bicknell Collection.*

door off Soledad Street, and up the stairway where he found the bodies of the dead gunfighters. He immediately checked their wounds finding, "Fisher was shot in the right leg below the knee … [he] also had a wound in the left breast near the heart, and one in the left eye, which went through and came out under the left ear." Thompson was shot in the right side of his abdomen, and Emerson found another shot above the left eye. Two more shots had struck his forehead with one more striking the left side of his chin.[21]

The Alamo City was thrown into a state of the wildest excitement when the news of the tragedy became known on the street. An immense crowd rushed to the town's Main Plaza and surged around the doors of the Vaudeville Theatre. Many tried to enter, or in some cases, reenter the house they had fled only a few minutes before. The crowd was estimated at about fifteen hundred people, and they swelled against the doors in vain, denied admission by City Marshal Shardein and his officers who had taken possession of the building. The inside was almost empty, except for a handful of employees. Under Shardein's strict orders, only officers of the law and newspaper reporters were granted admission.[22]

A reporter for the *Statesman* noted when he reached the spectacle spread out on the Theatre's second level, that "the floor was flooded with their gore." He described how "the two bodies were weltering in blood, and were laid out side by side, their hair and faces carmined [*sic*] with the life fluid. The stairs leading up to the scene of the horror, were as slippery as ice [from Joe Foster's blood], and the walls were stained and the floor was tracked with bloody footprints." Looking down at Thompson, he saw how his "face wore a stern expression, and the upper lip is drawn tight across the teeth. The brain is visible through the wound in the eyebrow."[23]

The reporter for the *Express* was permitted to inspect both Thompson and Fisher's revolvers. Fisher's pistol, like Thompson's, was a Colt six-shooter of the same caliber, and the newsman later described it as having a black-gutta percha (hard rubber) handle, with cylinder and barrel of blue bronzed steel. It had one empty chamber, but this charge appeared to have been fired some time before, as the empty shell was not under the hammer.[24]

Justice of the Peace Anton Adam was notified of the double killing at once and he enlisted a half-dozen nearby men to serve on a jury of inquest. They proceeded to where Thompson and Fisher were lying to view the bodies, and to check the scene of the shooting. The justice and the members of the jury searched the pockets of the dead men and found that both had only small sums of money. Two dollars were found on Fisher, and Thompson had only six dollars on his person. The autographed photograph of Ben Thompson, given by Ben to Fisher earlier in the day, was found in one of Fisher's pockets covered with his blood. A hearing was scheduled for the following morning at 10 a. m. in Justice Adam's courtroom.[25]

Walton would later write, "This assassination caused a greater degree of sensation, than any murder that ever occurred in Texas. The daily papers were filled with dispatches, editorials written, and communications published."[26] The double tragedy brought a mass of newspapermen to the San Antonio Western Union office. All five of the firm's telegraphers were called into work, and years later one of them, J. F. Marshall, recalled the rush to use the wire service. For the three days following, Marshall stated that their services were in high demand. Food was brought in for the telegraphers, and they were forced to work through the night stopping only long enough so they could take short naps.[27]

Gossip ran rampant on the streets of San Antonio. At first, because of the well-known contempt John King Fisher once held for Ben Thompson, it was erroneously believed by many that it was Fisher who "had given Thompson his quietus." Then supposedly his own friends mistakenly killed Fisher during the melee. Next, many thought it a remarkable fact that two such desperate men, both famous for being dead center shots, could be so riddled with bullets and balls without having taken the lives of one or more of their antagonists. Some suspected that they had been cut down with double barrel shotguns. Officer Andres Coy, brother of Jacobo, admitted to one reporter that he thought, "that Ben never fired a shot." However it happened, Ben Thompson was shot down, and "when the smoke cleared away the pride of Austin was dead." Throughout the long night, on the tongues of many San Antonians could be heard, "Jack Harris is fully revenged."[28]

"Billy Thompson bore the death of his brother very hard," reported the San Antonio *Express*, "Their affection for each other from their childhood was unequalled by those who tread the paths of peace."[29] On the streets of the Alamo City, as men met in groups and discussed the event, Billy Thompson "walked slowly up and down the pavement till a late hour," showing understandable "signs of great grief." He had lost a good friend as well as his brother. But he made no demonstration or threat toward anyone. He remained in "an abstract mood, silent, grief-stricken and desolate."[30]

When the excitement began to quiet down, the undertaking firm of Henry Carter and Thomas Mullaly, located on Alamo Plaza,

Billy Thompson's final resting place. He is buried under the stone on the far right in the Gill family plot in Fairview Cemetery in Bastrop, Texas. His younger sister Mary Jane, her husband Robert Gill, and their son Walton Thompson Gill are buried alongside him. *Courtesy the Tom Bicknell Collection.*

were called to take possession of the bodies. They transported the dead men across Main Plaza, past the San Fernando Cathedral, to a building commonly called the "Bat Cave," but officially known as the San Antonio city jail. An assembly of people numbering in the thousands followed the two undertakers, hopeful they would catch a glimpse of the dead gunfighters. Carter and Mullaly worked through the night undressing and washing the remains, preparing them for burial, and redressing the bodies before finally placing them into matching coffins.[31]

When the news of Ben Thompson's death reached Austin, it was received "with surprise and astonishment, and it was some time before it could be realized that the man who had escaped death so often, and who the people had looked upon as having a charmed life had been killed." Ben Thompson held an "undeviating belief he would die with his boots on, a death which is considered genteel by desperate men, and he himself had said many times over that he expected to be suddenly killed." The *Houston Post* commented, "Ben Thompson played his last card and was cruelly robbed of his life as he had robbed others." The *Dallas Weekly Herald* proclaimed, "The two most celebrated desperadoes in Texas are dead and the people rejoice."[32]

Early the following morning, a crowd of over three thousand people, all still anxious to get a sight of Ben Thompson and John King Fisher, were on the plaza surrounding the Bat Cave. The two dead gunfighters were "laid out in the room adjoining the marshal's office, but only the county and state officials and members of the press were permitted the privilege of viewing them." The clothing worn by both men was piled in a corner of the room soaked with their blood. Ben Thompson's new hat had a bullet hole nearly in the center of the crown and the yellow satin lining was spotted with his brains. The large, brown, broad-brimmed hat that Fisher had been wearing was also bloody. The reporter for the *Express* "found both corpses encased in handsome metallic burial cases, the lids of which had not yet been placed on the caskets ... [T]he gaping wounds in the temples of both men were horrible, and King Fisher's left eye had been entirely destroyed. Both corpses had been attired in handsome black cloth suits and the hands of both were crossed across their breasts. Fisher's face wore a placid and peaceful expression, but the ghastly stare on the features of Thompson was a terrible sight to witness."[33]

The morning edition of the *Express* repeated what the average man of the street was saying, that Jack Harris had been avenged. In Austin, the *Dispatch* editor responded, complaining about a supposed powerful influence the owners of the Vaudeville held over the *Express*. "It leads one to believe that Journal is run and controlled by that notorious den of infamy and detestable hole, where the youth, not only of San Antonio, but of other parts, are started at a rapid gait on the pathway to hell, with never a hope of retracing their steps." The *Dispatch* acknowledged that Ben Thompson earned his livelihood as a professional gambler, "but they had known him and his history for a long time," and with an intimate knowledge of his many faults, the newspaper felt his greatest fault lay in the fact that he was always "quicker on the trigger than his antagonist" and he must have come to his death by "bold blooded treachery."[34]

The *Statesman* complimented the *San Antonio Light* on its professionalism in its reporting of the tragedy. However, like the *Dispatch*, ripped the *Express* for their headline, which read, "A Good Night's Work." Lecturing the San Antonio newspaper, the *Statesman* wrote how "the *Express* forgets that nothing justifies ... the cowardly, brutal way in which he was killed ... if it were wrong for Ben to kill people, surely it was wrong for Simms, Coy and others to do it." If Thompson would have been tried, convicted, and lawfully executed, perhaps that would be "good work." But the manner in which Thompson was killed was just another murder, and by men no better than Ben Thompson. The *Statesman* ended its diatribe telling the *Express* it owed society an apology for its article, and its "savage" and "barbarous" caption line.[35]

The following morning in Justice Anton Adam's courtroom, the members of the coroner's jury assembled to listen to the testimony of witnesses as scheduled. Orders were given by Adam that none of the crowd gathered outside was to be allowed to attend the proceedings, and only officers of the court and representatives of the press were to be admitted. Witnesses were called to testify in the following order, Bexar County Precinct No. 4 Constable Alfredo Casanovas, Vaudeville House Policeman Jacobo Santos Coy, who appeared to have received only a slight wound in the calf of the right leg, San Antonio Police Officer J. Chadwell, City Marshal Phillip Shardein, J. M. Emerson, and, lastly, William H. Simms.[36] Coy and Simms provided the most important testimony. Joe Foster was excused from testifying due to the severity of his wound.

Jacobo Coy recounted his version of the bloody event. He stated how, after Simms joined the group Fisher offered to treat for refreshments. After the drinks and cigars had been taken, the topic of conversation turned to the killing of Jack Harris, but Coy claimed, in tones so low he could not specifically understand what was being said. Fisher, tiring of the subject, "rose to his feet," saying "Mr. Thompson you told me we were going to have some fun; never mind talking about past times." Ben replied, "Be easy; we'll get it pretty soon." Still impatient, Fisher encouraged the group to move downstairs, but upon reaching the doorway before the stairwell, Thompson turned suddenly and said, "Billy ain't that Joe Foster?" Ben then said, "Joe will you take a drink with us?" Replying to the offer, Foster, who had shunned liquor for a number of years, told Thompson, "Ben, you know I wouldn't drink." Thompson next asked Foster to shake hands, but requesting to be left alone Foster refused to shake, saying how Thompson had mistreated him in the past. Growing angry, Thompson blurted out, "Yes, God Damn you, I'm glad that you don't drink and shake hands with me!" Coy, standing to Thompson's left side, asked Thompson to behave. His response was, "Get out of the way; let me settle this affair with Foster." Thompson then pushed Coy aside, who again told Thompson not to raise a disturbance. He claimed he was determined to stop Thompson if he continued. Coy started toward Thompson, who shoved him aside a second time, calling out how Joe Foster was a thief. He slapped Foster across the face with his left hand as he drew his revolver with his right. As soon as Thompson's pistol appeared, Coy grasped it around the cylinder as it fired a shot. Thompson screamed at Coy to turn it loose. Coy continued to hold on as Thompson yelled, "God Damn you, turn my pistol loose," and John King Fisher chimed in saying, "Turn that pistol loose." Keeping his grip on the weapon with both hands as Thompson kept firing, Coy claimed one shot passed by his right ear. Calling out to Joe Foster and Billy Simms for help, Coy pleaded, "Don't run, assist me." Scuffling together from the doorway down into a corner, Ben Thompson, King Fisher, and Jacobo Coy all fell to the floor in a heap. Thompson landed in the middle of the three men, and as he fell, he loosened his hold of the revolver while Coy never let go. Coy testified, "I never drew my pistol. I think there were some twelve or thirteen shots altogether fired, in all … The parties who were shooting were behind us. I do not know whether Fisher had his pistol out or not. Thompson kept shooting all the time I held his pistol until he fell. I was holding his pistol with both hands and he was twisting it around to fire … I was wounded slightly in the leg, but did not discover it until the shooting was over."[37]

As the inquest progressed that day, the condition of Joe Foster became more and more precarious. His wound was below the left knee. The pistol ball shattered bones, and by coincidence, had taken a similar course as an old Civil War wound. The artery in his leg was severely enlarged from this old wound, and the enlargement extended from his ankle all the way up to his thigh. Foster's doctors deemed it impossible to save the limb, and amputated his leg a short distance above the knee joint. Foster suffered from an acute loss of blood prior to the amputation, and his doctors feared he would bleed out if another hemorrhage ensued. To ease his pain, he was heavily sedated by opiates. While influenced by the drugs, Foster continually spoke of his friend John King Fisher with affection and said how he deeply regretted the death of his friend.[38]

At noon, while Foster's doctors were finishing the operation, Billy Thompson called upon City Marshal Shardein at his office in the Bat Cave, and asked for permission to take custody of his brother's remains. The casket was placed on the afternoon train to Austin.[39]

Deputy United States Marshal Ferdinand Niggli received a telegram from Fisher's wife asking him to accompany her husband's remains and return them to Uvalde for interment. Placed on board the 6:40 Sunset train by Niggli and other friends of the deceased, the remains of John King Fisher went home for burial.[40]

At the inquest, Billy Simms was last to be called as a witness, and not surprisingly his testimony, beginning after the 2 p.m. break, dominated the hearing. In essence, he stated that when Ben Thompson sent the boy to summon him he immediately obliged. Thompson said, "Simms, I want to talk to you and tell you I haven't anything against you, but you haven't treated me right." Because of Thompson's rambling manner, Simms felt him to be half-crazy. Thompson continued, "I'm rich now; I can get out of any trouble. People might think I was taking chances to come here, but I'm surrounded by my friends. I've got a six-shooter on, but I won't need to pull it, and if you move you will be killed." Simms told Thompson that he didn't want to have any trouble with him, but Simms felt he had heard so much from Thompson that he anticipated a difficulty at any moment. Thompson said a great deal about how he was devoid of fear and how rich he was now. Suddenly he stood up and began moving for the door. Once he reached it, Thompson turned around, clinched Simms by the arm and began talking about Jack Harris and how "Harris pushed himself in the way; that he did not want to kill him … Joe Foster is the [one] who ought to have been killed." Suddenly he asked, "Ain't that Joe Foster?" Thompson had Simms go to where he was sitting, and tell Foster he wanted to talk with him. Foster complied, and walked up to Thompson while adjusting his glasses with both hands. Foster ignored Thompson's attempt to shake his hand. When pressed by Thompson, Foster eventually admitted he would not shake hands with him, saying, "I never would put a straw in your way. The world is wide enough for both of us, Ben." Growing upset, Thompson replied, "You wronged me and I killed Jack Harris without cause … Don't treat me this way; don't force me to extreme measures. I'll bet you money you'll be sorry you didn't shake hands with me. I'll live a long time yet, Joe Foster, and I'll make you leave this country. I'll expose you as a thief." In answer to Ben's threats, Foster said, "Maybe so, Ben; I don't doubt it. [But] I have been here twenty-five years, and I haven't stolen anything yet." Becoming more loud and boisterous, both Thompson and Fisher were slowly backing up towards the partition wall separating the auditorium and the second-floor bar when Ben suddenly "jerked his six-shooter and stuck it … in Foster's mouth, and [as] he cocked it he pulled it back" out. House policeman Coy grabbed Ben's revolver as it clicked saying, "Ben, I'm an officer don't do that." Simms testified, "After the first fire another pistol was drawn and just as this pistol was drawn, Fisher said don't you draw that you son of a bitch. The firing commenced then on both sides … Thompson and Fisher had fallen by this time, and the firing had ceased … Thompson fired the first shot, and while Coy was holding it. I think Thompson fired twice, before any other pistol was fired. Coy held on to it like grim death ... I saw Joe Foster with a pistol out after three or four shots were fired, but I don't know whether he fired or not. I don't know whether the [house] policeman [Coy] fired or not. My impression is he drew his pistol but I was watching Thompson and taking right good care of Mr. Simms about that time ... I don't think Thompson slapped Foster, but he was gesticulating rapidly with his hands. I saw Foster cocking his pistol; don't know that he shot, but he ought to have done so. I am not sure if Fisher got his pistol out or not, but he reached for it, when Thompson said he had a pistol on."[41] Simms thought Fisher would have participated in the shooting but his holstered six-shooter had slipped too far behind him and he received his death wound before he could reach and grasp his revolver.[42]

None of the witnesses testifying at the inquest seem to have seen John King Fisher with a pistol in his hand before he died. The talk on the street was disbelief that he did not get his work in because he was noted to be "so quick in drawing and so self-possessed when in danger."[43]

While he was in the middle of presenting his testimony, Billy Simms was questioned by one of the jurors to clarify, "who drew a pistol just after Thompson had drawn his." Mr. Simms declined to provide an answer, and Justice Adam sustained Simms's objection. The reporter for the *Express* wrote, "While ... apparently suffering from severe nervous shock, [he] detailed his testimony clearly, coherently and graphically, depicting the scene of the tragedy with a vivid and realistic manner which caused his words to be listened to with intense interest."[44]

The jury was sequestered at the conclusion of the witness testimony, and within fifteen minutes, they returned to the jury box with a verdict. They ruled that "Ben Thompson and J. K. Fisher both came to their deaths on the 11th day in March, A. D. 1884, while at the Vaudeville Theatre, in San Antonio, Texas, from the effects of pistol shot wounds from pistols held in and fired from the hands of William Simms, Joseph C. Foster, and Jacob S. Coy, and we further find that the said killing was justifiable and done in self-defense in the immediate danger of life."[45] It is interesting to note that one of the six-member jury was an employee of the Vaudeville Theatre, English born barkeeper, Henry L. Ansell.[46]

The prominent newspapers of Austin, the *Dispatch,* the *Statesman,* and the *Capital* reacted in dismay and disbelief to the inquest's verdict. The *Dispatch* published: "The verdict of the coroner's jury is simply prepared to suit the case ... The evidence given before the jury is unworthy of credence, and was given merely by those who desired Thompson's death. That Thompson came to his death by shots from the pistols of [Simms,] Foster and officer Coy, is unworthy of belief."[47] The *Statesman* maintained, "Let the coroner's jury find as it may—the killing of Ben Thompson and King Fisher [was] a downright and premediated murders ... the strange circumstances presents itself that although police officers were present when the killing took place, and actually took part in the struggle [referring to house policeman Coy], no one was arrested." No man who took the stand at the inquest identified Simms, Coy, or Foster as the gunmen; in fact, it was never established through testimony as to who actually fired the fatal shots.[48] The *Capital* asserted, "When the two men had been thus shot down, and were lying on the floor weltering in each other's blood, so close had they fallen, the [Vaudeville house] policeman, Jacobo Coy, took Thompson's pistol and fired two bullets into his head and then turned on Fisher and shot him twice also, once in the head." Coy pressed the revolver so close the powder burned the dead men's faces and hair.[49]

It was soon "generally credited" in Austin that Ben Thompson did not fall in a fair fight but was instead lured into a trap, and brutally assassinated without any show. No words of revenge were spoken, but this caused a great deal of resentment and indignation among his friends.[50] Billy Thompson, in an interview with the *Austin Daily Dispatch*, was one of the first to explain how his brother and friend King Fisher came to their end. Billy, "declare[d] that Ben and Fisher were shot by parties [hidden] in the boxes or behind the scenes, hired to do the shooting."[51]

The San Antonio to Austin train carrying Thompson's body passed through the town of Kyle. The morning edition of the *Express* "sold like wildfire on the streets." Everyone in Kyle wanted to read the newspaper's account of the "Tuesday night tragedy." Wrought with excitement, the people of the town waited at the depot to greet the train, hoping they could gaze upon the casket carrying the famous man's remains. Perhaps Ben's longtime friend Thomas G. Martin, a Kyle saloon owner, sometime lawman, and longtime sport, stood waiting and remembering how he had warned his friend that he would fool around with the Vaudeville gang one time too many.[52] When the train from San Antonio arrived in Austin at 4 p. m., a vast throng of people was waiting at the depot. Members of the Knights of Pythias took charge of Ben Thompson's remains, and conveyed them to the family residence on University Avenue. Conspicuous among the following mourners were the two lawmen most embarrassed by Thompson's antics during the last few months of his life, Travis County Sheriff Malcom Hornsby and Austin City Marshal H. Grooms Lee. His funeral was scheduled for the following day, Thursday, March 13, at 3 p. m.[53]

A reporter for the *Houston Post* called at the Thompson family home intending to interview Ben's wife Catherine. He was informed that she "was not in a condition to see anyone. Although a lady usually of remarkable courage and bravery, she broke completely down when the reality of the horrible fate of her husband was thrust upon her. She was completely prostrated and required the offices of a physician." The reporter did find the house filled with sympathizing family friends, relatives, and acquaintances. Determined to find a story to file, the *Post* reporter learned that Billy Thompson was checked into Austin's Cloud Hotel. Feeling unwell, Billy had confined himself in his hotel room. The *Post* reporter spoke with him there later in the evening, and observed, "he talks very calmly, shows no disposition to discuss his future movements and was perfectly clear of threats of any nature." Billy expressed the opinion that he was lucky to get out of San Antonio alive, explaining that, knowing his brother was in town he left the White Elephant Saloon to investigate the gunfire coming from the Vaudeville Theatre. As he reached the entrance, Billy Simms and several other men met him. Simms held a cocked revolver, and the others had pistols drawn. The correspondent wrote how at that moment, City Marshal Shardein interfered, and took Billy aside, warning him "if he went on the street, armed or not, he would be killed, as he had given his men orders to shoot him down on sight." In his article, the *Post* reporter explained that people arriving from San Antonio that evening said the accounts of the affair as initially published were all wrong. Parties concealed in private boxes at the theatre shot down the two men. Thompson had nine wounds and Fisher thirteen. Far more bullets were fired than could have been loaded into the pistols handled by Foster, Simms, and Coy. In Billy's room were the clothes worn by his brother when he was slain and after examination by the reporter, he described them as being "fairly riddled."[54]

After reading the *Post* reporter's incriminating article, City Marshal Shardein emphatically denied the charge made against him in the Houston newspaper. On the contrary, Shardein insisted that, if it were not for his timely interference, Billy Thompson would have met the same fate as his brother. A reporter from the

San Antonio Light held a lengthy interview with Billy the morning after his brother's death, and not a word was spoken about any threats made against him by Shardein. The *Light* agreed with the outraged marshal calling him "an able, efficient and courageous officer and would never be guilty of the conduct charged to him." Believing the accusation "originated in the fertile brain" of the *Post's* correspondent, the *Light* stated the *Post's* article was "sadly, wildly wrong."[55]

Disappointed by the findings of Justice Anton Adam's inquest, many relatives and friends of the Thompson family determined to learn the truth surrounding Ben's death. To provide some answers, a post mortem was performed on his remains. Early in the morning on Thursday, March 13, Doctors Thomas D. Wooten and Charles N. Worthington performed the autopsy at Thompson's residence. Wooten, a future regent of the University of Texas, was considered "one of the most scientific gentlemen in Texas." Prominent Austin gentlemen and members of the press observed the examination. Most importantly, a ballistics expert was on hand. Congress Avenue gun shop owner Joseph C. Petmecky was there to identify any bullets the doctors might recover from Thompson's body.[56]

At the completion of the autopsy it became obvious that "the cold, hard facts of science" showed how "valueless is human testimony in a case like this." The examination of Ben's wounds proved his brother's accusation. Ben "was shot by men concealed above them." The San Antonio inquest determined that only three shots struck Thompson while the Austin autopsy revealed eight wounds, all of which were from bullets entering Thompson's left side, and five of which had entered his head. The doctors tracked the trajectory of each projectile and made a startling discovery. Four bullets had come from the same point before striking Thompson's head. They were fired from a position above Thompson and to his left. The balls were tracked coursing downward exactly parallel to each other. The doctors found that two bullets entered the trunk of his body, one first passing through the left arm and then his heart, and the second entering the left hip and moving upward. These two shots must have been fired after Thompson had fallen, and as he lay dying on the floor. His face was "thickly filled with powder buried in the skin." Also, the hair back of his temple was singed clearly indicating a pistol was placed close to his head and fired. Two of the bullets that struck him down still remained in Thompson's body. One was tracked, found lodged in his mouth, and removed. The second struck his jawbone on a downward course and lodged in his neck. Both were taken out by Doctor Wooten and given to Mr. Petmecky for identification. Petmecky stated they came from Winchester rifles and .44 calibre pistols. Six of the eight wounds, each by themselves, would have been fatal, and when struck by even one of them, Thompson would have been paralyzed and powerless the instant he was hit.[57]

The findings of the autopsy were, "First, Thompson was shot while standing erect by persons who were above him, and who were also a little to the left, armed with Winchester rifles and revolvers as shown by the bullets found and by the same general downward track ... and that he must have been standing still at the time, as is shown by the parallel courses of the bullets. Secondly, that five of the balls were fired by different persons and simultaneously, as is shown by the fact that he would have instantly fallen from the effect of any of them; and their courses being in the same general direction." The newspaper report ended with the thought, "it would be interesting to have a scientific investigation of Fisher's wounds to see what sort of evidence they would give." However, John King Fisher's remains were buried without a post mortem investigation.[58]

With the autopsy evidence proving outright murder, Austin's *Daily Dispatch* continued its editorial attacks upon the Alamo

City. "Ben Thompson was killed in San Antonio, and that city is welcome to all the glory there is in such a brutal and cowardly assassination. We had read in history that it was common in Italy and Spain to hire men to commit assassination, but it has been left to San Antonio to inaugurate this hellish business in this country." The editor of the *Dispatch* continued, "We hope never to hear anything said about lawlessness in Austin, again. There never was, and we trust there never will be, such a cowardly and brutal act committed in this city. San Antonio is alone in this great country where hired assassination is endured and approved by the people and the press and it is welcome to the glory." The article finished with the following claim. "No other city in Texas, nor do we believe in this whole land, has a human slaughterhouse like this den of hell, the Vaudeville theatre, or a press that would ... sustain such an infamous place."[59]

Lying in state at his home on West Mesquite Street in Uvalde, John King Fisher's casket was impressively "draped with magnificent wreaths of flowers." His many friends and most of the citizens of his hometown viewed his body. Fisher's funeral service took place on the same day as Ben Thompson's, and the services began at almost the exact same hour. Reverend J. W. Stovall conducted his funeral, and the ceremony was the largest ever attended in Uvalde. Almost every wagon, carriage and hack in town turned out to be part of the procession to the town cemetery, including two vehicles called "busses" by the newspaperman reporting on the event. "Mr. Fisher was regarded as a reformed man," the reporter continued "and enjoyed the confidence and respect of our people." His untimely end was deeply regretted by the citizenry he represented. He had been serving as a deputy sheriff and his chances as a prominent candidate for county sheriff had more than "fair prospects of success." Suspicious minds have often thought Fisher lured Thompson to his death and died by mistake in the crossfire. While his visit to the Vaudeville and his meeting with Foster and Simms just before traveling to Austin only a day or two before the tragedy may point to involvement in a conspiracy to murder Ben Thompson, he was a warm friend of both Joe Foster and Billy Thompson. Most likely, his actions were part of an honest desire to settle the animosity between the parties. While no one can possibly know now what was in Fisher's heart, those closest to him believed he escorted Ben Thompson to the Vaudeville Theatre in the role of a peacemaker.[60]

In Austin, Rev. Richmond K. Smoot, the pastor of the First Southern Presbyterian Church and Chaplain to the Texas Senate, was selected to conduct Thompson's funeral service. After the completion of the autopsy and the final placement of the body into an elegant coffin, Ben Thompson's remains were again under the auspices and care of his fellow Knights of Pythias from the Austin Mount Bonnell Lodge No. 34. The assembled mourners overflowed the Thompson residence as they listened to Reverend Smoot's eloquent prayer asking for "the blessing of the Heavenly Father upon the heart broken wife and the grief stricken children." After Smoot's solemn funeral sermon, Ben's casket was placed in the hearse and covered with many decorative floral bouquets. The cortege, formed of members of the Knights of Pythias in full uniform dress, marched at the head of the procession. The hearse followed next with eight Pythians, four on each side, serving as pallbearers. Immediately following in carriages, were Rev. Smoot, other gentlemen. Ben's family, wife Catherine, their daughter Katie, and son Ben Jr. followed behind them in a separate vehicle. The heartbreaking crying of his two children was pitiful to behold, with Ben's daughter loudly sobbing, "Oh, my papa! My papa!" Sixty-two carriages of mourners took the long ride through Austin's streets to the gravesite at Oakwood Cemetery. At the grave, the Knights of Pythias performed their order's mystic rites, and Ben's coffin was lowered into the ground near the graves of his mother Mary Ann, and his infant daughter Augustua Lorraine. Once Ben was in the ground and the prayers ended, the many mourners began to drift away as the gravediggers piled dirt on his casket. Ben Thompson's final public spectacle was over.[61]

A lengthy "testimonial to the worth of our deceased brother Benjamin" was adopted by the Pythians, and under their "official seal and attestation," it was presented to his family along with individual condolences and words of sympathy. The testimonial was published in full by newspapers in both San Antonio and Austin. His Pythian brothers resolved, "whereas, by the death of Benjamin Thompson this lodge has been deprived of a useful member in good standing, and [to] the universal order an honorable and zealous knight ... and that our loathing should be especially added to the prevalent and extreme abhorrence at his assassination." Ben Thompson died without a will, and a fellow brother of the Knights of Pythias, Royal B. Underhill, filed at the county court the application for administration of Ben's estate, which was approved. It was believed he left assets valued at about $13,000 or $14,000 with debts amounting to $5,000 or $6,000.[62]

The war of words between the Austin and San Antonio newspapers did not stop after the funerals. "We are not surprised that the people of Austin, or many of them at least should be a little 'touchy' on the Ben Thompson question," published the *Express*. "With a record as a reckless desperado second to no other in the country, and a manner of life that called for heartiest condemnation, [and though] notoriously well known in that community, he was twice elected marshal, showing that a majority of the people there were his friends, and that he should be buried with honors is not a matter of surprise. But this does not change the fact that his death was a matter on which the people of the state can well congratulate themselves." The editor of the *Express* readily admitted

In its March 20, 1884 issue, the *National Police Gazette* headlined this article, "Ben Thompson's Final Exit." The dramatic prose continued, "The last act of a fierce and desperate career, as performed in a San Antonio, Texas, Temple of the wild and untrammeled drama." The illustration was based upon Joseph Foster's inaccurate deathbed account of how he shot Ben Thompson.

Courtesy the Tom Bicknell Collection.

that Ben Thompson "was a man with many noble impulses," but felt his faults weighed heavier. When sober he was a "good hearted gentleman but a demon when drunk; and he would get drunk." The editor stated his newspaper "glories in the death of no man … and we are sorry that Ben Thompson was what he was," however there were "no regrets over the desperado's death."[63]

In response to the published autopsy results, the great sympathy created at the funerals, and the negative publicity in the Austin newspapers that decried the city of San Antonio, its press, the Vaudeville Theatre, its ownership and staff, efforts were made to win back public opinion. Billy Simms and Jacobo Coy met with a correspondent of the *Express.* They granted an interview to describe the fatal fight and to inspect the very spot at the Vaudeville where the tragedy took place. Throughout the entire interview Coy did not speak a word. The reporter assured Simms he would publish any statement he made just as spoken. Simms then said, "I would like to have you state that ever since I have been under the responsibility of the executorship of the Harris estate, and had charge, my aim and every endeavor has been to conduct this establishment and show in an orderly manner, and actuated by this motive I employed Coy as a special policeman, knowing him to be a cautious, careful and law-abiding officer, on whom reliance could be placed." Pleading his case, Simms disclosed, "the difficulty which occurred is one which has given me great pain, and has since it transpired caused me the deepest regret; but I believe that there was no power on earth which could have prevented it. It had to come, for Ben Thompson was determined upon it, and could not be appeased or prevented, and both myself and Joe Foster did all in our power to mollify and pacify him, and Joe pleaded with him to abstain from any trouble, even after Thompson had denounced him as a thief and said he would expose him as such."

Next, the reporter examined the scene where the affray unfolded. Similar to their testimony at the inquest, Simms and Coy did not identify who fired the shots that killed Thompson and Fisher. A bullet hole high on the wall left of the stage was attributed to the first shot fired by Thompson. His second shot, which shattered Foster's leg, passed "through the frame work of the auditorium opposite the door of the gallery." Thompson's third shot hit Coy in his leg and "struck the floor where they fell." The reporter surmised that the firing then increased in rapidity thanks to the other parties involved, with the shots fired in the direction of the struggling Thompson and Coy. They were all found and lodged nearby each other. A shot that passed through Thompson was found above where his body landed imbedded in the north wall. Blood on the wall above where Fisher landed indicated that his head struck the spot as the bullet passed into his left eye. Between Thompson's fire and the parties responding behind to him, the reporter felt that the "escape of Coy... was providential."

Simms declared, "on behalf of myself, Foster and Coy, I intend to ask the grand jury to prefer an indictment against us and to insist on it and have a trial … a trial by a jury and will abide by their decision … all of us mentioned in the coroner's verdict were acting entirely in defense of our lives. I have no desire to see this trouble come on and would have done, and believe I did, all that any man could have done to avert it, and so did Foster and Coy. The latter risked his own life by grabbing Thompson and … [I had nothing] … on earth against Fisher either and had a pleasant conversation with the latter a few days before the unfortunate tragedy." It seems strange that Simms somehow did not remember such a remarkable character as John King Fisher, but he explained, "I had met Fisher a long time ago when our relations were only formal but friendly, and had not seen him for some time until this occasion, when I met him on his way to Austin, when we both remarked that the appearance of each had almost passed out of the recollection of the other, such a long time having passed since our former meeting." With disbelief that he could ever have a conflict with Fisher, Simms stated, "King Fisher, I had no idea was ever to be confronted by me in a difficulty of any kind, and if I had been told so I should have scoffed at the idea, and while I was satisfied that Thompson might attack me on account of the Harris matter, I would not have had a quarrel with him, and had firmly resolved to avoid him as far as I could do so without deserting with cowardice my premises, and I even hoped firmly when we started to the stairs to go to the bar and drink, that all of his resentment had been buried." Simms stated since Thompson "and King Fisher had healed their differences ... I hoped that by going with him and drinking he would bury his animosity for me."[64]

Simms's perfectly scripted interview brought an instantaneous reply in the next issue of the *Statesman.* "In conversation ... with Billy Sims [*sic*] ... he stated that he desired to have the killing of the two men fully investigated by the grand jury, and that himself, Foster and Coy were ready to abide the result. Why Sims [*sic*] should make such a bluffing statement as this is not quite clear, unless it be born of a guilty conscience. Ben Thompson was certainly unpopular here, and was greatly feared, and under ordinary circumstances his death would not be much regretted, but the more the terrible affair is sifted the more convinced are the people becoming that the killing was simply a foul murder." Hinting that no one really believed Simms's story, the *Statesman* claimed, "It will require more than a hasty coroner's jury to remove this impression, and both Sims [*sic*] and his confederates have already realized a foretaste of this growing fact."[65]

On the same day Billy Simms met with the *Express* reporter, a *Statesman* correspondent interviewed two traveling businessmen, one a representative from a wholesale liquor house in Kentucky and the other a salesman from Chicago selling tobacco wholesale. Their names were Alex T. Raymond and John R. Sublett, and the reporter felt they appeared "like very candid and truthful men, and the story they give corresponds so closely with the post mortem examination that there can be no doubt but it is a correct statement of the tragedy." An old acquaintance of theirs, a native of San Antonio, insisted on showing Raymond and Sublett the more popular sights of the city. As with Thompson and Fisher, they took in Ada Gray's performance at the Turner Opera Hall. Next, they accepted their friend's proposal to take in the variety show on the

Main Plaza. This is how they came to be in the first-floor barroom of the Vaudeville as Thompson and Fisher strolled in. Their natural curiosity was aroused when their friend pointed out the notorious Ben Thompson, and said how it was strange he would be there since he had earlier killed Jack Harris, the one-time proprietor of the Vaudeville, and close friend of the current owners, in the very same building.

Their interest peaked, Raymond and Sublett, along with their unnamed friend, closely scrutinized the two deadly gunfighters. Both Thompson and Fisher looked sober, acted pleasantly and spoke normally in "an ordinary conversational tone of voice." Billy Simms emerged and greeted Thompson saying, "Hello, Ben; glad to see you." Thompson then invited Simms to shake hands with King Fisher. "Simms then said to Thompson: 'Ben, I am awful glad to see you here. Let us forget the past, and be friends in the future.' Thompson replied: 'I desire to be friends, and I have come here with my friend Fisher to talk the matter over, and have a perfect understanding. I have a perfect right to do that, have I not? Simms said: 'Yes, Ben, that is right, and I know we can all be friends.' Ben then said; I have nothing against you or Foster. I am not afraid of you. I am here surrounded by my friends, but I want to be friends with you, and I have come here to talk this over.' Simms replied: 'That is all right; come up stairs and see Foster.'"

Thompson and Fisher enjoyed one more drink and without Simms, they climbed the stairs to the theatre. Fascinated, Raymond, Sublett, and their unidentified friend followed and took seats near enough to overhear the conversation of the two desperadoes. With house policeman Coy accompanying him, Simms joined Thompson and Fisher, choosing to sit side by side next to them. Thompson ordered drinks for all from a waitress, and on her return teased her, saying he would not pay, but finally he pulled a roll of bills out of his pocket bragging, "I have lots of money. I have $20,000 in that roll," and paid the girl. Saying, "I thought you brought me up here to see Foster, Billy, don't you play any games on me. I did not come here for any fuss and I don't want any, but you must treat me fair." "I am, Ben," said Simms, "it's just as I told you, and I will go and tell Foster you want to have a friendly talk with him." King Fisher spoke up saying, "Yes, go and get him, I want to make [sure] you fellows are good friends before I leave. I have invited Thompson here; he did not want to come, but you are all friends of mine, and I want you to be friends. I told him to come and talk the matter over like gentlemen together, and bury the past; Thompson is willing to do it, and I want Foster to meet him half way." Simms agreed, "all right, I will go and get him." He returned with Foster and together they walked up to Ben Thompson who, seated, extended his right hand to shake with Foster. Fisher said, "I want you and Thompson to be friends. You are both friends to me and I want you to shake hands like gentlemen." Refusing, Foster stated, "I cannot shake hands with Ben Thompson, nor can he and I be friends, and I want him to keep out of my way." As Foster finished speaking, Simms and Coy quickly stepped away from Thompson and Fisher, as Foster also made a hasty move to the side. Suddenly springing up, Thompson and Fisher were hit with a volley of shots "fired from a box a little to the left and considerably above the doomed men. Neither Thompson nor Fisher drew their pistols, nor did they have time to do so." Falling on his right side, Thompson lay on the floor, and in the confusion, either Simms or Coy rushed up, took hold of Thompson's revolver, bent over him placing the muzzle by his ear, and fired. One man then fired two more shots into Thompson's head and body as the other man finished off Fisher in a similar manner.

Raymond and Sublett explained that, Foster reached for his self-cocking six-shooter when the volley downed the ill-fated men, but it caught, and he gave it an angry jerk discharging a bullet into his leg. Falling to the ground from his self-inflected wound, he cried out for help.

Raymond told the *Statesman* reporter, "It is monstrous the evidence those fellows gave at San Antonio, and the whole town seems to be in mortal fear of the tough crowd who have their headquarters at that den of infamy, the Vaudeville. Thompson, no doubt, was a bad man, but that crowd who murdered him ought to be hanged, for it was the coldest blooded murder ever committed."

When asked to provide the name of their San Antonio friend, Raymond and Sublett refused because they promised to keep his identity a secret. He feared the Vaudeville crowd, and thought, if he should be a witness against them, his life would be in jeopardy. Also, he was one of the leading gentlemen of the city, and did not want it known he visited such a den.

The newspaper proclaimed the interview was "given exactly as related to the STATESMAN representative," and corresponded with the facts shown by the autopsy. It concluded ominously that it was "no doubt as near the truth as the public will ever get."[66]

Recuperating at his home on Soledad Street, Joe Foster was very comfortable in his bed when a reporter from the *Express* called to request from him a "statement of facts" vis-à-vis the Vaudeville tragedy. On the night of the eleventh, Foster stated he was eager to see a new act, a Chinese dance. To get a view of the stage, he left the main gambling room and passed through the keno room, moving toward the gallery. It was then, he claimed, he overheard a conversation and learned that Ben was at the Turner Hall Opera House. Only a few moments later, he was told that Thompson was in his place of business, seated in the Vaudeville's gallery area. Foster said, not hearing a first name spoken, he imagined it must be Billy Thompson who came into his establishment. However, he soon saw it was not Billy; instead it was his brother Ben. Foster noticed his longtime friend John King Fisher was with

Ben, sitting together with the house policeman Coy and his business partner Billy Simms. Called to join them, Foster first refused Thompson's offer to take a drink, and then was adamant he would not shake Thompson's hand. Foster explained, "I told him again I would never place a straw in his way, and for God's sake to go away and let me alone." Insults flew out of Thompson's mouth as the melee began. Foster described how he was armed with a pistol in his waistband, and he looked for a chance to get it out and working. As Coy reached to take hold of Thompson's revolver, Ben jumped back and struck a chair behind him losing his balance and throwing up his arms to help regain it. This provided Foster the opportunity he wanted, but he admitted he had difficulty drawing his pistol. A moment or two passed before he managed to fire it at Thompson, striking him in the chest. The shock of the bullet knocked Thompson down. Because Coy and Fisher were struggling together, all three of them fell to the floor. Rushing up to Thompson, Foster pushed his pistol against Ben's left eye, and let loose with his second shot. It was then, Foster claimed, he received the wound in his leg. However he stated he had no idea who shot him. Falling to the floor, he grabbed one of the theatre benches and pulled himself up enough to level his weapon and fired his four remaining cartridges into the mass of struggling men before him.

"The trouble between Ben Thompson and myself is well known to all," Foster explained. He stated he knew the difficulty between them would end in the death of one or the other, and he was determined to bide his time and not make a fight until he was certain the odds were in his favor. Foster told the reporter, "That was the reason why I did not draw my pistol until Thompson backed against the chair." He did not learn of the death of John King Fisher until afterward. Foster expressed a sincere sorrow, for they were warm friends, and the reporter explained how years ago, when Fisher was incarcerated in the Bexar County jail, it was Foster who freely, at his own expense, furnished Fisher with everything he needed or wanted for his personal comfort, including all of his meals.[67]

With the publication of the Joe Foster interview, the *Express* claimed, "The question as to who killed Ben Thompson is forever at rest." In Austin, the *Statesman* disagreed, publishing a retort, "Foster has an interview in the San Antonio *Express*. He is certainly the boss liar, if correctly reported. He says 'he put his pistol against Thompson's breast and fired,' and the shock keeled Thompson and Fisher into the corner. At the post mortem examination not a scratch on Thompson's breast appeared. Foster ought to have read the results of that examination before he made his statement."[68]

Billy Thompson left Austin after his brother's funeral, and remained quiet and out of the public's eye for a handful of days. Perhaps he visited with his sister Mary Jane, husband Robert Gill, and their family in nearby Bastrop. Nine days after the assassination, on Thursday, March 20, he returned to Austin, but had little to say to the press about his brother's death. The next day, Billy boarded the train to San Antonio where he moved about the city "quietly and peacefully attending to and looking after his brother's business." He made no movement to have an encounter with Billy Simms or Jacob Coy. The reporter failed to comment on what Ben's unfinished business could be, perhaps debts needed to be paid or possibly Billy was seeking evidence, and was speaking to patrons of the Vaudeville the night his brother died.[69] While Billy was still in town, Joe Foster began to decline. At first, the doctors felt Foster, "was progressing very favorably with a fine prospect of recovery." However, his old war wound in the same leg began causing him pain. He then suffered a severe hemorrhage and another during the night. In the morning, he started bleeding a third time. In desperation, his doctors performed an operation to stem the hemorrhaging but they were unsuccessful. On Saturday morning at about 11 a. m., the news circulated through the streets of San Antonio that Joe Foster had finally succumbed to his wound and silently breathed his last. His funeral was scheduled for 3 p. m. the next day, Sunday, March 23.[70]

Foster's funeral was well attended with more than sixty carriages counted in the procession to the cemetery. Among the many mourners, were not just a large number of barflies, gamblers, and women of easy virtue, but also a number of San Antonio's most prominent citizens. Rev. John W. Neal, pastor of the First Presbyterian Church, officiated at the services, and similar to his sermon at the funeral of Jack Harris, Reverend Neal had another chance to convince the sinners within ear shot to turn away from the vices they so warmly embraced. The hearse headed the procession east down Commerce Street until it reached South Palmetto and the entrance to City Cemetery Number 1. Only a few feet away from Jack Harris's final resting place, a freshly dug grave awaited Foster's coffin. Financially, Foster was well off, having a half-interest in the theatre business of the Vaudeville. He also controlled the large faro room there, and along with valuable real estate, he owned several high-quality harness racing trotters. He left all this to his wife, Ida Ellen. Their long union did not produce any children. Unlike Harris, his grave was marked. Today an old obelisk, at least eight feet high looms over his grave providing little information on the risky life he led. Only the usual scant words about who lies below was carved into the stone, "Joseph C. Foster 1837 - 1884.[71]

The newspapers, in both San Antonio and Austin, printed what they knew of his life. In essence, Foster was a life-long professional gambler, having spent the last twenty-five years operating games and gambling houses in San Antonio. Not wanting to write ill of the dead, especially a fellow San Antonian, the *Express* lauded him as a "sober, peaceful, industrious and useful citizen." The *Light* admitted that Foster, while he had earned his livelihood in a business not recognized as legal or moral, he was a man well respected by all classes of society, and he remained above the usual addictions of people working in his trade. He did not indulge in either alcohol or tobacco. In Austin, the *Statesman* offered an altogether different assessment of the man. "It is our theory that a sober man who follows the line of life which poor Foster did is doubly damned. That a man cooly [*sic*] trades in the baser passions of men and panders to the lowest appetites ... for money and does it soberly, is almost incredible." To his friends, he was known to be a congenial companion. Yet, to those who knew him well, he had a deep vindictiveness in his nature. The editor of the *Statesman* believed he should have made a full and clear confession concerning the Thompson-Fisher murders instead of protecting the guilty with both his words and his silence.[72]

The fear that Billy Thompson would seek revenge was a topic that kept reappearing in the San Antonio newspapers. When the *Times* of Wednesday, March 27, published, "that Billy Thompson was in town bent on mischief," the report was discounted by both civic officials and the San Antonio police. Still, sensational rumors swirled regarding threats against the remaining Vaudeville crowd, especially Billy Simms.[73] In reality, Billy Thompson was nearly a hundred miles away in Bastrop enjoying the hospitality of his sister's family.[74] Reports kept appearing, here and there, in newspapers about the discovery of additional "disinterested" witnesses whose evidence could help bring the "Vaudeville murderers" to justice. The *Statesman* commented, "by the time they are tried no doubt the state will be in a position to rid the world of the rest of the worthless tribe who inhabit that strangely scented play house."[75] In the opinion of William M. Walton, "It is not to be hoped that the truth, surrounding this assassination of Thompson and Fisher, will ever be reached by judicial investigation or otherwise until some one or more of the cowardly conspirators—as will almost assuredly be the case—and each of them may live in daily fear and trembling, for such a result—turn traitor to the others, and divulge the machinery of the plot ... Murder will out."[76]

Friends of Ben Thompson retained attorneys to continue the investigation. Initially, they hoped that they would eventually "unravel the dark mystery of the Vaudeville tragedy" and see justice delivered to the guilty. One of Ben Thompson's relatives sent a telegram to San Antonio attorney T. T. Teel, Fisher's former defense attorney and Thompson's former legal adversary during the Harris trial, requesting that he travel to Austin and perhaps be enlisted to investigate the killing of Thompson and Fisher. However, William Walton, Thompson's friends and relatives, and the newspapers were eventually disappointed, because no county or city officials in San Antonio had any interest in pursuing the case. The astute editor of the *Brenham Banner* predicted, "In a few months people will cease talking about Ben Thompson and he will be forgotten." As time went by, the sensationalism of his death started to slowly ebb, and public interest in discovering who squeezed the fatal triggers was lost. The spring session of the Bexar County grand jury issued two hundred indictments, "some against many of the most prominent men of the city, including county and municipal officers." This was an attempt by honest officials to rid the city of gambling and prostitution, and to close establishments such as the notorious Vaudeville Theatre. However, the grand jury never investigated the Vaudeville killings and no one was ever indicted or placed on trial for their lives for the murders of Ben Thompson and John King Fisher.[77]

Some two years prior to Ben's death, Walton began to prepare a manuscript depicting the life and adventures of Ben Thompson. Walton acknowledged that he had been greatly aided by Ben and, "much of what was written was taken from his own lips." With Ben's passing, Walton intended on publishing quickly, and having a book available for sale by the end of April. Not everyone agreed

The repaired headstone of Ben Thompson as it appears today in Austin's Oakwood Cemetery. Strangely, the date of his birth is incorrect as he was born November 2, 1843. *Courtesy the Chuck Parsons Collection.*

with his plans. In nearby Luling, Texas, the editor of the *Newsboy & Signal* commented, "Instead of making Ben out a persecuted hero, generous and brave, but a little erratic, it is claimed that posterity would have been better off if the mantle of oblivion had been thrown over his grave, hiding alike his virtues and his faults." Others felt a Ben Thompson biography would prove to be a financial bonanza for the owners of the copyright. Walton arranged for the profits to go largely to benefit Ben's widow and children.[78]

Regardless of the varying opinions on whether or not Walton's biography of Ben Thompson should have been published, the *Statesman* acknowledged, "The headlines of the Texas papers on the Thompson killing would make a rare literary curiosity for a future generation. Who will undertake the task of their collection?"[79] (See Appendix F)

The March 29, 1884, issue of the *National Police Gazette*, self-proclaimed as America's leading illustrated sporting journal, remembered Ben Thompson by publishing both an article and illustrations depicting his "final exit." Based on Joe Foster's deathbed account, the artist inaccurately portrayed Ben's "last act of a fierce and desperate career" at the Vaudeville Theatre, "fighting to the end with his six-shooter as an antagonist's bullets were about to deliver their fatal blows." The *Statesman*, his hometown paper, in summation wrote, "The green curtain has dropped, the last scene in the tragedy has been played," and Ben Thompson "has made his last salute to the great audience before whom he appeared." Laid in his grave, Ben "with his faults and follies, his friendship and his charity, his recklessness, and his daring, his courtesy and his affability" went forward to "meet the mysteries of the unknown beyond."[80]

Chapter 17

EPILOGUE

Four days after the Vaudeville tragedy, the San Antonio *Express* said of John King Fisher, "He was known to have been a desperate man and free with his six-shooter, and was in the company of a man known to be bent on shedding blood. A moment's hesitation to see if Fisher intended evil might have cost the man who shot him his life. Under such circumstances, would any friend of King Fisher have hesitated[?]" Sarah Vivian-Fisher and her three small daughters went to live with her father. She would grow old having never remarried, and at the age of ninety, Sarah passed away on August 10, 1946.

The citizens of Uvalde were upset by the San Antonio *Express* and its description of Fisher's bloody history and dark past, and they sent a defense of their dead deputy sheriff's character. It stated in part, "In justice to the dead and in justice to his family we ask that this correction ... be made. While we do not propose to ... enter into a discussion of the early life of J. K. Fisher ... We feel that we do not exaggerate when we assert that King Fisher has accomplished as much for law and order within the last two and a half years as any man in Western Texas ... Instead of the 'bravado, desperado and terror' ... his character and deportment have been diametrically the opposite. [He was] kind, courteous, affable and generous, always ready and willing to ferret out crime and bring the criminals to justice." This declaration came with the signatures of two hundred and seventy-one citizens, including many of the most prominent individuals Uvalde County had to offer.[1]

Though not everyone was pleased with Fisher's performance as a lawman. Mrs. Hannehan, the grieving mother of the stagecoach robber who resisted arrest and was subsequently gun downed by Fisher, would travel for years to the cemetery in Uvalde on the anniversary of her son's death. There she would gather brush and build a fire on Fisher's grave, and as the kindling burned higher and hotter, she would dance around the flames with "devilish glee."[2]

Many decades later, Fisher's grave was almost lost to memory until Mrs. Florence Kellogg, Fisher's oldest daughter, was called on to help find and mark her father's resting place. About a decade later, in October of 1959, the city of Uvalde planned a new road through that original burial ground in order to ease the flow of traffic. The city fathers decided to move twenty known graves, and establish a "Pioneer" cemetery nearby. After seventy-five years, Fisher's casket was brought to the surface, and found to be in excellent condition. Several of his descendants attended his reinternment, and found their desire to look through the "removable window ... at the top of the casket" irresistible. They discovered Fisher's "body to be in a remarkable state of preservation." The original teardrop shaped cast iron coffin with ornamental brass handles was set inside a new steel casket. His resting place was moved east about half a block from the original gravesite. The gunfighter now lies under the shade of a large pecan tree and a wrought iron fence surrounds his grave. His flat granite marker stands alone and simply reads, "John King Fisher 1856–1884."[3]

Two Mexican men were seen hanging around the home of Jacobo Coy during the afternoon of Thursday, March 13. Two city policemen, officers Rife and Brown,[4] informed City Marshal

Shardein of their suspicions concerning the two men's actions. At once Shardein went in search of the suspects and found them relaxing at the Washington Saloon. He quietly took them into custody after searching them and finding them to be unarmed. One was identified as Cecelio Charo, a deputy sheriff of LaSalle County and also a Texas Ranger serving under a staunch and very warm friend of John King Fisher, Captain Joseph Shely. The second man was named Tijerina and was not known in San Antonio.[5] Charo claimed he was in town with Tijerina because they were summoned to serve as witnesses at the Federal court, which was in session. United States Marshal Hal Gosling vouched for their story and acknowledged he was in possession of Charo's revolver, which had been left with the marshal beforehand. When interviewed by the reporter for the *Express*, Antonio Paulino Coy, Jacobo's brother and a deputy sheriff of Neuces County, stated he knew Charo to be "a desperate and unscrupulous character, and capable of doing any act for a small sum of money."

The reporter continued his investigation at the Vaudeville Theatre, where he found and spoke with Jacobo Coy. Coy "unhesitatingly told the reporter that he believed a conspiracy had been formed to take his life." He declined to state with positive knowledge who exactly was behind the plans to have him murdered but he did point out how Captain Joe Shely had "openly declared that the killing of King Fisher was a cold-blooded murder." Captain Shely was not in San Antonio when Charo and Tijerina were arrested, and his friends vowed Shely would never resort to paying assassins in his search for vengeance. As for Coy, he declared to the reporter that he was not afraid of any conspiracy to harm him and that the night Thompson and Fisher died he "had only done his duty in attempting to preserve the peace."[6]

Captain Shely was furious with Coy's inference and demanded the affair be fully investigated. In response, Jacobo Coy filed an affidavit charging Charo and Tijerina with conspiring to commit murder. Before a full investigation could take place, the county court would have to wait while the two prisoners were placed in the hands of Marshal Gosling so they could fulfill their summons and testify in the United States Court. Once this obligation was satisfied on Monday, March 18, the grand jury listened to witnesses. Two well-known lawmen, C. B. McKinney and Dario Gonzales, testified on behalf of the two suspects and assured the court of their good character. McKinney was a former captain of the Texas Rangers and currently was serving as sheriff of LaSalle County. Gonzales was the sheriff of Webb County and also protected John King Fisher from a Laredo lynch mob in 1877. Their words carried great weight and the grand jury concluded there was no foundation in fact for the charge brought against Charo and Tijerina. They were subsequently freed from custody.[7]

Kansas historian Floyd Benjamin Streeter, the second biographer of Ben Thompson, wrote that Billy Simms helped to financially support Jacob Coy until Coy's death twenty-one years after the bloodbath at the Vaudeville Theatre. While it confirms nothing, Coy is listed in the San Antonio City Directory of 1889–1890 as a neighbor of Simms. Simms resided at 522 Buena Vista while Coy was living a few doors down the street at number 510. The directory, however, did not state the profession or business Coy was currently involved in. It is believed he continued working as a special policeman even though the old wound he received in his right calf during the Vaudeville affray had partially crippled him. He walked with a limp for the rest of his life. Jacobo Coy died at the age of sixty-four on August 17, 1905, and is buried in San Antonio's San Fernando Cemetery No. 1.[8]

Six weeks after the tragedy at the Vaudeville, a friend of Fisher's from Eagle Pass arrived at the Vaudeville's first floor bar room intoxicated and apparently bent on revenge. His name was

Dick Lombard, and he was an attorney and former newspaperman. Lombard loudly announced to all in the house that the "killing of the best friend he ever had" was a cowardly and cold-blooded murder. When informed of the accusations, a sober Billy Simms confronted Lombard, who pulled a double-action revolver. Lombard snapped off one shot and hit nothing but the wall on the far end of the room. He then turned tail and dashed out the front door. Simms pursued Lombard as he scurried away to the front of the bookstore one door to the west of the Vaudeville. Simms fired off three shots that all missed Lombard, his intended target. Two bullets struck a tin water downspout and created a hole, while the third chipped away at the stone casing supporting the bookshop's large display window. The gunfire brought out an alert police officer who grabbed hold of Simms, but both Lombard and Simms managed to discharge one more shot at each other. Luckily Lombard's bullet flew harmlessly across the plaza. Simms's fourth and final shot struck the door casing around the entrance to the book store. The bouncing slug grazed Lombard's forearm and superficially wounded him. Two other policemen arrived, and the gunfight, if you could call it that, was over. The fact that no innocent bystander was hurt defied most odds.[9] This event gave credence to the belief that Billy Simms simply did not possess the marksmanship that had recently been credited to him.

Refusing to believe it was Simms who gunned down Thompson, R. P. Smyth, captain of the Austin Grays drill team, avowed, "No one who knew Billy Sims [*sic*] would believe for a moment that Billy would stand up to a pistol fight with Ben Thompson."[10] The judgement of several Texas rangers who knew both Ben Thompson and John King Fisher was similar. Born and raised in Austin, James B. Gillett opined, "While I do not think Billy Sims [*sic*] was afraid of anyone, he knew he was no match for Ben Thompson in a pistol duel and few men that ever lived were."[11] George Durham asserted,

"Billy Simms, credited with the killing, wouldn't have lasted one small fraction of a second before King Fisher."[12]

Eager to rid himself of the Vaudeville, Simms openly proclaimed he wished to divest himself of the lease and the fixtures comprising the barroom and theatre. On July 24, an investor named John Strappenbeck paid Simms $1,753.25 for the lease of the entire building. A month later, the *Express* informed its readership that the site had been released to Mr. R. Bianchini. His intentions were to open a dining hall and a first-class restaurant. Shortly after, other legitimate businesses took spaces in the building. The bloody days of the Vaudeville as a theatre, saloon, and gambling hall had ended.[13]

When Simms rid himself of the notorious Vaudeville Theatre, the building that housed it did not survive for long. At 2:20 a.m. on March 3, 1886, a fire started in the rear of the fifty-year-old, two-story adobe structure. Patrolling police officers sounded the alarm and eventually three fire companies responded. Many volunteers joined them in fighting the blaze. However, once a stored can of kerosene exploded, the blaze became an inferno that quickly raged out of control. At that point, all efforts had to be focused on carrying out as much of the contents of the businesses housed inside, and even more importantly, preventing the flames from affecting the other establishments nearby. The fire was finally put out at nine in the morning, almost seven hours after its discovery. The ruins of the charred adobe walls were all that remained, and the building was declared a total loss. On the same day the old Vaudeville Theatre burned, the *Express* editor wrote in his evening edition, "Thus perished the walls that once resounded to the husky songs of threadbare divas, the guffaws of cowboys out for an evening, the rattle of dice, and the roar of gunfire."[14]

With the exception of the coroner's hearing, Billy Simms never entered another courtroom that was concerned with the murders of Thompson and Fisher. For his future, he decided he would continue in the profession of providing adult entertainment for public consumption. For the next several decades, Simms ran various enterprises, both with and without business partners. Among the places he either owned outright, or a portion thereof, were the Fashion Theatre on Military Plaza, the Pickwick Saloon and Restaurant, the Crystal Saloon on Commerce Street not far from where the Vaudeville once sat, and a gambling hall called the Crystal Turf Exchange.[15] His success in business made Billy Simms a very wealthy man, and by the time of his death, wise investments in commercial and residential real estate had amassed him a fortune worth more than $200,000. Throughout his life, Simms demonstrated that generosity was one of his greater virtues. He shared his good fortune and made large contributions to various charities. It was later reported that few knew the extent of his philanthropic pursuits.[16]

On Saturday night, January 9, 1909, Simms was admitted to Santa Rosa Hospital. He had been complaining of stomach pain for several days prior. The attending doctors diagnosed Simms with an appendicitis attack, and recommended immediate surgery. It was initially believed he would survive the operation, but his surgeons were mistaken. His malady had progressed too far, and in relatively short order, all hope for recovery was lost. Billy Simms died before dawn on January 10, and his funeral rites took place that same day. In a little more than a month, he would have celebrated his fifty-third birthday. One of the longest funeral processions ever seen in San Antonio at that time followed Simms's casket down Commerce Avenue to the Improved Order of Redmen Cemetery where he was laid to rest.[17]

Nearly one hundred years after Jack Harris was buried, a small group of San Antonians known as the "Do-Nothing Gang" discovered that his friends and business partners left his grave unmarked and forgotten. The "Do-nothing Gang," led by Alice Evert and Gary Yantis, decided to honor Jack Harris's eventful life and place a fitting memorial over his grave. Along with help from business sponsors and several local publications, a headstone was purchased. On the weekend of July 10 and 11, 1982, along with a re-enactment of the shooting which took his life, a wake, parade, and gravesite funeral was held, including a eulogy performed by the Mayor of San Antonio Henry G. Cisneros. When the weekend-long event came to an end, both a new headstone and a newly erected historical marker remembered the life and death of Jack Harris (see Appendix E).[18]

Ben Thompson's friend, trusted legal counsel, and first biographer, Major William Martin "Buck" Walton would live another thirty-one years after Thompson's death. Walton died of heart failure on July 17, 1915, at the age of eighty-three. He was buried in the family plot underneath an impressive obelisk in the "Old Grounds" of Oakwood Cemetery, not far from Ben Thompson's final resting place.[19]

Like the Thompson brothers, William Walton had his demons, and he was known to be a more than frequent visitor to the barrooms of Austin. The city marshal's Record of Arrests book is sprinkled with entries documenting his overindulgence, as well as the incidents arising from it.[20] In 1892, he admitted that, "I have for over twenty years, to my own great injury and greater unhappiness of others, been addicted to the use of alcoholic stimulates, often to excess." Unlike Ben Thompson, Walton overcame his problem and continued to have a very successful law career. A career so brilliant that the Travis County Bar Association issued a series of resolutions upon Walton's death that stated, in part, "he was a great criminal lawyer is but to disparage his ability in all the other branches of the law. More than one Justice on the Supreme Bench has said that he was the greatest 'all round' lawyer he ever came in contact with. He practiced in literally all the courts, from the lowest to the highest. As an advocate before a court or jury he had few equals. His clear, incisive and logical mind and discriminating insight into the character of men made him well-nigh invincible as a lawyer." Walton, himself, wrote a concise assessment of his legal skills and areas of specialization. "[M]y own particular sphere was confined to criminal law and land law, especially to Mexican land law. My own personal practice was very heavy. I suppose no lawyer in Texas or in the South has defended more men charged with murder than I have ... Success usually attended me. I do not say this in vain glory but state it because it is the simple truth." It was Ben Thompson's very good fortune to have a legal mind as splendid as Walton's on hand to repeatedly, and successfully, defend him from charges of murder.[21]

A mere six weeks after the death of Ben Thompson, his biography, authored by William Walton, was advertised for sale in newspapers across the state. The printer, Edwards & Church of Austin, offered a copy by return mail for the price of only fifty cents.

The *Life and Adventures of Ben Thompson, The Famous Texan. Including a detailed and authentic statement of his birth, history and adventures, by one who has known him since a child* was described in one advertisement as "the most interesting biography ever published" and by another as "the story of Ben's life in an interesting and exciting manner, but the book is free from immorality and the sickening blood and thunder style that generally characterizes works of a similar nature. A person interested in Thompson can read the book without contamination, a quality which will insure its success, if that were ever problematical."[22]

Other comments were not as complimentary, "The Lockhart *Register* remarks: The Life of Ben Thompson, written by Major Walton, of Austin, is finding ready sale in this city. In fact, the demand is great. It is strange, in this age of literature, that people cannot find better reading material to supply their homes with.

No wonder lawlessness prevails to such an extent in our country, when the minds of youth are poisoned by such vicious literature. If Ben Thompson had been a man noted for his morality and piety, a few copies of his history would have satisfied the demand."[23]

More than a century later it is not known how well the book sold, but there is an indication it was not the success it was predicted to be. Today an Edwards & Church, 1884 First Edition is very scarce, and if one can be found, experts value the book at $6,000 plus or minus 20% depending on its condition.[24]

In the rush to get to the printer, Walton's manuscript was crammed full of factual mistakes. His verbose, nineteenth century writing style, though common for its time, failed to create a best-seller and thus failed to achieve lasting fame for its subject.[25]

Eventually, even "Buck" Walton soured and abandoned promoting Ben Thompson's life story. Shortly before his own death, Walton would write, "The only fighting that we had then was with pistols and many men went down not to get up again. But the names of the gamblers and their acts, their many exploits, mostly among themselves, have gone into the quiet of forgetfulness, and it is best to let them rest there. The gambler, as a distinctive trait, has left Austin. Let them go. I will not recall them—not even their memories." Thompson's legacy had lost its most important advocate.[26]

Two of Ben Thompson's most famous friends lived long into the Twentieth Century. The world-renowned showman William Frederick "Buffalo Bill" Cody rode into eternity at his sister's home in Denver, Colorado, six weeks shy of his seventy-first birthday. Cody's sister selected the exact place where he is buried atop Lookout Mountain. William Barclay "Bat" Masterson, the frontiersman turned Eastern newspaper columnist, died at his desk at the New York *Morning Telegraph* at the age of sixty-seven. He is buried in Woodlawn Cemetery in the Bronx, New York. In their own way, both the showman and the sporting man remembered

Ben Thompson forever, one through his story telling and the other with his writing ability.

Buffalo Bill Cody and Ben Thompson enjoyed a strong friendship. However, one has to ponder the questions which are now unanswerable. Why didn't the famous entertainer offer Ben Thompson a place in his troupe? And if Cody did offer, why did Thompson refuse? Later one of Cody's most popular acts was a shooting exhibition by Annie Oakley, one of the world's most famous experts in the handling of firearms. Near the end of her career, she gave an assessment of who were the finest marksmen in the world. "After traveling through fourteen countries, meeting and competing with the best marksman … I can safely say America leads the world in shooting … [however] … were we to believe all we read and hear, the cowboy and the "bad man" of the West were the greatest revolver shots in America. This, however, is far from being true. I can find more and better revolver shots right in New York [City] than any other place I know of. The cowboy and bad man have had their day, but when they were a plenty they were very much over-rated. There were … exceptions to this, however, one of whom was Ben Thompson, a Texan. He was an exceptionally fine shot, and so quick was he with the revolver that his opponent had little if any chance." Since Oakley never saw Thompson shoot, she must have learned of his skill with a pistol from the showman who for years witnessed the finest marksman in the world perform and compete. It could only have been Ben Thompson's good friend, Buffalo Bill Cody.[27]

Arguably "Bat" Masterson could be considered the most successful of all the men who participated in the "sporting life" of the nineteenth century. Masterson lived a long and healthy life, survived many exploits and dangers, and while he never attained great wealth, he did attain the friendship of many of the most prominent men of the times, including that of President Theodore Roosevelt. "Bat" was born from humble origins, and he wisely changed careers as the world changed around him. He moved from being a buffalo hunter, Indian fighter, sheriff, hired gun, gambler, bodyguard, and deputy United States marshal to ultimately becoming a bona-fide member of the press. Approached by his friend, journalist Alfred Henry Lewis, Masterson agreed to write a series of portraits of exceptional shootists with whom he was acquainted during his years west of the Mississippi River. Entitled "*Famous Gunfighters of the Western Frontier,*" published in *Human Life* magazine, Masterson's work appeared in installments beginning with Ben Thompson in January 1907. In his preamble, Masterson explained to his readers the indispensable triumvirate essential to success in a gunfight, "Any man who does not possess courage, proficiency in the use of fire-arms, and deliberation had better make up his mind at the beginning to settle his personal differences in some other manner than by an appeal to the pistol." In chronicling his friend's life, Masterson expressed his opinion of the man and showed how Ben Thompson conducted himself in deadly affrays.[28]

> Ben Thompson was a remarkable man in many ways and it is very doubtful if in his time there was another man living who equaled him with the pistol in a life and death struggle. Thompson in the first place possessed a much higher order of intelligence than the average 'gun fighter' or man killer of his time.
>
> He was more resourceful and a better general under trying conditions than any of that great army of desperate men who flourished on our frontier thirty years ago. He was absolutely without fear and his nerves were those of the finest steel. He shot at an adversary with the same precision and deliberation than he shot at a target. He was a past master in the use of the pistol and his aim was as true as his nerves were strong and steady. He had during his career more deadly encounters with the pistol than any man living and won out in every single instance.
>
> The very name of Ben Thompson was enough to cause the general run of 'man killers,' even those who had never seen

> him, to seek safety in instant flight. Thompson killed many men during his career, but always in an open and manly way. He scorned the man who was known to have committed murder, and looked with contempt on the man who sought for unfair advantages in a fight.
>
> The men whom he shot and killed were without exception men who had tried to kill him; and an unarmed man or one who was known to be a non-combatant, was far safer in his company than he would be right here on Broadway at this time. He was what could be properly termed a thoroughly game man, and like all men of that sort never committed murder ...
>
> Such men as 'Wild Bill' Hickok, Wyatt Earp, Billy Tilghman, Charley Bassett, Luke Short, Clay Addison, Joe Lowe, and Jim Curry were all men with nerves of steel who had often been put to the test—any one of whom would not have hesitated a moment to put up his life as the stake to be played for. Those men, all of them, lived and played their part and played it exceedingly well on the lurid edge of our Western frontier at the time Ben Thompson was playing his, and is safe to assume that not one of them would have declined the gage of battle with him had he flung it down to any one of their number.
>
> In making this admission, however, I am constrained to say that little doubt exists in my mind but that Thompson would have returned the winner of the contest. Ben Thompson was murdered along with his personal friend, King Fisher, in a vaudeville theatre in San Antonio, Texas, in March 1884.
>
> Both he and King Fisher were killed from ambush by a number of persons ... and neither ever knew what happened ... It was a cold-blooded, cruel and premeditated murder, for which no one was ever punished by law.[29]

Ben Thompson died without a Last Will and Testament, and his estate was placed into the care of the Travis County Probate Court.[30] His family very often lived on a financial edge, supplementing income when luck turned against Ben with the help of temporary loans secured by their personal items from Leonard Eck's Pawn Shop, on Pecan Street (6th Street). With the family belongings tied up in probate court, the use of a pawnbroker was no longer a viable option. As provided by law, Ben's widow Catherine asked the court to issue to her a monetary stipend to help support both her and her children. In August, five months after Ben's death, Royal B. Underhill, the court appointed administrator of Ben's estate, succeeded in having a $600 allowance granted to Mrs. Catherine (Kate) Thompson to cover the family's first year of support. As the probate proceedings lingered on, Catherine, again in need of money, was helped in late February 1885 when her husband's jewelry, a "solitaire ring and cluster scarf pin and ring," was raffled off for her benefit.[31]

The probate records provide a detailed list of the Thompson family homestead, including additional real estate holdings in the towns of Austin, Bastrop, and Mobeetie, shares of stock in a Savings & Loan Association, and an equal ownership share in a partnership with Robert Holman and Benjamin F. Marshall running the gambling hall above the Iron Front Saloon. The long list of belongings also included household furniture and personal property, however no firearms are to be found in the probate records. According to oral family history, Ben Thompson's weapons were given away to family members and friends in order to avoid probate taxes. Ben's double-barrel shotgun, manufactured by James Braddell & Sons of Belfast, Ireland, was presented to their young neighbor, Frank Hamer, the future legendary Texas Ranger and detective who would track down and end the infamous careers of depression era robbers and murderers Bonnie and Clyde.[32]

In July 1887, Ben and Kate's home on University Avenue was finally sold. After the mortgage was satisfied, the remaining proceeds enabled Kate to continue covering her living expenses. She remained in Austin for at least another five years after her husband's death. The city directory last listed her name in their 1889 - 1890 publication.[33] Exactly what became of Ben's wife remains a mystery. One unlikely story comes from Mrs. Jennie Stewart, the daughter of pawnbroker Leonard Eck, who after almost seventy years, recalled how Kate sold a portion of her furniture, and with the little bit of cash she received, moved to Virginia.[34] No facts support this theory.

In a brief, simple sworn statement containing few details, Kate's younger sister, Sarah, claimed Kate married a second time and her husband's name was Baker. Ben's sister, Mary Jane confirmed Sarah's story decades later. She stated Kate did marry a man named Baker, and with her new husband, moved to Paris, Texas. The couple had no children together, and by 1894, Kate had passed away from an unknown malady. Intensive research has been unable to discover the date of her passing, the cause of her death, or the location of her gravesite.[35]

Kate's troublemaking younger brother, James Moore, like his brother-in-law Ben Thompson, originally entered the printer's trade before he ultimately became a professional gambler and lived the life of a sporting man. His continuous arrests for gaming, assault, intoxication, and disorderly conduct implicate a pattern of unmanageable habits that James never successfully quelled.[36] He prospered for years as a gambler and was once reputedly worth $40,000, though this was most likely an exaggeration. Moore's long addiction to cocaine and alcohol irrevocably robbed him of his prosperity and his health, and at the age of fifty-seven, he was seriously ill, deeply dependent on substances, and financially broke. He was admitted to Austin's Insane Asylum where he briefly rallied thanks to the excellent care he received at the institution, but complete recovery was beyond hope. He relapsed and was taken to the city hospital where he died on Friday, June 9, 1905. His funeral was held the same day at Weed Undertaking Parlors. James Moore's remains were buried the next day in an unmarked grave in the pauper grounds of Oakwood Cemetery. The cemetery's administration has no record of his grave's exact location.[37]

Ben and Billy Thompson's two younger sisters married fine, respectable law-abiding men, had children, and lived long, productive lives. Both of their husbands earned their livelihood as merchants operating dry goods stores.

The youngest sister, Frances "Fannie" Thompson, married Leopold Rudolph Fink and their union produced three children, two sons, and a daughter. In 1918, Leo Fink passed away and Fannie spent the next thirty-six years as a widow. She died on March 3, 1954, in Palestine, Texas, shortly before her ninety-fifth birthday. Fannie often referred to her older brothers, Ben and Billy, as the "Bad Boys."[38]

Robert Gill, Mary Jane's husband, was always there to help his brothers-in-law and was instrumental in selecting the attorneys that successfully defended Billy in Ellsworth, Kansas. When Ben faced a jury for the Harris killing, Gill again was at the forefront in supporting his brother-in-law. Mary Jane and Robert had three sons and one daughter. Gill died on June 15, 1918. Mary Jane followed him on December 1, 1940, and was laid next to her husband of fifty-one years. They rest in Bastrop's Fairview Cemetery.

Kate Thompson struggled emotionally and financially after Ben's death, so the Gills helped to care for Katie. They cared so much they ensured Katie's future by helping her to attend Cedar Bluff Female College of Woodburn, Kentucky, during the late 1880s. Then on January 30, 1895, Kathryn Florence "Katie" Thompson married Bastrop County Judge Joseph Barton Price. Judge Price served the people of the county for twenty-five years, and Katie gave birth to a son. Judge Price died of a stroke on February 27, 1934, and Katie followed him on September 19, 1938.[39]

The ladies of the Thompson family were ashamed of the life their brothers chose to live, and they never spoke of Ben and Billy's exploits inside or outside of the family. During the decades-long fascination the media and public had with America's Wild West, the Thompson family shunned any newspapermen, researchers, or writers who showed up at their doorstep looking for information about the "Bad Boys." Shortly before her death, Katie was fearful of how her father would be portrayed in books and film, so she asked her son to burn what memorabilia, letters, and photographs of her father and Uncle Billy she still had in her possession. He complied with her wish.[40]

Ben Thompson was always chasing that next moment of exhilaration, but his dependency on gambling did not blind him from its destructiveness. Even though he refused to shed the life of a sporting man, Ben declared, "so help me God, I never have and never will countenance and assist, encourage, influence any boy, youth or man to engage in the hell-earning business." Despite this determination, and though he asserted, "I have a son, and I had rather follow him to the grave than see him contact the habit of gambling," Ben tried to provide his son with a private education that would prepare him for a bright, respectable future, but he failed in his endeavor to prevent his boy from following his example.[41] Ben Jr. was fifteen when his father was gunned down at the Vaudeville Theatre, and he was under the tutelage of his Uncle Billy before his twentieth birthday. Old newspaper records provide a small glimpse at Ben Jr.'s sporting life. Billy and his nephew were at the Park Variety Theatre together in the Texas border town of Laredo in February 1888. Ben Jr. was working there as a bartender when he mishandled his revolver while removing cartridges and accidently discharged the weapon. The bullet found the thigh of the leader of the theatre's orchestra, inflicting a painful, but not life-threatening wound.[42] They soon left Laredo for San Antonio, where on March 21, it was reported they were staying in the fast side of town at the St. Leonard Hotel on Main Plaza. A local newspaper noted the arrival of the brother and son of the dead Austin desperado.[43] No confrontation was ever recorded between them and Billy Simms.

Over the years, Billy Thompson and his nephew often visited their relatives in Bastrop and Austin as they moved about the gambling circuit.[44] During the early days of 1892, Billy and Ben Jr. were in Houston. The Wells Fargo Office there was robbed during the night of January 4-5. Fred Dodge, an investigator for Wells Fargo, was called upon to work the case, and within two or three days, he "knew all the men who were in on the robbery. I had several pretty good friends among the Gamblers in Houston—men whom I had known in the Tombstone days. Among whom was Billy Thompson, Brother of Ben Thompson, and from Billy I got my first tip." Two other professional gamblers also aided Dodge in gathering information, and they confirmed the stolen money was soon lost over the Houston faro tables during the first couple of nights after the robbery. More and more, Houston became Billy Thompson's favorite haunt throughout his final years.[45]

By the late fall of 1892, Ben Jr. and his uncle's wanderings landed them in the Pecos River Valley of southeastern New Mexico Territory. They were attracted to a boomtown named Eddy and a wild, unsavory offshoot sprouting up outside of Eddy's jurisdiction to avoid any rule of law, otherwise known as Phenix, or "Jagville." Mostly inhabited by saloon men, ladies of the demimonde and their pimps, gamblers and outlaws of various origins, Phenix, was for a few short years one of the most hell-raising places along the Mexican/United States border.[46] Harry A. Bennett opened the first barroom in Phenix in the spring of 1892, and many others soon followed. Two of Eddy's newspapers, the *County Citizen* and the *Current*, took notice of the two Thompsons and reported they were working at Bennett's Legal Tender. They continued to be residents living in Phenix as late as the spring of 1893.[47]

Soon Ben Thompson Jr.'s name appeared in the newspapers again, though this time it would be to announce his death. On September 9, 1893, at the age of twenty-four, he apparently succumbed to consumption, a disease quite common to the dissipated existence of members of the sporting crowd. His death occurred at 12:30 in the afternoon at his Aunt Sarah's home in Austin, on the corner of San Jacinto and Nineteenth streets. The house was one of his boyhood homes. His funeral was held in the home where he died the following afternoon, and he was laid to rest near his father in the Oakwood Cemetery family plot. His grave remains unmarked.[48]

Billy Thompson's eventual fate was long unsubstantiated. Wild rumors swarmed about Billy during his life, and it is no surprise rumors surround his death. The most popular one alleges he became embroiled in a difficulty at a fandango south of the border in Nuevo Laredo. Two Mexicans trailed Billy back across the Rio Grande, following him first through Laredo and then southeast on the old military road leading to nearby Zapata County. On this lonely stretch, Billy reined in his horse and confronted the Mexicans. Gunfire quickly commenced and in the wild shoot-out, the Mexicans were soon stretched out in the road dead. Billy, too, slipped out of his saddle and succumbed to his wounds. It would have been a fitting end for such a reckless life, but not a word of the above story is true.[49]

Bill Tucker's shotgun blast, and years of heavy drinking had shattered his health, and he never again showed the violent streak so prevalent in his youth. He most likely learned a lesson from his older brother's sudden death and he decided to put his days of getting into serious trouble behind him.

Billy showed interest in Houston as early as July 1884.[50] Houston, and occasionally Galveston, became his home during his final years. He continued on as a gambler, unable to do anything else for a livelihood. About a year before he died, he tried his luck at Cripple Creek, Colorado but he soon returned to Texas. During the late summer of 1897, Billy was sick and ailing from an abscess in his stomach, and he was taken to a Catholic hospital in Houston named Saint Joseph's. The hospital occupied an entire city block at 1910 Crawford Street and was staffed by twenty-five Sisters of Charity of the Incarnate Word. The facility offered the most modern comforts: steam heat, electric lights, hot running water, and large well-ventilated rooms. Even with this care, Billy's end came quickly. He died on Monday afternoon, September 6, at the age of fifty-two. Robert and Mary Jane Gill were notified by telegram of his passing. Robert telephoned requesting his remains be shipped to Bastrop for burial, and on Tuesday afternoon, his pallbearers, family, and friends met Billy's coffin at the town's railroad depot. His wake took place at the Gill's home at 709 Pecan Street and his funeral services were directed by Reverend D. H. Hotchkiss of the Bastrop Methodist Church. A long cortege of friends and relatives followed the hearse to Fairview Cemetery where his body was consigned to the earth in the Gill family plot. His exact gravesite is in Section C, Row 1, Number 19.[51]

Perhaps out of respect for his younger sisters, the Bastrop *Advertiser* made no mention of his violent past. In addition, the *Advertiser* wrote nothing of Billy ever marrying or having a family. If he did father any children, they never knew enough about where they came from to answer to the name of Thompson.[52] Surprisingly, the Austin *Statesman* took no notice of his passing, but other Texas newspapers drew attention to Billy's end. Remembering him with a memory far fonder then the facts suggest, the San Antonio *Express* correctly called Billy a "tough proposition" and wrote "though no means recognized as hard a citizen as his elder brother, [he] was still a man who carried half a dozen notches on his gun. His career as a gambler is hard to follow, it was one of travel and adventure. He had a roving spirit and, in his ramblings, traveled from the California slopes to the Mississippi river. Those were wild days, and a rover must have met with many thrilling incidents." The *Express* explained how Billy could be merciful. "He could have had a much longer record as a killer than he achieved, if he so desired as several men tried him out at different times, but were allowed to go after Thompson could have killed them." The Houston *Post* told its readers, "He was a man of nerve and courage, generous and true to a friend and unlike his brother, he was even forgiving of an enemy."[53]

Esteemed historian Joseph G. Rosa and expert on western gunfighters expressed his thoughts on Billy Thompson, "Mean, vicious, vindictive and totally unpredictable, Billy's survival was remarkable."[54] His skill in dodging the law for so many years and his ability to escape from custody at least four times, was indeed, remarkable. Billy Thompson must have also had a charming nature too. His avoidance of a hangman's noose, or a bullet in the back, may have been due to his popularity among a large portion of his fellow sports. He received their assistance in tight situations many times. How else could Billy have survived so many tribulations only to die with his boots off in a nice, clean hospital bed? His older brother's unrelenting love and assistance was a strong factor in his survival, and perhaps a tremendous quantity of luck must have been part of it too.

The editor of the *Statesman* acknowledged this maxim two days after Thompson and Fisher were murdered, "It is he who is in danger when he causes others to fear him ... Had their ... reputations not been so bloody; had there been less fear of them, they had not died thus."[55] Ben moved himself outside the protection of the law with his ceaseless misbehavior and growing unpopularity during the early months of 1884. His enemies at the Vaudeville knew that if Thompson came to his end under almost any circumstance no law enforcement officials would pursue those responsible for his death. Such was his decline, and Joseph Foster appears to have attempted to act on this opportunity when he invited Ben in a failed design to get him to visit the Vaudeville Theatre the week before Thompson went there with King Fisher. When Thompson did arrive in San Antonio, Simms and Foster knew of it and wisely used the time gained by the warning to make the arrangements necessary to protect themselves with all of the advantages they could devise. Thompson's autopsy confirmed what many professed to believe, that he was shot down by assassins he never saw. In Walton's final chapter of his Ben Thompson biography, he failed to name the gunmen who murdered Thompson, and at the same time the many newspaper reporters on the scene failed in their investigations to discover, or if they knew who they were, to publish the names of the true killers.[56]

Now, more than one hundred and thirty years separates Thompson's assassination from the present, and naming his killers may be a mystery beyond the reach of certainty. However, various theories can be examined. Many years from the tragedy, three prominent San Antonio newspapermen left their version of who did it.

Johnny Lunsford, a veteran newspaperman working for the San Antonio *Light* in 1884 failed to mention the identities of whom he thought pulled the triggers. Almost fifty years after the fact, Lunsford wrote about how the Vaudeville house policeman Jacobo Coy grasped Thompson's gun arm as Ben fired the shot that fatally wounded Foster in the leg and "in a second or less, there was a fusillade of pistol shots and both Thompson and Fisher fell dead in their tracks." Disappointingly, for a second time, Lunsford, who was a crack reporter, failed to identify who fired the fatal fusillade.[57]

Charles Merritt Barnes served as the court recorder at Justice Anton Adam's coroner's hearing, and has been identified as the reporter who also wrote the first day's story about the Vaudeville

Tragedy for the San Antonio *Express*. Similar to Johnny Lunsford's account, Barnes, while writing in 1910, recounted how Coy held Thompson as Ben wounded Foster in the leg but added that Foster then fired and struck Ben in the head. Per Barnes, "Shooting then became general at both Thompson and Fisher," with bartender Bob Churchill, "who with a shotgun fired several times at both Thompson and Fisher ... Both Thompson and Fisher fell riddled with bullets, which struck their heads and breasts ... The floor where they fell had many bullet holes in it, showing even after they were down those firing at them gave them no chance to do any further shooting." Two portions of Barnes's version unravels when compared to the known facts. The testimony from City Marshal Phillip Shardein at the coroner's inquest places Bob Churchill behind the bar on the ground floor with a shotgun aimed at the stairway leading down from where the fatal gunfire erupted. Also, buckshot was not discovered during the autopsy. Instead the doctors found wounds created by large calibre bullets and removed them from Ben's body. These were identified as such by gunsmith Joseph Petmecky and, in addition, the examination did not reveal any wounds in Thompson's breast. However, Barnes was correct about additional shots being fired into Thompson and Fisher after they were down. Powder burns discolored their faces and singed the hair of both dead men, but his version of Foster placing a head-shot into Thompson simply does not match the trajectory of the bullets discovered during Thompson's autopsy.[58]

In 1886, twenty-year old Frank H. Bushick arrived in San Antonio from Rockport, Texas, and joined the reporting staff of the *Express*. He excelled and was promoted in 1892 to be the editor of the newspaper until he resigned in 1905. Bushick enjoyed a long and varied career and in 1923, he was elected San Antonio's Tax Commissioner and for the next sixteen years became a key member of the town's dominate political machine, the People's party.[59] In the early 1930s, he began to write his reminiscences of Old San Antonio recalling the pioneers, politicians, pistol fighters, restaurants, architectural landmarks, gambling dens, and fellow newspaper men. Bushick published his work in book form in 1934 and titled it, *Glamourous Days.* One of the historical events he covered at length was presented in "Chapter XVI—Who Killed Ben Thompson? Friends of Thompson have always claimed that he was assassinated by parties concealed in the boxes. Simms was reputed to have killed Thompson, but sporting men in the know, related years afterward that the real slayers were three hangers-on at the theatre, a bartender named McLaughlin, Canada Bill, a gambler, and an English Jew variety performer named Harry Tremaine. It was said they were armed with Winchesters and fired from a nearby box, having been stationed there for that purpose … McLaughlin, Canada Bill, and Tremaine all left town immediately." Bushick acknowledged how the guilty also escaped the law. "No evidence of ambush or assassination came out at the inquest and no charges or indictments were ever filed against anybody. The local officials were friendly with the local gamblers and the coroner's inquest was perfunctory."[60]

According to the number of bullets that struck Thompson down during the initial volley, it appears it would have taken more than three shooters but Bushick only names three men. A search through available documentation for the variety performer Harry Tremaine revealed nothing.[61] The famous Old West gambler "Canada Bill" Jones could not have been one of the killers. He died in 1878.[62] It must have been another lesser known man with the same moniker. But McLaughlin is a name that briefly weaves through the peripheral surrounding the story of Ben Thompson until the name became part of what ended Ben's life. The made-up rumor that Ben Thompson had been killed started as a lark in late August 1883 by a couple of young Galveston men. By strange coincidence they falsely named Ben's killer as one "McLaughlin."[63] During the legal investigations and maneuvering after Ben fatally shot Jack Harris, an employee at the Vaudeville Theatre named John L. McLaughlin, a bartender and all-around-handy man, after some thought decided to come forward and be deposed by William M. Walton. His evidence was beneficial to Ben Thompson's defense. After Thompson and Fisher were gunned down, McLaughlin did not skip town; his name was listed as a hack driver in the 1885-1886 San Antonio City Directory. Soon after, however, he did disappear and scatter into the unknown just like Harry Tremaine and Canada Bill.[64]

Frank Bushick's explanation is by far the most credible. Walton ended his Thompson biography with, "It is confidently hoped that justice will eventually be dealt out to all concerned, as new facts are constantly coming to light which bid fair to unravel the dark mystery of thc Vaudeville tragedy." Since so many years have passed, it is doubtful anything further will ever be learned.[65]

Veteran Texas ranger George Durham left one final detail as to how much the killers were paid. "I am not bragging when I say that I was in a position to know the facts ... King Fisher was assassinated by paid killers. I know exactly how much they got. Them assassins was paid to get Ben Thompson. They didn't want King. But King stuck by Ben as he always stuck by a friend ... It was an ambush—a $200 ambush."[66]

It is not known exactly when Ben's tombstone was placed in the Thompson family plot in Oakwood Cemetery. It must have been well after he died because it was erected in the center of the plot and not directly over his actual grave. Surprisingly, his tombstone has a mistake engraved on it. Ben's birthdate is incorrect. In 1977, the co-author of this biography, Chuck Parsons, visited Oakwood Cemetery and was disturbed to see the condition of the gunfighter's headstone. For many years the marker over Thompson's grave was encrusted making it virtually unreadable. It was also loose from its setting and in danger of being broken into unrepairable pieces or perhaps even easily picked up and carried away by a relic or souvenir hunter. As president of the National Association Organization for Outlaw and Lawman History Inc., (NOLA) Parsons with the help of a local resident and fellow NOLA member Gaines Kincaid, took the initiative to have the stone permanently repaired. Their sole motivation was to preserve a historic site. Volunteers joined in to help with the restoration project. Headstone expert John Curly determined the stone was Vermont marble and provided his knowledge to Kincaid who properly cleaned and polished it until the carved lettering was again legible. A concrete base was poured by Austin builder Earl Truil and concrete expert Joe Nejek with the additional help of Terry Gray and Ronald Reid. The old stone was securely placed as wire and other metal was mixed with the concrete to further strengthen it. As the concrete was about halfway poured, Gaines Kincaid, self-admittedly, "got a sentimental streak and picked a couple of bluebonnets [the Texas State flower] and put them inside" the new concrete base. Sentimentality may have struck Mr. Kincaid but when they learned of the project friends of his pointedly asked, "Why do you want to honor that old bleep." A brief newspaper article reporting the work on the tombstone ran a headline above it, "Stone for Ben doesn't mean we like him." On Tuesday, June 17, 1980, former Austin Deputy Chief of Police R. B. Laws unveiled the repaired tombstone and spoke about the life of Ben Thompson to a small crowd of attendees.[67]

Evidently Ben Thompson's reputation as "Bad Ben" had not changed for the better over the many years after his death, even with countless Texas newspaper and magazine articles published about him. The many authors of these articles endlessly recalled Ben's dangerous mix of gentlemanly charm and volatile ruthlessness. But like William M. Walton, no one characterized

Thompson's actions during his life as anything other than that of a saloon brawler. Unlike Billy the Kid, Jesse James, and Wyatt Earp, Ben Thompson did not benefit from an advocate who stationed virtue at the core of his adventures. Thus, the fame he achieved in his lifetime ebbed, while the legends of the Wild West icons soared at the behest of their historical advocates.[68]

As to what manner of man Thompson may have been, one Austin newspaper wrote, "What a career and what a sad failure."[69] Ben carried with him so many blessings, but had in turn, good many curses. "Willful, passionate at times when excited, he was yet patient, mild and just."[70] Ben was a very fallible man full of contradictions and a mass of inconsistencies. In many respects, Ben Thompson was a remarkable man. He had in his possession a great physical courage, and for better or worse, he was a fitting representation of what the times in which he lived could produce. Ben would never forget a friend, and yet once while drunk, he publicly horsewhipped one of the state's most prominent citizens. He freely shared his good fortune with the downtrodden along with his relatives and many friends yet Ben would not hesitate to become embroiled in a feud and spill blood over a trivial amount of money. He had supreme self-confidence and was utterly ruthless with a pistol in his hand, yet he could be infinitely compassionate and helpful to the unfortunate. One Austin newspaperman wrote, "A terror himself to the officers of the law in Austin, when, in the position of city marshal, he was likewise a terror to evil doers, and made one of the best officers the city ever had."[71]

Author George MacDonald Fraser made the following observation: "It is a remarkable thing that a single redeeming quality in a black sheep wins greater esteem than all the virtues in honest men—especially if the quality is courage." Ben Thompson greatly benefited from this phenomenon throughout his adventurous life. The Austin newspaper *Texas Siftings* commented: "He was 'a very popular desperado. His pleasant manner, his honesty and reliability in business transactions, his natural wit and humor, his unwillingness to take any unfair advantage of his enemies, and his good looks, caused him to be popular with men who abhorred his dissolute life, and depreciated his lawless career.'"[72]

Ben's sister Mary Jane was often heard to repeat Proverbs 22:1 from the King James *Bible,* "A good name is rather to be chosen than great riches, and loving favor than silver and gold."[73] If Ben Thompson's fiery personality had taken a slightly different bent he might have stood well to the forefront in public estimation. He had the opportunity, and for a short period he realized this potential. His career as a successful and popular lawman could have rivaled or excelled those of his most admired contemporaries in Austin such as his friend James E. Lucy (city marshal 1885-1890) and Alden Jackson Thorp, a veteran policeman and Austin's city marshal for more than a decade (city marshal 1890-1901). Perhaps Ben might have surpassed the finest among them all, longtime lawman John Chenneville, who served the Austin community conscientiously for more than thirty years. The intelligent and effective Chenneville never had the need to resort to his revolver. However, with Ben Thompson, a personal spite meant a duel to the death was as inevitable as the abrupt end to his rising career in law enforcement, which brought an end to the admiration he so dearly desired from the worthwhile citizens of Austin.

With his killing of Jack Harris and his subsequent resignation as city marshal, "he went to the dogs very fast, and at, and even before his death, he could hardly be called sane … and acted more like a maniac then a reasonable human being." For Ben, fear and remorse were never a part of his nature. He was very fatalistic, and that undoubtedly influenced his wild behavior during the months leading up to his death.[74] He understood the road he had chosen and what was waiting for him at the end of it. Several years before he died he admitted as much,

> Whether by nature or not, I am from habit a gambler, willing to take the delights of the excitement that belongs to such character, and yet not afraid to meet and contend with the adversities that in due and natural course meet such men. Sooner or later, however prosperous a gambler may be, he meets with an untimely death; if not from the pistol or dagger, then from fatal disease contracted by dissipation and exposure consequent on such life. Every time a man sits down to a card table to gamble he takes his life in his hands and lays it down between him and his adversary. Fatal difficulties arise from cause and from no cause; men are killed in their difficulties and in those of others ... Yet I continue in that line of life ... which I will probably follow until I am dead.[75]

Bullets took Ben's life, disease claimed his son, and a combination of the two probably brought an end to his brother Billy.

The editor of the Austin *Statesman* commented when describing Ben Thompson's funeral wrote, "He has been a leading character in the Texas drama for the last thirty years."[76] Despite the slight exaggeration, the portrait is essentially just. From the age of fourteen, when he first fired a gun at another human being until his violent death, Thompson's wild, reckless career ran for almost twenty-six years. On Thursday, March 13, 1884, the editor of the Austin *Capital* expressed his thoughts about Ben Thompson and the life he led, "He possessed many good traits of character—if bad ones, let them sleep in the bloody grave where rest the immortal remains." He said Ben Thompson's "life of excitement ... fed on excitement," that, "[Ben was] one of the most remarkable men of the times and upon whose life a generation may not look again." But Ben lived in a time and place that is now long extinct. When he died, America's Wild West faded alongside him and a life to rival the one Ben Thompson lived could never hope to be replicated.

APPENDIX A

From the E. P. Lamborn Collection, No. 156, Box No. 2, Folder 9. at the Kansas State Historical Society, Topeka.

Mr. Edward Parker Lamborn's (1890-1978) extreme interest in lawmen and criminals encouraged him to spend a virtual lifetime collecting, researching and corresponding with others concerning crime and all those involved in committing or solving it. Among his papers is a letter he received from Ben Thompson researcher and author Floyd B. Streeter.

Feb. 28, 1935

Mr. E. P. Lamborn
R.R. 2
Leavenworth Kansas

Dear Mr. Lamborn:

Thank you for your letter of Feb. 26. Under separate cover I am sending you a copy of my article on Ellsworth in which I wrote up the shooting of Sheriff Whitney.[1]

I read Stuart Lake's book about the time I began collecting data for the Ellsworth story. I believe I have proven that Wyatt Earp had nothing to do with the incidents the day Sheriff Whitney was killed. If he was in town that day no mention is made of him in the contemporary records. Five eyewitnesses, whom I interviewed, state that he had no part in the shooting episode.[2] That tragedy has been told time and again in the homes of Ellsworth and a number of those who have heard the stories from the old timers, tell me that they never heard Wyatt Earp's name connected with it until Lake's account came out. I have found no one who says that Earp was there. Besides, I went through all the contemporary newspapers in the Kansas Historical Society's collection; the police court and the other city records at Ellsworth; the testimony before the coroner's jury and at Bill Thompson's trial in the district court in 1877; and the State records at Topeka and Austin, Texas. I tried to allow for the fact that witnesses under oath cannot tell exactly what happened because they are excited at such a time. (i.e. a shooting scrape) I feel that after three years of investigation, I have everything and that my account is the most accurate written so far.

I have checked the Lake book with contemporary sources for Wichita and Dodge City and have found evident inaccuracies.

I have nothing but the story in Bob Wright's book on the rescue of Bill Thompson in Nebraska. So far I have only Siringo's and Dane Coolidge's stories of Clay Allison's activities. In time I hope to check each story with contemporary sources. Tom Masterson's statements to you give a new angle—one that I have not heard. I do not have information on Jeff Carr and "Doc" Middleton and don't know what became of Dave Mathers.

We have quite a collection of western books, newspaper clippings, copies of articles, and pictures. Our pictures are mainly of Hays though we have pictures of Ellsworth, Dodge City, and other places.

We have pictures of Ben and Billy Thompson and Sheriff Whitney, but not of the other Ellsworth men mentioned or of Jim Currie.

I have not visited the Beeson Museum but intend to one of these days.

I shall be glad to hear from you anytime about these early western incidents and characters. The collection of these stories is a hobby. The work goes slow and is expensive.

If you ever come to Hays please hunt me up. I am here most of the time except in August.

Very Sincerely
Floyd B. Streeter
Librarian

APPENDIX B

Austin Daily Democratic Statesman, March 26, 1879.

LETTER FROM BEN. THOMPSON

Editors Democratic Statesman:

A day or two after writing to you from Denver we started for this place where we arrived about a week ago. Our troubles commenced at Denver, we had to handle our own baggage and have it weighed and had to pay one cent per pound from Denver to terminus of the south park railroad where we arrived about 2 o'clock p. m., leaving Denver at 9 o'clock A. m. Here we had sure enough trouble; the stages were crowded, and they won't haul any trunks, so we were in a fix. Well, we got everything expressed through for about seven cents a pound and our things came through all right a few hours after our arrival at Leadville. Our trip out on the Denver and South Park Railroad about seventy miles, and seven dollars fare, was very pleasant. At Webster, the place where we took the stage, we got a good dinner for one dollar. Webster is in the mountains. One side of the valley is all snow and the other nice green pine trees. One side looks like mid winter, the trees are all dead, and the other side looks about like the cedar mountains above Austin in summer time. Leaving Webster we had a nice, bright sunshine evening, but we had not gone more than three miles until we was right in the midst of a real snow storm, which we had to travel through all the evening and until 11 o'clock that night to Fair Play, where we stayed all night and had a good supper, breakfast and dinner and bed for two dollars. Next morning about 9 o'clock the stage (or rather stages, for there was ten of them loaded with from eight to twenty passengers each at ten dollars fare from the Railroad to Leadville) started and the ride was enjoyable for the first fifteen miles, when we stopped for dinner just at the timber line, where we commenced to make the ascent crossing the range. I never want to cross the range again. The dinner stand was left about 12 o'clock and by 2 o'clock we were on top of the range, thirteen thousand and some feet above the sea level. The driver told Frank Cotton and I that as we had never been in the mountains before that we had better not get out, as he could pull two of us up the mountain, so we rode up, and would have ridden down, but as we started down the wagon, horses and all come near going over an embankment several hundred feet high, so we got out and walked about seven miles before the outfit overtook us. After 9 o'clock that evening Leadville was sighted, and you bet that Frank Cotton and I [were] glad of it. Nothing that has been written, so far as I can judge, is any exaggeration. The mines around this place must be the richest ever before discovered; that is what all the old California miners and gamblers say about them, and they are investing their all in prospecting and developing mines they discover. It is impossible for me to describe this City fully. It is a City of ten or fifteen thousand inhabitants, of which about twenty-five hundred are ladies. Leadville has a water works and it is soon to have gass [*sic*] and a street railroad. Several churches and schools are already in operation; also two variety establishments and a theatre. One variety man pays for his house seventeen hundred dollars per month rent and at least two thousand a week for performers. He takes in about six or seven hundred a night for drinks at five dollars a bottle in the conversational parlors, where the visitors are entertained by the lady performers. Of gambling houses it is useless to speak as there is so many and all so crowded you cannot pass through them from morning till morning as they never close. Houses for sporting and saloon business rent for five to ten hundred per month, which shuts out all chances for legitimate business, as most anything you want is nearly as cheap here as in any frontier town [in] Texas. Drinks are twenty-five cents, twenty-five cents for a shave, water is fifty cents a barrel. Bed rooms, ten by twelve in size, scantily furnished, rent readily for sixty dollars a month. There is here at present several thousand brooken [*sic*] men that cannot find work, nor will there be anything for them to do until the snow is off the ground, then there will be work for all. The trouble now is that the mines already discovered, all but a few, are not sufficiently developed to be worked in winter. Men with money or machinery can come here and make all the money they want in six months, and not take many chances, all others had better stay away until some time about the last of May or the first of June. People are coming at the rate of one hundred a day, so you see how it will be if things continue this way. Building is going on as fast as lumber can be had, which, at present, is very scarce and selling at one hundred dollars per thousands. Mr. Pink Binford, formerly of Austin, and a nephew of Mrs. McCall, is here and has fine prospects for soon becoming a millionaire. Mr. Binford owns a one-fourth interest [in] an [*sic*] mine that they have been offered $90,000 for a one-half interest, which they refused.[1] Mr. Binford tells me that he and his partners have sent to Chicago for an engine to work their mine. At the present it is not being worked, on account of the inclemency of the weather. The Galveston gentlemen who have been here for several days prospecting don't seem to like Leadville on account of the high price at which real estate is held, and it being a matter of impossibility to rent in a good location, they speak of going down to Denver to open up business. Captain Owens will leave here in a few days for Texas to bring out his stock for freighting, as the opening for that business is good. Freights from the end of the track seventy-five miles is three cents per pound, and the trip is made in three days. It has been snowing all day, and in fact it has snowed every few hours since our arrival, still the sun shines nearly all the time and we don't suffer any from the cold. In fact I never felt better in my life than since my stay here. There is no sickness here except pneumonia and diphtheria, caused from exposure. I am told by experienced miners that if all the force that could be worked in the mines now operated was put on [,] that the ore now in sight could not be taken out in three years. Frank Cotton and I will stick it out with them for a few months any way. We do not advise any of our friends to come out here under six weeks except those who have plenty of means to go into business. [Illegible] … Poindexter … [illegible] … could do well here and I like to see him come out.

Yours Respectfully, BEN THOMPSON.

P. S.—I enclose you the following slip from the Leadville *Chronicle*, a very good weekly paper:

> Jack Calhoun and Ike Hosier have struck it rich in their mine—the Black Prince—on Bald Mountain, four or five miles from Leadville. The mine is a true fissure vein, fifteen feet between Walls, assaying about five hundred ounces. They were offered $130,000 for the mine, but refused to Consider the proposition. The owners are John E. Calhoun and Isaac H. Hosier, the young photographers opposite the *Democrat* office, and H. M. Wheelock and S. L. Munroe."

APPENDIX C

Austin Statesman, April 14, 1881.

"March Police Pickings.

Not withstanding the fact that the legislature was in session during the month of March, the police pickings were smaller than usual, and business in the police department was comparatively dull. The following arrests were made during the month: Intoxication 30, disturbing the peace 19, assault and battery 13, vagrancy 10, disturbing public worship 9, sleeping in a public place 4, firing a pistol within the city limits 3, malicious mischief 2, contempt of court 1, fast driving 2, fast riding 1, carrying a pistol 1, miscellaneous 2. Total number of arrests 97. Of this number 67 were white, 30 colored. There were 76 males and 21 females. The amount of fines collected by the city marshal, Thompson, was $351, and the amount worked out on the streets was $164."

Austin Statesman, June 3, 1881.

"May police Pickings.

During the month of May, the police made the following arrests: Disturbing the peace 40, intoxication 31, assault 10, asleep in a public place 7, vagrancy 5, keeping bawdy house 3, fighting 2, fast riding 4, carrying a pistol 2, butchering without a license 1, resisting an officer 1, other offenses 6; total number of arrests 112:

males 82, females 30; whites 72, colored 40. Of the number arrested there were 88 natives of the United States, 9 of Germany, 8 of Ireland, 5 of Mexico, 1 of England, and 1 of Switzerland. Of the number of the arrests, 83 were made during the day, and 29 during the night. Among the number scooped were 43 laborers, 5 stockman, 4 vagrants, 1 shoemaker, 3 printers, 1 newsboy, 1 express agent, 1 cowboy, 2 hackmen, 2 farmers, 1 bartender, 2 artists, 1 constable, 1 deputy sheriff, 1 variety performer, and 43 in various other trades. The total amount of fines was $729.25; paid in cash, $472.50; worked out, $256.75."

Austin Statesman, February 3 and 5, 1882.
The January 1882 record of seventy-seven arrests are, "classified and subdivided ... as follows: THE CHARGES. Vagrancy, 20; Intoxication, 27; asleep in a public place, 6; assault, 3; keeping a disorderly house, 1; discharging firearms, 4; disturbing the peace, 13; removing contents of a sink contrary to law, 1; carrying a pistol, 2. Total, 77. SEX AND COLOR. Males, 70; females, 7. White, 54; Mexican, 2; colored, 21. OCCUPATION. Laborers, 27; farmers, 5; saloon keepers, 3; student, 1; railroad men, 3; painters, 2; teamsters, 3; bootblacks, 3; miner, 1; prostitutes, 8; gamblers, 3; no occupation, 17; a German baron's son, 1. NATIVITY. United States, 50; Mexico, 2; Germany, 4; Ireland, 17; Sweden, 3; Italy, 1. NUMBER OF ARRESTS BY EACH OFFICER. E.R.Oberwetter, 27; C. H. Randolph, 2; J. L. Watts, 4; L.C. Lock, 10; Sergeant John Chenneville, 4; H.G. Madison, 3; L. Morris, 6; George Hutchinson, 3; J.W. Larue, 4; R.J. Stewart, day clerk, 3; Howe, special officer, 8; O.H. Binkley, 0; Ford, special officer, 3. Nine cases dismissed."

APPENDIX D

BEN THOMPSON AT THE BAR.

Continuance Granted Until the Next Term of Court.

The case of the state of Texas vs. Ben Thompson, charged and indicted for the murder of Jack Harris, was called for trial in the district court yesterday morning, before the Hon. Judge Geo. H. Noonan.

The prosecution announced that the state was ready to proceed with the trial.

Judge A. Y. [*sic*] Walton, of Austin, the leading attorney for the defense, announced that they were not ready for trial and asked for further time to prepare the affidavit on which he based application for a continuance until the next term of court.

The request for time was granted, and the district court adjourned until three o'clock.

The court room in the upper story of the city court house was crowded to overflowing with witnesses and spectators, showing in the clearest manner that general interest has not flagged any since the case was first opened.

Shortly after 3 o'clock, the district court was convened, when the following affidavit was read by Judge Walton.

At the conclusion, Judge Noonan granted the continuance without the slightest hesitation:

The state of Texas vs. Ben Thompson, in Bexar county district, September, 1882:

And now comes the defendant, Ben Thompson in person, and being first duly sworn, says, under his said oath, that he cannot safely go to trial at this, the present term of the court, for the want of testimony material to his defence [*sic*], viz: that of the following witnesses: John J. McLaughlin, A. L. Cashel [*sic*], Thomas G. Martin, Joseph A. Smith, L. Rouvant, Jack Cummings, R. Branan, J. C. Cummings, J. W. Alexander, Wm. Henderson, Geo. Shoof, ---- O'Brien, ---- Lastew, Geo. G. Lester, Tom Hughes, the two Mauri sisters, Lieutenant Hickey, Dr. Maurice, W. S. Ellis, ---- Hilliard, ---- Viles. The said McLaughlin, Jas. A. Smith, L. Rouvant, Frank Sparrow, Jack Cummings, Geo. G. Lester and Tom Hughes are citizens of and reside in the city of San Antonio, county of Bexar, as he is informed I believe. The said A. L. Cashiel [*sic*], and Thomas G. Martin are citizens of Hays county, Texas, and reside at the town of Kyle. The said H. A. Burbank is a citizen of Webb county, and resides at the city of Laredo. The said Mauri sisters are transient persons, variety theatre actresses, who frequently, as he is informed and believes, change their place of abode. The said Lieutenant Hickey is an officer of the United States army, Dr. Maurice a surgeon in the same army, and are stationed at Brackett, in the county of Kinney, as he is informed and believes. The said Hillard [*sic*] resides at the same place. The said W. S. Ellis and Viles are citizens of the county of Atascosa, Texas.

Affiant says that he has used due diligence to obtain the personal presence of said witness—or rather he would say, that he has used every possible diligence that it was in his power to use—having in view, both the law governing the issuance of subpoenas and attachments. He, affiant, says:

1. That the indictment in this case was returned by the grand jury of Bexar county, Texas, and filed in this court on the 6th day of September, A. D. 1882.
2. That he was served with a copy of said indictment on the same day, Viz: 6th September, 1882.
3. The court set the case for final trial on the 12th day of September, 1882.
4. The indictment is for a capital felony.
5. That he applied for and obtained from the clerk of the district court of Bexar county, Texas, returnable on this, the 12th day of September, A. D., 1882., process in the shape of subpoenas on the 7th day of September, 1882, for all of the witnesses whose residence is stated to be in Bexar county, Texas, directed to the sheriff of said Bexar county, and in the shape of attachments for all of the witnesses who reside otherwheres [*sic*] than in Bexar county, directed to the sheriff of the counties respectively, where said and each of said witnesses respectively reside and have their several and respective homes, except for the witness Ellis, which was issued on the 9th day of said month—no effective process could be issued for the said two Mauri sisters, whose exact whereabouts could not be learned, and is not now known; nor was any process issued for the witness Viles, because the materiality of his evidence was not known, until yesterday evening, at an hour too late to procure service of process on him, and his attendance at the hour when this case was called for trial.
6. That all of the processes issued for said witnesses as aforesaid, when issued to the officers of Bexar county, was placed in the hands of the sheriff of said county, and were issued to the officers of Webb, Kinney, Hays and Caldwell counties. The same was duly and promptly forwarded

through the United States mail to the sheriffs of said counties respectfully, with United States rates of postage fully paid on the said 7th day of September, 1882. Except as to the witness Ellis, and for him the attachment was duly issued and promptly forwarded by mail on said 9th day of September, 1882.

7. Of said processes so issued and placed in the hands of the sheriff of Bexar county, and forwarded by mail (the attachments as aforesaid) to the sheriffs of the counties respectively, where said several witness [*sic*], herein mentioned, reside, the following has been received, executed and returned into court, viz.: that for the witnesses—John J. McLaughlin, A. L. Cashell, Thos. G. Martin, Jos. A. Smith, Jack Cummings, Lasher, Geo. G. Lester, Tom Hughes, Lieut. Hickey, Doctor Morris, W. S. Ellis.
8. Affiant solemnly swears that he believes that the testimony of each, all, and every one of said witnesses is material to his defense.
9. The defense of affiant is self- defense, which, under the facts and circumstances, attendant on the alleged killing, is made up—is sustained and necessarily is made up , and must be sustained by a great variety of small facts; but which taken together, establish the defense, as he believes, beyond cavil or doubt.
10. He believes that he will be able to establish a conspiracy entered into by the deceased, W. H. Sims [*sic*] and others, to take his affiant's life at the time and place, when, to save his own life, it is charged that he took the life of the said Harris.
11. The several witnesses—viz: A. L. Cashell, Thomas G. Martin, Joseph A. Smith and L. Rouvant—were examined on a trial of a writ of habeas corpus before the judge of this honorable court, on the 25th, 26th, 27th, and 28th days of

August, 1882, who then and there, under their several corporal oaths, deposed to material facts, which being written down in their presence and read over to them, they severally signed with their names, and affirmed under their several oaths, the very truth of what was so, then an[d] there written down, which said several statements are here and now referred to, and made part thereof, as fully, completely and perfectly as if the same was herein *haec verba* set out and embodied herein, and he asks that said several statements of said witnesses may be taken and be considered as part of this application, being embodied in this document hereto appended, and marked exhibit "A." Affiant says that he expects to prove, and believes that he will be able to prove, by said witnesses as named, the very identical facts as set out in their said several sworn statements as aforesaid, on the trial of this case before the jury.

12. Affiant says that he expects to prove, and that he will be able to prove by the witness, John J. McLaughlin, the exact facts stated in his affidavit, attached to exhibit "A," heretofore referred to and made part hereof, which said affidavit was, under oath, made by the said McLaughlin deliberately and calmly, after due and thorough consideration. Affiant here refers specially to said affidavit of the said McLaughlin, and the same as part of exhibit "A" is here referred to, and made part hereof, as fully as if the same were set out herein line for line and word for word, and he asks that it be so received and considered by the court.
13. As to the two Mauri sisters, affiant says that he expects to prove by them and each of them, that after the said Jack Harris was shot he, as part of the very *res gestae* [statements given that may be exempt from hearsay rules] of the transaction, in which he lost his life, asked the ques-

tion of said two Mauri sisters, "is Thompson killed?" and being answered in the negative, then asked, "Are any of my friends killed?"—thus showing that he, the said Jack Harris, and his friends had concerted measures to kill and murder affiant, as he, affiant, verily believes.

14. That he, affiant, expects to prove by the witness, Ellis, heretofore mentioned, that Jack Harris, in the city of San Antonio, Texas, county of Bexar, sought to bribe, and did offer to bribe, him, the said Ellis, with and for the sum of five hundred dollars, to kill murder this affiant. That said offer to bribe was made in the city of San Antonio, about two months prior to the death of said Harris at the store of one Wolfson, a vender of matresses [*sic*] in said city of San Antonio
15. By the said witness Viles, (an Englishmen) affiant expects to prove, and fully believes he will be able to prove, at that moment the shot was fired that killed the said Jack Harris, he, the said Harris, was raising his shot gun into a shooting position, aiming in the direction of affiant, and that from the action of the said Harris, at the very moment he was shot, was about to shoot affiant and in the very act of doing so. Affiant is informed and believes that the said Viles, is an honorable and worthy citizen. The affiant, on yesterday evening, as soon as he heard of what the said Viles would swear, sent a special messenger for him, offering and proposing to pay any reasonable expense not limited by what the law allows as compensation, but the actual expenses of said witness Viles, for him to come and testify on the trial of this case, but he has not been able, even by this extra exertion to procure the attendance of said witness up to this hour.
16. Affiant expects to prove and believes that he will be able to prove by the witnesses Lieutenant Hickey and Dr. Maurice,

that on the night Jack Harris was on the streets of San Antonio armed with a shot-gun (which exact time will be fixed by witnesses, who are now present in court, or who answered to their names when called by the sheriff this morning) hunting affiant, for the openly declared purpose of shooting him, affiant—he, affiant, was sick at the Menger hotel, in the city of San Antonio, under the personal professional treatment of the said witness, Dr. Maurice.

17. Affiant expects to prove and believes that he will be able to prove, by the witness, Geo. Shoof, that Jack Harris, at his place of business, in the city of San Antonio, county of Bexar—his place of business being the Vaudeville variety Theatre, saloon and gambling house, openly declared that he would kill this affiant, if he, affiant, came to this, the city of San Antonio, and this when the affiant was not in the city of San Antonio.
18. Affiant expects to prove and believes will be able to prove, by the witness Alexander, that the said Harris, deceased, was getting ready to shoot affiant, and was in the act of shooting affiant, at the very moment when he (Harris) was shot, and that affiant neither touched or drew his pistol, until the said Harris had his gun up and was either ready, or getting ready to shoot him, affiant. His information is direct and from credible sources. That the ... [illegible] ... will be proven on trial before the jury, by the absent witness Braman.
19. Affiant says that he expects to be able to procure the attendance of each and all and every of said witnesses, save the two Mauri sisters, at the next term of court. And as to the said two Mauri, if he shall not be able to procure their and each of their and personal attendance at the next term of this court, he believes that he will be able to prove and

have in attendance their and each of their depositions, duly taken, in form of law, at and by the next ensuing term of this court.

20. That said witnesses, nor any of them, are absent, by the procurement or the consent of affiant.
21. That this application for a continuance is not made for delay, but, that justice may be done.
22. Affiant swears that there is no reasonable prospect, or expectations that the attendance of said witnesses can be secured during the present term of the court by a postponement of the trial to a future day of this said term.
23. Affiant says that he has been in the jail of Bexar county, Texas, since the day after the alleged killing of Jack Harris, that bail has been refused to him by the judge of this court on a hearing of a portion of the evidence for which a postponement of this trial is now sought.

Ben Thompson

Sworn to and subscribed before me, on this 12th day of September, A. D., 1882.

Geo. R. Dashiell.,

Clerk, District Court, Bexar Co., Texas.[1]

APPENDIX E

Jack Harris Historical Marker

(Note that the marker is all in upper case.)

D.A. (Jack) Harris

1834-1882

Jack Harris was born in Connecticut in 1834 and ran away to sea at the age of 12. In 1856 he was a member of William Walker's Nicaragua Expedition where he was captured and put in front of a firing squad before being rescued by Walker. Harris escaped to Texas and in 1860 he joined the police force of San Antonio. He served with the Confederacy during the Civil War and returned to San Antonio and the police department.

In 1868 he and Police Captain Penaloza started a saloon on Market Street. In 1872 Harris opened the Jack Harris Bar and Billiards Room on Main Plaza on Soledad and Commerce Streets. The name was changed to Jack Harris Vaudeville Theatre and Saloon three years later.

Harris headed the Democratic Party in San Antonio and dictated who ran for office for city and county government for many years. He also reigned supreme over the "Sporting Community."

Harris was shot in the Vaudeville Theatre on July 11, 1882, by Ben Thompson, City Marshall [*sic*] of Austin, as a result of arguments over a gambling debt two years earlier. At Jack Harris' funeral on July 12, 1882, there were 47 carriages in the procession out East Commerce Street. He died a single man at the age of 48.

The notoriety of his theatre, which reached the front page of "The New York Times," is believed to have popularized the term "Vaudeville" for variety theatres in the United States.

[Then at base in smaller letters]

This marker was erected on the centennial of the shooting of Jack Harris, through the efforts of the "Friends of Jack Harris" committee and the contributions of the citizens of San Antonio, July 11, 1982.

APPENDIX F

"The headlines of the Texas papers on the Thompson killing would make a rare literary curiosity for a future generation. Who will undertake the task of their collection?" *Austin Statesman,* March 20, 1884.

Wednesday, March 12, 1884.

Austin Statesman, "BEN THOMPSON, The Hero of Many a Bloody Fight, has fought his Last and Died Last Night. King Fisher Faithful to the End Yields Up His Life to Save His friend! Full and Graphic Account of the Death of Both Men at San Antonio."

San Antonio Express, "A Good Night's Work" and "Jack Harris Avenged."

Austin Daily Dispatch, "HE MEETS HIS DOOM. Ben Thompson Killed in San Antonio. THE VICTOR OF MANY BLOODY FIGHTS REMOVED FROM EARTH. Great Excitement Prevails and More Trouble Expected. HOW IT WAS RECIVED IN AUSTIN."

Austin Daily Capital, "BEN THOMPSON KILLED. At the Vaudeville in San Antonio. King Fisher Slain. Billy Simms Reported as Doing the Bloody Work. Great Excitement Prevails, And More Trouble is Expected To-Day."

San Antonio Light, "BLOODY TRAGEDY. Ben Thompson and King Fisher Killed—Joe Foster Wounded. A Real Tragedy at the Vaudeville—The Slayer of Jack Harris Dies Beneath the Same Roof—Coroner's Inquest."

San Antonio Times, and reprinted on March 16, 1884 in the *Corpus Christi Caller,* "A TERRIBLE TRAGEDY. Ben Thompson and King Fisher, noted Texas Desperadoes, Riddled with Bullets."

Houston Post, "MET HIS MAN. BEN THOMPSON AT LAST BITES THE DUST. The Hero of Many battles at Length Meets His Match, And Goes Down with Him In A Terrible And Deadly Fight. A Regular Fusilade [*sic*] in One of the San Antonio Theatres. Thompson Dies in the Same House Where He Murdered Jack Harris—The Details."

New York Herald, "A TEXAN TRAGEDY."

Thursday, March 13, 1884.
San Antonio Daily Express, "THE DEAD DESPERADOES. The last of Ben Thompson and King Fisher. Conclusion of the Testimony at the Inquest—Verdict of Self-Defense—The Bodies of the Dead Men Taken to their Home."

Austin Statesman, "THE VERDICT. A CORONER'S JURY PRONOUNCE THE SAN ANTONIO HORROR JUSTIFIABLE! Foster Has a Limb Amputated, and May Die of His Injuries. LATEST PARTICUARS OF THE TRAGEDY BY SPECIAL TELEGRAPH TO THE STATESMAN."

Austin Statesman, "SKETCH. A SKETCH OF THE CAREER OF THOMPSON WHO MET HIS DEATH IN SAN ANTONIO, A

Wonderful Career of a Remarkable Man Briefly Told by Those Who Knew Him."

Austin Statesman, "JUDGEMENT. At last poor Ben Thompson has taken the same bloody route to the Great Beyond upon which he has sent many another trembling traveler."

Austin Daily Capital, "From San Antonio. The Vaudeville Butchery—Testimony of J. S. Coy. The Coroner's Verdict. Joe Foster Dying."

Austin Daily Capital, "THOMPSON. The Deep Damnation of His Taking Off. Telegraph Accounts—Newspaper Accounts and the 'Reliable Gentleman.' EYEWITNESSES TELL WHAT THEY DIDN'T SEE. Biographical Sketch of Ben Thompson."

Galveston Daily News, "THOMPSON—FISHER TRAGEDY. Full Particulars Of The Terrible Affray. The Alamo City Tragedy. The Coroner's Jury Render's Verdict that Joe Foster, William Simms and J. S. Coy Did the Killing in Self-Defense."

Dallas Daily Herald, "AS SHEEP IN SHAMBLES Died Ben Thompson and King Fisher of Bloody Fame. So at Least Would the Coroner's Verdict Imply. Thompson's Pistol Kills Him in Another Man's Hands."

Gatesville Advance, "IN HELL."

Brenham Daily Banner, "BEN THOMPSON DIES IN HIS BOOTS."

Luling Signal, "DEATH IN A VARIETY DIVE. Exit Ben Thompson and King Fisher."

Houston Post, "BEN FINIS. THE CLOSING CHAPTER IN A BLOODY HISTORY. The Facts in Full in Reference to the Terrible San Antonio Tragedy. Thompson's Body Said To Have Been Riddled With Buckshot. Belief That He Was Led into a Trap and Killed by Unseen Foes. THE CORONER'S INQUEST FAILS TO SOLVE THE MYSTERY. Scenes on the Arrival of the Remains at the Home in Austin. A Sketch of the Life of the Dead Man and Something of His Bloody Tragedies—His Slayers Held Guiltless by the Coroner."

Chicago Tribune, "A DEAD DESPERADO. Particulars of the Killing of Ben Thompson—Honors to His Remains" and "HONORS TO A DEAD DESPERADO."

Chicago Daily News, "Fitting End of Two Desperadoes."

New York Times, "SHOOTING IN A THEATRE. TWO MEN KILLED AND A THIRD MORTALLY WOUNDED. AN AUDIENCE WHICH QUICKLY DISPERSED AND HASTILY DEMANDED READMISSION TO THE HOUSE. San Antonio, Texas, March 12. -Ben Thompson and [K]ing Fisher were shot dead in the Vaudeville Theatre last night."

Friday, March 14, 1884.

Austin Statesman, "AUTOPSY. THE POST MORTEM EXAMINATION OF THOMPSON AND WHAT IT DISCLOSED. Some Interesting Tales Told by the Silent Wounds and Leaden Messengers."

Austin Daily Capital, "LAID IN HIS GRAVE. Funeral of Ben Thompson Yesterday. Pythian Rites at the Dead's Man's Grave. The Autopsy Made Before the Funeral—What the Press Says of the Deceased."

San Antonio Express, "UVALDE. KING FISHER'S FUNERAL- HIS CHARACTER AND PROSPECTS."

San Antonio Daily Express, "THE THOMPSON—FISHER TRAGEDY. MORE ABOUT THE TRAGEDY AND THE INCIDENTS THERETO. A Dramatic Description of the Fight and Death of the Two Men by an Eye Witness. Yesterday Afternoon an *Express* reporter went to the Vaudeville and there met two of the parties present at the tragedy, Wm H. Simms ... and Jacob S Coy."

Sunday, March 15, 1884.

Austin Statesman, 'BEN THOMPSON'S MURDER. Simms Feigns a Desire for a Grand Jury Investigation."

Austin Daily Capital, "THE LATE TRAGEDY. Another version by an Eye Witness. Who Says Ben Thompson and King Fisher Never Saw the Men Who Shot Them. After They Were Shot Policeman Coy Gets in His Work—How Billie [*sic*] Simms Describes the Fatal Affair."

San Antonio Light, "AN INJUSTICE. Charging Marshal Shardein with ordering Bill Thompson Killed."

San Antonio Express, "SENSASIONAL SLANDER. Billy Thompson Indebted to Marshal Shardein for the Protection of His Life."

San Antonio Daily Express, "Testimonial to King Fisher."

Monday, March 16, 1884.

Austin Statesman, "THE FACTS. AN INTERESTING INTERVIEW WITH TWO GENTLEMEN WHO SAW THE SHOOTING. A Far Different Story From The One Told by Those Who Planned The

Murderous Work. A Fearful Den of Iniquity and Vice Where the Bloody Work Was Done."

Tuesday, March 18, 1884.
Austin Statesman, "Ben Thompson. The Opinion Gains Ground That He Was Deliberately Murdered!"

San Antonio Express, "Public Opinion on the Subject." *Bracket News,* "Thus ends the lives of two of the boldest desperadoes and homicides that Texas had ever known."

Belton Journal, "It Is Well. Few if any men in the state were more noted than Ben Thompson and King Fisher. None were more feared and dreaded than they. None could count more victims than they could from their ever ready pistols."

Waco News, "We have only time to pay a passing tribute to Ben Thompson's memory, which is that he can be spared about as well as any man we know of."

Wednesday, March 19, 1884.
San Antonio Express, "THE VAUDEVILLE TRAGEDY. The Question as to Who Killed Ben Thompson Set Forever at Rest—A Plain Statement of the Facts From Mr. Joe Foster."

Thursday, March 20, 1884.
Austin Daily Statesman, "Foster has an Interview in the San Antonio *Express*. He is Certainly the Boss Liar."

Friday, March 21, 1884.

Austin Statesman, "Billy Thompson Returned to the City Last Night. He has little to Say about His Brother's Murder."

Saturday, March 22, 1884.

San Antonio Light, "JOE FOSTER. His Death This Morning From His Wounds—His Funeral at 3 O'clock To-Morrow."

Bastrop Advertiser, "A SKETCH OF THE CAREER OF MAJOR BEN THOMPSON."

Sunday, March 23, 1884.

Austin Statesman, "EXIT, FOSTER."

Monday, March 24, 1884.

San Antonio Light, "Foster's Funeral."

Saturday, March 29, 1884.

THE NATIONAL POLICE GAZETTE; NEW YORK, "BEN THOMPSON'S FINAL EXIT. THE LAST ACT OF A FIERCE AND DESPERATE CAREER, AS PERFORMED IN A SAN ANTONIO, TEXAS TEMPLE OF THE WILD AND UNTRAMMELED DRAMA." Ben Thompson's Death. The noted Ex-Marshal of San Antonio, Texas, Dies at Last With His Boots On."

Tuesday, April 8, 1884.

Austin Statesman, "The Ben Thompson Cases in the County Court were Dismissed."

Friday, April 25, 1884.
Austin Statesman, "Life of Ben Thompson. Yesterday the Life of Ben Thompson was handed to us by Edwards & Church, the publishers. Major Walton, the author, has told the story of Ben's life in an interesting and exiting manner."

Austin Statesman, "THE DEVIL'S DEN. Once more the crack of the revolver is heard in the Vaudeville! And Sims [*sic*] of Unsavory Memory, Gets the Best of his Antagonist!"

San Antonio Daily Express, "MORE SHOOTING AT THE VAUDEVILLE. DICK LOMBARD SHOT IN THE ARM BY BILLY SIMMS. All on Account of the Fisher—Thompson Tragedy—Some Very Poor Shooting at Close Quarters."

Thursday, March 4, 1886.
San Antonio Light, "THE FIRE. A Business Corner Burned this Morning. Great Loss of Property—Four Hours Hard Work for the Brave and Gallant Firemen."

Saturday, March 6, 1886
San Antonio Express, "JACK HARRIS CORNER. Every Stone Bathed in Human Blood … just destroyed by fire."

ENDNOTES

Chapter 1

1 C. P. Dearden. Birth information for Ben Thompson is from certificate Ca 530175. Curate George Stewart baptized Ben on November 13, 1843, at St. Botolph's Church, Knottingley. William and Mary Ann Thompson's marriage solemnized at the Parish Church of Pontefract, County of York, number 326, on October 21, 1840.

2 Ibid. Mr. Dearden transcribed the Custom House of Goole shipping records, which document that Ben Thompson's grandparents, William Thompson and his wife Mary of Knottingley, invested in full or partial ownership of trading vessels beginning on December 14, 1836. He would eventually invest in eleven different sloops and had an interest in two vessels at the time of his death. Cited hereafter as Goole Shipping Records. The English Census of April 1841 discloses on Shepherd's Bridge, Knottingley, the business and residence of William Thompson, grocer, forty-five; wife Mary, forty; sons Benjamin, twelve; John, ten; Samuel, four and Sarah, a female servant, age fifteen. The same census shows the profession of Ben Thompson's father William as "mariner" and places his home near his father's grocery store. Anne Beck provided the information that mariner William Thompson was born December 17, 1816. The exact birthdate of his wife Mary Ann (Baker) Thompson is not known, but she was probably born between the years 1816-1818.

3 Ibid. William "Billy" Thompson's birthdate is from certificate C1 53017. He was born "twenty minutes to 8 p.m." On September 10, 1845, at St. Botolph's Church Curate George Stewart baptized Billy.

4 Ibid. The annuity information is from the Last Will and Testament of William Thompson, grocer, and his exact date of death appears on his gravestone.

5 *San Antonio Daily Express*, March 13, 1884.

6 C. P. Dearden. Goole Shipping Records. *Austin Daily Statesman*, March 13, 1884. The *Statesman* mistakenly reported that the father of Ben and Billy "was an English officer in the British Navy." Dale T. Schoenberger pointed out the statement of his being an officer was suspect in his book *The Gunfighters*, 147. C.P. Dearden also researched the question and determined only one Knottingley resident did serve in the Royal Navy as an officer during the 1840s and his name was not Thompson.

7 This information is from the Gill-Thompson Family Bible which shows Mary Jane Thompson's birth date and an English certified copy of an entry of birth.

8 C.P. Dearden provided copy of the Last Will and Testament of Mary Thompson.

9 Ibid. The English census of April 1851 shows William Thompson, mariner and wife Mary Ann, both thirty-three years of age; sons Benjamin, age seven and William, age five with daughter Mary Jane, age two years. Benjamin and William were both listed as "scholars" indicating they were both attending a formal school.

10 The Bakers sailed from Liverpool arriving on August 18, 1834, on the ship *Constitution*. Listed on the ship's manifest: William Baker, age twenty-five, occupation "joiner"; wife Matilda, age twenty-one and son John. In September 1850, William Baker, then forty-one, earned his living as a carpenter. Their eldest child, John, then seventeen, was born in England. Ann, then fourteen, and Richard, age twelve, were born in New York. Their other children, William, age ten; Matilda, age eight and Jane, age three, were born in Texas. Travis County 1850 census, 320.

11 *Texas State Gazette*, July 12, 1851.

12 Ibid.

13 Ibid. July 19, 1851.

14 Ibid. August 2, 1851. The *Austin Statesman* of January 17, 1878, in its popular column "Texas Facts and Fancies" incorrectly reported: "[Ben Thompson's] family came to this country in 1851, and had scarcely arrived here when his uncle and aunt were killed by a runaway negro [*sic*], who was lynched."

15 New Orleans Passenger Lists 1820–1945, National Archives Series, Number M259-36. This information was discovered by Ken Aaron and Lisa Lach.

16 Eva Karling, "Reminiscences of the Life of One of Bastrop's Pioneers," *Bastrop Advertiser*, March 1932, newspaper interview. The article outlines the life of Mary Jane (Thompson) Gill.

17 Ibid.

18 Ibid.

19 Letters of Guardianship approved and signed by Travis County Chief Justice John B. Costa, on May 1, 1855, appointing William C. Reager, guardian of the person and estate of William Baker, Richard Baker and Jane Baker, minors. Reager, born in Virginia, was in 1860, a thirty-seven-year-old farmer living with his wife, Ann, twenty-four, their natural born son, William, two years-of-age. Others in the household were William Baker, nineteen, Matilda Baker, seventeen, and Jane Baker, twelve. Travis County 1860 census.

20 *San Antonio Light*, March 12, 1884. *San Antonio Daily Express*, March 13, 1884.

21 John A. Green was the younger brother of confederate Civil War hero General Tom Green.

22 *San Antonio Daily Express*, March 13, 1884. J.B. Gillett, "Ben Thompson and Billy Sims" in *Frontier Times*, October, 1934, Vol. 12, No. 1. Gillett wrote that Ben Thompson attended Professor Swancoat's private school. Evidence suggests otherwise as Austin historian Mary Starr Barkley found that Swancoat's school for boys and girls was in Austin from 1860 to 1870. Barkley. *History of Travis County and Austin, 1839-1899*. Austin: The Steck Company, 167. J.B. Gillett grew up in Austin, but in 1860 he was only three years old so it is doubtful that he would have had first-hand knowledge of the schools Ben Thompson attended. Also, other evidence exists that Thompson was serving with the Texas Rangers for most of 1860 and in 1861 he enlisted in the Confederate Army remaining in the service for the duration of the war.

23 *San Antonio Daily Express*, March 13, 1884. In the *Galveston Daily News* of March 3, 1884, Ben is quoted as saying: "I am an old printer myself. I worked in the old *Gazette* office under [John] Marshall and [W.S.] Oldham, and before that

I had been in the old *State-Times* office under Rip Ford and Joe Walker. I was at one time on A.B. Norton's *Intelligencer*, and was working the old *Sentinel*, under Colonel Gibson, at the time of [the] Gibson-Paschal imbroglio." Barkley, *History of Travis County and Austin, 1839-1899*, 210-11. Thompson's most famous employer was John Salmon "Rip" Ford. Ford arrived in Texas at the age of twenty-one, shortly after the fall of the Alamo. The following next two years he served under legendary Texas Ranger Jack Hays. As Hays's adjutant during the Mexican War, he acquired his famous nickname. In his casualty reports, Ford would always neatly print "Rest In Peace" above the names of the slain. Later, when battle conditions hurried him, he shortened his message to "R.I.P." In the years following his discharge, Ford alternately practiced medicine, taught Sunday school, and became a newspaper publisher and in partnership with Joe Walker, an old Ranger friend, he published the *Austin State Times* until 1857. His career included temperance leader, route surveyor, he served as a member of both the Texas House of Representatives and Senate. Ford was elected mayor of Austin. His fame rose throughout the state as he performed as a successful Indian fighter and Civil War commander. For a superior biography of Ford see *Fighting Stock: "Rip" Ford of Texas* by Richard B. McCaslin (Fort Worth: TCU Press, 2011).

24 In the 1880 United States Census from Keith County, Nebraska, Billy Thompson gave his occupation as "printer." Of course, by 1880 Billy was a longtime professional gambler, the printer trade long since forgotten.

25 *Galveston Daily News*, February 3, 1905. Judge Alexander Watkins Terrell's speech.

26 *San Antonio Light*, March 12, 1884. *San Antonio Daily Express*, March 13, 1884.

27 Texas gunmen Cullen Baker, John Wesley Hardin and William P. Longley all shot their first victim as teenagers.

28 Subsequent evidence reported in Thompson's obituaries has indicated Ben was involved in more than one shooting incident as a youth. One of his hometown newspapers, Austin's *Statesman*, March 13, 1884, related what may have been the first time he fired his gun at another.

> As early as 1858-59, he had his first shooting scrape. In company with a number of other boys he went hunting geese. The party divided, and one division went down one side of the Colorado [River] and the other the oposite [*sic*]. A flock of geese were seen on an island in the stream and both parties tried to crawl up to them and get within shooting distance, the boys on the other side from Thompson shot first and only scared the geese away. This made Thompson and the boys with him angry and they began to shoot at the others. The other side returned the fire and a regular battle ensued. Finally, Thompson proposed to the leader of the other side ... to settle it by a duel. This was agreed to and the two placed themselves forty paces apart and blazed away at each other with shotguns. Both were wounded, and Thompson's opponent had to be carried home by his comrade.

The *Statesman* did not name his opponent. However, it did state he was "still living and a most highly respected citizen."

Texas Siftings, March 29, 1884 (Austin): A variation of the hunting story has both brothers defending their father's honor. Ben and Billy "were returning from hunting, when two elegantly dressed young gentlemen in a buggy drove past them. As they did so, one of them remarked that the two boys were the sons of that old drunkard Thompson, where upon Ben elevated his gun, and filled the cuticles of those young men with No. 7 bird shot."

San Antonio Daily Express, March 13, 1884. Another Texas newspaper published that Ben Thompson's first shooting episode "is of record in the minds of the residents of the city of Austin." The paper went on to describe how Ben, about the age of fifteen, on July 4, while employed driving a water cart, "got into a difficulty with a youth, and to assert his manhood and soothes [*sic*] his injured feelings, procured a shot-gun, loaded with bird shot and emptied it into the body of the offending youth." The boy was only wounded and soon recovered.

29 *Statesman*, January 17, 1878.

30 William M. Walton, *Life and Adventures of Ben Thompson, the Famous Texan* (Austin, TX: Edwards and Church, 1884. Facsimile edition by The Steck Company, Austin, Texas, 1956), 5. Hereafter, cited as Walton, *Thompson*. On the title page, the publisher made the claim, "Including a detailed and authentic statement of his birth, history and adventures, by one who has known him since a child." It is not known exactly when Walton and Thompson first met each other. Ben was seven years old when he immigrated to Austin, Texas. Almost two years later, at the age of twenty-one, Walton arrived in Austin on February 9, 1853, and immediately began to practice law. The October 1858 Smith shooting may have been the incident which resulted in the first meeting of Thompson and Walton. In the spring of 1859, Walton added his name to the petition asking the governor to pardon Thompson for wounding Smith. Later mutual acquaintances may have helped to establish their relationship further. Returning to his law career after the Civil War, Walton practiced law with William de Normandie, a former mayor of Austin and one-time-neighbor of the Thompson family, and subsequently, he also entered into a law partnership with attorney John A. Green, the gentleman whose earlier sponsorship continued the formal education of both Ben and Billy Thompson. Walton's biography of Thompson cannot be used without much skepticism. It is certainly prejudicial and sympathetic towards Thompson, and Walton's assertions of fact are often refuted by other contemporary sources. However, Walton's close relationship with Ben Thompson does provide a valuable insight into Thompson's character and behavior unavailable from any other source.

31 Floyd B. Streeter. *Ben Thompson: Man with a Gun*, (Frederick Fell, Inc., New York, 1957), 22. Posthumously published, in the Introduction historian William F. Kelleher wrote in his introduction to the Fell edition, "serves as a monument to the author." Hereafter, cited as Streeter, *Thompson*.

32 *Southern Intelligencer*, December 8, 1858. In 1860, the North Carolina born Browning was a twenty-eight-year-old lawyer with a wife and two children. 1860 Travis County census, 774. Browning would lose his life while serving the Confederacy. Judge Terrell later recalled Ben's appearance when he stood before him. "When I first saw him he was brought from jail with face bleached by long conferment [*sic*]. With his flazen [*sic*] curls and blue eyes, I thought him the handsomest child I had ever seen." *Galveston Daily News*, February 3, 1905. Terrell was instrumental in promoting the factual study of early Texas history by serving on the publication committee of the *Quarterly* of the Texas State Historical Association. The Texas County of Terrell is named in his honor.

33 A prominent banker, James H. Raymond, later served as President of the Texas State Lunatic Asylum in Austin. In 1849, Doctor C. G. Keenan was elected to the Third Texas Legislature, where he was selected as the Speaker of the House of Representatives.

34 Walton, *Thompson*, 7-8. The legal documents on file at the Texas State Archives list both January 11 and 13 as the date Ben Thompson was convicted of wounding James Smith. Docket No: 1185: *The State of Texas v. Benjamin Thompson.*

35 The petition is on file at the Texas State Archives. A close examination of the document reveals an impressive list of signers including the original judge involved in the affair, E. F. Calhoun, plus the following: P. DeCordova, E. Raven and F. T. Duffau, city aldermen; Charles S. West, attorney and state legislator who would rise to become an associate justice of the Texas Supreme Court; S. G. Sneed, teacher; N. G. Shelley, attorney, state senator and future Confederate brigadier general; Dennis Corwin, civil engineer and future Travis County sheriff; Business man John T. Miller, livery stable owner and father of Monroe Miller, a close lifelong friend of Ben Thompson; William Oliphant, pioneer photographer whose pictures captured many scenes of early Austin; Charles F. Millet, Austin's first volunteer fire chief, lumber dealer, contractor and builder of the opera house bearing his name, and finally William M. Walton, Ben Thompson's most noted defense lawyer and his first biographer.

36 Austin's jail dated from 1856 and was considered one of the most secure in the state. It was, however, often so overcrowded with inmates the jail was referred to as the "Black Hole of Calcutta," based upon the recent atrocity during the 1857 Sepoy Mutiny in British India. The building was eventually razed in 1906.

37 Gov. Hardin R. Runnels's Records, Texas State Archives.

38 *Statesman*, March 13, 1884. The newspaper added some details in what appears to be the same affair. The brief description it published erred by changing the wounded boy's name to Johnson. However, Thompson's victim was identified as a black youth and also incorrectly stated that Ben's time in jail stretched to "about six months."

39 Walton, *Thompson*, 8-10.

40 Ibid., *Thompson*, 12.

41 *Daily Capitol* (Austin), March 13, 1884. The *Dallas Daily Herald* and the *Houston Daily Post*, of Thursday, March 13, 1884, also published the following identical report carried by the *Daily Capitol* of why a teenage Ben Thompson left Austin for New Orleans. "A year or two before the War Between the States Ben was in New Orleans, where he had gone to work with a Bookbinder that had formerly carried on business in Austin." Samuel Webster Slater was born in 1813 at Hartford, Connecticut. Evidence indicates Slater's stay in Austin was short-lived. Beginning in 1849 his name and business is listed in the New Orleans city directory and continues every year until 1862 when publication temporarily ceased during the Civil War. The only exception is the city directory of 1860, where the page that should display his entry is missing. Slater carried on his bookbinding business until his death on November 15, 1882. His obituary appeared the next day in the New Orleans's leading newspaper, *The Daily Picayune.* Walton stated while in New Orleans Thompson worked "as a printer at the Commercial job office." The New Orleans City Directories for 1858, 1859 and 1861 list Samuel Slater's address as 23 Commercial Place.

42 *Statesman*, March 13, 1884.

43 Walton, *Thompson*, 12. During an interview with a reporter of the *Galveston Daily News* published March 3, 1884 Ben Thompson spoke of his time in the 1850s when he worked as a printer for various newspapers in Austin. After listing his hometown employers, he stated, "I was in New Orleans for a while, also,

working on the *True Delta*." He made no mention of Slater, perhaps because he was only discussing his work experience with newspapers.

44 Walton, *Thompson*, 12-18. The question has to be asked: Did Ben Thompson participate in a knife duel in New Orleans? A search through New Orleans city directories for the years 1853-1860 for an Emil or Emile de Tour, de la Tour, or la Tour was unsuccessful. If he was a member of the aristocracy and a permanent resident of New Orleans a listing should have been found. However, once again Ben Thompson's actions as described by Walton fit Ben's personality, but without additional corroborating contemporary evidence the authenticity of the episode remains suspect.

45 *Austin Daily Capitol*, March 13, 1884.

46 Pekka Hamalainen, *The Comanche Empire* (Yale University Press, 2008), 301-307.

47 Hardin Runnels earned the distinction of being the only man to have ever defeated Sam Houston in an election before Texas voters. Runnels, a veteran politician, had served three terms in the Texas House of Representatives, once as the speaker of that body. In 1855, he was elected lieutenant-governor and two years later he won the governorship over Houston. After losing his re-election bid to Houston in 1859, Runnels retired from politics.

48 Captain Edward Burleson Jr. experiences as an Indian fighter dated back more than a decade. He had previously served twice as an officer in the rangers. His famous father was elected as vice-president of the Republic of Texas.

49 Walton, *Thompson*, 164-68. At this time Ben Thompson began to look "to gambling, women and ... intoxicants" for enjoyment. Apparently, the seventeen-year old desired even more excitement than the previous mentioned pastime and decided to become a ranger per the *San Antonio Daily Express*, March 13, 1884. A search of records at the Texas State Archives by Donaly E. Brice and at the Texas Ranger Hall of Fame and Museum by Dan Agler failed to uncover any enlistment documentation concerning Ben Thompson. Mr. Agler offered a brief explanation on why, perhaps nothing could be found: "I could not find any record of a Ben Thompson during the 1847-1900 period. There have been many disasters befall the original records since the days of the Texas Republic and we are aware that information is lacking in the early period of Ranger history." Thompson's memoir depicting his service under Burleson along with Hall's later writings provide the best evidence that he did serve as a Ranger. In addition, Ben Thompson was not counted in the Federal census with his family when they were enumerated in Austin on August 3, 1860. Plus his account matches the formation of Burleson's command, and the enlistment period of Buckskin Sam Hall. Oddly, Walton's placement of this episode in his biography of Thompson was chronologically set in 1879-1880. This probably was an oversight due to Walton's rush to provide a manuscript to his publisher. At the time of Thompson's death it was falsely reported he once rode with a Mexican border leader that Texans feared and hated more than any other, Juan Nepomuceno Cortina. The authors could find no evidence to support this claim and believe it was merely to inflate his already notorious reputation.

50 Samuel Stone Hall, age twenty-one, was mustered in as a private in the Mounted Rangers on February 8, 1860, by Captain Edward Burleson in San Antonio. Ranger Muster Roll.

51 Walton, *Thompson*, 168 -172. Born on a farm outside Leominster, Massachusetts, on July 23, 1838, and seeking a more exciting life than farming offered, Samuel Stone Hall sailed to Texas. He was sixteen years old when he arrived, and hired on

as a bullwhacker, but this proved to be too tame. Being a Ranger was more to his liking, and besides serving under Burleson, he also served under Ben McCulloch. In February 1861 Hall sided with Texas and the Confederacy and enlisted in Colonel John Ford's command. After the Civil War, he owned and operated a San Antonio hotel named the Moodie House before he began writing poems under the pen name of "Buckskin Sam." The *Dallas Weekly Herald* published one of the first poems on Saturday, May 1, 1875, entitled "Ranging the Chaparral, or the Midnight Bugler." Burleson, Cortina, and others he met or knew of along the border are mentioned in it. Eventually Hall returned home to his family in Massachusetts but his wild drinking bouts and general rowdy behavior shocked his relatives, and he once again moved on to New York. He returned to the hotel business, and while working as a clerk he was recognized by author Colonel Prentiss Ingraham and Buffalo Bill Cody. Later during the early 1880s, Ingraham, always seeking inspiration for Beadle and Adams's weekly *Boys Library of Sport, Story and Adventure*, used Hall as a subject. One of the more entertaining tales Ingraham penned about Hall was *Plaza and Plain; or, Wild Adventures of 'Buckskin Sam,' (Major Sam S. Hall,) The Noted Texan Ranger, Scout, Guide, Ranchero and Indian-Fighter of the South-west Border.* Cody and Ingraham encouraged Hall to write about his experiences in Texas. This resulted in his first novel entitled *Kit Carson Jr., the Crack Shot of the West. A Romance of the Lone Star State.* Beatle and Adams published it on June 7, 1877. The following excerpt is from *Kit Carson Jr.*, is an example of Buckskin Sam's early writing style.

> All the Rangers, who were just ready to mount and rejoin the main command, now turned their eyes and attention up the stream toward the fast-approaching horseman, whom all recognized as Daring Bill, the brother of Fighting Ben. Dashing down toward them, at times causing his horse to bound so near the bank of the river that, as the hoofs of the animal spurned the turf, for the next spring, the earth upon which the horse stood an instant before would be detached and fall with a great splash down into the stream—the bank above projecting over the water-line below. Riding with as wild, careless, and graceful a manner as a Comanche brave, this young man, showing, by his dare-devil style, by his near approach to the edge of the dangerous bank, by the yell that burst from his lips as he saw the Rangers, a perfect type of the young Texan, who fears nothing, and glories in braving danger, no matter of what form or from what quarter. Billy Thompson was the dandy Ranger of the Rio Grande. He was always dressed in such nobby style, and no amount of scouting could set him back any, or prevent his looking neat and tidy. He was just as eager for a fight as his brother Ben, and you often hear speak of the fighting Thompsons, no matter in what portion of the State of Texas you may be traveling. A costly sombrero, trimmed with gold, a golden-snake [skin] for a band, sat jauntily upon Bill's well-shaped head; a fancy embroidered jacket of buckskin and leggings of the same, to match, glittering with the buttons which ran thickly down the seams, amid the long fringes; top boots, silver spurs, and red silk sash completed his make-up in the way of clothing; while the ivory butts of two large-sized Colt's revolvers projected from the ornamental scabbards, and a huge bowie-knife was stuck in the left side of his belt. A Sharp's carbine hung from his saddle-horn, and the bridle and saddle of his

> horse were one mass of exquisite stamped leather, and silver filagree-work. The horse seemed created for the rider—a beautiful mustang, black as midnight, and graceful as a prairie fawn. Take them, rider and horse together, they were as fine a sight as one would wish to see, as they came dashing down the banks of the Rio Grande, and into the midst of our Ranger friends. Bill Thompson's hands were extended, right and left, to all, as he said. "Howde, Pards! Is the big game over? Am I too late to take a hand? Howde, Ben! Shake, old boy!" "Yer a little late, fur this deal, Bill; thar are the last keerds what was slung out," said Big Foot, pointing toward the swaying forms of the executed bandits.

Hall earned a solid reputation as a yarn spinner as he authored at least sixty-five novels and countless magazine articles featuring adventures and romances set in Texas and the Southwest. In 1882, Hall moved to Wilmington, Delaware, to live with an old friend from his Texas days. He died there of pneumonia four years later. His remains were shipped to his boyhood home, and he is buried in Leominster. When informed of his passing, Beadle and Adams paid for his funeral expenses.

52 Capt. Ed Burleson and Pvt. Samuel Stone Hall were officially discharged on September 7, 1860. Texas Ranger Muster Rolls.

53 Enumerator S. J. Woods visited the Thompson household on August 3, 1860. Head of Household is shown to be "W. Thompson," age 42, whose profession is listed as mariner. He had $50 of personal estate. His wife, M.A. Thompson, is also listed as forty-two-years-old. Others were son W. Thompson, age fifteen, and daughters M. J. Thompson, age twelve, F. Thompson, age two. The two older children, as were the parents, are shown to be natives of England and both had attended a formal school within the year. The two-year-old was born in Texas. Others in the household were John Cole, a twenty-five-year-old farmer from Indiana, listed as a pauper, and a Carol Hamner, a forty-year-old native South Carolinian who is shown to be insane. 1860 Travis County census, 540.

54 *San Antonio Daily Express*, March 13, 1884.

55 The 1860 census confirms the family oral history that the Thompson family time and again lived with other relatives and/or boarders. In the 1850s, funds were released by a commissioner's court for the care of insane people and paupers. Mary Starr Barkley, *History of Travis County and Austin 1839 - 1899*, 241.

56 C. P. Dearden. Last Will and Testament of Mary Thompson.

57 Eva Karling, "Reminiscences of the Life of One of Bastrop's Pioneers," *Bastrop Advertiser*, March 1932, newspaper interview. The article outlines the life of Mary Jane (Thompson) Gill.

58 Walton, *Thompson*, 19-20.

Chapter 2

1 *Austin State Gazette*, June 15, 1861. Curiously, the *Gazette* reprinted a report entitled "Russell's Letters to the Times. The Fall of Sumter" which originally appeared in the *London Times* of May 11, 1861. Russell was the great British war correspondent, William Howard "Bull Run" Russell, who saw and reported so much of the American Civil War to the English people.

2 Service Records of Benjamin F. Thompson, Second Regiment Texas Cavalry, C. S. A. Old Military Records Division, National Archives. Often, official records such as the one above provided Ben Thompson with one of a variety of middle initials.

Anne Beck confirms that he did not have a middle name and any listing of middle initial is a clerical error.

3 Confederate Muster Roll Records. George W. Hagler, age forty-eight, was an officer in Thompson's company, and he was later discharged at the end of his enlistment.

4 Walton, *Thompson*, 21-23. A brief telling of the legendary shooting was first published in New York's *The World*, January 6, 1878 in an article entitled "Shooting Men of Texas." The *Austin Statesman* reprinted the Ben Thompson portion of the article eleven days later on January 17. *Austin Daily Capitol* of March 13, 1884. At the time of Thompson's death, in addition to the *Daily Capitol*, many other Texas newspapers inaccurately recounted Thompson's shooting of two fellow Confederate soldiers while on duty at Fort Clark.

5 *Austin Daily Capitol*, March 28, 1884. "From a Comrade-in-Arms." Confederate Muster Roll Records for William D. Vance and George W. Hagler state that both enlisted on April 13, 1861 at Weatherford, Texas, and on May 23 at San Antonio transferred into the Confederate States Army, Company H, Second Regiment Texas Mounted Riflemen. Colonel John S. Ford, Commanding.

6 Nathan Browner, age twenty-one, enrolled in April 1861, as a member of the Second Texas State Troops and was mustered in as a private in H. A. Hamner's Company H of the Second Texas Mounted Rifles, C. S .A. on May 23, 1861, in San Antonio for a period of twelve months. Evidence substantiating that he was accidentally wounded by Ben Thompson does not appear in his existing service records. The wound must not have been very serious because in September and October 1861, he was serving on scout duty and on December 12 of that same year, he was promoted to corporal. Confederate Research Center, Hillsboro, Texas.

7 Charge and Specifications preferred against Private Benjamin Thompson, H Company, 2nd Regiment Texas Mounted Rifles, Records Division, War Department, Rebel Archives. National Archives, Index To Compiled Service Records Of Confederate Soldiers Who Served In Organizations From The State Of Texas Microfilm M227, Roll 36. The criminal charge was signed by Colonel John S. Ford, First Lieutenant George W. Hagler, Lieutenant William D. Vance and by Corporal Nathan Browner. William Dennis Vance, born in Illinois in 1842, prior to the advent of the Civil War, his family moved to Arkansas where they lived for a number of years. Vance initially enlisted in the Second Regiment Texas Cavalry on March 15, 1861, and was assigned to Company H and given the initial rank of corporal. He was mustered out attaining the rank of 3rd Lieutenant. After the war he returned to Arkansas, where he served the community of Vaugine Township, Jefferson County as a justice of the peace for twelve years. Well respected, Judge Vance died on his seventieth birthday on October 26, 1912. United States Civil War Soldier Records and Profiles. *Pine Bluff* [Arkansas] *Daily Commercial*, October 26, 28, 1912.

8 Military Service records of Benjamin F. Thompson, Old Military Records Division, National Archives.

9 Ibid.

10 Walton, *Thompson*, 24.

11 Chuck Parsons, *Phil Coe: Texas Gambler* (Wolfe City, Texas: Henington Publishing Company, 1984), 5, 20. Philip H. Coe enlisted in Company D, Woods Regiment Texas Cavalry on March 24, 1862, at Belmont, Gonzales County, Texas. Later that same year on September 21, records list him as a 1st Lieutenant of Company F, Second Texas Regiment Cavalry. Records frequently list Coe as absent, sick, or absent without leave and a regimental return dated November 1862 has Private

Coe again listed as absent without leave. In March 1863, the popular Coe would again be a 1st Lieutenant for Company F, Second Texas Regiment.

12 Walton, *Thompson*, 25-26.

13 Thomas North, *Five Years In Texas; or, What You Did Not Hear During The War From January 1861 To January 1865. A Narrative Of His Travels, Experiences, and Observations, in Texas and Mexico* (Cincinnati: Elm Street Printing Co., 1870), 71-72, 104-5.

14 Eva Karling, "Reminiscences of the Life of One of Bastrop's Pioneers," *Bastrop Advertiser*, March 1932, newspaper interview. The article outlines the life of Mary Jane (Thompson) Gill. Mary Jane informed the reporter that her brother Ben "was severely wounded in the battle of the '*Harriot* [*sic*] *Lane*.'"

15 In the fall of 1862, William G. Tobin formed a company for the Second Texas Cavalry and became its captain. He previously served in the Texas Rangers, first as a captain and later elected to the rank of major. In 1859-60, Tobin participated in driving Juan Cortina and his partisans out of the lower Rio Grande Valley.

16 Walton, *Thompson*, 26.

17 Streeter, *Thompson*, 46. In San Antonio on April 15, 1861 forty-two-year old Charles L. Pyron enlisted in Colonel John S. Ford's Second Regiment, Texas Mounted Volunteers for a period of one year. When he enlisted Pyron was appointed a captain and throughout the war he was promoted through the ranks: first to major, then lieutenant colonel and finally he became the colonel in command of the regiment. *Galveston Daily News*, March 3, 1884. During an interview with a Galveston reporter Ben Thompson confirmed, "during the late war I was in Pyron's regiment."

18 Walton, *Thompson*, 27- 8. The Confederate Muster Rolls at the Harold Washington Public Library, Chicago, list a William Thompson, private, Company F, Second Texas Cavalry. Records indicate the same man also served with Woods' Regiment, Thirty-Second Texas Cavalry.

19 Walton, *Thompson*, 28.

20 Military service records of Benjamin Thompson, Old Military Records Division, National Archives.

21 Anne Beck. Kate's correct name was Catherine L. Moore. Her brother James was born in 1848 and was two years younger than Kate. Their sisters, Louisa, Mary (called Mollie) and Sarah were born in 1853, 1854 and 1856, respectively.

In 1866, Elizabeth Moore sold the farmstead to John Hancock, a very prominent Austin resident and staunch Unionist whose public life included serving four terms as a United States Congressman. Hancock purchased the farm as an investment but never lived on the property; instead his former slaves worked the farm for him. Over the years, subsequent owners made many changes to the buildings before they fell into disrepair.

The Moore-Hancock Farmstead's address is 4811 Sinclair Avenue, Austin and is currently owned by Michael and Karen Collins. The one hundred fifty years old log home and surrounding buildings are on the National Register of Historic Places and are a Texas Historical Landmark. In 1989, Karen Collins noticed a condemned, dilapidated old house. Curious as to what might be under the pink asbestos siding she inspected the building with her husband Michael, an archeologist with the Texas Archeological Research Laboratory, and together they discovered it was a log home dating back to the pioneer period of Texas. Michael and Karen Collins then spent the next five years researching the history of the house and lovingly restored it as close as possible back to the original condition. It is a rare example of pioneer architecture dating from the 1840s. The *Austin-American Statesman*, May 27, 1999. "Little House in the City."

22 Anne Beck. St. David's Episcopal Archives, Marriage Records, Vol. 1, microfilm roll #5.

23 Military Service records of Benjamin Thompson, Old Military Records Division, National Archives.

24 Ibid.

25 Only Gillett's reminiscence of this episode survives and his story is not corroborated by any other documentation. J.B. Gillett, "Ben Thompson and Billy Sims," *Frontier Times*, Vol. 12, No. 1 (October 1934), 2. James Buchanan Gillett was born in Austin on November 4, 1856. The 1860 Census of the City of Austin lists the Gillett family at dwelling 583; at that time the Thompson family was residing at dwelling 540. From 1861-1867, Mrs. F. M. Foster, a longtime Austin educator, was running a primary school for younger children.

26 Walton, *Thompson*, 31-57.

27 On February 10, 1864, Colonel Ford ordered Captain Ware, "to arrest any [deserters] who come within your reach." Spotting Ben Thompson on the Mexican side of the river may have raised Ware's suspicions as to whether or not Ben Thompson was absent without leave.

28 The *Galveston News*, June 27, 1864, published a telegraphed account of the attempted robbery of the Customhouse at Eagle Pass. "On the 19th at one o'clock p.m., the renegades, about one hundred strong, attacked Eagle Pass, and after a fight our men withdrew to the custom house with the loss of three horses, one man killed and five wounded. At last accounts, the enemy had withdrawn and our forces re-occupied the fort and custom house, which were being fortified. The enemy were in position on the Texas side of the river above Eagle Pass, with the Federal flag displayed. Capt. Weir [*sic*] commanded in the fight. Twenty-three of his men were armed ... The citizens had organized and reinforced Capt. Weir. Reinforcements had been sent from San Antonio. Capt. Weir says he will hold out until succor can reach him, if possible."

29 Julius' father was Major John Henry Brown (1820-1895), newspaper editor, Indian fighter, Confederate officer, politician, legislator and historian. Brown spent the last years of his eventful life authoring *Indian Wars and Pioneers of Texas* and *The History of Texas from 1685 to 1892,* both works are considered the standard in their respective field.

30 In 1855, Colonel B. Riddle, along with John S. Ford, was selected as agent for Texas to deal with Mexican General Santiago Vidauri, who one year earlier was successful in his rebellion against Santa Anna's national government. General Vidauri gained control of the State of Nuevo Leon. Riddle had strong ties to Mexico. He married a Mexican woman and lived in Chihuahua where he ran a merchandising business.

31 Santos Benavides (1827-1891), born in Laredo, he spent his life there fighting Indians, Juan Cortina and his partisans as well as Union soldiers. He served as mayor of Laredo, chief justice of Webb County and in 1860 was selected to be a captain of Texas State Troops. He later raised a cavalry regiment and was eventually promoted to the rank of brigadier general. The highest rank achieved by a Mexican-American serving the Confederacy.

32 Records indicate that Martino (Martin) Gonzales enlisted at Laredo in April 1861 in Captain Santos Benavides' Texas State Troops of the Rio Grande District. His initial rank was first corporal and in January 1862 he re-enlisted as a first sergeant.

In February 1864, with the rank of first lieutenant, he led a twenty-five-man patrol on a 200-mile long reconnaissance down the Rio Grande valley towards the Federals at Fort Brown. He discovered a Federal movement in time for Santos Benavides to successfully defend Laredo and repulse the attack. Confederate Muster records on file at the Texas State Archives and the Confederate Research Center, Hillsboro, Texas. Jerry Thompson, *Laredo-A Pictorial History*, (Donning Company/Publishers, Norfolk, Virginia, 1986), 159.

33 A search of available Confederate military records failed to discover a listing for a Miguel Zertuche.

34 Walton, *Thompson*, 46. In his biography of Thompson, Walton called Joe Owens "captain" giving an indication that many of his readers would be familiar with the man. In his letter published in the Austin *Statesman* during March 1879, Ben Thompson also addressed Owens as "captain" providing evidence he was a man of prominence. Like Thompson, Owens (by then a resident of Galveston) was in Leadville during its boom period looking for opportunity and he contemplated opening a fast freight line from the railroad head into Leadville. Austin *Statesman*, March 19, 27, 1879.

35 Ibid.

36 At this time a Lieutenant C. B. Gardiner, in command of a section of artillery, was part of Colonel Ford's forward movement against Fort Brown.

37 A saying primarily used in Great Britain, "a Daniel come to judgment," was written by William Shakespeare in his play, *The Merchant of Venice*. It alludes to the Biblical character Daniel, who was renowned for having excellent faculties of judgment.

38 It appears Ben Thompson was mistaken. Gonzales did not die in the shootout as he was listed as present for duty in August 1864. His name also appears on a roll of prisoners of war when General E. K. Smith, C. S. A. surrendered his command on June 2, 1865. He lived into the 1900s and applied for a Confederate pension when Texas began to honor requests in May 1899. Nothing has been found on a Juan Rodriguez under Santos Benavides' command. Confederate Research Center, Hillsboro, Texas.

39 Frank Brown, *Annals of Travis County and the City of Austin (from the Earliest Times to the Close of 1875)*, 60-63. A second description of this event is mentioned in the *Annals of Travis County*; claiming an alliance between the Willis family and the Comanche, originally came from J. W. Wilbarger, *Indian Depredations in Texas*, (Austin, Texas: Hutchings Printing House, 1889) 538-39. Facsimile edition in 1985 by Eakin Press of Austin, Texas.

40 *Statesman*, March 13, 1884.

41 Military Service records of Benjamin Thompson, Old Military Records Division, National Archives.

42 Walton, *Thompson*, 58-60. There was a John Combs, private, in the Travis Mounted Rifles, 26th Brigade, Texas Militia, who enlisted in June 1861. Texas State Archives, Confederate Muster Roll records.

43 Born in Kentucky in 1820, Dr. James M. Litten was among the many pro-unionists who lived in Austin at the outbreak of the Rebellion, and one of the few who chose to remain in the city during the war. His unpopular political views apparently did not slow his medical career or service to the community. In February 1864, Dr. Litten was listed as a certified physician by the Travis County commissioner's court. By 1871, his home and office was in the First Ward at the northeast corner of Colorado and Bois d'Arc streets, and at this time he was the official city

physician and chairman of Austin's Board of Health. Dr. Litten was a corporate officer for the Austin Electric Company when it was formed in January 1879, and in 1888 he served as a member of the city's school board.

44 The Miller stable was near the corner of Congress Avenue and Bois d' Arc (present day 7th street).

45 W. H. Sharp was born in Tennessee, as was his wife and two children. Census records indicate he arrived in Texas sometime after 1858. He served from 1863-1865 but he was not a career lawman. He normally earned his living as a house painter. 1860 Travis County census, 644.

46 Walton, *Thompson*, 57-64. Travis County Courthouse Records, State of Texas v. John Rapp and Ben Thompson, Austin History Center. A newspaper of the time describing the Coombs affair has not been discovered. The first mention of the event did not appear in print until a *New York World* article, dated January 6, 1878, entitled "Shooting Men of Texas." The *Statesman*, January 17, 1878, reprinted the portion of the *World's* article featuring Ben Thompson. "One night Captain Rabb appeared at his house, wounded in both hands, and appealed for assistance against over a dozen men, led by Lieutenant Coombs. Ben's mother and wife begged him to remain at home, but armed with his revolver he came down into the main street of Austin, and was immediately fired upon by Coombs. Thompson, who is one of the quickest and most unerring of pistol shots, killed Coombs and a horse, and the whole party galloped out of town. This was in 1864." At the time of Ben's death Austin's *Daily Capitol*, March 12, 1884, gave a few additional details in describing the fatal Thompson-Coombs encounter under the "Biographical Sketch" portion of the article. "The next serious affray was with John Coombs, whom he killed here in Austin. It was a general street fight, and the difficulty originated about the captaincy of a military company. Capt. Rapp was in the fight, which took place near Miller's livery stable. Another man was seriously wounded at the same time. He was admitted to bail in the case by Justice McLaughlin, stood trial and the jury acquitted him." *Statesman*, March 13, 1884. The newspaper reported, "[I]n the year 1862, John Rapp and a man named Combs had a fuss near where Mr. Brahl's cigar store now is and Thompson came to the rescue of his friend Rapp and shot Combs. He was not tried for this." *San Antonio Daily Express*, March 13, 1884. The *Express* reported "About 1863 the exact time not directly remembered, he became involved in a difficulty with a lieutenant and two privates, which affair Ben and another party forced on them, and although it is said he caused the Lieutenant to make the attack, he killed him and wounded one of the privates. With the good luck which seemed to attend him up to the hour of his demise, he got out of the difficulty with little punishment, if any, and an abundance of notoriety."

47 *San Antonio Daily Express*, March 13, 1884.

48 Service Records of Benjamin F. Thompson, Second Regiment Texas Cavalry, C. S. A., Old Military Records Division, National Archives.

49 Travis County Courthouse Records, Indictment for gambling at euchre and Docket No. 1528, Austin History Center. *Statesman*, July 5, 1990. James R. Jackson was interred in Austin's Oakwood Cemetery. He was born February 27, 1818 and died March 18, 1865. List of Marshals and Police Chiefs of City of Austin, Texas furnished by the Austin Police Department.

50 Walton, *Thompson*, 64, 66 -67.

51 Travis County Courthouse Records, Indictment for Theft, May 25, 1865. Austin History Center.

52 San Antonio Genealogical & Historical Society, Austin Cemetery Records, Alexander Eanes, City Sexton, forty-one. The cemetery is now named Oakwood. The details concerning the death of the Italian teamster are from the *Statesman* and *San Antonio Daily Express*, both dated March 13, 1884. The *Statesman* did not name the man while the *Express* called him Costia. Evidence of Ben Thompson being prosecuted for the fatal shooting of the Italian teamster has yet to be found. There was probably no investigation due to the lack of civil authority and the breakdown of the Confederate military. The affair, if not forgotten, was most likely ignored and Thompson escaped without any trouble, legal or otherwise.

Chapter 3

1 San Antonio Genealogical & Historical Society, Austin Cemetery Record, Alexander Eanes, City sexton, 41; "June 13[, 1865,] Cammel [*sic*] shot while Robbin [*sic*] Treasury age 23 Native of Texas."

2 Rapp had joined the Confederacy in 1861, had endured the agony of Sibley's fiasco in New Mexico, been wounded and made prisoner during the war, but was back in Texas in 1862. He was discharged at war's end. In 1860, Missourian John Rapp was twenty-five-years-old. He had married nineteen-year-old Kentucky-born Elizabeth Sower Rapp on November 17, 1858, but as yet had no children. Rapp claimed to have $1,920 in real estate and $2,250 in personal estate. At that time, they lived in the eastern side of Travis County.

Mike Cox, "The Great Texas Treasury Raid," www.truewesmagazine.com post March 31, 2015. Patrick Cox, "The Great Texas Treasury Robbery, June 11, 1865." *Journal* of the East Texas Historical Association, 51-53, Vol. 30, No. 2, 1992; *Galveston Daily News*, June 16, 1865, printing a report from William H. Prouse who was in Austin and gave first hand news of the robbery. George R. Freeman, born June 25, 1830 had been a Confederate captain in Company D, 23rd Texas Cavalry. Freeman became an attorney after the war. He died December 14, 1910 in Hamilton, Texas and is buried in Oakwood Cemetery in Austin. Aldevine "Al" L. Musgrove, born May 12, 1844, near Clarksville, Texas was a second lieutenant in Company D, 11th Texas Infantry. He became Doorkeeper of the Texas House of Representatives and served as policeman in Austin. He died May 9, 1919, in the Austin Confederate Home and was buried in Oakwood Cemetery. Frederick August "Fred" Sterzing, born April 9, 1844, in Siegene, Prussia served as a private in Company G, 16th Texas Infantry. He served as an Austin city official for fifty-five years, including forty-three years as tax assessor. He died February 26, 1928, in Austin and is buried in Oakwood Cemetery. James A. Mundie Jr., *et al. More Texas Burial Sites of Civil War and Reconstruction Era Notables*, Freeman, 182; Musgrove, 354; Sterzing, 462. Fred Sterzing was one of the Austin officials in the group photograph when Thompson was the newly elected city marshal. Lafayette Rogers "Reminiscences," p. 7, Call Number 2-23/1054, Texas State Archives.

3 Walton, *Thompson*, 66. St. David's Episcopal Church Archives, Austin. Vol. I., Microfilm role #5, 60.

4 The *Weekly Southern Intelligencer* of Austin, on August 1, 1865, published an appeal to all citizens to support and cooperate with the First Louisiana Cavalry, U.S.A., then stationed in Austin.

5 The United States Provost Marshal stationed at Galveston paroled Private Ben Thompson from Company I, Second Regiment Texas Cavalry. Old Military Records Division, National Archives.

6 Walton, *Thompson*, 66. The *Austin Daily Capitol*, March 13, 1884, substantiates Walton's version, publishing: "We were then under military rule and officers of the United States army did pretty much as they pleased with citizens."

7 *Austin Daily Capitol*, March 28, 1884. In this article, W. D. Vance, who had an earlier altercation with Ben but became friends after, stated: "The treatment he [Ben Thompson] received at the hands of the federal colonel in 1865 may have been and doubtless was the cause, to a great extent at least, of his subsequent career."

8 Walton, *Thompson*, 67. Walton stated the following pro-union men were approached to intervene on Ben Thompson's behalf including provisional Governor A. J. Hamilton, future United States Congressman John Hancock, also prominent candidates considered for the role as provisional governor: former Justice of the Texas Supreme Court James H. Bell, Dr. William C. Philips, and former and future Governor of Texas E. M. Pease.

9 Walton, *Thompson*, 67-69.

10 Andrew F. Rolle, *The Lost Cause: The Confederate Exodus to Mexico* (University of Oklahoma Press, Norman, 1965), Preface, 2-4.

11 *San Antonio Daily Express*, March 13, 1884, incorrectly stated in its review of Ben Thompson's life that he had "joined Cortinas [*sic*], the noted Mexican leader." Cortina's brief alliance with General Mejia and this episode in Ben Thompson's life may have been the basis for the false rumor that Thompson had ridden as one of Juan Cortina's men.

12 W. J. Gilly's: His first and middle initials are from the Austin *Statesman*, February 10. 1885.

13 Walton, *Thompson*, 68. William Walton provided the following description of the two men who agreed to help Ben Thompson escape to Mexico. "Gomez was a Louisiana raised Spaniard and adventurer, who held his place only because it paid him, he was accessible to the influence of money. Brickhouse was a Georgia scalawag of Connecticut birth, who floated on the surface of events and drifted into the First Louisiana regiment toward the close of the war, and in recompense for some dirty service to Badger was appointed a sergeant over better men, some of whom were Negroes. Such was the material Thompson had to use to accomplish his liberation from an imprisonment that daily became more unbearable."

14 *Statesman*, September 21, 1865.

15 Captain W.J. Gilly (Gilley), is a somewhat mysterious figure. He deserted from the Union Army and headed south where he fought for the Confederacy under Captain Raphael Semmes, the famed commander of the warship C.S.S. *Alabama*. Captured after the *Alabama* was sunk, he made an escape near the end of the war fleeing to Texas where he met Ben Thompson. Gilly moved south of the border and enlisted in the army of the ill-fated Emperor of Mexico, Maximilian. The *Statesman* published an obviously over dramatic account depicting Gilly and Thompson's friendship.

> In one of the engagements Gilly fell wounded and bleeding on the battlefield, and left for dead among the dying and the slain. He was literally shot and pierced to pieces with bayonets, and being sought out by Thompson, was discovered as described. Capt. Gilly, realizing his position and believing his time had come, made two requests—first that Ben Thompson should accept the sum of $4,000 which Gilly had in his possession, and with the money fly the country which threatened to give both of them graves; and secondly, that Ben should

> end the agony of his companion by at once blowing out the brains of the suffering and bleeding soldier. But Ben Thompson was too chivalrous to do either. Instead, he lifted the hacked and bruised body of his friend to his shoulders, carried him to a place of safety and nursed him into comparative health and strength by a tender devotion which was peculiarly his own.

With the fall of Maximilian's reign, Gilly remained in Mexico and declared that he eventually rose to the post of Marshal of Mexico City. *Austin Statesman*, January 22, 1885, "Ben Thompson's Friend. The Hero of Two Wars and the Boon Companion of Ben, Visits Austin. He pays His Respects to Gov. Ireland, and a Loving Tribute to the Dead Adventurer."

16 Walton, *Thompson*, 69, 70. The commanding officer of this company of contra-guerrillas was Captain Frank Mullins. He was reported to have been a former Confederate officer, originally from San Antonio. The *Daily Ranchero* of October 3, 1866, spoke highly of his character and reputation as an officer. He died of typhoid fever during the last week of September 1866. A search of military records at the Office of the Secretary of National Defense and of the National Archives of the Republic of Mexico failed to provide documentation proving Ben Thompson served in an official capacity with the Mexican Imperial Army. Schoenberger, *The Gunfighters*, 152, 183. Unofficial evidence exists of Thompson's time fighting on the behalf of the Imperial Army. Refer to the *Dallas Herald*, July 21, 1866, Contra-guerrillas's officers Captains Gille [*sic*] and Ben Thompson are named in an article.

17 Walton, *Thompson*, 70 - 71. *Daily Ranchero*, October 27, 1865. *Statesman*, November 30, 1865: "Ben Thompson 2nd Lieutenant in the Imperial Army." The Liberal commanders had made plans to capture Matamoros with more cunning than just a simple frontal assault. Throughout the war, many common soldiers changed their allegiance for the opportunity to plunder and loot. For officers, bribery proved to effectively motivate acts of treason. The commanding officers of one of the principal forts guarding the city—all of them Americans—were to be paid $20,000 to assassinate General Mejia and an additional $35,000 to surrender the fort they were assigned to defend. Mejia's secret police uncovered and foiled the plot. Captain W.W. Gholson was executed. He was described as being a tool of the real leader of the conspiracy, a Lieutenant Thomas A. Birch. Reported to have been an officer in the Union army, Birch was dishonorably discharged and he was known to have used several aliases. He often bragged he came all the way from Kentucky to sell himself to the highest bidder. Birch managed to escape Mejia's secret police and crossed over the Rio Grande to the safety of Texas where he disappeared.

18 Walton, *Thompson*, 70-71.

19 John Twohig was a famous Texas pioneer and patriot. He was born in Ireland and arrived in Texas in 1830 at the age of twenty-four, quickly becoming one of San Antonio's leading citizens. Twohig fought for Texas independence in 1835 and again resisted the Mexican invasion of 1842. He became a successful merchant, land speculator, and banker. His general store stood on Main Plaza. When Texas became a state, it was Twohig who unfurled an American flag from the tower of the San Fernando Cathedral in celebration of the event. He was renowned throughout Texas for his honesty and generosity. For many years until his death, Twohig personally financed a breadline for the poor and more unfortunate citizens of San Antonio.

20 Walton, *Thompson*, 70-72.

21 In an article entitled, "All Taken," the *Matamoros Daily Ranchero* of November 29, 1865, reported how, "General Mejia and his division have their picture taken by Louis De Planque the ambrotypist." An extensive search by the authors failed to locate this photograph. De Planque operated photography studios on both sides of the Rio Grande, in Brownsville and the sister city of Matamoros, Mexico. He made outstanding studio portraits of Mexican military leaders of both sides such as Tomas Mejia and Mariano Escobedo. *Handbook of Texas Online*, Lawrence T. Jones III, "Photography in Civil War Texas," accessed September 26, 2016, http://www.tshaonline.org/handbook/online/articles/kjp04.

22 Walton, *Thompson*, 72-74.

23 Ibid., 74, 75.

24 *San Antonio Daily Express*, March 13, 1884.

25 Walton, *Thompson*, 73-78.

26 *Dallas Herald*, July 21, 1866. In the newspaper's reporting of the surrender of Matamoros the editor listed among the contra-guerrillas's officers Captains Gille [*sic*] and Ben Thompson.

27 Walton, *Thompson*, 73-78.

28 Ibid., 78-9.

29 Ibid., 79-80.

30 General Mejia attempted an amazing and brilliant legal strategy. He shocked the court when he publicly called upon General Mariano Escobedo to act as his defense council. Earlier in the war, a captured Escobedo had been released by Mejia, who furnished him with money and a horse to make his escape. Escobedo now refused to defend Mejia, and the newspapers quoted him as saying he would see him "damned first." Convicted, Mejia was sentenced to face a firing squad. On the night before the scheduled executions, after saying goodbye to his young wife and new-born son, Tomas Mejia received one final visitor. General Escobedo stepped into Mejia's cell and made a miraculous offer. To repay Mejia's previous act of kindness to him, Escobedo offered money, a horse, and freedom. Mejia asked if the offer included Emperor Maximilian and General Miramon. Escobedo answered that it was not within his power to free the others. "Then I will stay and die with my Emperor," was Tomas Mejia's simple reply.

31 Walton, *Thompson*, 79-81.

32 Ibid., 80-81. The most complete biography of Throckmorton remains *Texas Confederate, Reconstruction Governor: James Webb Throckmorton* by Kenneth Wayne Howell (College Station: Texas A&M University Press, 2008).

33 St. David's Episcopal Church Archives.

34 Ben Thompson autographed and dated on July 5, 1867, a note to his first cousin Matilda "Tillie" (Baker) Roberts in her friendship album. He wrote, "As gold more splendid from the fire appears, Thus friendship brightens by the length of years. Ben Thompson Austin City Texas." The above information is from Sybil Patterson, Great Granddaughter of Abram & Matilda (Baker) Roberts and can be found posted on the website, www.pioneersandlegendsoftexas.com.

35 Brief article originally appearing in an undated *Houston Post* reprinted in the *Luling Signal*, September 20, 1883. In a little more than a decade, Ben Thompson would become one of the most widely-known men in Texas; occasionally he was known as "Captain Thompson." A Houston journal provided a "pen-picture" of the gunfighter-gambler that corroborated Ben's recollection of his adventures south of the Rio Grande, calling him "one of the most daring soldiers on Mexican soil." Ben, after joining the army of Emperor Maximilian, did "valiant service un-

der his adopted banner" until it was defeated. Ben commanded two companies of "bold riders—guerillas as some called them—and it is interesting to listen to the recitals of the daring exploits, splendid fighting and many narrow escapes of that band of men." The reporter told of how Ben held a check from Maximilian's government for $10,000 for his services, but one that could never be cashed, and that Ben "does not deserve the hard name he bears away from home." The newspaper finished his article by stating there were "plenty of worse men in the world than Ben Thompson."

36 Walton, *Thompson*, 82-86.

37 Ibid., 86. James B. Gillett, "Ben Thompson and Billy Sims," *Frontier Times*, 3. Elton R. Cude, *The Wild and Free Dukedom of Bexar*, p. 40, (Munguia Printers, San Antonio, Texas, 1978).

38 Anne Beck. The 1860 United States Census for Bastrop County, 247 B, Family #117 and the 1870 United States Census for Bastrop County, 5, Family # 34.

39 *Statesman*, March 13, 1884.

Chapter 4

1 Page, Bill. "Wine and Liquor Licenses in Brazos County, 1857-1871," 79. On March 1, 1861, a Mr. C.G. King paid for and was issued a county liquor license for his business located in the town of Bryan. This could be the King who later lost his establishment to Ben Thompson.

2 Walton, *Thompson*, 86-88.

3 Ibid., *Thompson*, 88-9.

4 *San Antonio Daily Express*, April 6, 1868.

5 *Flake's Daily Bulletin*, April 5, 1868.

6 Adjutant General Reconstruction Records Ledger #401-1133, Special Order 191, October 26, 1867, Headquarters District of Texas at Austin; *Flake's Daily Bulletin*, April 5, 1868.

7 *Weekly Austin Republican*, April 8, 1868.

8 Ledger #401- 1000, "Records of Murders and Assaults, 1867-1868," M[ar]ch [18]68, 246. Adjutant General Records, Texas State Archives.

9 *San Antonio Daily Express*, April 10, 1868.

10 *Flake's Daily Bulletin*, April 5, 1868.

11 Ibid.

12 Walton, *Thompson*, 89-91.

13 Ibid., *Thompson*, 89-94.

14 *Flake's Daily Bulletin*, June 12, 1868. In the spring of 1868, it wasn't just Billy Thompson's actions that brought him a small measure of notoriety. It was another young killer who contributed to Billy's growing repute as a gunman. In late March, a young man named James Tope was released from jail and, with two cohorts, started robbing ranchers near San Antonio. On Saturday, April 10, around 9 a.m., Tope rode alone into the little town of Oakville, in Live Oak County. It was halfway between San Antonio and Corpus Christi. Calling himself Billy Thompson, Tope was heavily armed with a double-barrel shotgun, six-shooter and at least one pocket pistol. He was very alert and "made many braggadocio remarks" about himself. He claimed he had escaped from San Antonio's Bexar County jail and although accused of several crimes, he made it clear to his audience that he was innocent of all of them. At the town's grocery, a group of men gathered, and even though it was early in the morning, everyone was drinking heavily. Seeking addi-

tional fun, they decided to start shooting their pistols at a mark, placing wagers on the outcome. James Minter, considered one of Live Oak County's better citizens, arrived in Oakville that morning, and stopped by the grocery store to do business. In conversation, the name of Tom Dodd came up, and Tope, who claimed to be a pal of Dodd's, threatened to whip any man who spoke derogatively of him. Minter then made the mistake of mumbling his opinion that Dodd was nothing better than a horse thief. Tope replied, "You are a damn liar," he then drew his pistol and began firing. The first bullet struck Minter in the shoulder, the second ripped through his chest, and as he fell to the ground, a third bullet tore into his back. Minter died without uttering another word. Firing promiscuously at his former drinking buddies, the killer leaped on his horse and sped off. A hastily formed posse failed to overtake him. The account of James Minter's killing first appeared in San Antonio's *Daily Herald*. The *Herald's* rival, the *Express*, reprinted the *Herald's* account two days later, and had the advantage of discovering that a man named Tope was running around under the alias of Billy Thompson. The correction was too late in the minds of many readers and even today Billy's name still remains in the Adjutant's General's Records, where he is officially, but mistakenly, accused of killing James Minter of Live Oak County. James Tope was on the run. He passed near a small community known as Dogtown (now Tilden) in McMullen County. There, he loudly threatened the life of William J. Walton (no relation to Austin attorney William M. Walton). On April 25, James Tope rode up to a house where Walton was staying with a friend. With his double-barrel shotgun resting across his saddle and a pistol holstered on his hip, Tope was, as usual, well-armed. Previously notified of the threats voiced against him, Walton armed himself before stepping out onto the porch and declaring, "I suppose I am the man that you are looking for." In response to Tope's next question, Walton freely stated his name. Uttering his last words, James Tope replied, "All hunkadora," as he raised his shotgun to fire. Walton, "well accustomed to the use of firearms, was too fast for him." Tumbling out of his saddle, the surprised and now dead Tope landed in the front yard of the house. Described as "peaceable," Walton immediately surrendered himself to the sheriff of Atascosa County and as word quickly spread about the killing many "law-abiding citizens ... crowded the office of the District Clerk, everyone wanting to sign Walton's bond." In its columns, the *San Antonio Express* kept trying to differentiate between Tope and Thompson, but in the *Herald's* reporting of Tope's violent ways and bloody end they continued to refer to him as Billy Thompson. *San Antonio Daily Express*, April 25, 1868. The letter sent to the *San Antonio Herald* describing the events leading to the death of James Minter was dated April 10, 1868, the same day the murder occurred. Ledger # 401-1000, "Records of Murders and Assaults, 1867-1868" [-] April [18]68, p. 247. Adjutant General Records, Texas State Archives. *San Antonio Herald*, March 25, 1868 and May 8, 1868. *San Antonio Daily Express*, June 11, 1868.

15 Scrivener, probably David D., was born in North Carolina around 1818. In 1870, he resided in Refugio County and worked as a retail grocer. His wife, Henrietta, was about twenty-eight-years-old and her vocation was listed as "Keeping House." At the time of the census, his children were Jeff Davis, age nine, Clara, age seven, and David, age two, all born in Texas. Living in the same household were his mother-in-law Henrietta Brown and her children, Bertha, age sixteen and Robert, age twenty-two. Robert Brown worked as a clerk in the family's grocery store. A twenty-one-year-old Texas native, Charles Ward, also clerked in the store. 1870 Refugio County Census, 160B.

16 *Galveston Daily News*, July 31, 1883 and Cause No. 22, *State of Texas vs. Wm. Thompson*, Grand Jury Indictment for Murder, Filed October 25, 1872.
17 Manuscripts Department, Kansas State Historical Society, Topeka. E. P. Lamborn Collection, Collection No. 156, Box No. 2, Folder B. Correspondence dated April 2, 1932 from Frank H. Bushick, San Antonio, Texas to E. P. Lamborn, Leavenworth, Kansas.
18 Cause No. 22, State of Texas vs. Wm. Thompson, Rockport, Aransas County, Texas.
19 Walton, *Thompson*, 97-8.
20 *Daily Austin Republican*, August 12, 1868.
21 General Orders No. 19, Headquarters, Fifth Military District, dated Austin, Texas, October 24, 1868, Texas State Archives. *Daily Austin Republican*, August 24, 1868. Walton, *Thompson*, 96. According to Walton, the messenger sent by Lieutenant Howe for reinforcements brought a note saying the Thompson brothers did the shooting. The unfounded story about Thompson killing Federal soldiers was continued by the *Statesman* years later (see March 13, 1884) when the newspaper carried an article reviewing his career, "[J]ust after the war and while the state was under military rule, he in company with others, killed some United States soldiers south of the city, and for this he was arrested and put into the 'Bullpen,' as it was called."
22 General Orders No. 17, Headquarters Fifth Military District, dated Austin, October 20, 1868. Texas State Archives.
23 Notarized answers to fifty-four cross interrogatories given by Ben Thompson on July 10, 1877 at Austin, Texas. Testimony and Records in the Case of State of Kansas vs. William Thompson, Records Division of the Ellsworth District Court. To question No. 40, Ben answered: "I was tried in Texas in 1868 by a military court for shooting a man who knocked my wife down with a gun."
24 Walton, *Thompson*, 94-102. In his version of the incident, Walton used the name Theophilus Brown as the man Ben Thompson shot and wounded and he did not mention the assault on Kate Thompson. This was probably done to prevent any embarrassment to the Thompson-Moore family. General Orders No. 17, Headquarters Fifth Military District, dated Austin, October 20, 1868. Texas State Archives.
25 Convict Record, Texas State Penitentiary at Huntsville. Prisoner #1286, John McGuire, 64-65, Ledger 1998/038-149. Texas State Archives.
26 Walton, *Thompson*, 88-99.
27 Ibid., *Thompson*, 102. General Orders No. 17. Ben Thompson, civilian, October 20, 1868 and General Orders No. 19, John McGuire, civilian, October 24, 1868. Headquarters Fifth United States Military District. Texas State Archives.
28 Convict Record, Texas State Penitentiary, 64-65, Ledger 1998/038-149, Prisoner #1285, Ben Thompson and Prisoner #1286, John McGuire.
29 Walton, *Thompson*, 102.
30 Only the birth year of 1869 is known for Ben Thompson Jr. per correspondence with Anne Beck dated December 2, 1996. Baptisms and Burials of St. David's Episcopal Church (1867-1870) Vol. II, No. 4, unlike the other children born to Ben and Kate Thompson, Ben Jr. does not appear in the church records.
31 Register of Letters Received and Letters Received of the Department of Texas. The District of Texas, and the 5th Military District, 1865-1870. Bastrop County Judge William T. Allen's correspondence dated April 13, 1869 to Major General James H. Carlton. Texas State Archives.

32 Information received about Moore's cocaine addiction from telephone conversation with Anne Beck, October 9, 1999. It is interesting to note that Ben Thompson often purchased the cocaine from an Austin pharmacist, also named Ben Thompson, for James Moore. Travis County Census, enumerated by Otto T. Zink, June 1870 shows the family: Elizabeth Moore, age forty-eight, Keeping House; James Moore, age twenty-one; Molly Moore, age sixteen; Kate Thompson, age twenty-three; Sarah Moore, age fourteen; and one-year-old Benjamin Thompson, 282. Molly, Kate, Sarah, and Benjamin were all listed as "at home." It is curious that enumerator Zink highlighted the "James Moore" name by placing quotation marks around it for reasons not now known.
33 1870 Walker County Census, Huntsville State Prison, 32.
34 Report from Special Officer C. S. Bell dated November 28, 1869, from Laredo to Captain C. E. Morse, Secretary of Civil Affairs, Austin. Barry A. Couch Collection.
35 Convict Record, Texas State Penitentiary, 64-78, Ledger 1998/038-149.
36 Correspondence with John Y. Simon, Ulysses S. Grant Association, Morris Library, Southern Illinois University, Carbondale, Illinois.
37 Notarized answers to fifty-four cross interrogatories given by Ben Thompson on July 10, 1877, at Austin, Texas. Testimony and Records in the Case of State of Kansas vs. William Thompson, Records Division of the Ellsworth District Court.
38 Walton, *Thompson*, 102.

Chapter 5

1 Lucille Ruby Elliott Gasper. *A Brief Sketch of the Life of Jacob J. Ellison, A Trail Driver's Record of the Old West*, Self-published, 21-2. "Big Jim" Ellison, a prominent rancher with a spread south of the town of San Marcos, which is located midway between Austin and San Antonio, sent two herds up the Chisholm Trail in the spring of 1871. Bill Thompson was not an uncommon name so it is not known for sure if he worked with Ellison but his son Jake recalled, "I went up that spring with Bill Thompson ... He was a fine man and a good boss, better than I thought, as he never had worked with cattle any, but he had lived a neighbor to Father and they were good friends, so my Father could not refuse letting him have a herd to Boss up the trail, as there was a hundred dollars a month in it. Thompson wanted to put in 50 steers of his own which he had bought ... that was also agreeable."
2 For a biography of Coe see *Phil Coe: Texas Gambler* by Chuck Parsons (Wolfe City, TX: Henington Publishing Co., 1984). Tom Bowles was born 1839 in Iowa, the son of John Walter Barnett and Louisa Frances Bowles. During the war he served as a private under Capt. James A. Thompson, mustering in on April 13, 1862. After the war, he apparently lived in Travis County, although he does not appear in the 1870 Travis County census. In 1880, he does appear to have resided with his sister, and other family members. He is shown to be forty-one-years-old with gambling as his profession. Tennessee State Marriage Records, 1780-2002, Provo, UT, Ancestry.com; Muster Roll Cards, 1838-1900, Provo, UT. Ancestry.com; 1880 Travis County Census lists Louisa Bowles as head of household, residing in the 4th Ward, 205. Bowles died in 1916 and was interred in Austin's Oakwood Cemetery on September 15. James B. Gillett's article "Ben Thompson and Billy Sims" in *Frontier Times*, 12:1, 3.
3 Walton, *Thompson*, 102-03.
4 Travis County Deed Records, Vol. U, 138. On January 14, 1871, Ben and Kate Thompson sold lot 77, division D, City of Austin, to Albert G. Budington, for

$250, Vol. U, 165-68, 183. On January 20, 1871, the Thompsons sold sections 4 and 5, Block 68 to John Hancock of Austin for $600 gold, Vol. U, 348. On March 20, 1871, they sold lot 4, block 182 to James Hickey for $600.

5 For the definitive work on Hickok see Joseph G. Rosa's *They Called Him Wild Bill: The Life and Adventures of James Butler Hickok* (Norman: University of Oklahoma Press, 1964 and second enlarged edition 1974), and *The West of Wild Bill Hickok* also by University of Oklahoma Press, 1982.

6 Richard O'Conner. *Wild Bill Hickok* (Garden City, NY: Doubleday & Co., Inc., 1959), 163.

7 In 1871, Stanley, while a correspondent for the New York *Herald,* went in search of British explorer Dr. David Livingstone, who left in quest of discovering the source of the Nile River four years previous. Following an eight-month trek through tropical forests Stanley found Livingstone near Lake Tanganyika, now part of Tanzania. Stanley later claimed he greeted him with the now famous line, "Doctor Livingstone, I presume?"

8 Walton, *Thompson,* 103-04.

9 Ibid., 105.

10 *Journal of Commerce* (Kansas City, MO), June 22 and 24, 1871.

11 Ibid.

12 Walton, *Thompson,* 105.

13 John Wesley Hardin. *The Life of John Wesley Hardin, As Written by Himself,* 44. Posthumously published in 1896 by Smith & Moore of Seguin, Texas; reprinted 1961 by the University of Oklahoma Press with an introduction by Robert G. McCubbin.

14 Quote is from a conversation between Leon Metz and co-author Bicknell.

15 Walton, *Thompson,* 106.

16 E. C. Little. "A Son of the Border" in *Topeka Mail and Breeze,* September 13, 1901.

17 "Minute Book of the City of Abilene, 1871." Microfilm copy at the Kansas State Historical Society, Topeka.

18 Ibid., The spelling of this man's name poses a problem. Rosa, in *They Called Him Wild Bill,* spells it "Sheran." The Abilene minute book spells it "Sharon." The 1870 Dickinson County census spells the name "Shearon."

19 *Abilene Chronicle,* September 14, 1871.

20 As yet, no contemporary evidence has been located that establishes who Jessie Hazel really was, if there was such an individual. The authors' conversations and correspondence with the great-grandniece of Coe, Marylyn Pense, has raised the question of Jessie Hazel being a member of the Hassell family of Gonzales County, the same county in which the Coe family resided. The names Hassell and Hazel could easily refer to the same family. See "Sarah Lee Hassell" by Tommie Nuinez, 341 in *The History of Gonzales County, Texas* by the Gonzales County Historical Commission, 1986, printed by the Curtis Media Corporation of Dallas.

21 *Austin Statesman,* October 12, 1871.

22 The cape Phil Coe wore that night is now in the possession of Marylyn (Portis) Pense, Willcox, AZ.

23 Ms. Pense has stated the Coe family's case concerning why and how Hickok killed their ancestor. "The real reason behind his [Hickok] actions was [a] woman named Jessie Hazel. She was a beautiful woman, and she loved Phil Coe. This infuriated Hickok because he wanted Jessie too. My family knew about the woman. They really did not approve of her, as she was a saloon girl [.] When Hickok saw Phil out on the street, he knew Phil had been drinking and was unarmed. ... The crowd

was unarmed also because of the law in the town. Hickok flew into a jealous rage and shot my Uncle Phil Coe in cold blood. Wild Bill Hickok was known to never miss his mark. When he shot my Uncle Phil below the belt, it was exactly where he meant to shoot him. This is proof that it was a crime of passion committed by a murderer." Marylyn Portis Pense, "A Crime of Passion, A Story About Phil Coe," *Tombstone Times*, December 2003, Issue 12, 1, 4-8.

24 *Abilene Chronicle*, October 12, 1871.

25 Little is known of Bud Cotton. The *Austin City Directory* of 1872-1873 lists a B.F. (Benjamin Franklin "Frank") Cotton and W. D. Cotton as residents on San Jacinto Street between Bois d' Arc (7th Street) and Pecan Street (6th Street), p. 40, 1872-1873. The Austin *Statesman* reported on July 11, 1874 Bud Cotton was elected an officer of the Hope Hook & Ladder Fire Company #2. The 1880 Travis County census shows a Frank Cotton, age forty-seven, profession "gambler" with wife Fanny, and children Jefferson, Lee "Dasy" and Elvira Cotton, the mother of Frank, age seventy. Frank Cotton was a native of Kentucky. Enumerated by Fritz Tegener, 204.

26 Walton, *Thompson*, 105-06, 109 and illustration between pages 174-75. Streeter, *Ben Thompson: Man with a Gun* (F. Fell, New York 1957), 85-91.

27 Telephone interview with Mrs. J.P. Lewis, June 7, 1984. See also *Phil Coe: Texas Gambler*, 39, n. 58.

28 *Brenham Daily Banner*, October 19, 1871. The Brenham City Cemetery is now known as the Prairie Lea Cemetery. Coe's standup marker adorned at the top with a handsome carving of clasped hands reads: "Gone but not Forgotten/ Philip H. Coe, Jr. Born July 18, 1839/Died October 9, 1871." He rests in range 2, section 2.

29 *Oxford Times*, October 21, 1871.

30 *Abilene Chronicle*, November 30, 1871.

31 "Minute Book of the City of Abilene, 1871" and Joseph G. Rosa, *They Called Him Wild Bill*, 204.

32 A copy of Ben Thompson's handwritten poem provided to the authors by Anne Beck.

Chapter 6

1 *Galveston Daily News*, February 2, 1872.

2 *Austin Daily State Journal*, January 26, 1872

3 Ibid., *San Antonio Daily Express*, March 11 and 13, 1884; *San Antonio Daily Express*, February 1, 1872; Walton, *Thompson*, 72.

4 *Austin Daily State Journal*, February 23, 1872. Judge W. Richard presided over this case on February 21, according to the criminal docket.

5 Jim Gray, *Desperate Seed: Ellsworth, Kansas on the Violent Frontier*, (Ellsworth: Kansas Cowboy Publications, 2009), 1-18. Hereafter cited as *Desperate Seed*; and Gray, "Chauncey Belden Whitney—Frontier Defender" in *The Kansas Cowboy* (newspaper), part one September-October 2014 and part two November-December 2015.

6 Ibid., Chauncey Belden Whitney was born in a rural wooded section of central Michigan in the early spring of 1842. His mother died before his sixth birthday and his father remarried before his seventh. According to family history, Chauncey enlisted in the Union army but before leaving for the war, he married for the first time on July 22, 1862. His wife was Ellen M. Norton. In camp, he soon contracted chronic dysentery, the war's deadliest killer. He returned home where his wife

nursed him until she too, was taken ill from the same bacterial disease and subsequently died. Whitney somehow recovered. A year later, Chauncey married again. There is confusion as to the young woman's name: Esther Ingraham or Ingersoll. In February 1864, twenty-two-year-old Chauncey Whitney traveled south to the town of Jackson, Michigan, and joined the proud, battle-hardened veterans of the 12th Michigan. Earlier, the unit had won fame at Shiloh and helped capture the Confederate Army at Vicksburg. He was placed in Company K and three months later, on May 15, he was promoted to corporal. Through most of 1864, the regiment was campaigning almost continuously, logging thousands of miles by marching and by moving by rail. Chauncey Whitney was with the regiment for two skirmishes during operations in Arkansas against Confederate General Shelby. The 12th Michigan Infantry settled down at Du Vall's Bluff for the last months of the war and performed guard duty for the rail-line there, with occasional scouting forays into southern Arkansas. Whitney was officially discharged from the service at Detroit, Michigan, on May 18, 1865. Whitney returned home after mustering out, but tragedy continued to stalk him. His mother and first wife had passed on, and his second wife died on September 22, 1865. The cause of her death is unknown. It is believed that both of Whitney's marriages were childless. He soon became romantically involved with a young lady by the name of Aramintha Dorriner Nichols whom everyone called "Dorm." The Michigan woods could not hold Whitney and he left in search of a life on the western frontier. He promised Dorm he would return for her once he was established, and for reasons now unknown he chose to set off for Kansas and settled at the fledging hamlet of Ellsworth.

7 Ibid., "Diary of Chauncey B. Whitney," Kansas Historical Collections, Vol. 12, 296-99. Without fear of retribution, Cheyenne war parties had been freely raiding small pioneer settlements north of Ellsworth. The state militia was poorly armed, poorly trained, and too inexperienced to properly deal with the fast-moving Cheyenne. The United States army was similarly unprepared. In response to the situation, Major George A. Forsyth received orders to recruit, organize, and equip a small mobile force of fifty frontiersmen to chase down the war parties. Eight members of the First Independent Kansas State Militia joined Major Forsyth and among them was Chauncey Whitney. He began to keep a diary describing their movements and experiences on the prairie and eventually the fight that was to come. In early September the small command tracked a war party moving northward through Kansas until they crossed the state line into Colorado. On September 16, Major Forsyth's company camped along the banks of the Arickaree River. At daylight the following morning a large force of mounted Cheyenne attacked the frontiersmen's camp, quickly arousing all. They captured seven of the horses, and then forced the soldiers onto an island. "About 500 attacked us on all sides, with their unearthly yells. The balls flew thick and fast." Colonel Forsyth was the first man wounded, then Lieutenant Beecher as well. Eight or ten men were wounded fairly quickly. The pinned down men were able to find some protection by digging into the sand with their knives and hands to create a breastwork. This saved them. They fought "the red devils all day till dark." For the next week the small command beat back the Cheyenne charges and withstood the siege eventually subsisting on putrid horse meat and a coyote they managed to kill. Scouts were sent out for help and several successfully passed by the Cheyenne camps surrounding their position. On the morning of September 25, the frontiersmen spotted an approaching column in the distance. It was the United States 10th Colored Cavalry, the

famed Buffalo soldiers, who came to their rescue. Whitney wrote in his diary. "Oh, the unspeakable joy: Shouts of joy and tears of gladness were freely comingled. Such a shaking of hands is seldom witnessed." The next day he set down his desire to leave the frontier behind. "Tomorrow we are to start for Fort Wallace, where I shall bid good-bye to our brave band of scouts to prepare to return east, where I will try to forget in a peaceful home the scenes of the past two years."

8 Undated letter from Nellie Henry-Whitney-Osborne Seaver to her daughter Mary Elizabeth Whitney Sutton on file in the Kansas State Historical Society.

9 Gray. "Chauncey Belden Whitney—Frontier Defender" in *The Kansas Cowboy*, September-October 2014, 1 and 9.

10 *Desperate Seed*, 43-4.

11 Chuck Parsons. "Eyewitness to Cowtown Violence" *Real West*, April 1980, 36-39, 49.

12 *Desperate Seed*, 46-7 and 52-54.

13 Ibid., 70.

14 "Three Generations of Fourth 'Estaters" in *Miami Daily News* (Kansas), January 23, 1927; *Desperate Seed*, 71-74 and 168-69; John Montgomery and Abbie M. Henry married on December 24, 1874.

15 *Desperate Seed*. 41, 67-68, 81; *Ellsworth Reporter*, May 2, 1872.

16 *Desperate Seed*. 111.

17 *Ellsworth Reporter*, June 6, 12, 20, 27, 1872.

18 Dale T. Schoenberger, *The Gunfighters* (Caldwell, ID: Caxton Printers, 1971), 154.

19 *"Report of Arrests,"* May-October 1872, 106 and 110. Texas State Archives. Ben was arrested several times both in Travis and Hopkins County; Aransas County District Court Records, Case # 22. This is the indictment of William Thompson for the murder of Remus Smith.

20 *Ellsworth Reporter*, December 23, 1872.

21 *Desperate Seed*, 116.

22 *Neosho Times* [Missouri], March 20, 1873; article originally appearing in Austin's *Daily State Journal*.

23 In 1870 Napoleon B. Mitchell was described as a white male, thirty-five years of age, with wife Emma, thirty. Mitchell's occupation is shown as "restaurateur." He was a native of Ireland. 1870 Travis County Census, 269.

24 *Austin Daily State Journal*, March 27, 1873. The saloon was owned by Matt Woodlief and William Wilson, located between Pecan and Bois d'Arc (modern 6th and 7th Streets). The bartender was R.D. Mitchell. In addition to being a saloon owner, Woodlief had a considerable reputation as a fighting man. He had fought for the Confederacy, earned a medical degree, and also became a heavy drinker. He was recognized as a fearsome gunfighter in Texas and Louisiana.

25 *Register of the Grand Central Hotel*, owner/proprietor Arthur Larkin. Microfilm available from the Kansas State Historical Society; Walton, *Thompson*, 112; *Desperate Seed*, 119.

26 Streeter, *Thompson*, 93.

27 From the Deposition of Witnesses, *State of Kansas v. William Thompson*, 54. Ben intended to go into the saloon business when he went to Ellsworth but found so many saloons already operating he decided against it. Question # 2. Ellsworth County Attorney Ira E. Lloyd deposed these witnesses. *Ellsworth Reporter*, May 15, 1873 noted: "Whiskey is an antidote against snake bites. With eight saloons in town there is no danger to be feared from snakes by our people." The number of saloons would soon increase to sixteen.

28 Jim Gray, "Chauncey Belden Whitney- Frontier Defender," Part 2, *The Kansas Cowboy*, Vol. 20, # 1. Nov.-Dec. 2014, 10. *Register of the Grand Central Hotel,* Ellsworth, Kansas. Among other noted characters who registered at the Grand Central were J.C. "Cad" Pierce and Neil Cane; Thomas G. Martin, one time captain of the Texas State Police; cattlemen John Good, Peter Murchison and B. F. "Bud" and Frank Cotton.

29 *Ellsworth Reporter*, June 26 and July 3, 1873.

30 Robert R. Dykstra, *The Cattle Towns* (Lincoln: University of Nebraska Press, 1868), 77.

31 Ibid., 134.

32 *Ellsworth Reporter*, July 3, 1873; *Desperate Seed*, 128.

33 *Abilene Chronicle*, February 1, 1872; *Ellsworth Reporter*, February 29, 1872. Tom Carson was arrested and jailed for shooting Norton; however, he escaped, disappeared, and was never heard from again. *Desperate Seed*, 85.

34 Ellsworth City Council Minutes, 87; Ellsworth Police Docket, 112, 115-21, 142; *Ellsworth Reporter*, September 11, 1873; Floyd B. Streeter, "Tragedies of a Cow Town," 90. (Hays, Kansas: *The Aerend*, Kansas State College, Spring 1934, Vol. 5, No. 2. In the City Council Minutes the name is spelled both Morco and Morcho. He himself was illiterate. The *Reporter* spelled his name Morco which is probably how it was pronounced.

35 *Desperate Seed*, 92, 98, 106, 128; Dan L. Thrapp. *Encyclopedia of Frontier Biography*, 668. (Lincoln: University of Nebraska Press, 1991). James D. Drees gives the name of the man Hogue killed in *Bloody Prairie*, Vol. 2, 1997. For a brief sketch of Hogue's life and career as a lawman, see *Why the West Was Wild: A Contemporary Look at the Antics of Some Highly Published Kansas Cowtown Personalities*, 217-21. Edited by Nyle H. Miller and Joseph W. Snell. Reprint of 1963 Kansas State Historical Society publication; reprint by University of Oklahoma Press, 2003. According to a June 9, 1877 report in the *Dodge City Times*, Hogue had died "not long since" from fever somewhere in the Wyoming Territory.

36 Streeter, *Thompson*, 92. Normally during the cattle season, June through October, a city marshal's salary was $150 per month, while his staff members received half that amount. All policemen could supplement their salary by earning a $2.50 bonus for each arrest they made, the bonus being created by the convicted lawbreaker who was forced to pay a fee to cover the court costs.

37 Ira E. Lloyd. *Exciting Early Day History of Ellsworth, Diary of Late Ira E. Lloyd Relates In Detail Early Day Lawless Cowtown*, 1-8. (Ellsworth: Ellsworth County Historical Society.)

38 *Ellsworth Reporter*, June 26 and July 3, 1873.

39 Jim Gray, "Chauncey Belden Whitney- Frontier Defender," Part 2, *The Kansas Cowboy*, Vol. 20, # 1. Nov.-Dec. 2014, 9.

40 The register of the Grand Central Hotel shows Ben registered on May 23, and again on August 14, 1873; brother Billy registered on April 18 and again on June 29, 1873. Ira E. Lloyd deposed Ben Thompson. During the deposition Ben responded that his wife was not with him in Ellsworth, that he did stay with Jenny Fields "and others." He also stated that Billy spent "a larger portion of his time" with Molly Brennan. Ben could not say specifically how much time; he knew that Billy boarded at the Grand Central. Interrogatives numbers 3-6.

41 *Ellsworth Reporter*, June 12, 1873.

42 Streeter, *Thompson*, 93. Old Police Docket Book, case # 118. During the many summers visiting Kansas from 1871 to 1880 this is the only known arrest of Ben Thompson.

43 *Ellsworth Reporter*, June 26, 1873; *Desperate Seed*, 130. William H. Brinkman abandoned the office of mayor.

44 Jim Gray. "Quiet Hero James B. Miller," *Kansas Cowboy*, p. 20-21, Vol. 9, No. 3, July–Aug. 2005. In Illinois, James B. Miller soon became acquainted with many prominent Illinois Republican politicians and was an intimate friend of many notable men of the time including Abraham Lincoln and Congressman E. B. Washburn, a political figure from Galena, Illinois and an early supporter of Ulysses S. Grant's Civil War military career. By 1868, Miller left his law practice in Chicago and sought a lucrative opportunity in western Kansas as a sales agent for the National Land Company's Ellsworth District. As agent he was responsible for all of the railroad lands in Ellsworth, Lincoln, Rice, and Barton Counties. Securing the rights from the Kansas Pacific Railroad, the National Land Company controlled all of the railroad town sites west of Junction City, Kansas. In 1869 alone, more than $1,000,000 worth of these lands were sold and more than 18,000 people settled these lands. Miller was also a ticket agent for the *Anchor* steam-ship line. Based out of New York, the line sailed to most major European ports. As early as 1869, James Miller began serving as the county's probate judge. Judge Miller was a staunch Episcopalian and lead a successful effort to build a church in Ellsworth. At the time of his election he was also serving as Clerk of the District Court.

He only served one term as mayor of Ellsworth, choosing not to run for reelection in 1874. Tragedy entered his life a few years later when his wife Francis died, and in 1879, he fractured his right leg near the hip joint in an accident from which he would never recover. Mayor Miller remained an invalid during his remaining fifteen years, and he passed away on January 29, 1894 in Chicago, Illinois. *Chicago Tribune*, January 30, February 15, 1894.

45 Floyd B. Streeter. "Tragedies of a Cow Town" *The Aerend*, Spring 1934, Vol. V, No. 2, 93. Old Police Court Docket, Case # 142.

46 John "High-Low Jack" Branham was the other policeman dismissed. Arrests were mainly for drunk and disorderly conduct or carrying a deadly weapon. Of the policemen at Ellsworth, Morco was especially active. See also *The Cattle Towns* by Robert R. Dykstra, 136-37.

47 Floyd B. Streeter, "Tragedies of a Cow Town" in *The Aerend*, 92. Information on J.C. Howard provided by Jim Gray.

48 Deposition by Ira E. Lloyd. State of Kansas vs. William Thompson, July 20, 1877. Questions 3 and 4. Testimony from Jennie Fields of Shawnee County, Kansas and Ben Warren of Webberville, Travis County, Texas, and James Goodwin and Moses Barber, both of Dodge City, Kansas all concur that the Thompson brothers and Sheriff Whitney were only on the best of terms during the summer of 1873.

49 Floyd B. Streeter. "Tragedies of a Cow Town" in *The Aerend*, 92.

50 Police Judge Vincent B. Osborn found Norton guilty of being drunk and disorderly; Norton claimed the pistol was discharged accidentally. Record of Ellsworth Municipal Court, August 15, 1873. *Desperate Seed*, 139; F.B. Streeter, "Tragedies of a Cow Town," *The Aerend*, 92. Norton paid his fine on September 8, 1873. Ira E. Lloyd. *Exciting Early Day History of Ellsworth*, 6.

51 Robert K. DeArment, *Knights of the Green Cloth: The Saga of the Frontier Gamblers* (Norman: University of Oklahoma Press, 1982), 58-76. Sterling was issued the Medal of Honor April 4, 1865.

52 Streeter, *Thompson*, 94; Deposition of Witnesses by Ira E. Lloyd. Interrogatives of C.C. Peppard, Bourbon County, Kansas; William Purdy, Atchison County, Kansas, Phillip Davis, Wyandotte County, Kansas, Ben Warren of Travis County, Texas and James Goodwin (Goodwyn), Ford County, Kansas.
53 Ibid., Interrogative of Ben Thompson.
54 The shotgun was stored in the back room of Jake New's saloon. Ben Thompson described the weapon as "a breech loading double barreled shot gun." The gun was a gift from J.C. Pierce and was valued at $150. Manufactured by George Gibbs & Co. of Bristol, England, it is a "snap-action, center-fire, breech-loading, 12 gauge weapon with a walnut stock. Six inches have been sawed off the standard barrel length. Thompson's shotgun is now part of the collection of the Boot Hill Museum, Dodge City, Kansas.
55 State of Kansas vs William Thompson, Ira E. Lloyd Deposition of Witnesses. Answer to interrogative # 11 by Ben Thompson.
56 Floyd B. Streeter. "Tragedies of a Cow Town," 94. Testimony of John Montgomery before Dr. W.M. Duck, the Ellsworth County Coroner. And answer to interrogatives from Ben Thompson, C.C. Peppard, William Purdy, Phillip Davis, Ben Warren and James Goodwin (Goodwyn). See note 52 above.
57 Ira E. Lloyd interrogative of Ben Thompson, question # 11. John DeLong was dismissed from the police force on August 12, 1873.
58 Floyd B. Streeter, "Tragedies of a Cow Town" in *The Aerend*, 94.
59 Ben Thompson answers to interrogatives in Ira E. Lloyd's Deposition of Witnesses, answers to questions 5 and 11; testimony from Ben Warren and James Goodwin.
60 Ibid., Ben Thompson answers to interrogative 5.
61 Walton, *Thompson*, 116. Walton wrote how Ben fired twice. Ben's first shot at Ed Hogue went through a wooden wall in the hope of striking the hiding Hogue. The second at Happy Jack, who like Hogue, "took advantage of a house" for concealment. See page 114, Walton, *Thompson*.
62 Ibid., and Ira E. Lloyd Deposition of Witnesses. Witness Ben Thompson answer to question 15.
63 Ira E. Lloyd Interrogatives. Witness Ben Thompson answer to question 5. *Ellsworth Reporter*, August 21, 1873. *Desperate Seed*, 142. Whitney's house was located on the northwest corner of Lincoln Avenue and 1st Street.
64 *Ellsworth Reporter*, August 21, 1873; Ira E. Lloyd Interrogatives. Witness Ben Thompson, answer to question 16.
65 Floyd B. Streeter, "Tragedies of a Cow Town," 145-146. (Hays, Kansas: *The Aerend*, Kansas State College, Spring 1934, Vol. 5, No. 2). Endnote 1, "John Montgomery told the Coroner's jury that Bill 'jumped back in Brennan's saloon after he fired the shot.'"
66 Ira E. Lloyd Interrogatives. Witness Ben Thompson, answer to questions 16 to 25.
67 Walton, *Thompson*, 117.
68 Ibid., *Ellsworth Reporter*, August 21, 1873; Ira E. Lloyd Interrogative, July 10, 1877. Witness Ben Thompson, answer to questions 7-10.
69 *Ellsworth Reporter*, August 21, 1873. "Floyd B. Streeter, "Tragedies of a Cow Town," *The Aerend*, 96. Jim Gray, "Chauncey Belden Whitney—Frontier Defender," Part 2, *The Kansas Cowboy*, Vol. 20, # 1. Nov.-Dec. 2014, 12.
70 Walton, *Thompson*,118-19; *Ellsworth Reporter*, August 21, 1873.
71 *Desperate Seed*, 143, 146. Streeter, *Thompson*, 102; *Ellsworth Reporter*, August 21, 1873, relates the death of J.C. Pierce.
72 Walton, *Thompson*,119.

73 *Desperate Seed,* 143; Floyd B. Streeter, "Tragedies of a Cow Town," 148.
74 Ira E. Lloyd Interrogatives. Witness Ben Thompson, answer to question 8.
75 Ibid., Witness Ben Thompson, answer to question 30.
76 Ibid., Witness Ben Thompson, answer to question 11 and 30. Testimony of witness James Goodwin. Walton, *Thompson,* 120-21.
77 *Ellsworth Reporter,* August 21, 1873; *Desperate Seed,* 147. South of the slowly flowing Smoky Hill River is the Ellsworth Cemetery. Sheriff C. B. Whitney's final resting place is marked by a large marble headstone and can be found in the extreme southwest portion of the cemetery only a few feet from the road. James A. Browning. *Violence Was No Stranger: A Guide to the Grave Sites of Famous Westerners* (Stillwater, OK: Barbed Wire Press, 1993), 275-76.

Chapter 7

1 The coroner's inquest testimony has been lost for decades. It was only through the research of Kansas historian Floyd B. Streeter, then Director of the Fort Hays State College Library, that a portion of the evidence survives. Streeter used this material from Coroner Duck's inquest in his article "Tragedies of a Cow Town" which appeared in *The Aerend* published by the Kansas State College of Hays in its Spring 1934 edition, and in his book *Prairie Trails & Cow Towns* first published in 1936 by Chapman & Grimes of Boston. It was reprinted in January 1963 by the Devin-Adair Company of New York. The complete title of the reprint was *Prairie Trails and Cow Towns: The Opening of the Old West.* Posthumously published as *Ben Thompson: Man with a Gun* by Frederick Fell, Inc. in 1957, Streeter's work, as historian William F. Kelleher wrote in his introduction to the Fell edition, "serves as a monument to the author."
2 *Ellsworth Reporter,* August 21, 1873.
3 Floyd B. Streeter, "Tragedies of a Cow Town," *The Aerend,* 145. Hereafter cited as Streeter, *The Aerend.*
4 *Nebraska City Press,* August 25, 1873, reprinted in the *Western Stock Journal* of Pleasanton, Texas, September 2, 1873; *Ellsworth Reporter,* August 21, 1873; Walton, 127-30.
5 Ira E. Lloyd, "Exciting Early Day History of Ellsworth: Diary of Ira E. Lloyd Relates in Detail Early Day Lawless Cowtown," 6. Printed by the Ellsworth Historical Society.
6 *Ellsworth Reporter,* August 21, 1873. Streeter, *The Aerend,* 149-51. *Desperate Seed,* 147.
7 Ibid.
8 *Nebraska City Press,* August 25, 26, 1873.
9 Ibid., August 26, 1873.
10 Streeter, *The Aerend,* 151-52.
11 Walton, 121-32. The Moore-Farrell wedding took place on September 2, 1873; the date was provided by Jane Summer in her *Some Early Travis County, Texas Records,* copy furnished by Anne Beck.
12 Streeter, *The Aerend,* 153.
13 *Nebraska City Press,* August 26, 1873. Ellsworth historian Jim Gray discovered the Pierce Family Cemetery was located at Webberville-Quad, 3097-214. However, officials authorized a housing subdivision to be erected on the site of where the cemetery once existed.
14 Streeter, *The Aerend,* 153.

15 Original proclamation in archives of the Kansas State Historical Society. On September 4, 1873 Governor Osborn appointed H.D. Stebbins sheriff of Ellsworth County who served until 1876.
16 *Ellsworth Reporter*, August 28, 1873; Streeter, *The Aerend*, 153.
17 Ira E. Lloyd diary. "Exciting Early Day History of Ellsworth," 7.
18 Register of the Grand Central Hotel, June 3, 1873.
19 *Ellsworth Reporter*, September 11, 1873. Streeter, *The Aerend*, 154.
20 Ibid.
21 *Desperate Seed*, 142, 146, Streeter, *Ben Thompson: Man With a Gun*, 149.
22 *Ellsworth Reporter*, September 11, 1873.
23 Ira E. Lloyd diary. "Exciting Early Day History of Ellsworth," 8.
24 Stuart N. Lake, *Wyatt Earp Frontier Marshal*, (Simon & Schuster, N.Y., N.Y., 1994), 88-91. The dramatic and controversial account of the arrest of Ben Thompson by Wyatt Earp is based upon Lake's correspondence with Earp. Their letters can be found among the Stuart N. Lake Papers at The Huntington Library, San Marino, California. Folder 39—Earp, Wyatt Berry Stapp to Stuart Nathaniel Lake. 1928-1929 Number of pieces: 16.
25 The newspaper article which appeared in the Winfield, Kansas, *Courier* and repeated here was provided by Wild West researcher and author Thomas Gaumer of Tucson, AZ. An important letter, also provided by Mr. Gaumer, from Streeter to a friend named E. P. Lamborn further clarifying the controversial incident appears in Appendix A. *Desperate Seed*, 143, 146. Streeter, *Thompson*, 144. For a thorough discussion of the Ellsworth episode see "The Ellsworth Incident" chapter in Lee A. Silva's *Wyatt Earp: A Biography of the Legend, Vol. 1. The Cowtown Years*, 191-244 and Jim Gray, "Wyatt Earp Was Never Here," *Kansas Cowboy*, Volume 9, January/February, 2005, Number 2, pp. 1, 3, 4, 16 -18.
26 *Ellsworth Reporter*, September 11 and 18, 1873.
27 *Ellsworth Reporter*, November 13, 1873. Ellsworth County Coroner's inquest testimony concerning the murder of Edward Crawford, November 8 and 10, 1873, Testimony of witnesses John DeLong, J. W. Nall, John Charles Brown and Charles Seward.
28 Ibid., Witnesses George Harris and Charles Seward.
29 *Ellsworth Reporter*, November 13, 1873. Ellsworth County Coroner's inquest testimony Charles Seward, J.W. Nall, L.W. Benson, Isaac Ziegler, George Harris, Lizzie Palmer, Suzie Hart, Alice Chambers.
30 Ibid., Isaac Ziegler, Charles Seward, J.W. Nall, John DeLong, John Charles Brown.
31 Ibid.
32 Ibid., Testimony of John Charles Brown and Mark Lambert Hopkins. On November 18, 1873, Brown was appointed city marshal of Ellsworth in which position he would serve until he resigned on July 20, 1875. He left Ellsworth and disappeared from history.
33 *Ellsworth Reporter*, November 13, 1873.
34 *Desperate Seed*, 152.
35 *Ellsworth Reporter*, November 13, 1873.
36 Ibid., *Ellsworth Reporter*, November 15, 1873.
37 *The State of Texas v. William Thompson*. Case # 1607 on file at DeWitt County Courthouse, Cuero.
38 *The State of Kansas v. William Thompson*. Information for murder in the first degree filed December 31, 1873. Witness list included Edward I. Hogue, John

Montgomery, Dr. William Fox, Dr. A. Gregg and William Nichols. Copy provided by Texas State Archives.

39 *Austin Statesman*, May 19, 1874.

40 *Galveston Daily News*, June 3, 1874; San Marcos (Texas) *West Texas Free Press*, June 13, 1874; *San Antonio Daily Express*, June 6, 1874.

41 Dale T. Schoenberger, *The Gunfighters*, 159.

42 Ira E. Lloyd. Deposition of witnesses, 54. Cross interrogatives July 10 and 13, 1877, City of Austin. Witness Ben Thompson response to question 42.

43 *San Antonio Daily Herald*, August 26, 1874. Mountain City was and is a small town in central Hays County, some twenty miles south of Austin on the road to San Marcos, the county seat of Hays County.

44 *San Antonio Daily Herald*, August 26, 1874.

45 The certification is dated September 12, 1874; the requisition dated October 16 and the arrest warrant dated October 30. Courtesy Texas State Archives.

Chapter 8

1 *New York Sun*, undated, quotation from James D. Horan's *The Authentic Wild West: The Gunfighters.* (New York: Crown Publishers, Inc., 1976), 142. *Freeborn County Standard*, [Albert Lea, Minnesota], July 21, 1881: "From the Philadelphia Press ... to the matter of pistols Ben is a phenomenon in this way. No man in Texas can draw quicker, and none is his superior in marksmanship ... He has taken risks which would be madness with anyone else ... 'When a man is bent on fighting,' he says, 'I reason with him and try to show him how foolish he is; but if there is no stopping him, why I let him fire first; that fixes me all fight on the plea of self-defense.' It has been Thompson's custom for years to follow this practice, which some day will prove fatal to him."

2 "Schedule of Inhabitants in the City of Austin, County of Travis, State of Texas, February 1875." All members of household # 891 were listed as "American," including the twenty-two-year-old female boarder identified as O. Doebbli. Farrell gave his nationality as Irish.

3 Matthias Woodlief has received little attention from western historians in spite of his reputation as a dangerous man during his lifetime. The only serious research in his life was done by Larry J. Woods and published in the "Gunfighters and Lawmen" column in *Wild West*, June 2005, 16, 71-73.

4 Caldwell County records. *Texas v. Ben Thompson* was case # 1303, "betting at a gambling bank" on January 12, 1875, and case #1394 "aggravated assault" on April 22, 1875. Bee County records show cause # 177 "Exhibiting a *monte* bank" indicted on February 16, 1875.

5 *Statesman*, August 29, 1875.

6 *San Antonio Daily Express*, November 28, 1875; Joseph Gallegly, *From Alamo Plaza to Jack Harris's Saloon: O. Henry and the Southwest He Knew* (Mouton, 1970), 85. Their stay in San Antonio was brief as their next stop on the tour was in Houston where they performed on November 30 and December 1. Hiram Robbins authored *Life on the Border* for Cody and Omohundro. Born in Virginia "Texas Jack" with his older brother Orville served in the regiment under the command of Confederate Colonel J. E. B. Stuart. The sixteen-year-old Omohundro was effective as a spy and scout earning his initial fame as "Boy Scout of the Confederacy."

7 Cantonment on the Sweetwater was renamed the following year to Fort Elliott. David E. Kyvig, "Fort Elliott" in *The New Handbook of Texas*, Vol. 2, 1099-1100.

8 The most complete work on Masterson remains that of Robert K. DeArment, especially his biography *Bat Masterson: The Man and the Legend* (Norman: University of Oklahoma Press, 1979) and for the later years, *Gunfighter in Gotham: Bat Masterson's New York City Years* (Revised edition, Norman: University of Oklahoma Press, 2013).

9 Stuart N. Lake. *Wyatt Earp: Frontier Marshal* (Boston: Houghton Mifflin Company, 1931; reprint New York: Simon & Schuster, 1994), 133.

10 Accounts differ as to the nature of Bat's wound, whether it was in the leg, stomach, or the pelvis. News accounts of the gunfight also reveal little substantial information. The *Denison News* (Texas) of February 10, 1876, provided an early version: "It is reported that a shooting scrape occurred in Contonment [*sic*], on the Sweetwater, last Sunday, in which a citizen, name unknown, Corporal King, Co. "H" 4th Cavalry and Mollie Brennan, formerly a Denison demimonde, were killed." The *Galveston Daily News* of the same date reported: "Last Sunday a shooting affair occurred at Cantonment, on Sweet Water. The participants were Corporal King, Co. H, Fourth Cavalry, and a citizen, also a prostitute named Mollie Brennan, who ran between the parties when firing." The Jacksboro, Texas, *Frontier Echo*, of February 11, 1876, provided the telegraphic news: "King, of H. Company, 4th Cavalry, and a woman, Molly Braman [*sic*], killed at San Antonio by a Citizen."

11 *Statesman*, February 3, 1876. The Sweetwater shooting actually occurred the night of Monday, January 24, 1876.

12 Gary L. Roberts. "Bat Masterson and the Sweetwater Shootout." *Wild West*, October 2000, 42-50.

13 *Statesman*, February 5 and 10, 1876. Walton, *Thompson*, 144-47. The Austin police record dates the incident as happening on February 4 at 3:30 p.m. Chenneville noted his arrest of Thompson was for "Assault with intent to kill one Wm Hannah." The record does not show that Hannah was arrested or charged. "Record of Arrests, [City of Austin] January 1, 1876-January 1, 1879. The original volumes are available at the Austin History Center. Mitchell's Saloon was on Congress Avenue between Bois d'Arc and Hickory Streets, present day 7th and 8th streets.

14 *Greenwood Advance* (Pennsylvania), February 24, 1876; *Richwood Gazette*, (Ohio), March 6, 1876.

15 *Austin Weekly Statesman*, February 10 and March 10, 1876. The victims were William H. Gazeley and his son Tom, killed by Aaron Burleson. Cardwell noted that the crime "begets great excitement in Bastrop County."

16 *Statesman*, March 14, 1884.

17 Ibid., March 16, 18, 30, 1876; *Daily State Gazette*, March 12, 17-18, 1876. Born Samuel Spencer Baldwin (1848 -1924), he circled the globe five times, performing before European royalty, Indian Rajahs, and Turkish sultans. In response to a question about spiritualism, Professor Baldwin explained: "I claim no occult or supernatural powers, I produced my effects by purely natural means." With his first wife Clara, he created the question and answer mentalist act; the same act where Ben Thompson was a participant, and is still being performed today. Baldwin, Professor Samri S. "The White Mahatma," *The Secrets of Mahatma Land Explained: Teaching and Explaining the Performances of The Most Celebrated Oriental Mystery Makers and Magicians in All Parts of the World* (Hartford, CT: Calhoun Printing Co., 1895.)

18 *San Antonio Daily Herald*, April 13, 14, 1876. *Galveston Daily News* of April 12, 1876. The details are sketchy. Cause #111, *State of Texas v. Ben Thompson* was

continued on December 11, 1876, and again on January 4, 1877, and finally on February 6, 1877, Thompson pled guilty and paid a fine of $25 plus court costs. Vol. A, Bexar County Criminal Court Minutes, 23, 29 and 34.

19 Case # 1607, *State of Texas v. William Thompson*, charged with the murder of Remus Smith. DeWitt County Courthouse, Cuero, Texas.

20 N. A. Jennings. *A Texas Ranger*. (Chicago: The Lakeside Press, R.R. Donnelley & Sons Company, 1992), 32-34.

21 Ibid., 133-34.

22 *Daily State Gazette*, August 29, 1876.

23 *Galveston Daily News*, August 12, 23, 1876. Southwest of Houston, near the town of Richmond in Fort Bend County, a difficulty resulting in a shooting took place on August 11 between one Joe Massie and a William Thompson. The cause of the trouble remains unknown, but early speculation was that the wound was mortal. A subsequent newspaper report agreed, but Massie's fate is unknown. Since "William Thompson" is such a common name it is uncertain if this was Ben's brother or another man.

24 *Statesman*, October 28, 1876.

25 Monthly Return of Company C, Capt. John C. Sparks, prepared by Sgt. Joseph Leverett, dated November 30, 1876. Sparks to Adj. Gen. William Steele, December 1, 1876. Gladden and Ringo had both participated in the Mason County War. See *The Mason County "Hoo Doo" War, 1874-1902*, (2006) and *John Ringo: King of the Cowboys: His Life and Times from the Hoo Doo War to Tombstone* (2008) both by David Johnson and published by the University of North Texas Press.

26 *Corsicana Observer*, December 2, 1876; *Burnet Bulletin*, December 8, 1876. McLennan County 1880 Federal Census shows Sparks with occupation listed as "Graindealer." His household consisted of his wife Amazon, thirty-five, and their five children ranging in age from fourteen years to nine months.

27 *Corsicana Observer*, December 2, 1876 and *Burnet Bulletin*, December 8, 1876.

28 *Statesman*, October 28, 1876.

29 Ibid., Monthly Return of Company C ending November 30, 1876.

30 Sergeant Leverett has received virtually no attention from historians. He was born in Clay County, Alabama on May 30, 1852, and died in Erath County, Texas. After his Ranger career he married R. L. Scroggins on December 7, 1884. Upon his death, he was buried in the Upper Greene Creek Cemetery in Stephenville, Erath County.

31 *Galveston Daily News*, October 28, 1876. *Statesman*, October 28, 1876.

32 The requisition from Governor Osborn to deliver William Thompson to Kansas is preserved today in the Texas State Archives.

33 *Galveston Daily News*, November 1, 1876.

34 Ira E. Lloyd, Deposition of Witnesses, 54. Cross Interrogatives, July 10 and 11, 1877. Witness Ben Thompson, answers to questions 49 and 50. Hereafter: Interrogatories.

35 *Statesman*, November 1, 1876; *Ellsworth Reporter*, November 16, 1876.

36 *Statesman*, November 5, 1876; *Galveston Daily News*, November 7, 1876. Monthly Return of Company C, Captain John C. Sparks commanding but prepared and signed by Sgt. Joe Leverett, for a month ending on November 30, 1876.

37 Ibid.

38 Ibid., November 17, 1876; *Galveston Daily News*, November 16, 1876; Monthly Return of Company C, Capt. John C. Sparks, November 30, 1876; *State of Texas v.*

William Thompson. Interrogatives, Witness Ben Thompson answer to question # 44.

39 Interrogatives, Witness Ben Thompson, Answer to questions 43-47.

40 *Corsicana Observer*, December 2, 1876.

41 Floyd B. Streeter, "Tragedies of a Cow Town," 160, *The Aerend*.

42 Today the old stone jail stands in ruins, although the remaining structure is listed on the Kansas Register of Historic Places and the National Register of Historic Places. It had been the county jail until 1909 and then sold to the city three years later and used for various purposes. Located at 6 North Court Street, the Ellsworth County Historical Society re-dedicated the 150-year-old building on October 11, 2003. The *Kansas Cowboy*, September-October 2003; *Dallas Daily Herald*, November 19, 1876; *Dallas News*, November 21, 24-25, 1876; *Galveston Daily News*, November 22, 26, 1876; *Ellsworth Reporter* November 30, 1876; *Corsicana Observer*, December 2, 1876.

43 *St. Louis Daily Globe-Democrat*, December 5, 1876; *San Antonio Daily Express*, December 19, 1876; *Burnet Bulletin*, December 22, 1876. The order to move Thompson to Leavenworth dated December 1, 1876, in District Court Records, Ellsworth. *Leavenworth Daily Times*, December 5, 1876.

Chapter 9

1 *Statesman*, October 8, 1876.

2 Ibid., January 4, 1876.

3 Ibid., February 2, 1877.

4 A search of the Travis County Clerk's records, by Rick Miller, including docket and minute books, found no cases involving Mark Wilson. However, Ben Thompson, the Burditt brothers and Billy Simms were noted numerous times.

5 *Galveston Daily News*, October 5, 1876.

6 "Schedule of Inhabitants in the City of Austin, County of Travis, State of Texas, February 1875," 50, shows the Wilson family in dwelling #322: Kate Wilson, single, [no age listed], Irish, Mark Wilson, single, 28, Irish, barkeeper Congress Avenue, and Lucy Wilson, single, 18, and Matilda Wilson, single 16, both American.

7 Walton, *Thompson*, 155-56.

8 *Statesman*, November 4-5, 1876. Joe Edgar Manry, *Curtain Call—The History of the Theater in Austin, Texas—1839 to 1905*, 38-40. (Austin: Waterloo Press, 1985). Hereafter cited as Manry, *Curtin Call*.

9 J.B. Gillett, "Ben Thompson and Billy Sims," in *Frontier Times*, 1-3, Vol. 12, No. 1, October 1934. "From childhood he was a trouble maker and often engaged in fist fights." James Burditt was constantly and consistently arrested on minor charges during the late 1870s and early 1880s. James Burditt's name appears in the Mayor's Court docket, Travis County Court Criminal Minutes and City of Austin Record of Arrests. Charges varied: discharging firearms, unlawfully bathing in the Colorado River, riding on sidewalk, assault, and fighting. Then, ironically, for five months from March 21, 1882 until August 1, 1882 James Burditt served Austin as a policeman. He was initially hired when Ben Thompson was the city marshal.

10 *Statesman*, December 31, 1876, and January 10, 1877. J.B. Gillett, "Ben Thompson and Billy Simms," *Frontier Times*, 2-3.

11 *Statesman*, January 9, 10, 1877.

12 Ibid. , December 25, 27, 28, 30, 1876; *Dallas Daily Herald*, December 30, 1876, reprinted from the *Austin State Gazette*, *Galveston Daily News*, December 27, 1876 and *San Antonio Daily Express*, December 27, 28, 1876.

13 *Statesman*, December 30, 1876 and January 9, 1877. Travis County District Court, Criminal Records, Cause No. 5005, *State of Texas v. Ben Thompson and James Burditt*, Charge: Murder; Walton, *Thompson*, 157-58.

14 *Statesman*, December 27-28, 1876.

15 *San Antonio Daily Express*, December 26, 28, 1876. *Galveston Daily News*, January 2, 1877.

16 John A. Green was the benefactor supporting the early education of Ben and Billy Thompson after they arrived in Austin (See Chapter One). Robert J. Hill joined Walton and Green circa 1876. In 1872, the law office of Walton, Green and Hill was one door west of Congress Avenue on Pecan Street.

17 Walton, *Thompson*, 160. *Statesman*, December 28, 1876.

18 *Statesman*, December 27, 29, 1876 and January 4, 1877.

19 Ibid., *San Antonio Daily Express*, December 27, 1876. *Indianapolis Journal*, August 31, 1877. Mathews went on to become a newspaper editor in Hot Springs, Arkansas, permanently settling there in 1877. His editorials at the *Sentinel-Star* angered several members of a rich and powerful clique of politicians and gamblers. On September 22, 1882, Charles Mathews was attacked in a street fight; he fought back against three key members of the clique: Civil War officer, railroad man, and hotel and spa builder Col. Samuel W. Fordyce, former U. S. Army officer and business associate of Fordyce, Col. DeWitt C. Rugg, and gambling den owner Frank Flynn. Mathews shot and wounded Rugg but was beaten with a cane by Fordyce and he received three pistol shots which proved fatal. His three assailants were charged with his murder; however, in separate trials all were eventually found not guilty. Dale T. Schoenberger. "Charles Mathews, Editor with a Gun" in *True West*, 26-29, January 1993.

20 *Statesman*, December 28-29, 1876. *Galveston Daily News*, December 27, 1876. Mark Wilson's grave is located in Section 2, Lot 403, Space 7. From *Oakwood Cemetery Burial Ledger, Book 1, July 1866 – Dec. 1880*. Austin History Center, 180 – 81. Reference notes that Wilson was buried December 28, was white and was thirty-one years of age and "Killed by being shot." Physician [Justice] James Neil "familie lot" No. 403 "Nativ[e] [of] Ireland." His grave is approximately 380 feet almost due east from that of Ben Thompson's final resting place. Today, Wilson's headstone is broken in three pieces and laying on the ground.

21 *Statesman*, December 28-29, 1876 and January 6, 1877. James W. LaRew would return and serve as an Austin police officer from December 1880 until February 1882. He served under City Marshal Ben Thompson, who was elected in December 1880.

22 Ibid., December 30, 1876.

23 Tom Bicknell. "Billy Simms, A Lover of Fair Play," 3-24, in *Quarterly* of the National Association for Outlaw and Lawman History, Inc., Vol. XXVIII, No.3 (July – September 2004).

24 *Statesman*, December 29, 1876.

25 Ibid., December 29, 1876 and January 5-6, 1877.

26 Ibid., January 6, 9-10, 1877.

27 Ibid., January 12, 1877.

28 Walton, *Thompson*, 160-161. Frederick E. "Fritz" Tegener served as a Justice of the Peace during 1876-1878, 1880-1884, and 1886-1888. At sixty-eight years of age,

Justice Tegener passed away on June 21, 1901 at 5:30 p.m., after a lingering illness. His funeral was held at his residence at 1903 South Congress Avenue on June 22 and he was interred at Oakwood Cemetery in Austin, Section 2, Lot 441, Space 1. *Austin Daily Statesman*, June 22, 1901.

29 *Statesman*, January 11, 17, 1877. *Galveston Daily News*, January 12, 1877

30 *Statesman*, January 12, 13, 14, 20, February 22, May 30, 1877. Manry, *Curtin Call*, 40-41.

31 *Statesman*, January 16, 21, 28, 1877. *Galveston Daily News*, January 21, 22, 26, 1877.

32 *Statesman*, January 24, 1877. *Galveston Daily News*, January 24, 26, 31, 1877.

33 Travis County District Court Records. The two orders are dated the January 20 and 24 of 1877.

34 *Statesman*, January 24, 30, 1877. *Galveston Daily News*, January 25, 30-31, 1877.

35 *Galveston Daily News*, January 31, 1877.

36 The 1876-1877 City of Galveston Directory, 50, 73, and 81.

37 *Statesman*, February 2, 1877.

38 Ibid., January 4, 11, February 1, 28, 1877.

39 Ibid., February 9, 11, 1877. "Schedule of Inhabitants in the City of Austin, County of Travis, State of Texas, Census. 1875." Vol. 2, Wards 9-10, 46. The Allen family entry is found on lines 1-7. A second witness also died on the same day Allen passed away. Described as a young man, his name was Charles Purcell, a bartender by trade and, similar to Mark Wilson, a member of the Volunteer Hope Hook and Ladder Firemen Company and the Hibernian Association. Cause of death was not reported in the February 11, 1877, issue of the *Statesman*. Earlier on January 8, 1877, the *Statesman* printed a synopsis of Purcell's testimony: "The first thing I heard was firecrackers; don't know where they came from; it was near where Thompson and Burditt were; I turned around and saw Wilson's face was black; Wilson asked Burditt what he did it for, and told Allen, policeman, to arrest him; Burditt then struck Wilson; and then Thompson struck at Wilson, when Wilson went to the bar and firing commenced."

40 Case Number 289, *The State of Kansas v. Wm. Thompson*. Records of the District Court, Ellsworth, Kansas. Hereafter cited as: Case Number 289.

41 Adj. Gen. William Steele to Ira E. Lloyd, Ellsworth, Kansas, April 5, 1877. Texas State Archives. Adj. Gen. Outgoing Correspondence, 225.

42 Mark Dugan, *Knight of the Road, The Life of Highwayman Ham White* (Athens, OH: Swallow Press/Ohio University Press, 1990), 18, 19, 24. Hereafter cited as: Dugan, *Knight of the Road*; *Statesman*, March 27, 1877. *Galveston Daily News*, March 27, 1877.

43 Dugan, *Knight of the Road*, 20, 24.

44 Cause 5005, *State of Texas v. Ben Thompson*, murder.

45 Hall's telegram to Steele, costing $1.40, is in "Special Forces Correspondence, 1876 [-1877]. Texas State Archives, Box 401-1157, folder 17. *San Antonio Daily Express*, May 25, 1877; *Galveston Daily News*, May 27, 1877. *Statesman*, May 27, 1877.

46 Cause 5005, *State of Texas v. Ben Thompson*. Walton, *Thompson*, 161.

47 Ibid.

48 *Statesman*, June 1, 1877.

49 *San Antonio Daily Express*, June 1, 1877.

50 *Statesman*, June 7, 1877. Travis County Clerk's Misdemeanor Records Division, Austin.

51 Cause 203, guilty and fined $25 on July 3, 1877, 55. Cause 204, 205, 206, 208 all dismissed on August 6, 1877, 59. Vol. A, County Court Criminal Minutes, Travis County, Austin.
52 Deposition of Witnesses, July 10 & 11, 1877, City of Austin, County of Travis, State of Texas, Witness Ben Thompson and Case Number 289.
53 Ibid., Witness W.A. Langford and Case Number 289.
54 Case Number 289.
55 Ira E. Lloyd. *Exciting Early Day History of Ellsworth, Diary of Late Ira E. Lloyd Relates In Detail Early Day Lawless Cowtown*, 5. (Ellsworth: Ellsworth County Historical Society.)
56 Case Number 289, September 3, 1877, Motion to Quash.
57 *Ellsworth Reporter*, September 13, 1877.
58 Ibid., September 6, 1877.
59 *Ellsworth Reporter*, September 20, 1877. *Statesman*, September 25, 1877. John Montgomery would leave the *Ellsworth Reporter* but he would remain in the Kansas newspaper business for sixty-five plus years. His son (John Jr.), grandson (Harry E.) and great-grandson (John) would also have prominent careers as "Fourth Estaters." Montgomery became the editor of the *Leavenworth Times*, then the *Manhattan Nationalist* and, lastly, in 1888 the owner and editor of the *Junction City Union*. He died at the age of eighty-seven on August 5, 1936, after several months of illness. Benjamin Floyd Streeter interviewed Montgomery prior to his death. Streeter did not record any mention Montgomery made of any role played by Wyatt Earp in Ellsworth on August 15, 1873.
60 Walton, *Thompson*, 127.

Chapter 10

1 The *Statesman* of March 3, 1877, listed the Golden Rule Billiard Room and Saloon available for rent for one year. "If interested," the ad advised, "see Mr. Oscar Sullivan at the premises." The establishment was on Congress Avenue at Bois d' Arc (7th) beneath the offices of the *Statesman*. The advertisement claimed it was the most popular establishment in the city.
2 Walton, *Thompson*, 150-54. Austin *Statesman*, October 3, 4, and 5, 1877. 1880 Census, Washington County, Texas. Enumerator B. J. Arnold found Lorraine and family living in the Crumpler Hotel of county seat Brenham. He was listed as "Without occupation" although he claimed a substantial personal estate of $4,000. His wife Frances, age thirty-two, was born in Tennessee and all three of their children were born in Texas: Claude, age five, William, age three, and daughter Georgia, age one.
3 Walton, *Thompson*, 152. Walton identifies Abram Simon, something the *Statesman* failed to do.
4 Austin *Statesman* October 6, 1877.
5 Ibid.
6 Record of Arrests Book, City of Austin, Austin History Center. *Statesman*, October 3, 4 and 5, 1877.
7 Ibid. October 5, 6, 1877. Record of Arrests Book, City of Austin. Austin History Center.
8 Ibid. Sparks was not the only Ranger from the Frontier Battalion to break the law in Austin during 1877. His sergeant, Joe Leverett, was arrested by Police Officer John Chenneville for assault on February 8.

9 *St. Louis Globe-Democrat*, October 7, 1877.

10 *Galveston Daily News*, November 18, 1877.

11 *Fort Worth Democrat*, January 19, 1878. "The accidental discharge of a pistol early yesterday morning in the Occidental Saloon led to the arrest of Billy Sims [*sic*], who was fined $10 and costs in the Mayor's Court for carrying the weapon."

12 Ibid., January 5, 1878. McClung and Thompson may have earlier met as Confederate soldiers. McClung, born February 18, 1835, had been a lieutenant in Coopwood's group of spies in John S. "Rip" Ford's regiment and part of Sibley's Brigade in the ill-fated New Mexico invasion. He later became a successful real estate agent in Tarrant County. McClung died November 22, 1919, in Fort Worth and is buried in Pioneers' Rest Cemetery. His death certificate indicated death was caused by hypostatic pneumonia. Ancestry.com and Tarrant County official death certificate # 33484.

13 *Fort Worth Democrat*: On Monday night, January 14, Ben Thompson raffled off his gold watch. On April 18, 1878, Ben Thompson raffled his $350 saddle, then on exhibition at the Occidental Saloon. The saddle was mounted with $140.00 worth of solid coin silver, and valued at $350.00. "All lovers of beauty and curiosity should not fail to examine the workmanship. The saddle will be raffled, 100 chances. See advertisement in another column." Ben Thompson had won this saddle at a raffle in Austin several years earlier. The winner of the saddle was not discovered. On February 2, 1878, "A team of five bays attached to a hack, valued at $300, were raffled off at the Cattle Exchange Thursday night [January 31, 1878] and were won by Ben Thompson, who threw 44 dice." On February 8, the *Democrat* informed its readers: "Mr. Ben Thompson, having no further use for his fine span of black horses, he will dispose of them at a very reasonable price. Anyone wishing to purchase an excellent team, this will be a rare opportunity. Call on either Ben Thompson, above the Occidental, or at John Leer's livery stable for further information."

14 *Fort Worth Democrat*, February 2, 1878.

15 Capt. B. B. Paddock, *History of Texas: Fort Worth and the Texas Northwest*, Vol. II, 875. (Chicago and New York: The Lewis Publishing Company, 1922).

16 *New York World*, January 6, 1878. "An account of the desperadoes of Texas would not be complete without mention of Ben Thompson, of Austin, who however, belongs to a different type altogether. There is nothing of the coward in his make up, and he generally gives his opponent the first shot never firing until self-defense demands it. Ben is one of the handsomest and best-dressed men in Austin, with a foot and hand as small as a lady's and a geniality and courtesy of manner which would lead any one to set him down as the most inoffensive of men. He is an Englishman by birth and is scarcely thirty five years of age." The *World* reviewed his life, in brief and often inaccurately in detail, beginning with his brother Billy fatally shot-gunning a Kansas sheriff. Next, it covered his family's arrival in Texas, the deaths of his aunt and uncle at the hands of a runaway slave, and Ben's first shooting and wounding of another boy in Austin in 1858. Ben Thompson's personal scrabbles as a Confederate soldier were presented as well as the exaggerated shooting incident at Fort Clark; the gambling den gunfight in Laredo and the killing of John Coombs in Austin in the defense of his friend John Rapp. The correspondent next described Thompson's time as a mercenary in Mexico fighting on behalf of the Emperor Maximilian and ended his story detailing the fatal gunplay at the Capital Theatre. The printing and reprinting of these newspaper features promoted in the public mind Thompson's notoriety of being a dangerous man.

Although his deadly reputation was becoming widely recognized, at the same time he was differentiated from such desperate men as Longley and Hardin, each portrayed as mindless murderers. Thompson's courage, gentlemanly behavior and honesty in business dealings countered his ruthlessness with a pistol.

17 *Fort Worth Democrat*, February 13, 1878.

18 *General City Directory of the Cities of Denison and Sherman for 1876 and 1877* (Denison: Mooney & Morrison), 41, 73, 91. Denison, Texas Genealogical Society. J. V. George clerked for the grocery firm of J. M. Sheeder & Brothers and he boarded at the European Restaurant. The Sheeder & Brothers Grocery firm was located at 215 Main, Denison, Texas. Another grocery store across the street at 208 Main was owned by E. B. Sims. It is not now known if this man was related to Billy Simms.

19 *Fort Worth Democrat* and *Austin Statesman*, February 14, 1878, and the *Denison Daily News*, August 3, 1878.

20 *Denison Daily Herald*, February 13, 1878. A transcript of the article was provided by Ann Lowry, Archive Librarian, *Sherman Herald-Democrat*, Denison, Texas. *Fort Worth Democrat*, February 14, 1878, and *Statesman*, February 15, 1878.

21 *Fort Worth Democrat*, February 17, 1878.

22 Record of Arrests Book, City of Austin. Austin History Center.

23 *Fort Worth Democrat*, March 3, 1878.

24 *Dallas Daily Herald*, April 3, "Ben Thompson and C. A. Rohrabocker, of Austin, are registered at the Windsor" and March 3, 1878, "Ben Thompson, Austin, is at the Le Grand."

25 *Fort Worth Democrat*, March 8, 1878.

26 *Statesman*, March 21, 1878.

27 Records of Oakwood Cemetery, Austin History Center.

28 *Fort Worth Democrat*, April 28, 1878.

29 *Austin American-Statesman*, July 19, 1936: Centennial Issue. Charles Cortissoz, AKA: Cuneo, Cunio, Coonie, Cunie, Coney, and even though he was of Italian descent, he was nicknamed "Mexican Charlie." Besides being a volunteer fireman, he was an Austin policeman for a two-month stint in September and October 1881. In 1874, he held two or three late night fandangos a week at his place of business which was well attended by prostitutes plying their trade. This was the beginning of Austin's First Ward neighborhood developing into the "fast" side of town and was first commonly referred to as the "Precincts of Mexico" or later more popularly: "Guytown." For decades the First Ward would be the center of Austin's vice district infamous throughout Texas for its saloons, gambling dens and bawdy houses.

30 Floyd B. Streeter, *Prairie Trails and Cow Towns*, 126. Per Streeter, the Dodge City papers in May 1878 reported: "Bill Thompson, well known on the cattle trail and in Texas and Kansas arrived in Dodge last week."

31 *Fort Worth Democrat*, July 23, 1878, in its Justice Court news noted, "Bill Thompson, brother of Ben Thompson, for carrying a pistol, was set for trial Wednesday; defendant furnishing bond for his appearance" and on July 25, issued in the Mayor's Court that Billy Thompson was fined $5 plus costs for carrying a six shooter.

32 *Galveston Daily News*, June 12, 1878. The fire department delegates hailed from Austin, Belton, Brenham, Calvert, Dallas, Galveston, Hempstead, Houston, Jefferson, Fort Worth, Marlin, Paris, Rockdale, San Antonio, Sherman, and Waco.

33 *Galveston Daily News*, June 12-16, 1878. Ben Thompson was selected to serve on a committee to study and report on incendiarism or arson; responsibilities of insurance companies and agents in connection therewith.

34 *Statesman*, August 4, 1878.

35 *San Antonio Daily Express*, July 30 and August 5, 1878, *Denison Daily News*, August 3, 1878 and *Statesman*, August 4, 1878; *San Antonio Express*, August 6, 1878.

36 John R. Lunsford, "How Ben Thompson Died With His Boots On," *Frontier Times*, Vol. 9, No. 2 (November 1931), 82-3.

37 J. B. Gillett, "Ben Thompson and Billy Sims," *Frontier Times*, Vol. 12, No. 1 (October 1934), and *Dallas Daily Herald*, Thursday, March 13, 1884. Gillett identified his two schoolmates as George Brush and Theodore Hillyer. The Brush Family owned a general merchandise store on Congress Avenue between Pecan and Pine Streets.

38 *General Directory of the City of San Antonio for 1879-1880* (Denison: Mooney and Morrison), 197, 239.

39 Testimony of W. H. Simms, *Habeas Corpus* hearing, *State of Texas vs. Ben Thompson*, 57. "I have been about the Vaudeville since 1878 … I was interested with Harris."

40 *San Antonio Light*, July 12, 1882. "Jack Harris and the Gambling Fraternity."

41 *Statesman*, August 11, 1878 and *Fort Worth Democrat*, August 17, 1878. Ben Thompson visited Hot Springs, Arkansas but it is difficult to date his time in this health resort town and mecca of gambling. The *Statesman* published a letter entitled, "Ben Thompson in the Role of a Newspaper Correspondent." In his communication with the newspaper editors, he speaks of being in Hot Springs, circa 1878, when a shooting scrape took place between the very argumentative and very violent dentist turned mayor; T. F. Linde and a "merchant tailor." Both men fired several ineffective shots at each other; however an unlucky "gentleman from Texas" was struck by a ricochet pistol ball causing a sizeable lump on his forehead. Unconscious, he was carried to a nearby drug store and the store soon filled with bystanders eager to see if he would recover. When the "supposed dead Texan" awoke "people scattered in all directions" to get "away from him as though he was some fierce wild beast." *Statesman*, July 3, 1880.

42 *San Antonio Daily Express*, November 7, December 17, 1878, *Bastrop Advertiser*, March 22, 1884.

43 *Statesman*, March 13, 1884. Jacob Carl DeGress, a Union cavalry commander during the Civil War, was afterwards an administrator of the Freedmen's Bureau in Texas and New Orleans. He was politically popular only among Radical Republicans. He became involved in local politics serving as an alderman and was twice elected mayor of Austin (1877-1880). Jacob DeGress died from complications from his Civil War wounds at the age of fifty-two in March of 1894, and was buried in Austin's Oakwood Cemetery.

44 *San Antonio Weekly Express*, November 14, 1878. A gap exists in the records of the *Statesman* from November 16-29, 1878.

45 *Statesman*, November 30, 1878.

46 Travis County Court Criminal Minutes, Vol. A, 104 –November 22, 1878. The indictment stated the alleged assault took place on November 1, 1878.

47 Anne Beck. The Finks established a large mercantile in New Ulm and the couple would eventually build a Texas curiosity known as "The Eyeglass House" due to the unique construction and paint colors which created the look of a large "pair

of spectacles" on the front of their home. Copy of undated *Dallas Morning News* article by Frank X. Tolbert. "Tolbert's Texas: 'Fink's Folly' In New Ulm."

48 Travis County Court Criminal Minutes, Vol. A, 98. On November 16, 1878, transferred to County Court: Keeping a gambling bank, Causes 5704, 5705, 5706, 5707, 5708 and aggravated assault and battery, Cause 5709. Transferred to Justice Court, carrying a pistol, Cause 5710.

49 A search of the index ledger at the Travis County Courthouse starting in 1878 lists sixty-nine causes for Ben and Billy Thompson. Travis County Court Criminal Minutes: Vol. A, 55 shows that on July 3, 1877, Ben Thompson pled guilty for Cause # 203 and was fined $25 plus costs. Thompson was committed to the county jail until the court was paid in full. Page 59 shows that on August 6, 1877 Causes # 204, 205, 206, 208 were all dismissed. Page 72 and 75 show that on October 3, 1877, Cause #260 was continued for service and was dismissed on November 7, 1877.

50 *Statesman*, November 30, December 3, 1878 and April 20, June 14, 1879. See Chapter 3, Endnote 28 for information concerning the 1864 lynching of the Willis Brothers.

51 Travis County Court Criminal Minutes, Vol. A, 139.

52 Gambolier (pronounced: "gambo-leer"). The origin of the word "is to frolic." Its first known usage was as a lyric in a Scottish drinking song. By the 1850s in America, a gambolier was otherwise known as a worthless individual given to carousing, gambling, and general moral depravity.

53 *San Antonio Daily Express*, December 17, 1878.

54 *Statesman*, December 19, 1878, "Ben Thompson as a Man of Peace—He Appeals to the Courts—He is a Reformer—He would Correct Bacon's Philosophy."

55 Ibid., *Galveston Daily News*, December 15, 17, 1878 and *San Antonio Daily Express*, December 15, 17, 18, 1878.

56 *Galveston Daily News*, December 19, 1878, *San Antonio Daily Express*, December 19, 1878, *Statesman*, December 21, 1878.

57 *Statesman*, December 21, 24, 1878.

58 Ibid., December 22, 1878.

59 *Galveston Daily News*, December 31, January 2, 11, 1879, *San Antonio Daily Express*, January 12, 1879.

60 *Galveston Daily News*, January 11, 1879, *San Antonio Daily Express*, January 12 and June 5, 1879, *Statesman*, June 7, 1879.

61 *Statesman*, January 7, 1879.

62 Travis County Court Criminal Minutes, Vol. A, 115 -116 shows that on January 6, 1879 Causes 413, 414, 415, 416 charges were dismissed. Page 118 shows that on January 7, 1879: Causes 417, 418, 419, 420, 421, 422 were all dismissed.

63 *San Antonio Daily Express*, June 5, 1879. Bacon's letter was dated April 23, 1879. *Statesman*, June 7, 1879, "the fellow Bacon, who wrote about Ben Thompson and was arrested therefor at San Antonio, got away and the last heard of him he was at Las Aguas Calientes in Central Mexico. Since Ben is coming down the silver line from New Mexico they may yet meet."

Chapter 11

1 *Statesman*, February 2, 1879.

2 *Bastrop Advertiser*, February 8, 1879. Although it was advertised that Ben Thompson of Austin had purchased the Dearden property opposite the Court

House and would erect a house there, it is doubtful he ever erected such a structure.

3 *Austin City Directory, 1877-1878*, 213. College is present day 12th Street. Apparently, Interstate 35 runs over the spot where the house once stood.

4 *Statesman*, February 19, 21, 1879.

5 Ibid., March 26, 1879.

6 Ibid.

7 Ibid., March 19, 26, 1879.

8 Walton, *Thompson*, 132. Walton reported the opposite in his biography of Thompson, stating that Ben could not remain due to the rarified air that affected his throat and lungs to such an extent he was forced to return to a lower elevation.

9 *Statesman*, March 26, 1879.

10 Walton, *Thompson*, 133.

11 *San Antonio Daily Express*, April 3, 1879. The newspaper did not name the letter writer.

12 *Statesman*, March 26, 1879. *San Antonio Daily Express*, April 6, 1879, stated a report from San Antonian Ed McElney refuted Ben Thompson's gambling losses and that his troubles in Leadville "were of no particular note."

13 *San Antonio Daily Express*, April 6, 1879. The newspaper identified the source as Ed McElney of San Antonio.

14 *Statesman*, April 4, 1879.

15 *Ford County Globe*, March 11, 25, 1879. *San Antonio Daily Express*, December 10, 1878. *Statesman*, December 7, 1878: "Billy Thompson Killed. [Austin] Marshal Creary received a dispatch yesterday from Waco stating that Billy Thompson was killed in that place [Knoblouch's Saloon] Thursday night [December 5, 1878] by Ben Gladdon [out on bail from a robbery charge]. "Deceased was a brother of Lath Thompson, for many years a policeman of this city [and bartender], and a brother-in-law of Pres Hopkins [another Austin bartender, gambler and friend of Ben Thompson]."

16 *Ford County Globe*, March 25, 1879 and the *Dodge City Times*, January 18, March 29, 1879.

17 DeArment, Robert K., *Bat Masterson, the Man and the Legend*, 148-50. Masterson was elected sheriff of Ford County, Kansas, by receiving three more votes than L.E. Deger, his nearest opponent. George G. Thompson, "Bat Masterson; The Dodge City Years," 19. (Fort Hayes Kansas State College Studies, Language and Literature Series No. 1, F. B. Streeter, Editor, General Series, Number Six, W.C. Austin, State Printer, Topeka, 1943.) The *Hays Sentinel*, in commenting on the election described Masterson as "cool, decisive and a 'bad man' with a pistol." *Dodge City Times*, November 24, 1877. *Ford County Globe*, April 8, 1879.

18 *Statesman*, April 24, 1879.

19 Ibid., May 4, 7, 1879. Tom Bowles would remain in Leadville until the second week of November. *Statesman*, November 13, 1879.

20 Eddie Foy and Alvin F. Harlow, *Clowning Through Life* (New York: E.P. Dutton & Co., 1928), 102-3. Hereafter cited as Foy, *Clowning Through Life*. Before appearing in book form, Foy's story first appeared in 1926-1927 serialized in *Collier's* magazine. Shortly before *Clowning Through Life* was published in hardcover, Foy would pass away at the age of seventy-one while performing in Kansas City. *Ford County Globe*, May 20, 1879.

21 Robert K. DeArment, *Bat Masterson, the Man and the Legend*, 148-50.

22 *Colorado Springs Weekly Gazette*, June 14, 1879.

23 *Pueblo Chieftain*, June 11, 1879.
24 *Colorado Springs Weekly Gazette*, June 14, 1979.
25 *Ford County Globe*, June 10, 1879. *Statesman*, June 17, 1879. Walton, *Thompson*, 133-34. Although Eddie Foy chose not to be part of Masterson's party, various sources list his brother Jim Masterson, Ben and Billy Thompson, Doc Holliday, Kinch Riley, John Joshua Webb, John Converse, Dave Rudabaugh, and Mysterious Dave Mather among the group.
26 *Dodge City Times*, June 14, 1879. *Colorado Springs Weekly Gazette*, June 14, 1879. *Pueblo Chieftain*, June 12, 1879.
27 *Pueblo Chieftain*, June 11, 12, 1879. Thomas Mead Bowen, a Union brevet brigadier general, would became a member of the Colorado House of Representatives in 1882 and resigned upon his election to the United States Senate. He served for six years from 1883 to 1889. In 1875, Bowen engaged in mining in the Summit District, north of Leadville, and developed rich and valuable gold properties.
28 DeArment, *Bat Masterson, The Man and the Legend*, 148-54.
29 *Colorado Springs Weekly Gazette*, June 14, 1879.
30 Ibid., June 14, 1879; *Pueblo Chieftain*, June 12, 1879
31 *Colorado Springs Weekly Gazette*, June 14, 1979. *Pueblo Chieftain*, June 12, 1879.
32 *Colorado Springs Weekly Gazette*, June 14, 1979.
33 On Thursday morning, June 12, Masterson, Thompson, and their followers arrived in Dodge City. *Dodge City Times*, June 14, 1879. *Statesman*, June 17, 1879. General Palmer's Denver & Rio Grande Railroad resumed construction and on July 20, 1880, their tracks finally reached Leadville.
34 Foy, *Clowning Through Life*, 104,
35 *Ford County Globe*, July 22, 1879. "W. B. Masterson, last week, purchased a house and a lot of G. M. Hoover on 2nd avenue." *Statesman*, August 19, 1879. DeArment, Robert K., *Bat Masterson, the Man and the Legend*, 153. Walton, *Thompson*, 133-34. Streeter, *Thompson*, 139–40, 208. As a young man in 1880, railroad historian, journalist, editor, and poet Cyrus Warman began as a laborer and eventually became an engineer for the Denver & Rio Grande Railroad. An 1896 piece by Warman did not mention a Thompson bribe but related how treasurer R. L. Weitbrec approached Bat Masterson. Streeter searched and found no record of a payment made to Ben Thompson listed in the files of the Atchison, Topeka and Santa Fe Company nor did he find anything among the archives of the affiliates (Union Contract Company and Rio Grande Extension Company) of the rival Rio Grande Railroad, which paid the temporary employees used during the Railroad war. "Unable to find conclusive, evidence on this matter," Streeter wrote, "nor has any statement by parties or witnesses to a deal, or by any other person in a position to know the facts, been found."
36 *San Antonio Express*, March 13, 1884. At the time of Ben Thompson's death in 1884, the *Austin Daily Capital* and *Statesman* published that the Atchison, Topeka and Santa Fe Company paid him a fee of $5,000.
37 *Ford County Globe*, July 30, 1878.
38 Foy, *Clowning Through Life*, 109-10
39 Ibid., 110-11.
40 Gary P. Fitterer, "The Life and Death of Billy Thompson (1845–1897)," Part Two, *Quarterly* of the National Association for Outlaw and Lawman History 25, no. 2 (April–May 2001): 10. James C. Shaw, *North from Texas* (Evanston, IL: The Branding Iron Press, 1952), 51-52.
41 *Statesman*, July 4, 1879.

42 *San Antonio Daily Express*, July 18, 1879. John King Fisher's letter was dated June 26, 1879.

43 *Statesman*, August 19, 1879.

44 Cause 554, 558, guilty and fined $10, $25 plus costs on August 5, 1879, p. 143, 145. Cause 555, 556, 557, 559, 560, 561 all dismissed on September 9, 1879, p. 150. Vol. A, County Court Criminal Minutes, Travis County, Austin.

45 *Statesman*, August 13, 15, and September 5, 10, 1879. The improvements of the lot were valued at $500 with surrounding lots selling for $100 per acre. A stable, chicken coop, and water cistern were enclosed by a wooden plank fence. The property was one and a half miles from the city post office. The title was undisputed. Thompson was selling single chances for $2.50 each or five chances for $10 dollars. Tickets could also be purchased at Joe Nagle's bookstore on Congress Avenue.

46 *Statesman*, September 10, 1879

47 Ibid.

48 Walton, *Thompson*, 155.

49 *Statesman*, October 2, 1879.

50 Ibid., October 22, 24, 1879.

51 *Galveston Daily News*, October 29, 1879.

52 *San Antonio Daily Express*, October 9, 1879.

53 *Statesman*, November 4, 1879. *Galveston Daily News*, November 4, 1879.

54 *Dodge City Times*, November 8, 1879. Paula Mitchell Marks, *And Die in the West: The Story of the O.K. Corral Gunfight*, 129. First published by William Morrow and Co., New York, 1989, and reprinted by University of Oklahoma Press, 1996.

55 *Statesman*, November 18, 19, December 3, 1879. Ben Thompson returned to Austin on Tuesday, December 2, 1879.

Chapter 12

1 *Statesman*, December 9, 10, 1879. Information on Millett's Opera House from the *Statesman*, February 10, March 24, May 26, 1878. Charles F. Millett was a contractor and lumber dealer and his opera house stands today at 109 East Ninth Street.

2 Ibid., December 9, 11, 1879.

3 *San Antonio Daily Express*, December 13, 14, 16, 17, 1879 and July 12, 1882. The issue of December 16 noted: "Buffalo Bill may give the public an opportunity of witnessing some of his unrivaled rifle shooting at the springs between 3 and 4 o'clock this afternoon." And on July 12, 1882: "[Ben Thompson] is one of the best pistol shots in the United States, having held his own in a contest with Buffalo Bill, or William Cody, at Austin and in this city." The seating capacity for San Antonio's Casino Hall allowed for 400 and, in addition, the building contained a barroom, ballroom, reading room, billiards and poker room, ladies lounge and in the basement was a bowling alley.

4 Gallegly, Joseph. *Footlights on the Border: The Galveston and Houston Stage Before 1900*, 192, (Gravenhage, The Netherlands: Mouton & Co., 1962).

5 The two images are now part of the Robert G. McCubbin Collection of photographs of the Wild West. Both are dated December 17, 1879.

6 "Record of Arrests" ledger, Austin History Center. Thomas R. Johnson made the complaint against Thompson for discharging firearms. Johnson was the combination night clerk and police officer. *Austin City Directory 1879-1880*, 104.
7 *San Antonio Evening Light*, July 12, 1882.
8 *Statesman*, March 2, 1880. The incident occurred on February 27.
9 Ibid., March 2, 1880.
10 *Statesman*, March 23, 1884. Joseph K. Foster, born in Missouri, was forty-one years old when the feuding with Thompson started. As a young man, he caught gold fever and went to California. By 1856, he moved on to New Mexico where he enlisted in a Confederate cavalry company at the start of the Civil War. Led by Capt. Joseph Phillips, they were known as the Partisan Rangers, and Foster found himself surrounded by "a most dare-devil, wild and reckless set of fellows." A year into the war, the company disbanded in Houston and Foster, for a short time, opened a gambling house there. Upon his return to San Antonio, he reenlisted and till the end of the war stayed in the Confederate army. When the war ended, he took on several partners, one of whom was noted gunman Matt Woodlief. Together they opened a saloon and gambling den. A shrewd businessman, he eventually became the sole proprietor of the establishment. He invested his profits in real estate and several successful race horses, supposedly attaining a considerable fortune for the times. Some said his wealth was as much as several hundred thousand dollars. His nature, described as warm and friendly to his friends, also had a strong streak of vindictiveness, which he was never able to suppress
11 *San Antonio Express*, July 13, 1882.
12 Walton, *Thompson*, 186-88. *San Antonio Express*, July 12, 13, 1882.
13 Ibid., In 1852 LaFayette Rogers arrived in Austin, in 1880 he was forty-six years old and a resident of Cherokee County, Texas. In his retirement he recounted how Ben Thompson was cheated at the Vaudeville Theatre's gambling room; Foster and Harris knew Thompson "would visit their gambling house and play Faro so they sent for a big nose Jew by the name of Dryfus [*sic*] to deal faro for them so as to skin Thompson." Ben lost all his money, then his watch, a diamond ring and, lastly, he borrowed money on a diamond stud. He then switched games and began playing *monte*. The *monte* dealer was Bill Tong and when Thompson began to win Foster stopped the game. Tong told Thompson over a glass of whiskey in the downstairs barroom that he had been robbed. Thompson returned to the gambling room and retrieved his watch and diamond jewelry from Foster with the point of his pistol. "Reminiscences of LaFayette Rogers," Manuscript Collection of Texas State Archives, Call Number 2-23/1054. In 1878, Louis Dryfoos owned Austin's Metropolitan Saloon (*Statesman*, December 15, 1878) and later ran San Antonio's Menger Hotel's billiard room and the hotel bar. *Morrison & Fourmy's General Directory of the City of San Antonio 1879-1880*, 127 and *1881-1882*, 132.
14 *Statesman*, March 18, 1880. James Simms spent his last night in Austin First Ward vice district with two other sporting men, Chip Burlage and Red Ryan, visiting the brothels owned by Sallie Daggett and Blanche Dumont. The three ne'er-do-wells attempted to cheat and rob a former Blanco County deputy sheriff named "Frenchy" Shubert. In the fracas Shubert killed Simms in the Gem Saloon. 1880 Travis County Census, 254 B. The Simms family is shown as living on Trinity Street. James M. Simms, fifty-two, a policeman; his wife Bridget, forty-eight, keeping house. Others were William, twenty-four, printer; Mollie, twenty-two; Kate, nineteen; Regina, sixteen, and three boarders.
15 *Statesman*, April 6, 1880.

16 Robert Holman worked a "club room" in an establishment on Congress Avenue between Bois d'Arc and Pecan Streets (most likely this was the second floor of the Iron Front Saloon). When the city directory was published, Holman resided with his widowed mother. *Austin City Directory*, 1881, 98.

17 *Statesman*, April 23, 1880.

18 Feit, Rachel, "Gardens of Eden, How Austin Used to Celebrate," *Austin Chronicle*, January 26, 2001, provides a wonderful description of the city's German beer gardens of the nineteenth century.

19 In 1881, Isaac C. Simon was proprietor of the Imperial Restaurant at 118 Pecan Street (6th). By 1885 he was a partner with John B. Billeisen in Simon's Restaurant at 609 Congress Avenue. *Austin City Directory*, 1881 and 1885.

20 *Statesman*, April 23, 25, 1880.

21 Ibid., The *Austin City Directory of 1872-1873* listed Robert F. Holman as a printer, 60.

22 Subsequently a few years later Ben Thompson, Ben J. Marshall, an Austin house painter and Ben's good friend, along with the intimidated Robert Holman formed a partnership to run the gambling room above the Iron Front Saloon on Congress Avenue. See endnote 64 in the Epilogue for financial information concerning the Thompson, Marshall, and Holman partnership.

23 *Statesman*, April 23, 24, 25, 1880.

24 Ibid., April 25, 1880.

25 Ibid., April 25, 27, 1880.

26 *Galveston Daily News*, May 11, 1880.

27 1880 Ford County Kansas Census, 554A. Their post office is shown as Dodge City. Brother William Thompson, age thirty-five, was then listed in Ogallala, Keith County, Nebraska as a boarder in Samuel J. Roney's hotel, giving his profession as printer, 47B. Former Ellsworth lawman John "Long John" DeLong was also counted as a boarder, now a laborer, age thirty-three. His birthplace is shown as "Canida West."

28 Mahnken, Robert R., "Ogallala—Nebraska's Cowboy Capital in Nebraska History," 28: 2 (April–June 1947). The 1880 Keith County, Nebraska Census shows William H. Tucker, age thirty-one with profession as a saloon keeper. Listed with him are his Texas-born wife Maggie, age twenty; a cousin. Oscar, thirty-nine, tending bar; half-brother Thomas J., age thirty-six, also tending bar; and another half-brother, John, age fourteen, attending school. Hobart Huson, *Refugio, A Comprehensive History of Refugio County from Aboriginal Times to 1955*, vol. 2 (Woodsboro, TX: The Rooke Foundation, 1955), 202. In 1871, Aransas County was formed from Refugio County, Texas.

29 *North Platte Nebraskan*, October 15, 1881; *Cleveland Plain-Dealer*, August 26, 1884; Athens, Ohio *Messenger*, October 23, 1884; *Omaha Daily Bee*, June 14, 1883.

On October 10, 1881, Dan Ferguson, a future friend and business partner of Wyatt Earp in the Coeur D' Alene, Idaho, mining camp, "squeezed off four quick shots" at Bill Tucker. Luckily for Tucker, all proved ineffective and the only injury he incurred was a lacerated abdomen. Elmer D. McInnes, "Coeur D' Alene Comrade," *Old West*, Spring 1996, 51-53. Much of Ogallala's business district burned down in early August 1884. Tucker was quickly back in operation because Ed Worley was reportedly killed in his place on August 17. Tucker, his wife Margaret and their children, Sonora, age five, and William, age one, were counted at North Platte, Lincoln County, in the 1885 Nebraska State Census. At the close of the 1885 cattle season he may have traveled on to New Mexico. By May 1886, the building that housed his saloon was being used by another business. Found in the 1895 Kansas State Census residing in Topeka was Maggie Tucker and her two children. There was no mention of her husband Bill Tucker and Maggie was earning her living as a housekeeper for George Hammel, a tailor. By the 1900 census, Maggie was listed as a widow. However, a herder by the name of William H. Tucker was listed at Miles City, Montana. This was probably the son, who would have been sixteen years old at the time. The above information concerning Tucker courtesy researcher and author Chris Penn of Marsham, Norfolk, England.

30 Robert K. DeArment, *Bat Masterson, the Man and the Legend* (Norman: University of Oklahoma Press, 1979), 184-85. The 1880 Ford County Census enumerated Masterson on June 22, as residing in Dodge City. The teenaged Annie Ladue is listed as a "concubine" and "Keeping House." She was a native of Illinois but the census failed to indicate where her parents were born. Census, 562. *Dodge City Times*, June 5, 1880.

31 *Dodge City Times*, June 26, 1880, the *Times* reported that Billy "had a difficulty with a Texas man in Ogallala a few days ago, a number of shots were fired." *Atchison Globe*, June 24, 1880, the *Globe* enhanced Ben Thompson's reputation in Kansas as a gunfighter by publishing an article retelling, with errors, his February 4, 1876, Congress Avenue shooting with three Llano county men visiting Austin.

32 Edgar Beecher Bronson, *Reminiscences of a Ranchman* (Lincoln: University of Nebraska Press, 1962), 267-73. First published in 1908; the University of Nebraska Press 1962 edition is a reprint of the A. C. McClurg & Co. 1910 edition.

33 Ibid., *North Platte Western Nebraskan*, June 26, 1880. "Thompson got his back, which was covered with a Chin-Chili-Overcoat, filled with a doubled barreled [*sic*] dose of Goose-Shot." Correspondence of G. E. Lemmon to E. P. Lamborn, June 4, 1935, and May 14, 1936, in the Lamborn Collection, Kansas State Historical Society, Topeka). And Gary P. Fitterer, "The Life and Death of Billy Thompson (1845–1897)," Part Two, *Quarterly* of the National Association for Outlaw and Lawman History 25, no. 2 (April–May 2002): 12. A chinchilla is a small rodent, or an expensive soft gray fur, a heavy cloth of wool, or wool and cotton blend with a tufted, napped surface, used for making overcoats.

34 *Statesman*, June 22, 1880. *San Antonio Daily Express*, July 8, 1880.

35 *Statesman*, July 2, 1880.

36 W. B. (Bat) Masterson, *Famous Gunfighters of the Western Frontier*, Annotated and Illustrated by Jack DeMattos (Monroe, WA: Weatherford Press, 1982), 138.

37 Chloral hydrate was discovered in 1832; however its properties as a sedative were not published until 1869. It is a solid, colorless, organic compound soluble with the addition of water or ethanol. At first it was used as a minor sedative for dental or other medical procedures. Mixed with ethanol and secreted into an alcoholic drink it became famous at the end of the nineteenth century and until present day as a *Mickey Finn.* The name was adopted from a notorious Chicago barman famous for knocking out selected patrons in such a manner and then robbing them to such an extent he would often leave his victims dumped naked in an alley near the back of his establishment.

38 Masterson, *Famous Gunfighters of the Western Frontier*, 138-43

39 *Rockport Transcript*, reprinted in the *Colorado Citizen*: "Billy Thompson, well known here as the brother of the somewhat notorious 'Ben' Thompson, and the man who killed young Smith, opposite the Scrivner's store in this place in

1867," recently exchanged shots with a fellow Texan named Tucker, in Ogallala, Nebraska." The remainder of the article depicting the Ogallala shooting is verbatim to the *Statesman* account of July 2, 1880.

40 *Statesman*, July 31, 1880. *San Antonio Daily Express*, July 13, 1882. A copy of the original *St. Louis Republican* article has yet to be found. The *Daily Express* wrote, "Almost a year ago, while Mr. Thompson was in St. Louis, the *St. Louis Republican* published an article purporting to be an interview, in which it was stated that during his life Thompson killed twenty-one men."

41 *Statesman*, September 19, November 2, 5, 1880. *Austin City Directory 1883-1884*, 65.

42 The purchase was made on November 5, 1880 and the house's exact location was Lot 31, Block 36, of Hearst's Addition, Division D, city of Austin. Travis County. Deed Records, Vol. 49, 1; *Statesman*, December 17, 1880. *San Antonio Daily Express*, December 18, 1880. Modern maps do not show San Marcos Street running north of Mesquite (11th Street). The house would have stood where Interstate 35 now flows or just south of the roadway on the grounds north of the University of Texas' Disch-Falk Field Baseball Stadium.

43 *Statesman*, November 2, 4, 11 and December 5, 12, 17, 1880.

44 M. B. Davis, Witness Testimony September 12, 1882, 3,4,5. Curiously Mervyn Bathurst Davis had only a few years before served under Lieutenant N.O. Reynolds and was among the Texas Rangers guarding John Wesley Hardin during his trial for murder at Comanche, Texas. See *Texas Ranger N.O. Reynolds, The Intrepid* by Chuck Parsons and Donaly E. Brice. (Denton: University of North Texas Press, 2014).

45 *Statesman*, December 5, 1880.

46 Silver City, New Mexico, *Herald and Southwest*, December 13, 1880. This reported that J. Farrell has been appointed City Marshal in place of J. Gilmo who had resigned.

47 *Galveston Daily News*, December 17, 1880.

48 *Luling Newsboy & Signal*, October 28, 1999, from a reprint of an article appearing in the "Long Ago in Luling" column, the original of which is no longer extant.

49 *Galveston Daily News*, December 18, 1880.

50 *San Antonio Daily Express*, December 19, 1880

51 *Statesman*, December 18, 19, 1880.

Chapter 13

1 In 1870, Blanche Dumont rented a house in Austin with two other prostitutes. By 1882, she owned her own brothel and had nine women accommodating customers. Her career as a madam in Austin's "Guytown" would span four decades, virtually the entire lifetime of the first ward vice district.

2 Information concerning the city of Austin and its law enforcement history is plentiful. For some of the most useful resources. see Doug Dukes, *Ben Thompson: Iron Marshal of Austin*, (2010). Frank Brown, *Annals of Travis County and the City of Austin from the Earliest Times to the Close of 1875*, (Transcript on file at the Austin History Center); David C. Humphrey, *Austin: An Illustrated History*, (Austin: Windsor Publications, 1985); Katherine Hart, *Austin & Travis County: A Pictorial History, 1839-1939*, (Austin: Encino Press, 1975); Mary Starr Barkley, *History of Travis County and Austin, 1839-1899*, (Austin: The Steck Company, 1967); the O. Henry quotation appears on page 229. Anonymous, *Introduction*

to the History of the Austin Police Department;* S.A. Gray and W.D. Moore, *Mercantile and General City Directory of Austin, Texas---1872-3;* Larry Jay Gage, "The City of Austin on the Eve of the Civil War," in the *Southwestern Historical Quarterly,* January 1960, 428-37; David C. Humphrey, "Prostitution and Public Policy in Austin, Texas, 1870-1915," in the *Southwestern Historical Quarterly,* April 1983, 473-516; Paul D. Lack, "Slavery and Vigilantism in Austin, Texas, 1840-1860," in the *Southwestern Historical Quarterly,* July 1981, 1-20. Tom Bicknell, "'The Proper Sort of a Person to be Marshal'—The Notorious Ben Thompson Becomes A Peace Officer," *Quarterly* of the National Association for Outlaw and Lawman History Inc. (NOLA) 27, no. 2 (April – June 2003): 40-53.

3 *Statesman,* June 24, 1881.

4 Doug Dukes, *Ben Thompson: Iron Marshal of Austin,* 5-7, 39, (2010). Information on Austin's civic improvements, the description of Ben Thompson's personality and official duties beyond traditional police work is from Mary Starr Barkley, *History of Travis County and Austin, 1839-189.*

5 *Statesman,* December 18, 21, 22, 1880. L.M. Crocker replaced Jacob C. DeGress in August 1880 when De Gress lost a lawsuit questioning his eligibility to serve as mayor.

6 *Statesman,* December 18, 1880.

7 Ibid., January 5, 21, February 3, 4, 1881. *Record of Arrests* Book, February 4, 5, 17, 1881, archived at the Austin History Center.

8 *San Antonio Daily Express,* July 13, 1882. *Statesman,* January 14, 1881. "From a gold bar is suspended a large gold wreath, in the center of which is a Texas star, surrounded by the word Texas. On the face of the star is engraved the word City Marshal. The top bar bears the name of Ben Thompson, and is surrounded by a small but well executed gold eagle and the whole 'get up' is exceedingly beautiful and appropriate."

9 Case 805 was dismissed on February 8, 1881, 235. On September 6, 1880, Case 804 was dismissed for the same reason, 219, and finally Case 803 was settled with a plea of guilty and a fine of $25 plus court costs, 218-19. June 9, 1880, Vol. A, County Court Criminal minutes, Travis County.

10 *Dallas Weekly Herald,* January 20, 1881.

11 1880 Travis County Census, 1, shows John Cheneville [*sic*], John, a white male and single, age twenty-eight, born in Louisiana, residing at Christine Peterson's boardinghouse. Creary resigned the office of city marshal two weeks prior to the scheduled elections and Chenneville became acting city marshal until the replacement election was held. The *Statesman* reported this on December 21, 1880, stating he "performed his duties well, and made a most excellent officer."

12 *Statesman,* February 3, 1881.

13 Ibid., February 17, April 14, 1881. There were 133 arrests during the month of February. Fines collected was $534; $221 worked out on the streets. During the month ninety-three whites and forty blacks were arrested.

14 *Record of Arrests* Book, December 27, 1880, Case # 9833, shows James Brown, teamster, was charged with vagrancy. Austin History Center.

15 Chuck Parsons, *James Madison Brown, Texas Sheriff, Texas Turfman.* (Wolfe City, Texas: Henington Publishing Company, 1993).

16 *San Antonio Daily Express,* February 23, 1881.

17 *Fort Worth Daily Democrat,* March 2, 1881.

18 Leo Tarleton, Witness Testimony July 25-28, 1882, *State of Texas v. Ben Thompson,* Habeas Corpus, 115-16. Tarleton was a highly respected attorney of

the Alamo City. He resided in San Antonio for forty-five years but travelled over much of the state due to his legal responsibilities. He died September 21, 1921, and is buried in the City Cemetery in San Antonio. *San Antonio Light*, September 22 and 26, 1921.

19 The 1880 Travis County Census shows Augustus L. Cashell as a thirty-five year old native of Alabama with a wife and four children. His occupation is given as "Printer" and logically he and Ben became acquainted with both being in the printing trade. 1880 Travis County census, 223.

20 A. L. Cashell, Witness Testimony July 25-28, 1882, *State of Texas v. Ben Thompson*, Habeas Corpus, 83-5, 88.

21 T.P. McCall, Witness Testimony July 25-28, 1882; *State of Texas v. Ben Thompson*, Habeas Corpus, 111-12.

22 W. H. Simms, Witness Testimony July 25-28, 1882, *State of Texas v. Ben Thompson*, Habeas Corpus, 50-58, 112-15. Briscoe Center for American History.

23 *San Antonio Daily Express*, February 23, 1881. The Texas Legislature was back in-session on February 25, 1881. *Statesman*, February 25, 1881. "Yesterday complaint was made against a colored individual, charging him with theft of goods. Capt. Thompson, chief of police, ran across him during the day, and quietly proceeded to take him in. He will have a hearing to-day."

24 *Dallas Daily Herald*, February 24, 1881. *Fort Worth Daily Democrat*, March 2, 1881.

25 *Statesman*, July 12, 1882. *Bastrop Advertiser*, July 15, 1882.

26 W. H. Simms, Witness Testimony July 25-28, 1882, *State of Texas v. Ben Thompson*, Habeas Corpus, 50-58, 112-15.

27 *Statesman*, February 26, March 2, 7, 8, 1881. Ben Thompson made an arrest on these days; March 11, 14, 16, April 5, 6, 1881. "Record of Arrests" Book, Austin History Center.

28 *Statesman*, April 29, 1881.

29 Eck's daughter, Mrs. Jennie Stewart, owner of the Austin Motel stated she was in possession of some pawned Thompson furniture.

30 Officer Cary (or Carry) H. Randolph was born in Florida on July 21, 1853, the son of Arthur M. and Laura Harrison Duval Randolph. Randolph died December 26, 1935.

31 *Statesman*, April 6, 1881.

32 *Galveston Daily News*, April 20, 1881.

33 *San Antonio Daily Express*, July 6, 1881.

34 *Statesman*, April 14, 1881. In the "March Police Pickings," column one learns that even though the legislature was in-session, "the police pickings were smaller than usual, and business in the police department was comparatively dull."

35 *Statesman*, May 24, 1881.

36 Ibid., June 3, 1881.

37 Ibid., November 7, 1876. On the page of the arrest record the name is written out as "Ringold."

38 *Statesman*, May 3, 1881. "Record of Arrests" Book, May 2, 1881, Case # 111248 and 111249. A superior biography of the feudist remains *John Ringo: King of the Cowboys* by David Johnson (Denton: University of North Texas Press, 2008).

39 *Texas Siftings*, May 21, 1881. The first *Texas Siftings* edition was published on May 9, 1881.

40 *Statesman*, May 24, 1881.

41 *San Antonio Daily Express*, April 8, 1881. *Statesman*, April 15, 1881.

42 O.C. Fisher with J.C. Dykes, *King Fisher: His Life and Times*, 108-09, (Norman: University of Oklahoma Press, 1966).
43 *Fort Worth Daily Democrat*, May 15, 1881.
44 *Statesman*, June 3 and July 17, 1881.
45 *Statesman*, August 16, 24, 1881. Susan Billingsley earned her living as a servant; she paid her fine with cash. *Record of Arrests* book, August 22, 1881, Case # 111682.
46 *Statesman*, July 2, 1881. *San Antonio Daily Express*, July 2, 1881. The Turner Hall was located on the southeast corner of Chestnut (18th Street) and Lavaca Street. The Austin City Directory of 1872 lists Herman Lungkwitz as a photographer residing opposite the Turner Hall. The bartender was most certainly young Herman Lungkwitz Jr, while the photographer was sixty-eight year old Herman Lungkwitz Sr., who was also a renowned classically trained landscape artist. He both photographed and painted the nearby Texas Hill country.
47 R. L. Wilson, "L. D. Nimschke—Firearms Engraver," 20-22, *The American Rifleman*, January 1966. Kenneth L. Cope, *Stevens Pistols and Pocket Rifles*, 35, (Ottawa: Museum Restoration Service, 1971). Richard Rattenbury, "From Showman to Shootist: A Stevens-Lord Presentation Pistol," 12-14, *Man at Arms*, Vol. 10, # 6, November/December 1988. Natalie and Tom Bicknell, "The Cody-to-Thompson Stevens-Lord No. 36 Target Pistol was a Handsome Present," in "Guns of the West" column, *Wild West*, February 2002, 16, 65.
48 R. L. Wilson and Greg Martin. *Buffalo Bill's Wild West, An American Legend.* 38, (New York: Random House, 1998).
49 *Statesman*, June 30, July 6, 7, 9, 10, 13, 14, 1881. *Bastrop Advertiser*, July 16, 1881. Mary Ann (Baker) Thompson was interred in Section 1, Lot 71 of the Oakwood Cemetery in Austin.
50 *Statesman*, July 12, 1881. *San Antonio Daily Express*, July 12, 13, 1881. *Galveston Daily News*, July 12, 1881. *Records of Arrests* Book, July 12, 1881, Case # 10544 lists Mrs. Amelia Schooman's occupation as prostitute and her crime as being: "Dressed in Men's Clothes."
51 Doug Dukes, in "Gunfighters and Lawmen" column, "A Peace Officer with More Hip than Holster," 18-19, *Wild West*, October 2015.
52 *National Police Gazette*, July 30, 1881. "Ben Thompson who keeps a gambling hall at Austin, Tex., is soft in speech, small in stature, and usually mild in manner: yet he is one of the most noted desperadoes of the Southwest and has killed half a dozen men. He cannot however, be accused of downright murder for in every instance he technically acted in self-defense. That is his peculiarity. Whenever he gets into a fight in which pistols are drawn he recklessly waits until his opponent has fired and then deliberately shoots back. This plan affords him a clear defense in court, and has not yet resulted in his death, as it might reasonably be expected."
53 W. H. Simms, Witness Testimony July 25-28, 1882, State of Texas v. Ben Thompson, Habeas Corpus, 50-58, 112-15.
54 *San Antonio Daily Express*, August 6, 1881.
55 Ibid., July 30, 1881. *Statesman*, August 10, 1881. *Fort Worth Daily Democrat*, August 16, 1881.
56 *San Antonio Daily Express*, August 17, September 20, 1881.
57 *Statesman*, August 31, 1881.
58 *Statesman*, September 4, 1881.
59 Ibid., October 9, 11, 25, 1881.
60 Ibid., November 4, 1881.

61 Ibid., November 6, 1881.
62 Ibid., September 24, November 2, 1881.
63 Ibid., November 7, 10, 1881.
64 Ibid., November 10, 20, 22, December 5, 1881.
65 Cowan, E. D. "Memories of the Happy Bad Man," *Chicago Sunday Chronicle*, October 16, 1898. Reprinted in the *Denver Rocky Mountain News*, October 21, 1898.
66 Thomas G. Martin, Witness Testimony July 25-28, *State of Texas v. Ben Thompson*, Habeas Corpus, 92-96.
67 Letter to the author from Gary P. Fitterer dated September 1, 2001. "Record of Arrests" Book, October 21, 1879 – May 31, 1885. *Statesman*, September 10, 1879, and January 29, 1885. 1880 Travis County Census. Alexander Mack is identified as a black male, age twenty-three, a laborer living on Colorado Street. He was a stepson of Barney and Sally Cook, also black.
68 Joe Edgar Manry, *Curtain Call: the History of the Theatre in Austin, Texas 1839 to 1905*, 74-75, (Austin: Waterloo Press, 1985). Warde was a member of the Knights of Pythias.
69 Silver City, New Mexico, *New Southwest*, December 17, 1881. Sallie (Moore) Farrell would marry Fred R. Arlitt on May 25, 1889.
70 William M. Edwardy, witness testimony July 25 - 28, 1882, *The State of Texas v. Ben Thompson*, Habeas Corpus, 90- 91.
71 *Statesman*, December 28, 1881.
72 Ibid., December 12, 15, 18, 1881.
73 *Statesman*, January 10 and 11, 1882.
74 Ibid., February 4, 1882.
75 Ibid., January 8, February 3 and 5, 1882. The badge remains as a prize possession of the Chenneville family.
76 *Fort Worth Daily Democrat*, January 20, 1882.
77 L. E. Edwards, Witness Testimony July 25-28, *State of Texas v. Ben Thompson*, Habeas Corpus, 85-88. *Austin City Directory, 1872-1873*, 47, *San Antonio Daily Express*, September 13, 1882.
78 *Brenham Daily Banner*, March 17, 1881. Keith County District Court, Grand Jury Indictment, *The State of Nebraska v. William Thompson*, Indictment for shooting with intent to kill. Nebraska State Historical Society, Reference Archivist Chad Wall could not locate any record that the case was bound over to the court for prosecution.
79 *Dallas Daily Herald*, March 16, 1882.
80 *Statesman*, April 5, 1882. The *Rockport Transcript's* editor described Thompson's friend: George Pendexter as "a genial, good fellow, good lawyer, and a true friend."
81 *Statesman*, March 17, 19 and 30, 1882.
82 Ibid., July 8, 1882.
83 Ibid., July 20, 1882. Officer Sheehan's response was reported to have originally occurred in 1877.
84 David C. Humphrey, "Prostitution and Public Policy in Austin, Texas, 1870-1915," *The Southwestern Historical Quarterly*, April 1983, 473-516.
85 *San Antonio Daily Express*, March 4, 1882.
86 *Statesman*, March 17, 1882. The International Railroad fixed track to Laredo on Christmas Day 1881.

87 Thomas G. Martin, Witness Testimony July 25-28, *State of Texas v. Ben Thompson*, Habeas Corpus, 92-96. W. H. Simms, Witness Testimony July 25-28, *State of Texas v. Ben Thompson*, Habeas Corpus, 50-58, 112-15.

88 *Statesman*, April 22, 23, May 4, 10, 12, 26, 27, 31, 1882. *Austin Daily Dispatch*, June 17, 1882. Letter to the author from George Fox, Grand Secretary of the Knights of Pythias of Texas, dated May 16, 1996. Mr. Fox graciously provided a copy of the "Semi-Annual Report Term Ending June 30, 1882, of Mt. Bonnell Lodge, No. 34" of the Knights of Pythias. Fifty-four men had achieved the status of Knight including Ben Thompson. For Thompson the rank of Page was conferred on Saturday, June 3 and for Esquire and Knight on Saturday, June 10, 1882. 1880 Travis County Census. Kentucky-born Edward Oesch gave "Druggist" as occupation. He is listed as a white male, age twenty-eight, married with two daughters and one son.

89 *San Antonio Daily Express*, September 13, 1882. *Statesman*, September 13, 1882. *Bastrop Advertiser*, September 16, 1882.

90 Gary Fitterer, *Quarterly* of the National Association for Outlaw and Lawman History, Part Two, 25, no. 2 (April – May 2001): 14. George W. Baylor to Neal Coldwell, May 19, 1882. General Correspondence, Adjutant General's Record Group (RG 401).

91 *Statesman*, May 27, 28, 1882.

92 Ibid., May 28, 1882.

93 H. A. Burbank, Witness Testimony July 25-28, 1882, *State of Texas v. Ben Thompson*, Habeas Corpus, 96-7.

94 W. A. Pitts, Witness Testimony July 25-28, 1882, *State of Texas v. Ben Thompson*, Habeas Corpus, 89-90.

95 John Chenneville, Witness Testimony July 25-28, 1882, *State of Texas v. Ben Thompson*, Habeas Corpus, 104. *Galveston Daily News*, September 14, 1881.

96 Thomas G. Martin, Witness Testimony July 25-28, *State of Texas v. Ben Thompson*, Habeas Corpus, 92-96.

97 Walton, *Thompson*, 176.

98 W. H. Simms, Witness Testimony July 25-28, 1882, *State of Texas v. Ben Thompson*, Habeas Corpus, 50-58, 112-15.

Chapter 14

1 Frank Sparrow, the Vaudeville Theatre's business and stage manager, booked the Mauri sisters on March 17, 1882, for a four-week stint paying the girls one salary at $50. Sparrow continued to sign the sisters throughout the spring and early summer of 1882 and the comments he recorded in his schedule book provide an insight into their abilities: pages 60-61, May 15, 1882, "Fair to Middling 'Little off their Nest," pages 62-63, May 15, 1882 "Artistically off—as Hustlers best in Biz." Pages 64-65, "Depart with Old Man Comment not necessary. Closed on [July]11th [the night Jack Harris died] and went to Chicago." Page 64-65, "October 16 Kate + (May Mauri) Season jt. Serio Comics + Song + Dance Close 1883. Same as last Season $30/100 joint." And with this last entry Kate and May Mauri drifted on and disappeared. "Ledger Book of Frank Sparrow, business and stage manager of the Vaudeville Theater, 1875-1884," Texana Collection, Texana Department, San Antonio Public Library.

2 *The State of Texas v. Ben Thompson*, Witness Testimony July 25 - 28, 1882. W. H. Simms, 50-58, 112-15. Charles F. A. Hummel, 73, George Horner, 79-80. Hereafter cited as Witness Testimony.
3 Witness Testimony, Barney Mitchell, 32-37, M. Harris, 73-78.
4 Witness Testimony, Johnny D. Dyer, 38-50.
5 Witness Testimony, Jacob Ripps, 58-60.
6 Witness Testimony, W. H. Simms, 50-58,112-15. John J. McLaughlin, 6-10, Sworn Testimony August 7, 1882.
7 Witness Testimony, Jacob Ripps, 58-60.
8 Witness Testimony, L. Rouvant, 106-108.
9 Witness Testimony, Ramon L. Biencourt, 66-73, W. H. Simms, 113-14. John J. McLaughlin, 6-10, Sworn Testimony August 7, 1882.
10 Witness Testimony, Johnny D. Dyer, 38-50. W. H. Simms, 50-58, 112-15; Ramon L. Biencourt, 66-73.
11 Witness Testimony, L. Rouvant, 106-08.
12 Witness Testimony, Johnny D. Dyer, 38-50.
13 Witness Testimony, E. A. Hicks, 61-65; W. H. Simms, 50-58, 112-15; Pat Carney (aka Cavanagh), 97-100. *San Antonio Daily Express*, July 13, 1882: Simms's Coroner's Hearing Testimony.
14 Witness Testimony, Johnny D. Dyer, 38-50; Walton, *Thompson*, 185. Sunset arrived in San Antonio on July 11, 1882, at 7:45 p. m.
15 Witness Testimony, Thomas O'Conner, 99-103; E. A. Hicks, 61-65; Ramon L. Biencourt, 66-73; Joseph A. Smith, 104-05; Charles Hoffman, 105-06.
16 Witness Testimony, Barney Mitchell, 32-37; M. Harris, 73-78; Johnny D. Dyer, 38-50.
17 "Ben must have understood that a glancing ricochet striking off a flat, hard surface from a low velocity handgun cartridge will not bounce off at the same angle that the bullet approached. He knew his bullet would track at a shallower angle, hugging closer to the wall. Thus, Thompson's shot was able to strike Harris." Mohan Jauhari, M.Sc., F. A. F. Sc., Assistant Director (Ballistics), Approximate Relationship Between the Angles of Incidence and Ricochet for Practical Application in the Field of Criminal Investigation," *The Journal of Criminal Law, Criminology and Police Science*. (Copyright 1971 by Northwestern University School of Law), Vol. 62, No. 1, 122.
18 *San Antonio Daily Express*, July 14, 1882. *Dallas Daily Herald*, July 12, 1882. *Galveston Daily News*, July 12, 1882. Johnny D. Dyer, 38-50; Pat Carney (aka Cavanagh), 97-100. *Statesman*, March 13, 1882 and reprinted in the *Bastrop Advertiser*, March 22, 1884: "The most interesting thing about this killing is the accuracy with which he shot. Harris was screened from view, yet he so shot as to hit the vital part of the body, and in order to do this he had to glance the ball along the wall."
19 *San Antonio Evening Light*, July 12, 1882; Johnny D. Dyer, 38-50; *San Antonio Daily Express*, July 26, 1882.
20 Witness Testimony, Ramon L. Biencourt, 66-73.
21 Witness Testimony, Dr. Thomas R. Chew, 65-66; Frank Sparrow, 110-11; *Statesman*, July 18, 1882.
22 Witness Testimony, Joseph C. Foster, 81-82.
23 *San Antonio Daily Express*, July 12, 1882.
24 Witness Testimony, Frank Sparrow, 110-11; Ledger Book of Frank Sparrow, 65.
25 *Galveston Daily News*, July 12, 1882.

26 Ibid., July 12, 1882.
27 Witness Testimony, Charles F. A. Hummel, 73; George Horner, 79-80; L. C. Grothaus, 80-81. The *San Antonio City Directory* places Horner Saloon at 268 W. Commerce and Hummel & Sons Gunsmiths at 270 W. Commerce.
28 Witness Testimony, C. J. Beck, 78-79.
29 *Galveston Daily News*, July 13, 1882.
30 *Statesman*, July 12, 1881; *San Antonio Daily Express*, July 12, 1882.
31 *San Antonio Light*, July 13, 1882. Reprint from the *San Antonio Times*.
32 *San Antonio Daily Express*, July 13, 14, 1882; *Dallas Daily Herald*, July 13, 1882; *San Antonio Light*, July 12, 13, 1882; Witnesses included Johnny D. Dyer, Barney Mitchell, W. H. "Billy" Simms, Policeman Jacob Ripps, and Dr. Adolph Herff. Members of the jury were: A. B. Stephenson, August Krawitz, C. P. Smith, Henry Muller, Simon Frank and C. F. Frommer, *Statesman*, July 14, 1882.
33 *San Antonio Daily Express*, November 3, 1882; Gary P. Fitterer, "The Life and Death of Billy Thompson (1845 – 1897), Part Two, *Quarterly* of the National Association for Outlaw and Lawman History, Inc. 25, no. 2 (April – May 2001): 14.
34 *San Antonio Daily Express*, July 14, 1882.
35 *San Antonio Light*, July 12, 13, 1882; *San Antonio Daily Express*, July 13, 14, 1882.
36 *San Antonio Light*, July 13, 14, 17, 1882; *San Antonio Daily Express*, July 13, 14, 1882; *Galveston Daily News*, July 14, 1882; *Statesman*, July 18, 1882.
37 The *San Antonio Daily Express* informed its readers, "The funeral of Jack Harris will take place this afternoon at 5 o'clock, [Wednesday, July 12,] from his residence on Soledad Street, friends and acquaintances are invited to attend." *San Antonio Daily Express*, July 12, 13, 1882; *Statesman*, July 13, 18, 1882; *Galveston Daily News* July 14, 1882; "Ledger Book of Frank Sparrow, business and stage manager of the Vaudeville Theater, 1875-1884," 65, date of entry July 15, 1882. Texana Collection, Texana Department, San Antonio Public Library.
38 *San Antonio Light*, July 14, 23, 1882; *San Antonio Daily Express*, July 14, 1882. An amount of $1,700 does not seem like much but in the dollar value of 2015, that amount would be worth $42,119, according to Morgan Freeman's "Inflation Calculator."
39 *Statesman*, July 15, 1882.
40 Ibid., July 19, 1882.
41 From the collections in the Briscoe Center for American History, the University of Texas at Austin, 32-117. *The State of Texas v. Ben Thompson*, Habeas Corpus case, July 25-28, 1882, 22nd Judicial District Court of Texas, Judge George H. Noonan, presiding. W. H. Herron, Esq., appointed to take down the testimony, George R. Dashiell, Clerk of the District Court. Witnesses for the State were Anton Adam, 32; Barney Mitchell, 32-37; W. K. Dobson, 37-38; Johnny D. Dyer, 38-50; W. H. Simms, 50-58; recalled 112-115; Jacob Ripps, 58-60; E. A. Hicks, 61-65; Dr. Thos. R. Chew, 65-66; R. L. Biencourt, 66-73; Chas. F. A. Hammel, 73; M. Harris, 73-78; C. J. D. Beck, 78-79; George Horner, 79-80; J. C. Foster, 81-82; Henry Ansell, 82-83. Witnesses for the defense: A. L. Cashell recalled, 83-85; L. E. Edwards, 85-88; W. A. Pitts, 89; William M. Edwards, 90-92; E. B. Connell, 92; Thos. G. Martin, 92; H. A. Burbank, Pat Cavanaugh, signed; Pat Carney, 97-100; Thos. O'Conner, 100-03; John Chenneville, 104; Jos. A. Smith, 104-05, T. P. McCall, recalled, 105; Charles Hoffman, 105-06; L. Rouvant; George Pendexter, 110; Frank Sparrow, 110-11; Leo Tarleton, 115-16; Jack Cummings, 116-17.
42 *Galveston Daily News*, July 26, 1882.

43 *San Antonio Express,* July 26, 1882. *Galveston Daily News*, July 26, 1882. *Statesman*, July 27, 1882.
44 *Dallas Daily Herald*, July 26, 1882. "The State was represented by Fred Cocke, district attorney of the [Bexar] county; Tarleton and Boone, I. G. and M. G. Anderson, Judge Devine, T. T. Teel and W. R. Wallace district attorney of Medina county. The attorneys for Thompson were N. O. and J. A. Green, of San Antonio; Wm. Walton, of Walton & Hill, of Austin, and Geo. Poindexter [*sic*], of Austin." *San Antonio Express,* July 26, 1882; *Galveston Daily News*, July 26, 1882.
45 *Dallas Daily Herald*, July 26, 1882; *San Antonio Express,* July 26, 1882; *Galveston Daily News*, July 26, 1882. Copy of Architect Dobson's Vaudeville diagram courtesy of Jim and Theresa Earle, College Station, Texas. Witness Testimony, W. K. Dobson, 37-8.
46 *Galveston Daily News*, July 27, 1882; Pat (A.K.A. Cavanaugh) Carney, 97-100; Thomas O'Conner, 100-03.
47 Witness Testimony, W.H. Simms, 112-15; *Statesman*, July 29, 1882; *San Antonio Daily Express*, July 26, 1882; *Galveston Daily News*, July 27, 1882.
48 Witness Testimony, Jack Cummings, 116-17; *Statesman*, July 29, 1882.
49 Witness Testimony, George Pendexter, 110.
50 *Galveston Daily News,* July 29, 1882; *Dallas Daily Herald,* July 29, 1882; *Bastrop Advertiser*, August 5, 1882, July 28, 1882; Bexar County District Clerk Records, Criminal Journal, District Court, 1882, 360-61: Ben Thompson, *Ex Parte, vs. T.P. McCall*, Sheriff of Bexar County; Application for Bail.
51 *Dallas Daily Herald*, July 29, 1882; *Galveston Daily News*, July 29, 1882; *Statesman*, August 22, 1882.
52 *Statesman*, August 8, 22, 1882; *Bastrop Advertiser*, September 2, 1882.
53 On August 2, 1882, the *Galveston Daily News* reported: "Bill Thompson, the brother of the notorious Ben Thompson, who killed Jack Harris recently in San Antonio, is a resident of this city."
54 *Statesman*, August 15, 1882. The sworn affidavits were taken as follows: John J. McLaughlin, August 7; John Lamar and Daniel Morgan, August 15; M. B. Davis, September 12, 1882. Bexar County Court Records. Collections in the Briscoe Center of American History.
55 *Dallas Daily Herald*, August 29, 1882; *Statesman*, August 30, 1882.
56 Walton, *Thompson*, 188; *Statesman*, September 1, 1882; *Galveston Daily News*, September 1, 3, 1882.
57 *San Antonio Daily Express*, September 14, 1882; *Legendary Watering Holes, the Saloons that made Texas Famous,* compiled and edited by Richard Selcer. See chapter two, "Jack Harris's Vaudeville and San Antonio's 'Fatal Corner,'" 53-120, by David Bowser (College Station: Texas A&M University Press, 2004). The Vaudeville's fall season opened September 17 to enthusiastic reviews and continued to receive positive reviews throughout the fall.
58 Bexar County District Clerk Records, Criminal Journal, District Court, 1882, Case 2118, 364-65. Collections in the Briscoe Center of American History. *Statesman*, September 6, 7, 1882.
59 Bexar County Court Records, Copy of Judge Wilson's order, signed September 9, 1882. Collections in the Briscoe Center of American History. *San Antonio Light*, September 12, 1882. *Statesman*, September 12, 1882. *Galveston Daily News*, September 12, 1882.
60 *Statesman*, September 16, 1882.

61 Bexar County District Clerk Records, Criminal Journal, District Court, 1882, Case 2118, 367. Collections in the Briscoe Center of American History. Information on the birth of Walton Thompson Gill provided by the Gill Family Bible. *San Antonio Light,* September 12, 1882; *Dallas Daily Herald,* September 13, 1882; *Statesman,* September 13, 1882; *San Antonio Daily Express,* September 13, 1882; *Bastrop Advertiser*, September 16, 1882.

62 *Statesman*, September 16, 1882.

63 Bexar County District Clerk Records, Criminal Journal, District Court, Case 2118, 379-80, bail denied on September 13, 1882. Collections in the Briscoe Center of American History. O. C. Fisher and J. C. Dykes, *King Fisher, His Life and Times,* 100, 102, (Norman: University of Oklahoma Press, 1966); *San Antonio Daily Express,* September 15, 1883; *Statesman,* September 16, 1882.

64 *Statesman*, October 7, 1882

65 Ibid., October 17, 1882; *Dallas Daily Herald*, October 17, 19, 1882; *Galveston Daily News*, October 24,1882.

66 Monthly Return of Captain G.W. Baylor, Company A, for month ending October 31, 1882. Henry Orsay was the chief clerk in the adjutant general's office. Texas State Archives.

67 *Galveston Daily News*, October 30, 1882. General Correspondence, Adjutant General's Papers, Texas State Archives. P.P. Court to Adjutant General W. H. King, October 23, 1882. Gary P. Fitterer, "The Life and Death of Billy Thompson (1845–1897), Part Two, *Quarterly* of the National Association for Outlaw and Lawman History, Inc. 25, no. 2 (April – May 2001): 14-15.

68 *Dallas Daily Herald*, October 29, November 2, 1882; *Galveston Daily News*, October 29, 30, 1882; *Houston Daily Post*, October 31, 1882; *El Paso Herald*, November 8, 1882.

69 *Dallas Daily Herald*, October 29, 1882; *Beaumont Enterprise*, November 4, 1882; Letters sent, Adjutant General's Office, April 1, 1882 - November 6, 1883, Letter Press Book 168-69 Texas State Archives. Henry Orsay to Capt. George W. Baylor, October 30, 1882. Gary P. Fitterer, "The Life and Death of Billy Thompson"14-15.

70 *Statesman*, October 24, 1882.

71 Ibid., August 14, 1911. He began serving on November 13th and during his long career as a public servant and peace officer, besides being a Bexar County tax collector and deputy sheriff, Kirk would three times be elected Austin's city marshal.

72 *Austin Statesman*, October 25, 1882.

73 *Dallas Daily Herald*, November 1, 16, 23, 1882; *Statesman*, December 17, 1882.

74 Ibid., July 22, 1882.

75 *National Police Gazette*, December 12, 1882.

76 *Galveston Daily News,* December 28, 1882; *Brenham Daily Banner,* January 2, 1883; *Houston Daily Post,* May 15, 1883; Gary P. Fitterer, "The Life and Death of Billy Thompson" 15-16.

77 *Statesman*, January 9, 1883. Subpoena information *State of Texas v. Ben Thompson*, murder [– Jack Harris] from Noah H. Rose Collection, Western History Collections, University of Oklahoma at Norman.

78 *San Antonio Daily Express*, January 11, 1883; *San Antonio Light*, January 11, 1883.

79 *San Antonio Daily Express*, January 11, 1883.

80 *Texas Siftings*, March 29, 1884.

81 *San Antonio Light*, January 11, 1883.

82 *San Antonio Light*, January 15, 18, 1883. Among the witnesses for the prosecution were: Barney Mitchell, Womble, Architect Dobson, May Mauri, Joe C. Foster, W.H. Sims [*sic*], Captain Ed Stevens, Sheriff McCall, Dr. T.R. Chew, and J.O. Goodrich.

83 *Dallas Daily Herald*, January 13, 1883; *San Antonio Light*, January 13, 18, 1883; *San Antonio Daily Express*, January 18, 1883. Witnesses for the defense: A.L. Cashell, John Cheneville, T. G. Martin, Joe Byne, L.H. Byrn, W. M. Edwardy, Bones Cullimore, L.G. Edwards, Willis Adams, W.E. Beck, Pat Carney, Tom O'Conner, John Lamar, John M.C. Burmingen, H.A. Burbank, E.B. Cornell, Mr. Fowler of Bastrop, John McLaughlin, John Fogg of Abilene, Captain W.A. Pitts, Bexar County Deputy Sheriff Pensaloza, Charles Hoffman, Dave Morgan, and Whit Spearsy [*sic*].

84 Walton, *Thompson*, 189; *San Antonio Light*, January 20, 1883; *Dallas Daily Herald*, January 21, 1883.

85 Walton, *Thompson*, 189. Bexar County District Clerk Records, Criminal Journal, District Court, 1882, Case 2118, 428. Collections in the Briscoe Center of American History. The jury consisted of H. Tatum, foreman, T. C. Rine, Rols Neighbors, Walter B. Beck, John Terrill, John Creswell, Frank Gull, Michael Franger, Jas. B. Mann, J. S. Campbell, J. S. Woolsey, and G. W. Waltsberger.

86 *San Antonio Light*, January 22, 1883. *San Antonio Daily Express*, January 23, 1883. *Dallas Daily Herald*, January 27, 1883.

Chapter 15

1 *San Antonio Light*, January 13, 1883; *Austin Daily Capital*, March 13, 1884; Houston *Daily Post*, March 13, 1884.

2 *San Antonio Light*, February 4, 1883. The newspaper reported that J. S. Goldsmith, who was "for a number of years proprietor of the Comique Theatre in New Orleans," would be the business manager for the Vaudeville for the coming spring season.

3 *Dallas Daily Herald*, January 23, 1883; *Statesman*, January 23, 1883; *San Antonio Light*, January 25, 1883. Walton, *Thompson*, 195-96. "Diary of Gus Birkner 1835-1940," 23, typed transcript on file in the Caldwell County Genealogical & Historical Society Library, Luling, Texas.

4 *El Paso Lone Star*, February 3, 1883

5 *Austin City Directory, 1883-1884*, 149, gives Thompson's address as 2009 University Ave. In 1905, the house was sold to the Women's Board of Missions of the Christian Church and the building was dedicated as the Texas Bible Chair, an educational institution unrelated to the state university that was meant to instruct any interested student, restricting no denomination, in the meaning and use of their specific religious faith. Four years after the dedication, the structure was lifted from its foundation and moved so a larger brick building for the Texas Bible Chair could be erected. The old Thompson family home was taken to a lot at 2626 Wichita where it became the Gamma Phi Beta sorority house. The house no longer stands on Wichita Avenue; the date of its dismantling is not known. *Daily Texan*, December 11, 1946, "Old Ben Thompson, Desperado Built First Bible Chair Home." *Statesman*, September 20, 1953, "Thompson's Old Home Ain't the Same."

6 *Texas Siftings*, April 5, 1884.

7 *Dallas Daily Herald*, March 29, 1883. Walton, *Thompson*, 196.

8 *San Angelo Standard*, April 19, 1890.

9 "Tradition credits Ben with the invention of the shoulder-holster which, of all the hideouts, is the most practical for extended use. The original shoulder-holster was merely a modified belt-holster, the principal modification consisting of a shoulder loop cut to assure perfect hang of the holster and addition of a back strap. While this old style holster carries the gun handily, it is by no means a fast-draw harness." Eugene Cunningham, *Triggernometry, A Gallery of Gunfighters,* (The Caxton Printers, Ltd., Caldwell, Idaho, 1956), 431. "The earliest and most common type of shoulder holster employed in the West was the so-called 'Texas' pattern, perhaps popularized—though certainly not invented—by notorious Texas shootist Ben Thompson." Richard C. Rattenbury, *Packing Iron, Gunleather of the Frontier West,* 153, (Zon International Publishing, Springfield, Ohio, 1993). "The concealment that a shoulder holster afforded allowed Western shootists to be 'well heeled' while not attracting attention. The most common type of shoulder rig used on the frontier was the Texas Pattern, which made its debut sometime during the late 1870s and is believed to be the earliest style. Texas gunman Ben Thompson packed his pistol in such a manner." Phil Spangenberger, "Shoulder Holsters, These concealed-carry rigs were born on the frontier," 20, *True West,* May 2005, Volume 52, Issue 4, Monthly Feature: "Shooting From The Hip."

10 *Luling Signal,* September 20, 1883, reprinted from the *Houston Post.*

11 Walton, *Thompson,* 174. Walton did not identify which Austin newspaper.

12 *Fort Worth Daily Gazette,* April 8, 1883; *Waco Examiner,* April 10, 1883. The 1880 McLennan Census, 11B.

13 Aransas County District Court Records, Case No. 22, *The State of Texas v. Wm. Thompson,* murder; *Houston Daily Post,* May 15, 1883. Gov. John Ireland file, Texas State Archives. Gary P. Fitterer, "The Life and Death of Billy Thompson (1845 – 1897), Part Two, *Quarterly* of the National Association for Outlaw and Lawman History, Inc. 25, no. 2 (April – May 2001): 16.

14 Aransas County District Court Records, Case No. 22, *The State of Texas v. Wm. Thompson,* murder. Gov. John Ireland File, Texas State Archives.

15 Record of Arrest Book, City Marshal John P. Kirk, May 30, 1883, No. 13038, Austin History Center; *Houston Post,* March 12, 1884.

16 Ten witnesses were summoned and among them were F. H. Bushick of Bexar County, Oliver P. Reid, former Rockport saloon owner and a Laredo furniture dealer at the time of the hearing, and D.D. Scrivner, Remus Smith's employer. Aransas County District Court Records, Case No. 22, *The State of Texas v. Wm. Thompson,* murder; letter from Sterling Fontaine Grimes to Aransas District Clerk C. F. Bailey, June 30, 1883. DeWitt County Courthouse, Cuero, Texas. *State of Texas v. William Thompson,* murder. Case # 1607- Remus Smith. Walton, *Thompson,* 190. *Statesman,* August 14, 1883. *San Antonio Daily Express,* July 13, 26, 1883. *Laredo Times,* July 26, 1883. *Galveston Daily News,* July 31, 1883. *Fort Worth Daily Gazette,* August 2, 9, 1883.

17 Hobart Huson. *Refugio, A Comprehensive History of Refugio County From Aboriginal Times to 1955,* Vol. II, *Secession to 1955,* 201. (Woodsboro, Texas: The Rooke Foundation, Inc., 1955). Saint Mary's of Aransas was the county seat of Refugio County from 1850 to 1886. When the San Antonio and Aransas Pass railroad bypassed it the town began to decline and two severe storms in the early 1900s caused extensive damage from which the town struggled to recover.

18 *San Antonio Daily Express,* August 21, 22, 1883. *Laredo Times,* August 23, 1883.

19 *San Antonio Light,* August 13, 1883.

20 *Corpus Christi Caller-Times,* September 23, 1883.

21 Ibid., October 7, 1883.

22 *Statesman*, October 7, and November 27, December 12, 1883. On July 28, an Englishman pedaled a water velocipede across the English Channel from Dover to Calais in less than eight hours.

23 Clerk C. F. Bailey certified the Grand Jury Indictment on October 25, 1883; Aransas County District Court Records, Case No. 22, *The State of Texas v. Wm. Thompson*, murder. October 29, 1883, DeWitt County Court Records, Case 1607, *The State of Texas v. Wm. Thompson*, murder.

24 *The Daily Fair News*, Austin, Texas, October 18, 1883. Eric C. Caren, *Texas Extra—A Newspaper History of the Lone Star State 1835-1935* (Castle Books, Edison, New Jersey. 1999), 137.

25 Record of Arrests Book, Austin History Center. Arrest 137: William Walton and Ben Thompson charged with purchasing the services of prostitutes, fined $5 and paid cash. Arrest 13038: On May 30 at 4 p. m., Ben Thompson discharged a pistol within city limits and was arrested by police officer E. R. Oberwetter. Ben paid a $10 fine. Cause 1535, Vol. A, County Court Criminal Minutes, Travis County.

26 Archives of the Austin City Council Meetings, December 8, 1883, special meeting, 414. DeWitt County Court Records, Case 1607, *The State of Texas v. Wm. Thompson*, murder.

27 Walton, *Thompson*. 197, *Statesman*, December 20, 1883; *Galveston Weekly News*, December 20, 1883.

28 The Hannahan family in 1870 consisted of head of household Thomas, a fifty-two-year-old stock raiser born in Ireland, his wife Mary, thirty-five, also born in Ireland, and their children: John, eleven, James, ten, Margaret, eight, Mary, six, and Bridget, four years old. The children were all born in Texas. 1870 Uvalde County Census, 542. A decade later, two members of the family are in the county jail: James, charged with murder, and Mrs. Hannahan, charged with accessory to murder. 1880 Uvalde County Census, 524B. Thomas Hannahan's fate is uncertain, but Mary Sheedy Hannahan, born March 24, 1816, in Ireland, lived until April 18, 1905, and is today buried in the Uvalde Cemetery in Row 11, site G, lot 155. Perhaps Fisher killed Thomas Hannahan and not one of his sons. 1870 and 1880 Census Uvalde County, Ancestry.com and FindaGrave.com.

29 The names of John King Fisher's daughters were Florence, Eugenia (Ninnie), and Mittie. A fourth daughter, name unknown, died in her sixth week of life in January 1882. *Crystal City, Texas Sentinel*, November 6, 1959, "New Grave For King Fisher Recreates Interest In Former Deputy Sheriff," reprinted through the courtesy of the Uvalde *Leader-News*, Publisher Harry Hornby Jr. and the article's author Miss Florence Fenley. O. C. Fisher with J. C. Dykes, *King Fisher, His Life and Times* (Norman: University of Oklahoma Press, 1966), 114-15.

30 Alison A. Kelso was listed as a thirty-two-year-old deputy sheriff with a wife and two children in the 1880 Uvalde County census, 524. In the 1880 Zavala County census, J.K. Fisher was listed as a twenty-five-year-old Stockman, with wife Sarah, twenty-one, and two daughters: Fredonia, aged three years and Eugenia, six months old. All were Texas born. Fisher had one herder to help in the stock raising, William Stidham, twenty-five years of age, occupation herder. 1880 Zavala County census, 472. John R. Baylor was the Zavala County census enumerator.

31 Walton, *Thompson*, 197.

32 Ibid., 197-98.

33 *Statesman*, January 2, 4, 1884.

34 Record of Arrest Book, City Marshal H. G. Lee, January 7, 1884, Entry 129, Ben Thompson, Fine $18.30, paid cash. *Statesman*, January 8, 1884, and June 26, 1884. *San Antonio Daily Express*, January 16, 1884. Invoice dated May 10, 1884, submitted to Ben Thompson's Estate by J. C. Petmecky, Gunsmith.

35 Jesse Lee Hall managed the Dull Ranch from 1880 to 1885. *Austin American*, March 14, 1927; "Captain Lucy Explodes Ben Thompson Myth; a True Story," James E. Lucy interviewed by Hugh Nugent Fitzgerald. Lucy served under Texas Ranger Lee Hall as a private enlisting July 15, 1877. For years, he was a private detective and tracked down many notorious fugitives. He was a friend of William and Robert Pinkerton, sons of the founder of the detective agency. From 1885 to 1890, Lucy served Austin as city marshal. He died at his home in Austin on July 10, 1927, and is interred in Oakwood Cemetery.

36 *San Antonio Daily Express*, January 12, 1884.

37 *Statesman*, January 16, 1884, reprinted from the *San Antonio Daily Express*.

38 *Statesman*, January 12, 13, 15, 16, 17, 1884; "Record of Arrest Book," City Marshal H. G. Lee, January 14, 1884, Entry 161. Total fine with costs was $36.

39 *San Antonio Daily Express*, January 16, 1884.

40 Ibid., January 16, 17, 1884.

41 *Statesman*, February 2, 1884. *San Antonio Daily Express*, February 3, 1884. In 1877 William A. Bowen, married Ada Debardelebon, the daughter of German Doctor John F. Debardelebon of Bastrop, a renowned surgeon throughout Texas. As a lifelong newspaperman, Bowen became a writer with a national reputation. He was a reporter and a member of the editorial staff on many Texas newspapers and on newspapers in both Chicago and St. Louis.

42 *Statesman*, February 2, 3, 14, 1884.

43 Ibid., February 3, 1884.

44 Ibid., February 3, 5, 7, 1884. *San Antonio Light*, February 4, 1884. *San Marcos Free Press*, February 7, 1884. "Senator Burgess requests the publication of the facts that he did not tell Ben Thompson that the *Statesman* force had conspired to kill him at sight, but that he told Ben to go home and quiet down as the people were very much exercised at him ... Ben Thompson has recalled the statement and acknowledges speaking hastily and more than he meant." *San Antonio Daily Express*, February 5, 1884.

45 *Statesman*, February 7, 1884.

46 *New York Times*, February 4, 1884; *Chicago Tribune*, February 3, 1884.

47 *San Antonio Daily Express*, February 3, 1884.

48 *Statesman*, February 5, 1884.

49 Ibid., February 6, 1884.

50 Records of Arrest Book, H. Grooms Lee, City Marshal, Cause 274—complainant Jesse McIntyre, Ben Thompson declared not guilty, Cause 275—complainant Wm. Gaines, Ben Thompson fined $37.95 and appealed, Cause 276—complainant, Wm. Powell, Ben Thompson fined $16.60, paid $13.60.

51 *Statesman*, February 7, 1884.

52 Ibid., February 14, 1884.

53 Ibid., February 17, 1884. *Dallas Weekly Herald*, February 21, 1884.

54 *Dallas Weekly Herald*, February 28, 1884. Richard Harding Davis, *The West from a Car Window* (New York: Harper Brothers, 1892).

55 *Ellsworth Reporter*, January 27, 1910, "Old Tombstone Stake In Poker Game Discovered in Austin, Texas." *Houston Chronicle*, December 21, 1924. J. Marvin Hunter, "Ben Thompson Wins a Tombstone," *Frontier Times*, Volume 2, Number

6, March 1925, pp. 2-3. Chuck Parsons, "The 'Free-Hearted Fellows' Of The Iron Front (Austin), *Legendary Watering Holes, The Saloons That Made Texas Famous,* Compiled and Edited by Richard Selcer (Texas A & M University Press, College Station, 2004), pp. 200-02.

56 Invoice dated May 10, 1884 submitted to Ben Thompson's Estate by J. C. Petmecky, Gunsmith. Knights of Pythias Grand Treasurer of Texas and collector of Pythian jewelry, George Fox, has identified the watch fob worn by Ben Thompson. Ben Thompson's descendent, Anne Beck, owns this photograph. Captain Harvey R. Marks was one of the best-known citizens of Austin, Texas. Born in New York on January 6, 1821, he went to Texas in 1838 and served as a captain of a company of Texas Rangers. Sometime in the 1840s, Marks returned to New York; however, he eventually moved to Baltimore where he married and began his career as a daguerreotype artist until 1853. From 1855 to 1858, he was reported to be in Mobile, Alabama. During the Civil War he served in the Confederate Army and fought until the end of the war. Marks returned to Texas and settled in Houston in 1866 where he was active as a photographer until he moved to Austin four years later. From 1870 until his death on March 12, 1902, he made Austin his home and owned a studio on Congress Avenue during his thirty plus years there. In November 1881, he was awarded seventeen First Class Premiums by the Capital State Fair Association for unequaled excellence. The *Statesman* reported on November 13, 1883, "The famous Austin artist, H. R. Marks, has sent to our branch office in Washington, admirable pictures of the leading politicians and statesmen and jurists of Texas. By the way, Marks' pictures of Jefferson Davis, of Hood, Bragg and other Confederate leaders have been selected and preferred by the Bureau of Confederate War Records at Washington to all others and will be used in making engraved likenesses of these officials for the publications of this bureau." *Statesman*, November 4, 1881 and March 13, 1902.

57 *Statesman*, February 23, 24, 26, 28, March 25, April 25, 1884. *San Antonio Daily Express*, February 26, 1884. Record of Arrests Book, H. Grooms Lee, City Marshal, Ben Thompson, Cause 353, fined $18.80, 359, continued till March. Theo Hillyer, Cause 363, Dismissed.

58 J. Marvin Hunter, "Knew Ben Thompson," *Frontier Times*, Volume 16, Number 10, July 1939. Knight of Pythias Roster Report of December 13, 1882, Mount Bonnell Lodge, No. 34, Austin, Texas, lists R. P. Smyth as a member and Smyth's employer: Phil Abraham, Chancellor of the lodge. Copy of the report courtesy of George Fox.

59 *Statesman*, February 27, 1884; *Luling Signal*, February 28, 1884; *Dallas Weekly Herald*, February 28, 1884. Ben Thompson presented his friend Claude Douglas Johns a "handsome, dark wood cane, banded in gold." *Austin American Statesman*, March 11, 1973.

60 *Statesman*, February 24, 1884.

61 Walton, *Thompson*, 200.

62 *Statesman*, February 26, 1884.

63 *San Antonio Daily Express*, February 28, 1884.

64 Amalia Mignon "Minnie" Hauck (1851 - 1929), performed under the name Minnie Hauk. She was an American born mezzo-soprano prima donna. During November 1866, at the age of fifteen, she was deemed the "Wonder Child" when she first appeared and was a sensation on the New York stage. She performed during Mardi Gras season at Galveston's Tremont Opera House on February 29, March 1, 2, 1884. On March 6, she appeared in Austin at Millet's Opera House, however the

critic for the *Statesman* had a low opinion of her voice writing that she was "a tolerable good singer but not a great prima donna." (*Houston Post*, March 12, 1884.) Before leaving Texas, she appeared at Houston's Pilot House on March 7, 8, 1884. During her career she appeared in over one hundred roles, sang *Carmen* in four languages, and performed in London, Paris, and Vienna. World War I wiped out most of her fortune and when she died in Lucerne, Switzerland, she was impoverished and nearly blind.

65 In Ben Thompson's day, Clear Lake was an area perfect for a cattle ranch, but it was mainly a region of small farms and fishing communities twenty years later. With the coming of the railroads, Galveston and Houston increased in population, as did other smaller communities. In 1901, the oil gusher at Spindletop launched the oil industry and the town became popular as a vacation spot for wealthy oilmen. In 1963, NASA's Johnson Space Center was established in Clear Lake. Casey Edward Greene. "Clear Lake City, Texas" in *The New Handbook of Texas*, 153-54.

66 *Galveston Daily News*, March 3, 13, 1884.

67 *Statesman*, March 12, 1884.

68 *Statesman*, March 9, 1884.

69 Ibid., November 15, 1883.

70 Ibid., *Statesman*, November 30, 1883.

71 Ibid., December 28, 1883.

72 J. Marvin Hunter, "Knew Ben Thompson," 420, *Frontier Times*, Volume 16, Number 10, July 1939.

73 Odie Minatra, "Some exploits of Ben Thompson," *Frontier Times*, Vol. 18, No. 12, September 1941, 560. The Jules Glaser family was native to Germany, and they were living in Guadalupe County in 1880. Jules and his wife were listed as farmers by the census taker; of their five children the oldest was Benjamin, thirteen, and all at home. This young man was still a teen when working in Austin when he and Thompson met. 1880 Guadalupe County Census, 223.

74 Lafayette Rogers Reminiscences, Call Number 2-23/1054, Manuscript Collection, Archives Division, Texas State Archives. On December 18, 1878, Austin policeman John Chenneville arrested Lafayette Rogers at 3 p.m. and charged him with vagrancy. Rogers was described as a United States citizen and a white male with "laborer" listed as his occupation. Austin Police Record of Arrests, Austin History Center.

75 *Statesman*, March 13, 1884.

76 *Uvalde Leader-News*, April 20, 1928. "Death of Ben Thompson and King Fisher Described," by A. H. Gregory, *Texas Argus*, San Antonio. *Texas Siftings*, April 5, 1884. O. Clark Fisher, "King Fisher—Texas Lawman, *Corral Dust* (Potomac Corral of the Westerners, Vol. IV, No. 1, Washington, D. C., March, 1959), 1-5; O. C. Fisher with J. C. Dykes, *King Fisher, His Life and Times,*124 (Norman: University of Oklahoma Press, 1966). Boatright was under indictment since October 1, 1883.

77 R. D. Holt, "The Introduction of Barbed Wire into Texas and the Fence Cutting War," *West Texas Historical Association Year Book*, June 1930, 65-79; Wayne Gard, "The Fence Cutters," *Southwestern Historical Quarterly* 51, no. 1 (July, 1947): 1-15. Joseph Gallegly, *From Alamo Plaza to Jack Harris's Saloon, O. Henry and the Southwest He Knew,* 136, (Publisher: The Hague Mouton, January 1970).

78 O. C. Fisher with J. C. Dykes, *King Fisher, His Life and Times,* 118.

79 A west Texas friend of Fisher's, Vinton L. Lee, saw him on the corner of Commerce Street and Main Plaza outside the Vaudeville Theatre. Fisher informed Lee he was on his way to Austin to interview Governor Ireland in regard to the new fence cut-

ting law and how to stop the lawlessness. Victor Lee James. *Frontier and Pioneer Recollections of Early Days in San Antonio and West Texas*, 76, published by the author, San Antonio, 1938.

80 O. C. Fisher with J. C. Dykes, *King Fisher, His Life and Times*, 124.

81 Ibid., 126.

82 McCubbin, Robert G. "A Blood-Stained Memento," 138-39, *True West*, Vol. 53, Issue 2, April 2006. During the first week of June 2004 San Antonio attorney Mark Eisenhauer contacted co-author Tom Bicknell and wanted to verify the 1884 vintage photograph purported to be Ben Thompson, given to him by a client, was in fact the notorious marshal of Austin. It was easily verified as being authentic. Mr. Eisenhauer had the photograph in his possession for thirteen years after having received it, with thanks, from an elderly Hispanic lady, for whom he performed work planning her estate. Bicknell contacted Robert McCubbin, owner of one of the most extensive and valuable collections of original Old West photographs, after he realized the historical value of the photo; in particular, the revelation of the dried brown stains of John King Fisher's blood on the back side. Bicknell wanted the photograph to find a home in a prominent and permanent collection, so he helped place Eisenhauer and McCubbin together. On June 11, 2004, they negotiated a mutually beneficial transaction. This photograph, which uniquely touches the lives and deaths of two notable western gunfighters, now safely resides in the McCubbin Collection.

83 *Statesman*, March 13, 1884. Thompson last wrote out his name when he signed a pledge for $50 to his Knights of Pythias Lodge at W. C. Denny and W. R. Brown's Cosmopolitan Saloon.

84 *Statesman*, March 13, 20, 1884. *San Marcos Free Press*, March 13, 1884. Joseph Shely, Company F, Frontier Battalion, Lieutenant from March 1, 1883, to March 1, 1884, and Captain March 1, 1884, to May 31, 1885, Texas Ranger Muster rolls, Texas State Archives. Ex-Medina County Sheriff, Deputy U. S. Marshal Ferdinand Niggli was shot and mortally wounded during a private difficulty by the current Medina County sheriff. He died five days later on August 31, 1885.

85 Walton, *Thompson*, 200.

86 *Dallas Daily Herald*, March 13, 1884.

87 Lunsford, John R. "How Ben Thompson Died With His Boots On," *Frontier Times*, Vol. 9, No. 2 (November 1931.) and *San Antonio Express*, September 6, 1931. Streeter, *Ben Thompson, Man with a Gun*, p. 193.

88 *Dallas Daily Herald*, March 13, 1884.

89 Walton, *Thompson*, 200. *Statesman*, March 13, 1884. *San Antonio Light*, March 12, 1884.

Chapter 16

1 Walton, *Thompson*, 200-01. *San Antonio Light*, March 12, 1884. *Statesman*, March 13, 1884. Thirty-two-year-old Harrington Lee "Hal" Gosling was the United States Marshal for the Western District of Texas and a member of the San Antonio Lodge of the Knights of Pythias. Marshal Gosling died in the line of duty on February 21, 1885, when outlaws Charles Yeager and James Pitts, with help from family members, murdered the trusting Gosling during an escape attempt while transporting these prisoners to the jail in San Antonio.

2 Walton, *Thompson*, 201. *San Antonio Light*, March 12, 1884. *Statesman*, March 13, 1884. *Galveston Daily News*, March 13, 1884. A. J. Thorpe often told his neph-

ew R. D. "Boss" Thorpe, also a future Austin Chief of Police (1928-1958) that he was unable to convince Ben Thompson not to go to San Antonio the night he was shot dead. Information provided by Sybil Paterson, great granddaughter of Abram Roberts and Matilda "Tillie" (Baker) Roberts—Jane Baker's sister. www.pioneersandlegendsoftexas.com.

3 *Statesman*, March 13, 1884. *San Antonio Light*, June 2, 1882.

4 Lunsford, John R. "How Ben Thompson Died With His Boots On," *Frontier Times*, Vol. 9, No. 2 (November 1931.) and *San Antonio Express*, September 6, 1931.

5 According to the 1880 Census, Bexar County, Jacobo Coy was a white male, age forty, who could neither read nor write. His occupation was day laborer and was born in Mexico. He and his wife were the parents of four children

6 *San Antonio Daily Express*, March 13, 1884. Billy Simms Coroner's Hearing Testimony.

7 Streeter, *Thompson*, 190. This information was provided by cowboy Pink Simms, a cousin to Billy Simms.

8 *San Antonio Light*, February 16, 18, and 25, 1884.

9 Elton R. Cude, *The Wild and Free Dukedom of Bexar*, 113-14. O. C. Fisher with J. C. Dykes, *King Fisher, His Life and Times*, 128. Years later, Tom Vanderhaven, a San Antonio attorney, who was a personal friend of King Fisher, told Terrell Kellogg, the King's grandson, that he had warned King of the possibility of tragedy that evening if he remained with Thompson.

10 *San Antonio Light*, March 12, 1884. The *San Antonio Daily Express* of March 13, 1884, described Billy Thompson's revolver slightly different: "White ivory handled nickel-plated six-shooter, handsomely ... engraved. It was a six-shooter .44 calibre Colt." The opening of the White Elephant Saloon and Club Parlors on Main Plaza at 315 West Commerce Street was reviewed in the *San Antonio Daily Express*, on Wednesday, August 8, 1883. Proprietors Fowler, Berliner & Co., provided San Antonio "one of the most elaborately appointed and elegantly furnished [establishments] to be found anywhere in the South."

11 *San Antonio Daily Express*, March 11, 1884—theater advertisement. *San Antonio Daily Express*, March 13, 1884. *Statesman*, March 13, 1884. Lunsford, John R. "How Ben Thompson Died With His Boots On," *Frontier Times*, Vol. 9, No. 2 (November 1931.) and *San Antonio Express*, September 6, 1931. Douglas W. Ellison, "Edge of Darkness: The Final Days of Ben Thompson," *Brand Book*, English Westerners' Society, London. Vol. 48, No. 3 (Summer 2015), 1-20. Douglas provides new information concerning the two gunmen's reason for leaving the Turner Opera Hall before the final curtain came down: "They were asked to leave by theatre manager Ernest Rische when some ladies objected to their presence. Rische and Charles Watkins, husband-manager of Ada Gray, then joined them for a drink at a nearby saloon." *San Antonio Daily Express*, August 30, 1902.

12 *San Antonio Daily Express*, June 3, 1906. "Risches's Reminiscences of the Thespian Temples, Actors and Actresses Who Played and Sang Here—Many Who Rode In Walked Out—Earnest [*sic*] Recalls Thompson, Foster, Fisher Tripple [*sic*] Tragedy."

13 Andres S. Coy Sr. served San Antonio as a police officer for thirty years rising to the rank of captain. Well known throughout the state as an excellent officer, he was acknowledged for being fair, even-handed and kind to the prisoners he held in custody. In 1913 at the age of sixty-nine, he passed away and was buried in San Antonio's San Fernando Cemetery. In the 1884 newspapers his name appears as Andreas however his headstone spells his name as Andres.

14 *San Antonio Light,* March 12, 1884, *San Antonio Daily Express,* March 13, 1884, *Galveston Daily News,* March 13, 1884, *Houston Post,* March 13, 1884, City Marshal Shardein, J. M. Emerson and J. B. Chadwell 's Coroner's Hearing Testimony. Walton, *Thompson,* 201.
15 Ibid., Billy Simms, Jacobo S. Coy's Coroner's Hearing Testimony.
16 *Statesman,* March 12, 1884.
17 *San Antonio Light,* March 11, 1884. *Texas Siftings,* April 5 1884. *Statesman,* March 12, 1884. *San Antonio Light,* March 12, 1884, *San Antonio Daily Express,* March 13, 1884, *Galveston Daily News,* March 13, 1884, *Houston Post,* March 13, 1884, Billy Simms, Jacobo S. Coy, and J. M. Emerson's Coroner's Hearing Testimony.
18 *San Antonio Light,* March 12, 1884, *San Antonio Daily Express,* March 13, 1884, *Galveston Daily News,* March 13, 1884, *Houston Post,* March 13, 1884, A. Casanovas (also spelled: Cosonovas), Billy Simms, City Marshal Phillip Shardein Coroner's Hearing Testimony.
19 Ibid., Phillip Shardein Coroner's Hearing Testimony.
20 Ibid., J. B. Chadwell Coroner's Hearing Testimony.
21 *San Antonio Light,* March 12, 1884, *San Antonio Daily Express,* March 13, 1884, *Galveston Daily News,* March 13, 1884, *Houston Post,* March 13, 1884, J. M. Emerson Coroner's Hearing Testimony.
22 *San Antonio Light,* March 12, 1884. *Statesman,* March 13, 1884. *New York Times,* March 13, 1884.
23 *Statesman,* March 12, 13, 1884. *San Antonio Lig*ht, March 12, 1884.
24 *San Antonio Daily Express,* March 13, 1884.
25 *San Antonio Light,* March 12, 1884. *Statesman,* March 13, 1884. *San Antonio Daily Express,* March 13, 1884. Robert G. McCubbin, "A Blood-Stained Memento," 138-139, *True West,* Vol.53, Issue 2, April 2006. Per McCubbin: "Triumvirate in Old West Photographs. Among the most sought-after collectibles of Old West outlaws and lawmen are original photographs, autographs and relics documented as having belonged to them. This cabinet card of Ben Thompson fits all three. Even more exciting, the card is tied to another Old West gunfighter-Thompson inscribed it to his pal John King Fisher, on the day both of them were killed. Inscribed by one, and with the blood of the other." Robert G. McCubbin and *True West* Editors, "The 65 Most Important Historical Photos from the Robert C. McCubbin Collection," 39, *True West,* Vol. 65, Issue 1, January 2018.
26 Walton, *Thompson,* 202. The *Statesman* agreed publishing on March 15, 1884: "The killing of Ben Thompson is the leading sensation in all the history of Texas. It was, indeed, a most tragic affair."
27 O. C. Fisher with J. C. Dykes, *King Fisher, His Life and Times,* 132.
28 *Statesman,* March 12, 1884. *Austin Daily Dispatch,* March 12, 1884. *San Antonio Light,* March 12, 1884, *Dallas Weekly Herald* March 13, 1884. *Houston Post,* March 13, 1884. *Austin Daily Capital,* March 13, 1884. *San Antonio Daily Express,* November 17, 1910.
29 *San Antonio Express,* March 14, 1884.
30 *Austin Daily Capital,* March 13, 1884.
31 *San Antonio Light,* March 12, 1884. *Statesman,* March 13, 1884.
32 *Austin Daily Capital,* March 12, 1884. *Austin Daily Dispatch,* March 12, 1884. *Houston Post,* March 13, 1884. *Dallas Weekly Herald* March 13, 1884.
33 *San Antonio Daily Express,* March 13, 1884.
34 *Austin Daily Dispatch,* March 12, 1884.

35 *Statesman*, March 16, 20, 1884.
36 *Statesman*, March 13, 1884. *San Antonio Light*, March 12, 1884. *San Antonio Daily Express*, March 13, 1884.
37 *San Antonio Light*, March 12, 1884, *San Antonio Daily Express*, March 13, 1884, *Galveston Daily News*, March 13, 1884, *Houston Post*, March 13, 1884, Jacobo S. Coy's Coroner's Hearing Testimony.
38 *Galveston Daily News*, March 13, 1884. *San Antonio Daily Express*, March 13, 1884. The *Austin Daily Capital*, March 13, 1884 reported, "Foster received two shots, one below the knee, shattering the bone of the leg, and the other a flesh wound in the thigh."
39 *Austin Daily Dispatch*, March 12, 1884. *San Antonio Daily Express*, March 13, 1884. *Houston Post*, March 13, 1884.
40 *San Antonio Daily Express*, March 13, 1884.
41 *San Antonio Light*, March 12, 1884, *San Antonio Daily Express*, March 13, 1884, *Galveston Daily News*, March 13, 1884, *Houston Post*, March 13, 1884, Billy Simms Coroner's Hearing Testimony. Lunsford, John R. "How Ben Thompson Died With His Boots On," *Frontier Times*, Vol. 9, No. 2 (November 1931.) and *San Antonio Express*, September 6, 1931.Mr. Lunsford was a reporter for the *San Antonio Light* on March 11, 1884. Almost fifty years later Lunsford wrote how Simms suggested that the party take a trip "across the creek" which was slang to visit one of the many houses of ill repute east of San Pedro Creek in the hope that he could lure Thompson away from his place, and thus avoid almost certain bloodshed. Thompson demurred and insisted on going up into the balcony. San Pedro Creek flows southward almost at the western boundary of Military Plaza. In the early 1880s it was also the boundary of where the many brothels openly operated in San Antonio. The *Austin Daily Capital* of March 13, 1884 quoted an unidentified witness, "Simms, he is quite sure, fired several shots in quick succession, and, as he was facing King Fisher, the direction from which he was shot, there was no doubt that he aimed the fatal shots that piled Fisher on his dead friend's bosom."
42 *Houston Post*, March 13, 1884.
43 *San Antonio Daily Express*, March 13, 1884. *San Antonio Light*, March 12, 1884.
44 *San Antonio Daily Express*, March 13, 1884.
45 *Statesman*, March 13, 1884. *Austin Daily Capital*, March 13, 1884. *San Antonio Daily Express*, March 13, 1884. *Galveston Daily News*, March 13, 1884. *Dallas Daily Herald*, March 13, 1884.*Chicago Tribune* March 13, 1884. *New York Times*, March 13, 1884. *New York Herald*, March 13, 1884.
46 The inquest verdict was signed by George Hilgers, H. L. Ansell, J. A. Bennett, E. J. Gaston, J. M. Martin, and B.W. Wallace, who comprised the coroner's jury.
47 *Austin Daily Dispatch*, March 13, 1884.
48 *Statesman*, March 13, 1884.
49 *Austin Daily Capital*, March 13, 15, 1884.
50 *Dallas Daily Herald*, March 13, 1884. *Brenham Daily Banner*, March 16, 1884.
51 *Austin Daily Dispatch*, March 13, 1884. Bob Boze Bell, based on the research by Tom Bicknell, "Classic Gunfights: Ben Thompson & King Fisher vs Joe Foster & Billy Simms," 54-57, *True West*, Vol. 53, Issue 2, March 2006. "Tom Bicknell believes, 'once Thompson insisted on speaking to Fisher, he sealed his doom.' Bicknell also concludes, "Maybe if Ben hadn't pushed for a meeting with Foster, he may have gotten out of the Vaudeville alive. The shooters must have been ready to react to a given signal, and I believe this would have been when Simms

and Coy moved quickly out of the way. Joe Foster was careful to be out of the line of fire. I doubt any argument had time to develop."

52 *San Antonio Daily Express, March 14, 1884.* Born in Missouri, the 1870 Census listed Thomas G. Martin's occupation as a member of the State Police and is believed to have served with the famous Ranger Captain Leander H. McNelly.

53 *Austin Daily Dispatch*, March 12, 1884, *San Antonio Daily Express*, March 13, 14, 1884. *Houston Post*, March 13, 1884. *Chicago Tribune*, March 13, 1884.

54 *Houston Post*, March 13, 1884.

55 *San Antonio Light*, March 15, 1884.

56 Dr. Thomas Dudley Wooten was also the father of Austin City Attorney Dudley Goodall Wooten. Dr. Charles N. Worthington, for the twenty-five years prior, was well known throughout Texas for his heavily advertised and popular "Cholera & Diarrhoea [*sic*] Medicine. The Great Cholera Cramp and Diarrhoea Cure." Advertisements also claimed it to be "Unfailing as a cure for Cramps, Indigestion and Dyspepsia." Austin gunsmith, firearm dealer and shop owner Joseph Carl Petmecky was an iconic Austin businessman for decades. His most famous customers were Sam Houston and legendary Texas rangers Ben McCulloch, Big Foot Wallace, and Lawrence "Sul" Sullivan Ross.

57 *Statesman*, March 14, 1884. *Austin Daily Dispatch*, March 14, 1884. *Austin Daily Capital*, March 14, 1884. *San Antonio Daily Express*, March 14, 1884. More than one hundred years later, author and historian Charley Eckhardt in his column for the Seguin, Texas, *Gazette-Enterprise* on November 13, 1991 wrote, "In the body of Ben Thompson, Dr. Wooten found … the distinctive flat-based, flat-nosed 200 grain slugs from the Winchester or .44-40 cartridge, which, in Texas, meant they came out of rifles or carbines, not six-shooters."

58 *Austin Daily Dispatch*, March 14, 1884. O. C. Fisher with J. C. Dykes, *King Fisher, His Life and Times*, 139.

59 *Austin Daily Dispatch*, March 13, 1884.

60 *San Antonio Daily Express*, March 14, 1884. *Brenham Daily Banner*, March 15, 1884.

61 Ben Thompson was interred in Oakwood Ceremony, Section 1, lot 71, space unknown [possibly No. 2]. Oakwood Cemetery information courtesy of Kay Ann Yaklin, InterCare Corporation Superintendent of Operations, San Marcos, Texas. Records of Oakwood Cemetery, City of Austin, p. 121, Date: March 13, 1884, Ben Thompson, age forty-two, "remains brought here from St [*sic*] Antonio [, cause of death] shot [, buried in] Lot 71 [, by] friends." Austin History Center. His pallbearers were police officer John Chenneville; A. J. Thorpe—police officer and future Austin Chief of Police and husband of Jane Baker, first cousin to the Thompson brothers; Milas M. Miller—brother of Thompson's close friend Monroe Miller; F. M. Kain, James L. White, Charles Bullian, W. R. Brown and C. Cooper. Also buried in Lot 71 is Ben's sister-in-law, Mollie [Moore] Conner, wife of Harry D. Conner, married March 19, 1873, interred April 28, 1886, age twenty-nine, "Disease = Hemorehage [*sic*] of bowel." *Austin Daily Dispatch*, March 13, 1884. *Statesman*, March 14, 1884. *Austin Daily Capital*, March 14, 1884. *San Antonio Daily Express*, March 14, 1884. *Brenham Daily Banner*, March 15, 1884.

62 *San Antonio Express*, March 22, 1884. *Statesman*, March 21, 28, 29, 1884.

63 *San Antonio Express*, March 14, 1884.

64 *Austin Daily Capital*, March 15, 1884.

65 *Statesman*, March 16, 1884.

66 Ibid., March 16, 20, 1884. *Austin Daily Capital*, March 15, 1884.

67 *San Antonio Express*, March 19, 1884.
68 *San Antonio Express*, March 19, 1884. *Statesman*, March 20, 1884
69 *Statesman*, March 21, 1884. *San Antonio Daily Express*, March 23, 1884.
70 *San Antonio Light*, March 22, 1884. *San Antonio Express*, March 23, 1884.
71 *San Antonio Light*, March 22, 1884. *San Antonio Express*, March 23, 1884. *Statesman*, March 23, 1884. *San Antonio Express – News*, July 9, 1982.
72 *San Antonio Express*, March 23, 1884. *San Antonio Light*, March 24, 1884. *Statesman*, March 23, 25, 1884.
73 *San Antonio Daily Express*, March 19, 1884.
74 *Bastrop Advertiser*, March 27, 1884.
75 *Statesman*, March 26, 1884.
76 Walton, *Thompson*, 228.
77 Ibid., 229. *San Antonio Express*, March 16, 18, 1884, "The grand jury has refused to indict Messrs. Simms, Foster and Coy for the killing of Ben Thompson and King Fisher. When the grand jury adjourns an effort will be made to get some of the friends Ben Thompson to make an affidavit before a justice of the peace in order that a full rehearing may be had once and for all. All the parties implicated are anxious for such a course." No evidence exists to indicate that such a course was taken. *San Antonio Express*, March 23, 1884, "Major Buck Walton, it is said, has been paid $7500 to push the prosecution of Simms and Coy, and he will do so, it is said." The rumor reported by the *Express* was obviously wrong as to the retainer paid, if indeed, any amount was given to Walton. *Brenham Daily Banner*, March 13, 1884. *Dallas Herald*, April 3, 1884. *Austin Statesman* reported on March 15, 1884: "It is said by parties from San Antonio, that letters have been received from King Fisher's friends to the fact that unless the law is permitted to deal out, justice to King Fisher's murderers, they will be taken care of. Parties in Austin who know Fisher's followers are certain, the murder of him and Thompson is but the beginning of serious tragedies sure to follow."
78 Walton, *Thompson*, Preface. *San Antonio Express*, March 14, 1884. *Statesman*, April 1, May 2, 1884. *Luling Newsboy & Signal*, June 5, 1884.
79 *Statesman*, March 20, 1884.
80 *Statesman*, March 14, 1884. *National Police Gazette*, March 29, 1884, published in New York, N. Y. by Richard K. Fox, editor and proprietor.

Chapter 17

1 Sarah Sallie Elizabeth (Vivian) Fisher is buried in Mount Hope Cemetery, Carrizo Springs, Texas. *San Antonio Express*, March 15, 20, 1884. *Austin Statesman*, March 20, 1884. O. C. Fisher, "King Fisher—Texas Gunman, Lawman," *Corral Dust*, (Potomac Corral of the Westerners, Vol. IV, No. 1, Washington, D. C., March, 1959), 1-5.
2 O. C. Fisher with J. C. Dykes, *King Fisher, His Life and Times* (Norman: University of Oklahoma Press, 1966), 115.
3 *Uvalde Leader-News*, October 11, 1959, "New Grave for King Fisher Recreates Interest In Former Deputy Sheriff." Author: Florence Fenley. In 1966, the Uvalde Pioneer Cemetery was renamed Frontier Cemetery.
4 The policemen's full names were Thomas C. Rife and Andrew Brown
5 In different editions of the *Express* Cecelio Charo was called Cecilia Ochoa and his last name also appeared as Charos. Tijerina's name was also alternately spelled as Tijerino and Tejerina. Lawman Charo was serving as a deputy under LaSalle

County Sheriff Charles Brown McKinney. Information about the two suspects and their story was graciously supplied by John King Fisher researcher and author Larry G. Shaver of Fincastle, Virginia from his manuscript, "This is King Fisher's Road."

6 Shaver manuscript, "This is King Fisher's Road." *San Antonio Express*, March 14, 15, 1884.

7 Ibid., *San Antonio Express*, March 15, 16, 17, 1884.

8 Streeter, *Thompson*, 202. Tom Bicknell, "Billy Simms, A Lover of Fair Play, "22-3, *Quarterly* of the National Association for Outlaw and Lawman History, Inc. 28, no. 3 (July-Sept. 2004). Born in Coahuila de Zaragoza, Mexico on January 2, 1841, Coy was related to a prominent Spanish military family dating back to the early settlement of San Antonio. His full name was Jose Jacobo de los Santos Coy. He married Maria Preciliana Garza on February 9, 1869, and fathered twelve children with Garza. Preciliana died July 27, 1895. In 1905, shortly before his death, Jacobo Coy married Virginia Gomez.

9 *Statesman*, April 25, 1884. *San Antonio Express*, April 25, 26, 1884.

10 J. Marvin Hunter, "Knew Ben Thompson," *Frontier Times*, Vol. 16, No. 10, July 1939, 420.

11 Captain J. B. Gillet, "Ben Thompson and Billy Sims," *Frontier Times*, Vol. 12, No. 1, October 1934, 1-3.

12 O. C. Fisher with J. C. Dykes, *King Fisher, His Life and Times* (Norman: University of Oklahoma Press, 1966), 141.

13 *San Antonio Express*, July 23, 1884. *San Antonio Light*, July 24, 1884.

14 *San Antonio Express*, March 3, 5, 6, 1886 and November 15, 1914. *San Antonio Light*, March 4, 1884. *Legendary Watering Holes, The Saloons That Made Texas Famous*, Compiled and Edited by Richard Selcer. David Bowser, Chapter Two, 113, "Jack Harris's Vaudeville and San Antonio's 'Fatal Corner,'" (Texas A&M University Press, College Station, 2004.) Charles Ramsdell, "Song and Dance—and Gunfire," *San Antonio Express Magazine*, January 4, 1948, 4-5. *San Antonio Express*, March 6, 1886. Alice Evertt, 28 – 32, "Fatal Corner," San Antonio Monthly, July 1982. Clarence J. La Roche, "Booze, Bullets and Bad Bad Ben, Powder Smell Clings to Harris Corner," *San Antonio Express-News*, Saturday, January 1, 1966. David Bowser, *West of the Creek, Murder, Mayhem and Vice in Old San Antonio* (Maverick Publishing Company, 2003), 17 – 22. Elton R. Cude, *The Wild and Free Dukedom of Bexar* (San Antonio: Munguia Printers, 1978), 45-46. Frank W. Jennings, *San Antonio, The Story of an Enchanted City*, 143-45 (San Antonio Express-News, 1998). *San Antonio Express*, March 6, 1886. *San Antonio Light*, February 8, 1884.

The San Fernando Cathedral on the west side dominates San Antonio's Main Plaza and the twin towers of this holy place have looked down for centuries on many other less than holy structures. Where the Vaudeville Theatre stood, citizens of San Antonio during most of the second half of the nineteenth century commonly called it "Jack Harris' Corner." Over many decades this infamous intersection, with the single exception of the Alamo Mission, was considered the bloodiest place in San Antonio due to the many shootouts, stabbings, and suicides that occurred there more often than anywhere else in the otherwise nicknamed Enchanted City. The *Express* declared, "Every square inch of the ground and every stone in the walls, almost is bathed in human blood, and could they rise up and tell the tale, the bloody details would far outrival the bloodiest dreams of a Ben Thompson." Without a doubt, the culmination of Ben Thompson's quarrel with the Vaudeville gang spilled more blood than any other single event. In modern times, the name evolved from "Jack Harris' Corner" to what twentieth century writers refer to as, "The Fatal Corner." It is known that since 1847 a barroom stood at the corner of Soledad and Commerce and the American gamblers loved to congregate, drink whiskey, chew and smoke tobacco, and play cards, usually Spanish Monte, even though poker had its place. It was a favorite rendezvous for hardcases. One of the first and cruelest scenes to occur here was enacted by the ever-bloodthirsty John Joel Glanton, the infamous scalp-hunter. Called a "desperado of desperadoes," it was said everyone who knew him was afraid of him. One afternoon in 1848, a drink was accidently spilled on Glanton's freshly polished boots. The poor culprit was a Mexican porter and apparently his apology wasn't good enough. Senselessly enraged, Glanton pulled his Bowie knife from his boot, grabbed the porter, and began cutting and slashing him, though he did not deliver a fatal blow. As the screaming victim ran frantically down Commerce Street struggling to get away, Glanton continued to slash the poor man until he was completely covered in blood from the thirty or more deep cuts on his back, chest, arms, shoulders, head, and face. Glanton finally ended the attack. While horribly scarred, the victim did eventually recover. As for John Joel Glanton, no one, not even the county sheriff or city marshal attempted to restrain or arrest him. Glanton soon went into New Mexico Territory and scalped anyone who came his way with hair dark enough to collect the bounty authorities were paying for hostile Apache scalps. Glanton carried on for several years until he was killed by a war party of revenge seeking Yuma Indians. Of course, he suffered the same fate of his hundreds of victims. He, too, was scalped.

By the 1850s, the corner building had been expanded and it also housed the pharmacy of Devine, Attwater, and McDonald. John McDonald was a noted lawyer and prominent politician. During an election campaign for city offices, a good deal of excitement and hard feelings were erupting. McDonald had a political difference of opinion with one of his business partners in the pharmacy, Dr. J. M. Devine. Angry words turned into gunfire and his former friend, Dr. Devine gunned down John McDonald. Enraged friends would have lynched Devine, had it not been for the timely intervention of the county sheriff and his deputies. In a subsequent trial, Dr. Devine was acquitted of the charge of murder and set free.

The next shooting affray was also due to an election. William "Big" Henry was well known in San Antonio since he once unsuccessfully served as the Bexar County Sheriff. After he was tossed out of office, Henry still often enjoyed the accommodations of the county jail. He was placed under arrest time and time again; the cause was usually illegal gambling, however drinking and brawling also got him into trouble. In late March of 1862, while out on bail for yet another offense, he entered his name for consideration as captain of a newly forming Confederate company. In the ensuing election, he lost by a significant margin to a more solid, responsible, and popular citizen by the name of William Adams (one source gives his first name as Warren). Angry, Henry resolved to kill Adams on sight and he told anyone who would listen of his intentions. During the afternoon of April 8, 1862, he saw Adams walking across the wide dirt plaza towards the northwest corner. Stepping out of the Plaza House, Henry called out for Captain Adams to stop. Walking up to Adams, "Big" Henry loudly proclaimed, "I can whip you on any ground, on this Plaza or anywhere else. I am a fighting man and as brave as Julius Caesar." Adams calmly admitted, "I believe you could, I am not a fighting man and I do not want a fuss" and began to turn and walk away. Placing his hand on his revolver, Henry screamed after Adams, "You are a god-damned coward and I am going to put two balls through your brain anyhow!" Adams had taken about six paces before slowly turning around and inquiring, "What did you say?" Henry repeated his insulting threat. Placing his hand on his pistol, Adams told "Big" Henry, "I will fight you now, pull away and go to shooting." Big Henry, quick with the mouth was also quick on the trigger; he fired the first shot but missed. Adams coolly took aim and shot twice striking his opponent first in the head and then the chest. Before his body hit the ground, Big Henry was dead. Captain Adams immediately turned himself in to the sheriff and was quickly exonerated by the statements of witnesses and released. Court records listed one final entry about Henry, "the defendant William R. Henry, unable to appear before the court forfeits his bond, having been killed in a recent affray."

On virtually the same spot where Adams ended Big Henry's life, two officers in the Confederate Army named Hunter and Phillips exchanged shots at each other for a long-forgotten reason. Phillips lost the fight and fell dead in the plaza dirt.

Lesser incidents included Major Neighbors shooting and wounding "Big" Jim Young in his side. While standing on the corner, Pete Brady snapped off a shot across the street at Buck Bennett but missed him, killing an innocent bystander instead.

On December 31, 1874, the corner building was advertised as Jack Harris's Saloon and Vaudeville Theater for the first time. It was billed as a place of fun and laughter. Singers, comic sketches, and comedians dominated the stage but sadness and despair also had their place in this old building. It was not uncommon for people to commit suicide in this building, for instance. There were also suicides among the variety women who earned their living at the Vaudeville. They may have been seeking a haven from a life that imposed notions of sin and shame onto their very being. On April 1, 1880, Miss Alice Hughes, was found dead at the Vaudeville. Among her other duties, she was mostly employed as a waitress and chair warmer who convinced lonely patrons to purchase expensive drinks. Perhaps she had grown so weary of life the embrace of poison felt warmer. One young man from South Carolina by the name of Warren Davis after a night of drinking with a number of variety women shot himself in the theatre box to the left of the main stage on Thursday night, February 7, 1884. Miss Lena Hazel, a "bibulous charmer," was the last to entertain Davis and he was dead for fifteen minutes or more before his body was discovered. The blaring music and the laughter of the audience covered the sound of the fatal gunshot. Though of course the most sensational deaths, and the culmination of tragedies at the "Fatal Corner," were the murders of Thompson and Fisher.

15 Tom Bicknell, "Billy Simms, A Lover of Fair Play," 22 -23, *Quarterly* of the National Association for Outlaw and Lawman History, Inc. 28, no. 3 (July-Sept. 2004). *San Antonio Daily Express,* August 6, 1885. *San Antonio Express,* April 21, 1886, *San Antonio Express,* June 17, 1886. *San Antonio Express,* July 3, 4, 14, 1886. *San Antonio Express,* July 14, 1886. *San Antonio Light,* January 11, 1909, "Funeral Draws Great Throng." *San Antonio Express,* January 12, 1909, "Scraps of History, Billy Simms Life." *General Directory of the City of San Antonio for 1892-1893,* p. 697.

16 *San Antonio Light,* January 11, 1909, "Funeral Draws Great Throng." *San Antonio Express,* January 12, 1909, "Scraps of History, Billy Simms Life."

17 Ibid., The Improved Order of Redmen Cemetery was later absorbed into the city cemetery system of San Antonio, per correspondence from Hope Brown, Records

Custodian. From records page 250: The Simms family plot is located in City Cemetery #4, Lot: South 1/2 of 6, Section One, Grave 1- William, Grave 2- his wife Lydia, Grave 4- their only child William Jr. Lydia Simms would remarry a man named Carl David Pollock. Mr. Pollock died November 30, 1931, Lydia followed him in death at the age of seventy-eight on October 29, 1950. She is buried next to both of her husbands and adjacent to her son.

18 Information provided by Gary W. Yantis.

19 The Walton Family Plot is on the far southwestern end of Oakwood Cemetery. Besides the obelisk, another substantial marker for William and his wife Letitia Ann is above them in spaces 13 and 14.

20 Record of Arrests Book on file at the Austin History Center: May 29, 1883, No. 13037, Buck Walton, Disturbing the Peace, 6 p.m., white, male, lawyer, U.S., Complainant [Policeman] A. J. Thorp, fine $5, paid cash and October 23, 1883, No. 14026, Intoxicated & No. 14027, Disturbing the Peace, Wm. M. Walton, 4 p.m., white, male, lawyer, U. S., Complainant, [Policeman] E. R. Oberwetter, Total fine for both offenses $10, paid cash.

21 William M. Walton Biography File. Quotation taken from newspaper clipping dated April 24, 1892. Austin History Center. William M. Walton, *Major Buck Walton, An Epitome of My Life, Civil War Reminiscences* (Austin: Waterloo Press, a Division of the Austin History Center, 1965), 18.

22 *Statesman*, April 25, May 2, 1884. *Corpus Christi Caller*, May 4, 1884.

23 *Galveston Daily News*, May 15, 1884.

24 Allen and Patricia Ahearn, *Collected Books: The Guide to Identification and Values, Fourth Edition.* (Quill & Brush Press, Comus, 2011). World Cat, the world's largest library catalog, states 112 copies of Walton's biography (all editions) can be found in libraries and archives around the world. Most are in North America however two copies, surprisingly, are available in Malaysian library collections. One is at the National Library in Kuala Lumpur and the second at Jabatan Pendidikan Tinggi, Putrajaya, Malaysia. Five editions of Walton's work including facsimiles are as follows: Edwards & Church, Austin, 1884: Frontier Times, Bandera, Texas, 1926; Frontier Press of Texas, Houston, 1954; The Steck Co., Austin, 1956; annotated edition self-published by Lisa Lach, 2016.

25 Seventy-three years would pass before a second biography of Ben Thompson appeared. Floyd Benjamin Streeter (1888-1956), historian, author, editor and librarian at Hays City Kansas State College (The school at Hayes City is now named Fort Hayes State University) took an interest in the Kansas history of the Old West. Streeter researched the death of Ellsworth County Sheriff C. B. Whitney during the early 1930s. His article on the subject first appeared in the quarterly magazine *The Aerend*, in the spring edition of 1934. Two years later, he published his in-depth study entitled, *Prairie Trails & Cow Towns: The Opening of the Old West.* Over the next twenty years he continued his research and writing on the history of early Kansas until his death at the age of sixty-eight in 1956. The following year, his notes and articles were compiled by others and formulated into a manuscript and published under the title, *The Complete and Authentic Life of Ben Thompson: Man with a Gun.* Mr. Streeter's excellent research of primary sources was the first professional look into Ben's life and it presented a biography full of new facts while explaining away many legends and falsehoods. Sadly, *Man with a Gun* appears slapped together and poorly edited. To its credit, and similar to Walton's first effort, it did not place Ben Thompson's life and actions, as adventurous as they were, within a false greater noble meaning.

26 William M. "Buck" Walton, "Major Buck Walton Interestingly Weaves Many Dramatic Incidents of Half A Century Of His Career, With Stirring History Of Olden Austin," From the Austin Public Library Walton File, undocumented newspaper article, copy donated by Miss Dot Thornton, June, 17, 1958.

At the age of twenty, celebrated short story author William Sydney Porter (O. Henry) arrived in central Texas. He took many different jobs until finally becoming a popular columnist for the *Houston Post.* In 1882, Porter lived in Austin and he did take note of then City Marshal Ben Thompson as well as other infamous Texas desperadoes using their quirks, personalities, behavioral traits and history in a number of his stories. In *The Reformation of Calliope,* the main character is a drunken reveler known for benders that include a little pistol play. In the twist ending O. Henry was famous for; Calliope Catesby snatches the badge off the town marshal he had knocked out and pins it on himself while pretending to be the lawman in front of his visiting mother. In a show of sympathy, the true town marshal goes along with the hoax during the duration of Calliope's mother's stay. John King Fisher influences Porter in the portrayal of two characters: King James in *The Last of the Troubadours* & Bud King in *The Passing of Black Eagle,* the Cisco Kid is based on John Wesley Hardin in *The Caballero's Way.* Gallegly, J. S., "Background and Patterns of O. Henry's Texas Badman Stories." *Rice Institute Pamphlet*—Rice University Studies, 42, no. 3 (1955), 1 – 31.

27 Natalie Bicknell and Thomas Bicknell, 16, 65, "The Cody - to - Thompson Stevens – Lord No. 36 Target Pistol Was A Handsome Present," *Wild West,* Monthly Feature: Guns of the West, February 2002.

28 Other "gunfighters" Masterson presented were Wyatt Earp, Luke Short, Billy Tilghman, Doc Holliday, and Buffalo Bill Cody.

29 W. B. (Bat) Masterson. "Ben Thompson," *Human Life,* Vol. 4, No. 4 (January 1907). W. B. (Bat) Masterson. *The 75th Anniversary Edition of Famous Gunfighters of the Western Frontier,* Annotated and Illustrated by Jack DeMattos (Monroe, WA: Weatherford Press, 1982), 11-25.

30 Travis County Probate Records, File Number 972, Notice of Application, Dated: March 17, 1885. Microfilm Reel # 975856 (Austin History Center) Vol. K, Estate of Ben Thompson, 113, 114, 234, 235, 236, 237, 238, For years 1885-1886: Probate Minutes, Vol. L, 107, 127, 133, 151, 249, 250, 368, 369, 381, 382, 392-400, 441-444, 507-511, 518-522, 523-529. Hereafter cited as Probate Records.

31 Probate Records, 368, 369. *Austin Statesman,* February 25, 1885. It is not known what became of his custom-made Knights of Pythias watch fob.

32 Probate Records, 237, Partners Robert Holman, Benjamin F. Marshall and Ben Thompson—Clubroom over 611 Congress, [The clubroom would be the gambling hall above the Iron Front Saloon which the Austin *Statesman* called, "the chief place of entertainment in the city."] furniture in business rooms—total value $672, Thompson's 1/3 share $224. R. L. Wilson, *The Peacemakers: Arms and Adventure in the American West* (New York: Random House, 1992), 159. The Thompson—Hamer shotgun is part of the Western Memorabilia Collection of James and Theresa Earle of College Station, Texas.

33 *Austin Statesman,* July 7, 1887. Austin City Directory, 1889 – 1890, 221: "Thompson Kate (*wid* [*sic*] Benjamin), r. 1606 Congress ave"

34 Marilyn Miller, "Old Safe Is Reminder of Gambling Marshal," unknown newspaper dated August 9, 1960. Ben Thompson Biography File, The Center for American History, the University of Texas, Austin.

35 Jane Summer (compiler). *Some Early Travis County, Texas Records* (Easley, S. C., Southern Historical Press, 1979). pp. 35, 53, Austin Genealogical Society Summer. Catherine L. "Kate" (Moore – Thompson) Baker's younger sister's full name: Sarah Isabella "Sallie" (Moore – Farrell) Arlitt. She married Fred R. Arlitt on May 25, 1889. Sarah's statement was made on August 16, 1894 and Mary Jane (Thompson) Gill's on November 15, 1920. The General Directory of the City of Paris 1891-92, p. 54, (Published by Morrison & Fourmy), lists eleven men named Baker residing in the town, two of which are identified as "colored." The directory is on file at the Texas State Archives, Austin.

36 Austin Records of Arrest book, entries for James Moore: February 16, 1880, 8842, Printer, Intoxication; May 19, 1883, 12988, Sport, Assault; August 25, 1883, 13444, Sport, Disturbing the Peace. *Austin Statesman,* August 7, 1884, "Jim Moore, gaming, two cases; fined $10 and costs in one case and the other dismissed."

37 Unidentified newspaper article, June 10, 1905. Federal Census 1850, Travis County, P. 146 A. Enumerated September 12, 1850. Dwelling/family #191. Martin Moore 36, M, Merchant, $8,000, Ireland, Elizabeth Moore, 28, F, Alabama, Catherine Moore, 06, F, Texas, James Moore, 02, M, Texas. Letter dated October 12, 1997, Kay Ann Yaklin, Superintendent of Operations Oakwood Cemetery, InterCare Corporation, Austin Texas: "Jim Moore, 06/10/1905 burial date, fifty-seven years old, Disease—Acute Enteritis [inflammation of small intestine], Physician H. K. Sterzing, ... No record of [exactly] where in Oakwood he was buried."

38 Thompson family oral history. *Palestine Herald Press,* March 4, 1954.

39 Compiled by the *Bastrop Advertiser* and the Bastrop Historical Society, *In the Shadow of the Lost Pines: A History of Bastrop County and Its People* (Published 1955), 44, "County Officials who have served Bastrop County: County Judge J. B. Price, 1894-1904 and 1909-1924." Bastrop County Marriage License dated January 31, 1895, W. M. Sears. M. G. performed the ceremony. Copies of *Record of Deaths,* Texas State Department of Health Bureau of Vital Statistics Standard Certificate of Death, Book IV, page 341, Deceased: J. B. Price, Date of Death, February 27, 1934 and Book IV, 364, Deceased: Mrs. Katie F. Price, age sixty-five years, nine months, eleven days. Informant: Ralph Price [son]. Date of Death: September 19, 1938. Burial: Cremated at San Antonio, Texas.

40 Thompson Family oral history. February 12, 1997, letter from Anne Beck.

41 Jacob Bickler (1849 – 1902) was a well-respected educator in Austin. In 1876, he founded his German and English Academy and during his long career as an educator he would become the president of the Texas State Teacher's Association. Ben Thompson Jr. is listed among the student body in the school's enrollment records. The entry for "Bennie Thompson" states he enrolled at the age of eleven and attended the academy from 1880-1883. Mr. Bickler's descendants have preserved ten volumes of school records and these were first published in the Austin Genealogical Society Quarterly, Vol. 16, No. 1, 1975. Benjamin Jr.'s entry appears on page 29. www.austintxgensoc.org/records/texas-german-and-english-academy-1976-1902/

42 *San Antonio Express,* February 14, 1888.

43 *San Antonio Express,* March 21, 29, 1888

44 *Bastrop Advertiser,* August 24, November 9, 1889.

45 It is not known exactly when Billy Thompson was in Tombstone, Arizona Territory. Wells Fargo operative Fred Dodge, by his own account, arrived there on December 7, 1879, and stayed off and on in the Tombstone area until 1888. Fred Dodge, edited by Carolyn Lake, *Under Cover for Wells Fargo, The Unvarnished*

Recollections of Fred Dodge (Houghton Mifflin Company, Boston, 1969), 8, 9, 148-49.

46 Jan Devereaux, "Jagville," *Quarterly* of the National Association for Outlaw and Lawman History, Inc. 27, no. 1 (Jan. - March 2004): 3-19.

47 *Eddy County Citizen*, November 19, 1892. *Eddy Current*, March 31, 1893.

48 *Austin Statesman*, September 10, 1893, *San Antonio Express*, 10, 1893. His aunt, Mrs. Fred R. Orlitt, was Sarah "Sallie" (Moore – Farrell) younger sister to Ben Thompson's wife Catherine. Sarah remarried after the death of her first husband, Austin police officer and bartender J. K. Farrell, on May 25, 1889, to Fred R. Orlitt. The 1875 Austin city census listed Ben Thompson, his wife and children and the Farrell's all residing at the house on San Jacinto and 19th Street.

49 Dale T. Schoenberger, "Whatever Happened to Texas Billy Thompson," 6, *Real West*, March 1982. Joseph G. Rosa, *The Taming of the West: Age of the Gunfighter, Men & Weapons on the Frontier 1840-1900* (Smithmark Publishers, N. Y., N. Y., 1993), 147.

50 *Statesman*, July 25, 1884, "Mr. Bill Thompson has returned from a trip to Houston."

51 Billy Thompson's death was first published by researcher and author Gary P. Fitterer in his article, "The Life and Death of Billy Thompson (1845-1897), Part Two, *Quarterly*, National Association for Outlaw and Lawman History, Inc. 25, no. 2 (April-May 2000): 18-20. *Houston Post*, September 7, 1897. *Bastrop Advertiser*, September 11, 1897. Fairview Cemetery records courtesy of Joyce Schaefer, Bastrop, TX. Morrison & Fourmy's General Directory of the City of Houston, 1895-96, 12 and 298.

52 Beck. Laurence E. Gesell, *Saddle the Wild Wind: The Saga of Squirrel Tooth Alice and Texas Billy Thompson* (Coast Aire Publications, L. L. C., Chandler, AZ., 2002). In his book Arizona State University Professor Gesell claims his great-grandparents are Billy Thompson and Dodge City prostitute "Squirrel Tooth Alice," who Gesell writes is Mary Elizabeth "Libby" Haley. The Thompson descendants of Central Texas refute his claim and Professor Gesell does not present any genealogical documentation to boost his argument.

53 Ibid., *San Antonio Daily Express*, September 8, 10, 1897. *Houston Post*, September 8, 1897. Thomas C. Bicknell, "Whatever Became of Texas Billy Thompson," *Kansas Cowboy*, Part One, 1,4,6, Vol. 5, No. 2, January 2001 and Part Two, 6, 15, Vol 5, No. 3, March 2001. www.knottingley.org/history

54 Joseph G. Rosa, *The Taming of the West: Age of the Gunfighter, Men & Weapons on the Frontier 1840-1900*. (Smithmark Publishers, N. Y., N. Y., 1993), 178.

55 *Statesman*, March 13, 1884.

56 Frank H. Bushick, *Glamorous Days in Old San Antonio (A Never-to-be Forgotten City)* (The Naylor Company, San Antonio, Texas, 1934), 182-86. Paul Adams, 321-29, "The Unsolved Murder of Ben Thompson—Pistoleer Extraordinary," *Southwestern Historical Quarterly* 48, no. 3 (Jan. 1945). Walton, *Thompson*, 200-02.

57 *San Antonio Express*, September 6, 1931, "How Ben Thompson Died—With His Boots On ... John R. Lunsford, Reporter at Time Tells Story of Famous Tragedy." John R. Lunsford, 84, "How Ben Thompson Died with His Boots On," *Frontier Times*, Volume 9, Number 2, November 1931. Johnny Lunsford passed away on February 4, 1934, at the age of seventy-six.

58 Charles Merritt Barnes, *Combats and Conquests of Immortal Heroes* (Guessaz & Ferlet Company, San Antonio, Texas, 1910), 120. *Austin Statesman*, March

14, 1884. "Autopsy. The Post Mortem Examination of Thompson And What It Disclosed. Some Interesting Tales Told by the Silent Wounds and Leaden Messengers."

59 His father, Frank, was called as a witness in the Billy Thompson/Remus Smith murder trial. *San Antonio Light,* December 4, 1952; "Frank Bushick Dies." *San Antonio Evening News,* December 4, 1952; "Death Claims Frank Bushick."

60 Frank H. Bushick, *Glamorous Days in Old San Antonio (A Never-to-be Forgotten City),* (The Naylor Company, San Antonio, Texas, 1934), 182-86.

61 A search through stage manager Frank Sparrow's booking records for the Vaudeville Theatre failed to find any entry for a Harry Tremaine. An examination of the Vaudeville's Theatre troupe during February through March 1884 did not reveal a performer listed as Harry Tremaine. Charles Bennett Myler, 166, "A History of the English Speaking Theatre in San Antonio before 1900," PhD dissertation, University of Texas, 1968.

62 William B. Secrest, 20, "A Gamblin' Man," *Real West,* March 1979.

63 *Laredo Times,* August 23, 1883, originally published in the *Galveston Daily News.*

64 *State of Texas v. Ben Thompson,* murder: Testimony of John L. McLaughlin, August 7, 1882, pp. 6-10. The Center for American History, the University of Texas at Austin. McLaughlin, John, hack driver, *San Antonio City Directory 1885-86,* p. 223, Texas State Archives, Austin.

65 Walton, *Thompson,* 229. *San Antonio Express,* March 6, 1886, Alice Evertt, 28 – 32, "Fatal Corner," San Antonio Monthly, July 1982. *San Antonio Evening News,* December 4, 1952. *San Antonio Light,* December 4, 1952.

66 O. C. Fisher with J. C. Dykes, *King Fisher, His Life and Times* (Norman: University of Oklahoma Press, 1966), 141. George Durham, (As told to Clyde Wantland), "On the Trail of 5,100 Outlaws—Beyond the Nueces," *Valley Morning Star,* Harlingen, Texas, November 8, 1969. George Durham, *Taming the Nueces Strip* (Austin: University of Texas Press, 1962).

67 "Ceremonies at the Restoration of the Austin City Marshal Ben Thompson Headstone ... in Oakwood Cemetery Austin, Texas ... June 17th, 1980 at 4:00 o'clock in the afternoon ... Taped, Photographed, Transcribed and Compiled by Mulkey Owens, Member, Travis County Historical Commission." Program: "The Reparation of the Thompson Stone, Oakwood Cemetery, Austin, June 17, 1980." Austin History Center. *Austin Citizen,* June 18, 1980. [University of Texas] *Daily Texan,* June 18, 1980.

68 Author Evan S. Connell in *Son of the Morning Star,* his beautifully written, all-encompassing history of Custer and the Battle of the Little Bighorn, noted, "Some think such an advocate might be as necessary as the hero." This statement is true. All of the most famous icons of America's Old West, contemporaries of Ben Thompson, have become so because of the tireless efforts of an advocate or advocates who created a popular image and always a higher moral far exceeding the boundaries of reality. These advocates undeniably understood the old adage: Give a dog a good name and he will be everyone's friend.

Civil War bushwhacker Jesse James, a publicity craving bandit, was turned from being a ruthless killer not above shooting down unarmed employees of the banks and trains he robbed, into a popular hero who was continuing the fight for the Southern cause against Northern tyranny. The advocate who helped to accomplish this was John Newman Edwards, a Missouri newspaperman and former Confederate soldier. For years, Edwards fashioned the legend of outlaw Jesse James into a social bandit, a valiant hero who robbed from the rich to give to the poor. In reality, Jesse and his cohorts were the only people who enjoyed the stolen money, but the myth was born and continues to live on to this day in the mind of the general public.

The Saga of Billy the Kid by Walter Noble Burns first appeared in December 1926, decades after Billy's death. Burns, a former Chicago Newspaperman, produced a so-called non-fiction biography that was mostly historically inaccurate. When *The Saga* was first published, Billy the Kid (real name Henry McCarty) was largely forgotten outside of New Mexico, however Burns's romanticized prose portrayed the youthful but troubled Billy as unequaled with a six-shooter as he rode across the mesas of the Southwest in a quest to seek justice for his murdered older friend and mentor. Would "Henry the Kid" have been as popular? Since publication of *The Saga of Billy the Kid*, the ill-fated Henry McCarty's wonderfully crafted legend has never stepped down from the saddle. Instead he rides into the annals of pop-culture revolvers blazing. Burns's book was a huge success and it encouraged him to pen *Tombstone: An Iliad of the Southwest*. Doc Holiday and all of the Earp Brothers are central figures in the story, along with their adversaries the Clanton and McLaury Brothers, however it is the tall slim taciturn Wyatt Earp who Walter Noble Burns singled out as the "Lion of Tombstone."

Writer Stuart N. Lake sought to present the public with a larger than life Westerner, and so he selected Wyatt Earp. Initially published as a four part serial in *The Saturday Evening Post* magazine, Lake's *Wyatt Earp Frontier Marshal* appeared in book form in October 1931. It was an immediate best seller. The biography burned "The Gunfight at the O. K. Corral" into America's consciousness and projected Wyatt Earp as the greatest lawman of the Western Frontier, who as a knight-errant tamed the most lawless towns with his mythical long barreled "Buntline Special" six-shooter. Lake's biography was highly imaginative and filled with fictionalized dialog, however, it stood as the foundation for all future stories of this grossly exaggerated, iconic lawman.

John Newman Edwards, Walter Noble Burns, and Stuart N. Lake started the legends other countless writers continued until none were as famous as the noble bandit Jesse James, the unparalleled gunfighter Billy the Kid, and the esteemed lawman Wyatt Earp. Seventy plus years would pass before a second biography of Ben Thompson appeared after Floyd Benjamin Streeter's research was compiled and published by others as a biography entitled, *Ben Thompson, Man with a Gun*. While full of new facts and the debunking of falsehoods, *Man with a Gun*, was similar to Walton's work in that it too failed to romanticize Thompson's eventful life. In 1966, the prolific Western fiction writer Lauran Paine penned a paraphrasing of Walton's first biography. Westernlore Press published *Texas Ben Thompson*, and while some of his other books were made into motion pictures, Paine's tale about Ben Thompson failed to stir enough interest to produce a film adaptation. Ben was never presented as a man with a grand social purpose and a six-shooter, so the Motion Picture Industry has ignored Ben Thompson while simultaneously lighting up the silver screen with an endless number of films about Jesse James, Billy the Kid, and Wyatt Earp. A few television programs have mentioned Thompson by name but in these thinly veiled portrayals, the storyline has no real resemblance to the actual man. One B-grade television show kept only the names the same while changing all the facts: the 1954 "Ben Thompson" episode of LEGENDS of the OLD WEST, Stories of the Century, was historically false throughout with the exception of their cutting six word assessment of Ben's behavior: "Suave when sober, savage when drunk."

69 *Texas Siftings,* March 29, 1884.
70 *Austin Capital,* March 13, 1884
71 Ibid.
72 *Texas Siftings*, April 5, 1884.
73 Eva Karling, "Reminiscences of the Life of One of Bastrop's Pioneers," *Bastrop Advertiser*, March 1932, newspaper interview. The article outlines the life of Mary Jane (Thompson) Gill.
74 *Texas Siftings*, April 5, 1884.
75 Walton, *Thompson*, 32.
76 *Statesman*, March 14, 1884.

Appendix A

1 F. B. Streeter, "Tragedies of a Cowtown," *The Aerend, a Kansas Quarterly* 5, no. 2 (Spring 1934): 81-96 and 145-162.
2 "Tragedies of a Cowtown," in endnote 11, 93. Mr. Streeter listed, "personal interviews with the following eyewitnesses: John Montgomery, Ernest Cunningham, Ed Schermerhorn, Charles Larkin. The story has also been gotten from other eyewitnesses through a third party, and from those who have heard eyewitnesses tell the story many times on the streets and in the homes of Ellsworth."

Appendix B

1 According to the 1879 directory, Pink Binford's occupation was mining and he resided on Lafayette Avenue between Spruce and Leiter avenues. Directory published by the Daily Times Steam Printing House.

Appendix D

1 *San Antonio Daily Express,* September 13, 1882

BIBLIOGRAPHY

PRIMARY SOURCES—ENGLAND

C. P. DEARDON COLLECTION, KNOTTINGLEY

Certified copy of an Entry of Birth Pursuant to the Births and Deaths Registration Act 1953—No. CI 530175 (Ben), CI 530176 (Billy) and CI 942950 (Mary Jane).

Certified Copy of an Entry of Marriage, Pursuant to the Marriage Act 1949—(AA 054588). Registration District Pontefract, 1840. William and Mary Ann (Baker) Thompson.

Custom House of Goole Shipping Records.

Last Will and Testament of William Thompson, grocer.

Last Will and Testament of Mary Thompson, widow of William Thompson, grocer.

PRIMARY SOURCES—UNITED STATES

Adjutant General Reconstruction Records Ledger #401-1133, Special Order 191, October 26, 1867, Headquarters District of Texas at Austin.

Adjutant General Records, Ledger #401- 1000, "Records of Murders and Assaults, 1867-1868," M[ar]ch [18]68. Texas State Archives, Austin.

Aransas County District Court Records, Case No. 22, *The State of Texas v. Wm. Thompson*, murder.

Gov. John Ireland File, Texas State Archives, Austin.

Archives of the Austin City Council Meetings, December 8, 1883, special meeting.

Austin Cemetery Records [renamed Oakwood], San Antonio Genealogical & Historical Society.

Travis County, Texas, Deed Records, Vol. 49.

Bee County, Texas, District Court records, Ben Thompson, Case # 177.

Ben Thompson's Estate, invoice dated May 10, 1884, submitted by J. C. Petmecky, Gunsmith, Austin.

Ben Thompson Biography File, Briscoe Center for American History, the University of Texas, Austin.

Bexar County Criminal Court Minutes, Vol. A, Ben Thompson, Cause #111.

Bexar County District Clerk Records, Criminal Journal, District Court, 1882. 360-61: Ben Thompson, Ex Parte, v. T.P. McCall, Sheriff of Bexar County; Application for Bail and Case 2118, 364-65, 367, Copy of Judge Wilson's order, signed September 9, 1882 and 379-80, bail denied on September 13, 1882, and 428. Briscoe Center of American History, University of Texas, Austin.

Bexar County Court Records, sworn affidavits of John J. McLaughlin, August 7; John Lamar and Daniel Morgan, August 15; M. B. Davis, September 12, 1882. Briscoe Center of American History, University of Texas, Austin.

Caldwell County, Texas, District Court records, Ben Thompson, Case # 1303.

"Ceremonies at the Restoration of the Austin City Marshal Ben Thompson Headstone... in Oakwood Cemetery Austin, Texas... June 17th, 1980 at 4:00 O'clock in the afternoon... Taped, Photographed, Transcribed and Compiled by Mulkey Owens, Member, Travis County Historical Commission." Program: "The Reparation of the Thompson Stone, Oakwood Cemetery, Austin, June 17, 1980." Austin History Center.

Confederate Muster Rolls, Harold Washington Public Library, Chicago, Il.

Confederate Muster Rolls, Texas State Archives, Austin.

Confederate Muster Rolls, Confederate Research Center, Hillsboro, Texas.

Convict Record, Texas State Penitentiary at Huntsville, Walker County, Texas, 64-65, Ledger 1998/038-149, Prisoner #1285, Ben Thompson and Prisoner #1286, John McGuire, Texas State Archives, Austin.

Coroner's Inquest Testimony, November 8, 1873, Murder of Edward Crawford. Ellsworth, County, Kansas Court Records.

E. P. Lamborn Collection, No. 156, Box No. 2, Folder 9. Manuscripts Department, Kansas State Historical Society, Topeka. Correspondence dated February 28, 1935, Floyd B. Streeter to Mr. Lamborn.

Correspondence dated December 1, 1876 from Texas Ranger Captain John C. Sparks to Texas Adj. Gen. William Steele. Texas State Archives, Austin.

Deposition of Witnesses and Interrogatory questions by Ira E. Lloyd, Ellsworth County attorney, *State of Kansas v. William Thompson*, murder. Ellsworth County, Kansas, District Court records.

DeWitt County District Court Records, Cuero, Texas. Case # 1607. *State of Texas v. William Thompson*, murder.

Diary of Chauncey B. Whitney, Historical Collections, Vol. 12, Kansas State Historical Society, Topeka.

District Court of Travis County, Docket No: 1185: *The State of Texas v. Benjamin Thompson.*

Docket No. 1528, *State of Texas v. John Rapp and Ben Thompson.* Austin History Center.

District Court Records, Case Number 289, *The State of Kansas v. Wm. Thompson*, murder.

Extradition papers for William Thompson, murder in the first degree, Call number 2-10/434, Texas State Archives, Austin.

Fairview Cemetery records, Bastrop, Texas.

General Correspondence, Adjutant General's Record Group (RG 401), George W. Baylor to Neal Coldwell, May 19, 1882. Texas State Archives, Austin.

General Correspondence, Adjutant General's Papers, P.P. Court to Adjutant General W. H. King, October 23, 1882. Texas State Archives, Austin.

General Correspondence, Adjutant General's Office, April 1, 1882 – November 6, 1883, Letter Press Book 168-69. Henry Orsay to Capt. George W. Baylor, October 30, 1882. Texas State Archives, Austin.

General Directory of the City of Austin for 1872-1873, 1877-1878, 1879-1880, 1881-1882, 1883-1884, 1885-1886, 1889-1890, Austin History Center.

General City Directory of the Cities of Denison and Sherman for 1876-1877 (Mooney & Morrison). Denison Genealogical Society.

General Directory of the City of Houston for 1879-1880, 1895-896 (Published by Morrison & Fourmy), Texas State Archives, Austin.

General Directory of the City of Paris for 1891-1892 (Published by Morrison & Fourmy), Texas State Archives, Austin.

*General Directory of the City of San Antonio for 1879-1880, 1881-1882, 1892-1893 (*Published by Morrison & Fourmy), Texas State Archives. Austin.

General Orders No. 17, Headquarters Fifth Military District, Ben Thompson, civilian, dated Austin, October 20, 1868. Texas State Archives, Austin.

General Orders No. 19, Headquarters, Fifth Military District, John McGuire, civilian, dated Austin, Texas, October 24, 1868. Texas State Archives, Austin.

Gill-Thompson Family Bible, information provided by Anne Beck.

Gov. Hardin R. Runnels's Records, Texas State Archives, Austin.

Habeas Corpus Testimony, *The State of Texas v. Ben Thompson*, murder. Briscoe Center for American History, University of Texas, Austin.

Heller's Galveston City Directory, 1876-1877. Rosenberg Library, Galveston.

"Introduction to the History of the Austin Police Department"; S.A. Gray and W.D. Moore, *Mercantile and General City Directory of Austin, Texas---1872-3.* Austin History Center.

Keith County District Court, *The State of Nebraska v. William Thompson*, Indictment for shooting with intent to kill. Nebraska State Historical Society, Lincoln.

Knight of Pythias Roster Report of June 30, 1882, and December 13, 1882 of the Mount Bonnell Lodge, No. 34, Austin, Texas.

Lafayette Rogers Reminiscences, Call Number 2-23/1054, Manuscript Collection, Texas State Archives, Austin.

Ledger Book of Frank Sparrow, business and stage manager of the Vaudeville Theater, 1875-1884, Texana Collection, San Antonio Public Library.

List of Marshals and Police Chiefs of City of Austin, Texas. Austin Police Department.

Minute Book of the City of Abilene, 1871, Kansas State Historical Society, Topeka.

Monthly Return of Company A, [Texas Ranger] Captain G.W. Baylor, for month ending October 31, 1882. Henry Orsay was the chief clerk in the adjutant general's office. Texas State Archives, Austin.

Monthly Return of Company C, [Texas Ranger] Captain John C. Sparks, prepared by Sgt. Joseph Leverett, dated November 30, 1876. Texas State Archives, Austin.

National Archives, Index To Compiled Service Records Of Confederate Soldiers Who Served In Organizations From The State Of Texas, Microfilm M227, Roll 36.

New Orleans City Directories 1849 through and including 1860. Williams Research Center, New Orleans Public Library.

The Albert Johannsen and Edward T. LeBlanc Collections of Nickel and Dime Novels, Rare Books/Special Collections of Founders Memorial Library, Northern Illinois University, DeKalb.

Oakwood Cemetery Records, InterCare Corporation, San Marcos, Texas.

Oakwood Cemetery Burial Ledger, Book 1, July 1866 – Dec. 1880. Austin History Center.

Original proclamation of Governor Thomas A. Osborn appointment of H.D. Stebbins, sheriff of Ellsworth County. Kansas State Historical Society, Topeka.

Passenger manifest of the ship *Constitution*, Microfilm roll 24, list #676. National Archives and Records Administration.

Passenger manifest of the ship *Granada*, New Orleans Passenger Lists 1820 – 1945. National Archive Series Number M259_36.

Ranger Muster Rolls, Texas State Archives, Austin.

Ranger Muster Rolls, Texas Ranger Hall of Fame and Museum, Waco.

Record of Arrests Book, City of Austin. Austin History Center and Texas State Archives, Austin.

Records and Papers of Ulysses S. Grant Association, Morris Library, Southern Illinois University, Carbondale, Illinois.

Register of the Grand Central Hotel, owner/proprietor Arthur Larkin, microfilm. Ellsworth, Kansas, Kansas State Historical Society, Topeka.

Register of Letters Received of the Department of Texas, the District of Texas, and the 5th Military District, 1865-1870. Bastrop County Judge William T. Allen's correspondence dated April 13, 1869 to Major General James H. Carlton. Texas State Archives, Austin.

Report from Special Officer C. S. Bell dated November 28, 1869, from Laredo to Captain C. E. Morse, Secretary of Civil Affairs, Austin. Barry Couch Collection.

Reminiscences of LaFayette Rogers, Call Number 2-23/1054, Manuscript Collection, Texas State Archives, Austin.

San Antonio City Cemetery System Records, San Antonio, TX.

Saint David Episcopal Church Archives, Baptisms and Burials (1867-1870) and (1871-1879) Vol. II, microfilm roll # 4, Marriage Records, Vol. 1, microfilm roll #5, Austin, TX.

Seaver, Nellie (Henry-Whitney-Osborne), undated letter from her to her daughter Mary Elizabeth (Whitney Sutton). Kansas State Historical Society, Topeka.

Service Records of Benjamin F. Thompson, Second Regiment Texas Cavalry, C.S.A., Old Military Records Division, National Archives, Washington D. C.

Subpoena information *State of Texas v. Ben Thompson*, murder, from Noah H. Rose Collection, Western History Collections, University of Oklahoma at Norman.

Telegram from Adj. Gen. William Steele to Charles Williams, Revenue Office, Galveston, October 27, 1876. Texas State Archives, Austin.

Texas Adj. Gen. William Steele, Outgoing Correspondence Ledger, 401-623, letter to B. Melasky, foreman, Travis County Grand Jury, October 28, 1876, 436 and letter to Ira E. Lloyd, Ellsworth County attorney, November 16, 1876. 467. Texas State Archives, Austin.

Texas Ranger Lieutenant Jesse Lee Hall's telegram to Texas Adj. Gen. William Steele, "Special Forces Correspondence, 1876 [-1877]." Box 401-1157, folder 17, Texas State Archives, Austin.

Travis County Clerk's Misdemeanor Records Division, Austin.

Travis County Court Criminal Minutes, Vol. A, Austin

Travis County Deed Records, Vol. U, 138, 165-68, 183, 348, Austin.

Travis County District Court, Criminal Records, Cause No. 5005, *State of Texas v. Ben Thompson and James Burditt.*

Travis County guardianship documents for William C. Reager, assigned guardianship of William, Richard and Jane Baker, minors as ordered by John B. Costa, Chief County Judge, May 1, 1855.

Travis County Probate Records, File Number 972, Notice of Application, Dated: March 17, 1885. Microfilm Reel # 975856, Estate of Ben Thompson. Austin History Center.

Vaudeville Theatre diagram of Ben Thompson/Jack Harris shooting by Architect Dobson, courtesy of Jim and Theresa Earle, College Station, Texas.

William M. Walton Biography File, Austin History Center.

WEBSITES

www.austintxgensoc.org/records/texas-german-and-english-academy-1876-1902/

www.brazosgenealogy.org/data/liquor.txt

www.findagrave.com

www.knottingley.org/history

http://www.pioneersandlegendsoftexas/

www.tcsheriff.org/about/agency-history/history

www.tshaonline.org/handbook/online/articles

ENGLISH CENSUS

April 1841

April 1851

CITY CENSUS

1875 Austin, Texas

FEDERAL CENSUS

KANSAS

1870 Ellsworth County

1880 Ford County

NEBRASKA COUNTIES

1880 Buffalo County

1880 Keith County

TEXAS COUNTIES

1850 Travis County

1860 Bastrop County

1860 Travis County

1870 Bastrop County

1870 Bexar County

1870 Refugio County

1870 Travis County

1870 Uvalde County

1870 Walker County

1880 Bell County

1880 Bexar County

1880 Guadalupe County

1880 McLennan County

1880 Travis County

1880 Washington County

1880 Uvalde County

1880 Zavala County

1910 Kinney County

STATE CENSUS

KANSAS

1875 Ellsworth County

NEBRASKA

1885 Lincoln County

INTERVIEWS and PERSONAL CORRESPONDENCE

Anne Beck, descendent of Ben Thompson

C.P. Dearden, Knottingley Historian

Mark Eisenhauer, San Antonio attorney

Gary P. Fitterer, researcher and author

George Fox, Grand Secretary of the Knights of Pythias of Texas

Mrs. J.P. Lewis

Robert McCubbin, collector, historian, publisher and author

Leon Claire Metz

Marylyn (Portis) Pense, great-grandniece of Phil Coe

NEWSPAPERS—MEXICO

Matamoros Daily Ranchero

NEWSPAPERS—UNITED STATES

ARKANSAS
Pine Bluff Daily Commercial
Hot Springs Sentinel-Star

COLORADO
Colorado Springs Weekly-Gazette
Denver Rocky Mountain News
Pueblo Chieftain

FLORIDA
Miami Daily News

ILLINOIS
Chicago Sunday Chronicle
Chicago News
Chicago Tribune

KANSAS
Abilene Chronicle
Atchison Globe
Dodge City Times
(Ellsworth) *Kansas Cowboy*
Ellsworth Messenger
Ellsworth Reporter
Ford County Globe
Hays Sentinel
Junction City Union
Leavenworth Daily Times
Manhattan Nationalist
Oxford Times
Winfield Courier

INDIANA
Indianapolis Journal

LOUISIANA
(New Orleans) *The Daily Picayune*

MINNESOTA
(Albert Lea) *Freeborn County Standard*

MISSOURI
(Kansas City) *Journal of Commerce*
St. Louis Daily Globe-Democrat
St. Louis Republican
Neosho Times

NEBRASKA
Nebraska City Press
North Platte Nebraskan
North Platte Western Nebraskan
Omaha Daily Bee
Sidney Telegraph

NEW MEXICO
Eddy County Citizen
Eddy Current

Silver City Herald and Southwest
(Silver City) *New Southwest*

NEW YORK
National Police Gazette
New York Herald
New York Sun
New York Times
New York World

OHIO
Athens Messenger
Cleveland Plain-Dealer
Richwood Gazette

PENNSYLVANIA
Greenwood Advance

TEXAS
Austin-American Statesman
Austin Chronicle
Austin Citizen
Austin Capitol
Austin Daily Dispatch
(Austin) *Daily Fair News*
Austin State Journal
Austin Republican
(Austin) *Southern Intelligencer*
Austin State Gazette
Austin Statesman
(Austin) *Texas Siftings*
(Austin) *Texas State Gazette*
(Austin) *Texas State Times*
Bastrop Advertiser
Beaumont Enterprise
Brenham Daily Banner
Burnet Bulletin
Colorado [County] *Citizen*

Corpus Christi Caller
Corpus Christi Caller-Times
Corsicana Observer
Crystal City, Texas Sentinel
(University of Texas, Austin) *Daily Texan*
Dallas Herald
Dallas News
Denison Herald
Denison News
El Paso Herald
El Paso Lone Star
Fort Worth Gazette
Fort Worth Democrat
Galveston Daily News
(Galveston) *Flake's Daily Bulletin*
Houston Chronicle
Houston Post
Jacksboro Frontier Echo
Laredo Times
Luling Newsboy & Signal
Luling Signal
Palestine Herald Press
Rockport Transcript
San Angelo Standard
San Antonio Daily Express
San Antonio Express-News
San Antonio Herald
San Antonio Light
(San Antonio) *Texas Argus*
San Marcos West Texas Free Press
(Seguin) *Gazette-Enterprise*
Sherman Herald-Democrat
(Uvalde) *Leader-News*
Waco Examiner
(Pleasanton) *Western Stock Journal*

BOOKS, PAMPHLETS, AND ARTICLES

Adams, Paul. "The Unsolved Murder of Ben Thompson—Pistoleer Extraordinary." *Southwestern Historical Quarterly* 48, no. 3 (January 1945).

Ahearn, Allen and Patricia Ahearn. *Collected Books: The Guide to Identification and Values.* 4th Edition. NP: Quill & Brush Press, Comus, 2011.

Asbury, Herbert. *Gem of the Prairie: An Informal History of the Chicago Underworld.* Garden City, New York: Garden City Publishing Co., Inc., 1942.

Barkley, Mary Starr. *History of Travis County and Austin, 1839-1899.* Austin, Texas: The Steck Company, ND.

Bastrop Historical Society. *In the Shadow of the Lost Pines: A History of Bastrop County and Its People.* NP, 1955.

Barnes, Charles Merritt. *Combats and Conquests of Immortal Heroes.* San Antonio, Texas: Guessaz & Ferlet Company, 1910.

Bell, Bob Boze. "Classic Gunfights: Ben Thompson & King Fisher vs Joe Foster & Billy Simms." *True West* 53, no. 2 (March 2006).

Bell, Bob Boze. "Classic Gunfights: Billy Thompson vs Chauncey 'Cap' Whitney." *True West* 53, no. 10 (December 2006).

Bicknell, Natalie and Tom Bicknell. "The Cody-to-Thompson Stevens-Lord No. 36 Target Pistol was a Handsome Present." *Wild West* 14, no. 5 (February 2002).

Bicknell, Thomas C. "Ben Thompson—Mercenary for the Emperor." *Quarterly* of the National Association for Outlaw and Lawman History 22, no. 2 (April-June 1998).

Bicknell, Thomas C. "Ben Thompson, Gambler, Gunfighter… Poet." *Quarterly* of the National Association for Outlaw and Lawman History 23, no. 3 (July-September 1999).

Bicknell, Thomas C. "'The Proper Sort of a Person to be Marshal'—The Notorious Ben Thompson Becomes A Peace Officer." *Quarterly* of the National Association for Outlaw and Lawman History 27, no. 2 (April-June 2003).

Bicknell, Thomas C. "Whatever Became of Texas Billy Thompson." *Kansas Cowboy* 5, no. 2 (January 2001), and 5, no.3 (March 2001). http://www.knottingley.org/history.

Bicknell, Thomas C. "Billy Simms, A Lover of Fair Play." *Quarterly* of the National Association for Outlaw and Lawman History 28, no.3 (July – September 2004).

Bowser, David. *West of the Creek, Murder, Mayhem and Vice in Old San Antonio.* NP: Maverick Publishing Company, 2003.

Bronson, Edgar Beecher. *Reminiscences of a Ranchman.* Lincoln, Nebraska: University of Nebraska Press. 1962. First published in 1908.

Brown, Frank. *Annals of Travis County and the City of Austin (from the Earliest Times to the Close of 1875).* Transcript on file at the Austin History Center.

Browning, James A. *Violence Was No Stranger: A Guide to the Grave Sites of Famous Westerners.* Stillwater, OK: Barbed Wire Press, 1993.

Bushick, Frank H. *Glamorous Days in Old San Antonio (A Never-to-be Forgotten City).* San Antonio, Texas: The Naylor Company, 1934.

Caren, Eric C. *Texas Extra—A Newspaper History of the Lone Star State 1835-1935.* Edison, New Jersey: Castle Books, 1999.

Cope, Kenneth L. *Stevens Pistols and Pocket Rifles.* Ottawa, Canada: Museum Restoration Service, 1971.

Cowan, E. D. "Memories of the Happy Bad Man." *Chicago Sunday Chronicle,* October 16, 1898.

Cox, Mike. "The Great Texas Treasury Raid." *True West*, March 31, 2015, www.truewestmagazine.com

Cox, Patrick. "The Great Texas Treasury Robbery, June 11, 1865." *Journal* of the East Texas Historical Association 30, no. 2 (1992).

Cude, Elton R. *The Wild and Free Dukedom of Bexar*. San Antonio, Texas: Munguia Printers, 1978.

Cunningham, Eugene. *Triggernometry, A Gallery of Gunfighters*. Caldwell, Idaho: The Caxton Printers, 1956.

Davis, Richard Harding. *The West from a Car Window*. New York: Harper Brothers, 1892.

DeArment, Robert K. *Knights of the Green Cloth: The Saga of the Frontier Gamblers*. Norman, Oklahoma: University of Oklahoma Press, 1982.

DeArment, Robert K. *Gunfighter in Gotham: Bat Masterson's New York City Years*. rev. ed., Norman: University of Oklahoma Press, 2013.

Devereaux, Jan. "Jagville." *Quarterly* of the National Association for Outlaw and Lawman History 27, no. 1 (January – March 2004).

Diary of Gus Birkner, 1835-1940. Luling, Texas: typed transcript on file in the Caldwell County Genealogical & Historical Society Library.

Dodge, Fred. *Under Cover for Wells Fargo: The Unvarnished Recollections of Fred Dodge*. Boston, Massachusetts: Houghton Mifflin Company, 1969.

Drees, James D. *Bloody Prairie Ellis County* no. 2. Hays, Kansas: Ellis County Historical Society, 1997.

Dugan, Mark. *Knight of the Road: The Life of Highwayman Ham White*. Athens, Ohio: Swallow Press/Ohio University Press, 1990.

Dukes, Doug. *Ben Thompson: Iron Marshal of Austin*. NP: 2010.

Dukes, Doug. "A Peace Officer with More Hip than Holster." *Wild West*, October 2015.

Durham, George. "On the Trail of 5,100 Outlaws—Beyond the Nueces." *Valley Morning Star*, November 8, 1969. Harlingen, Texas.

Durham, George. *Taming the Nueces Strip*. Austin, Texas: University of Texas Press, 1962.

Dykstra, Robert R. *The Cattle Towns*. Lincoln, Nebraska: University of Nebraska Press, 1968.

Ellison, Douglas W. "Edge of Darkness: The Final Days of Ben Thompson." *Brand Book*, English Westerners' Society 48, no. 3 (Summer 2015).

Evertt, Alice. "Fatal Corner." *San Antonio Monthly*, July 1982.

Feit, Rachel. "Gardens of Eden, How Austin Used to Celebrate." *Austin Chronicle,* January 26, 2001.

Fisher, O.C. and J.C. Dykes. *King Fisher: His Life and Times*. Norman: University of Oklahoma Press, 1966.

Fisher, O. C. "King Fisher—Texas Lawman." *Corral Dust*, Potomac Corral of the Westerners (Washington, D. C.) 4, no. 1 (March, 1959).

Fitterer, Gary P. *The Life and Death of Billy Thompson (1845 – 1897). Quarterly* of the National Association for Outlaw and Lawman History 25, no. 1 (January – March 2001), and no. 2 (April – May 2001).

Foy, Eddie, and Alvin F. Harlow. *Clowning Through Life.* New York: E.P. Dutton & Co., 1928.

Gage, Larry Jay. "The City of Austin on the Eve of the Civil War." *Southwestern Historical Quarterly* 63 (January 1960).

Gallegly, Joseph. *Footlights on the Border: The Galveston and Houston Stage Before 1900*. Gravenhage, The Netherlands: Mouton & Co., 1962.

Gallegly, Joseph. *From Alamo Plaza to Jack Harris's Saloon: O. Henry and the Southwest He Knew*. Gravenhage, The Netherlands: Mouton & Co., 1970.

Gallegly, Joseph. "Background and Patterns of O. Henry's Texas Badman Stories." *Rice Institute Pamphlet* 42, no. 3 (1955).

Gard, Wayne. "The Fence Cutters." *Southwestern Historical Quarterly* 51, no. 1 (July 1947).

Gasper, Lucille Ruby Elliott. *A Brief Sketch of the Life of Jacob J. Ellison, A Trail Driver's Record of the Old West*. NP: Self-published, ND. Copy found in Texana Collection, San Antonio Public Library.

Gesell, Laurence E. *Saddle the Wild Wind: The Saga of Squirrel Tooth Alice and Texas Billy Thompson*. Chandler, Arizona: Coast Aire Publications, 2002.

Gillett, J.B. "Ben Thompson and Billy Sims." *Frontier Times* 12, no. 1 (October 1934).

Gray, Jim. *Desperate Seed: Ellsworth, Kansas on the Violent Frontier*. Ellsworth, Kansas: Kansas Cowboy Publications, 2009.

Gray, Jim. "Ellsworth's Circle Cemetery." *Kansas Cowboy* 4, no. 3 (March 2000).

Gray, Jim. "Wyatt Earp Was Never Here." *Kansas Cowboy* 9, no. 2 (Jan. - Feb. 2005).

Gray, Jim. "Quiet Hero James B. Miller." *Kansas Cowboy* 9, no. 3 (July – Aug. 2005).

Gray, Jim. "Those Wild Millett Cowboys!" *Kansas Cowboy* 11, no. 1 (Nov. – Dec. 2006).

Gray, Jim. "Frontier Ellsworth Was Shaped by Men of War." *Kansas Cowboy* 14, no. 3 (Mar. – April. 2010).

Gray, Jim. "Chauncey Belden Whitney—Frontier Defender." *Kansas Cowboy* 19, no. 6 (Sept.- Oct. 2014), and 20, no. 1 (Nov.- Dec. 2015).

Greene, Casey Edward. "Clear Lake City, Texas." *The New Handbook of Texas*. www.tshaonline.org/handbook/online/articles

Gregory, A. H. "Death of Ben Thompson and King Fisher Described." *Texas Argus*. San Antonio, Texas. ND.

Hardin, John Wesley. *The Life of John Wesley Hardin, As Written by Himself*. Seguin, Texas: Smith & Moore, 1896. Reprinted by the University of Oklahoma Press in 1961.

Hart, Katherine. *Austin & Travis County: A Pictorial History, 1839-1939*. Austin, Texas: Encino Press, 1975.

Horan, James D. *The Authentic Wild West: The Gunfighters*. New York: Crown Publishers, 1976.

Holt, R. D. "The Introduction of Barbed Wire into Texas and the Fence Cutting War." *West Texas Historical Association Year Book*. NP: June 1930.

Howell, Kenneth Wayne. *Texas Confederate, Reconstruction Governor: James Webb Throckmorton*. College Station, Texas: Texas A&M University Press, 2008.

Humphrey, David C. *Austin: An Illustrated History*. Austin, Texas: Windsor Publications, 1985.

Humphrey, David C. "Prostitution and Public Policy in Austin, Texas, 1870-1915." *Southwestern Historical Quarterly* 86, April 1983.

Hunter, J. Marvin. "Ben Thompson Wins a Tombstone." *Frontier Times* 2, no. 6 (March 1925).

Hunter, J. Marvin. "Knew Ben Thompson." *Frontier Times* 16, no. 10 (July 1939).

Huson, Hobart. *Refugio, A Comprehensive History of Refugio County From Aboriginal Times to 1955*, and Vol. 2, *Secession to 1955*. Woodsboro, Texas: The Rooke Foundation, 1955.

Jauhari, Mohan. "Approximate Relationship Between the Angles of Incidence and Ricochet for Practical Application in the Field of Criminal Investigation." *The Journal of Criminal Law, Criminology and Police Science* 62, no. 1.

James, Victor Lee. *Frontier and Pioneer Recollections of Early Days in San Antonio and West Texas*. San Antonio, TX: NP, 1938.

Jennings, Frank W. "San Antonio, The Story of an Enchanted City." *San Antonio Express-News*, 1998.

Jennings, N.A. *A Texas Ranger*. Chicago, Illinois: The Lakeside Press, 1992.

Johnson, David. *John Ringo: King of the Cowboys: His Life and Times from the Hoo Doo War to Tombstone*. Denton, Texas: University of North Texas Press, 2008.

Johnson, David. *The Mason County "Hoo Doo" War, 1874-1902*. Denton, Texas: University of North Texas Press, 2006.

Josselyn, N.W. *St. Louis to Denver for 1870*. Business directory published in St. Louis, Missouri. NP, ND.

Katzenmeier, Dennis. "Memoirs of a Lawless Cowtown." *Kansas Cattle Towns of the Chisholm Trail*. Special issue of *Tour Kansas* guide, 2000.

Kyvig, David E. "Fort Elliott." *The New Handbook of Texas*. ND. www.tshaonline.org/handbook/online/articles

Lack, Paul D. "Slavery and Vigilantism in Austin, Texas, 1840-1860." *Southwestern Historical Quarterly* 83 (July 1981).

Lake, Stuart N. *Wyatt Earp, Frontier Marshal*. Boston, Massachusetts: Houghton Mifflin Company, 1931.

La Roche, Clarence J. "Booze, Bullets and Bad Bad Ben, Powder Smell Clings to Harris Corner." *San Antonio Express-News*, January 1, 1966.

Lloyd, Ira E. "Exciting Early Day History of Ellsworth, Diary of Late Ira E. Lloyd Relates In Detail Early Day Lawless Cowtown." Ellsworth, Kansas: Ellsworth County Historical Society, ND.

Lunsford, John R. "How Ben Thompson Died With His Boots On." *Frontier Times* 9, no. 2 (November 1931).

McCaslin, Richard B. *Fighting Stock: "Rip" Ford of Texas*. Fort Worth: Texas Christian University Press, 2011.

McCubbin, Robert G. "A Blood-Stained Memento." *True West* 53, no. 2 (April 2006).

McCubbin, Robert G. "The 65 Most Important Historical Photos from the Robert C. McCubbin Collection." *True West* 65, no. 1 (January 2018).

McInnes, Elmer D. "Coeur D' Alene Comrade." *Old West*, Spring 1996.

Mahnken, Robert R. "Ogallala—Nebraska's Cowboy Capital." *Nebraska History* 28, no. 2 (April – June 1947).

Manry, Joe Edgar. *Curtain Call—The History of the Theater in Austin, Texas—1839 to 1905*. Austin, Texas: Waterloo Press, 1985.

Marks, Paula Mitchell. *And Die in the West: The Story of the O.K. Corral Gunfight*. New York: William Morrow and Co., 1989.

Masterson, W. B. "Ben Thompson." *Human Life* 4, no. 4 (January 1907).

Masterson, W. B. and Jack DeMattos. *Famous Gunfighters of the Western Frontier*. Monroe, Washington: Weatherford Press, 1982.

Metz, Leon C. *John Wesley Hardin, Dark Angel of Texas*. El Paso, Texas: Mangan Books, 1996.

Miller, Nyle H. and Joseph W. Snell. *Why the West Was Wild: A Contemporary Look at the Antics of Some Highly Published Kansas Cowtown Personalities*. Norman: University of Oklahoma Press, 2003.

Miller, Rick. *Bloody Bell County: Vignettes of Violence and Mayhem in Central Texas*. Waco, Texas: Nortex Press, 2011.

Minatra, Odie. "Some exploits of Ben Thompson." *Frontier Times* 18, no. 12 (September 1941).

Mundie, Jr., James A. *More Texas Burial Sites of Civil War and Reconstruction Era Notables*. Hillsboro, Texas: Hill Country Press, 2002.

Myler, Charles Bennett. "A History of the English Speaking Theatre in San Antonio before 1900." Austin: University of Texas, 1968.

Nielsen, Elaine. *Ogallala: A Century On The Trail*, Ogallala, Nebraska: Keith County Historical Society, 1984.

Nolan, Oran Warder. "Tom Sullivan, Frontier Darkey." *Frontier Times* 28, November 1949.

North, Thomas. *Five Years In Texas; or, What You Did Not Hear During The War From January 1861 To January 1865. A Narrative Of His Travels, Experiences, and Observations, in Texas and Mexico*. Cincinnati, Ohio: Elm Street Printing Co., 1870.

Nuinez, Tommie for the Gonzales County Historical Commission. "Sarah Lee Hassell." *The History of Gonzales County, Texas*. Dallas, Texas: Curtis Media Corporation of Dallas, 1986.

O'Conner, Richard. *Wild Bill Hickok*. Garden City, NY: Doubleday & Co., 1959.

O'Neal, James B. *They Die But Once: The Story of a Tejano*. NP: Kessinger Publishing, 2010.

Paddock, Capt. B. B. *History of Texas: Fort Worth and the Texas Northwest* 2. Chicago and New York: The Lewis Publishing Company, 1922.

Page, Bill. "Wine and Liquor Licenses in Brazos County, 1857-1871." ND. http://www.brazosgenealogy.org/data/liquor.txt

Parsons, Chuck and Donaly E. Brice. *Texas Ranger N.O. Reynolds, The Intrepid.* Denton, Texas: University of North Texas Press, 2014.

Parsons, Chuck. *James Madison Brown, Texas Sheriff, Texas Turfman.* Wolfe City, Texas: Henington Publishing Company, 1993.

Parsons, Chuck. *Phil Coe: Texas Gambler.* Wolfe City, Texas: Henington Publishing Company, 1984.

Parsons, Chuck. "Eyewitness to Cowtown Violence." *Real West,* April 1980.

Pense, Marylyn. "A Crime of Passion, A story about Phil Coe." *Tombstone Times* 1, no. 12 (December 2003).

Ramsdell, Charles. "Song and Dance—And Gunfire." *San Antonio Express Magazine,* January 4, 1948.

Rattenbury, Richard C. "From Showman to Shootist: A Stevens-Lord Presentation Pistol." *Man at Arms* 10, no. 6 (Nov.- Dec. 1988).

Rattenbury, Richard C. *Packing Iron, Gunleather of the Frontier West.* Springfield, Ohio: Zon International Publishing, 1993.

Roberts, Gary L. "Bat Masterson and the Sweetwater Shootout." *Wild West,* October 2000.

Rosa, Joseph G. *They Called Him Wild Bill: The Life and Adventures of James Butler Hickok.* Norman: University of Oklahoma Press, 1964.

Rosa, Joseph G. *The West of Wild Bill Hickok.* Norman: University of Oklahoma Press, 1982.

Rosa, Joseph G. *The Taming of the West: Age of the Gunfighter, Men & Weapons on the Frontier 1840-1900.* New York: Smithmark Publishers, 1993.

Schoenberger, Dale T. *The Gunfighters*. Caldwell, Idaho: The Caxton Printers, 1983.

Schoenberger, Dale T. "Whatever Happened to Texas Billy Thompson." *Real West*, March 1982.

Schoenberger, Dale T. "Charles Mathews, Editor with a Gun." *True West*, January 1993.

Secrest, William B. "A Gamblin' Man." *Real West*, March 1979.

Selcer, Richard, *Legendary Watering Holes, the Saloons that made Texas Famous,* College Station: Texas A&M University Press, 2004.

Shaver, Larry G. "This is King Fisher's Road." Unpublished manuscript.

Shaw, James C. *North from Texas*. Evanston, Illinois: The Branding Iron Press, 1952.

Silva, Lee A. *Wyatt Earp: A Biography of the Legend, Vol. 1. The Cowtown Years*. NP: Graphic Publishers 2002.

Soodalter, Ron. "Gomorrah of the Plains." *Wild West* 30, no. 2 (August 2017).

Spangenberger, Phil. "Shoulder Holsters, These concealed—carry rigs were born on the frontier." *True West* 52, no. 4 (May 2005).

Streeter, Floyd B. *The Complete and Authentic Life of Ben Thompson: Man with a Gun*. New York: Frederick Fell, 1957.

Streeter, Floyd B. *Prairie Trails & Cow Towns: The Opening of the Old West*. New York: Devin-Adair Company, January 1963.

Streeter, Floyd B. "Tragedies of a Cow Town." *The Aerend* 5, no. 2. Hays, Kansas: Kansas State College, Spring 1934.

Summer, Jane. *Some Early Travis County, Texas Records*. Easley, South Carolina: Southern Historical Press, 1979. Austin Genealogical Society Summer Issue.

Terrell, Alexander Watkins. *From Texas to Mexico and the Court of Maximilian in 1865*. Dallas: The Book Club of Texas, 1933.

Thrapp, Dan L. *Encyclopedia of Frontier Biography*. Lincoln: University of Nebraska Press, 1991.

Thompson, George G. "Bat Masterson; The Dodge City Years." *Fort Hayes Kansas State College Studies, Language and Literature Series* no. 1, and *General Series* no. 6, 1943.

Thompson, Jerry. *Laredo—A Pictorial History*. Norfolk, Virginia: Donning Company/Publishers, 1986.

Tracey, Joshua L. *The Handbook for the Kansas Pacific Railway*. NP: Wiebusch & Sons Printers, 1870.

Walton, William M. *Life and Adventures of Ben Thompson, The Famous Texan*. Austin, Texas: Steck Company Publishers, 1884. Facsimile ed., 1956.

Walton, William M. *Major Buck Walton, An Epitome of My Life, Civil War Reminiscences*. Austin, Texas: The Waterloo Press, 1965.

Wilbarger, J. W. *Indian Depredations in Texas*. Austin, Texas: Hutchings Printing House, 1889.

Wilson, R. L. "L. D. Nimschke—Firearms Engraver." *The American Rifleman*, January 1966.

Wilson, R. L. *The Peacemakers: Arms and Adventure in the American West.* New York: Random House, 1992.

Wilson, R. L. and Greg Martin. *Buffalo Bill's Wild West, An American Legend*. New York: Random House, 1998.

Wright, Robert M. *Dodge City: The Cowboy Capital*. Wichita, Kansas: The Eagle Press, ND.

Woods, Larry J. "Gunfighters and Lawmen." *Wild West*, June 2005.

INDEX

—C—

—F—

—G—

—H—

—MC—

—M—

—N—

—O—

—P—

—R—

—T—

—U—

—V—

—W—

—Y—

—Z—